VISUAL QUICKSTART GUIDE

# MAC OS X 10.4
# TIGER

**Maria Langer**

**Peachpit Press**

Visual QuickStart Guide
# Mac OS X 10.4 Tiger
Maria Langer

Peachpit Press
1249 Eighth Street
Berkeley, CA 94710
510-524-2178 • 800-283-9444
510-524-2221 (fax)

Find us on the World Wide Web at: www.peachpit.com

Peachpit Press is a division of Pearson Education

Copyright ©2005 by Maria Langer

Editor: Clifford Colby
Technical Editor: Clifford Colby, Victor Gavenda
Indexer: Julie Bess
Cover Design: The Visual Group
Production: Maria Langer, David Van Ness

## Colophon

This book was produced with Adobe InDesign CS and Adobe Photoshop 7.0 on a dual-processor Power Macintosh G5. The fonts used were Utopia, Meta Plus, and PIXymbols Command. Screenshots were created using Snapz Pro X on an eMac. Screenshots reprinted by permission of Apple Computer, Inc.

## Notice of Rights

## Notice of Liability

The information in this book is distributed on an "As Is" basis, without warranty. While every precaution has been taken in the preparation of the book, neither the author nor Peachpit Press shall have any liability to any person or entity with respect to any loss or damage caused or alleged to be caused directly or indirectly by the instructions contained in this book or by the computer software and hardware products described in it.

## Trademarks

Visual QuickStart Guide is a registered trademark of Peachpit Press, a division of Pearson Education. Apple, Macintosh, Mac, iPod, eMac, PowerBook, AirPort, AirPort Extreme, AirPort Express, FireWire, SuperDrive, Mac OS, Aqua, Finder, iTunes, iPhoto, iMovie, iCal, iDVD, iSync, iChat, Sherlock, Apple-Script, QuickTime, ColorSync, Bonjour, AppleTalk, Carbon, Cocoa, Quartz, TrueType, AppleCare, Mac.com, and .Mac are either trademarks, registered trademarks, or service marks of Apple Computer, Inc. in the United States and/or other countries. Microsoft Internet Explorer is a trademark of Microsoft Corporation in the United States and/or other countries. PostScript is a trademark of Adobe Systems Incorporated. Other product names used in this book may be trademarks or registered trademarks of their respective owners.

Throughout this book trademarked names are used. Rather than put a trademark symbol in every occurrence of a trademarked name, we state we are using the names only in an editorial fashion and to the benefit of the trademark owner with no intention of infringement of copyright.

ISBN 0-321-30526-4

9 8 7 6 5 4 3 2 1

Printed and bound in the United States of America.

## Dedication

To Janet LeRoy
Happy Big Birthday

# Thanks!

To Cliff Colby, for his thorough review and editing of this book, which seems to get fatter with every edition. Also, a big thanks for Cliff for really not panicking.

To Victor Gavenda, for his help with a few technical questions I had during the writing process.

To Ron Hipschman for his technical assistance and guidance on the Unix chapter. Ron's Unix expertise is far better than mine will ever be.

To David Van Ness, for fine-tuning the book's layout and spotting all those shifting thumbtabs.

To Mike Shebanek and Chris Bourdon at Apple Computer, Inc., for getting me the information I needed to write this book. Without their help, it would be impossible for me to finish this book in time for Tiger's release.

To the developers at Apple, for continuing to refine the world's best operating system. As I worked with early versions of Tiger while writing this book, I found myself getting more and more excited. I couldn't wait to install it on my production Mac so I could use it every day!

To the folks at Ambrosia Software, for developing and continuing to update Snapz Pro X. I could not have taken the 2,000+ screen shots in this book without this great software program.

And to Mike, for the usual reasons.

www.marialanger.com

# Table of Contents

**TABLE OF CONTENTS**

# Introduction to Mac OS X

**Figure 1** The About This Mac window for Mac OS X 10.4.

## Introduction

Mac OS X 10.4 (**Figure 1**) is the latest version of the computer operating system that put the phrase *graphic user interface* in everyone's vocabulary. With Mac OS, you can point, click, and drag to work with files, applications, and utilities. Because the same intuitive interface is utilized throughout the system, you'll find that a procedure that works in one program works in virtually all the others.

This *Visual QuickStart Guide* will help you learn Mac OS X 10.4 by providing step-by-step instructions, plenty of illustrations, and a generous helping of tips. On these pages, you'll find everything you need to know to get up and running quickly with Mac OS X—and a lot more!

This book was designed for page flipping. Use the thumb tabs, index, or table of contents to find the topics for which you need help. If you're brand new to Mac OS, however, I recommend that you begin by reading at least the first two chapters. In them, you'll find basic information about techniques you'll use every day with your computer.

If you're interested in information about new Mac OS X features, be sure to browse through this **Introduction**. It'll give you a good idea of what you can expect to see on your computer.

## ✔ Tips

- The "X" in "Mac OS X" is pronounced "ten."

- Although this book is over 700 pages long, it doesn't cover every single aspect of using Mac OS X. You can find additional material that didn't make it into this book on the book's companion Web site, www.langerbooks.com/macosquickstart/.

# New Features in Mac OS X 10.4

Mac OS X 10.4 (Tiger) is a major revision to Mac OS X. Here's a look at some of the new and revised features you can expect to find.

## ✔ Tip

■ This book covers many of these features.

## System

■ **Spotlight (Figure 2)** is a new search feature that enables you to search available volumes from the Finder or while other applications are active. It even works within applications such as System Preferences to help you find what you're looking for.

■ **Dashboard (Figure 3)** introduces tiny applications called widgets, which appear onscreen with the push of a button. Mac OS X comes with a number of widgets you can use to perform simple tasks or get information.

■ **Automator (Figure 4)** makes it easy to create workflows to automate repetitive tasks. Use actions that come with Mac OS X 10.4 applications or write your own with AppleScript.

■ **Family Controls (Figure 5)** enable you to set up user accounts to protect kids from interacting with strangers or visiting unapproved Web sites on the Internet.

■ **VoiceOver** is Mac OS X's new built-in screen reader, which uses voice synthesis to read back whatever appears on screen, as well as what you type or click.

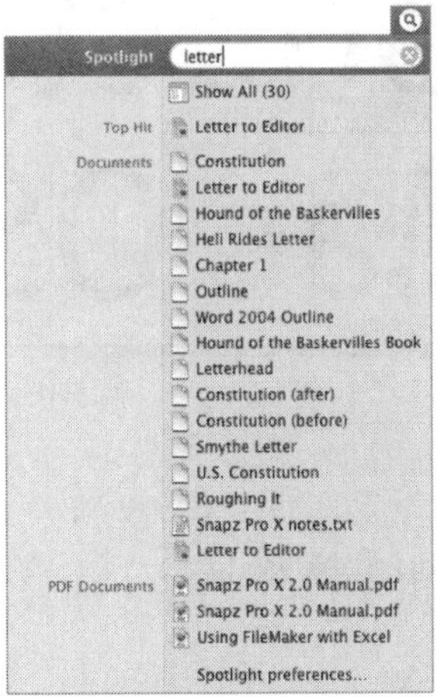

**Figure 2** One of Spotlight's features is a search results menu you can access when any application is active.

**Figure 3** Dashboard puts tiny applications called widgets on your screen when you press F12.

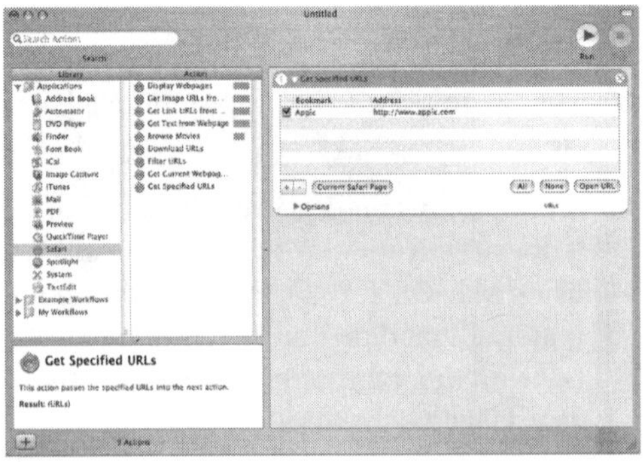

**Figure 4** You can use Automator to create custom workflows to automate tasks.

**Figure 5** Parental Controls enable you to limit the use of certain applications.

**Figure 6** Burn folders make it easy to organize files before burning them to CD.

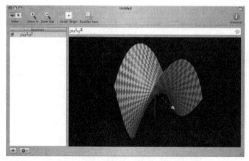

**Figure 7** Grapher is the Mac OS X version of Apple's old Graphing Calculator.

# Finder

- **Smart folders** work with Spotlight to create folders full of search results. Smart folders are constantly updated, thus automating the search process.

- **Burn folders (Figure 6)** make it easy to organize files to be burned onto a CD. Because burn folders contain aliases of items, there's no need to fill your hard disk with duplicate items. Best of all, when an item changes, the current version of the item is burned to CD.

# Applications

- **Dictionary** puts the Oxford American Dictionaries inside your Macintosh. Use it to get word definitions, pronunciations, synonyms, and antonyms. This feature is available as an application or as a Dashboard widget.

- **Grapher (Figure 7)**, the first Mac OS X version of Graphing Calculator, graphs complex formulas.

- Address Book has several new features, including **Smart Groups**, which automatically group contacts by search criteria you specify, and **Address Book Sharing**, which enables you to share contacts with others over a network or the Internet.

- **iCal** is better integrated with Address Book and Mail. You can now use iCal to send event invitations to Address Book contacts via Mail.

**NEW FEATURES IN MAC OS X 10.4**

## Printing

- The Print dialog now includes a **PDF menu (Figure 8)**, which offers options for creating or faxing document PDFs.

- The Finder now includes a Print command, which quickly prints documents selected in a Finder window.

## Internet

- Safari can now work as an **RSS reader (Figure 9)**, so you can browse syndicated sites. A new View All RSS Articles command displays recent RSS articles from a variety of sources in your Safari window.

- Mail has a number of new features, including **Spotlight** searching, **Smart Mailboxes**, and the ability to synchronize accounts, mailboxes, and other Mail features with other computers via a .Mac account.

- iChat now supports video conferencing with up to three other people or audio conferencing with up to nine other people.

## .Mac

- A .Mac account now makes it possible to synchronize bookmarks, calendars, contacts, keychains, mail account, mail rules, mail signatures, and smart mailboxes.

**Figure 8** The new PDF menu in Print dialogs lets you create or fax documents as PDFs.

**Figure 9** Safari is now an RSS article reader as well as a standard Web browser.

New Features in Mac OS X 10.4

# Setting Up Mac OS X 10.4

## Setting Up Mac OS X 10.4

Before you can use Mac OS X, you must install it on your computer and configure it to work the way you need it to. The steps you need to complete to do this depend on the software currently installed on your computer.

Use the Mac OS X 10.4 installer to do one of the following:

▲ Update an existing Mac OS X installation to Mac OS X 10.4.

▲ Install Mac OS X 10.4 to replace an existing Mac OS X installation.

▲ Install Mac OS X 10.4 on a computer with a Mac OS 9.2 or earlier installation and no version of Mac OS X.

Then restart your computer and use the Mac OS Setup Assistant to configure Mac OS X.

This chapter explains how to properly install and configure Mac OS X 10.4 on your computer.

## ✔ Tips

■ Not sure which version of Mac OS is installed on your computer? I explain how to find out on the next page.

■ To run Mac OS 9-compatible applications in the Classic environment, Mac OS 9.1 or later must also be installed on your computer. The Classic environment is discussed in **Chapter 18**.

# Determining Which Mac OS Versions Are Installed

In order to know which installation and configuration steps you need to perform, you must first learn which versions of Mac OS are installed. There are several ways to do this; the easiest is to consult the Startup Disk control panel (on Mac OS 9.2.2 or earlier) or the Startup Disk pane of System Preferences (on Mac OS X or later).

## ✔ Tips

■ If your computer is brand new and you haven't started it yet, chances are you have Mac OS X 10.4 installed. When you start your computer, it'll display the Mac OS Setup assistant. Skip ahead to the section titled "Configuring Mac OS X 10.4" later in this chapter.

■ A quick way to tell whether your computer is currently running Mac OS 9.2 or earlier or Mac OS X or later is to consult the Apple menu icon on the far left end of the menu bar. A six-color apple appears on Mac OS 9.2 or earlier; a blue apple appears on Mac OS X or later.

## To check the Startup Disk control panel on Mac OS 9.2 or earlier

1. Choose Apple > Control Panels > Startup Disk (**Figure 1**) to display the Startup Disk control panel.

2. If necessary, click the triangle beside the name of your hard disk to display the System folders installed on your computer (**Figures 2** and 3). The Version column indicates which versions of Mac OS are installed.

3. Click the Startup Disk control panel's close box to dismiss it.

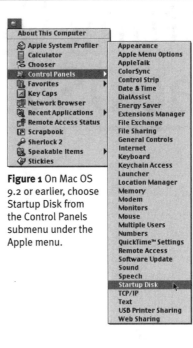

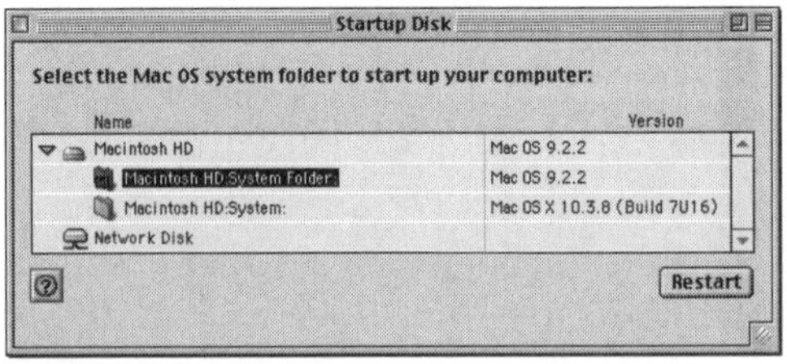

**Figure 1** On Mac OS 9.2 or earlier, choose Startup Disk from the Control Panels submenu under the Apple menu.

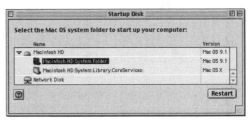

**Figure 2** Here's what the Startup Disk control panel might look like with Mac OS 9.1 and Mac OS X installed...

**Figure 3** ...and here's what the Startup Disk control panel might look like with Mac OS 9.2.2 and Mac OS X 10.3.8 installed.

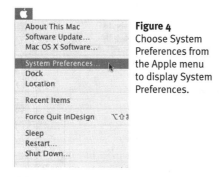

**Figure 4**
Choose System Preferences from the Apple menu to display System Preferences.

**Figure 5** The System Preferences window looks like this in Mac OS X 10.0.x...

**Figure 6** ...and like this in Mac OS X 10.2.8.

**Figure 7** Here's what the Startup Disk pane might look like with Mac OS 9.1 and Mac OS X 10.0 installed...

## To check the Startup Disk preferences pane on Mac OS X or later

1. Choose Apple > System Preferences (**Figure 4**) to display the System Preferences window (**Figures 5** and **6**).

2. Click the Startup Disk icon to display the Startup Disk preferences pane (**Figures 7** and **8**). The installed versions of Mac OS appear beneath each System folder icon.

3. Choose System Preferences > Quit System Preferences (**Figure 9**), or press ⌘Q to dismiss System Preferences.

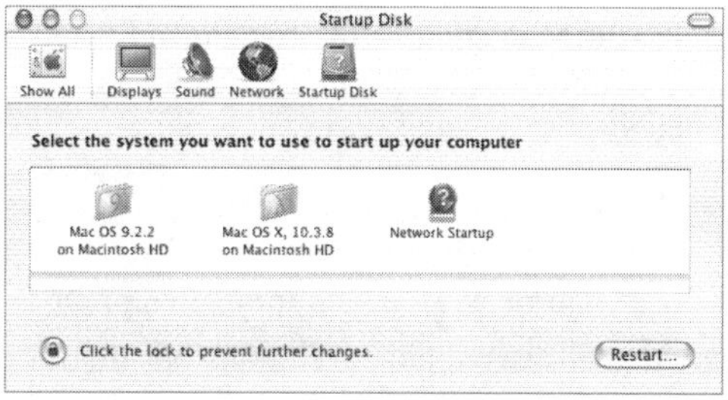

**Figure 8** ...and here's what it might look like with Mac OS 9.2.2 and Mac OS X 10.3.8 installed.

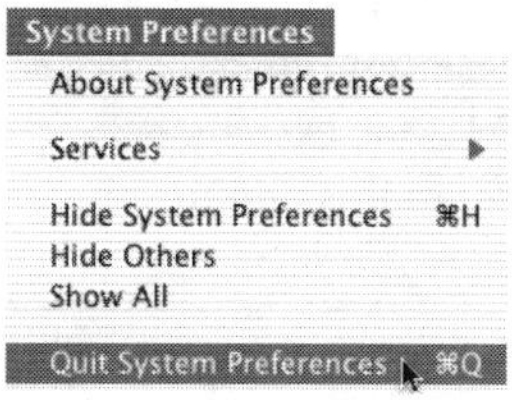

**Figure 9**
Choose Quit System Preferences from the System Preferences menu to dismiss System Preferences.

# Installing Mac OS X 10.4

Mac OS X's installer application handles all aspects of a Mac OS X installation. It restarts your computer from the Mac OS X Install DVD, then displays step-by-step instructions to install Mac OS X 10.4 from its install disc. When the installation process is finished, the installer automatically restarts your computer from your hard disk and displays the Mac OS Setup Assistant so you can configure Mac OS X 10.4 for your use.

This part of the chapter explains how to install and configure Mac OS X. Unfortunately, since there's no way to take screen shots of the Mac OS X installation and configuration procedure, this part of the chapter won't be very "visual." Follow along closely and you'll get all the information you need to complete the installation and configuration process without any problems.

## ✔ Tips

- The installation instructions in this chapter assume you know basic Mac OS techniques, such as pointing, clicking, double-clicking, dragging, and selecting items from a menu. If you're brand new to the Mac and don't know any of these techniques, skip ahead to **Chapter 2,** which discusses Mac OS basics.

- You can click the Go Back button in an installer window at any time during installation to change options in a previous window.

- Remember, you can skip using the Mac OS X 10.4 installer if Mac OS X 10.4 or later is already installed on your computer. Consult the section titled "Determining Which Mac OS Versions Are Installed" earlier in this chapter to see what is installed on your computer.

**Figure 10**
When you insert the Mac OS X Install DVD, its icon appears on the desktop...

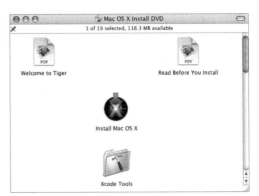

**Figure 11** ...and a Mac OS X Install DVD window opens.

**Figure 12** The Mac OS X installer prompts you to restart your computer.

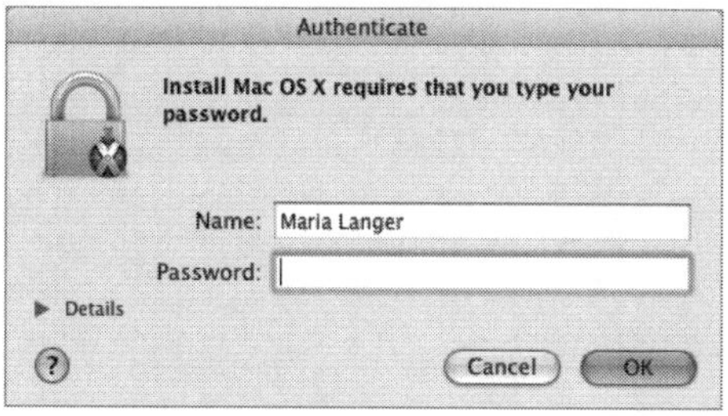

Authenticate

Install Mac OS X requires that you type your password.

Name: Maria Langer

Password:

▶ Details

(?)                    Cancel    OK

**Figure 13** If you're upgrading an existing installation of Mac OS X, you'll have to enter an administrator name and password to complete the installation.

**Figure 14** The installer comes with a file full of important information about Mac OS X 10.4 compatibility and other issues.

## ✔ Tips

- It's a good idea to open and read the file named Read Before You Install that's included on the Mac OS X Install DVD (**Figure 11**). This document (**Figure 14**) contains important information about compatibility and other installation issues.

- The Authenticate dialog (**Figure 13**) prevents someone without administrator privileges from installing system software. This is especially important on a computer used by more than one person.

## To launch the Mac OS X installer & select an installation language

1. Insert the Mac OS X Install DVD disc in your drive. A Mac OS X Install DVD icon should appear on your desktop (**Figure 10**), along with a Mac OS X Install DVD window (**Figure 11**).

2. Double-click the Install Mac OS X icon.

3. An Install Mac OS X dialog appears (**Figure 12**). Click Restart.

4. If you're using any version of Mac OS X, an authenticate dialog like the one in **Figure 13** may appear. Enter the name and password for an administrator and click OK.

5. Wait while Mac OS X and the installer load from the DVD disc.

6. In the first window that appears, select the primary language you want to use with the installer and Mac OS X.

7. Click the right arrow button.

8. Continue following the instructions in the section titled "To install Mac OS X" on the next page.

- These instructions assume you're installing in English. Obviously, the onscreen instructions will be different if you're installing in another language!

LAUNCHING THE MAC OS X INSTALLER

## To install Mac OS X

1. Read the information in the Introduction ("Welcome to the Mac OS X Installer") window.

2. Click Continue.

3. Read the information in the License ("Software License Agreement") window.

4. Click Continue.

5. Click the Agree button in the dialog sheet that appears.

6. In the Select Destination ("Select a Destination") window, click to select the icon for the disk on which you want to install Mac OS X. A green arrow appears on the disk icon. The installer automatically knows if it has to upgrade an existing Mac OS X installation or install Mac OS X 10.4 from scratch.

7. To set advanced installation options, click the Options button. A dialog sheet offers up to three options, depending on what is already installed on the destination disk. Select one of these options and click OK:

   ▲ **Upgrade Mac OS X** upgrades an existing Mac OS X installation to Mac OS X 10.4.

   ▲ **Archive and Install** moves existing Mac OS X System files to a folder named Previous System and installs Mac OS X 10.4 from scratch. You might want to use this option if you suspect there's something wrong with your Mac OS X installation and you want to force the installer to start fresh. If you select this option, you can turn on the Preserve Users and Networks Settings check box to automatically move all existing Mac OS X settings to the new installation. This also skips the Setup Assistant.

▲ **Erase and Install** completely erases the destination disk and installs Mac OS X 10.4 from scratch. Use this option only after backing up your data, since all data on the disk will be lost. If you select this option, choose a disk format from the "Format disk as" pop-up menu; your options are Mac OS Extended and Unix File System.

8. Click Continue.

9. In the Installation Type ("Easy Install") window, you have two options:

   ▲ To perform a standard Mac OS X 10.4 installation, click the Install button.

   ▲ To perform a custom Mac OS X 10.4 installation, click the Customize button. In the Custom Install window that appears, toggle check marks to specify which Mac OS X components should be installed. Then click Install.

10. Wait while software from the DVD is installed. A status area dialog tells you what the installer is doing and may indicate how much longer the installation will take.

   When the installer is finished, it ejects the disc, restarts the computer, and displays the first screen of the Setup Assistant.

**INSTALLING MAC OS X**

*Continued on next page...*

*Continued from previous page.*

## ✔ Tips

■ If necessary, in step 3 you can use the pop-up menu to select a different language for the license agreement.

■ In step 5, if you click the Disagree button, you will not be able to install Mac OS X.

■ A note beneath the disk icons in step 6 indicates how much space is available on each disk. You can see how much space a Mac OS X installation takes by looking at the bottom of the window. Make sure the disk you select has enough space for the installation.

■ Step 7 is optional. If you follow step 7 and don't know what to select, click Cancel to use the default installation option.

■ In step 7, if you select the Erase and Install option and don't know what disk format to choose from the pop-up menu, choose Mac OS Extended (Journaled). (If you wanted the Unix File System option, you'd know it.)

■ The Customize option in step 9 is provided for Mac OS X "power users" and should only be utilized if you have a complete understanding of Mac OS X components and features.

# Configuring Mac OS X 10.4

When your computer restarts after a Mac OS X installation, the Mac OS X Setup Assistant automatically appears. This program uses a simple question-and-answer process to get information about you and the way you use your computer. The information you provide is automatically entered in the various System Preferences panes of Mac OS X to configure your computer for Mac OS X.

## ✔ Tips

■ If you just bought your Macintosh and Mac OS X is installed, the first time you start your computer, you'll see the Mac OS X Setup Assistant described here. Follow these instructions to configure your computer.

■ If the Mac OS X Setup Assistant does not appear, Mac OS X is already configured. You can skip this section.

■ If you upgraded from a previous version of Mac OS X to Mac OS X 10.4 only some of the Mac OS X Setup Assistant screens will appear and many of them may already contain configuration information. Follow along with the instructions in this section if you need help entering missing information.

■ I managed to get some screen shots of the Mac OS X Setup Assistant when I upgraded Mac OS X on my production Mac. So although not all steps are illustrated here, there are enough screen shots to give you an idea of what you'll see when you configure Mac OS X.

## To configure Mac OS X

1. In the Welcome window that appears after installing Mac OS X, select the name of the country you're in. Click Continue.

2. In the Do You Already Own a Mac? window, select an options and click Continue:

   ▲ **Transfer my information from another Mac** enables you to use a FireWire cable to connect your Mac to another Mac and transfer configuration settings from the other Mac. If you choose this option, continue following the instructions that appear onscreen. You should be able to skip most of the rest of these steps.

   ▲ **Transfer my information from another partition on this Mac** transfers configuration settings from another disk partition on your computer. (This option is only available if Mac OS is installed on a second partition on your computer's hard disk.) If you choose this option, continue following the instructions that appear onscreen. You should be able to skip most of the rest of these steps.

   ▲ **Do not transfer my information** does not transfer any configuration information.

3. In the Select Your Keyboard window, select a keyboard layout. Click Continue.

4. The Mac OS Setup Assistant attempts to determine how you connect to the Internet by sensing connections. It then displays appropriate screens for configuring your connection. If the options that appear are correct for your setup, continue following the instructions in step 6. If the options are not appropriate for your setup, click the Different Network Setup button and continue following the instructions in step 5.

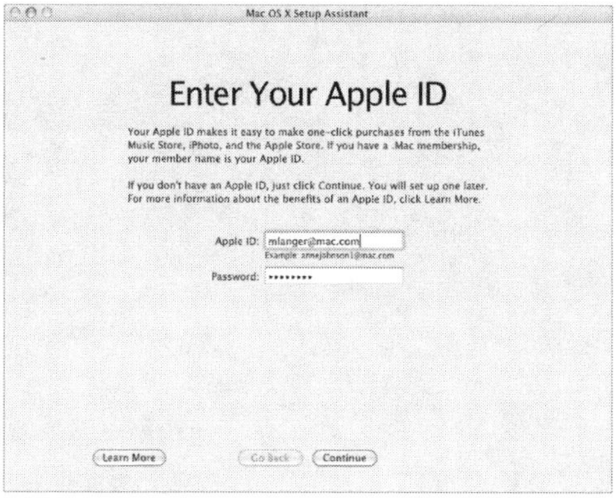

**Figure 15** The Mac OS X Setup Assistant prompts you to enter your Apple ID and password.

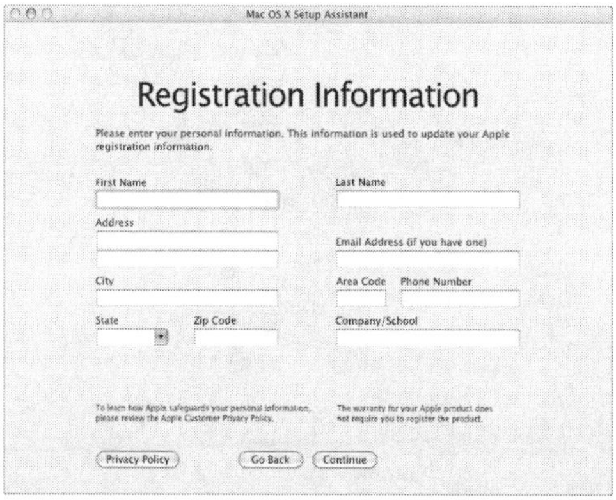

**Figure 16** You'll have to fill in this form with registration information.

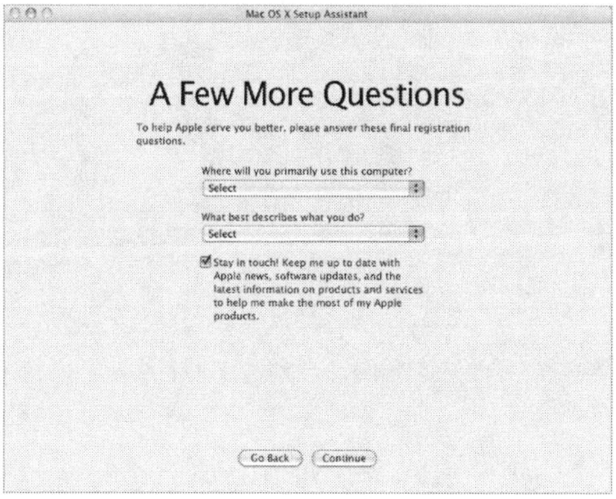

**Figure 17** Answer some marketing questions in this window.

5. In the How Do You Connect? window that appears, select one of the options for how you connect to the Internet and click Continue:

   ▲ **AirPort wireless** requires a wireless network and an AirPort card or base station attached to your computer.

   ▲ **Telephone modem** uses your computer's internal modem or an external modem.

   ▲ **Cable modem** uses a cable modem connected to your computer via Ethernet or USB cable.

   ▲ **DSL modem** uses a DSL modem connected to your computer via Ethernet.

   ▲ **Local network (Ethernet)** uses an Ethernet network. This option is common at workplaces.

   ▲ **My computer does not connect to the Internet** is for computers that are not connected to the Internet in any way. Skip ahead to step 8.

6. Enter information in the screen that appears to provide information about your Internet service or local area network and click Continue.

7. The Enter Your Apple ID window appears (**Figure 15**). If you have an Apple ID, enter it and your password. If you don't, leave both boxes blank. Then click Continue.

8. In the Registration Information window (**Figure 16**), fill in the form. You can press [Tab] to move from one field to another. Click Continue.

9. In the A Few More Questions window (**Figure 17**), use pop-up menus to answer two marketing questions. Turn on the check box to get information about Apple products via e-mail. Then click Continue.

*Continued on next page...*

**CONFIGURING MAC OS X**

*Continued from previous page.*

10. In the Create Your Account window, fill in the form to enter information to set up your Mac OS X account:

    ▲ **Name** is your full name.

    ▲ **Short Name** is a short version of your name that is used for networking. I usually use my first initial followed by my last name: *mlanger*.

    ▲ **Password** is a password you want to use with your account.

    ▲ **Verify** is the same password you entered in the Password box.

    ▲ **Password hint** is a hint that will remind you what your password is. Don't use this box to enter your password again, since it will appear when you cannot successfully log into your account.

    When you're finished entering account information, click Continue.

11. If you do not have an Internet connection, the Set Date and Time window may appear. Set the date and time and click Continue.

12. If you're a .Mac member, the Automatically Renew .Mac window may appear (**Figure 18**). To automatically renew your .Mac account, turn on the check box and click Continue. If you'd prefer not to automatically renew, just click Continue. Then click Continue in the Thanks for being a .Mac Member window.

13. Continue following the steps in the section titled "To finish the installation" on the next page.

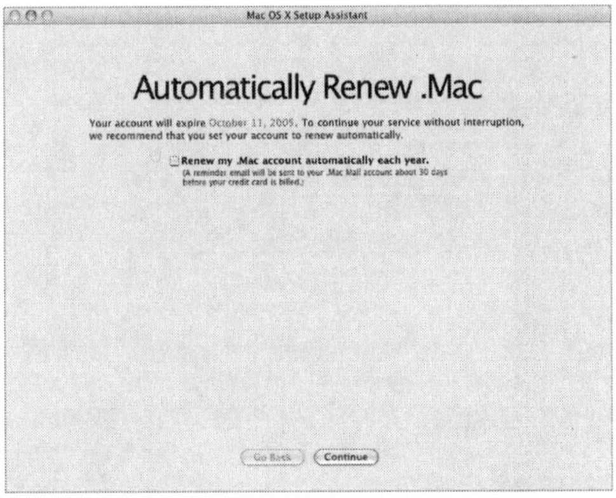

**Figure 18** If you're a .Mac member, you can turn on the check box to automatically renew .Mac every year.

## ✔ Tips

- If your country is not listed in step 1, turn on the Show All check box to display more options.

- In step 3, you can turn on the Show All check box to show additional keyboard layouts.

- In step 8, if you have a .Mac account and a connection to the Internet. your contact information may already be filled in based on data stored on Apple's .Mac server.

- In step 8, you can learn about Apple's privacy policy by clicking the Privacy button. When you're finished reading the information in the dialog sheet that appears, click OK to dismiss it and return to the Registration Information window.

- When you enter your password in steps 7 and 10, it displays as bullet characters. That's why you enter it twice: so you're sure you entered what you thought you did the first time.

- Remember the password you enter in step 10! If you forget your password, you may not be able to use your computer. It's a good idea to use the Password Hint field to enter a hint that makes your password impossible to forget.

CONFIGURING MAC OS X

## To finish the installation

In the Thank You window that appears, click Go.

The Mac OS X Desktop appears with your Home folder window and the Mac OS X Install DVD window open (**Figure 20**).

## ✔ Tips

- I explain how to work with the Mac OS Desktop and Finder in **Chapters 2 through 4**.

- To eject the Install DVD, press the Eject Media button on your keyboard or drag the DVD icon to the Trash icon in the Dock. I tell you more about ejecting discs in **Chapter 3**.

- The Software Update utility may run right after installing Mac OS X 10.4. If any software updates are available for your computer, a dialog with update information appears. I explain how to use Software Update in **Chapter 21**.

- If you chose the Install and Archive option when you installed Mac OS X 10.4, a folder named Previous Systems appears on your hard disk (**Figure 21**). You can move items you need out of that folder and into appropriate locations on your hard disk. Delete this folder if it is no longer needed. You may have to enter an administrator's password to delete it.

**Figure 19** This screen appears at the very end of the configuration process.

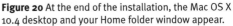

**Figure 20** At the end of the installation, the Mac OS X 10.4 desktop and your Home folder window appear.

**Figure 21** A Previous Systems folder appears on your hard disk if you performed a "clean" installation of Mac OS X 10.4 using the Archive and Install installation option discussed earlier in this chapter.

# Finder
# Basics

## The Finder & Desktop

The *Finder* is a program that is part of Mac OS. It launches automatically when you start your computer.

The Finder provides a graphic user interface called the *desktop* (**Figure 1**) that you can use to open, copy, delete, list, organize, and perform other operations on computer files.

This chapter provides important instructions for using the Finder and items that appear on the Mac OS X desktop. It's important that you understand how to use these basic Finder techniques, since you'll use them again and again every time you work with your computer.

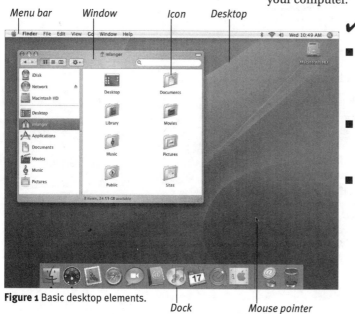

Menu bar    Window    Icon    Desktop

**Figure 1** Basic desktop elements.

Dock    Mouse pointer

## ✔ Tips

- You never have to manually launch the Finder; it always starts automatically.

- Under normal circumstances, you cannot quit the Finder.

- If you're new to Mac OS, don't skip this chapter. It provides the basic information you'll need to use your computer successfully.

# The Mouse

Mac OS, like most graphic user interface systems, uses the mouse as an input device. There are several basic mouse techniques you must know to use your computer:

◆ **Point** to a specific item onscreen.

◆ **Click** an item to select it.

◆ **Double-click** an item to open it.

◆ **Press** an item to activate it.

◆ **Drag** to move an item or select multiple items.

## ✔ Tip

■ Some computers use either a trackball or a trackpad instead of a mouse.

## To point

1. Move the mouse on the work surface or mouse pad.

   *or*

   Use your fingertips to move the ball of the trackball.

   *or*

   Move the tip of one finger (usually your forefinger) on the surface of the trackpad.

   The mouse pointer, which usually looks like an arrow (**Figure** 2), moves on your computer screen.

2. When the tip of the mouse pointer's arrow is on the item you want to point to (**Figure** 3), stop moving it.

## ✔ Tip

■ The tip of the mouse pointer is its "business end."

**Figure 2** The mouse pointer usually looks like an arrow pointer when you are working in the Finder.

Applications

**Figure 3** Move the mouse pointer so the arrow's tip is on the item to which you want to point.

USING THE MOUSE

**Figure 4**
Click to select
an icon...

**Figure 5** ...or an item in a list.

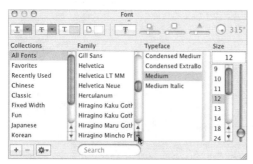

**Figure 6** Press a scroll bar arrow to activate it.

**Figure 7** Drag to move items
such as folders.

# To click

1.  Point to the item you want to click.

2.  Press (and release) the mouse button once. The item you clicked becomes selected (**Figures 4** and **5**).

# To double-click

1.  Point to the item you want to double-click.

2.  Press (and release) the mouse button twice quickly. The item you double-clicked opens.

## ✔ Tip

■   Keep the mouse pointer still while double-clicking. If you move the mouse pointer during the double-click process, you may move the item instead of double-clicking it.

# To press

1.  Point to the item you want to press.

2.  Press and hold the mouse button without moving the mouse. The item you are pressing is activated (**Figure 6**).

## ✔ Tip

■   The press technique is often used when working with scroll bars, as shown in **Figure 6**, where pressing is the same as clicking repeatedly.

# To drag

1.  Point to the item you want to drag.

2.  Press the mouse button down.

3.  While holding the mouse button down, move the mouse pointer. The item you are dragging moves (**Figure 7**).

**USING THE MOUSE**

# Menus

The Finder—and most other Mac OS programs—offers menus full of options. There are four types of menus in Mac OS X:

◆ A **pull-down menu** appears on the menu bar at the top of the screen (**Figure 8**).

◆ A **submenu** appears when a menu option with a right-pointing triangle is selected (**Figure 9**).

◆ A **pop-up menu**, which displays a triangle (or arrow), appears within a window (**Figures 10** and **11**).

◆ A **contextual menu** appears when you hold down [Control] while clicking an item (**Figure 12**).

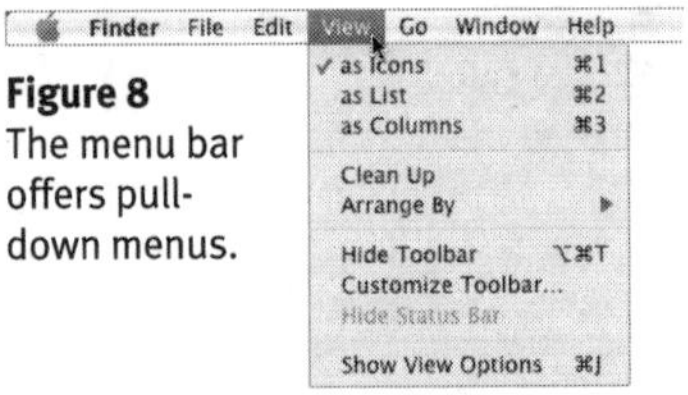

## ✔ Tips

■ A menu option followed by an ellipsis (…) (**Figure 8**) will display a dialog when chosen. Dialogs are discussed in detail in **Chapter 7**.

■ A menu option that is dimmed or gray cannot be chosen. The commands that are available vary depending on what is selected on the desktop or in a window.

■ A menu option preceded by a check mark (**Figure 8**) is enabled, or "turned on."

■ A menu option followed by a series of keyboard characters (**Figure 8**) has a keyboard shortcut. Keyboard shortcuts are discussed later in this chapter.

■ Contextual menus only display options that apply to the item you are pointing to.

■ In Mac OS X, menus are slightly translucent. Although this makes them look cool on screen, it doesn't always look good when illustrated on paper.

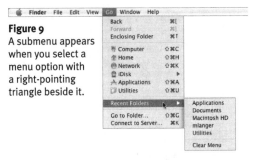

**Figure 8**
The menu bar offers pull-down menus.

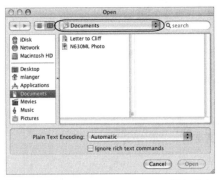

**Figure 9**
A submenu appears when you select a menu option with a right-pointing triangle beside it.

**Figure 10** Pop-up menus can appear within dialogs.

**Figure 11** To display a pop-up menu, click it.

**Figure 12**
A contextual menu appears when you hold down [Control] while clicking.

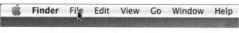

**Figure 13** Point to the menu name.

**Figure 14** Click (or press) to display the menu.

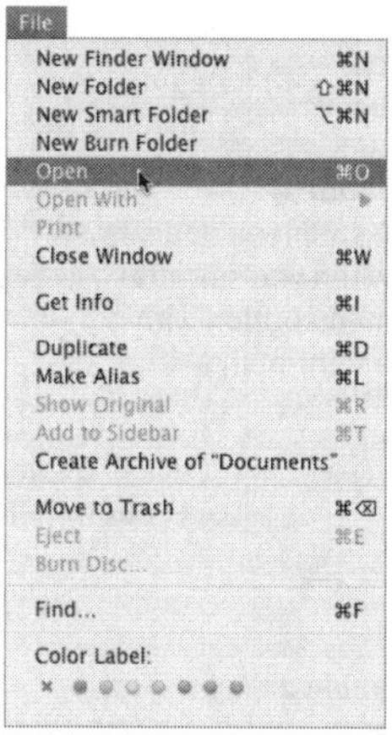

**Figure 15** Click (or drag) to choose the menu option you want.

**Figure 16**
Hold down Control while pointing to an item.

Users

**Figure 17** A contextual menu appears when you click.

**Figure 18** Click (or drag) to choose the option you want.

## To use a menu

1. Point to the name of the menu (**Figure 13**).

2. Click. The menu opens, displaying its options (**Figure 14**).

3. Point to the menu option you want (**Figure 15**).

4. Click to choose the option. The menu disappears.

## ✔ Tips

■ Mac OS X's menus are "sticky menus"— each menu opens and stays open when you click its name.

■ To close a menu without choosing an option, click outside the menu.

■ This book uses the following notation to indicate menu commands: *Menu Name* > *Submenu Name* (if necessary) > *Command Name*. For example, the instructions for choosing the Documents command from the Recent Folders submenu under the Go menu (**Figure 9**) would be: "choose Go > Recent Folders > Documents."

## To use a contextual menu

1. Point to the item on which you want to act.

2. Press and hold down Control (**Figure 16**).

3. Click. A contextual menu appears at the item (**Figure 17**).

4. Click the menu option you want (**Figure 18**).

## ✔ Tip

■ Contextual menus are similar to the Action pop-up menu. I tell you about this Mac OS X feature later in this chapter.

**USING MENUS**

# The Keyboard

The keyboard offers another way to communicate with your computer. In addition to typing text and numbers, you can use it to choose menu commands.

There are three types of keys on a Mac OS keyboard:

◆ **Character keys**, such as letters, numbers, and symbols, are for typing information. Some character keys have special functions, as listed in **Table 1**.

◆ **Modifier keys** alter the meaning of a character key being pressed or the meaning of a mouse action. Modifier keys are listed in **Table 2**.

◆ **Function keys** perform specific functions in Mac OS or an application. Dedicated function keys, which always do the same thing, are listed in **Table 3**. Function keys labeled (F1) through (F15) on the keyboard can be assigned specific functions by applications. (The number of function keys vary depending on the keyboard model.)

## ✔ Tips

■ (⌘) is called the *Command key* (not the Apple key).

■ Contextual menus are discussed on the previous page.

Table 1

| Special Character Keys | |
|---|---|
| Key | Function |
| (Enter) | Enters information or "clicks" a default button. |
| (Return) | Begins a new paragraph or line or "clicks" a default button. |
| (Tab) | Advances to the next tab stop or the next item in a sequence. |
| (Delete) | Deletes a selection or the character to the left of the insertion point. |
| (Del) | Deletes a selection or the character to the right of the insertion point. |
| (Esc) | "Clicks" a Cancel button or ends the operation that is currently in progress. |

Table 2

| Modifier Keys | |
|---|---|
| Key | Function |
| (Shift) | Produces uppercase characters or symbols. Also works with the mouse to extend selections and to restrain movement in graphic applications. |
| (Option) | Produces special symbols. |
| (⌘) | Accesses menu commands via keyboard shortcuts. |
| (Control) | Modifies the functions of other keys and displays contextual menus. |

Table 3

| Dedicated Function Keys | |
|---|---|
| Key | Function |
| (Help) | Displays onscreen help. |
| (Home) | Scrolls to the beginning. |
| (End) | Scrolls to the end. |
| (Page Up) | Scrolls up one page. |
| (Page Down) | Scrolls down one page. |
| (←)(→)(↑)(↓) | Moves the insertion point or changes the selection. |

## To use a keyboard shortcut

1. Hold down the modifier key(s) in the sequence. This is usually (⌘ ⌘), but can be (Option), (Control), or (Shift).

2. Press the letter, number, or symbol key in the sequence.

For example, to choose the Open command, which can be found under the File menu (**Figure 15**), hold down (⌘ ⌘) and press (O).

## ✔ Tips

- You can learn keyboard shortcuts by observing the key sequences that appear to the right of some menu commands (**Figures 8**, **9**, and **14**).

- Some commands include more than one modifier key. You must hold all modifier keys down while pressing the letter, number, or symbol key for the keyboard shortcut.

- You can find a list of all Finder keyboard shortcuts in **Appendix A**.

- Some applications refer to keyboard shortcuts as *keyboard equivalents* or *shortcut keys*.

# Icons

Mac OS uses icons to graphically represent files and other items on the desktop, in the Dock, or within Finder windows:

◆ **Applications** (**Figure 19**) are programs you use to get work done. **Chapters 7** through **9** discuss working with applications.

◆ **Documents** (**Figure 20**) are the files created by applications. **Chapter 7** covers working with documents.

◆ **Folders** (**Figure 21**) are used to organize files. **Chapters 3** and **4** discuss using folders.

◆ **Volumes** (**Figure 22**), including hard disks, CDs, DVDs, iPods, and network disks, are used to store data. **Chapter 3** covers working with volumes.

◆ The **Trash** (**Figure 23**), which is in the Dock, is for discarding items you no longer want and for ejecting removable media. The Trash is covered in **Chapter 3**.

## ✔ Tip

■ Icons can appear a number of different ways, depending on the view and view options chosen for a window. Windows are discussed later in this chapter; views are discussed in **Chapter 3**.

TextEdit       Preview       Microsoft Word

**Figure 19** Application icons.

Letter       Picture.gif       Note

**Figure 20** Document icons, including a TextEdit document, a Preview document, and a Word document.

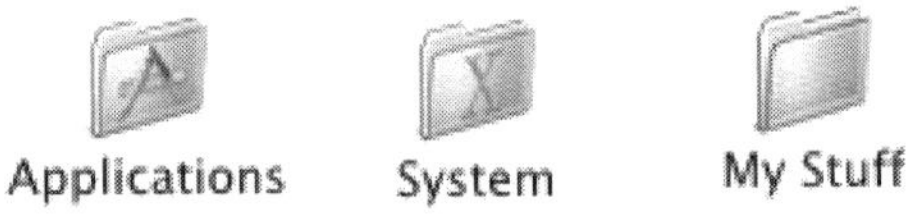

Applications       System       My Stuff

**Figure 21** Folder icons.

Macintosh HD       iDisk       Network

**Figure 22** Three different volume icons: hard disk, iDisk, and Network.

**Figure 23** The three faces of the Trash icon in the Dock: empty, full, and while dragging removable media.

Figure 24 To select an icon, click it.

Figure 25 Hold down ⌘ ⌘ while clicking other icons to add them to a multiple selection.

## To select an icon

Click the icon that you want to select. The icon darkens, and its name becomes highlighted (**Figure 24**).

## ✔ Tip

- You can also select an icon in an active window by pressing the keyboard key for the first letter of the icon's name or by pressing (Tab), (Shift)(Tab), ←, →, ↑, or ↓ until the icon is selected.

## To deselect an icon

Click anywhere in the window or on the Desktop other than on the selected icon.

## ✔ Tips

- If you select one icon and then click another icon, the originally selected icon is deselected and the icon you clicked becomes selected instead.

- Windows are discussed later in this chapter.

## To select multiple icons by clicking

1. Click the first icon that you want to select.

2. Hold down ⌘ ⌘ and click another icon that you want to select (**Figure 25**).

3. Repeat step 2 until all icons that you want to select have been selected.

## ✔ Tip

- Icons that are part of a multiple selection must be in the same window.

## To select multiple icons by dragging

1. Position the mouse pointer slightly above and to the left of the first icon in the group that you want to select (**Figure 26**).

2. Press the mouse button, and drag diagonally across the icons you want to select. A shaded box appears to indicate the selection area, and the items within it become selected (**Figure 27**).

3. When all the icons that you want to select are included in the selection area, release the mouse button (**Figure 28**).

### ✔ Tip

■ To select multiple icons by dragging, the icons must be adjacent.

## To select all icons in a window

Choose Edit > Select All (**Figure 29**), or press Ⓒ ⌘Ⓐ.

All icons in the active window are selected.

### ✔ Tip

■ Activating windows is covered later in this chapter.

## To deselect one icon in a multiple selection

Hold down Ⓒ ⌘ while clicking the icon that you want to deselect. That icon is deselected while the others remain selected.

**Figure 26** Position the mouse pointer above and to the left of the first icon that you want to select.

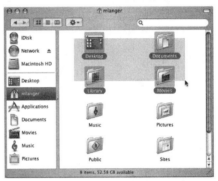

**Figure 27** Drag to draw a shaded selection box around the icons that you want to select.

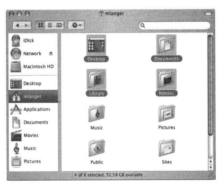

**Figure 28** Release the mouse button to complete the selection.

**Figure 29** Choose Select All from the Edit menu to select all items.

**Figure 30** Point to the icon that you want to move.

**Figure 31** Drag the icon to the new location.

**Figure 32** Release the mouse button to complete the move.

# To move an icon

1.  Position the mouse pointer on the icon that you want to move (**Figure 30**).

2.  Press the mouse button, and drag the icon to the new location. As you drag, a shadowy image of the icon moves with the mouse pointer (**Figure 31**).

3.  Release the mouse button when the icon is in the desired position (**Figure 32**).

# ✔ Tips

■  You cannot drag to reposition icons within windows set to list or column view. Views are discussed in **Chapter 3**.

■  You move icons to rearrange them in a window or on the desktop, or to copy or move the items they represent to another folder or disk. Copying and moving items is discussed in **Chapter 3**.

■  You can also move multiple icons at once. Simply select the icons first, then position the mouse pointer on one of the selected icons and follow steps 2 and 3 above. All selected icons move together.

■  To force an icon to snap to a window's invisible grid, hold down ⌃⌘ while dragging it. The grid, which I tell you more about in **Chapter 4**, ensures consistent spacing between icons, so your window looks neat.

**MOVING ICONS**

**25**

## To open an icon

1. Select the icon you want to open (**Figure 33**).

2. Choose File > Open (**Figure 34**), or press ⌃⌘O.

*Or*

Double-click the icon that you want to open.

## ✔ Tips

- Only one click is necessary when opening an item in a Finder window toolbar or the Dock. The toolbar and Dock are covered in detail later in this chapter.

- What happens when you open an icon depends on the type of icon you open. For example:

  ▲ Opening a disk or folder icon displays the contents of the disk or folder in the same Finder window (**Figure 35**). Windows are discussed next.

  ▲ Opening an application icon launches the application so that you can work with it. Working with applications is covered in **Chapter 7** and elsewhere in this book.

  ▲ Opening a document icon launches the application that created that document and displays the document so you can view or edit it. Working with documents is covered in **Chapter 7**.

  ▲ Opening the Trash displays items that will be deleted when you empty the Trash. Using and emptying the Trash is discussed in **Chapter 3**.

- To open a folder or disk in a new Finder window, hold down ⌃⌘ while opening it.

- The File menu's Open With submenu, which is discussed in **Chapter 7**, enables you to open a document with a specific application.

**Figure 33** Select the icon.

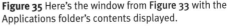

**Figure 34** Choose Open from the File menu.

**Figure 35** Here's the window from **Figure 33** with the Applications folder's contents displayed.

OPENING ICONS

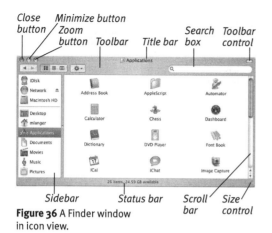

Close button / Minimize button / Zoom button / Toolbar / Title bar / Search box / Toolbar control

**Figure 36** A Finder window in icon view.

Sidebar / Status bar / Scroll bar / Size control

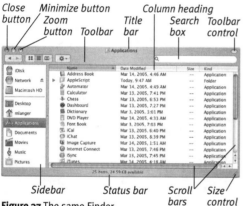

Close button / Minimize button / Zoom button / Toolbar / Title bar / Column heading / Search box / Toolbar control

**Figure 37** The same Finder window in list view.

Sidebar / Status bar / Scroll bars / Size control

## ✔ Tips

- By default, when you open a folder or disk icon, its contents appear in the active window. As discussed in **Chapter 4**, you can use Finder Preferences to tell Mac OS X to open folders in new windows.

- I cover the Finder's three window views in **Chapter 3**, the toolbar and Sidebar later in this chapter, the status bar in **Chapter 4**, and Spotlight in **Chapter 5**.

# Windows

Mac OS makes extensive use of windows for displaying icons and other information in the Finder and documents in other applications. **Figures 36** and **37** show two different views of a Finder window.

Each window includes a variety of controls you can use to manipulate it:

- The **close button** closes the window.

- The **minimize button** collapses the window to an icon in the Dock.

- The **zoom button** toggles the window's size between full size and a custom size.

- The **toolbar** displays buttons and controls for working with Finder windows.

- The **title bar** displays the window's icon and name.

- The **Search box** enables you to search for files using Spotlight.

- The **toolbar hide control** toggles the display of the toolbar.

- The **Sidebar**, which is customizable, shows commonly accessed volumes and folders, including the default folders in your Home folder.

- The **status bar** provides information about items in a window and space available on disk.

- The **size control** enables you to set a custom size for the window.

- **Scroll bars** scroll the contents of the window.

- **Column headings** (in list view only) display the names of the columns and let you quickly sort by a column. (The selected column heading is the column by which the list is sorted.)

## To open a new Finder window

Choose File > New Finder Window
(**Figure 38**), or press ⌘N. A new
Home folder window for your account
appears (**Figure 39**).

### ✔ Tip

■ The Home folder is discussed in **Chapter 3**.

## To open a folder or disk in a new Finder window

Hold down ⌘ while opening a folder or
disk icon. A new window containing the
contents of the folder or disk appears.

### ✔ Tip

■ Opening folders and disks is explained
earlier in this chapter.

## To close a window

Click the window's close button (**Figures 36
and 37**).

*Or*

Choose File > Close Window (**Figure 40**), or
press ⌘W.

## To close all open windows

Hold down Option while clicking the active
window's close button (**Figures 36** and **37**).

*Or*

Hold down Option while choosing File > Close
All (**Figure 41**), or press ⌘Option W.

### ✔ Tip

■ The Close Window/Close All commands
(**Figures 40** and **41**) are examples of
*dynamic menu items*—pressing a modifier key (in this case, Option) changes the
menu command from Close Window
(**Figure 40**) to Close All (**Figure 41**).

**Figure 38**
Choose New Finder
Window from the
File menu.

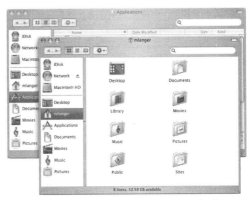

**Figure 39** The active window appears atop all other
windows and the buttons on the left end of its title bar
appear in color.

**Figure 40** Choose Close
Window from the File
menu...

**Figure 41** ...or hold down
Option and choose Close
All from the File menu.

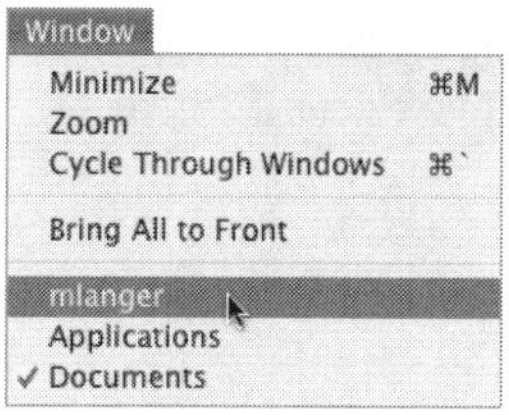

**Figure 42** Choose the name of the window you want to activate from the Window menu.

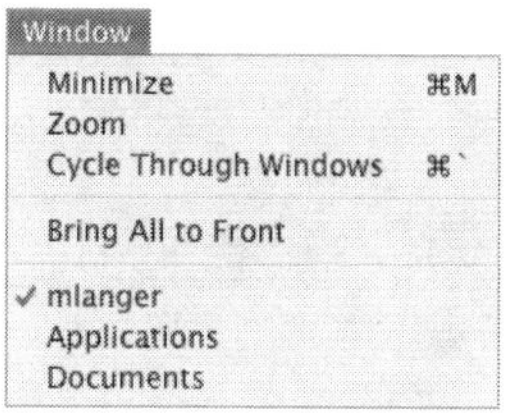

**Figure 43** A check mark appears beside the active window's name.

## To activate a window

Click anywhere in or on the window.

*Or*

Choose the name of the window you want to activate from the Window menu (**Figure 42**).

## ✔ Tips

- Make sure that the window you want to work with is open and active *before* using commands that work on the active window—such as Close Window, Select All, and View menu options.

- You can distinguish between active and inactive windows by the appearance of their title bars; the buttons on the left end of an active window's title bar are in color (**Figure 39**). In addition, a check mark appears beside the active window's name in the Window menu (**Figure 43**).

- When two or more windows overlap, the active window will always be on top of the stack (**Figure 39**).

- You can use the Cycle Through Windows command (**Figure 43**) or its handy shortcut, ⌃ ⌘ `, to activate each open window, in sequence.

## To bring all Finder windows to the top

Choose Window > Bring All to Front (**Figure 43**). All open Finder windows that are not minimized are moved in front of any windows opened by other applications.

## ✔ Tip

- Finder windows can be intermingled with other applications' windows. The Bring All to Front command gathers the windows together in the top layers. This command is useful when working with many windows from several different applications.

ACTIVATING WINDOWS

## To move a window

1. Position the mouse pointer on the window's title bar (**Figure 44**) or border.

2. Press the mouse button and drag the window to a new location. As you drag, the window moves along with your mouse pointer (**Figure 45**).

3. When the outline of the window is in the desired position, release the mouse button.

## ✔ Tip

■ As discussed later in this chapter, hiding the toolbar and Sidebar removes window borders. If window borders are not showing, the only way to move a window is to drag its title bar.

## To resize a window

1. Position the mouse pointer on the size control in the lower-right corner of the window (**Figure 46**).

2. Press the mouse button and drag. As you drag, the size control moves with the mouse pointer, changing the size and shape of the window (**Figure 47**).

3. When the window is the desired size, release the mouse button.

## ✔ Tips

■ The larger a window is, the more you can see inside it.

■ By resizing and repositioning windows, you can see inside more than one window at a time. This comes in handy when moving or copying the icons for files and folders from one window to another. Moving and copying files and folders is covered in **Chapter 3**.

**Figure 44** Position the mouse pointer on the title bar.

**Figure 45** As you drag, the window moves.

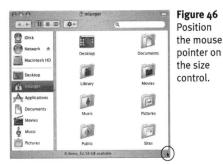

**Figure 46** Position the mouse pointer on the size control.

**Figure 47** As you drag, the window's size and shape changes.

**Figure 48**
The Minimize Window command minimizes the active window.

**Figure 49** Minimized windows shrink down into icons in the Dock.

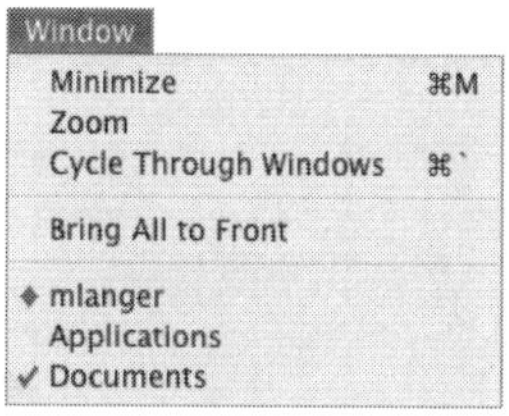

**Figure 50**
A diamond beside a window name indicates that the window has been minimized.

## To minimize a window

Click the window's minimize button (**Figures 36** and **37**).

*Or*

Choose Window > Minimize (**Figure 48**), or press ⌃ ⌘ M.

*Or*

Double-click the window's title bar.

The window shrinks into an icon and slips into the Dock at the bottom of the screen (**Figure 49**).

## ✔ Tip

■ To minimize all windows, hold down Option and choose Windows > Minimize All, or press Option ⌃ ⌘ M.

## To redisplay a minimized window

Click the window's icon in the Dock (**Figure 49**).

*Or*

Choose the window's name from the Window menu (**Figure 50**).

## To zoom a window

Click the window's zoom button (**Figures 36** and **37**).

Each time you click the zoom button, the window's size toggles between two sizes:

◆ **Standard state** size is the smallest possible size that would accommodate the window's contents and still fit on your screen (**Figure 1**).

◆ **User state** size, which is the size you specify with the size control (**Figure 47**).

**MINIMIZING & ZOOMING WINDOWS**

# To scroll a window's contents

Click one of the scroll bar arrows (**Figure 51**) as follows:

◆ To scroll the window's contents up, click the down arrow on the vertical scroll bar.

◆ To scroll the window's contents down, click the up arrow on the vertical scroll bar.

◆ To scroll the window's contents to the left, click the right arrow on the horizontal scroll bar.

◆ To scroll the window's contents to the right, click the left arrow on the horizontal scroll bar.

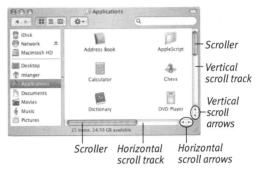

**Figure 51** Scroll bar components.

## ✔ Tips

■ If you have trouble remembering which scroll arrow to click, think of it this way:

▲ Click down to see down.

▲ Click up to see up.

▲ Click right to see right.

▲ Click left to see left.

■ You can also scroll a window's contents by either clicking in the scroll track on either side of the scroller or by dragging the scroller to a new position on the scroll bar. Both of these techniques enable you to scroll a window's contents more quickly.

■ Scroll bars only appear when necessary—when part of a window's contents are hidden. In **Figure 36**, for example, it isn't necessary to scroll from side to side so the horizontal scroll bar does not appear. In **Figure 46**, all of the window's contents are displayed so no scroll bars appear.

■ The scrollers in Mac OS X are proportional—this means that the more of a window's contents you see, the more space the scroller will take up in its scroll bar.

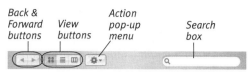

*Back & Forward buttons*    *View buttons*    *Action pop-up menu*    *Search box*

**Figure 52** The toolbar.

**Figure 53** The Action pop-up menu offers commands for working with selected items in a window.

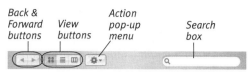

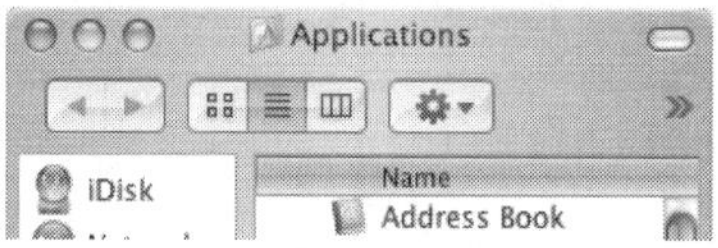

**Figure 54** When the window is narrow, some toolbar items may be hidden.

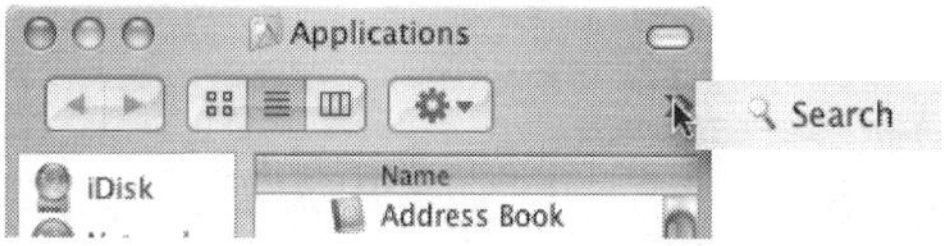

**Figure 55** Click the double arrow to display a menu of hidden items.

# The Toolbar

The toolbar (**Figure 52**) offers navigation tools and view buttons within Finder windows:

◆ The **Back button** displays the previous window's contents.

◆ The **Forward button** displays the window that was showing before you clicked the Back button.

◆ **View buttons** enable you to change the window's view.

◆ The **Action pop-up menu** (**Figure 53**) offers commands for working with an open window or selected object(s) within the window.

◆ **Search box** enables you to quickly search the window for a file by name.

## ✔ Tips

■ The toolbar can be customized to show the items you use most; **Chapter 4** explains how.

■ Does the Action pop-up menu in **Figure 53** look familiar? It should! It's very similar to the contextual menu shown in **Figure 17**.

■ Views are covered in **Chapter 4**, using the Search box is covered in **Chapter 5**, and file management and navigation are discussed in **Chapter 3**.

■ If the window is not wide enough to show all toolbar buttons, a double arrow appears on the right side of the toolbar (**Figure 54**). Click the arrow to display a menu of missing buttons (**Figure 55**), and select the button you want.

## To hide or display the toolbar

Click the toolbar control button (**Figure 56**).

One of two things happens:

◆ If the toolbar is displayed, it disappears (**Figure 56**).

◆ If the toolbar is not displayed, it appears (**Figure 57**).

## ✔ Tip

■ As shown in **Figure 56**, hiding the toolbar also hides the Sidebar (which is discussed on the next page) and window borders and moves the status bar so it appears right beneath the title bar. This makes the window smaller and more like the windows in Mac OS 9 and earlier.

## To use a toolbar button

Click the button once.

## To use the Action pop-up menu

1. If necessary, select the icon(s) for the items you want to work with.

2. Click the Action pop-up menu to display a menu of commands (**Figure 53**).

3. Choose the command you want to use.

*Toolbar control*

**Figure 56** The toolbar control button can hide the toolbar...

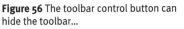

**Figure 57** ...or display it.

WORKING WITH THE TOOLBAR

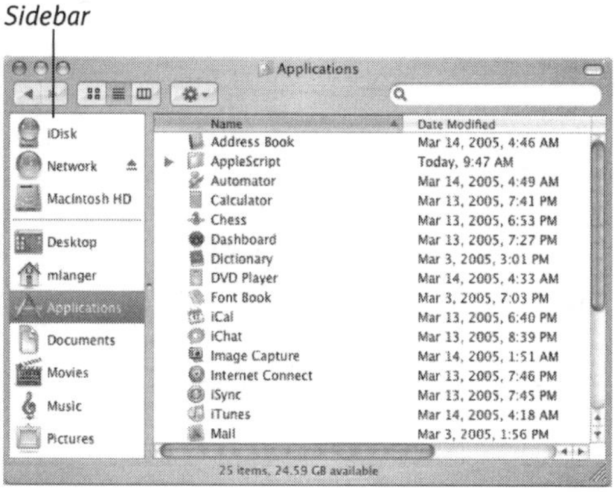

*Sidebar*

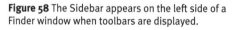

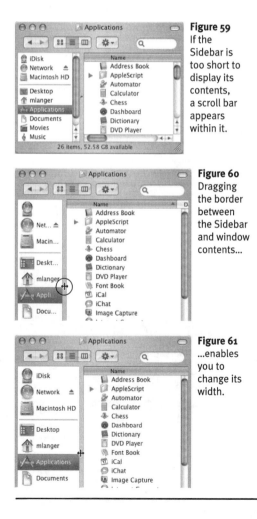

**Figure 58** The Sidebar appears on the left side of a Finder window when toolbars are displayed.

**Figure 59** If the Sidebar is too short to display its contents, a scroll bar appears within it.

**Figure 60** Dragging the border between the Sidebar and window contents...

**Figure 61** ...enables you to change its width.

# The Sidebar

The *Sidebar* appears on the left side of Finder windows when toolbars are displayed (**Figure 58**). It offers quick access to the items you use most.

The Sidebar has two parts:

◆ The upper part of the Sidebar displays icons for volumes that are accessible by your computer, such as your hard disk, iDisk, network disks, and CD and DVD discs.

◆ The lower part of the Sidebar displays icons for the Desktop, your Home folder, and several commonly accessed folders within your Home folder.

## ✔ Tips

■ You can customize the lower part of the Sidebar to display whatever items you want. I explain how in **Chapter 4**.

■ I tell you about your Home folder and volumes in **Chapter 3**.

■ When a window is resized, the size of the Sidebar may also change. If the Sidebar is too short to display its contents, a vertical scroll bar appears within it (**Figure 59**).

■ You can change the width of the Sidebar by dragging the divider between it and the window contents (**Figures 60** and **61**).

## To use the Sidebar

Click the icon for the item you want.

One of two things happens:

◆ If the item was a volume or folder, the window's contents change to display the contents of the item you clicked.

◆ If the item was an application or document, the item opens in its own application window.

# The Dock

The Dock (**Figure 62**) offers easy access to often-used applications and documents, as well as minimized windows.

**Figure 62** The Dock displays often-used applications and documents.

## ✔ Tip

■ The Dock can be customized; **Chapter 6** explains how.

## To identify items in the Dock

Point to the item. The name of the item appears above the Dock (**Figure 63**).

**Figure 63** Point to an icon to see what it represents.

## To identify items in the Dock that are running

Look at the Dock. A triangle appears beneath each item that is running, such as the Finder in **Figures 62**, **63**, and **64**.

**Figure 64** An item's icon bounces while it is being opened.

## To open an item in the Dock

Click the icon for the item you want to open. One of four things happens:

◆ If the icon is for an application that is running, the application becomes the active application.

◆ If the icon is for an application that is not running, the application launches. While the application launches, the icon in the Dock bounces (**Figure 64**) so you know something is happening.

◆ If the icon is for a minimized window, the window is displayed.

◆ If the icon is for a document that is not open, the application that created the document launches (if necessary) and the document opens.

## ✔ Tip

■ Using applications and opening documents is discussed in greater detail in **Chapter 7**; minimizing and displaying windows is discussed earlier in this chapter.

**Figure 65**
Four commands under the Apple menu let you change the work state of your computer.

# Sleeping, Restarting, & Shutting Down

The Apple menu (**Figure 65**) offers several options that change the work state of your computer:

◆ **Sleep** puts the computer into a state where it uses very little power. The screen goes blank and the hard disk may stop spinning.

◆ **Restart** instructs the computer to shut down and immediately start back up.

◆ **Shut Down** closes all open documents and programs, clears memory, and cuts power to the computer.

◆ **Log Out** *User Name* closes all open documents and programs and clears memory. Your computer remains running until you or someone else logs in.

I discuss all of these commands on the following pages.

## ✔ Tips

■ If your computer's keyboard includes a power key, pressing it displays a dialog with buttons for the Restart, Sleep, and Shut Down commands. If your keyboard does not include a power key—most don't these days—you can display the same dialog by holding down Control while pressing the Media Eject button at the top-right corner of the keyboard.

■ Do *not* restart or shut down a computer by simply flicking off the power switch. Doing so prevents the computer from properly closing files, which may result in file corruption and related problems.

■ Mac OS X also includes a screen saver, which automatically starts up when your computer is inactive for five minutes. Don't confuse the screen saver with System or display sleep—it's different. To display the screen again, simply move the mouse or press any key. You can customize screen saver settings with the Desktop & Screen Saver preferences pane, which is covered in **Chapter 21**.

## To put your computer to sleep

Choose Apple > Sleep (**Figure 65**).

## ✔ Tips

■ When you put your computer to sleep, everything in memory is preserved. When you wake the computer, you can quickly continue working where you left off.

■ Sleep mode is an effective way to conserve the battery life of a PowerBook or iBook without turning it off.

■ By default, Mac OS X automatically puts a computer to sleep when it is inactive for 10 minutes. You can change this setting in the Energy Saver preferences pane, which is discussed in **Chapter 21**.

## To wake a sleeping computer

Press any keyboard key. You may have to wait several seconds for the computer to fully wake.

## ✔ Tips

■ It's much quicker to wake a sleeping computer than to restart a computer that has been shut down.

■ On some computer models, pressing Caps Lock or certain other keys may not wake the computer. When in doubt, press a letter key—they always work.

**Figure 66** This dialog appears when you choose the Restart command from the Apple menu.

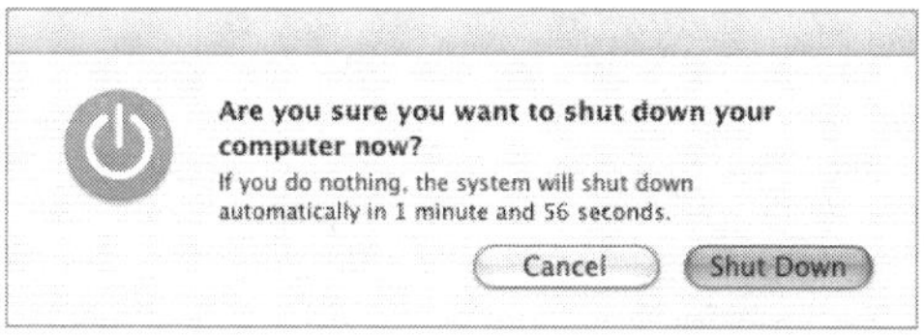

**Figure 67** This dialog appears when you choose the Shut Down command from the Apple menu.

## To restart your computer

1. Choose Apple > Restart (**Figure 65**).

2. In the dialog that appears (**Figure 66**), click Restart or press Return or Enter.

   *or*

   Do nothing. Your computer will automatically restart in 2 minutes.

## ✔ Tip

■ Restarting the computer clears memory and reloads all system files.

## To shut down your computer

1. Choose Apple > Shut Down (**Figure 65**).

2. In the dialog that appears (**Figure 67**), click Shut Down or press Return or Enter.

   *or*

   Do nothing. Your computer will automatically shut down in 2 minutes.

RESTARTING & SHUTTING DOWN

# Logging Out & In

If your computer is shared by multiple users, you may find it more convenient to log out when you're finished working. The Log Out command under the Apple menu (**Figure 65**) closes all applications and documents and closes your account on the computer. The computer remains running, making it quick and easy for the next person to log in and get right to work.

## ✔ Tips

- If you are your computer's only user, you'll probably never use the Log Out command. (I hardly ever do.)

- Mac OS X's *fast user switching* feature makes it quicker and easier to switch from one user account to another. I explain how this feature works in **Chapter 17**.

## To log out

1. Choose Apple > Log Out *User Name* (**Figure 65**), or press Shift ⌃ ⌘ Q.

2. A confirmation dialog like the one in **Figure 68** appears. Click Log Out or press Return or Enter.

   *or*

   Do nothing. Your computer will automatically log you out in 2 minutes.

   Your computer closes all applications and documents, then displays the Login Screen.

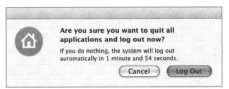

**Figure 68** A dialog like this one confirms that you really do want to log out.

## To log in

1. If the Login Screen displays icons for user accounts, click the icon for your account.

2. Enter your password in the Password box that appears.

3. Click Log In.

*Or*

1. If the Login Screen displays only Name and Password boxes, enter your full or short account name in the Name box and your password in the Password box.

2. Click Log In.

Your Mac OS desktop appears, looking the same as it did when you logged out or shut down your computer.

## ✔ Tips

■ The appearance of the Login Screen varies depending on how the Accounts preference pane has been configured by the system administrator. (Unfortunately, Mac OS X does not allow me to take screen shots of these screens, so I can't show them to you.) Account options are discussed in **Chapter 17**.

■ Your user name and short name are created when you use the Mac OS Setup Assistant to configure Mac OS X, as discussed in **Chapter 1**. You can use either name to log in.

LOGGING IN

# File Management

## File Management

In Mac OS, you use the Finder to organize and manage your files. You can:

- View the contents of your disks in windows in a variety of ways.

- Automatically sort items by name, kind, creation date, or other criteria in ascending or descending order.

- Rename items.

- Create folders to store related items.

- Move items stored on disk to organize them so they're easy to find and back up.

- Copy items to other disks to back them up or share them with others.

- Delete items you no longer need.

- Mount and eject disks.

- Write to, or "burn," data CDs.

## ✔ Tip

- If you're brand new to Mac OS, be sure to read the information in **Chapter 2** before working with this chapter. That chapter contains information and instructions about techniques that are used throughout this chapter.

# Mac OS X Disk Organization

Like most other computer operating systems, Mac OS X uses a hierarchical filing system (HFS) to organize and store files, including system files, applications, and documents.

The top level of the filing system is the computer level, which corresponds to the top section of the Sidebar (**Figure 1**). This level shows the computer's internal hard disk, any other disks the computer has access to (including iDisk, if you are a .Mac member), and the Network icon.

The next level down is the computer's hard disk level. You can view this level by clicking the name of your hard disk in the Sidebar (**Figure 1**) or on the desktop. While the contents of your hard disk may differ from what's shown in **Figure 2**, some elements should be the same:

◆ **Applications** contains Mac OS X applications.

◆ **System** and **Library** contain the Mac OS X system files.

◆ **Users** (**Figure 3**) contains individual folders for each of the computer's users, as well as a Shared folder.

The following folders may also appear if you upgraded to Mac OS X from Mac OS 9.x or if you installed Mac OS 9.x on your computer after installing Mac OS X:

◆ **Applications (Mac OS 9)** contains applications that run under the Classic environment.

◆ **System Folder** contains the Mac OS 9.x system files for running the Classic environment.

◆ **Documents** contains documents you saved on your hard disk before upgrading to Mac OS X.

**Figure 1** The top level of your computer shows all mounted disks and a Network icon.

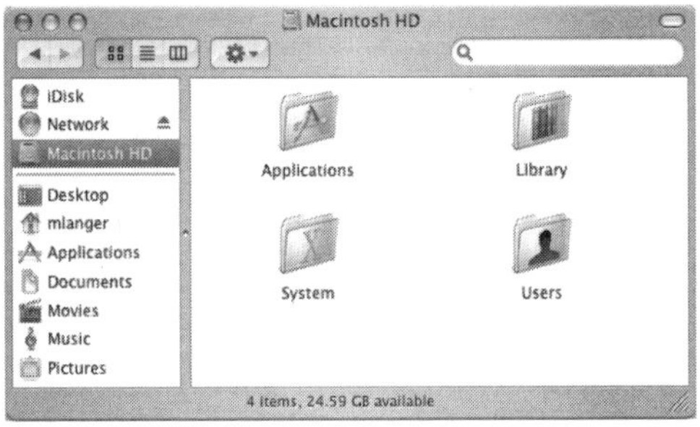

**Figure 2** A typical hard disk window might look like this.

**MAC OS X DISK ORGANIZATION**

**Figure 3** The Users folder contains a home folder for each user, as well as a Shared folder.

**Figure 4** Your home folder is preconfigured with folders for storing a variety of item types.

◆ **Desktop (Mac OS 9)** contains items that appear on the desktop when you start your computer with Mac OS 9.x.

By default, a Mac OS X hard disk is organized for multiple users. Each user has his or her own "home" folder, which is stored in the Users folder (**Figure 3**). You can view the items inside your home folder by opening the house icon with your name on it on the Sidebar or inside the Users folder (**Figure 3**). Your home folder is preconfigured with folders for all kinds of items you may want to store on disk (**Figure 4**).

## ✔ Tips

- When you install new applications on your computer, you should install Mac OS X–compatible applications in the Applications folder and Mac OS 9.x–compatible applications in the Applications (Mac OS 9) folder.

- If you upgraded from a previous version of Mac OS to Mac OS X, you may want to move the contents of the Documents folder on your hard disk (**Figure 2**) to the Documents folder inside your home folder (**Figure 4**) to keep your documents together and easier to find. As you can see, these are different Documents folders.

- Unless you are an administrator, you cannot access the files in any other user's home folder except those in the user's Public and Sites folders.

- If you place an item in the Shared folder inside the Users folder (**Figure 3**), it can be opened by anyone who uses the computer.

- I discuss applications in **Chapter 7**, the Classic environment in **Chapter 18**, sharing computers in **Chapter 17**, and networking in **Chapter 16**.

**MAC OS X DISK ORGANIZATION**

# Pathnames

A *path* or *pathname* is a kind of address for a file on disk. It includes the name of the disk on which the file resides, the names of the folders the file is stored within, and the name of the file itself. For example, the pathname for a file named *Letter.rtf* in the Documents folder of the mlanger folder shown in **Figure 4** would be: Macintosh HD/Users/mlanger/Documents/Letter.rtf

When entering a pathname from a specific folder, you don't have to enter the entire pathname. Instead, enter the path as it relates to the current folder. For example, the path to the above-mentioned file from the mlanger folder would be: Documents/Letter.rtf

To indicate a specific user folder, use the tilde (~) character followed by the name of the user account. So the path to the mlanger folder (**Figure 4**) would be: ~mlanger. (You can omit the user name if you want to open your own user folder.)

To indicate the top level of your computer, use a slash (/) character. So the path to eMac 800 (**Figure 1**) would be: /

When used as part of a longer pathname, the slash character indicates the *root level* of your hard disk. So /Applications/AppleScript would indicate the AppleScript folder inside the Applications folder on your hard disk.

Don't worry if this sounds confusing to you. Fortunately, you don't really need to know it to use Mac OS X. It's just a good idea to be familiar with the concept of pathnames in case you run across it while working with your computer.

**Figure 5**
The Go menu.

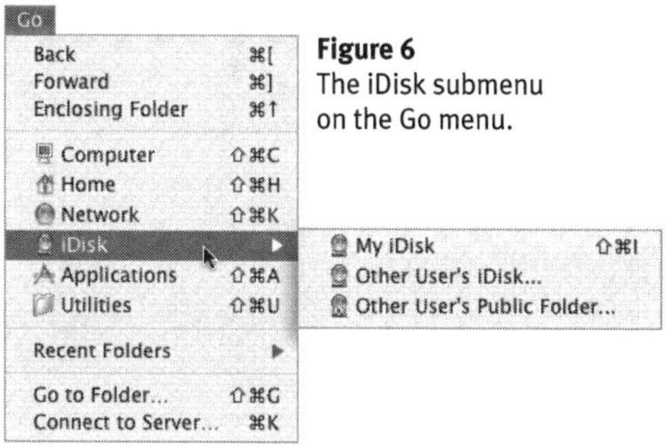

**Figure 6**
The iDisk submenu
on the Go menu.

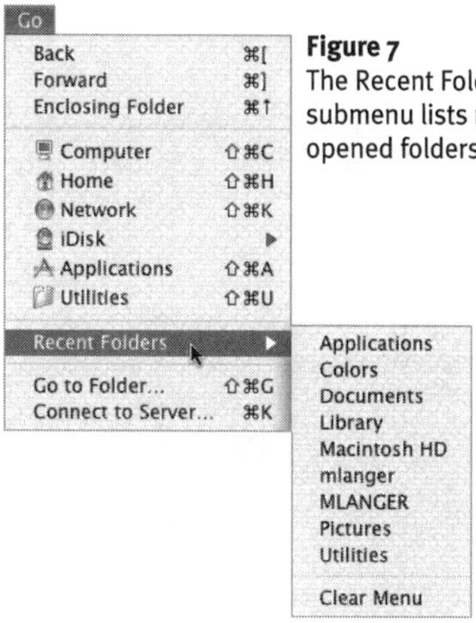

**Figure 7**
The Recent Folders
submenu lists recently
opened folders.

## ✔ Tip

■ I discuss iDisk in **Chapter 14** and connecting to network servers in **Chapter 16**.

# The Go Menu

The Go menu (**Figure 5**) offers a quick way to
open specific locations on your computer:

◆ **Back** ([⌃ ⌘ [ ]) displays the contents of the
folder or disk you were looking in before
you viewed the current folder or disk.
This command is only active if the current window has displayed the contents
of more than one folder or disk.

◆ **Forward** ([⌃ ⌘ ] ]) displays the contents of
the window you were viewing before you
clicked the Back button. This command
is only available if a window is active and
if the Back button has been clicked.

◆ **Enclosing Folder** ([⌃ ⌘ ↑]) opens the
parent folder for the active window's
folder. This command is only available if
a window is active and if the window was
used to display the contents of a folder.

◆ **Computer** ([Shift ⌃ ⌘ C]) opens the top
level window for your computer (**Figure 1**).

◆ **Home** ([Shift ⌃ ⌘ H]) opens your home
folder (**Figure 4**).

◆ **iDisk** displays a submenu of options for
accessing iDisk accounts and folders on
Apple's .Mac server via the Internet
(**Figure 6**).

◆ **Applications** ([Shift ⌃ ⌘ A]) opens the
Applications folder.

◆ **Utilities** ([Shift ⌃ ⌘ U]) opens the Utilities
folder inside the Applications folder.

◆ **Recent Folders** displays a submenu of
recently opened folders (**Figure 7**).

◆ **Go to Folder** ([Shift ⌃ ⌘ G]) lets you open
any folder your computer has access to.

◆ **Connect to Server** ([⌃ ⌘ K]) enables you
to open a server accessible via a network.

## To open a Go menu item

Choose the item's name from the Go menu (**Figure 5**) or one of its submenus (**Figures 6** and **7**).

## To go to a folder

1. Choose Go > Go to Folder (**Figure 5**), or press Shift ⌃ ⌘ G.

2. In the Go to Folder dialog that appears (**Figure 8**), enter the pathname for the folder you want to open.

3. Click Go.

   If you entered a valid pathname, the folder opens in a Finder window.

   *or*

   If you did not enter a valid pathname, an error message appears in the Go to Folder dialog (**Figure 9**). Repeat steps 2 and 3 to try again, or click Cancel to dismiss the dialog.

## ✔ Tip

■ If a window is open when you use the Go to Folder command, the Go to Folder dialog will appear as a dialog *sheet* attached to the window (**Figure 10**). The pathname you enter must be from that window's folder location on your hard disk.

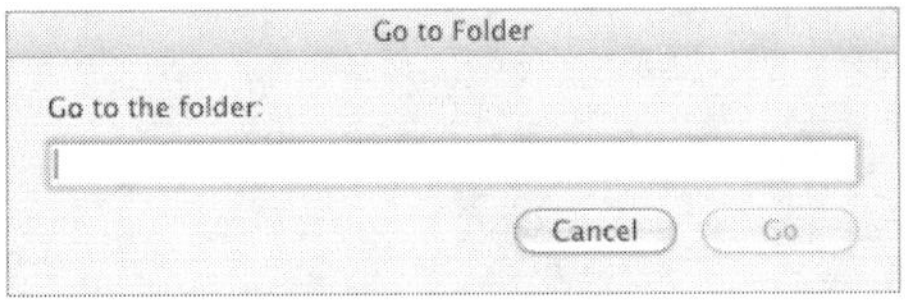

**Figure 8** Use the Go to Folder dialog to enter the pathname of the folder you want to open.

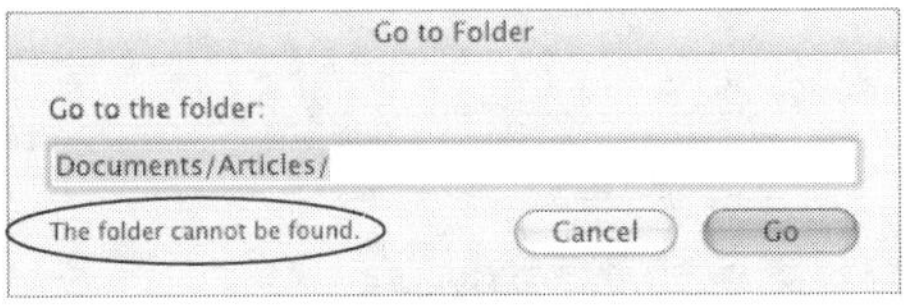

**Figure 9** An error message appears in the Go to Folder window if you enter an invalid pathname.

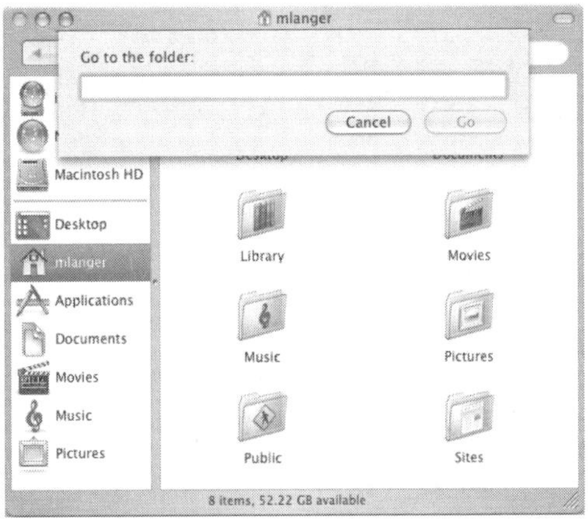

**Figure 10** If a window is active when you use the Go to Folder command, the dialog appears as a sheet attached to the window.

**Figure 11** You can display a window's contents as icons,...

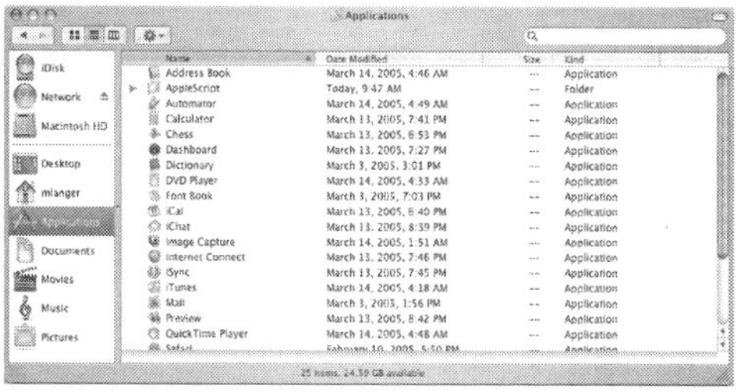

**Figure 12** ...as a list,...

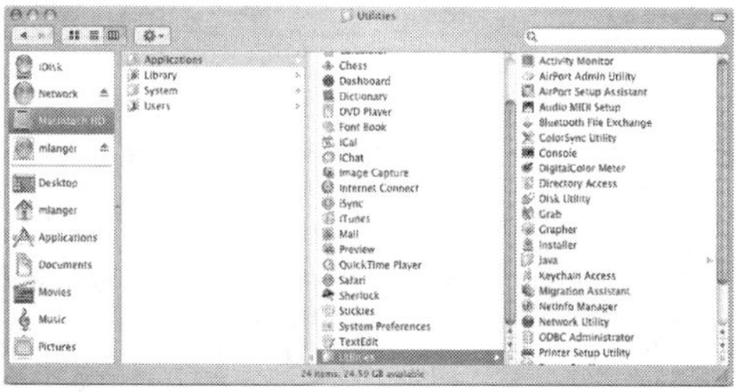

**Figure 13** ...or as columns.

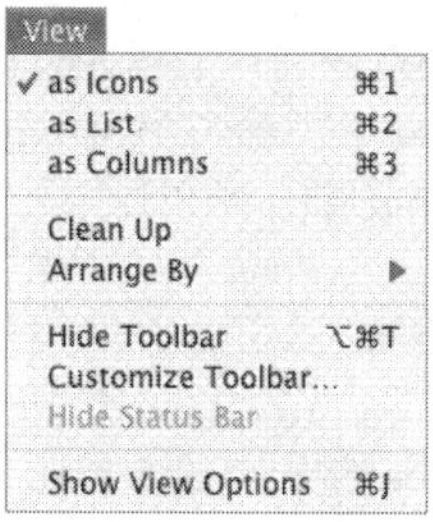

**Figure 14**
The View menu offers a variety of options for changing a window's view, along with three new command key equivalents for switching from one view to another.

*Icon List Column
view view view*

**Figure 15** The view buttons in the toolbar.

# Views

A Finder window's contents can be displayed using three different views:

◆ **Icons** displays the window's contents as small or large icons (**Figure 11**).

◆ **List** displays the window's contents as a sorted list (**Figure 12**).

◆ **Columns** displays the window's contents with a multiple-column format that shows the currently selected disk or folder and the items within it (**Figure 13**).

## ✔ Tip

■ You can customize views by setting view options globally or for individual windows. I explain how in **Chapter 4**.

## To change a window's view

1. If necessary, activate the window whose view you want to change.

2. Choose the view option you want from the View menu (**Figure 14**) or press the corresponding shortcut key.

   *or*

   Click the toolbar's view button for the view you want (**Figure 15**).

The view of the window changes.

## ✔ Tips

■ Commands on the View menu (**Figure 14**) work on the active window only.

■ A check mark appears on the View menu beside the name of the view applied to the active window (**Figure 14**).

■ You can set the view for each window individually.

**SETTING VIEWS**

**49**

## To neatly arrange icons in icon view

1. Activate the window that you want to clean up (**Figure 16**).

2. Choose View > Clean Up (**Figure 14**). The icons are arranged in the window's invisible grid (**Figure 17**).

   *or*

   Choose one of the commands from the Arrange By submenu under the View menu (**Figure 18**):

   ▲ **by Name** arranges the icons alphabetically by name (**Figure 11**).

   ▲ **by Date Modified** arranges the icons chronologically by the date they were last modified, with the most recently modified item last.

   ▲ **by Date Created** arranges the icons by the date they were created, with the most recently created item last.

   ▲ **by Size** arranges the icons in size order, with the largest item last. (Folders have a size of 0 for this option.)

   ▲ **by Kind** arranges the icons alphabetically by the kind of file.

   ▲ **by Label** arranges the icons by color-coded label (if applied).

   The icons are arranged in the window's invisible grid in the order you specified (**Figure 11**).

## ✔ Tips

■ A window's invisible grid ensures consistent spacing between icons.

■ You can manually position an icon in the window's invisible grid by holding down ⌘ while dragging it within the window.

**Figure 16** Start with a messy window like this one...

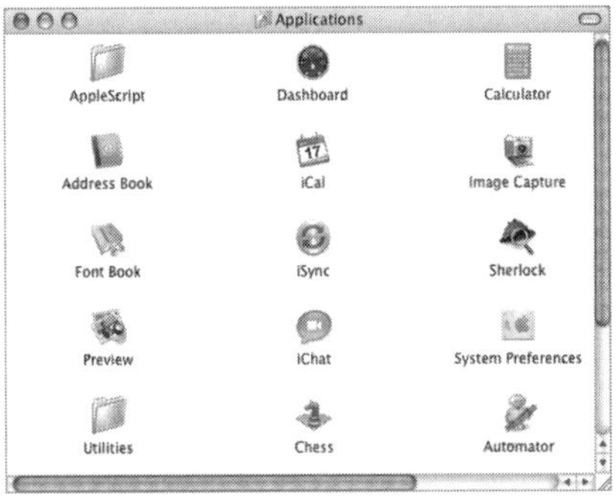

**Figure 17** ...and use the Clean Up command to put the icons in place.

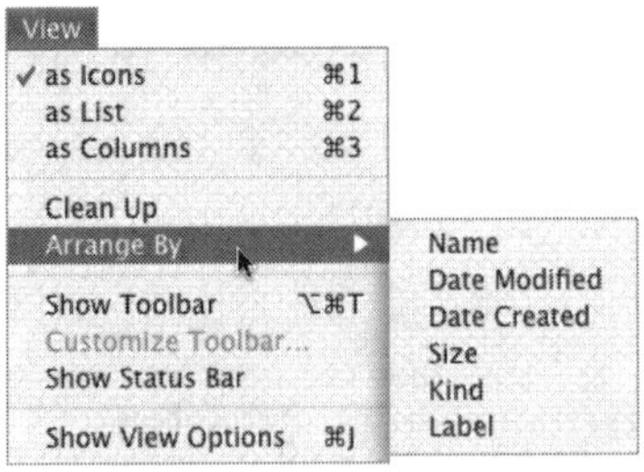

**Figure 18** The Arrange by submenu offers several options for neatly arranging icons.

■ When one or more icons are selected, the Clean Up command becomes the Clean Up Selection command. Choosing it arranges just the selected icons.

■ I tell you how to apply and customize labels in **Chapter 4.**

*ARRANGING ICON VIEW WINDOW CONTENTS*

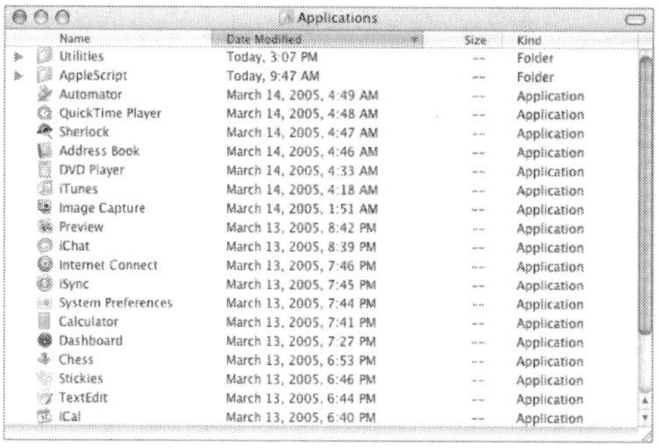

**Figure 19** Click a column heading to sort by that column.

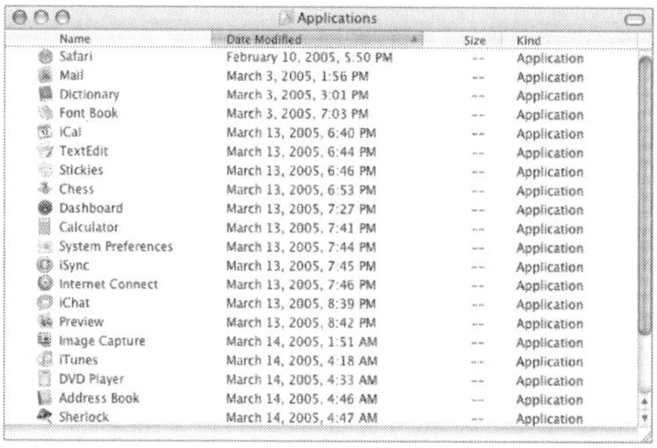

**Figure 20** Click the same column heading to reverse that column's sort order.

## To sort a window's contents in list view

Click the column heading for the column you want to sort by. The list is sorted by that column (**Figure 19**).

## ✔ Tips

■ You can identify the column by which a list is sorted by its colored column heading (**Figures 12**, **19**, and **20**).

■ You can reverse a window's sort order by clicking the sort column's heading a second time (**Figure 20**).

■ You can determine the sort direction by looking at the arrow in the sort column. When it points up, the items are sorted in ascending order (**Figure 20**); when it points down, the items are sorted in descending order (**Figure 19**).

■ To properly sort by size, you must turn on the Calculate all sizes option for the window. I explain how in **Chapter 4**.

■ You can specify which columns should appear in a window by setting View Options. I explain how to do that in **Chapter 4**, too.

# Icon Names

Mac OS X is very flexible when it comes to names for files, folders, and disks.

◆ A file or folder name can be up to 255 characters long. A disk name can be up to 27 characters long.

◆ A name can contain any character except a colon (:).

This makes it easy to give your files, folders, and disks names that make sense to you.

## ✔ Tips

■ Normally, you name documents when you save them. Saving documents is covered in **Chapter 7**.

■ A lengthy file name may appear truncated (or shortened) when displayed in windows and lists.

■ Since Mac OS 9.x and earlier cannot recognize very long file names, it's not a good idea to use them to name files you may work with in Mac OS 9. Instead, stick to file names of 31 characters or less.

■ No two documents in the same folder can have the same name.

■ Because slash characters (/) are used in pathnames, it's not a good idea to use them in names. In fact, some programs (such as Microsoft Word) won't allow you to include a slash in a file name.

■ Working with and naming disks is covered later in this chapter.

**Figure 21**
Start by selecting the icon.

**Figure 22**
When you click, an edit box appears around the name.

**Figure 23**
Type a new name for the icon.

**Figure 24**
When you press Return, the name changes.

# To rename an icon

1. Click the icon to select it (**Figure 21**).

2. Point to the name of the icon, and click. After a brief pause, a box appears around the name and the name becomes selected (**Figure 22**).

3. Type the new name. The text you type automatically overwrites the selected text (**Figure 23**).

4. Press Return or Enter, or click anywhere else. The icon is renamed (**Figure 24**).

## ✔ Tips

- Not all icons can be renamed. If the edit box does not appear around an icon name (as shown in **Figure 22**), that icon cannot be renamed.

- You can also rename an icon in the Info window, which is covered in **Chapter 4**.

RENAMING ICONS

# Folders

Mac OS uses folders to organize files and other folders on disk. You can create a folder, give it a name that makes sense to you, and move files and other folders into it. It's a lot like organizing paper files and folders in a file cabinet.

Mac OS X 10.4 support three different kinds of folders:

◆ A standard **folder** is for manually storing files on disk. You create the folder, then move or copy items into it. Throughout this book, I'll use the term *folder* to refer to this kind of folder.

◆ A **smart folder** works with Mac OS X 10.4's new integrated searching feature to automatically organize folders that meet specific search criteria. I explain how to work with Smart folders in **Chapter 5**.

◆ A **burn folder** is for organizing items you want to save or "burn" onto a CD. I explain how to create and use burn folders later in this chapter.

## ✔ Tips

■ A folder can contain any number of files and other folders.

■ It's a good idea to use folders to organize the files on your hard disk. Imagine a file cabinet without file folders—that's how your hard disk would appear if you never used folders to keep your files tidy.

■ As discussed earlier in this chapter, your home folder includes folders set up for organizing files by type. You'll find that these folders often appear as default file locations when saving specific types of files from within software programs. Saving files from within applications is covered in **Chapter 7**.

| File | | |
|---|---|---|
| New Finder Window | ⌘N | |
| New Folder | ⇧⌘N | |
| New Smart Folder | ⌥⌘N | |
| New Burn Folder | | |
| Open | ⌘O | |
| Open With | ▶ | |
| Print | | |
| Close Window | ⌘W | |
| Get Info | ⌘I | |
| Duplicate | ⌘D | |
| Make Alias | ⌘L | |
| Show Original | ⌘R | |
| Add to Sidebar | ⌘T | |
| Create Archive | | |
| Move to Trash | ⌘⌫ | |
| Eject "Macintosh HD" | ⌘E | |
| Burn Disc... | | |
| Find... | ⌘F | |
| Color Label: | | |
| × ● ● ● ● ● ● | | |

**Figure 25**
Choose New Folder from the File menu.

## To create a folder

1.  Choose File > New Folder (**Figure 25**), or press (Shift) (⌘) (N). A new untitled folder (**Figure 26**) appears in the active window.

2.  While the edit box appears around the new folder's name (**Figure 26**), type a name for it (**Figure 27**) and press (Return).

## ✔ Tips

■   You can rename a folder the same way you rename any other icon. Renaming icons is discussed on the previous page.

■   Working with windows is discussed in **Chapter 2**.

**Figure 26**
A new folder appears.

**Figure 27**
Enter a name for the folder while the edit box appears around it.

CREATING FOLDERS

# Moving & Copying Items

In addition to moving icons around within a window or on the desktop (see **Chapter 2**), you can move or copy items to other locations on the same disk or to other disks by dragging them:

◆ When you drag an item to a location on the same disk, the item is moved to that location.

◆ When you drag an item to a location on another disk, the item is copied to that location.

◆ When you hold down Option while dragging an item to a location on the same disk, the item is copied to that location.

The next few pages provide instructions for all of these techniques, as well as instructions for duplicating items.

## ✔ Tips

■ You can move or copy more than one item at a time. Begin by selecting all of the items that you want to move or copy, then drag any one of them to the destination. All items will be moved or copied.

■ You can continue working with the Finder or any other application—even start more copy jobs—while a copy job is in progress.

■ In Mac OS X, you can also copy Finder items using the Copy and Paste commands under the Finder's Edit menu. I explain how to use Copy and Paste in **Chapter 9**.

**Figure 28** Drag the icon onto the icon for the folder to which you want to move it...

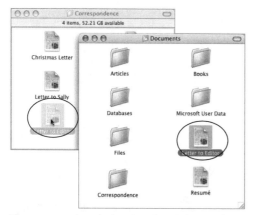

**Figure 29** ...or drag the icon into the window in which you want to move it.

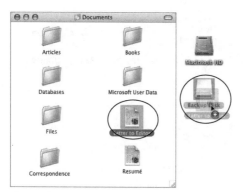

**Figure 30** Drag the icon to the destination disk's icon...

## To move an item to another location on the same disk

1. Drag the icon for the item that you want to move as follows:

   ▲ To move the item into a specific folder on the disk, drag the icon onto the icon for the folder. The destination folder icon becomes selected when the mouse pointer moves over it (**Figure 28**).

   ▲ To move the item into a specific window on the disk, drag the icon into the window. A border appears around the inside of the destination window (**Figure 29**).

2. Release the mouse button. The item moves.

## ✔ Tip

■ If the destination location is on another disk, the item you drag will be copied rather than moved. To move (rather than copy) an item to another disk, hold down ⌘ while dragging it to the disk.

MOVING ITEMS TO ANOTHER DISK LOCATION

## To copy an item to another disk

1. Drag the icon for the item that you want to copy as follows:

   ▲ To copy the item to the top (or *root*) level of a disk, drag the icon to the icon for the destination disk (**Figure 30**).

   ▲ To copy the item into a folder on the disk, drag the icon to the icon for the folder on the destination disk (**Figure 31**).

   ▲ To copy the item into a specific window on the disk, drag the icon into the window (**Figure 32**).

   When the item you are dragging moves on top of the destination location, a plus sign in a green circle appears beneath the mouse pointer. If the destination is an icon, the icon becomes selected.

2. Release the mouse button. A Copy window like the one in **Figure 33** appears. When it disappears, the copy is complete.

## ✔ Tips

- You cannot copy items to a disk that is write protected or to a folder for which you don't have write privileges. When you try, the green plus sign changes to a circle with a line through it. I tell you about write-protected disks later in this chapter.

- If a file with the same file name already exists in the destination location, an error message appears in the Copy window (**Figure 34**). Click Stop to dismiss the window without making the copy, or click Replace to replace the existing file with the one you are copying.

- Because copying small files happens so quickly in Mac OS X, you probably won't see the Copy window (**Figure 33**) very often. It doesn't have time to appear!

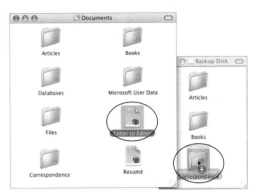

**Figure 31** ...or to a folder icon in a window on the destination disk, ...

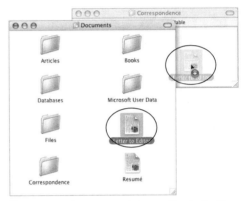

**Figure 32** ...or to an open window on the destination disk.

**Figure 33** A window like this indicates copy progress.

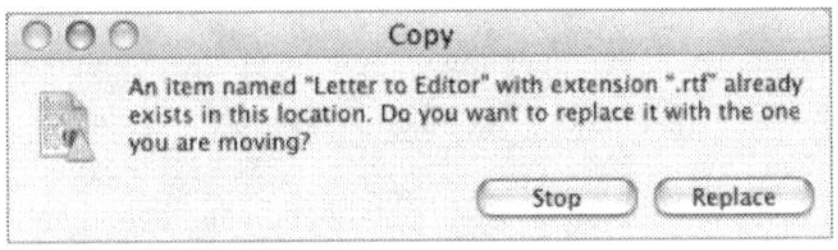

**Figure 34** If a file with the same name already exists in the destination, Mac OS tells you.

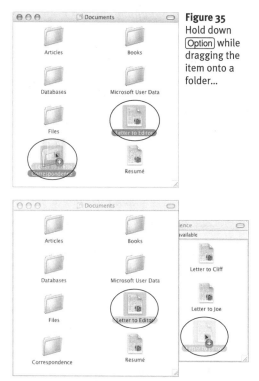

**Figure 35**
Hold down (Option) while dragging the item onto a folder...

**Figure 36** ...or into a window on the same disk.

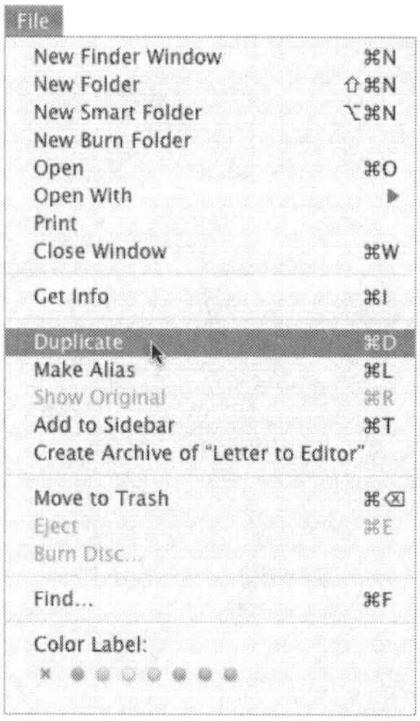

**Figure 37**
Choose Duplicate from the File menu.

Letter to Editor copy

**Figure 38**
A duplicate appears with the original.

## To copy an item to another location on the same disk

1. Hold down (Option) while dragging the icon for the item that you want to copy onto a folder icon (**Figure 35**) or into a window (**Figure 36**).

   When the mouse pointer on the item you are dragging moves on top of the destination location, a plus sign in a green circle appears beneath it. If the destination is an icon, the icon becomes highlighted.

2. Release the mouse button. A Copy window like the one in **Figure 33** appears. When it disappears, the copy is complete.

## ✔ Tips

- When copying an item to a new location on the same disk, you *must* hold down (Option). If you don't, the item will be moved rather than copied.

- If a file with the same file name already exists in the destination location, an error message appears in the Copy window (**Figure 34**). Click Stop to dismiss the window without making the copy, or click Replace to replace the existing file with the one you are copying.

## To duplicate an item

1. Select the item that you want to duplicate.

2. Choose File > Duplicate (**Figure 37**), or press ⌘ D.

   *Or*

   Hold down (Option) while dragging the item that you want to duplicate to a different location in the same window.

   A copy of the item you duplicated appears beside the original. The word *copy* is appended to the file name (**Figure 38**).

# The Trash & Deleting Items

The Trash is a special place on your hard disk where you place items you want to delete. Items in the Trash remain there until you empty the Trash, which removes them from your disk. In Mac OS X, the Trash appears as an icon in the Dock.

## To move an item to the Trash

1. Drag the icon for the item you want to delete to the Trash icon in the Dock.

2. When the mouse pointer moves over the Trash icon, the Trash icon becomes selected (**Figure 39**). Release the mouse button.

*Or*

1. Select the item that you want to delete.

2. Choose File > Move To Trash (**Figure 40**), or press ⌘ Delete.

## ✔ Tips

- The Trash icon's appearance indicates its status:
  - ▲ If the Trash is empty, the Trash icon looks like an empty wire basket.
  - ▲ If the Trash is not empty, the Trash icon looks like a wire basket with crumpled papers in it (**Figure 41**).

- You can delete more than one item at a time. Begin by selecting all the items you want to delete, then drag any one of them to the Trash. All items will be moved to the Trash.

- Moving a disk icon to the Trash does not delete or erase it. Instead, it *unmounts* it. Working with disks is covered a little later in this chapter.

- You cannot drag an item to the Trash if the item is locked. I tell you about locking and unlocking items in **Chapter 4**.

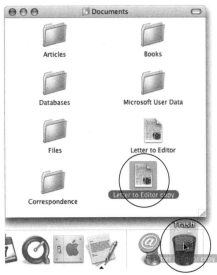

**Figure 39** To move an item to the Trash, drag it there...

**Figure 40**
...or select the item and choose Move To Trash from the File menu.

**Figure 41**
When an item has been moved to the Trash, the Trash icon looks full.

**Figure 42** Opening the Trash displays the Trash window.

**Figure 43** If the last thing you did was to put an item in the Trash, you can use the Undo command to take it back out.

**Figure 44**
The Finder menu includes two commands for emptying the Trash.

**Are you sure you want to remove the items in the Trash permanently?**
You cannot undo this action.

Cancel    OK

**Figure 45** The Trash warning dialog asks you to confirm that you really do want to delete the items in the Trash.

## To move an item out of the Trash

1. Click the Trash icon in the Dock to open the Trash window (**Figure 42**).

2. Drag the item from the Trash window to the Desktop or to another window on your hard disk.

   The item is moved from the Trash to the window you dragged it to.

*Or*

Choose Edit > Undo Move of "*Item Name*" (**Figure 43**), or press ⌃⌘Z. The item is moved back to where it was before you moved it to the Trash.

## ✔ Tip

■ The Undo command (**Figure 43**) will only take an item out of the Trash if the last thing you did was put it in the Trash.

## To empty the Trash

1. Choose Finder > Empty Trash (**Figure 44**), or press Shift ⌃⌘Delete.

2. A Trash warning dialog like the one in **Figure 45** appears. Click OK to delete all items that are in the Trash.

*Or*

1. Point to the Trash icon, press the mouse button, and hold it down until a menu appears (**Figure 46**).

2. Choose Empty Trash. The contents of the Trash are deleted. No warning appears.

## ✔ Tip

■ You can disable the Trash warning dialog (**Figure 45**) in the Finder Preferences window. I explain how in **Chapter 4**.

**MOVING ITEMS FROM & EMPTYING THE TRASH**

## To permanently remove items in the Trash from your disk

1. Choose Finder > Secure Empty Trash (**Figure 44**).

2. A Trash warning dialog like the one in **Figure 47** appears. Click OK to permanently remove all items that are in the Trash.

## ✔ Tips

- The Secure Empty Trash command makes it impossible to use special data recovery software to unerase deleted files.

- You may want to use the Secure Empty Trash command to erase personal files on a shared computer or a computer you plan to give away or sell.

- Deleting files from disk with the Secure Empty Trash command may take longer than using the Empty Trash command, especially when deleting large files.

- You can disable the Trash warning dialog (**Figure 47**) in the Finder Preferences window. I explain how in **Chapter 4**.

**Figure 46** When you point to the Trash icon in the Dock and hold the mouse button down, a menu with an Empty Trash option appears.

> Are you sure you want to erase the items in the Trash permanently using Secure Empty Trash?
>
> If you choose Secure Empty Trash, you cannot recover the files.
>
> Cancel    OK

**Figure 47** Using the Secure Empty Trash command displays a warning dialog like this.

**Table 1**

| Terminology for Storage Media Capacity | | |
|---|---|---|
| Term | Abbreviation | Size |
| byte | byte | 1 character |
| kilobyte | KB | 1,024 bytes |
| megabyte | MB | 1,024 KB |
| gigabyte | GB | 1,024 MB |

**Figure 48** A write-protected icon appears in the status bar of CD-ROM discs and other write-protected media.

## ✔ Tips

- Don't confuse storage media with memory. The term *memory* usually refers to the amount of RAM in your computer, not disk space. RAM is discussed in **Chapter 7**.

- At a minimum, all new Macintosh computers include a hard disk and CD/DVD drives.

- Storage devices can be internal (inside your computer) or external (attached to your computer by a cable).

- Some external storage devices must be properly connected and turned on *before* you start your computer or your computer may not recognize the device.

# Storage Media

A Macintosh computer can read data from, or write data to, a wide range of storage media, including:

- **Hard disks**—high capacity magnetic media.

- **CD-ROM, CD-R, DVD, and DVD-R discs**—high capacity, removable optical media.

- **Zip, or other disks or cartridges**—high capacity, removable magnetic media.

- **Floppy disks or diskettes**—low capacity, removable magnetic media.

To use storage media, it must be:

- **Mounted**—inserted, attached, or otherwise accessible to your computer.

- **Formatted** or **initialized**—specially prepared for use with your computer.

All of these things are covered in this section.

- Disk storage media capacity is specified in terms of bytes, kilobytes, megabytes, and gigabytes (**Table 1**).

- If a disk is *write-protected* or *locked*, files cannot be saved or copied to it. A pencil with a line through it appears in the status bar of write-protected or locked disks (**Figure 48**). I tell you more about the status bar in **Chapter 4**.

- You cannot write data to a CD-ROM. But if your Mac has a CD-Recordable (CD-R) drive or SuperDrive, you can use special software to create or *burn* your own CDs.

STORAGE MEDIA

# Mounting Disks

You *mount* a disk by inserting it in the disk drive so it appears in the top level computer window (**Figure 49**). When a disk is mounted, your computer "sees" it and can access the information it contains.

## ✔ Tips

- You must mount a disk to use it.

- To learn how to mount disks that are not specifically covered in this book, consult the documentation that came with the disk drive.

- Mounted disks appear in the top-level window for your computer (**Figure 49**). You can display this window by choosing Go > Computer (**Figure 5**), as discussed earlier in this chapter.

- Mounted disks may also appear on the desktop, as shown in **Figure 49**, depending on how Finder preferences are set for the display of items on the desktop. I explain how to set Finder preferences in **Chapter 4**.

- You mount a network volume by using the Connect to Server command under the Go menu (**Figure 5**) or by browsing the network and opening the disk you want to mount. I explain how to access network volumes in **Chapter 16**.

**Figure 49** Here's a desktop with an internal hard disk, CD-ROM disc, floppy disk, and network volume mounted.

## To mount a CD or DVD disc

Insert the CD or DVD disc into the CD or DVD slot.

*Or*

1. Follow the manufacturer's instructions to open the CD or DVD disc tray or eject the CD or DVD caddy.

2. Place the CD or DVD disc in the tray or caddy, label side up.

3. Gently push the tray or caddy into the drive. After a moment, the disc icon appears in the top-level computer window. **Figure 49** shows a mounted CD-ROM (FileMaker Pro 7).

## ✔ Tip

■ If your CD or DVD drive does not use a disc tray or caddy, consult its documentation for specific instructions.

## To mount a Zip disk

Insert the disk in the Zip drive, label side up, metal side in. After a moment, the disk icon appears in the top-level computer window.

## To mount a floppy disk

Insert the disk in the floppy disk drive, label side up, metal side in. The disk's icon appears in the top-level computer window. **Figure 49** shows a mounted floppy disk (Untitled).

# Ejecting Disks

When you eject a disk, the disk is physically removed from the disk drive and its icon disappears from the top-level computer window.

## ✔ Tip

- When the disk's icon disappears from the top-level computer window, it is said to be *unmounted*.

## To eject a disk

1. Click the disk's icon once to select it.

2. Choose File > Eject "*Disk Name*" (**Figure 50**), or press ⌘ ⌘ E.

*Or*

1. Select the name of the disk in the Sidebar.

2. Click the eject button to the right of the disk name (**Figure 51**).

*Or*

1. Drag the disk's icon to the Trash (**Figure 52**). As you drag, the Trash icon turns into a rectangle with a triangle on top (**Figure 53**).

2. When the mouse pointer moves over the Trash icon, it becomes selected (**Figure 52**). Release the mouse button.

*Or*

Press the Media Eject key on the keyboard.

## ✔ Tips

- If you try to eject a disk that contains a file that is in use by your computer, a dialog like the one in **Figure 54** appears. Click OK to dismiss the dialog, then quit the open application. You should then be able to eject the disk. Working with applications is covered in **Chapter 5**.

- Not all keyboards include a Media Eject key. Check the documentation that came with your computer for more information.

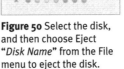

**Figure 50** Select the disk, and then choose Eject "*Disk Name*" from the File menu to eject the disk.

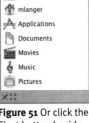

**Figure 51** Or click the Eject button beside the item's name in the Sidebar.

**Figure 52** Or drag the disk icon to the Trash.

**Figure 53** When you drag a disk icon, the Trash icon changes into an icon like this.

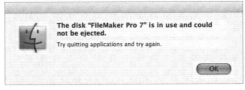

The disk "FileMaker Pro 7" is in use and could not be ejected.

Try quitting applications and try again.

OK

**Figure 54** A dialog like this appears if you try to eject a disk that contains open files.

**Ejecting Disks**

# Burning CDs

If your Macintosh includes a Combo drive, CD-R/CD-RW drive, or SuperDrive, you can write, or *burn*, files onto blank CD-R media. This is a great way to archive important files that you don't need on your computer's hard disk and to share files with other computer users.

The Mac OS X 10.4 Finder offers two ways to burn a CD:

◆ Create a burn folder, fill the folder with the files you want to include on the CD, and use the Burn Disc command to burn the CD. Burn folders are a new feature of Mac OS X 10.4.

◆ Insert a blank CD, name the CD, then drag the icons for the files you want to include on the CD onto the CD's icon on the desktop. Then use the Burn Disc command to burn the CD.

On the following pages, I explain how to use both techniques.

## ✔ Tip

■ You can also burn CDs or DVDs from within iTunes, iDVD, or other third-party utilities, such as Roxio Toast. iTunes is discussed in **Chapter 8**.

## To burn a CD from a burn folder

1. Choose File > New Burn Folder (**Figure 55**). A burn folder icon named *Burn Folder* appears in the active window (**Figure 56**).

2. While the folder name is selected, enter a new name for the folder and press [Return]. The folder's name changes (**Figure 57**).

3. Use techniques discussed earlier in this chapter to copy the files you want to include on the CD to the burnable folder. You can create regular folders inside the burnable folder to organize the files you add to it. **Figure 58** shows an example of the contents of a burn folder that includes both files and folders.

4. When you are finished adding files, click the Burn button near the top of the burn folder's window (**Figure 58**) or select the burn folder icon and choose File > Burn Disc (**Figure 59**).

5. A Burn Disc dialog appears (**Figure 60**). Insert a CD in your computer. You may need to press the Media Eject button to open the CD tray and then press it again to slide the tray and CD back into the computer.

6. A dialog like the one in **Figure 61** appears next. Set options as desired:
   - ▲ **Disc Name** is the name you want to give the disc.
   - ▲ **Speed** (**Figure 62**) is the burn speed.

7. Click Burn.

   A Burn status dialog appears as the disc is burned (**Figure 63**). When the dialog disappears, the CD appears on the desktop and in the Sidebar (**Figure 64**) and is ready to use.

**Figure 55** Choose New Burn Folder from the File menu.

**Figure 56** An icon for the burn folder appears in the active window.

**Figure 57** The name you give the folder is the name that will be given to the CD.

**Figure 58** The contents of a burn folder.

| File | |
|---|---|
| New Finder Window | ⌘N |
| New Folder | ⇧⌘N |
| New Smart Folder | ⌥⌘N |
| New Burn Folder | |
| Open | ⌘O |
| Open With | ▶ |
| Print | |
| Close Window | ⌘W |
| Get Info | ⌘I |
| Duplicate | ⌘D |
| Make Alias | ⌘L |
| Show Original | ⌘R |
| Add to Sidebar | ⌘T |
| Create Archive of "File Backup" | |
| Move to Trash | ⌘⌫ |
| Eject | ⌘E |
| Burn Disc... | |
| Find... | ⌘F |
| Color Label: | |
| ✕ ● ● ● ● ● ● ● | |

**Figure 59**
Choose Burn Disc
from the File menu.

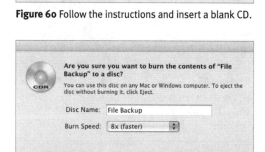

Figure 60 Follow the instructions and insert a blank CD.

**Figure 61** Set burning options in this dialog.

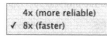

**Figure 62** Use the Speed pop-up menu to choose a burn speed.

**Figure 63** This dialog appears while the disc is being burned.

## ✔ Tips

- When you copy files to a burn folder, Mac OS creates aliases to the original files. When it burns the disc, however, it copies the original files rather than the aliases to the disc. I tell you about aliases in **Chapter 4**.

- Use the burn folder feature to create a backup folder for periodically backing up important files to CD. Just create a burn folder and fill it with the files you want to back up. Burn a CD each time you want to back up the files. Be sure to retain the burn folder each time you burn a CD. Because the burn folder contains aliases rather than original files, the latest versions of the files will always be burned onto the CD.

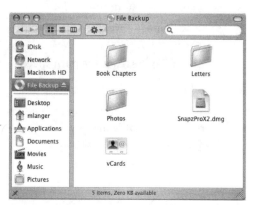

**Figure 64** The finished CD contains all of the files and folders you copied to the burnable folder.

## To burn files directly to a blank CD

1. Insert a blank CD into your computer.

2. A dialog like the one in **Figure 65** appears. Make sure Open Finder is chosen from the Action pop-up menu (**Figure 66**) and click OK.

   An Untitled CD icon appears on the desktop and in the Sidebar (**Figure 67**).

3. If desired, rename the CD icon as instructed earlier in this chapter. The name that appears on the icon is the name that will be burned onto the disc.

4. Use techniques discussed earlier in this chapter to copy the files you want to include on the CD to the CD icon. You can create regular folders inside the CD to organize the files you add to it. **Figure 68** shows an example of a recordable CD that includes both files and folders.

5. Click the Burn button beside the CD's icon in the Sidebar or near the top of the CD's window (**Figure 68**).

   *or*

   Choose File > Burn Disc (**Figure 59**).

6. A dialog like the one in **Figure 61** appears next. Set options as desired:

   ▲ **Disc Name** is the name you want to give the disc.

   ▲ **Speed** (**Figure 62**) is the burn speed.

7. Click Burn.

   A Burn status dialog appears as the disc is burned (**Figure 63**). When the dialog disappears, the CD is ready to use.

**Figure 65** This dialog appears when you insert a blank CD.

**Figure 66** The Action pop-up menu enables you to choose the application you want to use to burn the CD.

**Figure 67** An Untitled CD icon appears on the desktop and in the Sidebar.

**Figure 68** Here's what the contents of a recordable CD might look like when ready to burn.

## ✔ Tip

■ If you choose a different application from the Action pop-up menu (**Figure 66**) in step 2, Mac OS X will open that application so you can use it to burn the disc. The remaining steps do not apply.

# Advanced Finder Techniques

**4**

## Advanced Finder Techniques

In addition to the basic Finder and file management techniques covered in **Chapters 2** and **3**, Mac OS X offers more advanced techniques you can use to work with windows and manage files:

◆ Use hierarchical outlines and select items in multiple folders in list view.

◆ Use spring-loaded folders to access folders while copying or moving items.

◆ Use Exposé to quickly view open applications or documents.

◆ Apply color-coded labels to Finder items.

◆ Use aliases to make frequently used files easier to access without moving them.

◆ Quickly reopen recently used items.

◆ Use the Info window to learn more about an item or set options for it.

◆ Create archives to save space on disk or minimize data transfer time.

◆ Undo actions you performed while working with the Finder.

## ✔ Tip

■ If you're brand new to Mac OS, be sure to read the information in **Chapters 2** and **3** before working with this chapter. Those chapters contain information and instructions about techniques that are used throughout this chapter.

# Working with List View

Windows displayed in list view have a feature not found in icon or column views: They can display the contents of folders within the window as an outline (**Figures** 73 and 74). This makes it possible to see and select the contents of more than one folder at a time.

## ✔ Tip

- Views are discussed in detail in **Chapter 3**.

## To display or hide a folder's contents in outline list view

- To display a folder's contents, use one of the following techniques:
  - ▲ Click the right-pointing triangle beside the folder (**Figure 1**).
  - ▲ Click the folder once to select it, and press ⌃ ⌘ →.

  The items within that folder are listed below it, slightly indented (**Figure 2**).

- To hide a folder's contents, use one of the following techniques:
  - ▲ Click the down-pointing triangle beside the folder (**Figure 2**).
  - ▲ Click the folder once to select it, and press ⌃ ⌘ ←.

  The outline collapses to hide the items in the folder (**Figure 1**).

## ✔ Tip

- As shown in **Figure 3**, you can use this technique to display multiple levels of folders in the same window.

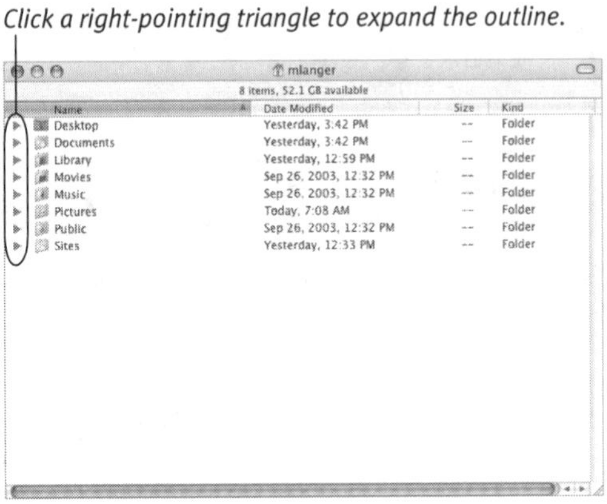

*Click a right-pointing triangle to expand the outline.*

**Figure 1** Right-pointing triangles indicate collapsed outlines.

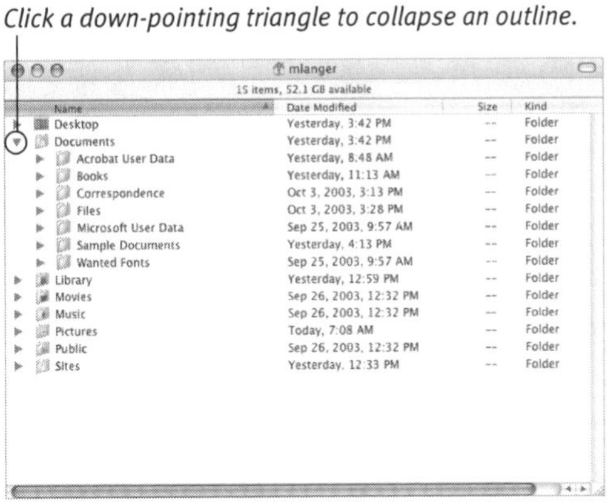

*Click a down-pointing triangle to collapse an outline.*

**Figure 2** Folder contents can be displayed as an outline...

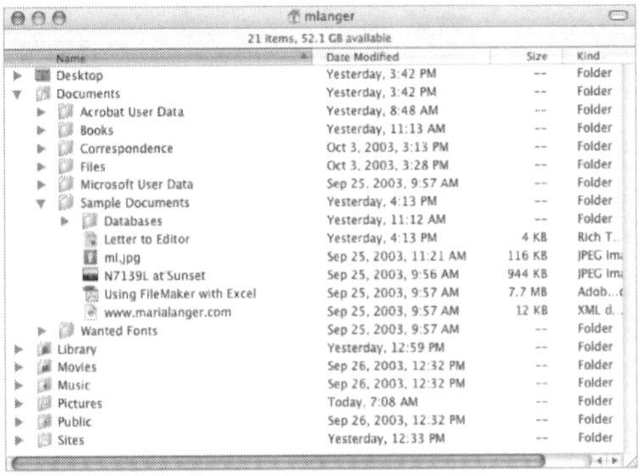

**Figure 3** ...that can show several levels.

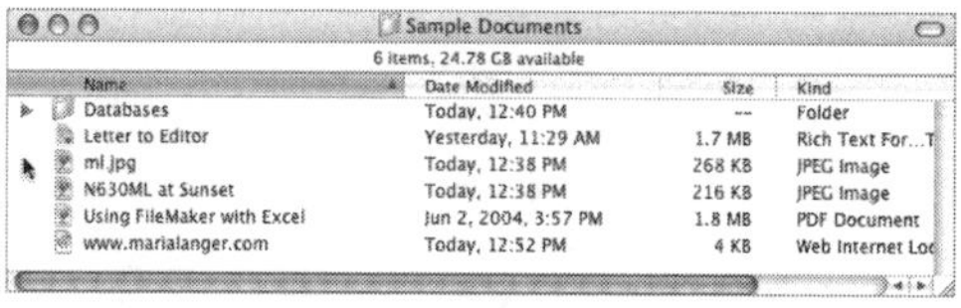

**Figure 4** Position the mouse pointer in front of the first icon you want to select.

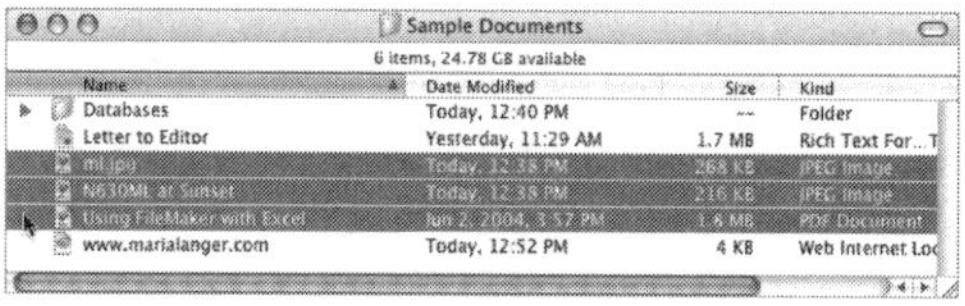

**Figure 5** Drag over the other icons you want to select.

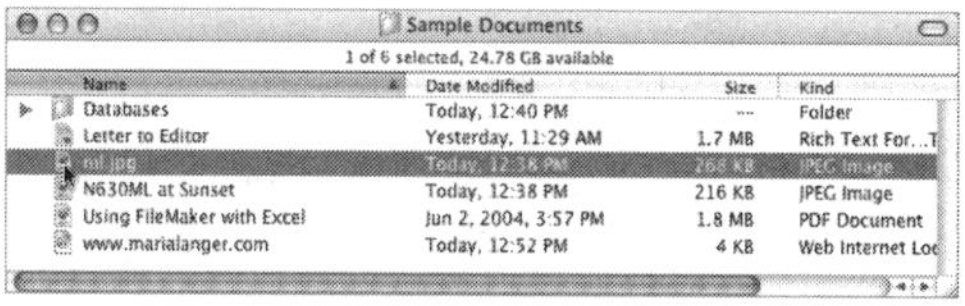

**Figure 6** Select the first icon.

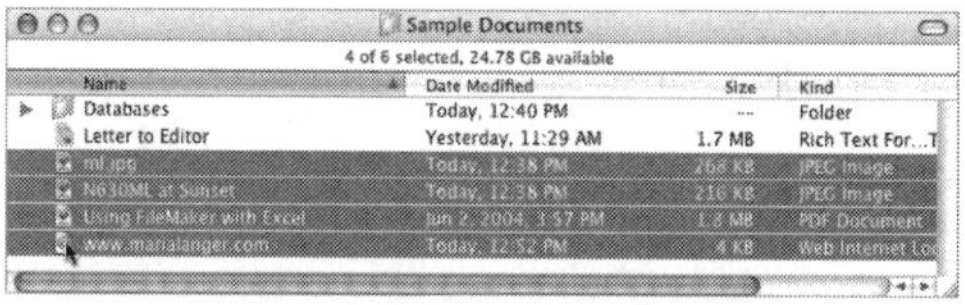

**Figure 7** Hold down (Shift) and click the last icon.

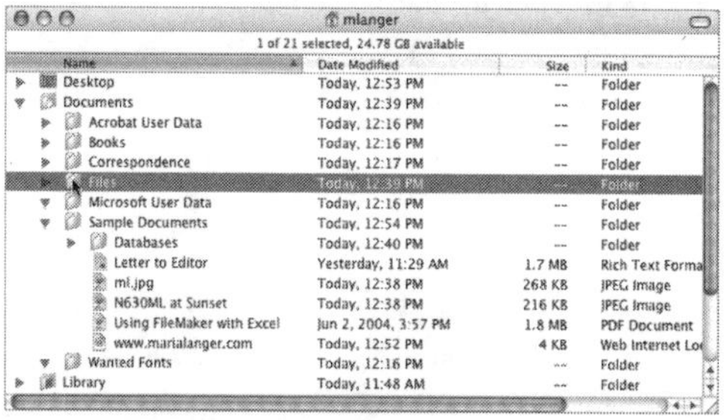

**Figure 8** Select the first

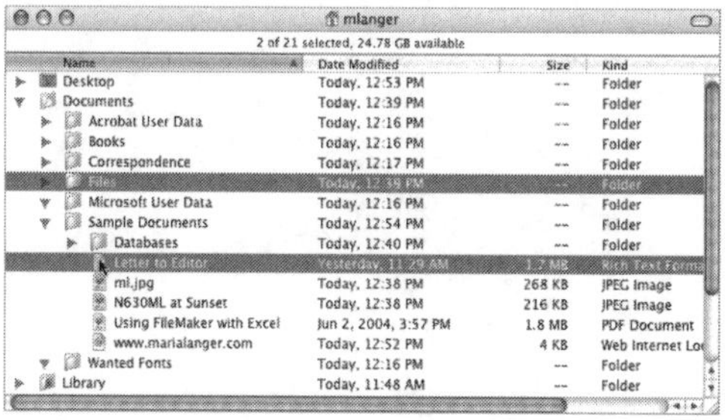

**Figure 9** Hold down (⌘) and click another icon.

# To select multiple contiguous icons in list view

1. Position the mouse pointer in front of the first icon you want to select (**Figure 4**).

2. Hold the mouse button down and drag over the other icons you want to select (**Figure 5**).

*Or*

1. Click to select the first icon you want to select (**Figure 6**).

2. Hold down (Shift) and click the last icon in the group you want to select (**Figure 7**).

# To select multiple noncontiguous icons in list view

1. Click to select the first icon you want to select (**Figure 8**).

2. Hold down (⌘) and click the next icon you want to select (**Figure 9**).

3. Repeat step 2 until all icons have been selected (**Figure 10**).

# To deselect icons

Click anywhere in the window other than on an icon's line of information.

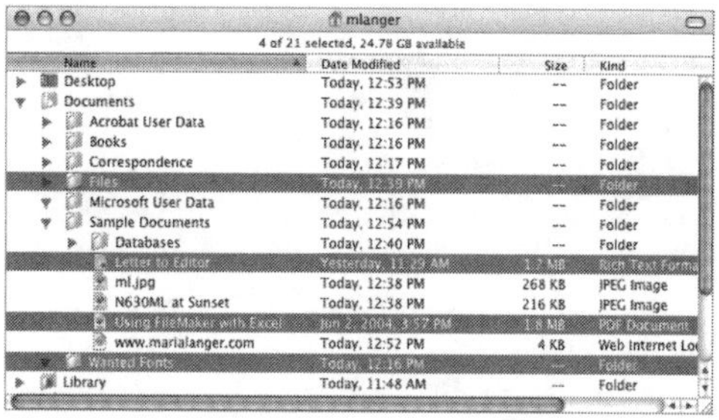

**Figure 10** Continue holding down (⌘) and clicking icons until you're finished selecting the icons you want.

**SELECTING ICONS IN LIST VIEW**

**75**

# Spring-Loaded Folders

The spring-loaded folders feature lets you move or copy items into folders deep within the file structure of a disk—without manually opening a single folder. Instead, you simply drag icons onto folders (**Figures 11** and **13**) and wait as they're automatically opened (**Figures 12** and **14**). When you drop the icon into the final window, all windows except the source and destination windows automatically close (**Figure 15**).

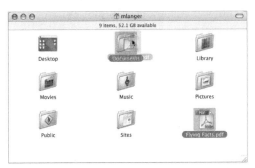

**Figure 11** Drag an icon onto a folder and wait...

## ✔ Tips

- The spring-loaded folders feature is sometimes referred to as *spring-open folders.*

- Using the spring-loaded folders feature requires a steady hand, good mouse skills, and knowledge of the location of folders on your disk.

- To use the spring-loaded folders feature, it must be enabled in the Finder preferences. Although this feature is normally turned on by default, if it's not, you can learn how to enable it in **Chapter 6.**

- To use the spring-loaded folders feature to move or copy more than one item at a time, select the items first, then drag any one of them.

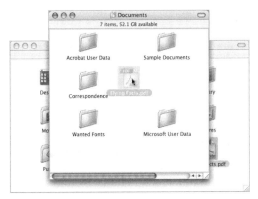

**Figure 12** ...until the folder opens.

**Figure 13** Continue to drag the icon onto a folder in that window and wait...

**Figure 14** ...until that folder opens.

**Figure 15** When you're finished, only the source window (which is active) and the destination window remain open.

## To move an item using spring-loaded folders

1. Drag the item you want to move onto the folder to which you want to move it (**Figure 11**), but do not release the mouse button. After a moment, the folder blinks and opens (**Figure 12**).

2. Without releasing the mouse button, repeat step 1. The destination folder becomes selected (**Figure 13**), then blinks and opens (**Figure 14**). Do this until you reach the final destination.

3. Release the mouse button to place the item into the destination window. All windows other than the source and destination windows close; the source window remains active (**Figure 15**).

## ✔ Tips

■ In steps 1 and 2, to open a folder immediately, press Spacebar while dragging an item onto it.

■ To close a folder's window so you can open a different folder in the same window, drag the item away from the open window. The window closes so you can drag the item onto a different folder and open it.

## To copy an item using spring-loaded folders

Hold down Option while following the above steps.

## ✔ Tip

■ If the destination folder is on another disk, it is not necessary to hold down Option to copy items; they're automatically copied.

**USING SPRING-LOADED FOLDERS**

# Exposé

If you're like most Mac OS X users, you probably have multiple applications and windows open at the same time while you work. The result can be a cluttered screen, with many layers of windows hiding other windows and the desktop.

Exposé helps solve the problem of screen clutter by making it easy to see all open windows in all applications (**Figure 16**), all open windows in a single application (**Figure 18**), or the entire desktop (**Figure 20**) at once. Simply press one of Exposé's shortcut keys (**Table 1**) to see what you need to see.

## ✔ Tips

- You can customize Exposé's shortcut keys or add additional Exposé triggers. I explain how in **Chapter 21**.

- You can use Exposé while copying or moving items. Begin dragging the item you want to move or copy, then use the appropriate Exposé keystroke for the view you need and complete the drag and drop while Exposé is active.

## To see all open windows at once

1. Press F9.

   All open windows resize so you can see into each one (**Figure 16**).

2. To activate a window, point to it to highlight its name (**Figure 17**) and click it or press F9 again. Exposé is released and the window comes to the front.

   *or*

   To release Exposé without activating a specific window, press F9 again.

**Table 1**

| Standard Shortcut Keys for Exposé ||
|---|---|
| Key | Description |
| F9 | Displays all open windows at once. |
| F10 | Displays all open windows for the current application at once. |
| F11 | Displays the desktop. |

**Figure 16** Pressing F9 displays all open windows.

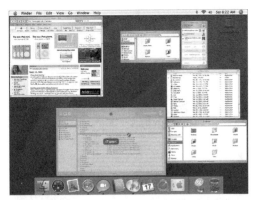

**Figure 17** Point to a window to highlight its name.

**Figure 18** Pressing F10 displays all of the windows in the currently active application—in this case, Finder.

**Figure 19** Point to a window to highlight its name.

**Figure 20** Pressing F11 displays the desktop.

## To see all open windows in the current application

1. Press F10.

   All open windows in the current application resize so you can see into each one and other application windows are dimmed (**Figure 18**).

2. To activate a window, point to it to highlight its name (**Figure 19**)and click it or press F10 again. Exposé is released and the window comes to the front.

   *or*

   To release Exposé without activating a specific window, press F10 again.

## To see the desktop

1. Press F11.

   All open windows shift to the edges of the screen so you can see the desktop (**Figure 20**).

2. To release Exposé, press F11 again.

## To switch from one Exposé view to another

Press the shortcut key for the other view.

# Labels

Mac OS X's Labels feature enables you to assign color-coded labels to Finder icons. You can then sort list view windows by label or search for items based on the assigned label. With a little imagination, labels can be a useful file management tool.

## ✔ Tips

- You can only sort a window by labels if the Label column is displayed in that window. I explain how to customize a list view window in **Chapter 6**.

- You can change the name associated with a label or its color. I tell you how in **Chapter 6**.

## To assign a label to an item

1. In a Finder window, select the icon(s) you want to apply a label to (**Figure 21**).

2. From the File menu, choose the color of the label you want to apply (**Figure 22**).

   The name of the icon is enclosed in an oval in the color you choose (**Figure 23**).

## To remove a label from an item

1. In a Finder window, select the icon you want to remove a label from (**Figure 24**).

2. From the File menu, choose the X beneath Color Label (**Figure 25**).

   The label is removed.

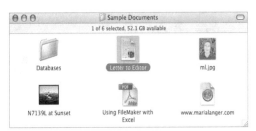

**Figure 21** Select the icon you want to apply a label to.

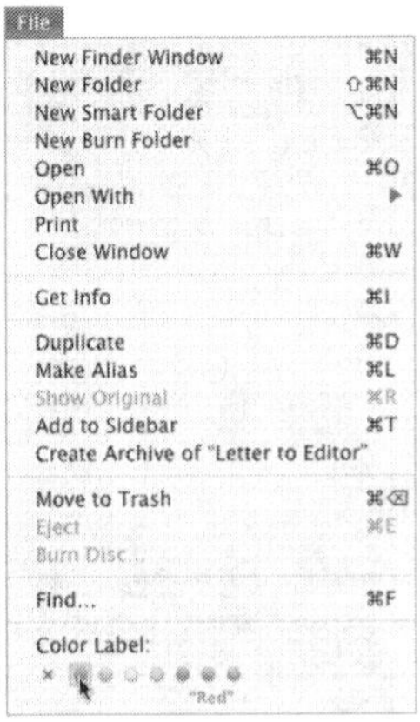

**Figure 22** Choose a label color from the bottom of the File menu.

**Figure 23** The color you chose is applied to the icon's name. (I know it doesn't look red here, but it is.)

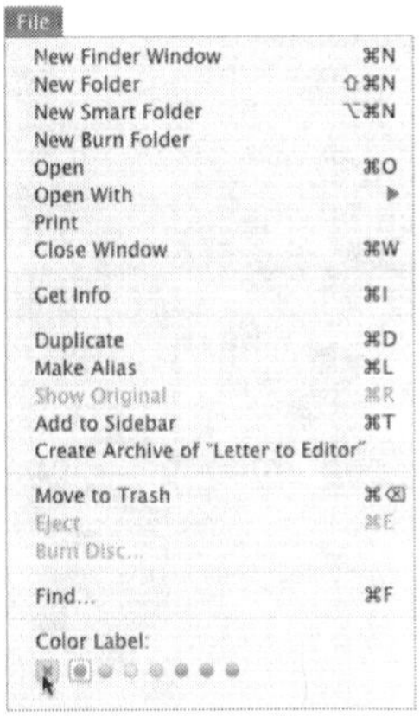

**Figure 25** Choosing the X under Color Label removes the label from selected icons.

**Figure 24** Select the icon you want to remove the label from.

iTunes

iTunes alias

**Figure 26**
The icon for an alias looks like the original item's icon but includes a tiny arrow.

# Aliases

An *alias* (**Figure 26**) is a pointer to an item. You can make an alias of an item and place it anywhere on your computer. Then, when you need to open the item, just open its alias.

## ✔ Tips

- It's important to remember that an alias is not a copy of the item—it's a pointer. If you delete the original item, the alias will not open.

- You can use the Select New Original dialog (**Figure 46**) to reassign an original to an alias, as explained later in this chapter.

- By putting aliases of frequently used items together where you can quickly access them—such as on your desktop—you make the items more accessible without actually moving them.

- The Favorites and Recent Items features work with aliases. These features are discussed a little later in this chapter.

- You can name an alias anything you like, as long as you follow the file naming guidelines discussed in **Chapter 3**. An alias's name does not need to include the word *alias*.

- The icon for an alias looks very much like the icon for the original item but includes a tiny arrow in the bottom-left corner (**Figure 26**).

- You can move, copy, rename, open, and delete an alias just like any other file.

ALIASES

## To create an alias

1. Select the item you want to make an alias for (**Figure 27**).

2. Choose File > Make Alias (**Figure 28**), or press ⌘ L.

   The alias appears right beneath the original item (**Figure 29**).

   *Or*

   Hold down ⌘ Option and drag the item for which you want to make an alias to a new location. The alias appears in the destination location.

## ✔ Tip

■ An alias's name is selected right after it is created (**Figure 29**). If desired, you can immediately type a new name to replace the default name.

## To find an alias's original file

1. Select the alias's icon.

2. Choose File > Show Original (**Figure 30**), or press ⌘ R.

   A window for the folder in which the original resides opens with the original item selected (**Figure 31**).

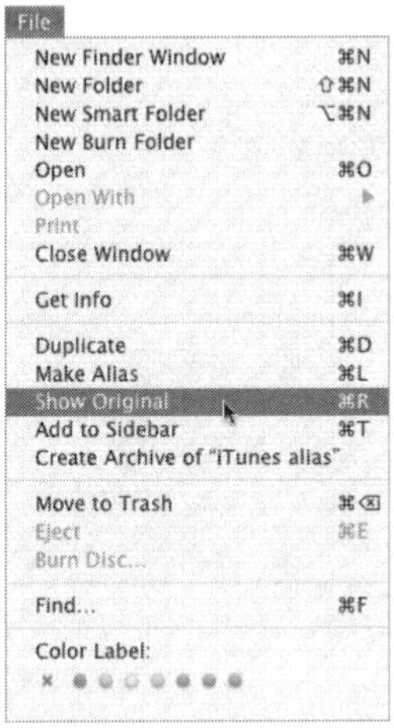

**Figure 27**
To create an alias, begin by selecting the item for which you want to make an alias.

**Figure 28**
Choose Make Alias from the File menu.

**Figure 29** The alias appears with the original.

**Figure 30**
Choose Show Original from the File menu.

**Figure 31** The original item appears selected in its window.

**Figure 32** Adding the Favorites folder to the Sidebar is one good way to make Favorite items easily accessible.

**Figure 33** The Dock is another good place for the Favorites folder.

# Favorites

The Favorites feature, which was introduced in the first release of Mac OS X, enabled you to add frequently accessed items to a Favorites submenu under the Go menu, in Open and Save As dialogs, and in a Favorites folder in Finder window toolbars. In Mac OS X 10.3, Apple began phasing out the Favorites feature, encouraging users to take advantage of the Sidebar instead.

If you're already using the Favorites feature and don't want to give it up, read on to learn more about how it works.

## ✔ Tips

- If you're brand new to Mac OS X or you are not already using Favorites, my advice is to skip this section. It's never a good idea to start using a feature that's being phased out.

- The Favorites feature works with aliases, which are discussed on the previous two pages.

- To take full advantage of Favorites, consider adding your Favorites folder to the Sidebar (**Figure 32**) or Dock (**Figure 33**) to make its contents more accessible. I explain how to add items to the Sidebar and Dock in **Chapter 6**.

## To add a favorite item

1. In the Finder, select the icon for the item that you want to add as a favorite item (**Figure 34**).

2. Hold down Shift and choose File > Add to Favorites (**Figure 35**), or press Shift ⌃ ⌘ T.

   The item is added to your Favorites folder (**Figure 36**).

## ✔ Tip

■ Favorite items are stored in the Favorites folder in the Library folder inside your home folder (**Figure 36**). You can learn more about your Home folder in **Chapter 3**.

## To remove a favorite

1. Open the Favorites folder in the Library folder inside your Home folder (**Figure 36**).

2. Drag the item that you want to remove out of the window.

3. Close the Favorites folder window.

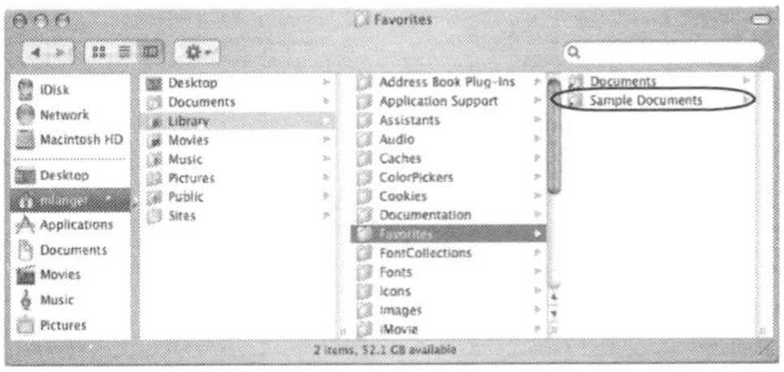

## ✔ Tip

■ Once you have removed an item from your Favorites folder, you can delete it if you no longer need it. Remember, it should be an alias to another item on disk. Deleting it does not remove the original.

**Figure 34**
Select the item that you want to add as a favorite item.

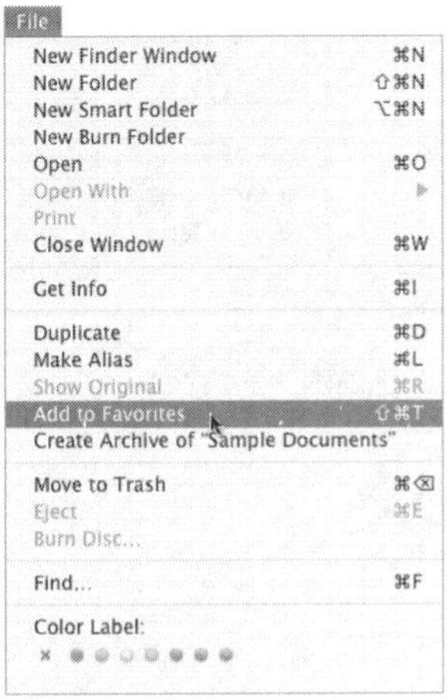

**Figure 35** Hold down Shift and choose Add to Favorites from the File menu.

**Figure 36** The item is added as an alias to the Favorites folder inside the Library folder in your Home folder.

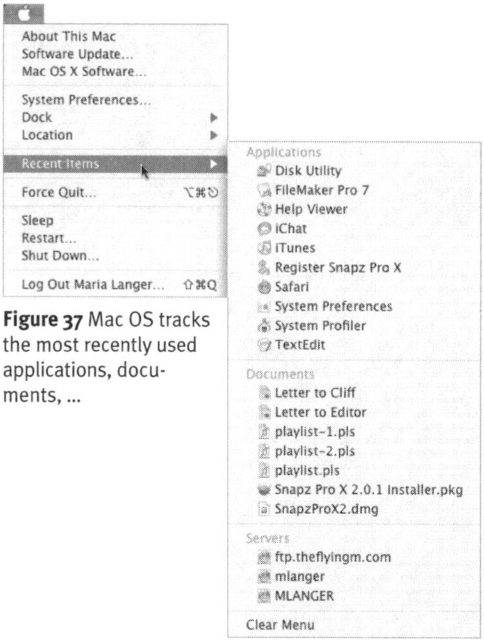

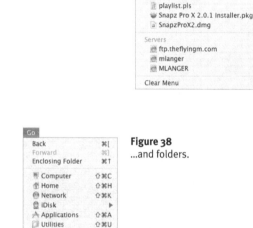

**Figure 37** Mac OS tracks the most recently used applications, documents, ...

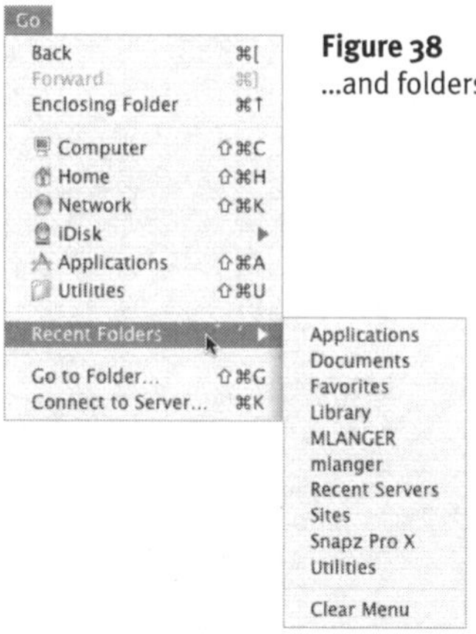

**Figure 38**
...and folders.

# Recent Items

Mac OS automatically tracks the things you open. It creates submenus of the most recently opened items in four categories—applications, documents, servers, and folders—making it quick and easy to open them again.

## ✔ Tip

■ You can specify how many recent applications and documents Mac OS X should track in the Recent Items submenu (**Figure 37**) by setting options in the Appearance preferences pane. I explain how in **Chapter 21**.

## To open recent items

To open a recently used application, document, or server, choose its name from the Recent Items submenu under the Apple menu (**Figure 37**).

*Or*

To open a recently used folder, choose its name from the Recent Folders submenu under the Go menu (**Figure 38**).

## ✔ Tips

■ Recent Items works with aliases, which are discussed earlier in this chapter.

■ Working with applications and documents is discussed in **Chapter 7**; working with servers is discussed in **Chapter 16**.

## To clear the Recent Items submenu

Choose Apple > Recent Items > Clear Menu (**Figure 37**).

## ✔ Tip

■ Clearing the Recent Items submenu does not delete any application or document files.

## To clear the Recent Folders submenu

Choose Go > Recent Folders > Clear Menu (**Figure 38**).

## ✔ Tip

■ Clearing the Recent Folders submenu does not delete any folders.

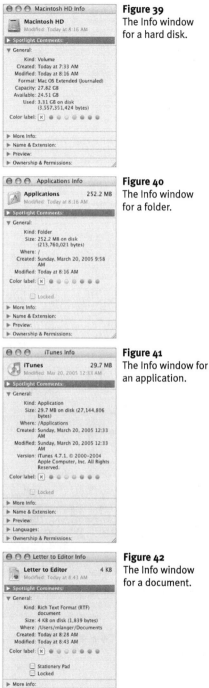

**Figure 39**
The Info window
for a hard disk.

**Figure 40**
The Info window
for a folder.

**Figure 41**
The Info window for
an application.

**Figure 42**
The Info window
for a document.

# The Info Window

You can learn more about an item by opening its Info window (**Figures 39** through **42**). Depending on the type of icon (disk, folder, application, document, alias, and so on), the General information in the Info window will provide some or all of the following:

- ◆ **Kind** or type of item.

- ◆ **Size** of item or contents (folders and files only).

- ◆ **Where** item is on disk.

- ◆ **Created** date and time.

- ◆ **Modified** date and time.

- ◆ **Format** of item (disks only).

- ◆ **Capacity** of item (disks only).

- ◆ **Available** space on item (disks only).

- ◆ **Used** space on item (disks only).

- ◆ **Version** number or copyright date (applications only).

- ◆ **Original** location on disk (aliases only).

- ◆ **Color label** assigned to the item.

- ◆ **Stationery Pad** check box (documents only) to convert the file into a stationery format file, which is like a document template.

- ◆ **Locked** check box to prevent the file from being deleted or overwritten (folders and files only).

## ✔ Tip

- ■ Other types of information available for a disk, folder, or file can be displayed by clicking triangles at the bottom of the info window (**Figures 39** through **42**).

THE INFO WINDOW

## To open the Info window

1. Select the item for which you want to open the Info window (**Figure 24**).

2. Choose File > Get Info (**Figure 43**), or press ⌃⌘Ⅰ.

   The Info window for that item appears (**Figure 42**).

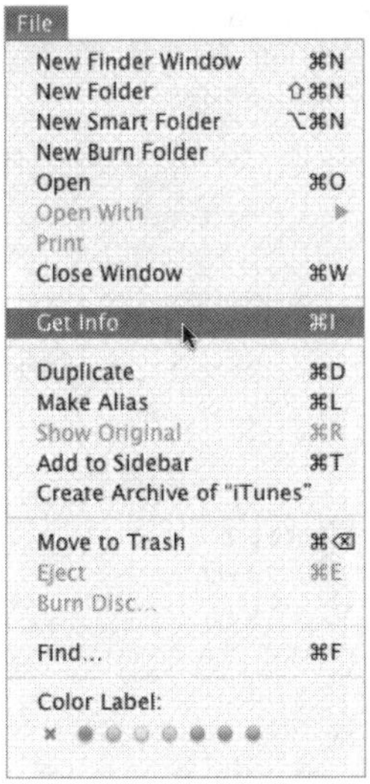

## To enter Spotlight comments in the Info window

1. Open the Info window for the item for which you want to enter comments (**Figure 42**).

2. If necessary, click the triangle beside Spotlight Comments near the top of the window. The window expands to show the Spotlight Comments box.

3. Type your comments into the Spotlight Comments box (**Figure 44**). They are automatically saved.

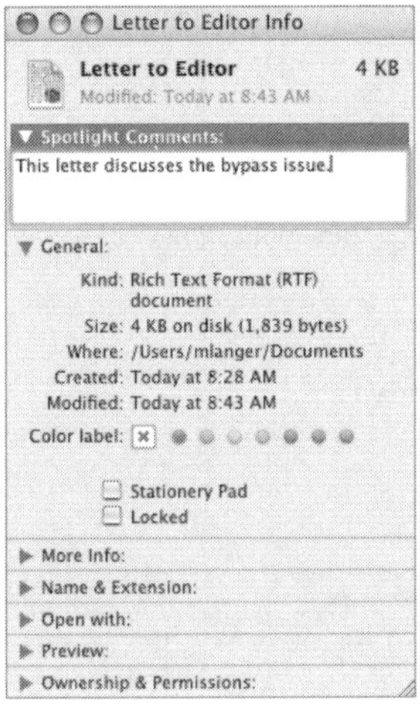

## ✔ Tips

- Mac OS X's new Spotlight feature can find files based on the comments you enter in the Spotlight Comments field. I explain how to use Spotlight in **Chapter 5**.

- As discussed in **Chapter 6**, you can set a window's list view to display comments entered in the Info window.

## To lock an application or document

1. Open the Info window for the item you want to lock (**Figures 40** through **42**).

2. Turn on the Locked check box.

## ✔ Tip

- Locked items cannot be deleted or overwritten. They can, however, be moved.

**Figure 43**
Choose Get Info from the File menu.

**Figure 44**
You can enter information about the item in the Spotlight Comments box.

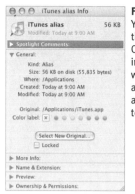

**Figure 45**
You can click the Select New Original button in the Info window for an alias to assign a new original to the alias.

## To select a new original item for an alias

1. In the Info window for the alias (**Figure 45**), click the Select New Original button.

2. Use the Select New Original dialog that appears (**Figure 46**) to locate and select the item that you want to use as the original for the alias.

3. Click Choose. The item you selected is assigned to the alias.

## ✔ Tips

- The Select New Original dialog is similar to an Open dialog, which is covered in **Chapter 7**.

- If you try to open an alias for which the original cannot be found, a dialog like the one in **Figure 47** appears. Click Fix Alias to display the Select New Original dialog (**Figure 46**), and select a new original.

- I discuss Aliases earlier in this chapter.

**Figure 46** Use the Select New Original dialog to locate and choose a new original for an alias.

**Figure 47** This dialog appears when you attempt to open an alias for which the original cannot be found.

# Working with Archives

Mac OS X's archive feature enables you to create compressed copies of items called *archived files* or *archives*. Archives take up less space on disk than regular files. You may find them useful for backing up files or for sending files to others over a network or via e-mail.

## ✔ Tip

■ The archive feature uses ZIP format compression, which was originally developed as a DOS and Windows PC format. As a result, document archives created with this feature are fully compatible with DOS and Windows PCs.

## To archive a file or folder

1. Select the item you want to archive (**Figure 48**).

2. Choose File > Create Archive of "*Item Name*" (**Figure 49**).

3. Wait while your computer creates the archive. While it works, a Copy status dialog appears (**Figure 50**). When the dialog disappears, the archive file appears in the same location as the original as a .zip file (**Figure 51**).

## ✔ Tip

■ You can archive multiple items at once. Select the items, then choose File > Create Archive of *n* items (where *n* is the number of selected items). When the archive appears, it will be named *Archive.zip*.

## To open an archive

Double-click the archive file. The archive's contents are uncompressed and appear in the same window as the archive file.

**Figure 48** Select the item you want to archive.

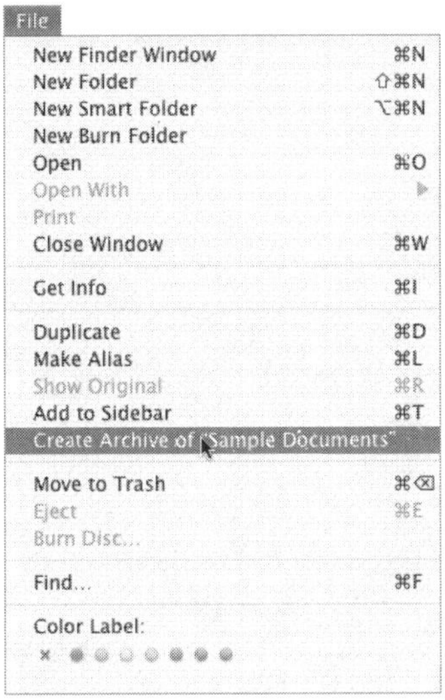

**Figure 49** Choose Create Archive from the File menu.

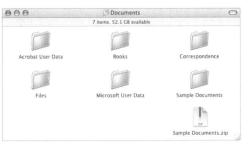

**Figure 50** A Copy progress dialog appears while the file is being compressed.

**Figure 51** An archive file has a .zip file extension.

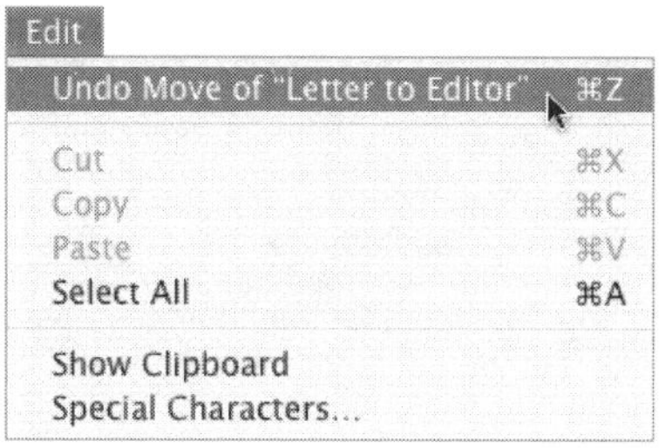

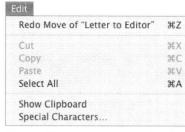

**Figure 52** The Undo command enables you to undo the last action you performed.

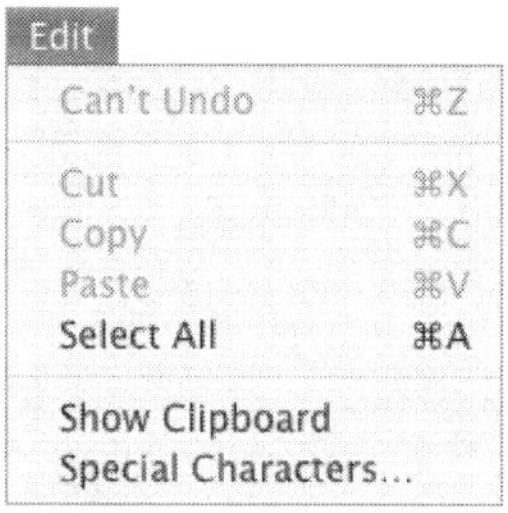

**Figure 53**
If an action cannot be undone, the words *Can't Undo* will appear at the top of the Edit menu in gray.

**Figure 54** The Redo command undoes the Undo command.

# Undoing Finder Actions

The Mac OS X Finder includes limited support for the Undo command, which can reverse the most recently completed action. Say, for example, that you move a file from one folder to another folder. If you immediately change your mind, you can choose Edit > Undo Move (**Figure 52**) to put the file back where it was.

## ✔ Tips

■ Don't depend on the Undo command. Unfortunately, it isn't available for all actions (**Figure 53**).

■ The exact wording of the Undo command varies depending on the action and the item it was performed on. In **Figure 52**, for example, the command is Undo Move of "Letter to Editor" because the last action was to move a document icon named *Letter to Editor*.

■ The Undo command is also available (and generally more reliable) in most Mac OS applications. You'll usually find it at the top of the Edit menu.

## To undo an action

Immediately after performing an action, choose Edit > Undo *action description* (**Figure 52**), or press ⌘Z. The action is reversed.

## To redo an action

Immediately after undoing an action, choose Edit > Redo *action description* (**Figure 54**). The action is redone—as if you never used the Undo command.

## ✔ Tip

■ Think of the Redo command as the Undo-Undo command since it undoes the Undo command.

# Using Mac OS Search Features

## Search Features

Mac OS X offers a number of ways you can search for files or folders:

◆ The Finder's built-in search feature enables you to initiate a search based on file name or content from a Finder window. Search results appear within the window, sorted by file type.

◆ The Finder's Find command takes Finder searching a step further by offering additional search options, including the ability to find files based on kind, dates, labels, size, and other criteria.

◆ Spotlight, which is new in Mac OS X 10.4, enables you to perform a search without activating the Finder. Search results can appear in a special Spotlight menu or as a customizable list in a window.

Once you have a list of found files, opening the file you want to view is as easy as double-clicking it.

Mac OS X 10.4 also introduces Smart Folders. This feature, which works with the Finder's Find command, enables you to create a special folder that is automatically updated based on search criteria you specify for it.

This chapter takes a closer look at all of these search features so you'll never have to worry about misplacing a file.

# The Search Field

The Finder's Search field appears in the top-right corner of a Finder window's toolbar (**Figure 1**). You can use it to initiate a search based on item name or contents. Simply enter a word or phrase in the field and Mac OS X displays a list of matches.

## ✔ Tip

- A window's toolbar must be displayed to use the Search field. If the toolbar is not displayed, click the toolbar control button (**Figure 1**) to display it.

## To find files with the Search field

1. Click in the Search field of a Finder window to position the blinking insertion point there (**Figure 1**).

2. Enter the word or phrase you want to search for (**Figure 2**).

   As soon as you begin typing, the window turns into a Searching window. Mac OS begins displaying results sorted by item type (**Figure 2**).

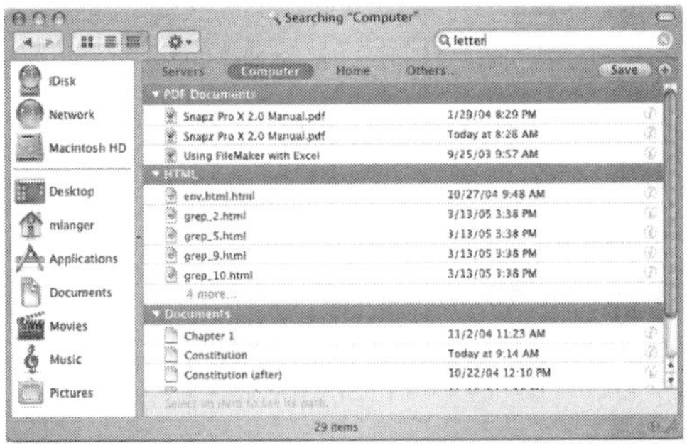

## ✔ Tips

- You can specify a search location by clicking one of the location buttons above the search results in the Searching window (**Figure 2**). I tell you more about search locations on the next page.

- Remember, the search feature searches by name or contents. If you're not sure of a file's name, search for some text you expect to find in the document. **Figure 3** shows an example.

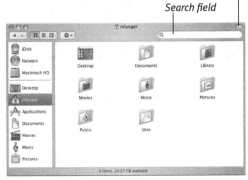

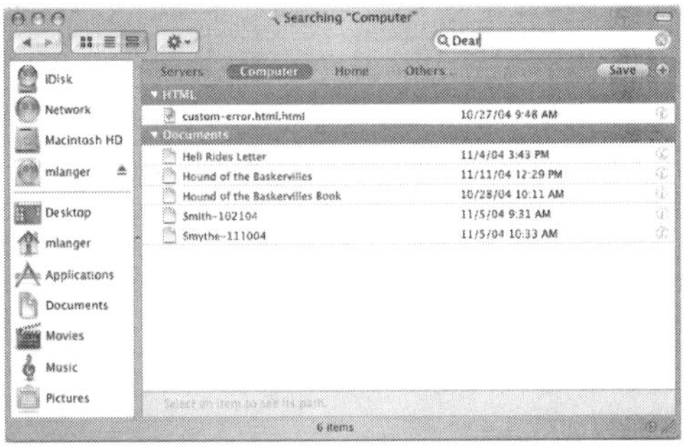

Toolbar control button

Search field

**Figure 1** The Search field appears in the toolbar of a Finder window.

**Figure 2** When you enter a search word, Mac OS X immediately begins displaying search results.

**Figure 3** Remember, the search feature searches by contents, too. In this example, I found two other letters by searching for the word *Dear*—which appears as part of the text in most letters—rather than *letter*.

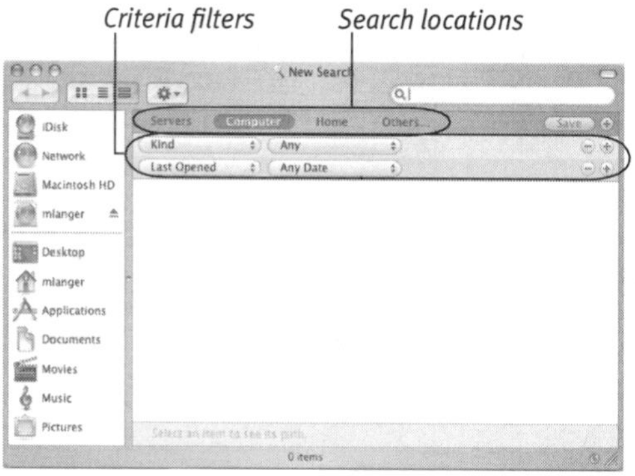

Criteria filters          Search locations

**Figure 4** Choosing the Find command displays a New Search window with additional options.

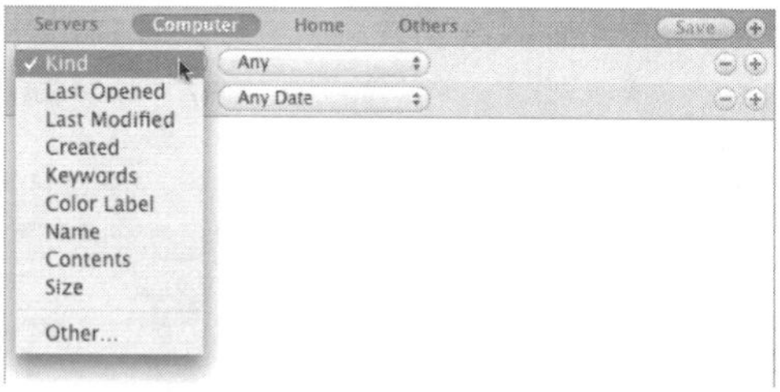

**Figure 5** There are several categories of Criteria filters.

# The Find Command

Mac OS X's Find command also works with the Search field, but it automatically offers additional search options (**Figure 4**):

◆ **Search locations** appear as buttons beneath the Search field. Click a button to search just that location. By default, four buttons appear:

▲ **Servers** are network volumes your computer is connected to.

▲ **Computer** is the top level of your computer, which includes all hard disks and inserted media.

▲ **Home** is your Home folder.

▲ **Others** enables you to select specific locations.

◆ **Criteria filters** appear as pop-up menus (**Figure 5**) in rows above the search results area. You can set options with these filters to narrow down the search results. There are several basic categories of criteria filters:

▲ **Kind** is the type of item.

▲ **Last Opened** is the date the item was last opened.

▲ **Last Modified** is the date the item was last changed.

▲ **Created** is the date the item was created.

▲ **Keywords** are keywords associated with the item.

▲ **Color Label** is the label assigned to the item.

▲ **Name** is the item's name.

▲ **Contents** is the contents of the item.

▲ **Size** is the size of the item.

▲ **Other** enables you to set more advanced criteria filter options.

## ✔ Tip

■ You can display criteria filters when using the Search field as discussed on the previous page. Click the Add (**+**) button near the top of the New Search window (**Figure 2**) to add a filter row.

## To find files with the Find command

1. If necessary, activate Finder.

2. Choose File > Find (**Figure 6**), or press ⌃ ⌘ F.

   A New Search window like the one in **Figure 4** appears.

3. Enter a search word or phrase in the Search field.

4. Click a location button to choose one of the search locations.

5. Set up criteria filters by choosing options from the pop-up menus (**Figure 5**).

Search results appear in the Searching window (**Figure 7**).

## ✔ Tips

- You can perform any combination of steps 3 through 5. Each step you perform adds criteria that narrows the search results.

- The search results must match all search criteria specified in steps 3 through 5.

- To add additional criteria filters, click the Add (+) button at the right end of a criteria row.

- To remove a criteria filter, click the Remove (–) button at the right end of its row.

- Clicking the Save button near the top of the New Search window creates a smart folder. I tell you about smart folders a little later in this chapter.

**Figure 6**
The Finder's File menu.

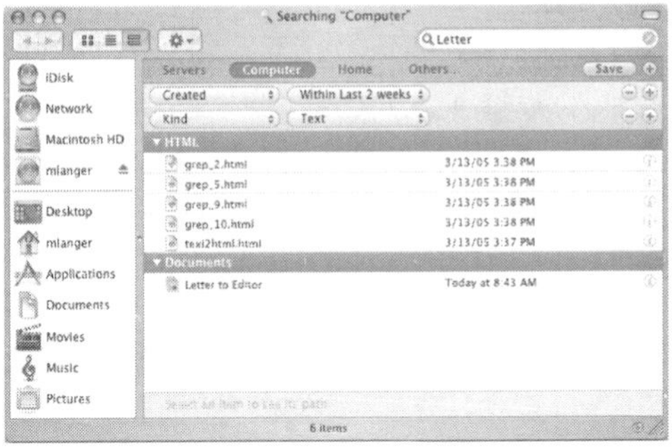

**Figure 7** When you set criteria at the top of the window, search results will appear in a list.

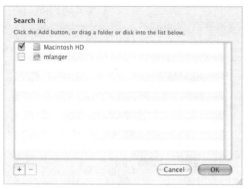

**Figure 8** The Search in dialog sheet lists specific locations you can search.

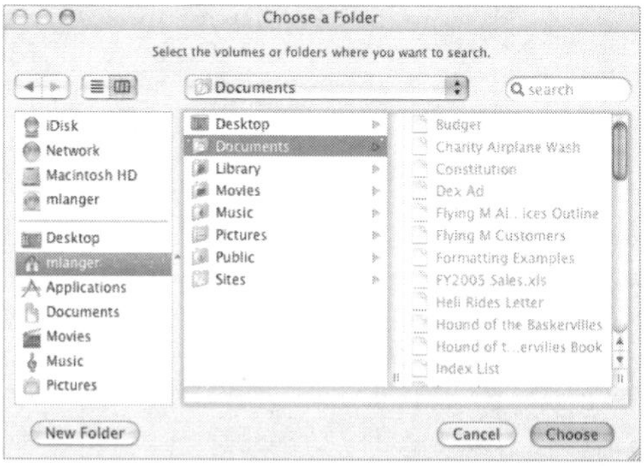

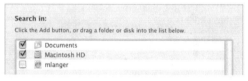

**Figure 9** Use the Choose a Folder dialog to add a folder or volume to the Search in dialog.

**Figure 10** The location you added appears in the list.

**Figure 11** A new button for the number of places you will search appears in the New Search or Searching dialog.

# To set specific search locations

1. Near the top of the New Search (**Figure 4**) or Searching (**Figure 7**) window, click the Others button. A Search in dialog sheet appears (**Figure 8**).

2. To add a location to the list, click the + button at the bottom of the list, use the Choopse a File dialog that appears (**Figure 9**) to locate, select, and choose a folder or volume. The location you selected appears in the list (**Figure 10**).

3. To remove a location from the list, select the location and click the – button at the bottom of the list. The location you selected is removed from the list.

4. Toggle the check boxes beside locations to indicate which locations should be searched.

5. Click OK. The location buttons change to indicate the number of other places to be searched (**Figure 11**).

## ✔ Tips

- Another way to add a location to the Search in dialog is to simply drag the folder or volume icon into the window.

- The locations you add to the Search in dialog (**Figure 8**) remain there until you remove them. The search location buttons, however, return to default values each time you open a New Search window.

SETTING SPECIFIC SEARCH LOCATIONS

# Smart Folders

Smart folders, which is a new feature in Mac OS X 10.4, takes the Find command one step further. It enables you to save search criteria as a special folder. Opening the folder automatically performs a search and displays matching items. So the smart folder's contents always contain items that match search criteria, even if the files and folders on your computer change.

## To create a smart folder

1. Choose File > New Smart Folder (**Figure 6**) or press Option ⌘ N. A New Smart Folder window, which looks a lot like a New Search or Searching window, appears (**Figure 12**).

2. Follow steps 3 through 5 in the section titled "To find files with the Find command" to set up search criteria for the smart folder. The search results appear in the window (**Figure 13**).

3. Click the Save button near the top of the New Smart Folder window.

4. Set options in the dialog that appears (**Figure 14**):

   ▲ **Save As** is the name of the smart folder. Give it a name that describes what the folder will contain.

   ▲ **Where** is the location in which the smart folder will be saved. Your choices are Saved Searches, the Desktop, or your Home folder.

   ▲ **Add To Sidebar** instructs Mac OS X to add an alias of the folder to the Sidebar (**Figure 15**).

5. Click Save. The name you gave the smart folder appears in the window's title bar (**Figure 15**) and the smart folder is saved for future use.

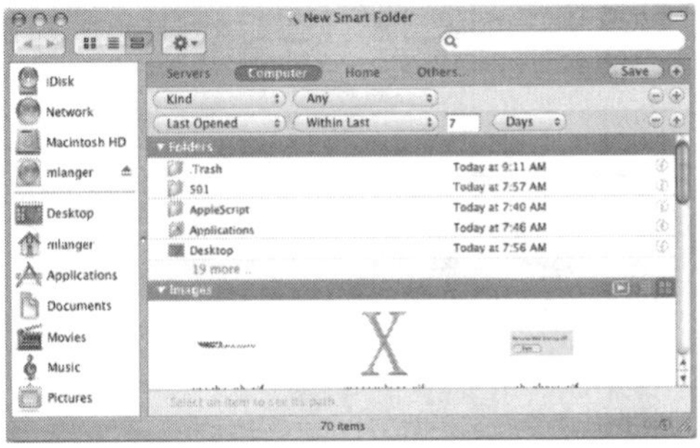

**Figure 12** The New Smart Folder window.

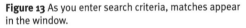

**Figure 13** As you enter search criteria, matches appear in the window.

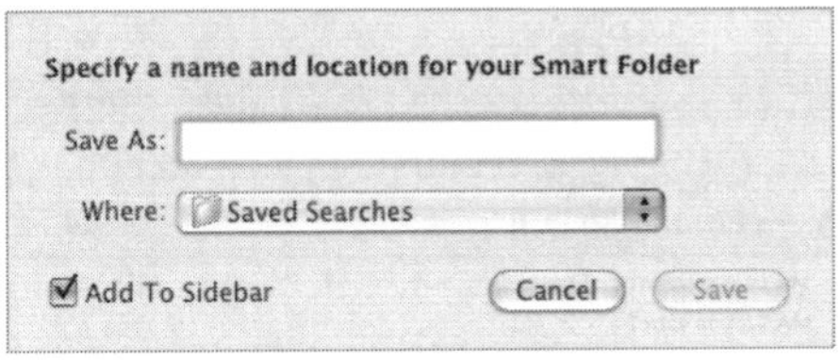

**Specify a name and location for your Smart Folder**

Save As:

Where: Saved Searches

☑ Add To Sidebar      Cancel      Save

**Figure 14** Use this dialog to set options for saving a smart folder.

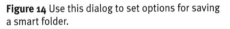

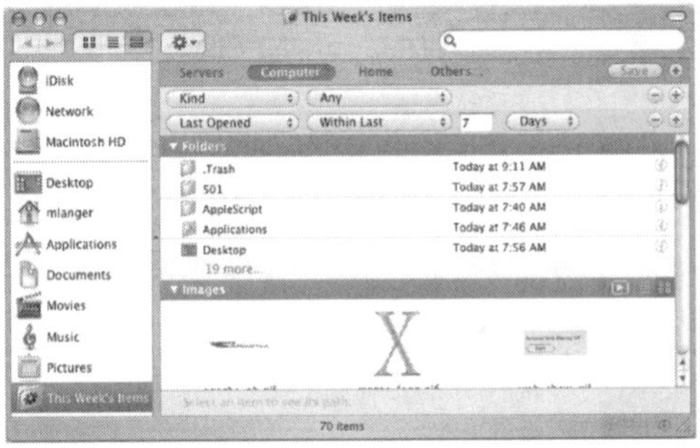

**Figure 15** The name of the smart folder appears in the title bar. In this example, the smart folder has also been added to the Sidebar.

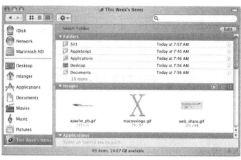

**Figure 16** The contents of a smart folder displayed after it has been saved.

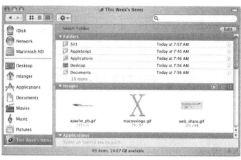

**Figure 17** Smart folder icons in the Saved Searches folder.

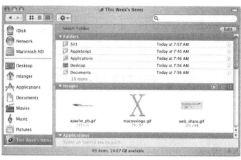

**Figure 18** The Saved Searches folder is in the Library folder in your Home folder.

# To open a smart folder

If the smart folder has been added to the Sidebar, click the name of the smart folder in the Sidebar (**Figure 16**).

*Or*

If the smart folder has not been added to the Sidebar, open the icon for the smart folder (**Figure 17**).

The contents of the smart folder appear in a window like the one in **Figure 16**.

## ✔ Tip

- The Saved Searches folder is in the Library folder in your Home folder (**Figure 18**).

# To edit a smart folder

1. Open the smart folder you want to edit (**Figure 16**).

2. Click the Edit button near the top of the window. The search criteria appears near the top of the window (**Figure 15**).

3. Make changes as desired to search criteria. The search results in the window change accordingly.

4. Click the Save button. The changes are saved to the smart folder's definition.

# To delete a smart folder

Drag the smart folder's icon to the Trash.

## ✔ Tip

- Deleting a smart folder does not delete the contents of the smart folder. It simply deletes the search criteria that displays those contents. The original items remain on disk.

# Spotlight

Spotlight, which is brand-new in Mac OS X 10.4, makes Finder searching available in the menu bar, no matter which application is active. Simply click the Spotlight icon in the menu bar (**Figure 19**) and enter a search word or phrase. Spotlight displays a menu of matches (**Figure 20**) or a window that lists all of the matches (**Figure 21**).

**Figure 19** Clicking the Spotlight icon in the menu bar displays Spotlight's search field.

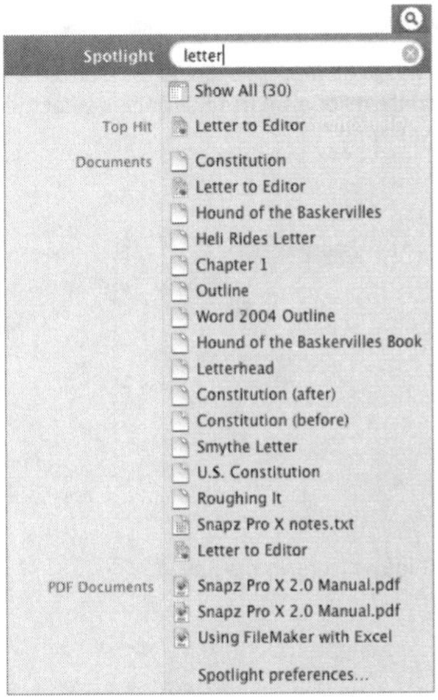

## ✔ Tips

■ The new Spotlight preferences pane enables you to set options to control the types of files that appear in Spotlight results. I tell you more about these options in **Chapter 21**.

■ Spotlight also works within certain Mac OS X applications, such as System Preferences. I explain how to use Spotlight with System Preferences in **Chapter 21**.

## To find items with Spotlight

1. Click the Spotlight icon on the far right end of the menu bar. The Spotlight search field appears (**Figure 19**).

2. Enter a search word or phrase in the search field. Spotlight immediately begins displaying matches for what you enter in a menu beneath the search field (**Figure 20**).

3. To open one of the items in the menu, click that item.

    *or*

    To display a window that lists all of the items Spotlight found (**Figure 21**), choose Show All from Spotlight's menu of found items.

## ✔ Tip

■ In step 1, you can press ⌃ ⌘ Spacebar to activate the Spotlight search field.

**Figure 20** As you enter a word or phrase in the search field, Spotlight displays results in a menu.

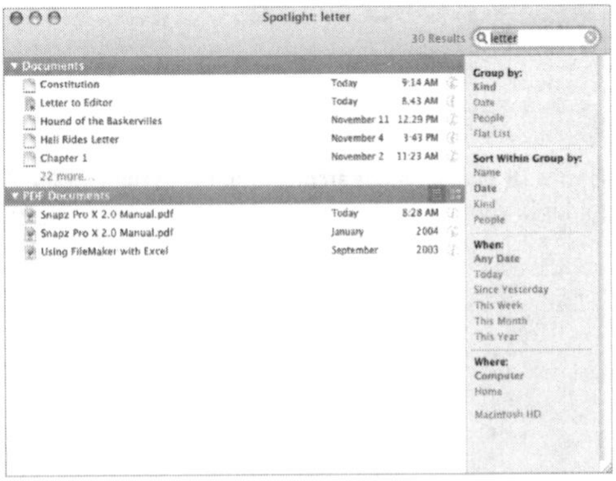

**Figure 21** Choosing Show All from Spotlight's menu of found items displays the items in a window like this.

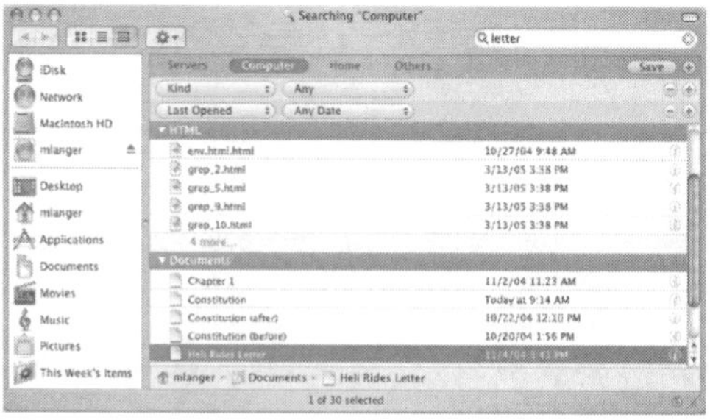

**Figure 22** The path to an item appears in the bottom a Finder search results window when the item is selected in the list.

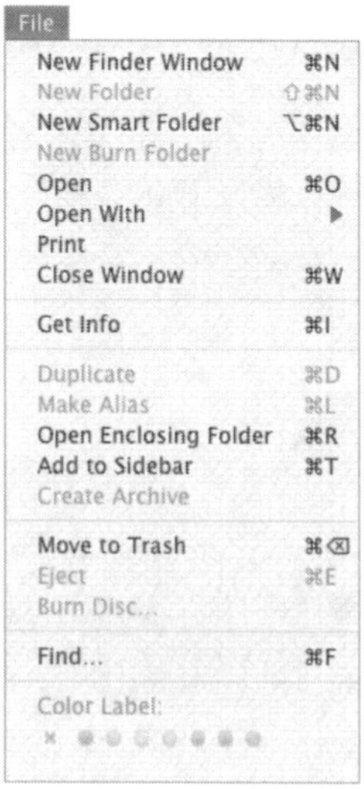

**Figure 23**
You can use options on the Finder's File menu to work with any selected item.

# Working with Search Results

Whether you search for items with a Finder window's search field (**Figure 1**), the Find command and New Search window (**Figure 4**), smart folders (**Figure 12**), or Spotlight (**Figure 19**), you will eventually wind up with a list of found items. **Figures 2**, **11**, **16**, and **21** show examples. Here's what you can do with these lists.

## ✔ Tip

- In addition to the tasks listed here, you can also use available Finder menu commands on any selected item in a list of found items.

## To open a found item

In the list of found items, double-click the item you want to open.

## To see where an item resides on disk

In the list of found items, select the item. Its location on disk appears at the bottom of the window (**Figure 22**).

## ✔ Tip

- This does not work with a Spotlight window of found items.

## To open the folder in which an item resides

1. In the list of found items, select the item for which you want to open the enclosing folder (**Figure 22**).

2. Choose File > Open Enclosing Folder (**Figure 23**) or press ⌘ ⌘ R.

   The folder in which the item resides opens.

## To get more information about an item

Click the tiny "i" button to the far right of the item you want more information about. The line for that item expands to show additional information (**Figures 24** and **25**).

### ✔ Tips

- To collapse the line for the item, click the triangle button to the far right of the item's name.

- You can also use the File menu's Get Info command (**Figure 23**) or the More info button in a Finder search results window (**Figure 24**) to display the Info window for any item in a list. I tell you about the Info window in **Chapter 4**.

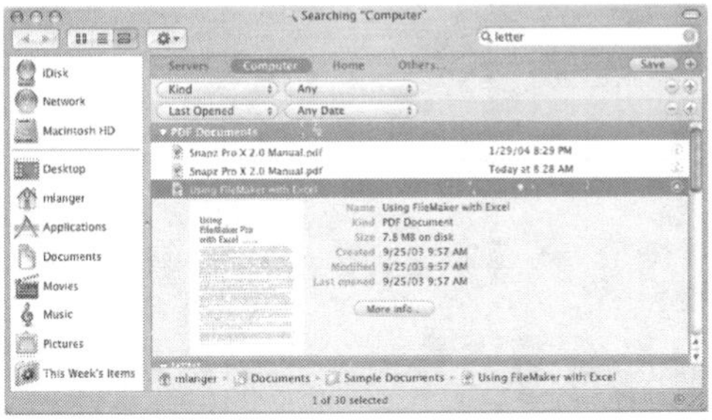

## To change the way items are listed in a Spotlight window

Click options on the far right side of the Spotlight window (**Figure 21**):

- ◆ **Group by** determines how search results are grouped.

- ◆ **Sort Within Group by** determines how search results are sorted within each group.

- ◆ **When** narrows down the search results by modification date.

- ◆ **Where** narrows down the search results by item location.

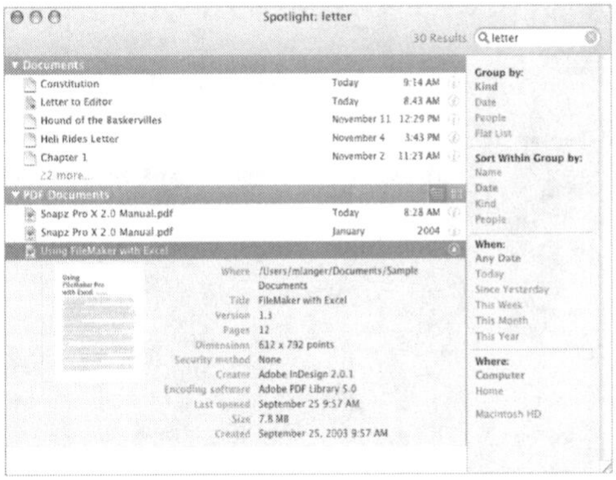

**Figure 24** Information about an item, including a preview, in a Finder's search results window.

**Figure 25** You can also display information about an item in Spotlight's search results window.

# Customizing the Finder

## Customizing the Finder

One of the great things about Mac OS is its user interface flexibility. Although the Mac OS X Finder looks the same on every computer when installed, it is highly customizable, making it possible for every Mac user to set up the Finder so it looks and works just right.

This chapter covers a number of Finder customization features, including:

◆ **Finder Preferences** enable you to set general Finder options, as well as text for labels, Sidebar contents, and advanced options.

◆ **Toolbar customization** enables you to specify what icons appear in the toolbar and what order they appear in.

◆ **Sidebar customization** enables you to add, remove, and shuffle Sidebar contents.

◆ **Dock customization** enables you to add, remove, and shuffle Dock contents and to set options that control the way the Dock looks and works.

◆ **View Options** enable you to customize the appearance of window contents.

◆ **Window customization** enables you to change column width, shuffle columns around, and show or hide the status bar.

# Finder Preferences

Finder preferences enables you to customize several aspects of the desktop and Finder. The Finder's preferences window is organized into four different panes of options:

◆ **General** lets you set basic options for the desktop and Finder windows.

◆ **Labels** enables you to set label names for the Finder's label feature, which is discussed in **Chapter 4**.

◆ **Sidebar** lets you set options for the Sidebar.

◆ **Advanced** enables you to set options for the display of file extensions and the Trash warning.

## To open Finder Preferences

Choose Finder > Preferences (**Figure 1**) or press ⌘,. The Finder Preferences window opens, displaying the last pane of options you accessed.

## To set General Finder Preferences

1. In the Finder Preferences window, click the General button to display General options (**Figure 2**).

2. Toggle check boxes to specify what items should appear on the desktop:

  ▲ **Hard disks** displays icons for mounted hard disks.

  ▲ **CDs, DVDs, and iPods** displays icons for removable media, including CDs and DVDs, as well as iPods.

  ▲ **Connected servers** displays icons for mounted server volumes.

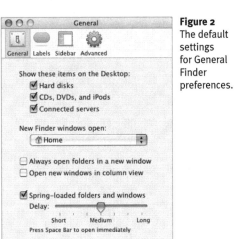

**Figure 1**
Choose Preferences from the Finder menu.

**Figure 2**
The default settings for General Finder preferences.

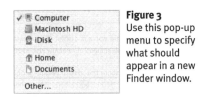

**Figure 3**
Use this pop-up menu to specify what should appear in a new Finder window.

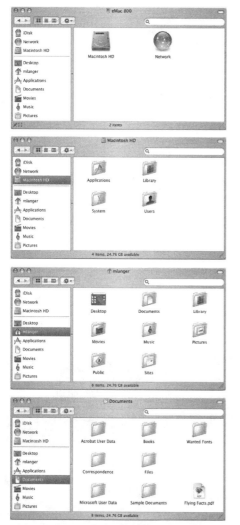

**Figures 4, 5, 6, & 7** A new Finder window can display the top-level computer window, your hard disk contents, your Home folder contents, or your Documents folder contents.

**Figure 8** Use a dialog like this to display a specific folder when you open a new Finder window.

3. Choose an option from the pop-up menu (**Figure 3**) to determine what should appear in a new Finder window (the window that appears when you choose File > New Finder Window):

▲ **Computer** displays the icons for the network and all mounted volumes (**Figure 4**).

▲ *Hard Disk name* displays the root level of your hard disk (**Figure 5**).

▲ **iDisk** displays the top level of your iDisk. (This option only appears if you are a .Mac subscriber and use iDisk.)

▲ **Home** displays the contents of your Home folder (**Figure 6**).

▲ **Documents** displays the contents of the Documents folder inside your Home folder (**Figure 7**).

▲ **Other** displays the Choose a Folder dialog (**Figure 8**), which you can use to select a different folder to display.

4. Toggle check boxes to set other options:

▲ **Always open folders in a new window** opens a new window to display the contents of the folder you open. This makes Mac OS X work more like Mac OS 9.2 and earlier.

▲ **Open new windows in column view** opens all new windows in column view, regardless of which view was last used to view the window.

▲ **Spring-loaded folders and windows** enables the spring-loaded folders feature. You can use the slider to set the delay time for this feature.

## ✔ Tip

■ I discuss disks, mounting disks, and views in **Chapter 3**, spring-loaded folders in **Chapter 4**, and iDisk in **Chapter 14**.

**SETTING GENERAL FINDER PREFERENCES**

## To customize labels

1. In the Finder Preferences window, click the Labels button to display Labels options (**Figure 9**).

2. To change the name of a label, select the text for the label you want to change (**Figure 10**) and enter new text (**Figure 11**).

3. Repeat step 2 for each label you want to change.

## ✔ Tip

■ The names of labels appear on the File menu when you point to a label (**Figure 12**) and in a list view window when the Label column is displayed (**Figure 13**). I explain how to display specific columns in list view later in this chapter.

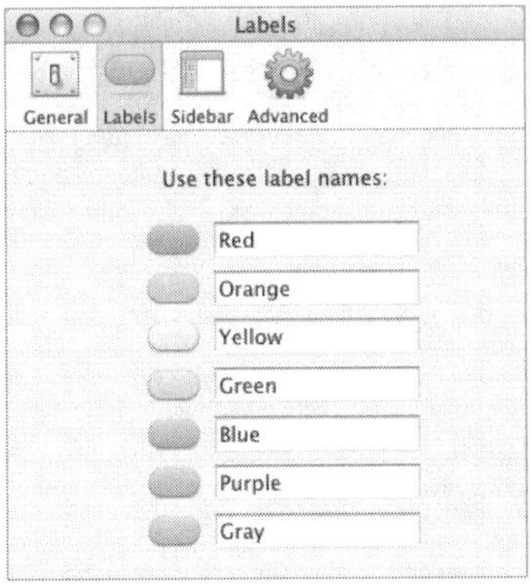

**Figure 9** The default settings in the Labels window of Finder preferences.

**Figure 10** To change a label, select it...

**Figure 11** ...and enter a new label.

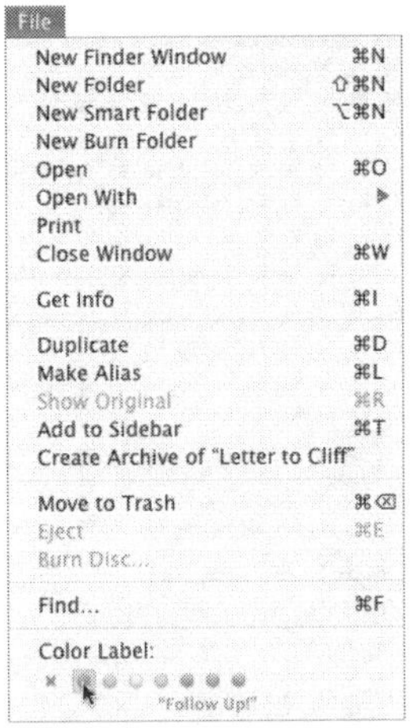

**Figure 12** The new label appears on the File menu.

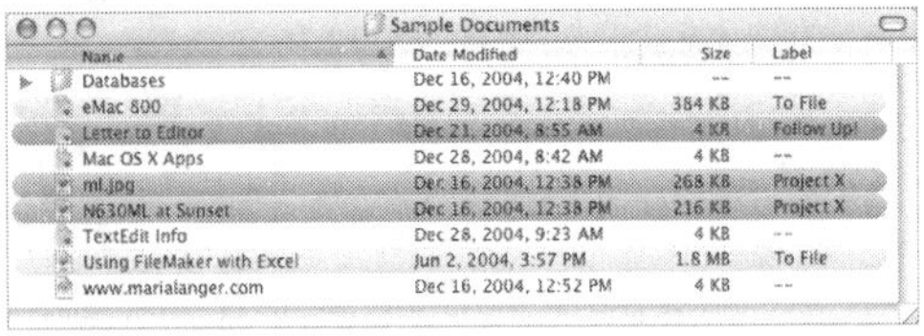

**Figure 13** Here's what labels look like in list view. Three different customized labels have been applied and the Label column is displayed.

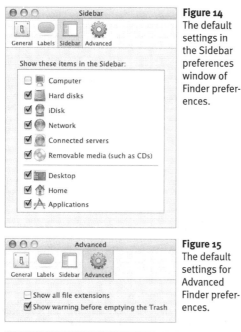

**Figure 14**
The default settings in the Sidebar preferences window of Finder preferences.

**Figure 15**
The default settings for Advanced Finder preferences.

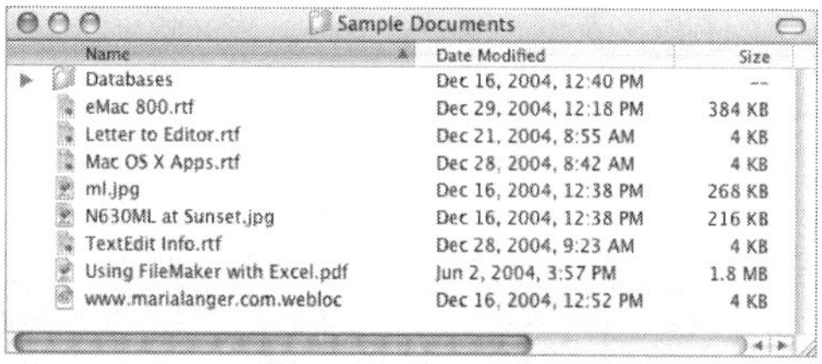

**Figure 16** You can set up the Finder so it always displays file extensions as part of an item's name.

**Figure 17**
The Hide extension check box in a file's Info window determines whether the file's extension appears in Finder windows.

## To set Sidebar preferences

1. In the Finder Preferences window, click the Sidebar button to display Sidebar options (**Figure 14**).

2. Toggle check boxes to specify what items should appear in the Sidebar.

## ✔ Tip

- I tell you more about customizing the Sidebar later in this chapter.

## To set Advanced preferences

1. In the Finder Preferences window, click the Advanced button to display Advanced options (**Figure 15**).

2. Toggle check boxes to set options:

   ▲ **Show all file extensions** tells the Finder to display file extensions in Finder windows (**Figure 16**) for all files from that point forward. This option, in effect, turns off the Hide extension check box in the Name & Extension area of the Info window (**Figure 17**) for all files on a go-forward basis.

   ▲ **Show warning before emptying the Trash** displays a dialog like the one in **Figure 18** when you choose Finder > Empty Trash or Finder > Secure Empty Trash. Turning off this check box prevents the dialog from appearing.

## ✔ Tip

- I discuss the Info window in **Chapter 4** and the Trash in **Chapter 3**.

**Figure 18** The Trash warning dialog.

# Customizing the Toolbar

The toolbar, which is discussed in **Chapter 2**, can be customized to include buttons and icons for a variety of commands and items.

## ✔ Tips

■ When you customize the toolbar, your changes affect the toolbar in all windows in which the toolbar is displayed.

■ To display the toolbar, click the Toolbar control button in the upper-right corner of a Finder window, choose View > Show Toolbar, or press Option ⌃ ⌘ T.

## To customize the toolbar

1. With any Finder window open and the toolbar displayed, choose View > Customize Toolbar (**Figure 19**). The Customize Toolbar dialog sheet appears (**Figure 20**).

2. Make changes to the toolbar contents as follows:

   ▲ To add an item to the toolbar, drag it from the dialog sheet to the position you want it to occupy in the toolbar (**Figure 21**). When you release the mouse button, the item appears on the toolbar (**Figure 22**).

   ▲ To remove an item from the toolbar, drag it off the toolbar (**Figure 23**). When you release the mouse button, the item disappears in a puff of digital smoke (**Figure 24**).

   ▲ To rearrange the order of items on the toolbar, drag them into the desired position (**Figure 25**). When you release the mouse button, the items are rearranged (**Figure 26**).

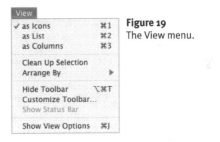

**Figure 19**
The View menu.

**Figure 20** The Customize Toolbar window.

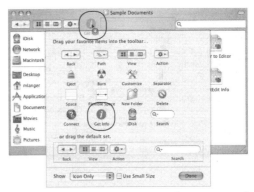

**Figure 21** To add an item, drag it from the center part of the dialog sheet to the toolbar.

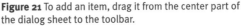

**Figure 22** When you release the mouse button, the item is added.

**Figure 23**
To remove an item, drag it off the toolbar.

**Figure 24** When you release the mouse button, the item is removed.

**Figure 25** To rearrange toolbar items, drag them around the toolbar.

**Figure 26** When you release the mouse button, the items are rearranged.

| Icon & Text |
| ✓ Icon Only |
| Text Only |

**Figure 27**
Show pop-up menu options.

**Figures 28 & 29** You can also display the toolbar as icons and text (above) or as text only (below).

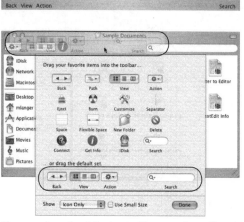

**Figure 30** Drag the default set of icons to the toolbar.

3. To specify how items should appear on the toolbar, choose an option from the Show pop-up menu at the bottom of the window (**Figure 27**):

   ▲ **Icon & Text** displays both the icon and the icon's name (**Figure 28**).

   ▲ **Icon Only** displays only the icon (**Figure 26**).

   ▲ **Text Only** displays only the name of the icon (**Figure 29**).

4. To display smaller size toolbar buttons, turn on the Use Small Size check box.

5. When you are finished making changes, click Done.

## ✔ Tip

■ You don't have to use the Customize Toolbar dialog to rearrange or remove toolbar items. Just hold down ⌃ ⌘ and drag the item you want to move to a new position or drag the item you want to remove off the toolbar.

## To restore the toolbar to its default settings

1. With any Finder window displaying the toolbar open, choose View > Customize Toolbar (**Figure 19**). The Customize Toolbar dialog sheet appears.

2. Drag the group of items in a box near the bottom of the window to the toolbar (**Figure 30**). When you release the mouse button, the toolbar's default items appear (**Figure 20**).

3. Click Done.

# Customizing the Sidebar

In addition to using Finder preferences to specify what standard items should appear in the Sidebar (as discussed earlier in this chapter) you can customize the toolbar a number of ways:

◆ Change the width of the Sidebar to better display long item names or just show icons.

◆ Add or remove folders, files, and other items in the bottom half of the Sidebar.

## ✔ Tip

■ The Sidebar only appears if the toolbar is displayed. I tell you more about the toolbar earlier in this chapter and in **Chapter 2**.

**Figure 31** Position the mouse pointer on the border between the Sidebar and the rest of the window...

**Figure 32** ...and drag to move the border, thus changing the Sidebar's width.

**Figure 33** If you make the Sidebar very narrow, you can display just the icons for Sidebar items.

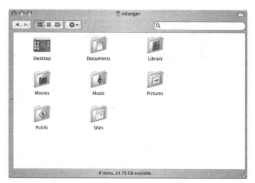

**Figure 34** Double-clicking the divider between the Sidebar and the rest of the window hides the Sidebar from view.

## To change the Sidebar width

1. Position the mouse pointer on the divider between the Sidebar and the rest of the Finder window. The mouse pointer turns into a line with two arrows coming out of it (**Figure 31**).

2. Press the mouse button down and drag. As you drag, the Sidebar's width changes (**Figure 32**).

3. When the Sidebar is the desired width, release the mouse button.

## ✔ Tips

■ The Sidebar's border may "snap" to a certain width as you drag. This width will be wide enough to fully display all Sidebar item names. You can continue to drag to change this width if desired.

■ You can drag the divider to the left until it "snaps" to display only Sidebar icons (**Figure 33**).

■ To hide the sidebar without hiding the toolbar (**Figure 34**), double-click the divider in the Finder window. To redisplay the Sidebar, double-click the left border of the window.

## To add an item to the Sidebar

1. Drag the icon for the item you want to add to the Sidebar. A blue line indicates where it will appear (**Figure 35**).

2. Release the mouse button. The item appears on the Sidebar (**Figure 36**).

### ✔ Tips

■ Adding an item to the Sidebar does not move it from where it resides on disk. Instead, it creates and adds a pointer to the original item to the Sidebar.

■ Be careful when adding an icon to the Sidebar. If you drag the icon on top of a folder or disk icon already on the Sidebar, the icon will be moved into that folder or disk.

## To remove an item from the Sidebar

1. Drag the item off the Sidebar (**Figure 37**).

2. Release the mouse button. The item disappears in a puff of digital smoke (**Figure 38**).

### ✔ Tip

■ Removing an item from the Sidebar does not delete it from disk. Instead, it removes the pointer to the original item from the Sidebar.

**Figure 35** To add an item to the Sidebar, drag it on.

**Figure 36** The item appears where you positioned it.

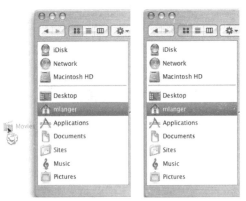

**Figure 37** To remove an item from the Sidebar, drag it off. **Figure 38** The item is removed.

Figure 39 Pressing the mouse button on a Dock item often displays a menu. These examples show the menu for iChat when the application is not running (left) and when it is running (right).

# Customizing the Dock

The Dock, which is discussed in **Chapter 2**, can be customized to include icons for specific documents and applications that you use often. This makes them quick and easy to open any time you need them.

## ✔ Tips

- When you press the mouse button down on a Dock icon, a menu with commands or other options that apply to that icon appears (**Figures 39a** and **39b**). You can select a command like any other menu command.

- When you press the mouse button down on a folder in the Dock, it appears as a menu. Choose an item to open it or point to a folder within the menu to display a submenu of items within it. **Figure 40** shows an example of how you can use this feature.

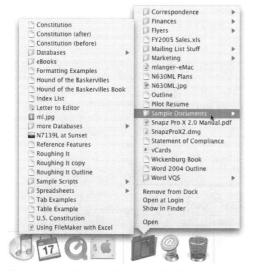

Figure 40 Creative use of folders in the Dock can put all your frequently used files at your fingertips—without turning the Dock into a cluttered mess. (As this example shows, however, the menus themselves can become cluttered messes!)

## To add an icon to the Dock

1. Open the window containing the icon you want to add to the Dock.

2. Drag the icon from the window to the Dock. Items on the Dock shift to make room for the new item (**Figure 41**).

3. Release the mouse button. The icon appears (**Figure 42**).

### ✔ Tips

- Dragging an icon to the Dock does not remove it from its original location.

- When dragging items to the Dock, drag applications to the left of the divider and documents, folders, Web sites, and servers to the right of the divider.

## To remove an icon from the Dock

1. Drag the item from the Dock to the desktop (**Figure 43**).

2. Release the mouse button. The icon disappears in a puff of digital smoke.

### ✔ Tips

- Removing an icon from the Dock does not delete it from disk.

- If you try to remove an icon for an application that is running, the icon will not disappear from the Dock until you quit the application.

**Figure 41** Drag an icon from the window to the Dock.

**Figure 42** The icon appears in the Dock.

**Figure 43** Drag an icon off the Dock.

About This Mac
Software Update...
Mac OS X Software...

System Preferences...
Dock ▶ — Turn Hiding On ⌥⌘D
Location ▶ — Turn Magnification On
Recent Items ▶ — Position on Left
Force Quit... ⌥⌘⎋ — ✓ Position on Bottom
— Position on Right
Sleep
Restart... — Dock Preferences...
Shut Down...
Log Out Maria Langer... ⇧⌘Q

**Figure 44** The Dock submenu under the Apple menu offers options for customizing the way the Dock looks and works.

**Figure 45** When magnification is turned on, pointing to an icon enlarges it.

**Figure 46** You can position the Dock on the side of the screen instead of the bottom.

**Figure 47** You can resize the Dock by pointing to the divider line and dragging.

## To set basic Dock options

Choose options from the Dock submenu under the Apple menu (**Figure 44**):

◆ **Turn Magnification On** magnifies a Dock icon when you point to it (**Figure 45**). With this option enabled, the command changes to **Turn Magnification Off**, which disables magnification.

◆ **Turn Hiding On** (Option ⌃ ⌘ D) automatically hides the Dock until you point to where it is hiding and it should appear. This is a great way to regain screen real estate normally occupied by the Dock. With this option enabled, the command changes to **Turn Hiding Off**, which displays the Dock all the time.

◆ **Position on Left**, **Position on Bottom**, and **Position on Right** move the Dock to the left side, bottom, or right side of the screen. The option that is not available (Position on Bottom in **Figure 46**) is the one that is currently selected. When positioned on the left or right, the Dock fits vertically down the screen (**Figure 39**).

◆ **Dock Preferences** displays the Dock preferences pane, which includes a few additional options for customizing the Dock. I cover the Dock preferences pane in **Chapter 21**.

## ✔ Tip

■ To change the size of the Dock, point to the divider line. When the mouse pointer turns into a line with two arrows (**Figure 47**), press the mouse button and drag up or down to make the Dock bigger or smaller.

SETTING BASIC DOCK OPTIONS

# Customizing Window & Desktop Views

As discussed in **Chapter 3**, a window's view determines how icons and other information appear within it. Mac OS X remembers a window's view settings and uses them whenever you display the window.

You can customize views a number of ways:

◆ Change the settings for the default view for icon, list, and column views.

◆ Change the settings for an individual window's icon or list view.

◆ Change the view for the desktop.

View settings offer a number of options:

◆ Icon view settings include icon size, label text size and position, display options, arrangement, and background.

◆ List view settings include icon size, text size, columns, date format, and item size calculation, as well as column width and the order in which columns appear.

◆ Column view settings include text size, icon appearance, and preview column.

◆ Desktop view settings include icon size, label text size and position, display options, and arrangement.

You can also display a status bar with disk information in any Finder window.

## ✔ Tip

■ The only time the Finder does not use a window's custom view is when you have the "Open new windows in column view" option set in the Finder preferences' General window (**Figure 2**). I tell you about this option earlier in this chapter.

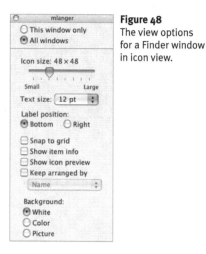

**Figure 48**
The view options for a Finder window in icon view.

| | |
|---|---|
| 10 pt | |
| 11 pt | |
| ✓ 12 pt | |
| 13 pt | |
| 14 pt | |
| 15 pt | |
| 16 pt | |

**Figure 49**
The Text size pop-up menu enables you to set the size of the type for icon labels.

**Figures 50 & 51** You can place icon labels beneath the icons (above), which is the default setting, or to the right of icons (below).

# To set icon view options

1. To set icon view options for a specific window, activate that window and make sure it is displayed in icon view.

   *or*

   To set default icon view options, activate any window that is displayed in icon view.

2. Choose View > Show View Options (**Figure 19**), or press ⌃⌘J to display the view options window (**Figure 48**).

3. Select the radio button for the type of option you want to set:

   ▲ **This window only** customizes the settings for the active window.

   ▲ **All windows** sets options for all icon view windows that do not have custom settings.

4. Use the Icon size slider to set the size of icons:

   ▲ Drag the slider to the left to make the icon size smaller.

   ▲ Drag the slider to the right to make the icon size larger.

5. Choose a type size from the Text size pop-up menu (**Figure 49**).

6. Select a Label position radio button to specify where icon labels should appear:

   ▲ **Bottom** displays labels below the icons (**Figure 50**).

   ▲ **Right** displays labels to the right of the icons (**Figure 51**).

*Continued on next page...*

SETTING ICON VIEW OPTIONS

*Continued from previous page.*

7. Toggle check boxes to specify how icons should appear:

▲ **Snap to grid** forces icons to snap to the window's invisible grid, thus ensuring consistent spacing between icons.

▲ **Show item info** displays information about the item beneath its name. **Figure 52** shows an example with graphic file size, in pixels, displayed.

▲ **Show icon preview** displays a document's preview, if available, in place of its standard icon. **Figure 52** shows a preview icon for a graphic file.

▲ **Keep arranged by** automatically arranges icons in a certain order. If you select this option, choose a sort order from the pop-up menu beneath it (**Figure 53**).

8. Select a Background option:

▲ **White** makes the background white.

▲ **Color** enables you to select a background color for the window. If you select this option, click the color well that appears beside it (**Figure 54**), use the Colors palette (**Figure 55**) to select a color, and click OK.

▲ **Picture** enables you to set a background picture for the window. If you select this option, click the Select button that appears beside it (**Figure 56**), use the Select a Picture dialog to locate and select a background picture (**Figure 57**), and click Select.

9. When you're finished setting options, click the view option window's close button to dismiss it.

**Figure 52** You can display information about an item beneath its label.

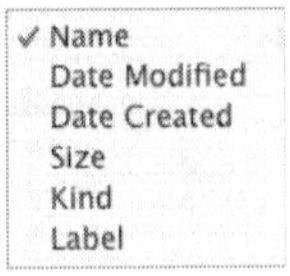

**Figure 53** Use this pop-up menu to specify an automatic arrangement order.

**Figure 54** When you select the Color radio button, a color well appears.

**Figure 55** Use the Colors palette to select a new background color.

**Figure 56** When you select the Picture radio button, a Select button appears.

Setting Icon View Options

**Figure 57** Use the Select a Picture dialog to locate and select a background picture.

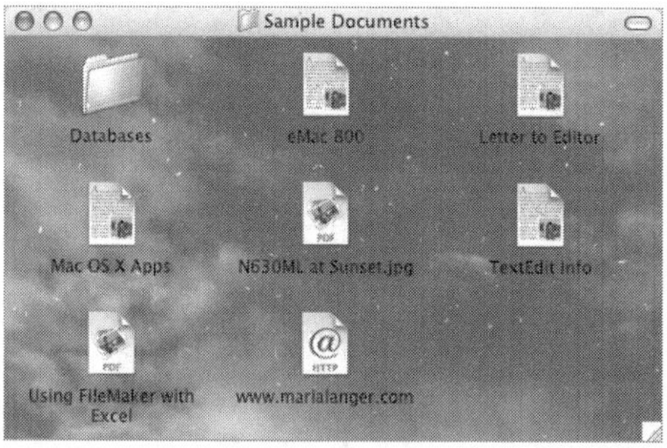

## ✔ Tips

■ To restore the current window's options to the default settings for all icon view windows, select the All windows radio button in step 3.

■ I explain how to select a color with the Colors palette in **Chapter 11**.

■ Working with dialogs is discussed in **Chapter 7**.

■ A background picture fills the window's background behind the icons (**Figure 58**).

**Figure 58** A background picture appears behind icons.

# To set list view options

1. To set list view options for a specific window, activate that window and make sure it is displayed in list view.

   *or*

   To set default list view options, activate any window that is displayed in list view.

2. Choose View > Show View Options (**Figure 19**) or press ⌃⌘J to display the view options window (**Figure 59**).

3. Select the radio button for the type of option you want to set:

   ▲ **This window only** customizes the settings for the active window.

   ▲ **All windows** sets options for all list view windows that do not have custom settings.

4. Select an Icon size option by clicking the radio button beneath the size you want.

5. Choose a type size from the Text size pop-up menu (**Figure 49**).

6. Select the columns you want to appear in list view by turning Show columns check boxes on or off:

   ▲ **Date Modified** is the date and time an item was last changed.

   ▲ **Date Created** is the date and time an item was first created.

   ▲ **Size** is the amount of disk space the item occupies.

   ▲ **Kind** is the type of item. I tell you about types of items in **Chapter 2**.

   ▲ **Version** is the item's version number.

   ▲ **Comments** is the information you entered in the Spotlight Comments field of the Info window. I tell you about the Info window in **Chapter 4**.

   ▲ **Label** is the label assigned to the item.

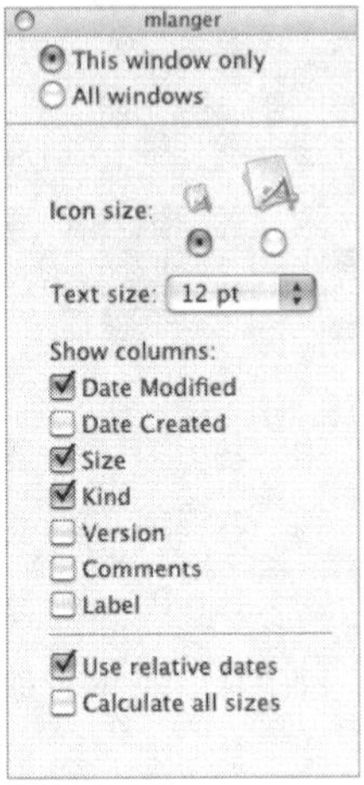

**Figure 59**
The view options for list view.

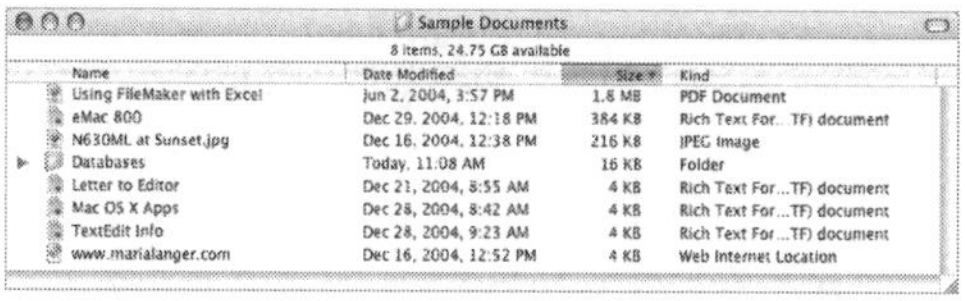

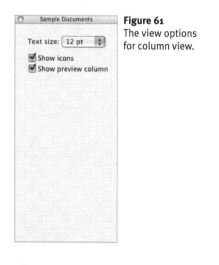

**Figure 60** When you turn on the Calculate all sizes in the list view options for a window, you can sort the window's contents by size. This example also shows the Use relative dates option enabled.

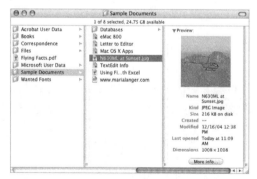

**Figure 61**
The view options for column view.

**Figure 62** With the Show preview column option enabled, selecting an item that includes a preview displays the preview in the far right column.

7. To display the date in relative terms (that is, using the words "today" and "yesterday"), turn on the Use relative dates check box.

8. To display the disk space occupied by items and the contents of folders in the list, turn on the Calculate all sizes check box.

9. When you're finished setting options, click the view option window's close button to dismiss it.

## ✔ Tip

- Turning on the Calculate all sizes check box in step 8 makes it possible to sort all of a window's contents by size, including folders (**Figure 60**). Sorting window contents is covered in **Chapter 3**.

## To set column view options

1. Activate any window that is displayed in column view.

2. Choose View > Show View Options (**Figure 19**) or press ⌃⌘J to display the view options window (**Figure 61**).

3. Choose a type size from the Text size pop-up menu (**Figure 49**).

4. To display icons beside item names, turn on the Show icons check box.

5. To display previews (when available) for selected items (**Figure 62**), turn on the Show preview column check box.

6. When you're finished setting options, click the view option window's close button to dismiss it.

**SETTING LIST & COLUMN VIEW OPTIONS**

## To set desktop view options

1. Click anywhere on the desktop to activate it.

2. Choose View > Show View Options (**Figure 19**) or press ⌘J to display the Desktop view options window (**Figure 63**).

3. Use the Icon size slider to set the size of icons:

   ▲ Drag the slider to the left to make the icon size smaller.

   ▲ Drag the slider to the right to make the icon size larger.

4. Choose a type size from the Text size pop-up menu (**Figure 49**).

5. Select a radio button to specify where icon labels should appear:

   ▲ **Bottom** displays labels below the icons.

   ▲ **Right** displays labels to the right of the icon.

6. Toggle check boxes to specify how icons should appear:

   ▲ **Snap to grid** forces icons to snap to the desktop's invisible grid, thus ensuring consistent spacing between icons.

   ▲ **Show item info** displays information about the item beneath its name.

   ▲ **Show icon preview** displays a document's preview, if available, in place of its standard icon.

   ▲ **Keep arranged by** automatically arranges icons in a certain order. If you select this option, choose a sort order from the pop-up menu beneath it (**Figure 53**).

7. When you're finished setting options, click the view option window's close button to dismiss it.

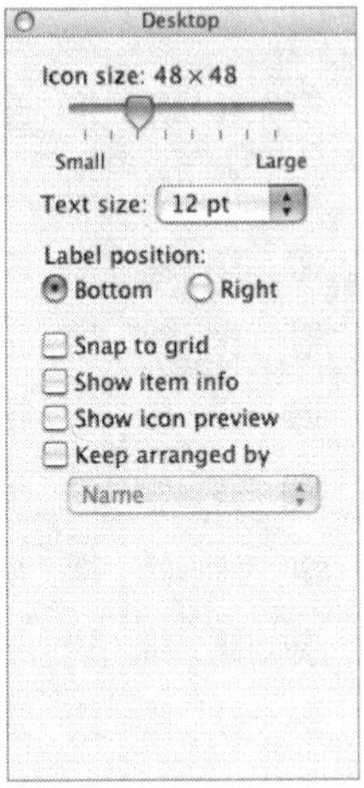

**Figure 63**
View options for the desktop.

## ✔ Tip

■ You can set the desktop color or picture in the Desktop & Screen Saver preferences pane, which I cover in **Chapter 21**.

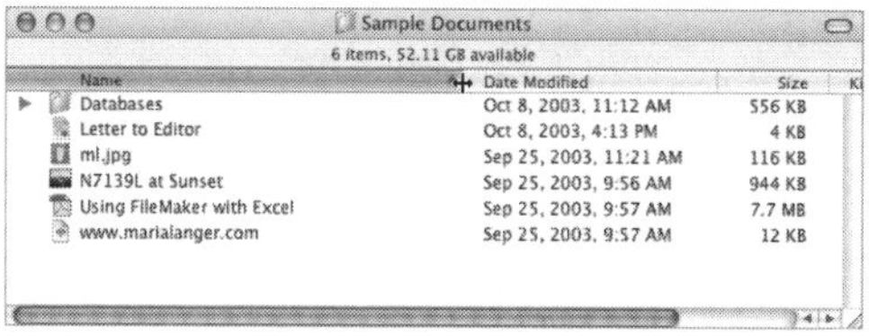

**Figure 64** Position the mouse pointer on the column border.

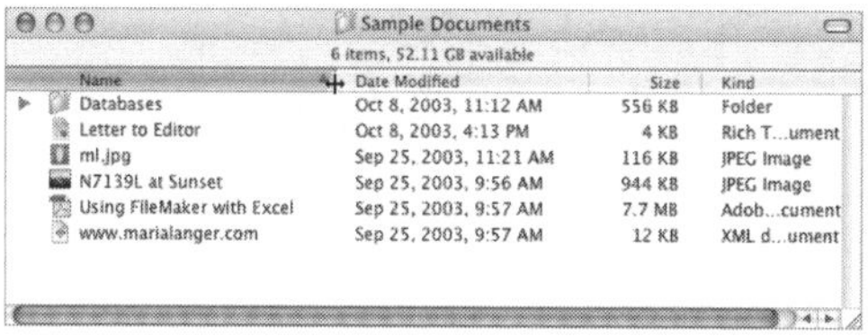

**Figure 65** When you press the mouse button down and drag, the column's width changes.

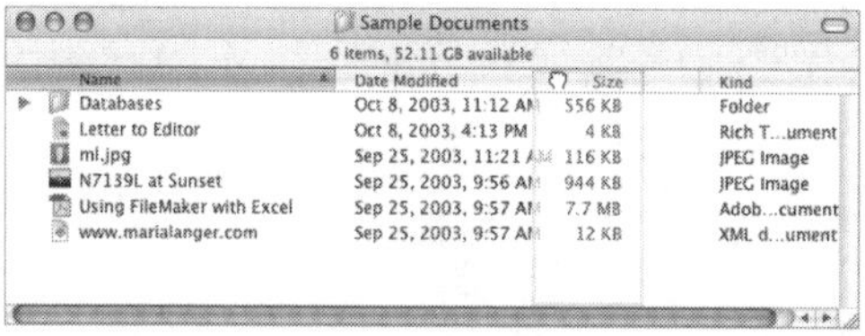

**Figure 66** Drag a column heading...

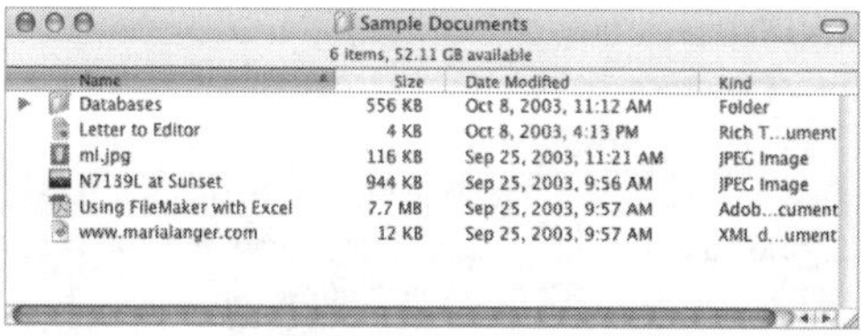

**Figure 67** ...to change the column's position.

## To change a column's width

1. Position the mouse pointer on the line between the heading for the column whose width you want to change and the column to its right.

2. Press the mouse button down. The mouse pointer turns into a vertical bar with two arrows (**Figure 64**).

3. Drag as follows:
   - ▲ To make the column narrower, drag to the left (**Figure 65**).
   - ▲ To make the column wider, drag to the right.

4. When the column is displayed at the desired width, release the mouse button.

## ✔ Tip

- If you make a column too narrow to display all of its contents, information may be truncated or condensed.

## To change a column's position

1. Position the mouse pointer on the heading for the column you want to move.

2. Press the mouse button down and drag:
   - ▲ To move the column to the left, drag to the left (**Figure 66**).
   - ▲ To move the column to the right, drag to the right.

   As you drag, the other columns shift to make room for the column you're dragging.

3. When the column is in the desired position, release the mouse button. The column changes its position (**Figure 67**).

## ✔ Tip

- You cannot change the position of the Name column.

**CHANGING COLUMN WIDTH & POSITION**

## To display the status bar

Choose View > Show Status Bar (**Figure 68**).

The status bar appears above the window's contents (**Figure 69**).

## ✔ Tips

- The status bar always appears when the toolbar is displayed (**Figure 70**).

- As shown in **Figures 69** and **70**, the status bar shows the number of items in the window and the total amount of space available on the disk.

- If one or more items are selected in a window, the status bar reports how many items are selected (**Figure 71**).

- When the status bar is displayed, it appears in all Finder windows.

## To hide the status bar

Choose View > Hide Status Bar (**Figure 72**).

The status bar disappears.

## ✔ Tip

- The status bar cannot be hidden when the toolbar is displayed.

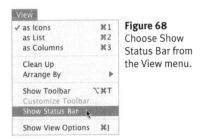

**Figure 68**
Choose Show Status Bar from the View menu.

*Status bar*

**Figure 69** When the toolbar is not displayed, the status bar appears above the window's contents.

*Status bar*

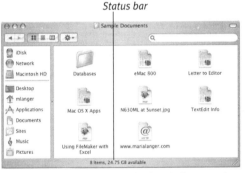

**Figure 70** When the toolbar is displayed, the status bar appears at the bottom of the window.

**Figure 71** The status bar can also report how many items are selected in a window.

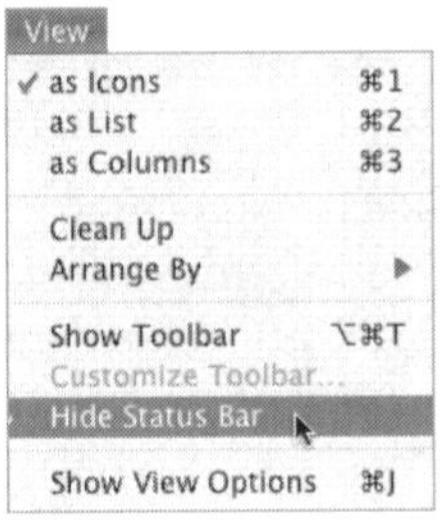

**Figure 72**
When the status bar is displayed, the Hide Status Bar command appears on the View menu.

**DISPLAYING & HIDING THE STATUS BAR**

# Application Basics

## Applications

*Applications*, which are also known as *programs*, are software packages you use to get work done. Here are some examples:

- ◆ **Word processors**, such as TextEdit, iWork's Pages, and Microsoft Word, are used to write letters, reports, and other text-based documents.

- ◆ **Spreadsheets**, such as Microsoft Excel, have built-in calculation features that are useful for creating number-based documents such as worksheets and charts.

- ◆ **Databases**, such as FileMaker Pro, are used to organize information, such as the names and addresses of customers or the artists and titles in a record collection.

- ◆ **Graphics** and **presentation** programs, such as Adobe Photoshop and Microsoft PowerPoint, are used to create illustrations, animations, and presentations.

- ◆ **Communications** programs, such as Internet Connect and Safari, are used to connect to other computers via modem or to the Internet.

- ◆ **Integrated** software, such as AppleWorks, combines "lite" versions of several types of software into one application.

- ◆ **Utility** software, such as Disk Utility and StuffIt Expander, performs tasks to manage computer files or keep your computer in good working order.

## ✔ Tips

- ■ Your Macintosh comes with some application software, most of which is discussed throughout this book.

- ■ Make sure the software you buy is Mac OS-compatible, and if possible, labeled "Built for Mac OS X." You may see Mac OS X applications referred to as *Carbon* or *Cocoa* applications. (Carbon and Cocoa are two methods for writing Mac OS X software.)

- ■ If Mac OS 9.x is installed on your computer, your computer can also run *Classic applications*—those applications written for Mac OS 9.x or earlier. This chapter discusses Mac OS X applications only; to learn about using Classic applications, consult **Chapter 18**.

# Multitasking & the Dock

Mac OS uses a form of *multitasking,* which makes it possible for more than one application to be open at the same time. Only one application, however, can be *active.* You must make an application active to work with it. Other open applications continue running in the background.

Mac OS X uses *preemptive multitasking,* a type of multitasking in which the operating system can interrupt a currently running task to run another task, as needed.

## ✔ Tips

- Mac OS 9 uses *cooperative multitasking,* a type of multitasking in which a running program can receive processing time only if other programs allow it. Each application must "cooperate" by giving up control of the processor to allow others to run.

- Mac OS X also features *protected memory,* a memory management system in which each program is prevented from modifying or corrupting the memory partition of another program. This means that if one application freezes up, your computer won't freeze up. You can continue using the other applications that are running.

- One application that is always open is Finder, which I cover in detail in **Chapters 2** through **6**.

- The active application is the one whose name appears at the top of the application menu—the menu to the right of the Apple menu—on the menu bar (**Figure 3**). The application menu is covered a little later in this chapter.

## To learn what applications are running

Look at the Dock. A tiny triangle appears beneath each application that is running (**Figure 1**).

**Figure 1** A tiny triangle appears beneath each open application. Click an icon to make its application active.

**Figure 2** When you hold down ⌥⌘ and press [Tab], icons for each open application appear onscreen.

**Figure 3** The name of the active application appears at the top of the application menu.

## To switch from one open application to another

In the Dock (**Figure 1**), click the icon for the application you want to activate.

*Or*

1. Hold down ⌥⌘ and press [Tab]. A large icon for each open application appears onscreen (**Figure 2**).

2. While holding down ⌥⌘, press [Tab] repeatedly to cycle though the icons until the one you want to activate is selected. Release the keys.

   *or*

   Click the icon for the application you want to activate.

The windows for the application you selected come to the front and the application name appears on the Application menu (**Figure 3**).

## ✔ Tips

- Another way to activate an application is to click any of its windows. This brings the window to the foreground onscreen and makes the application active.

- You can also use Exposé to activate an application's windows. I explain how to use Exposé in **Chapter 4**.

# Using Applications & Creating Documents

You use an application by opening, or *launching*, it. It loads into the computer's memory. Its menu bar replaces the Finder's menu bar and offers commands that can be used only with that application. It may also display a document window and tools specific to that program.

Most applications create *documents*—files written in a format understood by the application. When you save documents, they remain on disk so you can open, edit, print, or just view them at a later date.

For example, you may use Microsoft Word to write a letter. When you save the letter, it becomes a Word document file that includes all the text and formatting you put into the letter, written in a format that Microsoft Word can understand.

Your computer keeps track of applications and documents. It automatically associates documents with the applications that created them. That's how your computer is able to open a document with the correct application when you open the document from the Finder.

## ✔ Tips

■ You can launch an application by opening a document that it created.

■ A document created by an application that is not installed on your computer is sometimes referred to as an *orphan* document since no *parent* application is available. An orphan document usually has a generic document icon (**Figure 4**).

**Figure 4**
An orphan document often has a generic document icon like this one. This example shows an Adobe InDesign document copied to a computer that does not have InDesign installed.

Chapter 5

**Figure 5**
Select the icon for the application that you want to open.

TextEdit

| File | |
|---|---|
| New Finder Window | ⌘N |
| New Folder | ⇧⌘N |
| New Smart Folder | ⌥⌘N |
| New Burn Folder | |
| Open | ⌘O |
| Open With | ▶ |
| Print | |
| Close Window | ⌘W |
| Get Info | ⌘I |
| Duplicate | ⌘D |
| Make Alias | ⌘L |
| Show Original | ⌘R |
| Add to Sidebar | ⌘T |
| Create Archive of "TextEdit" | |
| Move to Trash | ⌘⌫ |
| Eject | ⌘E |
| Burn Disc... | |
| Find... | ⌘F |
| Color Label: | |
| ✗ ● ● ● ● ● ● ● | |

**Figure 6**
Choose Open from the File menu.

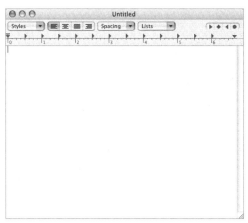

**Figure 7** When you launch TextEdit by opening its application icon, it displays an empty document window.

**Figure 8**
Select the icon for the document you want to open.

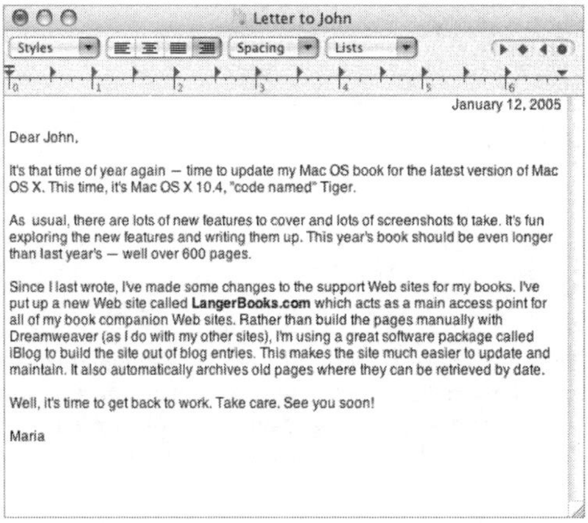

**Figure 9** When you launch TextEdit by opening one of its documents, it displays the document.

## To launch an application

Double-click the application's icon.

*Or*

1. Select the application's icon (**Figure 5**).

2. Choose File > Open (**Figure 6**), or press ⌃ ⌘ O.

*Or*

If an icon for the application is in the toolbar or the Dock, click that icon once.

The application opens (**Figure 7**).

## To open a document & launch the application that created it at the same time

Double-click the icon for the document that you want to open.

*Or*

1. Select the icon for the document that you want to open (**Figure 8**).

2. Choose File > Open (**Figure 6**), or press ⌃ ⌘ O.

*Or*

If an icon for the document is in the Sidebar or the Dock, click that icon once.

If the application that created the document is not already running, it launches. The document appears in an active window (**Figure 9**).

LAUNCHING APPS & OPENING DOCS

## To open a document with drag & drop

1. Drag the icon for the document that you want to open onto the icon for the application with which you want to open it.

2. When the application icon becomes selected (**Figure 10**), release the mouse button. The application launches and displays the document (**Figure 9**).

## ✔ Tips

- Drag and drop is a good way to open a document with an application other than the one that created it.

- Not all applications can read all documents. Dragging a document icon onto the icon for an application that can't open it either won't launch the application, will open the document but display only gibberish, or will display an error message.

- In step 1, the application icon can be in a Finder window (or the desktop), in the Sidebar, or on the Dock.

## To open a document with the Open With command

1. Select the icon for the document that you want to open (**Figure 8**).

2. Choose File > Open With to display the Open With Submenu (**Figure 11**) and choose the application you want to use to open the file. The application you chose opens and displays the document.

## ✔ Tip

- The Open With submenu (**Figure 11**) will only list applications that are installed on your computer and are capable of opening the selected document.

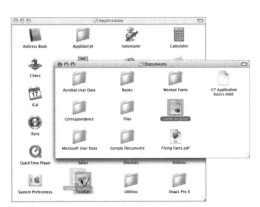

**Figure 10** Drag the icon for the document you want to open onto the icon for the application you want to open it with.

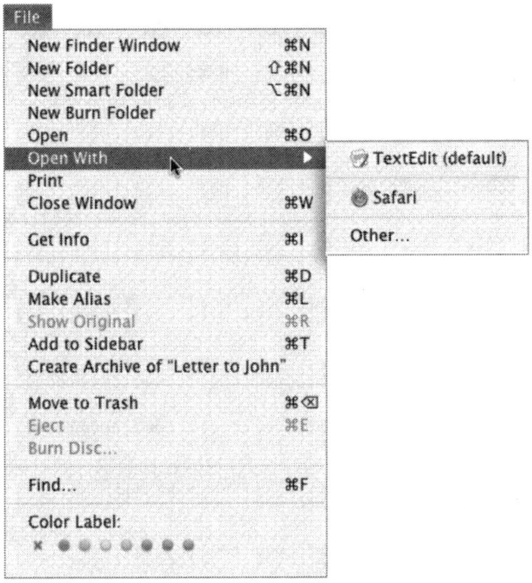

**Figure 11** The Open With submenu lists installed applications that can open a selected document. The options that appear depend on what type of document is selected and what applications are installed on your computer.

# Standard Application Menus

Apple's Human Interface Guidelines provide basic recommendations to software developers to ensure consistency from one application to another. Nowhere is this more obvious than in the standard menus that appear in most applications: the application, File, Edit, Window, and Help menus. You'll see these menus with the same kinds of commands over and over in most of the applications you use. This consistency makes it easier to learn Mac OS applications.

The next few pages provide a closer look at the standard menus you'll find in most applications.

## ✔ Tips

■ The Finder, which is covered in **Chapters 2** through **6**, has standard menus similar to the ones discussed here.

■ The Finder rules regarding the ellipsis character (…) and keyboard shortcuts displayed on menus also apply to applications. **Chapter 2** explains these rules.

# The Application Menu

The application menu takes the name of the currently active application—for example, the TextEdit application menu (**Figure 12**) or the iTunes application menu (**Figure 13**). It includes commands for working with the entire application.

## To learn about an application

1. From the application menu, choose About *application name* (**Figures 12** and **13**).

2. A window with version and other information appears (**Figure 14**). Read the information it contains.

3. When you're finished reading about the application, click the window's close button.

## To set application preferences

1. From the application menu, choose Preferences (**Figures 12** and **13**).

2. The application's Preferences window (**Figure 15**) or dialog appears. Set options as desired.

3. Click the window's close button.

   *or*

   Click the dialog's OK or Save button.

## ✔ Tip

■ Preference options vary greatly from one application to another. To learn more about an application's preferences, check its documentation or onscreen help.

**Figures 12 & 13**
The TextEdit application menu (left), and the iTunes application menu (right).

**Figure 14** The About window for TextEdit provides its version number and other information.

**Figure 15** TextEdit's Preferences window offers two panes of options you can set to customize the way TextEdit looks and works.

## To hide an application

From the application menu, choose Hide *application name* (**Figures 12** and **13**) or press ⌃ ⌘ H. All of the application's windows, as well as its menu bar, are hidden from view.

## ✔ Tip

- You cannot hide the active application if it is the only application that is open (the Finder) or if all the other open applications are already hidden.

## To hide all applications except the active one

From the application menu, choose Hide Others (**Figures 12** and **13**) or press Option ⌃ ⌘ H.

## To hide the active application and display another application

Hold down Option while switching to another application.

## To display a hidden application

Click the application's icon (or any of its document icons) in the Dock (**Figure 1**).

## To unhide all applications

From the application menu, choose Show All (**Figures 12** and **13**).

## To quit an application

1. From the application menu, choose Quit *application name* (**Figures 12** and **13**), or press ⌃ ⌘ Q.

2. If unsaved documents are open, a dialog appears, asking whether you want to save changes to documents. The appearance of this dialog varies depending on the application that displays it. **Figure 16** shows an example from TextEdit when a single unsaved document is open. Click the appropriate button to save the document(s) or quit without saving (Cancel).

   The application closes all windows, saves preference files (if applicable), and quits.

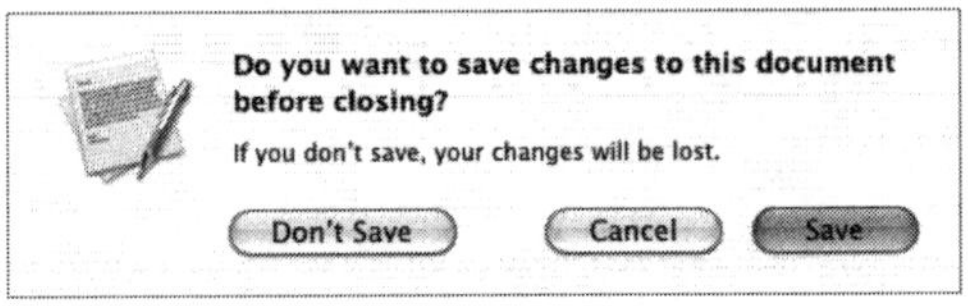

## ✔ Tips

- Closing all of an application's open windows is not the same as quitting. An application normally remains running until you quit it.

- I tell you more about saving documents later in this chapter.

- If an application is unresponsive and you cannot access its menus or commands, you can use the Force Quit command to make it stop running. I explain how near the end of this chapter.

**Figure 16** This dialog appears when you close a TextEdit document that contains unsaved changes.

**File**

| New | ⌘N |
| Open... | ⌘O |
| Open Recent | ▶ |
| Close | ⌘W |
| Save | ⌘S |
| Save As... | ⇧⌘S |
| Save All | |
| Revert to Saved | |
| Show Properties | ⌥⌘P |
| Page Setup... | ⇧⌘P |
| Print... | ⌘P |

**File**

| New Window | ⌘N |
| Open File... | ⌘O |
| Open Location... | ⌘L |
| Close Window | ⌘W |
| Save As... | ⌘S |
| Mail Contents of This Page | ⌘I |
| Mail Link to This Page | ⇧⌘I |
| Import Bookmarks... | |
| Export Bookmarks... | |
| Page Setup... | ⇧⌘P |
| Print... | ⌘P |

**File**

| New Card | ⌘N |
| New Group | ⇧⌘N |
| New Group From Selection | |
| New Smart Group... | ⌥⌘N |
| Close | ⌘W |
| Save | ⌘S |
| Import | ▶ |
| Export vCard... | |
| Back up Address Book... | |
| Revert to Address Book Backup... | |
| Subscribe to Address Book... | |
| Send Updates... | |
| Print... | ⌘P |

**Figures 17, 18, & 19**
The File menu in Text-Edit (top left), Address Book (bottom left), and Safari (above).

**Figure 20** Safari's New Window command opens a new Web browser window displaying the default Home page.

# The File Menu

The File menu (**Figures 17**, **18**, and **19**) includes commands for working with files or documents. This section discusses the commands most often found under the File menu: New, Open, Close, and Save.

## ✔ Tip

■ The Page Setup and Print commands are also found on the File menu. These commands are discussed in detail in **Chapter 12**.

## To create a new document or window

Choose File > New (**Figure 17**).

*Or*

Choose File > New Window (**Figure 19**).

*Or*

Press ⇧⌘N.

A new untitled document (**Figure 7**) or window (**Figure 20**) appears.

## ✔ Tip

■ As shown in **Figures 17**, **18**, and **19**, the exact wording of the command for creating a new document or window varies depending on the application and what the command does. This command, however, is usually the first one on the File menu.

## To open a file

1. Choose File > Open (**Figure 17**) or press ⌃⌘O to display the Open dialog (**Figure 21**).

2. Use any combination of the following techniques to locate the document you want to open:

   ▲ Use the From pop-up menu (**Figure 22**) to backtrack from the currently displayed location to one of its enclosing folders or to a recently accessed folder.

   ▲ Click one of the items in the Sidebar list on the left side of the dialog to view the contents of that item.

   ▲ Press ⇧⌃⌘H to view the contents of your Home folder.

   ▲ Click one of the items in either list to view its contents in the list on the right side of the window. (The list containing the item you clicked shifts to the left if necessary.)

   ▲ Use the scroll bar at the bottom of the two lists to shift lists. Shifting lists to the right enables you to see your path from the item selected in the Sidebar list.

3. When the name of the file you want to open appears in the list on the right side of the window, use one of the following techniques to open it:

   ▲ Select the file name and then click Open or press [Return] or [Enter].

   ▲ Double-click the file name.

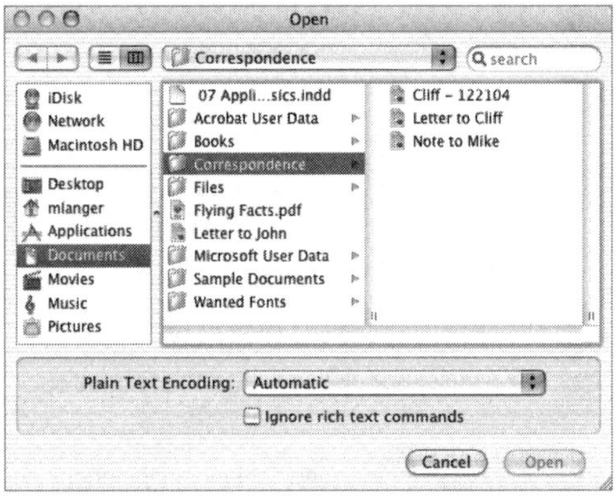

**Figure 21** TextEdit's Open dialog includes all of the elements found in a standard Open dialog.

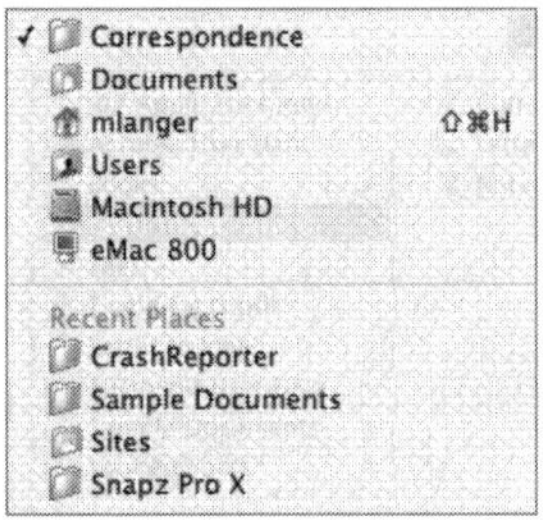

**Figure 22**
The From (and Where) pop-up menu enables you to backtrack from the currently displayed location to the folders in which it resides or a recently accessed folder.

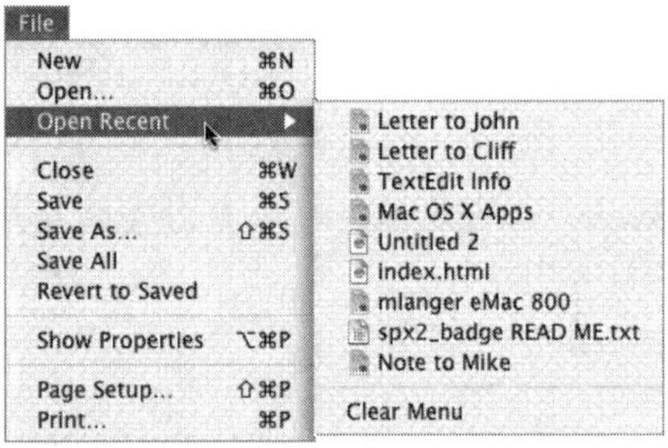

**Figure 23** TextEdit's Open Recent submenu makes it easy to reopen a recently opened document.

**Figure 24** When you select a file in the Open dialog, the file's icon or a preview and other information for the file appears. This example shows Preview's Open dialog with a JPEG format file selected. The image in the right side of the dialog is the file's custom icon, which was created automatically by Photoshop when the image was saved.

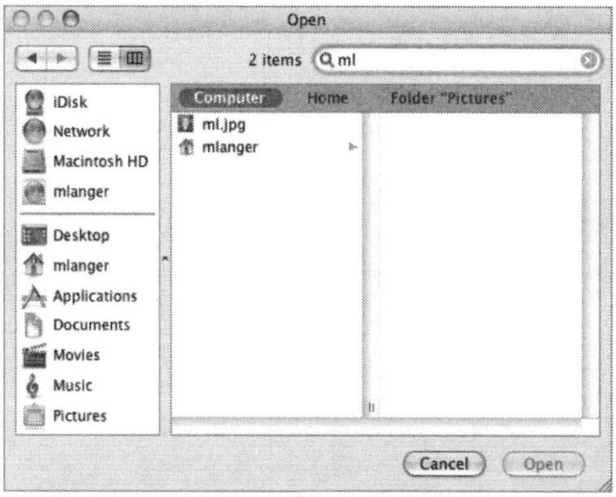

**Figure 25** Mac OS X 10.4's new Spotlight feature works within the Open dialog, too.

## ✔ Tips

- The exact wording of the Open command varies depending on the application and what you want to open. For example, the Open command on Safari's File menu (**Figure 19**) is Open File.

- The Open Recent command, which is available on the File menu of some applications (**Figure 17**), displays a submenu of recently opened items (**Figure 23**). Choose the item you want to open it again.

- As illustrated in **Figures 21** and **24**, the Open dialog has many standard elements that appear in all Open dialogs.

- In step 3, you can only select the files that the application can open; other files will either not appear in the list or will appear in gray. Some applications, such as Microsoft Word, include a pop-up menu that enables you to specify the types of files that appear in the Open dialog.

- In step 3, selecting a file's name in the Open dialog displays its icon or a preview and other information for the file on the right side of the dialog (**Figure 24**).

- Mac OS X 10.4 adds Spotlight to the Open dialog. Simply enter a part of the file's title or contents in the Search field within the Open dialog and a list of files that match appears in the dialog (**Figure 25**). Select a file and click Open to open it. I tell you more about Spotlight in **Chapter 5**.

- The Sidebar is covered in **Chapter 2**, file paths are discussed in **Chapter 3**, and iDisk is covered in **Chapter 14**.

**OPENING FILES**

## To close a window

1. Choose File > Close (**Figures 17** and **18**), File > Close Window (**Figure 19**), or press Ⓖ ⌘ Ⓦ.

   *or*

   Click the window's close button.

2. If the window contains a document with changes that have not been saved, a dialog sheet similar to the one in **Figure 16** appears.

   ▲ Click Don't Save to close the window without saving the document.

   ▲ Click Cancel or press Esc to keep the window open.

   ▲ Click Save or press Return or Enter to save the document.

## ✔ Tip

■ The exact appearance of the dialog sheet that appears when you close a document with unsaved changes varies depending on the application. All versions of the dialog should offer the same three options, although they may be worded differently. **Figure 16** shows the dialog that appears in TextEdit.

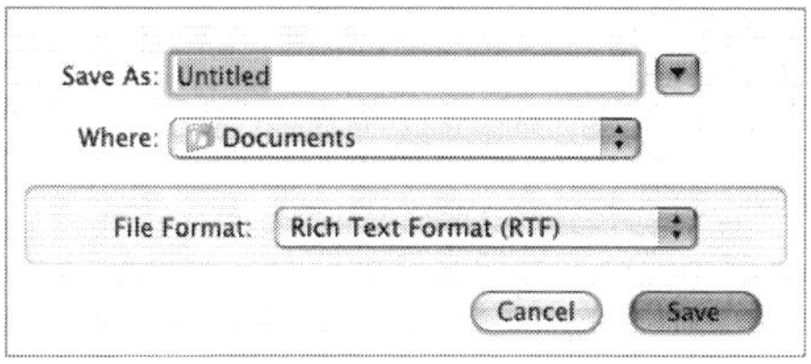

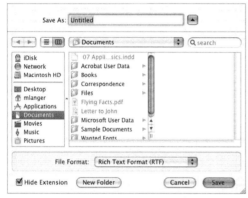

**Figure 26** The Save dialog sheet can be collapsed to offer fewer options...

**Figure 27** ...or expanded to offer more options.

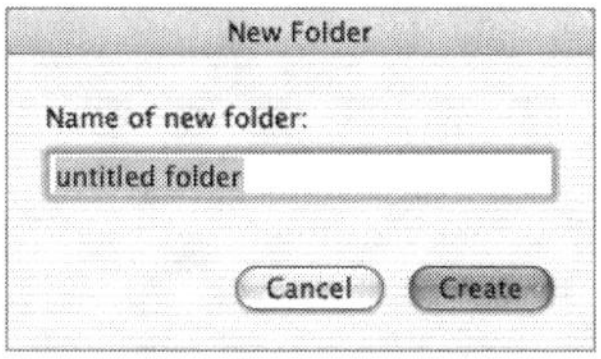

**Figure 28** Use the New Folder dialog to enter a name for a new folder.

**Figure 29** The name of the newly saved file appears in the window's title bar.

## To save a document for the first time

1. Choose File > Save (**Figure 17**) or press ⌃⌘S to display the Save dialog (**Figure 26** or **27**).

2. Use the Where pop-up menu (**Figure 22**) to select a location in which to save the document.

   *or*

   If necessary, click the triangle beside the Where pop-up menu (**Figure 26**) to expand the dialog (**Figure 27**). Then use any combination of the following techniques to select a location in which to save the document:

   ▲ Use the Where pop-up menu (**Figure 22**) to backtrack from the currently displayed location to one of its enclosing folders or a recently accessed folder.

   ▲ Click one of the items in the Sidebar list on the left side of the dialog to view the contents of that item.

   ▲ Press Shift⌃⌘H to view the contents of your Home folder.

   ▲ Click one of the items in either list to view its contents on the right side of the dialog. (The list containing the item you clicked shifts to the left if necessary.)

   ▲ Use the scroll bar at the bottom of the two lists to shift lists. Shifting lists to the right enables you to see your path from the item selected in the Sidebar.

   ▲ Click the New Folder button to create a new folder inside the currently selected folder. Enter a name for the folder in the New Folder dialog that appears (**Figure 28**), and click Create.

*Continued on next page...*

*Continued from previous page.*

3. When the name of the folder in which you want to save the document appears on the Where pop-up menu, enter a name for the document in the Save As box and click Save.

   The document is saved in the location you specified. The name of the file appears in the document window's title bar (**Figure 29**).

## ✔ Tips

- Not all applications enable you to save documents. The standard version of QuickTime Player, for example, does not include a Save command on its File menu.

- The Save dialog (**Figures 26** and **27**) is also known as the Save Location dialog because it enables you to select a location in which to save a file.

- In step 1, you can also use the Save As command. The first time you save a document, the Save and Save As commands do the same thing: display the Save dialog.

- Some applications automatically append a period and a three-character *extension* to a file's name when you save it. Extensions are used by Mac OS X and Windows applications to identify the file type. You can toggle the display of file name extensions in Finder preferences, which I discuss in **Chapter 6**.

- The Sidebar is covered in **Chapter 2**, file paths are discussed in **Chapter 3**, and iDisk is covered in **Chapter 14**.

**SAVING DOCUMENTS**

*Close button*

**Figure 30** A bullet in the close button of a document window indicates that the document has unsaved changes.

# To save changes to a document

Choose File > Save (**Figure 17**), or press ⌃⌘S.

The document is saved in the same location with the same name, thus overwriting the existing version of the document with the new version.

## ✔ Tip

- Mac OS X includes three ways to indicate whether a window contains unsaved changes:

  ▲ A bullet character appears in the close button on the title bar of the window for a document with unsaved changes (**Figure 30**).

  ▲ The document icon appears faded on the title bar of the window for a document with unsaved changes (**Figure 30**).

  ▲ In some applications, a bullet character appears in the Window menu beside the name of the window for a document with unsaved changes (**Figure 34**). The Window menu is discussed a little later in this chapter.

SAVING CHANGES TO DOCUMENTS

## To save a document with a new name or in a new location

1. Choose File > Save As (**Figures 17** and **19**) to display the Save dialog sheet (**Figure 26** or **27**).

2. Follow steps 2 and 3 in the section titled "To save a document for the first time" to select a location, enter a name, and save the document.

## ✔ Tips

■ Saving a document with a new name or in a new location creates a copy of the existing document. The open document is the copy, not the original. Any further changes you make and save for the open document are saved to the copy rather than the original.

■ If you use the Save dialog to save a document with the same name as a document in the selected location, a confirmation dialog like the one in **Figure 31** appears. You have two options:

▲ Click Cancel or press (Esc) to return to the Save dialog and either change the document's name or the save location.

▲ Click Replace or press (Return) or (Enter) to replace the document on disk with the current document.

**Figure 31** This dialog appears when you try to save a file with the same name as another file in a folder. This is what the dialog looks like in TextEdit.

**Edit**

| | |
|---|---|
| Undo Cut | ⌘Z |
| Redo Typing | ⇧⌘Z |
| Cut | ⌘X |
| Copy | ⌘C |
| Paste | ⌘V |
| Paste and Match Style | ⌥⇧⌘V |
| Delete | |
| Complete | ⌥⎋ |
| Select All | ⌘A |
| Insert | ▶ |
| Find | ▶ |
| Spelling | ▶ |
| Speech | ▶ |
| Special Characters... | ⌥⌘T |

**Edit**

| | |
|---|---|
| Undo Add To Group | ⌘Z |
| Redo Add To Group | ⇧⌘Z |
| Cut | ⌘X |
| Copy | ⌘C |
| Paste | ⌘V |
| Delete | |
| Remove From Group | |
| Select All | ⌘A |
| Find | ▶ |
| Rename Group | |
| Edit Smart Group... | |
| Edit Card | ⌘L |
| Edit Distribution List... | |
| Special Characters... | ⌥⌘T |

**Figures 32 & 33**
The Edit menus for TextEdit (top) and Address Book (bottom).

# The Edit Menu

The Edit menu (**Figures 32** and **33**) includes commands for modifying the contents of a document. Here's a quick list of the commands you're likely to find, along with their standard keyboard equivalents:

◆ **Undo** (⌘Z) reverses the last editing action you made.

◆ **Redo** (Shift ⌘Z) reverses the last undo.

◆ **Cut** (⌘X) removes a selection from the document and puts a copy of it in the Clipboard.

◆ **Copy** (⌘C) puts a copy of a selection in the Clipboard.

◆ **Paste** (⌘V) inserts the contents of the Clipboard into the document at the insertion point or replaces selected text in the document with the contents of the Clipboard.

◆ **Clear** or **Delete** removes a selection from the document. This is the same as pressing Delete when document contents are selected.

◆ **Select All** (⌘A) selects all text or objects in the document.

## ✔ Tips

■ Not all Edit menu commands are available in all applications at all times.

■ Edit menu commands usually work with selected text or graphic objects in a document.

■ Most Edit menu commands are discussed in greater detail in **Chapter 9**, which covers TextEdit.

THE EDIT MENU

# The Window Menu

The Window menu (**Figures** 34 and 35) includes commands for working with open document windows as well as a list of the open windows.

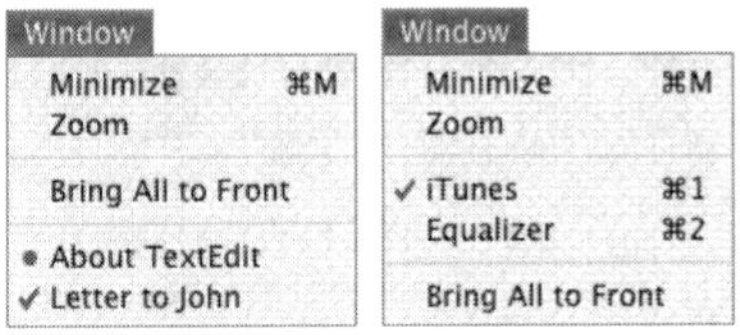

## ✔ Tips

- The windows within applications have the same basic parts and controls as Finder windows, which are discussed in detail in **Chapter 2**.

- A bullet character beside the name of a window in the Window menu (**Figure 34**) indicates that the window contains a document with unsaved changes.

## To zoom a window

Choose Window > Zoom (**Figures** 34 and 35).

The window toggles between its full size and a custom size you create with the window's size control.

## ✔ Tip

- I explain how to resize a window with the size control in **Chapter 2**.

## To minimize a window

Choose Window > Minimize (**Figures** 34 and 35), or press ⌃ ⌘ M.

*Or*

Click the Minimize button on the window's title bar.

The window shrinks down to the size of an icon and slips into the Dock (**Figure 36**).

**Figures 34 & 35** The Window menus for TextEdit (left) and iTunes (right).

**Figure 36** The icon for a minimized window appears in the Dock. If you look closely, you can see a tiny icon for the application in which it is open.

## To display a minimized window

With the application active, choose the window's name from the Window menu (**Figures 34** and **35**).

*Or*

Click the window's icon in the Dock (**Figure 36**).

The window expands out of the Dock and appears onscreen.

## To bring all of an application's windows to the front

Choose Window > Bring All to Front (**Figures 34** and **35**).

All of the application's open windows are displayed on top of open windows for other applications.

## ✔ Tip

■ Mac OS X allows an application's windows to be mingled in layers with other applications' windows.

## To activate a window

Choose the window's name from the Window menu (**Figures 34** and **35**).

# The Help Menu

The Help menu (**Figures 37** and **38**) includes commands for viewing onscreen help information specific to the application. Choosing the primary Help command (or pressing ⌘?) launches the Help Viewer application with help information and links (**Figure 39**).

## ✔ Tips

- Onscreen help is covered in **Chapter 20**.

- Although the Help menu may only have one command for a simple application (**Figures 37** and **38**), it can have multiple commands to access different kinds of help for more complex applications.

Help
| TextEdit Help    ⌘? |

Help
| iChat Help    ⌘? |

**Figures 37 & 38** The Help menu for Sherlock (left) and TextEdit (right).

**Figure 39** Choosing iChat Help from iChat's Help menu displays this Help Viewer window.

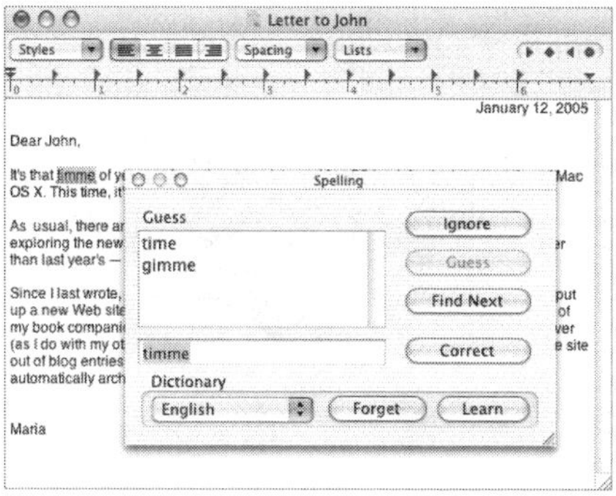

**Figure 40** This Spelling dialog in TextEdit is an example of a modeless dialog—you can interact with the document while the dialog is displayed.

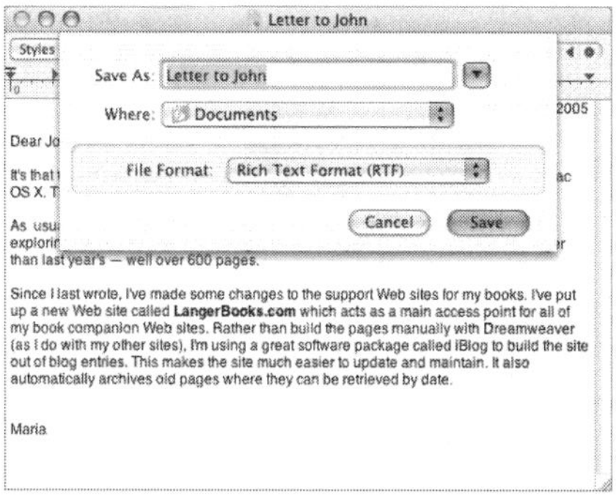

**Figure 41** A standard Save Location dialog sheet is an example of a document modal dialog—you must address and dismiss it before you can continue working with the document it is attached to.

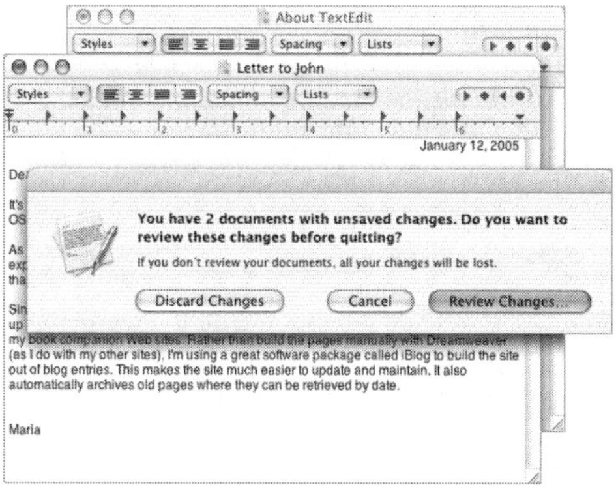

**Figure 42** An application modal dialog like this Quit dialog requires your attention before you can continue working with the application.

# Dialogs

Mac OS applications use *dialogs* to tell you things and get information from you. Think of them as the way your computer has a conversation—or dialog—with you.

Mac OS X has three main types of dialogs:

◆ *Modeless* dialogs enable you to work with the dialog while interacting with document windows. These dialogs usually have their own window controls to close and move them (**Figure 40**).

◆ *Document modal* dialogs usually appear as dialog *sheets* attached to a document window (**Figure 41**). You must address and dismiss these dialogs before you can continue working with the window, although you can switch to another window or application while the dialog is displayed.

◆ *Application modal* dialogs appear as movable dialogs (**Figure 42**). These dialogs must be addressed and dismissed before you can continue working with the application, although you can switch to another application while the dialog is displayed.

## ✔ Tips

■ You don't need to remember *modeless* vs. *modal* terminology to work with Mac OS X. Just understand how the dialogs differ and what the differences mean.

■ Some dialogs are very similar from one application to another. This chapter covers some of these standard dialogs, including Open (**Figure 21**), Save Location (**Figures 25, 26,** and **41**), Save Changes (**Figures 16** and **42**), and Replace Confirmation (**Figure 31**). Two more standard dialogs—Page Setup and Print—are covered in **Chapter 12**.

## To use dialog parts

◆ Click a *tab control* to view a *pane* full of related options (**Figure 43**).

◆ Use *scroll bars* to view the contents of *scrolling lists* (**Figure 44**). Click a list item once to select it or to enter it in a *combination box* (**Figure 44**).

◆ Enter text or numbers into *entry fields* (**Figure 45**), including those that are part of combination boxes (**Figure 44**).

◆ Click a *pop-up menu* (**Figures 44** and **45**) to display its options. Click a menu option to choose it.

◆ Click a *check box* (**Figure 46**) to toggle it on or off. (A check box is turned on when a check mark or X appears inside it.)

◆ Click a *radio button* (**Figure 46**) to choose its option. (A radio button is chosen when a bullet appears inside it.)

◆ Drag a *slider* control (**Figures 44** and **46**) to change a setting.

◆ Consult a *preview area* (**Figure 43**) to see the effects of your changes.

◆ Drag an image file into an *image well* (**Figure 45**).

◆ Click a *push button* (**Figures 43** and **45**) to activate it.

*Pane*        *Pane buttons*        *Preview area*

**Figure 43** The Screen Saver pane of Desktop & Screen Saver preferences.        *Push buttons*

*Scrolling lists*        *Scroll bar*   *Combination box*

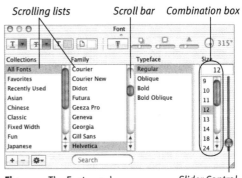

**Figure 44** The Font panel.        *Slider Control*

*Image well*     *Pop-up menu*   *Entry field (active)*  *Entry field (inactive)*

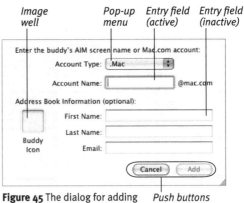

**Figure 45** The dialog for adding    *Push buttons*
buddy information to iChat.

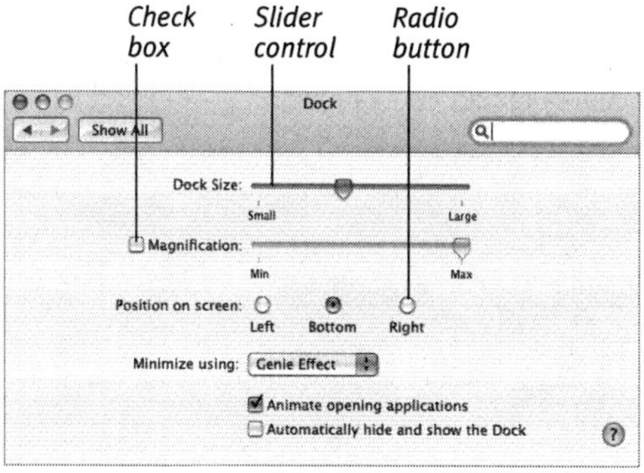

Check box    Slider control    Radio button

**Figure 46** Dock preferences.

## ✔ Tips

- An entry field with a dark border around it is the active field (**Figure 45**). Typing automatically enters text in this field. You can advance from one entry field to the next by pressing (Tab).

- If an entry field has a pair of arrows or triangles beside it you can click the triangles to increase or decrease a value already in the field.

- The default push button is the one that pulsates. You can always select a default button by pressing (Enter) and often by pressing (Return).

- You can usually select a Cancel button (**Figure 45**) by pressing (Esc).

- You can select as many check boxes (**Figure 46**) in a group as you like.

- One and only one radio button in a group can be selected (**Figure 46**). If you try to select a second radio button, the first button becomes deselected.

- If you click the Cancel button in a dialog (**Figure 45**), any options you set are lost.

- To select multiple items in a scrolling list, hold down (⌘) while clicking each one. Be aware that not all dialogs support multiple selections in scrolling lists.

- There are other standard controls in Mac OS X dialogs. These are the ones you'll encounter most often.

# Force Quitting Applications

Occasionally, an application may freeze, lock up, or otherwise become unresponsive. When this happens, you can no longer work with that application or its documents. Sometimes, you can't access any application at all!

The Force Quit command (**Figure 47**) enables you to force an unresponsive application to quit. Then you can either restart it or continue working with other applications.

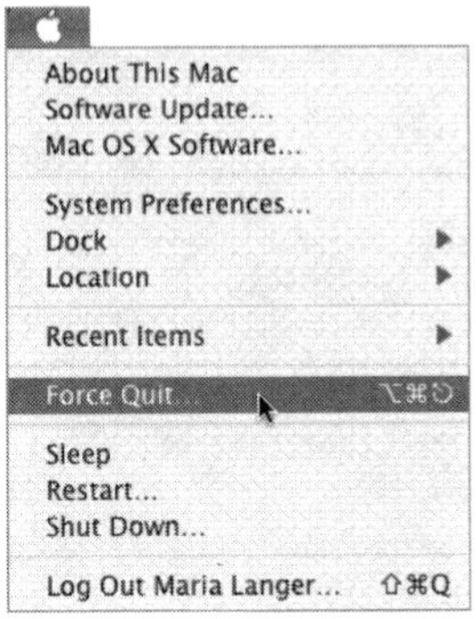

## ✖ Warning!

- When you use the Force Quit command to quit an application, any unsaved changes in that application's open documents may be lost. Use the Force Quit command only as a last resort, when the application's Quit command cannot be used.

## ✔ Tips

- Mac OS X's protected memory, which is discussed at the beginning of this chapter, makes it possible for applications to continue running properly on your computer when one application locks up.

- If more than one application experiences problems during a work session, you might find it helpful to restart your computer. This clears out RAM and forces your computer to reload all applications and documents into memory. You can learn more about troubleshooting Mac OS X in **Chapter 23**.

**Figure 47**
Choose Force Quit from the Apple menu.

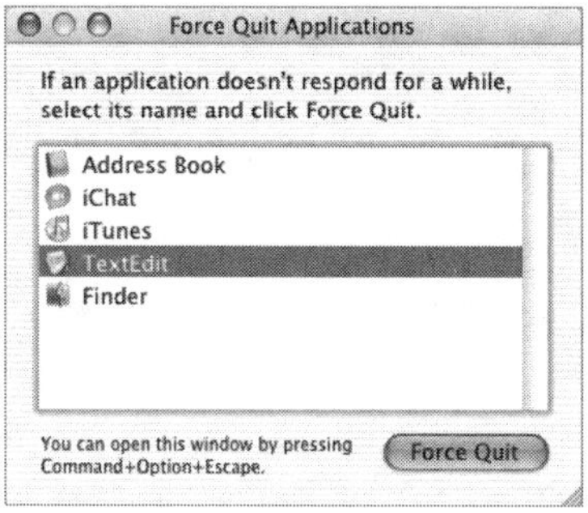

**Figure 48** Select the application you want to force to quit.

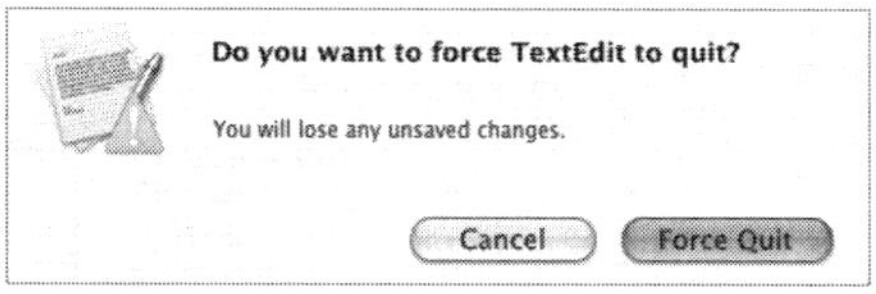

**Figure 49** Use this dialog to confirm that you really do want to force quit the application.

## To force quit an application

1. Choose Apple > Force Quit (**Figure 47**), or press Option ⌘ Esc.

2. In the Force Quit Applications window that appears (**Figure 48**), select the application you want to force to quit.

3. Click Force Quit.

4. A confirmation dialog like the one in **Figure 49** appears. Click Force Quit.

   The application immediately quits.

## ✔ Tip

■ If you selected Finder in step 2, the button to click in step 3 is labeled Relaunch.

**FORCE QUITTING APPLICATIONS**

# Using Mac OS X Applications

**8**

Figure 1 The contents of the Applications folder.

## Mac OS Applications

Mac OS X includes a variety of software applications that you can use to perform tasks on your computer.

This chapter provides instructions for getting started with the following Apple programs in the Applications folder (**Figure 1**):

◆ **Address Book**, which enables you to keep track of contact information for friends, family members, and business associates.

◆ **Calculator**, which enables you to perform calculations and conversions.

◆ **Chess**, which is a computerized version of the game of chess.

◆ **Dictionary**, which provides word definitions and synonyms.

◆ **DVD Player**, which enables you to play movies on DVD discs.

◆ **iCal**, which lets you keep track of appointments, events, and to-do lists.

◆ **Image Capture**, which enables you to download image files from a digital camera or import images from a scanner and save them on disk.

◆ **iSync**, which enables you to synchronize some data on your computer with another computing device.

*Continued on next page...*

*Continued from previous page.*

◆ **iTunes**, which lets you play CDs, record music from a CD to your hard disk, burn music CDs, or upload music to an iPod or other MP3 player.

◆ **Preview**, which enables you to view images and PDF files.

◆ **QuickTime Player**, which enables you to view QuickTime movies, sounds, and streaming video.

◆ **Stickies**, which enables you to place colorful notes on your computer screen.

## ✔ Tips

■ The Mac OS X 10.4 installer places icons for some Mac OS X applications in the Dock (**Figure 2**).

■ Mac OS X includes a number of other applications that are discussed elsewhere in this book:

▲ TextEdit is covered in **Chapter 9**.

▲ Dashboard is covered in **Chapter 10**.

▲ Font Book is covered in **Chapter 11**.

▲ iChat, Internet Connect, Mail, and Safari are covered in **Chapter 13**.

▲ Sherlock is covered in **Chapter 15**.

▲ Automator and AppleScript are covered in **Chapter 20**.

▲ System Preferences are covered in **Chapter 21**.

▲ Most applications in the Utilities folder are covered in **Chapter 22**.

**Figure 2** By default, the Dock is configured with icons for several Mac OS X applications.

MAC OS APPLICATIONS

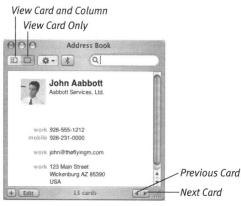

**Figure 3** The main Address Book window, with several records already created.

View Card and Column
    View Card Only

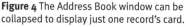

**Figure 4** The Address Book window can be collapsed to display just one record's card.

# Address Book

Address Book enables you to keep track of the names, addresses, phone numbers, e-mail addresses, and Web URLs of people you know. The information you store in Address Book's database can be used by Mail to send e-mail messages and iChat to send instant messages.

In this chapter, I provide enough information to get you started using Address Book for your contact management needs. You can explore the rest of Address Book's features on your own.

## ✔ Tips

- You must have an Internet connection to send e-mail or use iChat.

- Mail and iChat are covered in **Chapter 13**.

## To launch Address Book

Double-click the Address Book icon in the Applications folder (**Figure 1**) to select it.

*Or*

1. Click the Address Book icon in the Applications folder (**Figure 1**).

2. Choose File > Open, or press ⌘O.

*Or*

Click the Address Book icon in the Dock (**Figure 2**).

Address Book's main window appears (**Figure 3**).

## ✔ Tip

- If the Address Book window looks more like what's shown in **Figure 4**, you can click the View Card and Column button in its upper-left corner to expand the view to show all three columns (**Figure 3**).

# To add a new card

1. Click the Add New Person button (a plus sign) beneath the Name column in the main Address Book window (**Figure 3**).

   *or*

   Choose File > New Card (**Figure 5**), or press ⌘N.

   A *No Name* record is created in the Name column and a blank address card appears beside it, with the *First* field active (**Figure 6**).

2. Enter information about the contact into appropriate fields. When a field is active, text appears within it to prompt you for information (**Figure 7**). Press Tab or click on a field to move from field to field.

3. To change the label that appears beside a field, click the tiny triangles beside it (**Figure 8**) to display a menu (**Figure 9**), then choose the label you prefer.

4. To add more fields, click the green plus sign button beside a similar field (**Figure 8**). For example, to add another phone number field, click the plus sign beside a phone number. Then enter information and choose a field label as discussed in steps 2 and 3.

5. To remove a field, click the red minus sign button beside it.

6. When you are finished entering information, click the Edit button to view the completed card (**Figure 10**).

**Figure 5**
Address Book's File menu.

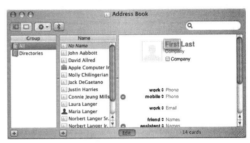

**Figure 6** When you click the Add New Person button, Address Book creates an unnamed card record and selects the first field for entry.

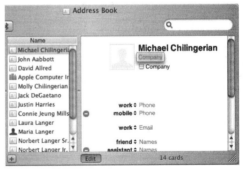

**Figure 7** Each active field prompts you for entry information.

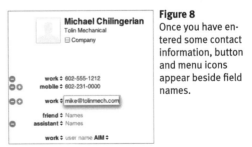

**Figure 8**
Once you have entered some contact information, button and menu icons appear beside field names.

**Figure 9**
Click the triangles to display a menu of applicable field labels.

**Figure 10** The completed contact record appears in the column on the right side of the window.

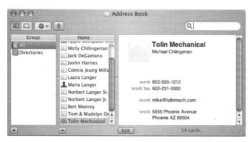

**Figure 11** You can choose to list a contact by its company name rather than the person's name.

**Figure 12** Address Book's Phone preferences pane lets you set up phone number formatting options.

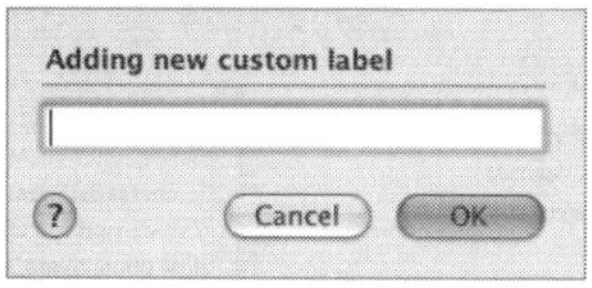

**Figure 13**
You can use this dialog to create a custom label for a record's card.

## ✔ Tips

■ You can enter information into any combination of fields; if you do not have information for a specific field, skip it and it will not appear in the completed card.

■ To list the entry by company name, rather than the person's name, as shown in **Figure 11**, turn on the Company check box beneath the Company field (**Figure 7**) when entering contact information. A contact that does not include a person's name is automatically listed by the company name.

■ By default, Address Book automatically formats telephone numbers to enclose the area code in parentheses. It doesn't matter how you enter a phone number; Address Book will change it to this format. You can turn off automatic phone number formatting in the Phone preferences pane (**Figure 12**); choose Address Book > Preferences and click the Phone button to display it.

■ In step 3, if you choose Custom from the pop-up menu, use the Adding new custom label dialog that appears (**Figure 13**) to enter a custom label and click OK.

## To delete a contact record

1. In the Name column of the Address Book window, select the contact you want to delete.

2. Press Delete.

3. In the confirmation dialog that appears, click Yes. The contact disappears.

## To edit a contact card

1. In the Name column of the Address Book window, select the contact you want to edit.

2. Click the Edit button.

3. Make changes as desired in the record's address card.

4. When you are finished making changes, click Edit again to save your changes and view the modified card.

## ✔ Tip

■ The Card menu (**Figure 14**) includes commands you can use to modify the currently selected card.

## To add an image to a contact card

1. In the Name column of the Address Book window, select the contact for which you want to add a picture or logo to display the contact card.

2. Drag the icon for the file containing the photo or logo you want to add from a Finder window to the image well in the address card window (**Figure 15**).

3. When you release the mouse button, the image appears in a dialog like the one in **Figure 16**. Click Set.

   The image appears in the card (**Figure 17**).

## ✔ Tips

■ Another way to add an image to a card is to choose Card > Choose Custom Image to display a dialog like the one in **Figure 16**. Then either drag the image into that dialog or click the Choose button to use another dialog to locate and select the image you want to use.

■ To remove a photo or logo from a contact record, select the contact and choose Card > Clear Custom Image (**Figure 14**).

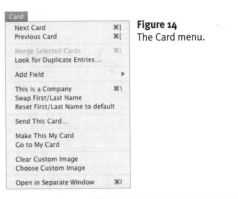

**Figure 14**
The Card menu.

**Figure 15** To add a picture for a record, simply drag its icon into the image well.

**Figure 16**
The image appears in a dialog like this one. (Yes, that's Mike, my significant other for the past 20+ years.)

**Figure 17**
The picture is added to the record's card.

**Figure 18** Drag a vCard file's icon into the Address Book window's Name column.

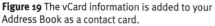

**Figure 19** The vCard information is added to your Address Book as a contact card.

**Figure 20** Drag the name of a contact from the Name column of the Address Book window to a Finder window.

**Figure 21**
A saved vCard file's icon looks like this.

## To add information from a vCard

1. Drag the icon for the vCard from a Finder window to the Name column in the Address Book window (**Figure 18**).

   *or*

   Double-click the icon for a vCard file.

2. A dialog box appears, telling you how many cards will be added. Click OK.

   An Address Book contact card is created based on the vCard contents (**Figure 19**).

## ✔ Tips

- *vCard,* or *virtual address card,* files are commonly used to share contact information electronically.

- When you import a vCard, Address Book creates (or modifies) a Last Import group. I tell you about groups on the next page.

## To save information as a vCard

Drag the name of a contact from the Name column of the Address Book window to a Finder window (**Figure 20**).

The vCard file's icon (**Figure 21**) appears where you dragged it.

## ✔ Tips

- You can save multiple vCards at once. Simply hold down ⌘ while clicking contact names to select multiple contacts and then drag any of them to a Finder window as discussed above.

- You can send your vCard via e-mail to anyone you like. This makes it easy for people to add your contact information to their contact database.

- The vCard format is recognized by most Mac OS and Windows contact management software.

**WORKING WITH VCARDS**

## To organize contact cards into groups

1. Click the Add New Group button (a plus sign) under the Group column of the Address Book window (**Figure 3**).

   *or*

   Choose File > New Group (**Figure 5**) or press Shift⌘N.

2. A new entry appears in the Group column. Its name, *Group Name*, is selected (**Figure 22**). Enter a new name for the group and press Return to save it (**Figure 23**).

3. Repeat steps 1 and 2 to add as many groups as you need to organize your contacts.

4. Select All in the Group column.

5. Drag a contact name from the Name column onto the name of the group you want to associate it with in the Group column. When a box appears around the group name (**Figure 24**), release the mouse button to add the contact to that group.

6. Repeat step 5 to organize contact cards as desired.

## ✔ Tips

- To see which contact cards are in a group, click the name of the group in the Group column. The Name column changes to display only those contacts in the selected group (**Figure 25**).

- A contact can be included in more than one group.

- The Directories entry in the Group column enables you to use an LDAP server to search for an e-mail address. This is an advanced feature that is beyond the scope of this book.

**Figure 22**
When you click the Add New Group button, a new group appears in the Group column, with its default name selected.

**Figure 23**
Enter a new name for the group and press Return to save it.

**Figure 24**
To add a contact to a group, simply drag its name to the group name.

**Figure 25**
To see which contacts are in a group, select the name of the group.

**Figure 26** This dialog confirms that you want to delete a record from a group...

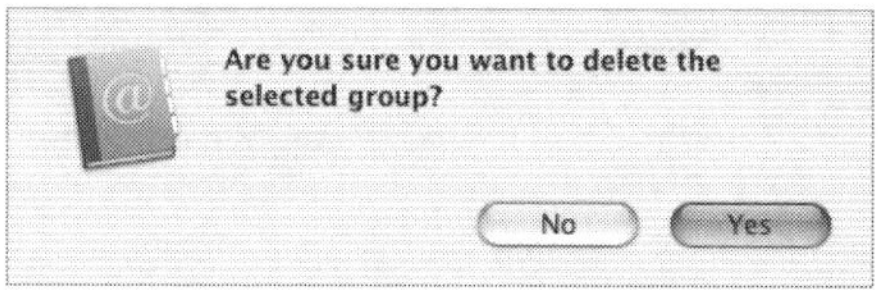

**Figure 27** ...and this dialog confirms that you want to delete a group.

## To remove a contact from a group

1. In the Group column, select the group you want to remove the contact from (**Figure 25**).

2. In the Name column, select the contact you want to remove.

3. Press ⌈Delete⌋.

4. Click the appropriate button in the confirmation dialog that appears (**Figure 26**):

   ▲ **Cancel** does not delete the contact.

   ▲ **Delete** deletes the contact from the Address Book database.

   ▲ **Remove from Group** removes the contact from the group. The contact remains in the Address Book database.

## ✖ Warning

- If you delete a contact from the All group, you will remove the contact from the Address Book database.

## To remove a group

1. In the Group column, select the group you want to remove (**Figure 25**).

2. Press ⌈Delete⌋.

3. In the confirmation dialog that appears (**Figure 27**), click Yes. The group is removed but all contacts within it remain in the Address Book database.

## ✔ Tip

- You cannot remove the All group.

**WORKING WITH GROUPS**

161

## To create a smart group

1. Choose File > New Smart Group (**Figure 5**). A dialog like the one in **Figure 28** appears.

2. Enter a name for the group in the Smart Group Name box.

3. Use options in the middle of the dialog to set criteria for matching contacts. **Figure 29** shows an example.

4. To add more matching criteria, click the + button at the far right end of the line of criteria you already set. The dialog expands to offer an additional line and a pop-up menu for matching options (**Figure 30**). Set options as desired.

5. Repeat step 4 as necessary to add more matching criteria.

6. Click OK.

   The smart group is created and populated with contacts that match the criteria you specified (**Figure 31**).

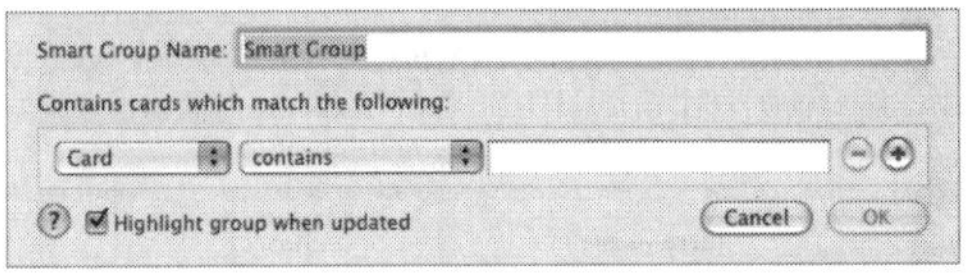

## ✔ Tips

- The smart group feature is brand new in Mac OS X 10.4.

- You can delete a smart group the same way you delete a regular group. I explain how on the previous page.

- You cannot manually remove a contact from a smart group. The only way a contact can be removed from a smart group is if it no longer matches the criteria you specified when you set up the smart group.

- To edit a smart group's matching criteria, select the group and choose Edit > Edit Smart Group (**Figure 32**). Then use the dialog that appears (**Figure 28**) to modify settings and click OK.

**Figure 28** Use this dialog to set options for a new smart group.

**Figure 29** You can use pop-up menus and a text box to set matching criteria.

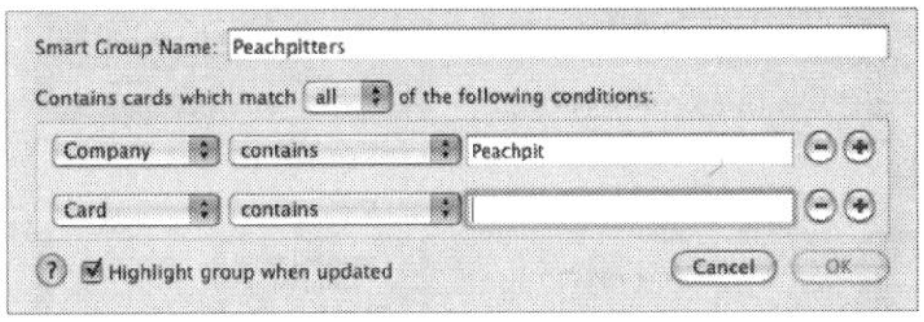

**Figure 30** Clicking a + button expands the dialog so you can set up additional matching criteria.

**Figure 31** In this example, the smart group matched all contacts in my Address Book data file that work for Peachpit Press.

**Figure 32** Address Book's Edit menu.

CREATING SMART GROUPS

**Figure 33** Enter all or part of a contact name in the Search box to find that contact.

# To search for a contact card

1. In the Group column, select the name of the group in which you expect to find the contact.

2. Enter all or part of the contact name in the Search box at the top of the Address Book window (**Figure 33**).

   The names of contacts that match what you typed appear in the Name column (**Figure 33**).

## ✔ Tips

- In step 1, if you're not sure which group a contact is in, select All.

- Search results begin appearing in the Name column as soon as you begin entering search characters in the Search box. The more you enter, the fewer results are displayed.

- If no contact cards match your search criteria, the Name column will be empty.

**SEARCHING FOR CONTACTS**

# To print Address Book records

1. In the Group column, select the group containing the records you want to print.

2. To print information for only some records in the group, hold down ⌘ and click in the Name column to select each record you want to print.

3. Choose File > Print (**Figure 5**) or press ⌘P. A Print dialog like the one in **Figure 34** appears.

4. Choose the name of the printer you want to use from the Printer pop-up menu.

5. Choose an option from the Style pop-up menu:

   ▲ **Mailing Labels** (**Figure 34**) enables you to print mailing labels.

   ▲ **Envelopes** (**Figure 35**) enables you to print envelopes.

   ▲ **Lists** (**Figure 36**) enables you to print contact lists.

   ▲ **Pocket Address Book** (**Figure 37**) enables you to print pocket-sized address books.

6. Set options in the dialog as desired:

   ▲ For mailing labels, click the Layout button (**Figure 34**) and set label layout options. Then click the Label button and set options for label content, sort order, color, and font.

   ▲ For envelopes, click the Layout button (**Figure 35**) and set envelope layout options. Then click the Label button and set options for envelope content, print order, color, and font. Finally, click the Orientation button and select an envelope print orientation.

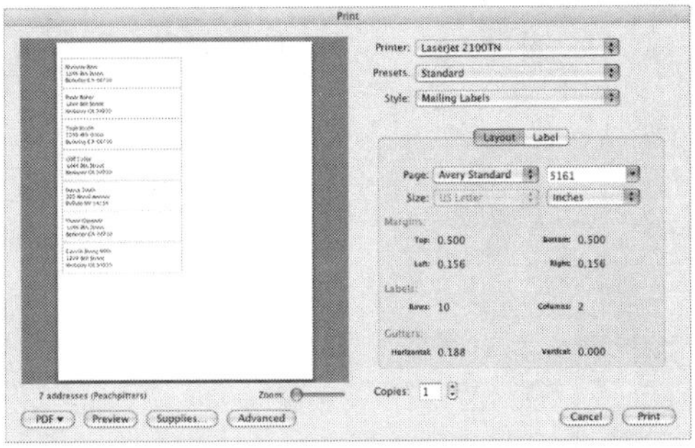

**Figure 34** The Mailing Labels Layout options.

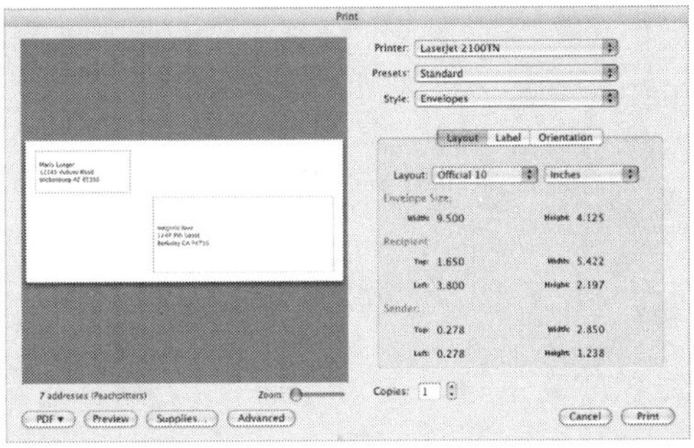

**Figure 35** The Envelopes Layout options.

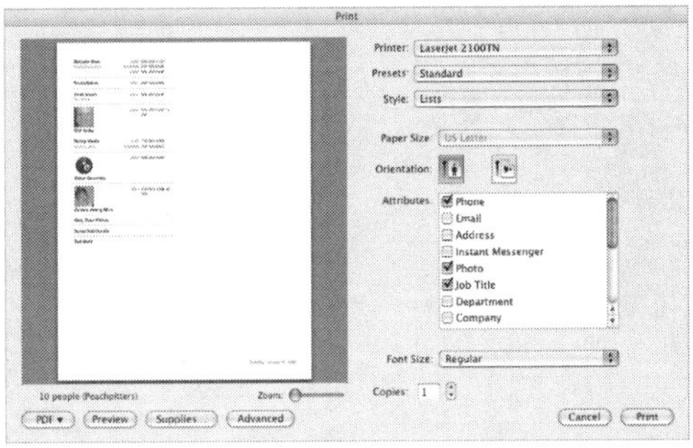

**Figure 36** The Lists options.

**Figure 37** The Pocket Address Book options.

▲ For lists (**Figure 36**), set Paper Size, Orientation, and Font Size options. Then turn on check boxes in the Attributes area to specify what information you want to print for each record.

▲ For pocket address books (**Figure 37**), set Orientation, Flip Style, and Font options. Then turn on check boxes in the Attributes area to specify what information you want to print for each record.

7. Click Print. Address Book sends the information to your printer and it prints.

## ✔ Tips

■ The Envelopes and Pocket Address Book options are brand new in Mac OS X 10.4.

■ I discuss printing in greater detail in **Chapter 12**.

# Calculator

Calculator displays a simple calculator that can perform addition, subtraction, multiplication, and division, as well as complex mathematical calculations and conversions.

## To launch Calculator

Double-click the Calculator icon in the Applications folder (**Figure 1**).

*Or*

1. Click the Calculator icon in the Applications folder (**Figure 1**) to select it.

2. Choose File > Open, or press ⌃ ⌘ O.

The Calculator window appears (**Figure 38**).

## To perform basic calculations

Use your mouse to click buttons for numbers and operators.

*Or*

Press keyboard keys corresponding to numbers and operators.

The numbers you enter and the results of your calculations appear at the top of the Calculator window.

## ✔ Tip

■ You can use the Cut, Copy, and Paste commands to copy the results of calculations into documents. **Chapter 9** covers the Cut, Copy, and Paste commands.

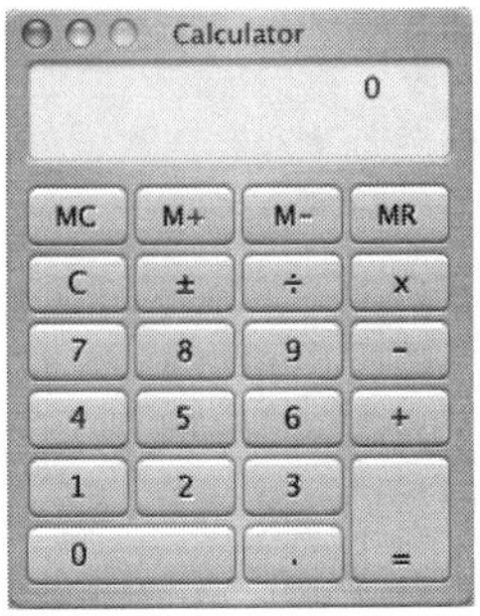

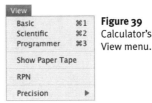

**Figure 38**
The Calculator looks and works like a $10 pocket calculator.

**Figure 39**
Calculator's View menu.

**Figure 40**
When you choose Show Paper Tape from the View menu, your entries appear in a separate window.

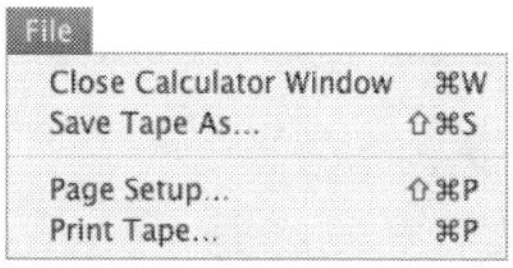

**Figure 41** The File menu includes commands for saving and printing the paper tape.

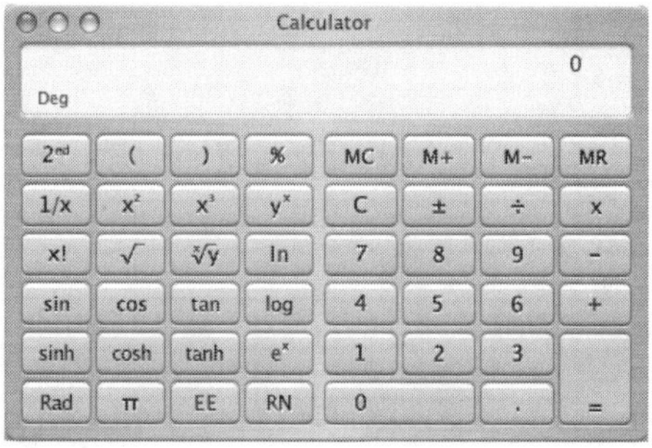

**Figure 42** Choosing Scientific from the View menu expands the Calculator to display scientific functions.

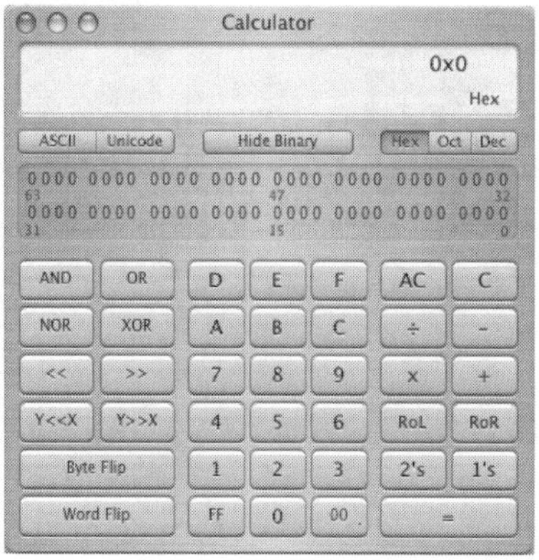

**Figure 43** Choosing Programmer from the View menu displays programming-related functions.

## To keep track of your entries

Choose View > Show Paper Tape (**Figure 39**). The Paper Tape window appears. It displays your entries as you make them (**Figure 40**).

## ✔ Tips

- To hide the Paper Tape window, choose View > Hide Paper Tape or click the Paper Tape window's close button.

- To start with a fresh tape, click the Clear button.

- You can use commands under the File menu (**Figure 41**) to save or print the paper tape.

## To perform scientific calculations

1. Choose View > Scientific (**Figure 39**) or press ⌃⌘2. The window expands to show a variety of functions used for scientific calculations (**Figure 42**).

2. Click buttons for the functions, values, and operators to perform your calculations.

## ✔ Tip

- To hide scientific functions, choose View > Basic (**Figure 39**) or press ⌃⌘1.

## To perform programmer functions

1. Choose View > Programmer (**Figure 39**) or press ⌃⌘3. The window expands to show a variety of programming-related functions (**Figure 43**).

2. Click buttons for the functions, values, and operators to perform your calculations.

## ✔ Tip

- To hide programmer functions, choose View > Basic (**Figure 39**) or press ⌃⌘1.

USING THE CALCULATOR

## To use Reverse Polish Notation

1. Choose View > RPN (**Figure 39**). The letters *RPN* appear in the calculator's window (**Figure 44**).

2. Click buttons for the functions, values, and operators to perform your calculations.

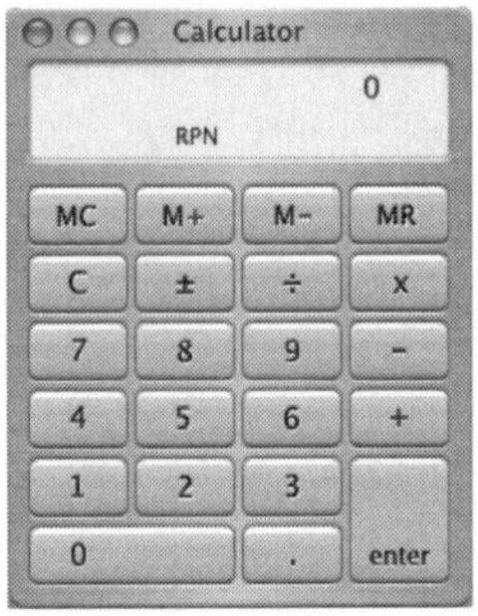

## ✔ Tips

■ Reverse Polish Notation, or RPN, is an alternative format for entering calculations. It is commonly used on Hewlett-Packard brand calculators.

■ If you don't know what Reverse Polish Notation is, you probably don't need to use it.

## To perform conversions

1. Enter the value you want to convert.

2. Choose the conversion you want from the Convert menu (**Figure 45**).

3. In the dialog that appears, set options for the conversion you want to perform. **Figure 46** shows an example that converts speed from miles per hour to knots.

4. Click OK. The original value you entered is converted and appears at the top of the Calculator window.

## ✔ Tips

■ The Convert menu's Recent Conversions submenu makes it easy to repeat conversions you have done recently.

■ If you have an Internet connection, you should choose Convert > Update Currency Exchange Rates before using the Convert menu to perform currency conversions.

**Figure 44**
The letters RPN indicate the calculator is configured for Reverse Polish Notation.

**Figure 45** The Convert menu lists a variety of common conversions.

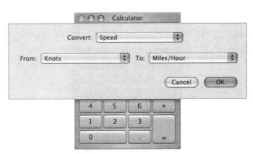

**Figure 46** Set conversion options in a dialog sheet like this.

**Figure 47** The Chess window displays a three-dimensional chess board.

**Figure 48**
Chess's Game menu.

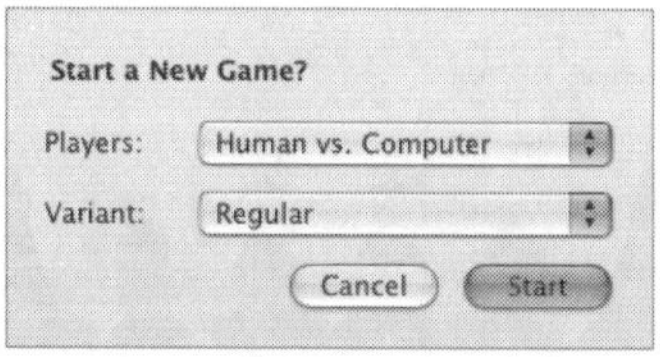

**Figure 49** A dialog sheet like this one appears when you choose New from the File menu.

**Figures 50 & 51**
The Players (top) and Variants (bottom) pop-up menus enable you to set options for a new game.

# Chess

Chess is a computerized version of the classic strategy game of chess. Your pieces are white and you go first; the computer's pieces are black.

## To launch Chess

Double-click the Chess icon in the Applications folder (**Figure 1**).

*Or*

1. Click the Chess icon in the Applications folder (**Figure 1**) to select it.

2. Choose File > Open, or press ⌃⌘O.

The Chess window appears (**Figure 47**).

## To move a chess piece

Drag the piece onto any valid square on the playing board.

## ✔ Tips

- The computer moves automatically after each of your moves.

- If you attempt to make an invalid move, an alert sounds and the piece returns to where it was.

- If Speakable Items is enabled, you can use spoken commands to move chess pieces. I tell you about Speakable Items in **Chapter 21**.

## To start a new game

1. Choose Game > New Game (**Figure 48**) or press ⌃⌘N. A dialog sheet like the one in **Figure 49** appears.

2. Choose an option from the Players pop-up menu (**Figure 50**).

3. If desired, choose an option from the Variant pop-up menu (**Figure 51**).

4. Click Start.

CHESS

# Dictionary

Dictionary, which is brand new in Mac OS X 10.4, has all the features of a dictionary and thesaurus, without all that paper. Simply type a word or phrase into the search box at the top of Dictionary's window. Dictionary comes up with a list of matches. Double-click the one that interests you to get definitions, pronunciations, and synonyms. You'll never have an excuse to use the wrong word again!

## To launch Dictionary

Double-click the Dictionary icon in the Applications folder (**Figure 1**).

*Or*

1.  Click the Dictionary icon in the Applications folder (**Figure 1**) to select it.

2.  Choose File > Open, or press ⌘O.

The Dictionary and Thesaurus window appears (**Figure 52**).

## To look up a word or phrase

1.  Enter the word or phrase you want to look up in the search box at the top of the Dictionary and Thesaurus window. As you type, Dictionary begins displaying a list of matches (**Figure 53**).

2.  Double-click the word or phrase that interests you. The window displays dictionary and thesaurus information for that entry (**Figure 54**).

## ✔ Tips

■ To change the size of font characters in the Dictionary and Thesaurus window, click one of the font size buttons in the window's toolbar.

■ To print a Dictionary entry, choose File > Print (**Figure 55**). I tell you more about printing in **Chapter 12**.

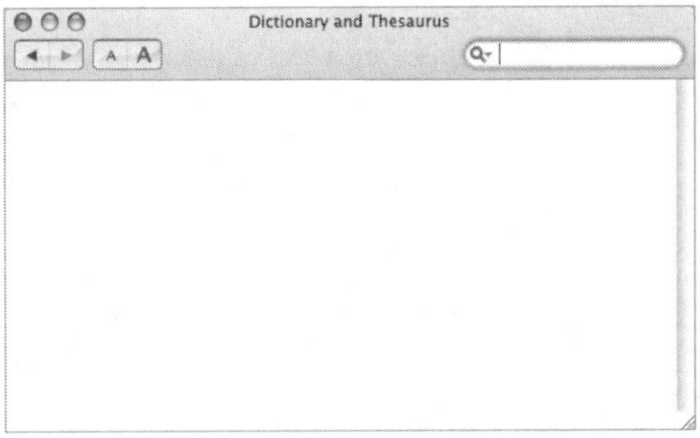

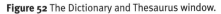

**Figure 52** The Dictionary and Thesaurus window.

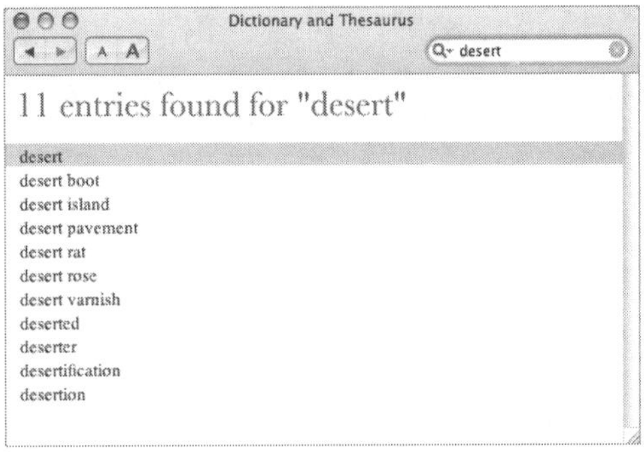

**Figure 53** Dictionary displays a list of words and phrases.

**Figure 54** Double-clicking a word displays its entry.

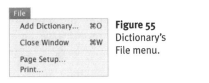

**Figure 55** Dictionary's File menu.

**Figure 56** DVD Player either starts with a blank Viewer window and Controller palette...

**Figure 57** ...or begins playing the DVD-Video. (This is the first DVD I created with iDVD. It didn't get any awards.)

# DVD Player

DVD Player enables you to play DVD-Video on your Macintosh.

## ✔ Tip

- To use DVD Player, your Macintosh must have a DVD-ROM drive or SuperDrive. For that reason, the Mac OS X installer only installs DVD Player on computers that have one of these drives. If you can't find DVD Player in your Applications folder, chances are that your computer can't play DVD-Video anyway.

## To launch DVD Player

Insert a DVD-Video into your computer. DVD Player should launch and do one of two things:

- Display a black Viewer window with a floating Controller palette (**Figure 56**).

- Immediately begin DVD play (**Figure 57**).

If DVD Player does not launch at all, then:

Double-click the DVD Player icon in the Applications folder (**Figure 1**).

*Or*

1. Click the DVD Player icon in the Applications folder (**Figure 1**) to select it.

2. Choose File > Open or press ⌘O.

## ✔ Tip

- If a Drive Region Code dialog appears the first time you play a DVD-Video, click the Set Drive Region button to set DVD Player's region to match that of the disc you inserted. Then click OK to dismiss the confirmation dialog that appears.

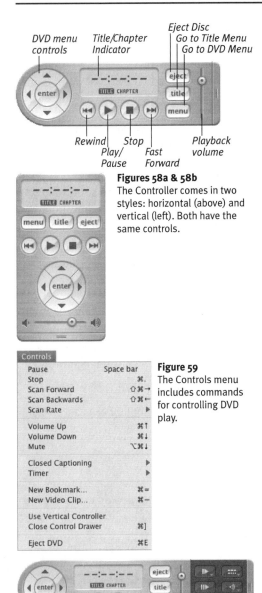

DVD menu controls
Title/Chapter Indicator
Eject Disc
Go to Title Menu
Go to DVD Menu

Rewind
Play/Pause
Stop
Fast Forward
Playback volume

**Figures 58a & 58b**
The Controller comes in two styles: horizontal (above) and vertical (left). Both have the same controls.

**Figure 59**
The Controls menu includes commands for controlling DVD play.

**Figure 60** A horizontal Controller, expanded to show additional control buttons. Point to a button to learn its name.

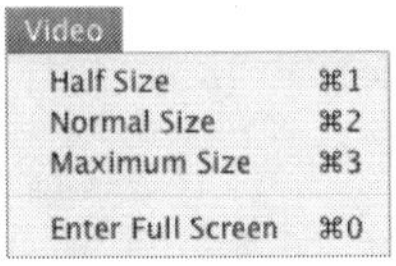

**Figure 61**
The Video menu enables you to set the size of the Viewer window.

## To display the Controller

Move the mouse while the DVD is playing.

*Or*

Choose Window > Show Viewer (the menu appears, if necessary, when you point to it), or press (Control)(C).

The Controller appears (**Figure 58a** or **58b**).

## ✔ Tips

■ You can change the appearance of the Controller from horizontal (**Figure 58a**) to vertical (**Figure 58b**) by choosing an option from the Controller Type submenu under the Controls menu (**Figure 59**).

■ To display additional DVD controls on the Controller, double-click the pair of tiny lines on the right (**Figure 58a**) or bottom (**Figure 58b**) of the Controller. **Figure 60** shows a horizontal Controller expanded to show these controls.

## To control DVD play

Click buttons on the Controller (**Figure 58a**, **58b**, or **60**).

*Or*

Choose a command from the Controls menu (**Figure 61**).

## ✔ Tip

■ The Pause button on the Controller (**Figures 58a** and **58b**) and the Pause command on the Controls menu (**Figure 59**) change into a Play button and a Play command when a DVD is not playing.

## To resize the Viewer window

Choose an option from the Video window (**Figure 61**) or press the corresponding short-cut key.

CONTROLLING DVD PLAY

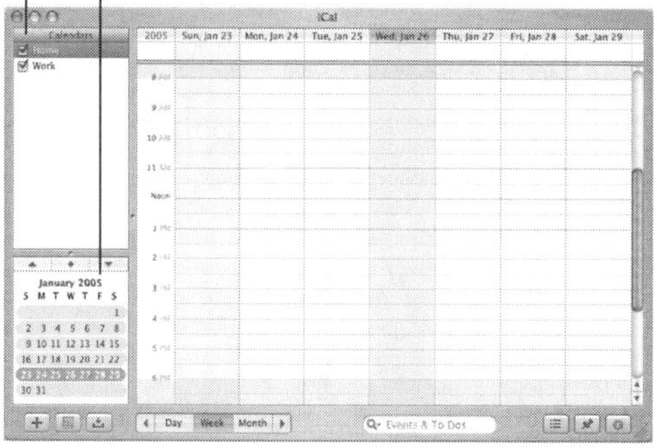

*Calendar list*

*Mini-month calendar*

**Figure 62** iCal's main window, showing a week at a glance view.

# iCal

iCal is a personal calendar application that enables you to keep track of appointments and other events. With iCal, you can:

◆ Create multiple color-coded calendars for different categories of events—for example, home, business, or school. You can view your calendars individually or together.

◆ View calendars by day, week, or month.

◆ Share calendars on the Web with family, friends, and business associates.

◆ Send e-mail invitations for events to people in your Mac OS X Address Book.

◆ Get notification of upcoming events on screen or by e-mail.

◆ Create and manage a priorities-based to-do list.

This part of the chapter provides basic instructions for setting up and using iCal.

## ✔ Tip

■ You can learn more about iCal's features and public calendars you can subscribe to at Apple's iCal Web site, www.apple.com/ical/.

## To launch iCal

Double-click the iCal icon in the Applications folder (**Figure 1**).

*Or*

Click the iCal icon in the Dock (**Figure 2**).

*Or*

1. Click the iCal icon in the Applications folder (**Figure 1**) to select it.

2. Choose File > Open, or press ⌃ ⌘ O.

iCal's main window appears (**Figure 62**).

iCAL

## To change the calendar view

Click one of the view buttons at the bottom of the calendar window (**Figure 63**).

◆ **Day** shows a day at a glance (**Figure 64**).

◆ **Week** shows a week at a glance (**Figure 62**).

◆ **Month** shows a month at a glance (**Figure 65**).

## To view a specific day, week, or month

1. Follow the instructions in the previous section to change the view.

2. Click the Next or Previous button (**Figure 66**) above the mini-month calendar until the date's month appears as one of the mini-month calendars. For example, to view June 30, 2005, you'd click the Next or Previous button until June 2005 appeared.

3. In the mini-month calendar, click the day, week, or month you want to view. It appears in the main calendar window.

*Or*

1. Choose View > Go to Date (**Figure 67**) or press Shift ⌘ T.

2. Enter the date you want to go to in the tiny dialog sheet that appears (**Figure 68**).

3. Click Show.

## ✔ Tip

■ To view today's date, click the Today button above the mini-month calendar, choose View > Go to Today (**Figure 67**), or press ⌘ T.

**Figure 63** Use these buttons to switch between Day, Week, and Month view or to go back or forward in the calendar.

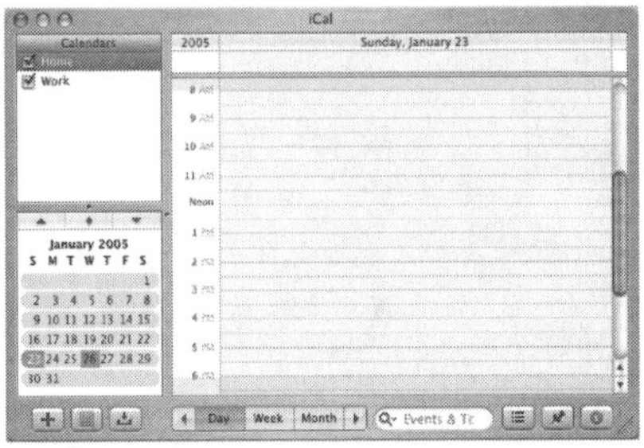

**Figure 64** Day view shows one day at a time.

**Figure 65** Month view shows a month at a

Previous month     Today     Next month

**Figure 66** The navigation buttons above the mini-month calendar.

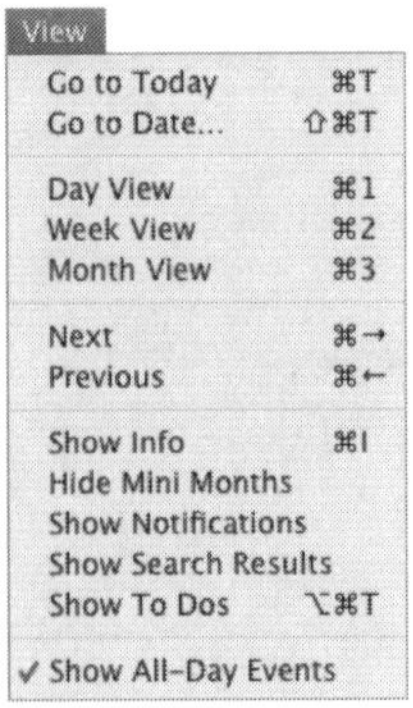

**Figure 67** iCal's View menu.

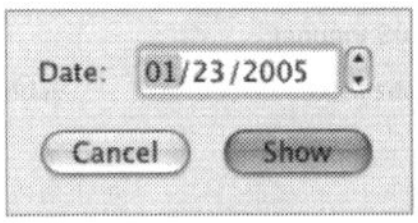

**Figure 68** Enter the date you want to view in this dialog.

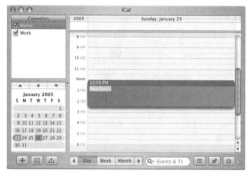

**Figure 69** Drag from the event's start time to end time.

**Figure 70** When you release the mouse button, the event box appears with its default name selected.

| File | |
|------|---|
| New Event | ⌘N |
| New To Do | ⌘K |
| New Calendar | ⌥⌘N |
| New Calendar Group | ⇧⌘N |
| Import... | |
| Export... | |
| Close | ⌘W |
| Back up Database... | |
| Revert to Database Backup... | |
| Print... | ⌘P |

**Figure 71**
iCal's File menu.

*Info drawer*

**Figure 72** A new event inserted in month view, using the New Event command.

## To create an event by dragging

1. In the Calendar list on the upper-left corner of the calendar window, click the name of the calendar you want to add the event to.

2. In Day or Week view, drag from the event's start time to end time (**Figure 69**). When you release the mouse button, a box for the event appears in the calendar window with its default name (New Event) selected (**Figure 70**).

3. Enter a new name for the event, and press (Return).

## ✔ Tip

- Another way to create an event is to double-click anywhere in the date box. This is almost the same as using the New Event command discussed next; it creates a new event with default settings and displays the Event Info window (**Figure 72**).

## To create an event with the New Event command

1. In any calendar view window, select the day you want to add the event to.

2. Choose File > New Event (**Figure 71**), or press (⌘ ⌘ N). A box for the event appears in the calendar window with its default name (New Event) selected (**Figure 72**).

3. Enter a new name for the event and press (Return).

## ✔ Tip

- The Info drawer automatically appears when you insert an event with the New Event command (**Figure 72**). I explain how to use the Info drawer to enter event details next.

# To set event details

1. In the calendar window, select the event you want to modify.

2. If necessary, click the Show Info button in the lower-right corner of the window, choose View > Show Info (**Figure 67**), or press ⌃ ⌘ I to display the Info drawer.

3. To enter an event name and location, click in the appropriate field at the top of the Info drawer and type what you want to appear (**Figure 73**).

4. To indicate that the event lasts all day (or more than one day), turn on the all-day check box. You can then enter an ending date in the to date area (**Figure 74**).

   *or*

   To specify starting and ending times for the event, make sure the all-day check box is turned off and then enter the starting and ending times in the two time areas (**Figure 75**).

5. To set the event to repeat on a regular basis, choose an option from the repeat pop-up menu (**Figure 76**). If none of the standard options apply, you can choose Custom and use the dialog that appears (**Figure 77**) to set a custom repeating schedule. Then, if necessary, set an ending option in the end field that appears (**Figure 78**).

6. To identify one or more people involved with the event, enter each person's name in the Attendees field. As you type, iCal attempts to match names to those in your Address Book database (**Figure 79**), but you can enter any name.

**Figure 73** To enter an event name or location, click the field and enter the information you want to appear.

**all-day** ☑
from 01/15/05
to 01/15/05

**Figure 74** When you turn on the all-day check box, you can enter starting and ending dates.

**all-day** ☐
from 01/15/05 at 7:00 AM
to 01/15/05 at 3:00 PM

**Figure 75** With the all-day check box turned off, you can enter starting and ending times.

repea ✓ None
every day
attendee every week
every month
calenda every year
alarm Custom...
url None

**Figure 76** Use the repeat pop-up menu to set an event to repeat regularly.

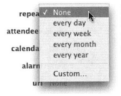

**Figure 77** Choosing Custom from the repeat pop-up menu displays this dialog.

repeat Custom... ⬍
every 2 weeks
end on date ⬍ 12/31/05

**Figure 78** An example of a custom repeating option with an end date.

attendees Celia Venegas
Celia Venegas
Celt John
repeat None ⬍

**Figure 79** As you enter a name in the attendees field, iCal attempts to match it to an Address Book entry.

calendar
Home
Work
alarm

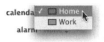

**Figure 80** You can add an event to any calendar.

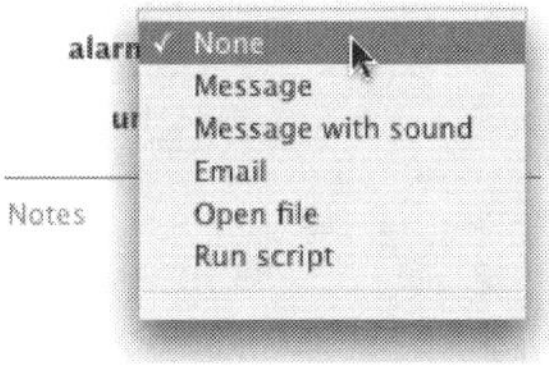
alarm
None
Message
Message with sound
Email
Open file
Run script
Notes

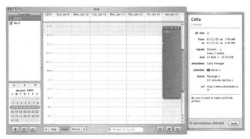

**Figure 81** Choosing an option from the alarm pop-up menu sets a reminder for the event.

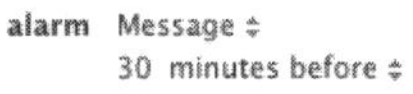
alarm
Message
30 minutes before

**Figure 82** If you choose an alarm, you must set how far in advance it should activate.

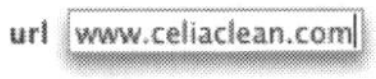
url
www.celiaclean.com

**Figure 83** You can associate a Web page's URL with an event.

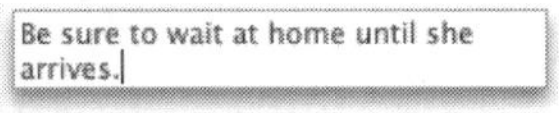
Be sure to wait at home until she arrives.

**Figure 84** Enter notes about the event in the notes field.

Celia

**Figure 85** Here's an example of a completed event with its details in Week view.

7. To specify a calendar to add the event to, choose a calendar from the calendar pop-up menu (**Figure 80**). The menu lists all calendars you have created.

8. To be reminded about the event, choose an option from the Alarm pop-up menu (**Figure 81**). Then set other alarm options as necessary (**Figure 82**).

9. To associate a Web page with the event, enter a URL in the url field (**Figure 83**).

10. To add notes about the event, click the Notes field and type what you want to appear (**Figure 84**).

**Figure 85** shows an example of an event with detailed information in the Info drawer.

## ✔ Tips

- You can use these steps to add settings for a new event or make changes to an existing event.
- The all-day event check box is handy for entering information about vacations and other events that span multiple days.
- In step 4, the ending date must be after the starting date. It may be necessary to change AM to PM *before* entering the second time.
- A quick way to change an event's date is to drag its event box from one date to another in the main calendar window. This automatically changes the date info in the Info drawer for the event.
- A quick way to change an event's time is to drag its top or bottom border in Day or Week view of the main calendar window. This automatically changes the time info in the Info drawer for the event.

*Continued on next page...*

*Continued from previous page.*

- If an event has attendees, you can click an attendee's name to access a menu of options for that attendee. **Figure 86** shows an example for an attendee from my Address Book database; note that iCal has automatically looked up the person's e-mail address.

- If you set an event to repeat, any time you change that event's details, a dialog like the one in **Figure 87** appears. Click the appropriate button for the change.

- Icons for some settings appear in the upper-right corner of the event box when viewed in Day or Week view (**Figure 85**).

- I tell you more about individual calendars later in this section.

## To delete an event

1. In the calendar window, select the event you want to delete.

2. Press Delete. The event disappears.

**Figure 86** When you click an attendee's name, iCal displays a menu of options for working with that attendee.

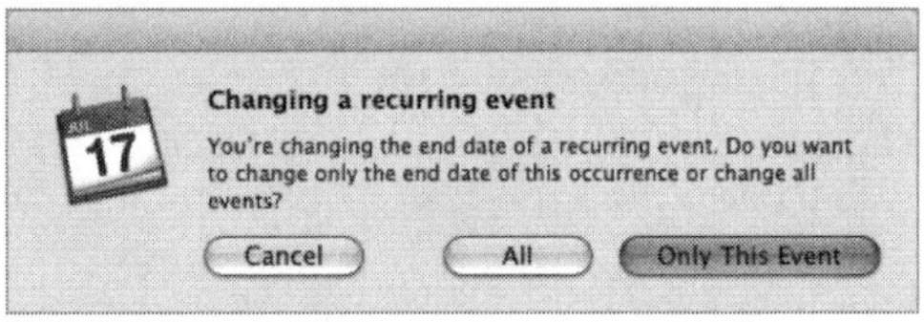

**Figure 87** A dialog like this appears when you make a change to a repeating event.

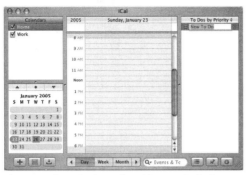

**Figure 88** The To Do items list with a new To Do item added.

**Figure 89** You can use the Info drawer to set options for a To Do item.

**Figure 90** Use the priority pop-up menu to prioritize To Do items.

**Figure 91** When you turn on the due date check box, you can enter a deadline for the item.

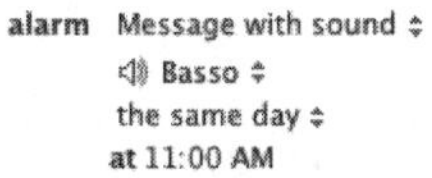

alarm   Message with sound ‡
           ◁) Basso ‡
           the same day ‡
           at 11:00 AM

**Figure 92** There are more alarm options for to do items than calendar events.

# To create a To Do item

1. Choose File > New To Do (**Figure 71**), or press ⌃ ⌘ K. If the To Do items list was not already showing, it appears. An untitled To Do item appears in the list with its default name (New To Do) selected (**Figure 88**).

2. Enter a name for the To Do item and press Return.

# To set To Do item details

1. If necessary, click the Show To Do list button in the lower-right corner of the window or press Option ⌃ ⌘ T to display the To Do items list.

2. In the To Do items list, select the item you want to modify.

3. If necessary, click the Show Info button in the lower-right corner of the window or press ⌃ ⌘ I to display the Info drawer (**Figure 89**).

4. To enter an item name, click in the field at the top of the Info drawer and type what you want to appear.

5. To mark the item as completed, turn on the completed check box.

6. To set a priority for the item, choose an option from the priority pop-up menu (**Figure 90**).

7. To set a due date for the item, turn on the due date check box and enter a date in the field beside it (**Figure 91**). You can then use the Alarm pop-up menu (**Figure 81**) and associated options (**Figure 92**) to set a reminder for the item.

*Continued on next page...*

**ADDING & SETTING OPTIONS FOR TO DO ITEMS**

**179**

*Continued from previous page.*

8. To specify a calendar to add the item to, choose a calendar from the calendar pop-up menu (**Figure 80**). The menu lists all calendars you have created.

9. To associate a Web page with the item, enter a URL in the url field (**Figure 83**).

10. To add notes about the item, click the Notes field and type what you want to appear (**Figure 84**).

**Figure 93** shows an example of a To Do item with several options set.

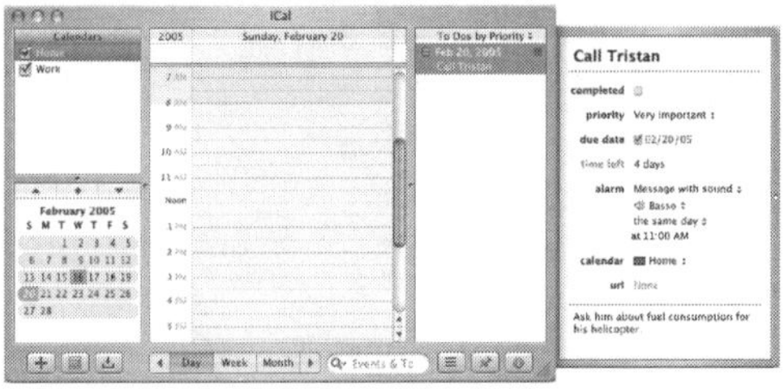

## ✔ Tips

■ You can mark a To Do item as complete by clicking its check box in the To Do items list (**Figure 93**).

■ The stack of lines on the button to the left of a To Do item's name in the To Do items list (**Figure 93**) indicates its priority: the more lines, the more important the item is. You can click this button to change the priority (**Figure 94**).

■ You can change the sort order of To Do items by clicking the arrows at the top of the To Do list to display a menu (**Figure 95**) and choosing a different option.

## To delete a To Do item

1. If necessary, click the Show To Do list button in the lower-right corner of the window or press ⌥Option ⌘T to display the To Do items list.

2. In the To Do items list, select the item you want to delete.

3. Press Delete. The item disappears.

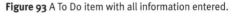

**Figure 93** A To Do item with all information entered.

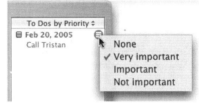

**Figure 94** Click the priority button to change an item's priority.

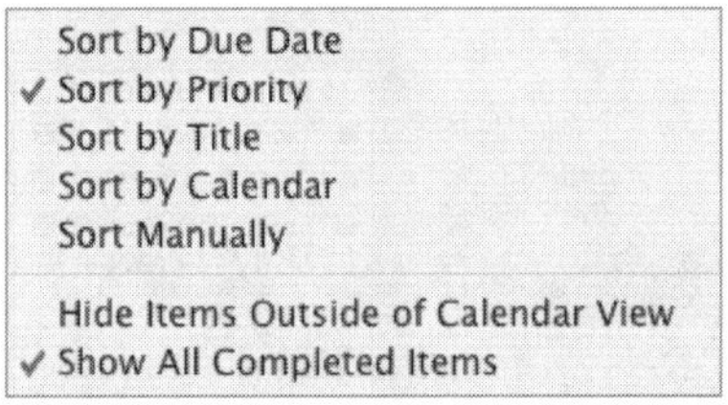

**Figure 95** Use this menu to change the sort order of To Do items.

**Figure 96**
A new calendar in the Calendars list.

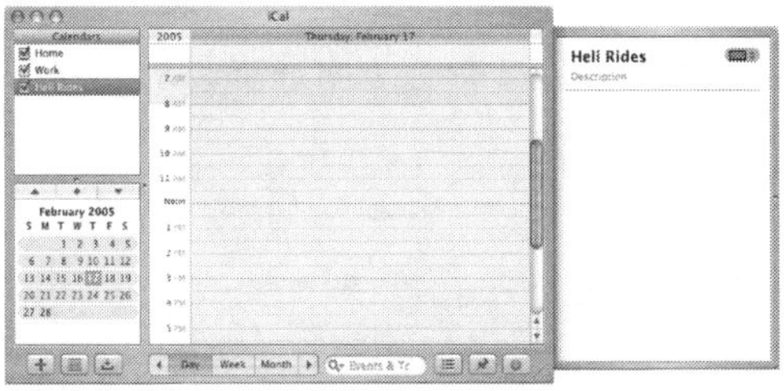

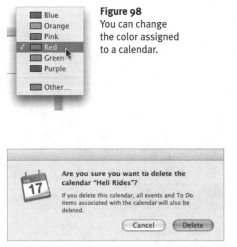

**Figure 97** Use the Info drawer for a calendar to change its name, add a description, or set its color.

**Figure 98**
You can change the color assigned to a calendar.

**Figure 99** A dialog like this confirms that you really do want to delete a calendar and all of its events.

# To create a calendar

1. Choose File > New Calendar (**Figure 71**) or press Option ⌘ N. An untitled calendar appears in the Calendars list with its default name selected (**Figure 96**).

2. Enter a name for the Calendar and press Return.

# To set calendar options

1. In the Calendars list, select the calendar you want to set options for.

2. If necessary, click the Show Info button in the lower-right corner of the window or press ⌘ I to display the Info drawer (**Figure 97**).

3. Click the Name or Description field or use the color pop-up menu (**Figure 98**) to modify calendar settings.

# ✔ Tips

■ Choosing Custom from the colors pop-up menu (**Figure 98**) displays the Colors palette, which you can use to select a custom color. I tell you how to use the Colors palette in **Chapter 11**.

■ To display events from only certain calendars, in the Calendars list, turn off the check boxes for the calendars you don't want to view.

# To delete a calendar

1. In the Calendars list, select the calendar you want to delete.

2. Press Delete.

3. If a confirmation dialog like the one in **Figure 99** appears, click Delete. The calendar and all of its events are removed.

# To publish a calendar

1. In the Calendars list, select the calendar you want to publish.

2. Choose Calendar > Publish (**Figure 100**).

3. A dialog sheet like the one in **Figure 101** appears. Set options as desired:

   ▲ **Publish calendar as** is the name of the calendar as it will be published.

   ▲ **Publish on** enables you to specify whether the calendar should be published on your .Mac account or on a private server. If you choose a Private Server, the dialog expands to offer more options (**Figure 102**).

   ▲ **Base URL** is the Web address for accessing your calendar. This option only appears if you are publishing to a private server.

   ▲ **Login** and **Password** is your login information for the server you are publishing on. These options only appears if you are publishing to a private server.

   ▲ **Publish changes automatically** updates the calendar online whenever you make changes to it in iCal.

   ▲ **Publish titles and notes** includes event or item names and notes in the published calendar.

   ▲ **Publish alarms** includes event or item alarms in the published calendar.

   ▲ **Publish To Do items** includes To Do items in the published calendar.

4. Click Publish.

5. Wait while your computer connects to the Internet and uploads the calendar.

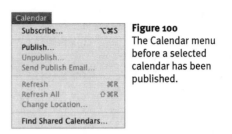

**Figure 100**
The Calendar menu before a selected calendar has been published.

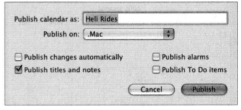

**Figure 101** Use this dialog to set options for publishing a calendar.

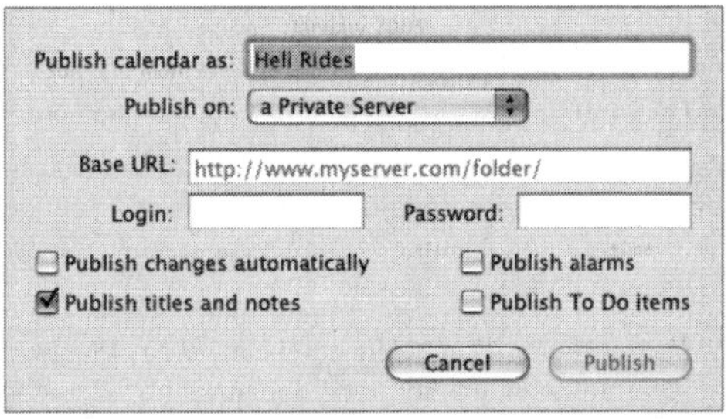

![Dialog with private server options]
**Figure 102** The dialog expands to offer additional options when you indicate that you want to publish on a private server.

![Calendar Published dialog]
**Figure 103** A dialog like this confirms that the calendar has been published and provides information about accessing it.

**Figure 104** Here's a calendar published on .Mac.

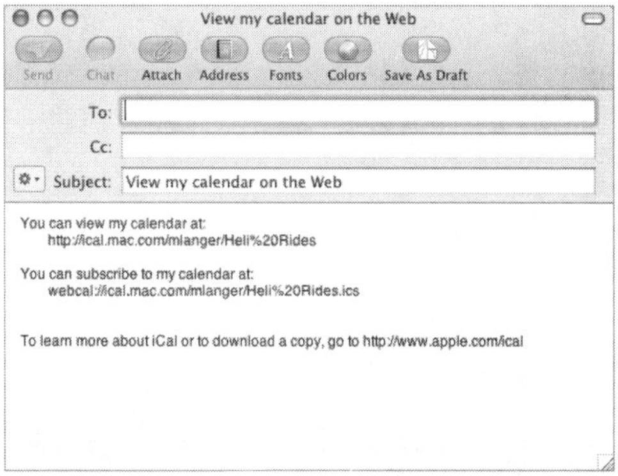

**Figure 105** If you click the Send Mail button, an e-mail message with access information is prepared automatically.

**Figure 106**
When you select a calendar that has been published, the Calendar menu changes to offer additional options.

6. When the upload is complete, a dialog like the one in **Figure 103** appears. You have three options:

   ▲ **Visit Page** launches your Web browser, connects to the Internet, and displays the calendar page (**Figure 104**).

   ▲ **Send Mail** launches your e-mail application and creates a message with the calendar's access information (**Figure 105**). You can address the message and send it to people you want to inform about the calendar.

   ▲ **OK** simply dismisses the dialog.

## ✔ Tips

■ You must have a connection to the Internet to publish a calendar.

■ You must have a .Mac account to publish a calendar on .Mac. I tell you more about .Mac in **Chapter 14**.

■ In step 3, if you choose not to automatically update the calendar, you can do so manually. Select the calendar in the Calendars list and choose Calendar > Refresh (**Figure 106**) or press ⌃⌘R.

■ To create a new e-mail message with information about accessing a calendar (**Figure 105**), select the calendar in the Calendars list and choose Calendar > Send Publish Email (**Figure 106**).

■ In the Calendars list, a curves icon appears beside the name of a calendar that has been published (**Figure 109**).

## To unpublish a calendar

1. In the Calendars list, select the calendar you want to remove from the Web.

2. Choose Calendar > Unpublish (**Figure 106**).

3. In the confirmation dialog that appears, click Unpublish.

PUBLISHING CALENDARS

## To subscribe to a calendar

1. Choose Calendar > Subscribe (**Figure 101** or **106**).

2. A dialog sheet like the one in **Figure 107** appears. Enter the URL for the calendar you want to subscribe to and click Subscribe.

3. After a moment, iCal displays a dialog like the one in **Figure 108**. Set options as desired:

   ▲ **Title** is the name of the calendar as it should appear in your Calendar list.

   ▲ **Refresh** instructs iCal to refresh the calendar periodically. Turn on this check box and select an option from the pop-up menu. You might want to use this option if you expect the calendar to change often.

   ▲ **Remove alarms** disables any alarms that have been set for and published with the calendar.

   ▲ **Remove To Do items** removes any To Do items that may have been published with the calendar.

4. Click OK.

   The calendar's events appear in the calendar window (**Figure 109**).

## ✔ Tips

■ In the Calendars list, an arrow icon appears beside the name of a calendar that has been subscribed to (**Figure 109**).

■ You cannot add, modify, or delete events on a calendar that you subscribe to.

■ To update the contents of a calendar you have subscribed to, select the name of the calendar in the Calendars list and choose Calendar > Refresh (**Figure 106**) or press ⌃ ⌘ R.

**Figure 107** Use this dialog to enter the URL for a calendar on the Web.

**Figure 108** Set options for a calendar you are subscribing to in this dialog.

**Figure 109** This example shows four calendars, including one that is published (Heli Rides) and one that is subscribed to (Sunrise & Sunset).

■ To unsubscribe from a calendar, delete it from the Calendars list. I explain how to delete calendars earlier in this chapter.

■ To find more calendars you can subscribe to, choose Calendar > Find Shared Calendars (**Figure 106**) or check out www.apple. com/ical/library. You can find everything from Apple Store events to professional sports game dates.

# Image Capture

Image Capture is an application that performs two functions:

◆ Download image files from a digital camera to your computer's hard disk.

◆ Operate your scanner to scan and save images.

In this part of the chapter, I explain how to download images from a digital camera with Image Capture.

## ✔ Tips

■ Some digital cameras and scanners require that driver software be installed on Mac OS X before the camera or scanner can be used. Consult the documentation that came with your scanner or camera or check the device manufacturer's Web site for Mac OS X compatibility and driver information.

■ Not all digital cameras or scanners are compatible with Image Capture. Generally speaking, if Image Capture does not "see" your camera or scanner when it is connected and turned on, the camera or scanner is probably not compatible with Image Capture and Image Capture cannot be used.

■ If you have Apple's iLife suite of products, you can also download images from a digital camera using iPhoto, which offers additional features for managing photos saved to disk. For more information about iPhoto and iLife, be sure to check out these great Peachpit Press books: *iPhoto 5 for Mac OS X: Visual QuickStart Guide, Robin Williams Cool Mac Apps*, and *The Macintosh iLife '05*.

## To download images from a digital camera

1. Attach your digital camera to your computer's USB or FireWire port, using the applicable cable.

2. If necessary, turn the camera on and set it to review mode. The main Image Capture window should appear (**Figure 110**).

3. To download all images on the camera, click the Download All button in the main Image Capture window (**Figure 110**).

    *or*

    To download some of the images on the camera, click the Download Some button in the main Image Capture window (**Figure 110**). A window full of thumbnail images appears (**Figure 111**). Select the images you want to download. To select more than one image, hold down Shift while clicking each image. Then click the Download button.

    A dialog sheet appears, showing the progress of the download (**Figure 112**). When it disappears, the download is complete and Image Capture displays the window(s) for the folder(s) in which it downloaded the pictures.

### ✔ Tips

- If Image Capture doesn't launch automatically after step 2, you can open it by double-clicking its icon in the Applications folder (**Figure 1**).

- If iPhoto is installed on your computer, it may launch instead of Image Capture when you connect a digital camera. If so, you must manually launch Image Capture by double-clicking its application icon (**Figure 1**) to open and use it.

**Figure 110** Image Capture's main window is named for the camera you have attached and turned on.

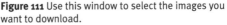

**Figure 111** Use this window to select the images you want to download.

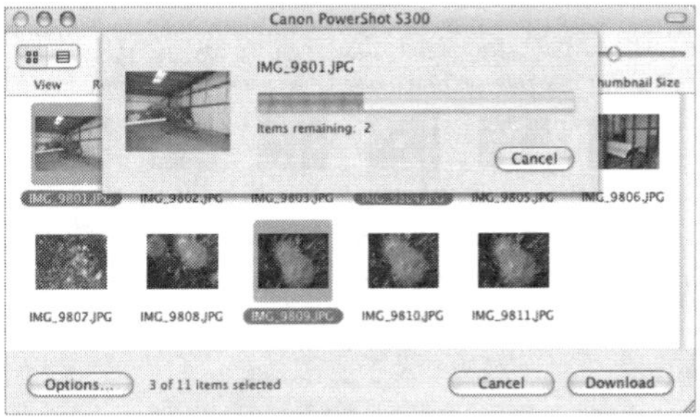

**Figure 112** A progress window appears as the pictures are downloaded.

- You can also use the thumbnail window (**Figure 111**) to delete images on the camera. Select the images you want to delete, click the Delete button, and click Delete in the confirmation dialog that appears.

**Figure 113** The iSync window before devices have been added.

**Figure 114** As explained here, you no longer use iSync to synchronize information across computers.

# iSync

iSync is synchronization software that keeps your iCal calendar information, Address book contact information, and Safari bookmarks up to date on your iPod, Bluetooth or USB mobile phone, and Palm OS device.

This part of the chapter provides instructions for using iSync to synchronize information between your computer and an iPod.

## ✔ Tips

■ Although the information here does not include specific instructions for using iSync with a mobile phone or Palm OS device, it should be enough to get you started using iSync with these devices.

■ To use iSync with a Bluetooth-enabled mobile phone, you must have a Bluetooth adapter connected to your Macintosh. You can learn more about Bluetooth in **Chapter 16**.

■ In Mac OS X 10.4, you no longer use iSync to synchronize information between Macintosh computers. Instead, use the .Mac pane of System Preferences, which is discussed in detail in **Chapter 14**.

■ For a complete list of devices that work with iSync, use your Web browser to visit www.apple.com/isync/devices.html.

## To launch iSync

Double-click the iSync icon in your Applications folder (**Figure 1**). iSync's main window appears (**Figure 113**).

## ✔ Tip

■ By default, iSync displays a .mac icon in its main window (**Figure 113**). Clicking this icon opens the window to display information about syncing with .Mac (**Figure 114**).

iSYNC

## To add a device

1. Choose Devices > Add Device (**Figure 115**), or press ⌥⌘N. The Add Device window appears and iSync begins looking for devices. When it is finished, it displays icons for all devices it found (**Figure 116**).

2. Double-click the icon for the device you want to add. An icon for the device appears in the iSync window and the window expands to show device synchronization options (**Figure 117**).

## ✔ Tip

■ The device you are trying to add must be accessible to your Macintosh to appear in the Add Device window (**Figure 116**). If a device does not appear, make sure it is properly connected (or within range, in the case of a Bluetooth-enabled mobile phone) and turned on. Then follow steps 1 and 2 above again.

## To configure an iPod for synchronization

1. If necessary, in the iSync window, click the iPod's device icon to show configuration options (**Figure 117**).

2. Turn on check boxes and choose other options to set synchronization preferences:

   ▲ Turn on *iPod Name* **synchronization** enables synchronization between the computer and the iPod.

   ▲ **Automatically synchronize when iPod is connected** automatically synchronizes data according to your settings each time the iPod is connected to the computer.

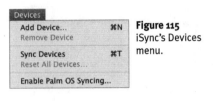

**Figure 115**
iSync's Devices menu.

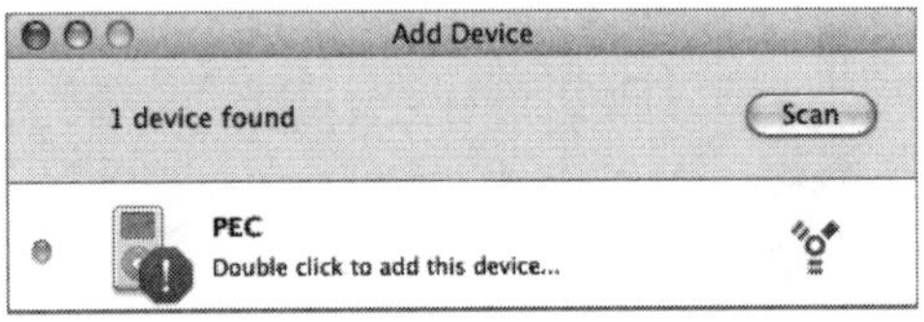

**Figure 116** Use the Add Devices window to add compatible devices to iSync.

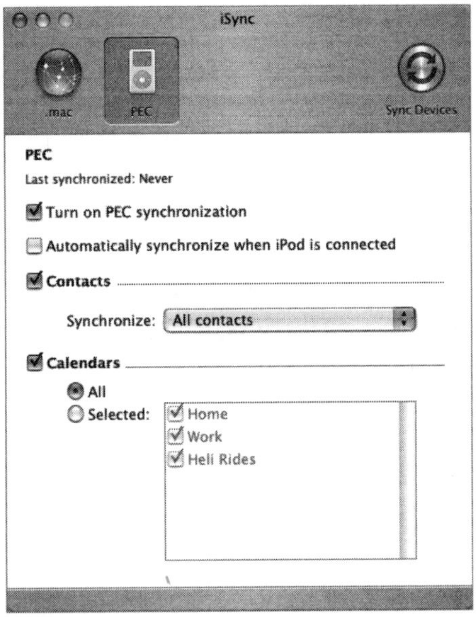

**Figure 117** Configuration options for an iPod.

**Figure 118** iSync displays a progress bar while it performs a synchronization.

▲ **Contacts** synchronizes Address Book contacts to the Contacts extra in the iPod. With this option turned on, you can select All contacts or a specific group name from the Synchronize pop-up menu to determine which contacts should be synchronized.

▲ **Calendars** synchronizes iCal calendars to the Calendar extra in the iPod. With this option turned on, if you have multiple calendars you can select the Selected radio button and toggle check marks to indicate which calendars should be synchronized.

**3.** Click the iPod icon to collapse the window and save your settings.

## To perform a synchronization

Click the Sync Devices button in the iSync window (**Figure 117**). As shown in **Figure 118**, a progress bar appears in the iSync window to indicate that a sync is in progress. In addition, the Sync Now button turns into a Cancel Sync button.

When the progress bar disappears from the iSync window, the synchronization is complete.

**CONFIGURING & SYNCHRONIZING iPODS**

# iTunes

iTunes is a computer-based "jukebox" that enables you to do several things:

◆ Play MP3 and AAC format audio files.

◆ Record music from audio CDs on your Macintosh as AAC and MP3 files.

◆ Buy music from the iTunes Music Store.

◆ Create custom CDs of your favorite music.

◆ Save AAC and MP3 files to an iPod and save MP3 files to other MP3 players.

◆ Listen to Internet-based radio stations.

The next few pages explain how you can use iTunes to record and play MP3 music, copy MP3 files to an iPod, and burn audio CDs.

## ✔ Tips

■ MP3 and AAC are standard formats for audio files.

■ Your computer must have a CD-R drive or SuperDrive to burn CDs.

## To set up iTunes

1. Double-click the iTunes icon in your Applications folder (**Figure 1**).

2. If a license agreement window appears, click Accept.

3. The iTunes Setup Assistant window appears (**Figure 119**). Read the welcome message, and click Next.

4. In the Internet Audio window (**Figure 120**), set options as desired and click Next:

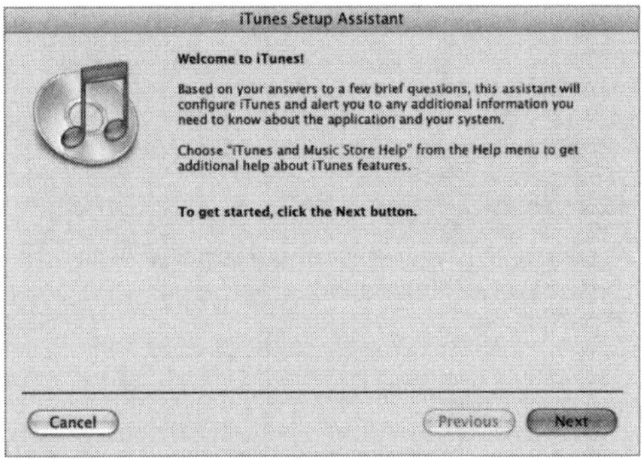

**Figure 119** The first screen of the iTunes Setup Assistant.

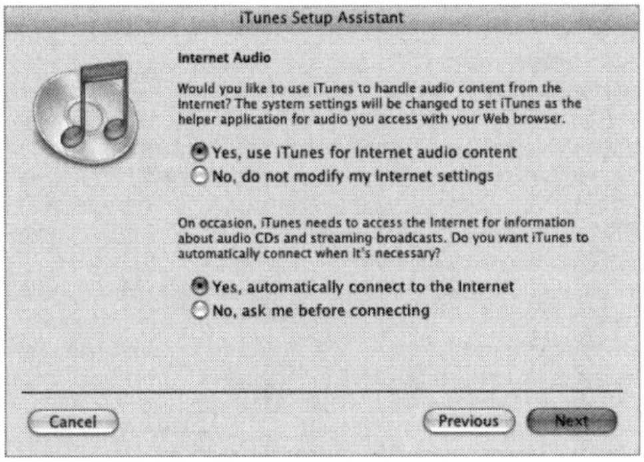

**Figure 120** Set options for Internet playback in this screen.

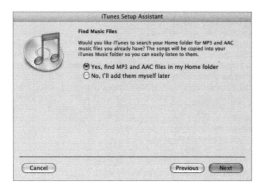

**Figure 121** The Find Music Files window of the iTunes Setup Assistant.

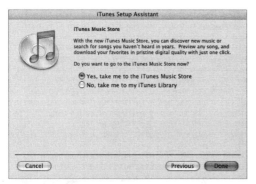

**Figure 122** The iTunes Music Store window of the iTunes Setup Assistant.

Playback controls
Source list   Song list

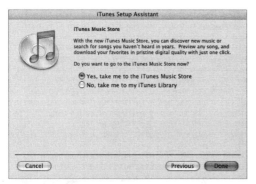

**Figure 123** The iTunes main window. In this example, iTunes has located some music files in my Home folder and automatically imported them. It's also found some shared music from another one of my computers.

▲ Select an Internet audio content option. **Yes, use iTunes for Internet audio content** instructs your computer to set your Web browser helper settings to use iTunes for all Internet audio playback. **No, do not modify my Internet settings** does not change your Web browser's helper settings.

▲ Select an Internet connection option. **Yes, automatically connect to the Internet** tells iTunes that it's okay to connect to the Internet anytime it needs to. **No, ask me before connecting** tells iTunes to display a dialog that asks your permission before connecting to the Internet.

5. In the Find Music Files window (**Figure 121**), select an option and click Next:

▲ **Yes, find MP3 and AAC files in my Home folder** tells iTunes to search your hard disk for music files in your Home folder (or any of its folders) and add them to you music library.

▲ **No, I'll add them myself later** tells iTunes not to look for music files.

6. In the iTunes Music Store window (**Figure 122**), select an option:

▲ **Yes, take me to the iTunes Music Store** connects to the Internet and displays the Home page of the iTunes Music Store when you click Done.

▲ **No, take me to my iTunes Library** displays the contents of your iTunes Music Library when you click Done.

7. Click Done.

iTunes completes its configuration and displays the iTunes main window with either the iTunes Music Store (**Figure 127**) or your iTunes Library (**Figure 123**).

# To view & listen to music by source

1. Click one of the items in the Source list (**Figure 124**) to display the contents of the source:

   ▲ **Library** displays all the music in your iTunes library (**Figure 123**).

   ▲ **Party Shuffle** (**Figure 125**) creates a dynamic, random playlist of songs from the Library or a specific playlist.

   ▲ **Radio** connects to the Internet and displays music streams organized by category. Click a triangle to the left of a stream category in the Song list to display a list of streams (**Figure 126**).

   ▲ **Music Store** connects to the Internet and displays the iTunes Music Store (**Figure 127**).

   ▲ *CD Name* displays the contents of an audio CD inserted in your computer's CD drive.

   ▲ *Shared Music Library Name* displays all the music available via network from a shared music library (**Figure 128**). This feature enables you to listen to music on other network users' computers. Click the triangle to the left of the shared library name to display individual playlists within that library.

   ▲ *Smart Playlist Name* displays music in a smart playlist.

   ▲ *Playlist Name* displays music in a playlist.

2. To play music from the library (**Figure 123**), party shuffle (**Figure 125**), audio CD, shared music library (**Figure 128**), or playlist, click the Play button above the Source list (**Figure 129**).

   *or*

**Figure 124** The Source list includes several different music sources.

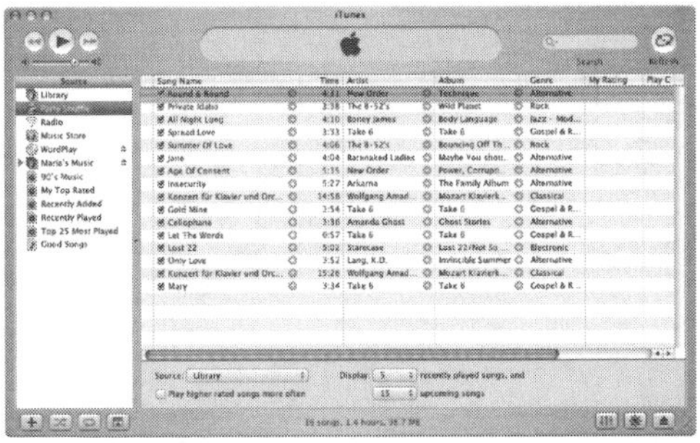

**Figure 125** The Party Shuffle feature enables you to create your own dynamic mix of music.

**Figure 126** The Radio source list offers access to streaming audio on the Internet.

VIEWING & LISTENING TO MUSIC BY SOURCE

**Figure 127** The iTunes Music Store is a great place to shop for music. (I think I might be its best customer.)

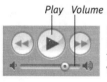

**Figure 128** If you're on a network and others have shared their libraries, you can listen to their music.

*Play   Volume*

**Figure 129** Use the playback controls to play music and set the volume.

*Stop*
*Backward   Forward*

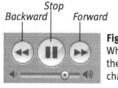

**Figure 130** When music is playing the playback controls change.

*New Playlist   Shuffle*
*Repeat        Song Artwork*

**Figure 131** Use buttons at the bottom of the Source list to work with the list and control music play.

To play music from a radio stream (**Figure 126**), double-click the name of the stream.

*or*

To browse music in the iTunes Music Store (**Figure 127**), follow the instructions in the section titled "To shop for music online" later in this section.

## ✔ Tips

- You must have access to the Internet to use the Radio and Music Store sources.

- You can listen to a specific song in a library or playlist by double-clicking the song in the Song list.

- Once you have begun playing music from a library or playlist, the Backward and Forward buttons become active and the Play button turns into a Stop button (**Figure 130**).

- You can use buttons at the bottom of the Source list (**Figure 131**) to work with the list and change the way music is played.

- To sort the song list by one of its columns, click the column heading. Clicking the same heading again reverses the sort.

- Clicking the Browse button in the corner of the iTunes window splits the window so you can browse a selected source by Genre, Artist, or Album (**Figure 132**).

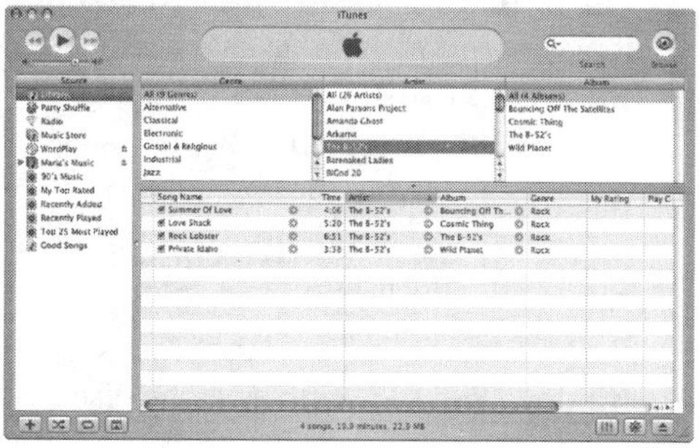

**Figure 132** Click the Browse button to browse music by genre, artist, or album.

**193**

## To add songs from an audio CD to the Library

1. Insert an audio CD in your CD drive. A dialog like the one in **Figure 133** appears briefly while your computer accesses the Internet to get song names. After a moment, the CD's name appears in the Source list and a list of the tracks on it appears in the song list (**Figure 134**).

2. Turn on the check box beside each song you want to add to the Library. (They should already all be turned on.)

3. Click the Import button. iTunes begins importing the first song. The status area provides progress information (**Figure 135**). The song may play while it is imported.

## ✔ Tips

■ Sometime during step 1, iTunes may ask your permission to connect to the Internet. It must do this to retrieve information about the songs on the CD. If you don't connect to the Internet, song names do not appear in the Song list.

■ You can specify whether a song plays while it is imported by setting iTunes preferences. Choose iTunes > Preferences and click the Importing button to get started.

■ When iTunes is finished importing songs, it plays a sound. In most cases, iTunes will finish importing songs from a CD before it finishes playing them.

■ When you are finished importing songs from a CD, select the CD name in the Source list and click the Eject button in the lower right corner of the iTunes window (**Figure 134**) to eject the disc.

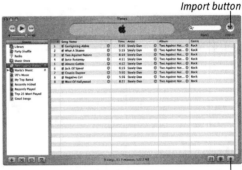

**Figure 133** iTunes accesses an Internet database to get information about the songs on a CD.

**Figure 134** When you insert a CD, it appears in the Source list and a list of its songs appear in the song list.

**Figure 135** iTunes shows the import progress at the top of its window and puts an importing icon beside the song currently being imported in the song list.

Figure 136 Importing an audio file on disk is as easy as dragging it into the iTunes window.

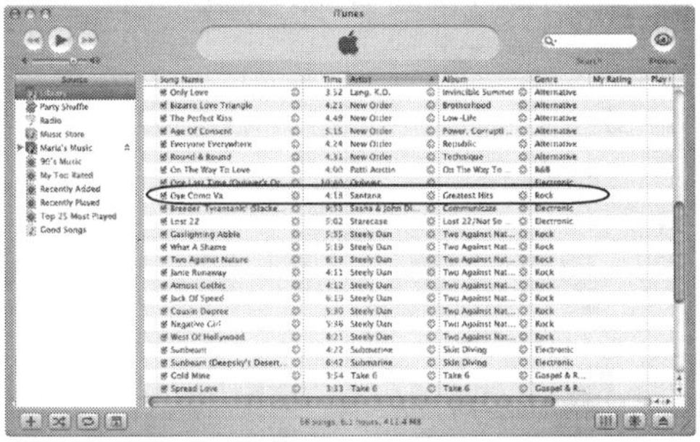

Figure 137 The song you dragged in appears in the iTunes Library window.

Figure 138 Exporting a song as an audio file is as easy as dragging it from the iTunes window to a Finder window.

04 Rock Lobster.mp3

**Figure 139**
An icon for the exported MP3 file appears where the song was dragged.

## To import music files on disk to the Library

Drag the icon for the music file from the Desktop or a Finder window to the iTunes window (**Figure 136**).

After a moment, the song appears in the Library window (**Figure 137**).

### ✔ Tips

- You can use this technique to add a bunch of music files at once. Simply select their icons and drag any one of them into the window. I explain how to select multiple icons in the Finder in **Chapter 2**.

- You could also use the Add to Library command on the iTunes File menu, but I think the drag-and-drop technique is quicker and easier.

## To export songs from the iTunes Library as audio files

Drag the name of the song you want to export from the iTunes Library window to the Desktop or a Finder window (**Figure 138**).

After a moment, an audio file icon for the exported song appears in the Finder (**Figure 139**).

### ✔ Tip

- You can use this technique to export a bunch of audio files at once. Simply hold down ⌃⌘ while clicking each song you want to select. Then drag any one of them into the Finder window.

## To create a playlist

1. Click the New Playlist button (**Figure 131**), choose File > New Playlist, or press ⌃ ⌘ N.

2. A new untitled playlist appears in the Source list (**Figure 140**). Type a name for the playlist, and press Enter (**Figure 141**).

## To add songs to a playlist

1. If necessary, select Library in the source window to display all music files.

2. Drag a song you want to include in the new playlist from the Song list to the playlist name in the Source list (**Figure 142**).

3. Repeat step 2 for each song you want to add to the playlist.

4. When you're finished adding songs, click the playlist name. The songs appear in the list.

## ✔ Tips

- In step 2, you can select and drag multiple songs. Hold down ⌃ ⌘ while selecting songs to select more than one, then drag any one of them.

- You can change the order of songs in a playlist by dragging them up or down.

- You can sort songs in a playlist by clicking a column heading. Clicking once sorts in ascending order; clicking twice sorts in descending order.

## To remove a song from a playlist

1. Select the song you want to remove.

2. Press Delete. The song is removed from the playlist.

## ✔ Tip

- Removing a song from a playlist does not remove it from the iTunes Library.

**Figure 140**
Clicking the New Playlist button creates a new, untitled playlist.

**Figure 141**
To give the playlist a name, simply type it in and press Enter.

**Figure 142** To add songs to a playlist, drag them from the Song list to the playlist name.

WORKING WITH PLAYLISTS

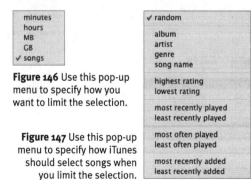

**Figure 143** The Smart Playlist dialog.

| Album |  |
|---|---|
| ✓ Artist | **Figure 144** |
| BPM | Use this pop-up menu to |
| Bit Rate | specify the type of criteria |
| Comment | you want to match. |
| Compilation | |
| Composer | |
| Date Added | |
| Date Modified | |
| Disc Number | |
| Genre | |
| Grouping | |
| Kind | |
| Last Played | |
| My Rating | |
| Play Count | |
| Playlist | |
| Sample Rate | |
| Size | |
| Song Name | |
| Time | |
| Track Number | |
| Year | |

**Figure 145** Here's an example of smart playlist settings with multiple criteria.

| minutes | ✓ random |
|---|---|
| hours | album |
| MB | artist |
| GB | genre |
| ✓ songs | song name |
| | highest rating |
| | lowest rating |
| | most recently played |
| | least recently played |
| | most often played |
| | least often played |
| | most recently added |
| | least recently added |

**Figure 146** Use this pop-up menu to specify how you want to limit the selection.

**Figure 147** Use this pop-up menu to specify how iTunes should select songs when you limit the selection.

## To create a smart playlist

1. Choose File > New Smart Playlist or press ⌥⌘N to display the Smart Playlist dialog (**Figure 143**).

2. Choose an option from the first pop-up menu (**Figure 144**), and set criteria using options on that line.

3. To add additional matching criteria, click the + button. The dialog expands to offer an additional line for criteria. Set criteria as desired in this line. You can repeat this step as necessary to set all criteria. **Figure 145** shows an example with multiple criteria set.

4. If you set up multiple criteria in step 3, choose an option from the Match pop-up menu:

   ▲ **All** matches all criteria you set. This narrows down the search and produces fewer matches. Keep in mind that if criteria is mutually exclusive (for example, "Genre contains Jazz" and "Genre contains New Age") no items will be found.

   ▲ **Any** matches any criteria. This expands the search and produces more matches.

5. To limit the size of the playlist by time, file size, or number of songs, turn on the Limit to check box, choose an option from the pop-up menu (**Figure 146**), and enter a value in the box beside it. You can also use the selected by pop-up menu in that line (**Figure 147**) to specify how songs should be chosen.

6. To match only songs that are checked in the song list, turn on the Match only checked songs check box.

*Continued on next page...*

*Continued from previous page.*

7. To automatically update the playlist each time songs are added or removed from the Library, turn on the Live updating check box.

8. Click OK.

9. A new smart playlist appears in the Source list with a suggested name based on what you entered. When the list is selected, you can see the songs iTunes selected (**Figure 148**).

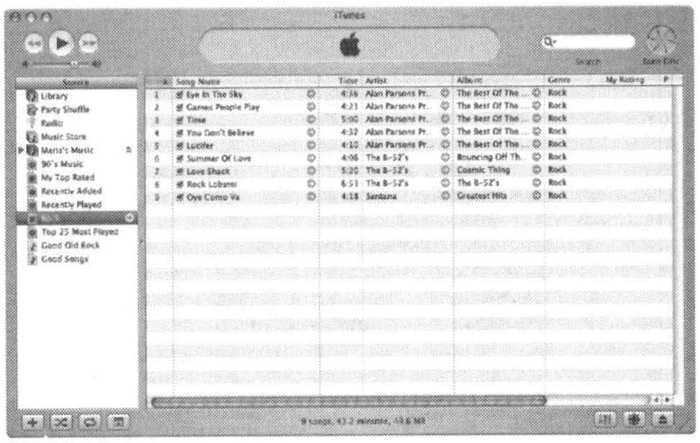

**Figure 148** iTunes selected these songs, based on the criteria shown in **Figure 150**.

## ✔ Tip

■ The types of criteria iTunes can use (**Figure 149**) are divided into two categories: information you can change and information you can't change. To see (and change) information for a song, select the song in the song list and choose File > Get Info or press ⌃⌘I. **Figures 149** and **150** show examples of two panes of information for a song. Explore this feature on your own.

## To delete a playlist

1. In the source window, select the playlist you want to delete (**Figure 148**).

2. Press ⌈Delete⌋.

3. In the confirmation dialog that appears, click Yes. The playlist is removed.

## ✔ Tip

■ Deleting a playlist does not delete the songs on the playlist from your music library.

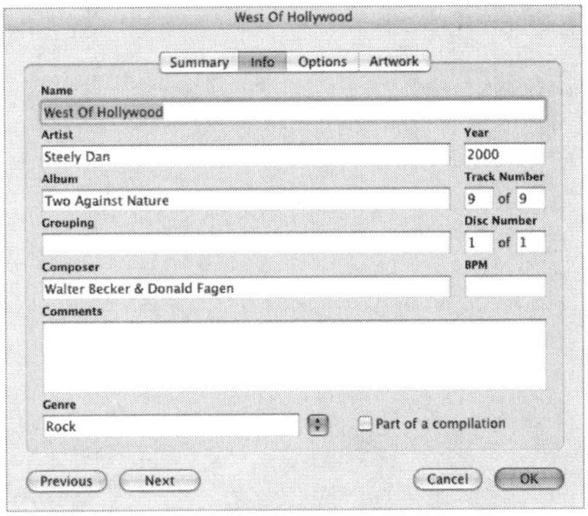

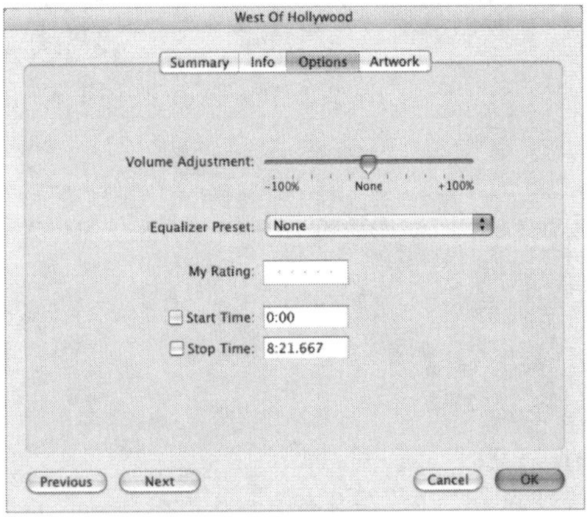

**Figures 149 & 150** Two examples of the Info window for a song: Info (top) and Options (bottom).

**Figure 151**
Your iPod or MP3 player should appear in the Source list, like my iPod photo, which I named "PEC" (short for "Personal Entertainment Center") does.

**Figure 152** Drag the song from the song list to the iPod or MP3 player.

## ✔ Tips

- If iTunes was already running when you connected your MP3 player and it did not list the MP3 player in the Source list, quit iTunes and relaunch it. If it still doesn't appear, your MP3 player may not be compatible with iTunes. Check the iTunes Web site for assistance: www.apple.com/itunes/.

- In step 3, you can select and drag multiple songs. Hold down ⌃ ⌘ while selecting songs to select more than one, then drag any one of them. You can only copy one playlist at a time.

## To manually copy songs or playlists to an iPod or other MP3 player

1. Using the USB or FireWire cable that came with your iPod or other MP3 player, connect it to your Macintosh and, if necessary, turn it on.

2. If iTunes is not already running or does not automatically open, launch it. After a moment, the MP3 player should appear in the Source list (**Figure 151**).

3. Drag the song(s) or playlist you want to copy to the iPod or MP3 player from the Song or Source list to the iPod or MP3 player in the Source list (**Figure 152**). The status area indicates copy progress.

4. Repeat step 3 for each song or playlist you want to copy.

5. When you are finished copying songs or playlists, you can select the iPod or MP3 player in the Source list and click the Eject button to unmount it. You can then disconnect it from your Macintosh.

- The number of songs you can copy to an iPod or MP3 player is limited by the amount of storage in the player and the size of the songs.

- When you copy a playlist, any songs in the playlist that are not already on the iPod are also copied.

- If your iPod is automatically updated when you connect it to your computer, you cannot manually copy songs to it using these steps. Follow the instructions in the section titled "To set iPod options" on the next page to set up your iPod so you can manage songs manually.

COPYING SONGS TO AN iPOD OR MP3 PLAYER

## To set iPod options

1. Using the FireWire or USB cable that came with your iPod, connect it to your Macintosh. If iTunes is not already running, it launches, and the iPod appears in the Source list (**Figure 151**).

2. Select the iPod in the source list and click the Display iPod Options button in the bottom-right corner of the iTunes window. The iPod preferences window appears.

3. If necessary, click the Music button to display music options (**Figure 153**).

4. Select one of the update radio buttons:

   ▲ **Automatically update all songs and playlists** automatically copies all songs in iTunes to your iPod when you connect it to your Macintosh.

   ▲ **Automatically update selected playlists only** automatically copies all songs in the playlists you select to your iPod when you connect it to your Macintosh. If you select this option, be sure to turn on the check box beside each playlist you want to copy.

   ▲ **Manually manage songs and playlists** enables you to manually copy songs and playlists from iTunes to your iPod when you connect it to your Macintosh. If you select this option, you'll have to follow the instructions on the previous page to copy songs and playlists to your iPod.

5. Toggle check boxes for other music options:

   ▲ **Only update checked songs** copies only the songs that are checked off in the iTunes Song list. This option can only be selected if one of the automatic update radio buttons is selected in step 4.

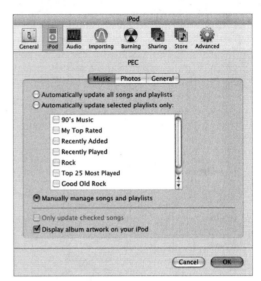

**Figure 153** Music options of iPod preferences.

SETTING iPOD OPTIONS

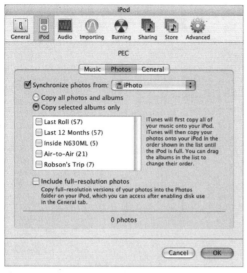

**Figure 154** Photos options in iPod preferences with iPhoto selected for synchronization.

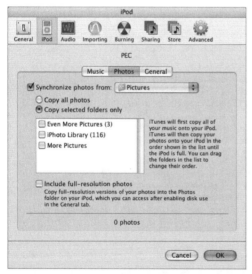

**Figure 155** Photos options in iPod preferences with the Pictures folder selected for synchronization.

▲ **Display album artwork on your iPod** displays album artwork for a song when your iPod plays the song. This option is only avaiable for iPod photo.

6. If you have an iPod photo, click the Photos button to display Photo options (**Figure 154**).

*or*

If you do not have an iPod photo, skip ahead to step 10.

7. To copy photos to your iPod photo, turn on the Synchronize photos from check box and choose a source location for the photos you want to copy from the pop-up menu.

8. If you chose iPhoto in step 7 (**Figure 154**), select a radio button for which photos should be copied:

▲ **Copy all photos and albums** copies all photos and all albums in iPhoto.

▲ **Copy selected albums only** copies only the photos and albums in the albums you select. Be sure to turn on the check box beside each album you want to include.

*or*

If you choose a folder in step 7 (**Figure 155**), select a radio button for which photos should be copied:

▲ **Copy all photos** copies all photos in the folder you selected, as well as in its subfolders.

▲ **Copy selected folders only** copies only the photos in the folders you select. Be sure to turn on the check box beside each folder you want to include.

*Continued on next page...*

**SETTING iPOD OPTIONS**

*Continued from previous page.*

9. To include a full-size copy of each photo in the disk space on your iPod, turn on the Include full-resolution photos check box.

10. Click the General button to display General options (**Figure 156**).

11. Toggle check boxes to set options:

▲ Open iTunes when this iPod is attached automatically launches iTunes when you connect your iPod.

▲ Enable disk use mounts the iPod on your desktop so you can copy files to it like any other disk. This option can only be selected if one of the automatic update radio buttons is selected in step 4.

12. Click OK to save your settings.

## ✔ Tips

■ If you have more songs in iTunes than will fit on your iPod, you should choose the second or third radio button in step 4 to automatically or manually update your iPod with less than all of the music in iTunes.

■ In step 8, iPhoto must be installed to appear in the pop-up menu. A discussion of iPhoto, which is part of Apple's iLife suite of products, is beyond the scope of this book.

■ I explain how to work with mounted disks in **Chapter 3**.

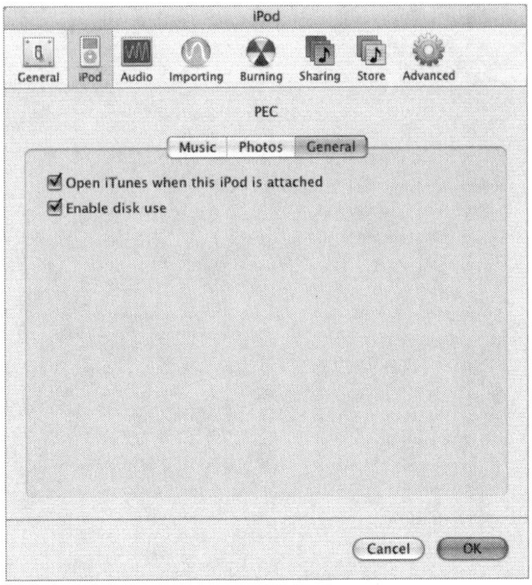

**Figure 156** General options in iPod preferences.

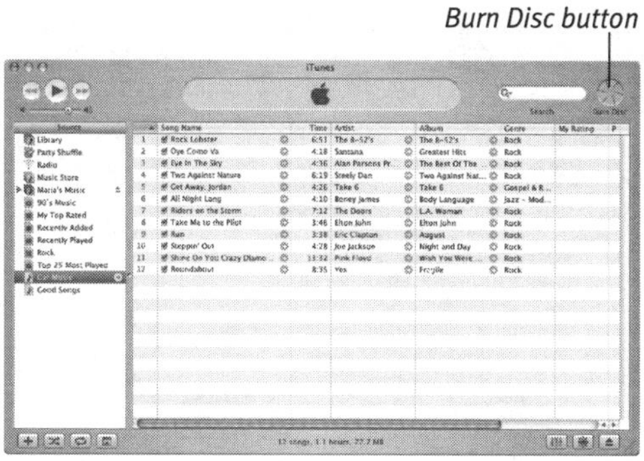

Burn Disc button

**Figure 157** Select the Playlist you want to burn to CD and click the Burn CD button.

**Figure 158** iTunes prompts you to click the Burn CD button again.

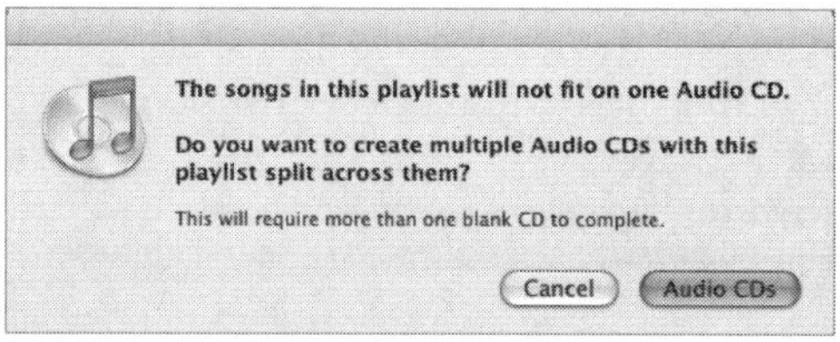

**Figure 159** This dialog appears if you try to put too many songs on an audio CD.

## To burn an audio CD

1.  Create a playlist that contains the songs you want to include on the CD.

2.  Select the playlist (**Figure 157**).

3.  Click the Burn Disc button.

4.  When prompted, insert a blank CD in your computer's CD-R drive or Super-Drive and close the drive.

5.  When prompted, click the Burn Disc button, which is now black and yellow (**Figure 158**).

6.  Wait while iTunes prepares and burns the CD. This could take a while; the progress appears in the status window at the top of the iTunes window. You can switch to and work with other applications while you wait.

7.  When iTunes is finished burning the CD, it makes a sound. The icon for the CD appears on your desktop.

## ✔ Tips

■  Your computer must have a compatible CD-R drive or SuperDrive to burn audio CDs. You can find a list of compatible devices on the iTunes Web site, www.apple.com/itunes/.

■  I explain how to create a playlist earlier in this section.

■  If the playlist you have selected will not fit on an audio CD, iTunes displays a dialog like the one in **Figure 159**. If you click Audio CDs, iTunes prompts you to insert a blank CD each time it needs one.

■  Do not cancel the disc burning process after it has begun. Doing so can render the CD unusable.

**BURNING AUDIO CDs**

# To share music with other network users

1. Choose iTunes > Preferences.

2. Click the Sharing button to display Sharing preferences (**Figure 160**).

3. To play music shared by other network users, turn on the Look for shared music check box. This displays any shared music libraries in the Source list (**Figure 124**) on your computer, so you can listen to it.

4. To share your music with other network users, turn on the Share my music check box. Then select one of the radio buttons:

   ▲ **Share entire library** shares all of your music.

   ▲ **Share selected playlists** enables you to toggle check boxes for individual playlists you want to share.

5. If you turned on the Share my music check box in step 4, enter a name for your library in the Shared name box.

6. To require other network users to enter a password to listen to your music, turn on the Require password check box and enter a password in the box beside it.

7. Click OK.

8. A dialog like the one in **Figure 161** may appear. Click OK.

## ✔ Tips

■ Once sharing is enabled, the Status area in the Sharing preferences dialog reports whether your music is being accessed by other users on the network (**Figure 162**).

■ I tell you more about Mac OS X's networking features in **Chapter 16**.

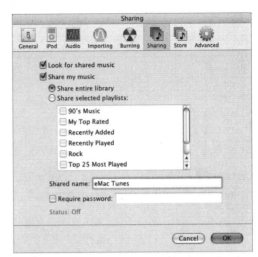

**Figure 160** Sharing preferences enable you to share iTunes music.

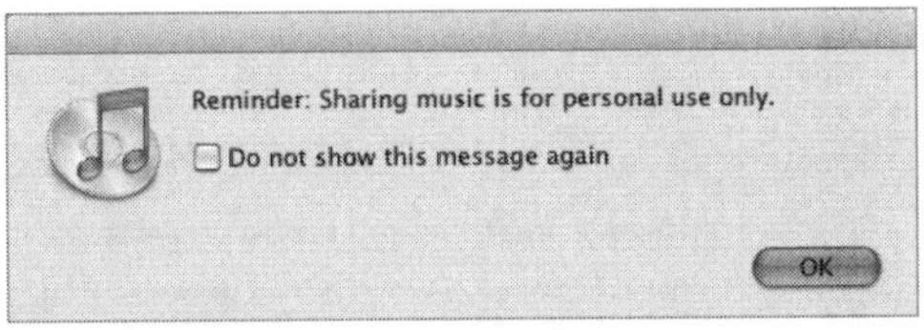

**Figure 161** This dialog appears when you enable sharing. (The Apple lawyers obviously had a hand in this one.)

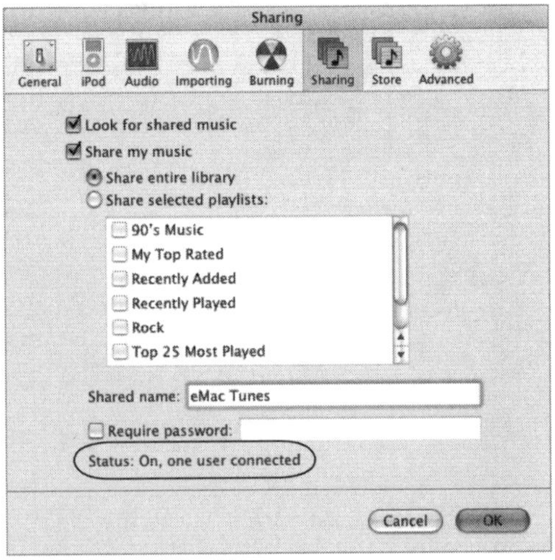

**Figure 162** Sharing status appears in the bottom of the Sharing preferences dialog.

**Figure 163** Search results for the word "Yes."

**Figure 164** Clicking an artist link displays all available albums for that artist.

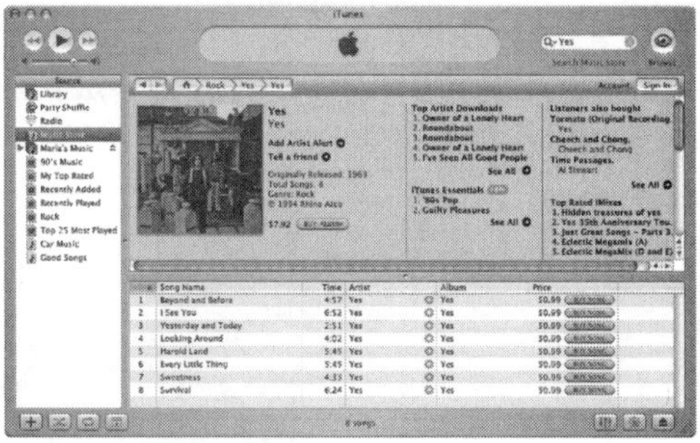

**Figure 165** Clicking an album link displays a list of songs in that album.

**Figure 166** You can monitor download progress of purchased songs at the top of the iTunes window.

## To shop in the iTunes Music Store

1. In the Source list, select Music Store.

   Your computer connects to the Internet and displays the Home page of the iTunes Music Store (**Figure 127**).

2. Use any combination of the following techniques to locate and sample songs:

   ▲ Click links in the window to browse through available albums and songs.

   ▲ To search for a specific album, song, or artist, enter a search word or phrase in the Search box at the top-right of the iTunes window and press [Return]. Search results appear in the window (**Figure 163**).

   ▲ To listen to a sample of a song, double-click its name in a search results list (**Figure 163**).

   ▲ To see matches for an artist (**Figure 164**), click an artist link or the arrow button beside the artist name in a search results list (**Figure 165**).

   ▲ To see matches for an album (**Figure 165**), click an album link or the arrow button beside the album name in a search results list (**Figure 163**).

3. To buy a song or album, click the Buy Song or Buy Album button for it. The song or album is downloaded to your computer (**Figure 166**) and appears in the Purchased Music playlist (**Figure 167**).

Continued on next page...

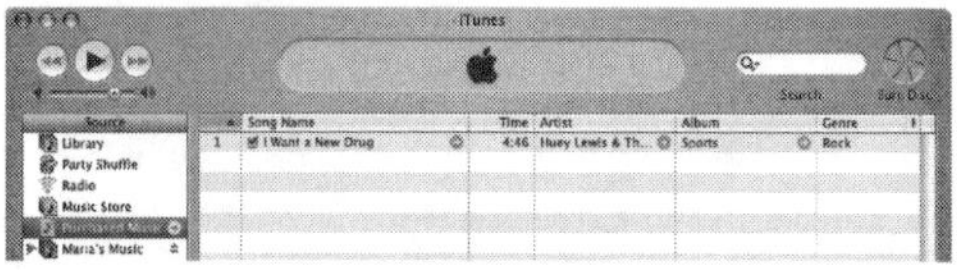

**Figure 167** iTunes records all your music purchases in a special Purchased Music playlist.

## ✔ Tips

- Step 2 covers only a handful of the ways you can browse the contents of the iTunes Music Store. There are far too many other navigation tools to cover here. Explore them on your own to find your favorite ways to get around the iTunes Music Store.

- In step 3, if you are not logged into the iTunes Music Store, a dialog like the one in **Figure 168** appears. If you have an Apple ID, enter it and your password and click Buy. If you don't have an Apple ID, click the Create New Account button and follow the instructions that appear onscreen to set up an Apple ID.

- Purchased music has some limitations:

  - ▲ You can only play purchased music on up to five authorized computers — iTunes will tell you if your computer isn't authorized to play a song and give you a chance to authorize it.

  - ▲ Although you can include a purchased song on any number of CDs that you burn, you can only burn up to seven CDs from an unchanged playlist.

- If you buy as many songs as I do at the iTunes Music Store (759 songs so far), you may want to set up a shopping cart so you can download purchased music all at once at the end of a shopping spree. Choose iTunes > Preferences and click the Store button (**Figure 169**) to get started.

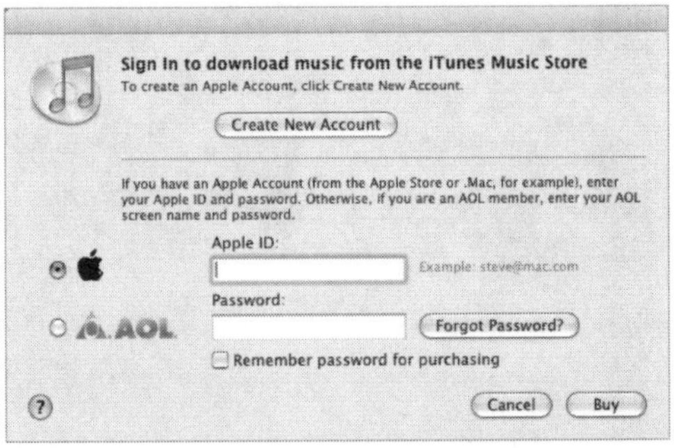

**Figure 168** If you are not logged in to the iTunes Music Store, a dialog like this appears when you buy music.

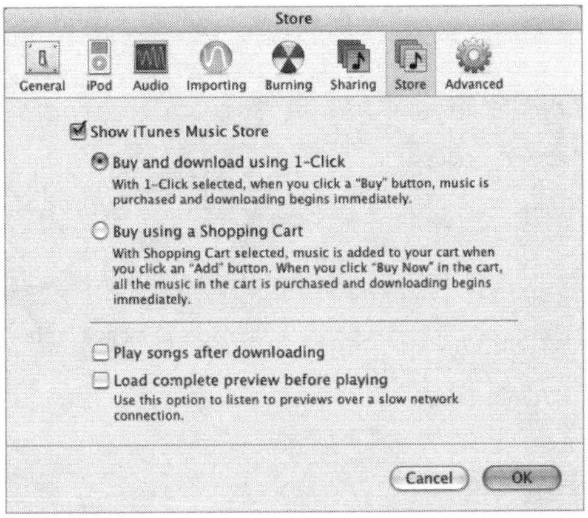

**Figure 169** Use the Store preferences dialog to customize the way the iTunes Music Store works.

**Figure 170** Here's an image file opened with Preview. (Gary-Paul Prince, in his Halloween costume—at least that's what he told me.)

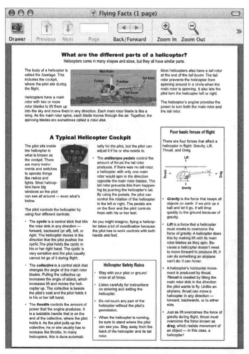

**Figure 171** Here's a PDF file opened with Preview. (Want to learn how helicopters fly? You can download this PDF from www.marialanger.com/articles/FlyingFacts.pdf.)

# Preview

Preview is a program that enables you to open and view two kinds of files:

◆ **Image files** (**Figure 170**), including JPG, GIF, HDR, TIF, PSD, PICT, PNG, BMP, and SGI.

◆ **PDF,** or **Portable Document Format, files** (**Figure 171**) created with Mac OS X's Print command, Adobe Acrobat software, or other software capable of creating PDFs.

## ✔ Tips

■ When you open PostScript (PS) or EPS format files, Preview automatically converts them to PDF files for viewing.

■ I explain how to create PDF files with the Print command in **Chapter 12**.

■ You can also open PDF files with Adobe Acrobat Reader software. You can learn more about Acrobat Reader—and download a free copy of the software—on the Adobe Systems Web site, www.adobe.com/products/acrobat/readstep.html.

PREVIEW

## To open a file with Preview

Drag the document file's icon onto the Preview icon in the Applications folder (**Figure 172**).

*Or*

Double-click the icon for a Preview document (**Figure 173**).

Preview launches and displays the file in its window (**Figures 170** and **171**).

## ✔ Tips

- You can also use Preview's Open command to open any compatible file on disk. I explain how to use an application's Open command in **Chapter 7**.

- To open multiple files at once, select all of their icons and drag any one of them onto the Preview icon.

- You can use options on a Preview window's toolbar (**Figures 170** and **171**) or Preview's View menu (**Figure 174**) to zoom in or out, rotate the window's contents, or view a specific page.

- If a document has multiple pages or if you opened multiple image files at once, you can click the Drawer button in the window's toolbar to display or hide a drawer with thumbnail images of each page (**Figure 175**) or image. Click a thumbnail to move quickly to that page or image.

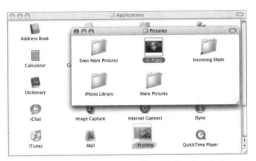

**Figure 172** One way to open a file with Preview is to drag the file's icon onto the Preview icon.

Flying Facts.pdf

**Figure 173**
You can also double-click a Preview document's file icon.

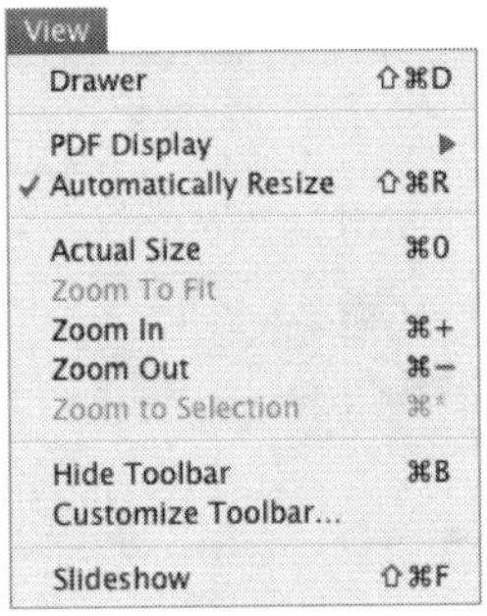

**Figure 174**
Preview's View menu.

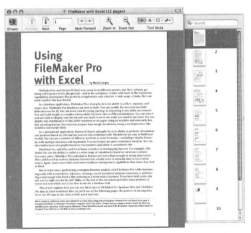

**Figure 175** You can display a Drawer with thumbnails for a multi-page document.

## To search for text in a PDF file

1. Open the PDF file you want to search.

2. If necessary, click the Drawer button to display the drawer.

3. Enter a search word or phrase in the Search box at the top of the drawer.

   As you type, Preview searches the document for the text you entered. It displays a list of sentences containing that text in the drawer, along with corresponding page numbers. It also highlights the first occurrence of the search text in the main document window. You can see all this in **Figure 176**.

## ✔ Tips

- To display a specific occurrence of the search text, click its reference in the drawer. A blue circle appears momentarily around the occurrence (**Figure 176**).

- To view thumbnails rather than search results in the drawer (**Figure 175**), clear the search text by clicking the tiny X icon on the right side of the Search box at the top of the drawer (**Figure 176**).

- The more text you enter in the Search box, the fewer matches Preview finds.

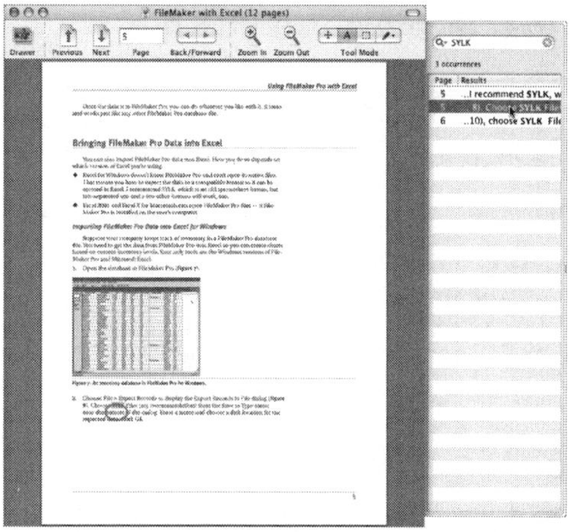

**Figure 176** When you enter search text in the Search box, Preview quickly displays matches. A blue circle appears momentarily around an occurrence in the document when you select it in the list.

SEARCHING FOR TEXT

## To select text in a PDF file

1. In Preview's toolbar, click the Text tool button (**Figure 177**), choose Tools > Text Tool, or press ⌃⌘2.

2. Position the mouse pointer over text in the document window. It turns into an I-beam pointer (**Figure 178**).

3. Press the mouse button down and drag to select text (**Figure 179**).

## ✔ Tip

■ Once text is selected, you can use the Copy command to copy it to the clip-board and use it in another document. I tell you about the Copy and Paste com-mands in **Chapter 9**.

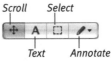

Scroll    Select    Text    Annotate

**Figure 177** Preview's tool buttons for a PDF file.

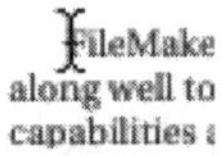

FileMaker along well to capabilities i

**Figure 178** The mouse pointer turns into an I-beam pointer.

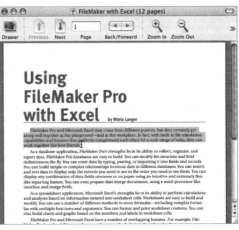

**Figure 179** Drag to select text.

SELECTING TEXT

**Figure 180** Position the mouse pointer where you want to begin the selection. (This is Connie Jeung-Mills from Peachpit Press. I'd like to think that this is a Halloween costume, too, but she didn't tell me it was, so I have to wonder.)

## To select part of a picture

1. Position the mouse pointer in the upper-left corner of the area you want to select (**Figure 180**).

2. Press the mouse button down and drag down and to the right. A selection box appears over the image (**Figure 181**).

3. Release the mouse button to complete the selection.

## ✔ Tips

- Once you have selected part of a picture, you can use the Copy command to copy it to the clipboard for use in another document. I tell you about the Copy and Paste commands in **Chapter 9**.

- To deselect document contents, click in the document window anywhere other than on the selection.

- You can use the Select tool to crop an image. Simply select the part of the image you want to keep and choose Tools > Crop Image or press ⌃ ⌘ K. The document is cropped (**Figure 182**).

**Figure 182** The Crop Image command removes everything except the selection.

**Figure 181** Drag to make the selection.

**211**

# QuickTime Player

QuickTime is a video and audio technology developed by Apple Computer, Inc. It is widely used for digital movies as well as streaming audio and video available via the Internet. QuickTime Player is an application you can use to view QuickTime movies and streaming Internet content.

## ✔ Tips

■ There are two versions of QuickTime Player: the standard version, which is included with Mac OS X, and the Pro version, which enables you to edit and save QuickTime files. You can learn about QuickTime Pro on Apple's QuickTime Web site, www.apple.com/quicktime/.

■ Internet access is covered in **Chapter 13**.

■ I explain how to set QuickTime preferences in **Chapter 21**.

## To launch QuickTime Player

Click the QuickTime Player icon in the Dock (**Figure 2**).

*Or*

Open the QuickTime Player icon in the Applications folder (**Figure 1**).

A QuickTime Player window appears (**Figure 183**).

## ✔ Tip

■ Clicking contents in a QuickTime Player window may display the What's On page of Apple's QuickTime Web site (**Figure 184**) or open iTunes to display the iTunes Music Store (**Figure 137**).

**Figure 183** When you launch QuickTime, it uses your Internet connection to obtain content from Apple's QuickTime Web site—in this case, an ad for video from the recent Grammy Awards ceremony. Clicking the "Click here for more content" button in this window takes you to the What's On page on Apple's QuickTime site (**Figure 184**).

**Figure 184** The What's On page of Apple's QuickTime Web site changes regularly.

**Figure 185**
A QuickTime movie file icon.

Batman Begins.mov

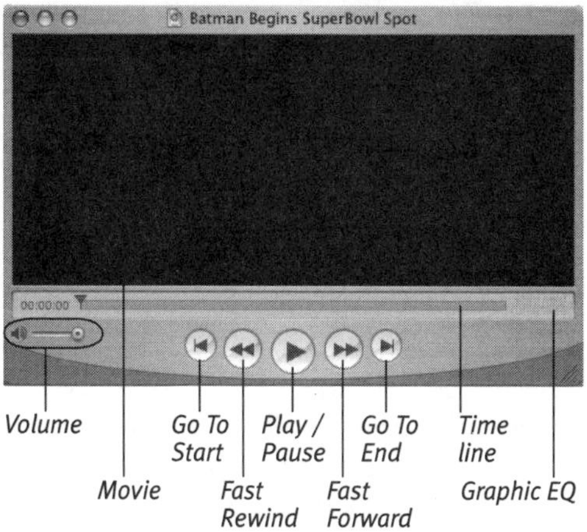

**Figure 186** The first frame of the movie appears in a QuickTime Player window.

Volume
Go To Start
Play / Pause
Go To End
Time line
Movie
Fast Rewind
Fast Forward
Graphic EQ

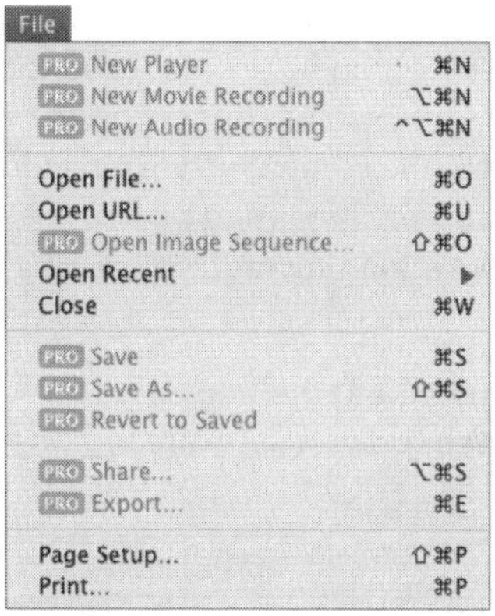

**Figure 187**
QuickTime Player's File menu. Gray command marked PRO are available in the Pro version only.

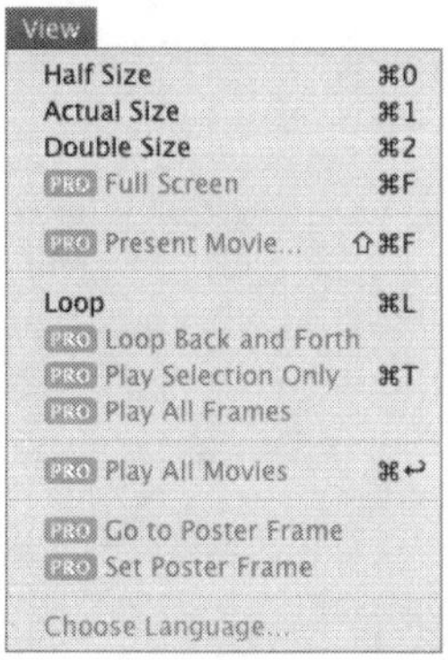

File
PRO New Player   ⌘N
PRO New Movie Recording   ⌥⌘N
PRO New Audio Recording   ⌃⌥⌘N
Open File...   ⌘O
Open URL...   ⌘U
PRO Open Image Sequence...   ⇧⌘O
Open Recent   ▶
Close   ⌘W
PRO Save   ⌘S
PRO Save As...   ⇧⌘S
PRO Revert to Saved
PRO Share...   ⌥⌘S
PRO Export...   ⌘E
Page Setup...   ⇧⌘P
Print...   ⌘P

**Figure 188**
Use the View menu to change the size of the movie's window.

View
Half Size   ⌘0
Actual Size   ⌘1
Double Size   ⌘2
PRO Full Screen   ⌘F
PRO Present Movie...   ⇧⌘F
Loop   ⌘L
PRO Loop Back and Forth
PRO Play Selection Only   ⌘T
PRO Play All Frames
PRO Play All Movies   ⌘↵
PRO Go to Poster Frame
PRO Set Poster Frame
Choose Language...

## To open a QuickTime movie file

Double-click the QuickTime movie file icon (**Figure 185**).

If QuickTime Player is not already running, it launches. The movie's first frame appears in a window (**Figure 186**).

## ✔ Tip

■ You can also open a QuickTime movie file by using the Open Movie in New Player command on QuickTime Player's File menu (**Figure 187**). The Open dialog is covered in **Chapter 7**.

## To control movie play

You can click buttons and use controls in the QuickTime Player window (**Figure 186**) to control movie play:

◆ **Go To Start** displays the first movie frame.

◆ **Fast Rewind** plays the movie backward quickly, with sound.

◆ **Play** starts playing the movie. When the movie is playing, the Play button turns to a **Pause** button, which pauses movie play.

◆ **Fast Forward** plays the movie forward quickly, with sound.

◆ **Go To End** displays the last movie frame.

◆ **Time line** tracks movie progress. By dragging the slider, you can scroll through the movie without sound.

◆ **Volume** changes movie volume; drag the slider left or right.

## To specify movie size

Select a size option from the View menu (**Figure 188**). The size of the movie's window changes accordingly.

OPENING & CONTROLLING QUICKTIME MOVIES

**213**

**Figure 189** QuickTime content can appear in a Web browser window, like this.

## To open QuickTime content on Apple's Web site

1. Use your Web browser to visit www.apple.com/quicktime/whatson/ (**Figure 184**).

2. Click buttons or links to open a Web page containing the content you want to view (**Figure 189**).

   The QuickTime content is downloaded from the Web and, after a moment, begins playing right in the Web browser window.

## ✔ Tips

- Apple's Web site isn't the only source of QuickTime content. As you explore the Web, you're likely to encounter Quick-Time movies and sounds on many other Web sites.

- QuickTime content available on the Web includes *streaming* audio or video *channels*. This requires a constant connection to the Internet while content is downloaded to your computer. Streaming content continues downloading until you close its window.

- I tell you more about the Internet and using Web browser software in **Chapter 13**.

Figure 190 The default windows that appear when you first launch Stickies tell you a little about the program.

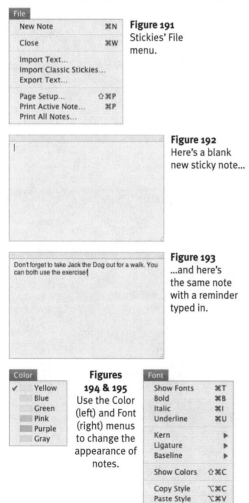

**Figure 191**
Stickies' File menu.

**Figure 192**
Here's a blank new sticky note...

**Figure 193**
...and here's the same note with a reminder typed in.

**Figures 194 & 195**
Use the Color (left) and Font (right) menus to change the appearance of notes.

# Stickies

Stickies is an application that displays computerized "sticky notes" that you can use to place reminders on your screen.

## To launch Stickies

Double-click the Stickies icon in the Applications folder (**Figure 1**).

*Or*

1. Click the Stickies icon in the Applications folder (**Figure 1**) to select it.

2. Choose File > Open, or press ⌘O.

The default Stickies windows appear (**Figure 190**).

## ✔ Tips

- Read the text in the default Stickies windows (**Figure 190**) to learn more about Stickies.

- Sticky notes remain on the desktop until you quit Stickies.

- When you quit Stickies, all notes are automatically saved to disk and will reappear the next time you launch Stickies.

## To create a sticky note

1. Choose File > New Note (**Figure 191**) or press ⌘N to display a blank new note (**Figure 192**).

2. Type the text that you want to include in the note (**Figure 193**).

## ✔ Tip

- You can use options under the Color and Font menus (**Figures 194** and **195**) to change the appearance of notes or note text. Common text formatting options are covered in **Chapters 9** and **11**.

## To print sticky notes

1. To print just one sticky note, click it to activate it and then choose File > Print Active Note (**Figure 191**) or press ⌃⌘P.

   *or*

   To print all sticky notes, choose File > Print All Notes (**Figure 191**).

2. Use the Print dialog that appears to set options for printing and click the Print button (**Figure 196**).

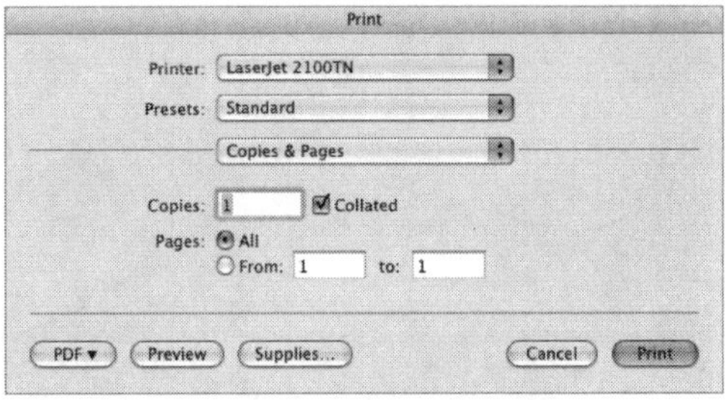

### ✔ Tip

■ **Chapter 12** covers the Print dialog and printing.

## To close a sticky note

1. Click the close box for the sticky note you want to close.

   *or*

   Activate the sticky note you want to close and choose File > Close (**Figure 191**) or press ⌃⌘W.

2. A Close dialog like the one in **Figure 197** may appear.

   ▲ **Don't Save** closes the note without saving its contents.

   ▲ **Cancel** leaves the note open.

   ▲ **Save** displays the Export dialog (**Figure 198**), which you can use to save the note as plain or formatted text in a file on disk. Enter a name and select a disk location for the note's contents, then choose a file format and click Save.

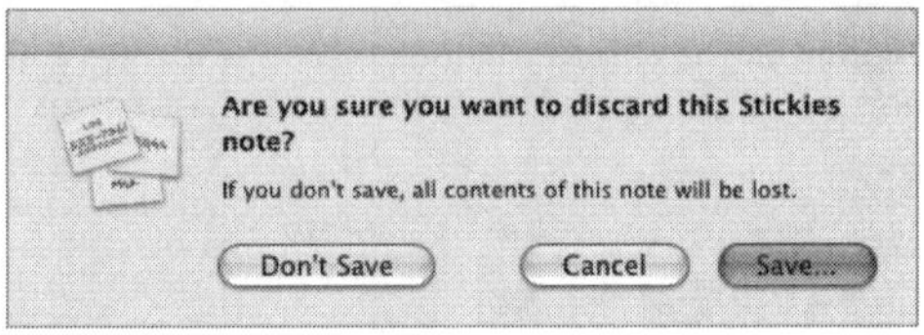

### ✔ Tip

■ Once a sticky note has been saved to disk, it can be opened and edited with TextEdit or any other program capable of opening text files.

**Figure 196** The Print dialog.

**Figure 197** The Close dialog asks if you want to save note contents.

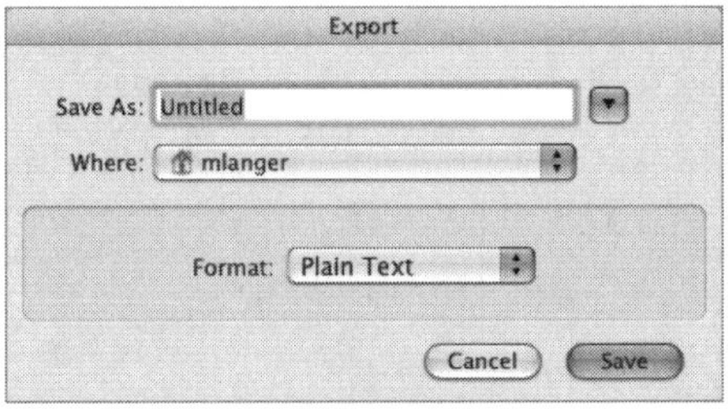

**Figure 198** Use the Export dialog to save a note as plain or formatted text in a file on disk.

USING STICKIES

# Using TextEdit

## TextEdit

*TextEdit* (**Figure 1**) is a text editing application that comes with Mac OS. As its name implies, TextEdit lets you create, open, edit, and print text documents (**Figure 2**), including the "Read Me" files that come with many applications.

This chapter explains how to use TextEdit to create, edit, format, open, and save documents.

**Figure 1**
The TextEdit application icon.

TextEdit

**Figure 2**
A TextEdit document's icon.

Letter

## ✔ Tips

- TextEdit can open and save Microsoft Word format files. This makes it possible to work with and create Microsoft Word documents, even if you don't have Microsoft Word.

- Although TextEdit offers many of the features found in a word processing application, it falls far short of the feature list of word processors such as Microsoft Word and the word processing components of iWork's Pages or integrated software such as AppleWorks.

- If you're new to computers, don't skip this chapter. It not only explains how to use TextEdit but provides instructions for basic text editing skills—such as text entry and the Copy, Cut, and Paste commands —that you'll use in all Mac OS-compatible applications.

# Launching & Quitting TextEdit

Like any other application, you must launch TextEdit before you can use it. This loads it into your computer's memory so your computer can work with it.

## To launch TextEdit

Double-click the TextEdit application icon in the Applications folder window (**Figure 3**).

*Or*

1. Select the TextEdit application icon in the Applications folder window (**Figure 3**).

2. Choose File > Open, or press ⌃⌘O.

   TextEdit launches. An untitled document window appears (**Figure 4**).

## ✔ Tip

■ As illustrated in **Figure 4**, the TextEdit document window has the same standard window parts found in Finder windows. I tell you how to use Finder windows in **Chapter 2**; TextEdit and other application windows work the same way.

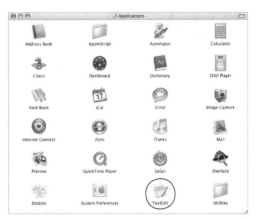

**Figure 3** You can find TextEdit in the Applications folder.

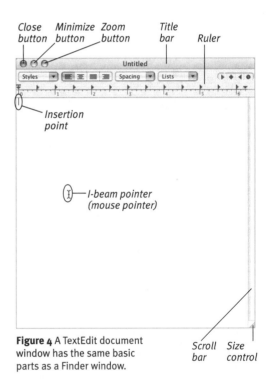

Close button, Minimize button, Zoom button, Title bar, Ruler, Insertion point, I-beam pointer (mouse pointer), Scroll bar, Size control

**Figure 4** A TextEdit document window has the same basic parts as a Finder window.

**Figure 5**
Choose Quit TextEdit from the TextEdit menu.

**Figure 6** A dialog sheet like this appears when you quit TextEdit with an unsaved document open.

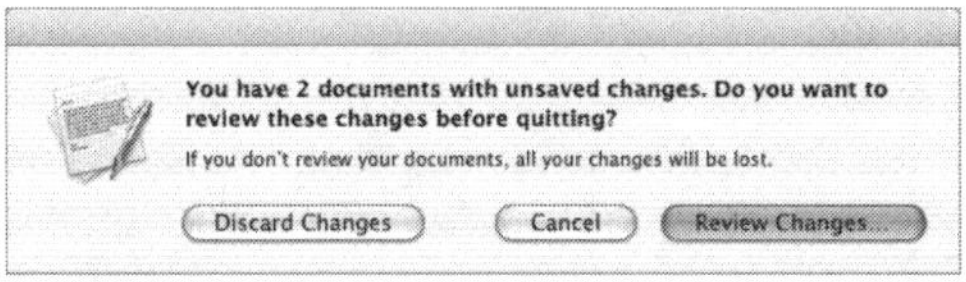

**Figure 7** A dialog like this appears when you quit Text-Edit with multiple unsaved documents open.

## To quit TextEdit

1. Choose TextEdit > Quit TextEdit (**Figure 5**), or press ⌃ ⌘Q.

2. If a single unsaved document is open, a dialog sheet like the one in **Figure 6** appears, attached to the document window.

   ▲ Click Don't Save to quit without saving the document.

   ▲ Click Cancel or press Esc to return to the application without quitting.

   ▲ Click Save or press Return or Enter to save the document.

   *or*

   If multiple unsaved documents are open, a dialog like the one in **Figure 7** appears:

   ▲ Click Discard Changes to quit Text-Edit without saving any of the documents.

   ▲ Click Cancel or press Esc to return to the application without quitting.

   ▲ Click Review Changes or press Return or Enter to view each unsaved document with a dialog like the one in **Figure 6** to decide whether you want to save it.

   TextEdit closes all windows and quits.

## ✔ Tip

■ You learn more about saving TextEdit documents later in this chapter.

QUITTING TEXTEDIT

# Entering & Editing Text

You enter text into a TextEdit document by typing it in. Don't worry about making mistakes; you can fix them as you type or when you're finished. This section tells you how.

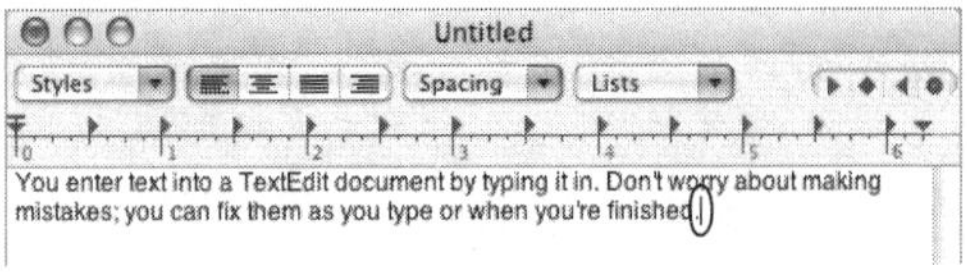

## ✔ Tip

- The text entry and editing techniques covered in this section work exactly the same in most word processors, as well as many other Mac OS applications.

## To enter text

Type the text you want to enter. It appears at the blinking insertion point (**Figure 8**).

## ✔ Tips

- It is not necessary to press Return at the end of a line. When the text you type reaches the end of the line, it automatically begins a new line. This is called *word wrap* and is a feature of all word processors. By default, in TextEdit, word wrap is determined by the width of the document window.

- The insertion point moves as you type.

- To correct an error as you type, press Delete. This key deletes the character to the left of the insertion point.

**Figure 8** The text you type appears at the blinking insertion point.

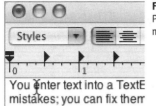

**Figure 9**
Position the mouse pointer...

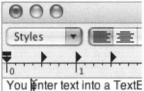

**Figure 10**
...and click to move the insertion point.

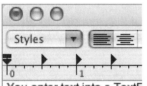

**Figure 11**
Position the insertion point...

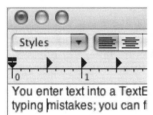

**Figure 12**
...and type the text that you want to appear.

# To move the insertion point

Press ⬅, ➡, ⬆, or ⬇ to move the insertion point left, right, up, or down one character or line at a time.

*Or*

1. Position the mouse pointer, which looks like an I-beam pointer, where you want the insertion point to appear (**Figure 9**).

2. Click the mouse button once. The insertion point appears at the mouse pointer (**Figure 10**).

## ✔ Tips

■ Since the text you type appears at the insertion point, it's a good idea to know where the insertion point is *before* you start typing.

■ When moving the insertion point with the mouse, you must click to complete the move. If you simply point with the I-beam pointer, the insertion point will stay right where it is (**Figure 9**).

## To insert text

1. Position the insertion point where you want the text to appear (**Figure 11**).

2. Type the text that you want to insert. The text is inserted at the insertion point (**Figure 12**).

## ✔ Tip

■ Word wrap changes automatically to accommodate inserted text.

MOVING THE INSERTION POINT, INSERTING TEXT

## To select text by dragging

Drag the I-beam pointer over the text you want to select (**Figure 13**).

## To select text with Shift-click

1. Position the insertion point at the beginning of the text you want to select (**Figure 14**).

2. Hold down [Shift] and click at the end of the text you want to select. All text between the insertion point's original position and where you clicked becomes selected (**Figure 15**).

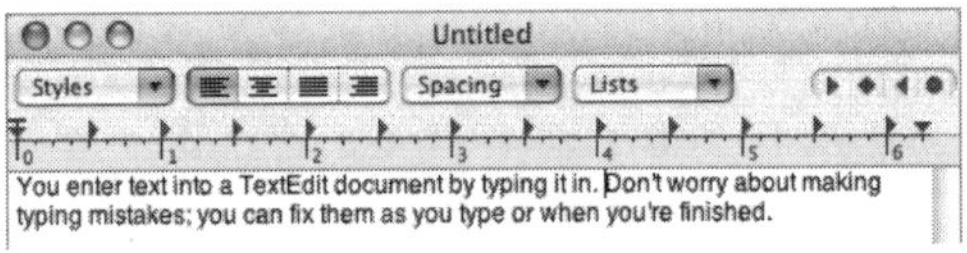

## ✔ Tip

■ This is a good way to select large blocks of text. After positioning the insertion point as instructed in step 1, use the scroll bars to scroll to the end of the text you want to select. Then Shift-click as instructed in step 2 to make the selection.

## To select a single word

Double-click the word (**Figure 16**).

## ✔ Tip

■ In some applications, such as Microsoft Word, double-clicking a word also selects the space after the word.

## To select all document contents

Choose Edit > Select All (**Figure 17**), or press [⌃][⌘][A].

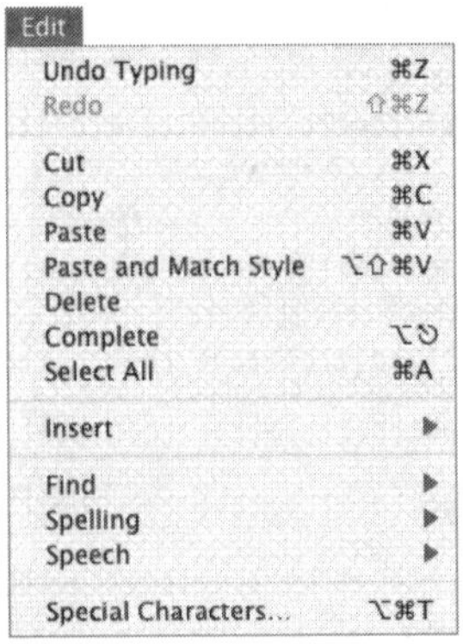

## ✔ Tip

■ There are other selection techniques in TextEdit and other applications. The techniques on this page work in every application.

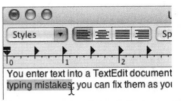

**Figure 13** Drag the I-beam pointer over the text that you want to select.

**Figure 14** Position the insertion point at the beginning of the text you want to select.

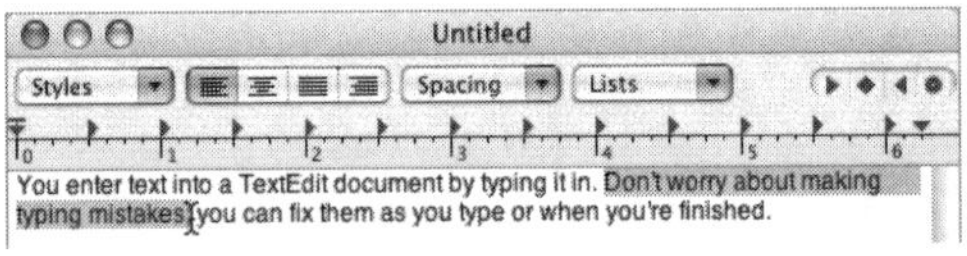

**Figure 15** Hold down [Shift] and click at the end of the text you want to select.

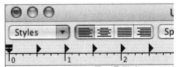

**Figure 16** Double-click the word that you want to select.

**Figure 17**
The Edit menu.

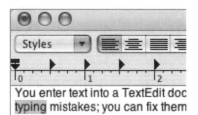

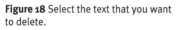

Figure 18 Select the text that you want to delete.

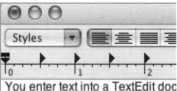

Figure 19 When you press Delete, the selected text disappears.

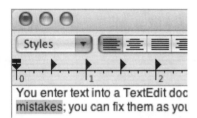

Figure 20 Select the text that you want to replace.

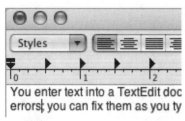

Figure 21 The text you type replaces the selected text.

## To delete text

1. Select the text that you want to delete (**Figure 18**).

2. Press Delete or Del. The selected text disappears (**Figure 19**).

## ✔ Tip

■ You can delete a character to the left of the insertion point by pressing Delete. You can delete a character to the right of the insertion point by pressing Del.

## To replace text

1. Select the text that you want to replace (**Figure 20**).

2. Type the new text. The selected text is replaced by what you type (**Figure 21**).

DELETING & REPLACING TEXT

# Basic Text Formatting

TextEdit also offers formatting features that you can use to change the appearance of text.

◆ **Font formatting** enables you to change the appearance of text characters. This includes the font typeface and family, character style, character size, and character color.

◆ **Text formatting** enables you to change the appearance of entire paragraphs of text. This includes the alignment, line spacing, and ruler settings such as tabs and indentation.

## ✔ Tips

■ This chapter introduces the most commonly used formatting options in TextEdit. You can further explore these and other options on your own.

■ Some text formatting options are on the ruler. If the ruler is not showing, you can display it by choosing Format > Text > Show Ruler or by pressing ⌃⌘R.

## To apply font formatting

1. Select the text you want to apply font formatting to (**Figure 22**).

2. Use any combination of the following techniques to apply font formatting:

   ▲ Choose Format > Font > Show Fonts (**Figure 23**), or press ⌃⌘T to display the Font panel (**Figure 24**). Set options in the Font panel as desired. You can immediately see the results of your changes in the document window behind the Font panel (**Figure 25**); make changes if you don't like what you see. You can also select different text and format it without closing the Font panel window.

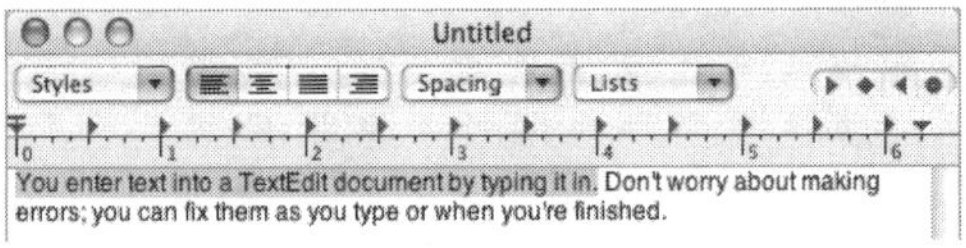

**Figure 22** Select the text you want to format.

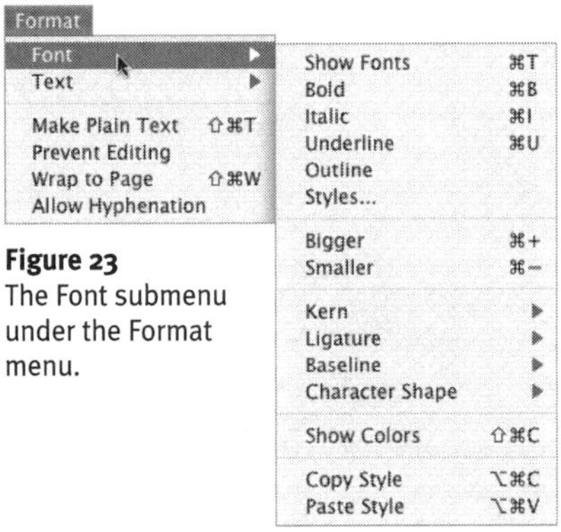

**Figure 23**
The Font submenu under the Format menu.

**Figure 24** The Font panel.

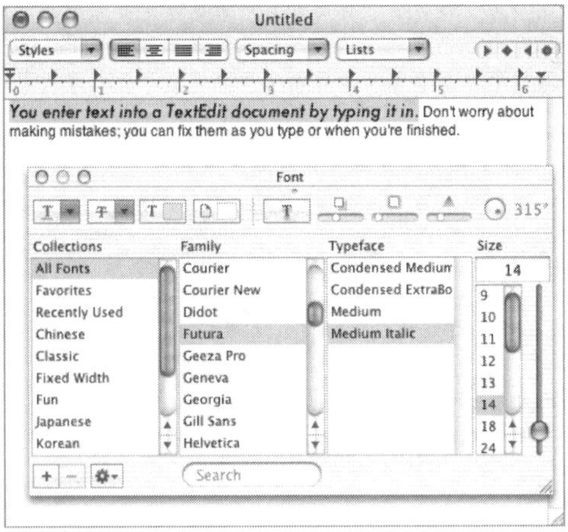

**Figure 25** The changes you make in the Font panel are immediately applied to the selected text.

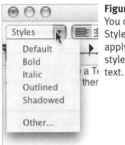

**Figure 26**
A check mark appears beside the name of each style applied to selected text.

**Figure 27**
You can use the Styles pop-up to apply certain font styles to selected text.

**Table 1**

**Shortcut Keys for TextEdit Font Formatting**

| Keystroke | Formatting Applied |
| --- | --- |
| ⌃ ⌘ B | Bold |
| ⌃ ⌘ I | Italic |
| ⌃ ⌘ U | Underline |
| ⌃ ⌘ + | Bigger |
| ⌃ ⌘ − | Smaller |

▲ Choose options from the Format menu's Font submenu (**Figure 23**) to apply formatting. You can choose any combination of options. A check mark appears beside the type of formatting applied to selected text (**Figure 26**).

▲ Choose an option from the Styles pop-up menu on the ruler (**Figure 27**). The Default option removes formatting applied with the Styles pop-up menu.

▲ Press the shortcut key for the type of formatting you want to apply. Consult **Table 1** for a list.

## ✔ Tips

■ Generally speaking, a *font* is a style of typeface.

■ You can apply more than one style to text (**Figure 26**).

■ A check mark appears on the Font submenu beside each style applied to a selection (**Figure 26**).

■ To remove an applied style, choose it from the Font submenu again.

■ Some styles are automatically applied when you select a specific typeface for a font family in the Font panel (**Figure 25**). Similarly, if you select a typeface in the Font panel, certain style options become unavailable for characters with that typeface applied. For example, if you apply Futura Medium Italic font, as shown in **Figure 25**, the Bold option on the Font submenu cannot be applied to that text.

■ I tell you more about fonts and explain how to use the Font panel in **Chapter 11**.

**APPLYING FONT FORMATTING**

## To apply text formatting

1. Select the paragraph(s) you want to format.

2. Use any combination of the following techniques to apply font formatting:

   ▲ Choose an option from the Format menu's Text submenu (**Figure 28**) to apply formatting.

   ▲ Click one of the alignment buttons on the ruler (**Figure 29**).

   ▲ Choose an option from the Line and paragraph spacing pop-up menu on the ruler (**Figure 30**).

   ▲ Choose an option from the Lists bullets and numbering pop-up menu on the ruler (**Figure 31**).

   ▲ Press the shortcut key for the type of formatting you want to apply. Consult **Table 2** for a list.

## ✔ Tip

■ Alignment and spacing options affect all lines in a paragraph.

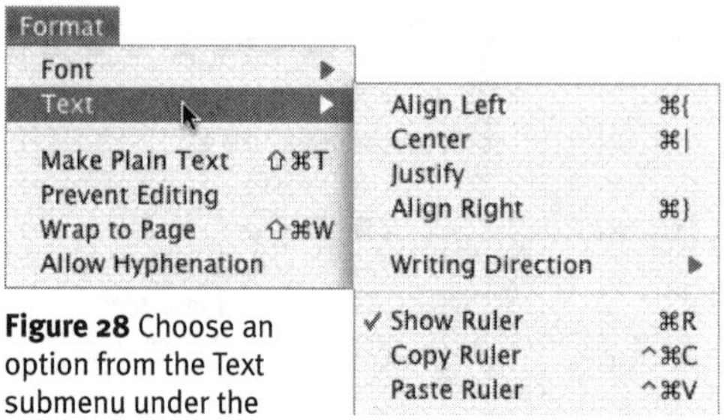

**Figure 28** Choose an option from the Text submenu under the Format menu.

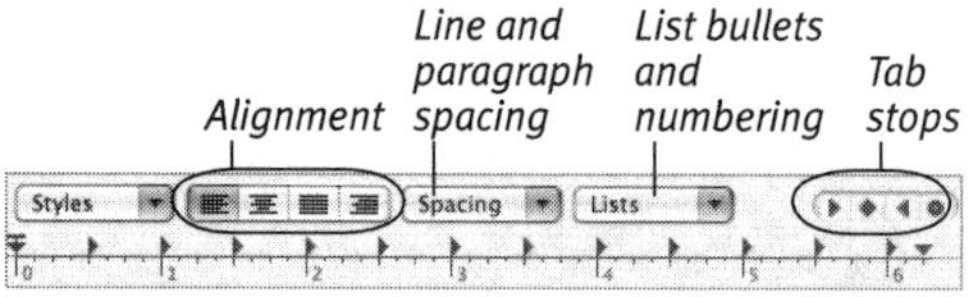

**Figure 29** You can use buttons and pop-up menus on the ruler to set alignment, line spacing, bullet and numbering formats, and tabs.

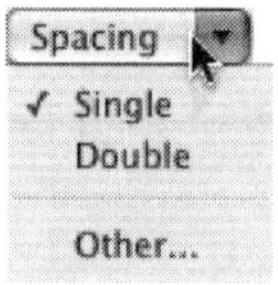

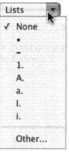

**Figure 30**
Use the Line and paragraph spacing pop-up menu to set line spacing for selected paragraphs.

**Figure 31**
Use the List bullets and numbering pop-up menu to set bullet or numbered list formatting for the selected paragraphs.

Table 2

| Shortcut Keys for TextEdit Text Formatting | |
|---|---|
| **Keystroke** | **Formatting Applied** |
| ⌃ ⌘ { | Align Left |
| ⌃ ⌘ | | Center |
| ⌃ ⌘ } | Align Right |

APPLYING TEXT FORMATTING

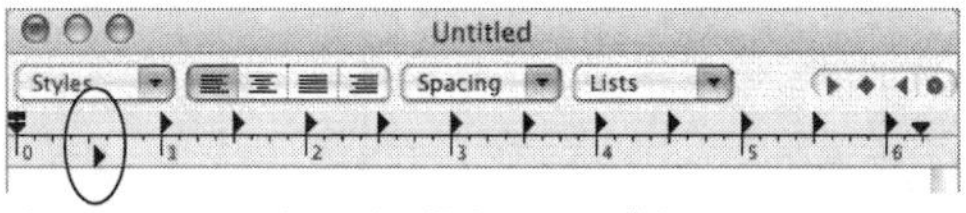

![Figure 32 ruler with tab being dragged off]

**Figure 32** Drag the tab off the ruler. (The mouse pointer disappears as you do this, so it isn't easy to illustrate!)

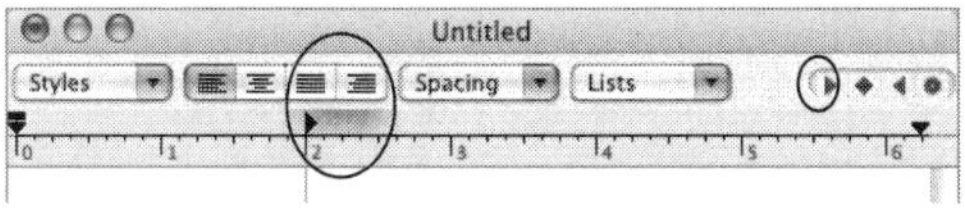

![Figure 33 ruler with tab icon being dragged into position]

**Figure 33** Drag one of the tab icons from the top half of the ruler into position on the ruler. Although the mouse pointer disappears as you drag, a tiny box with the tab location in it appears as you drag.

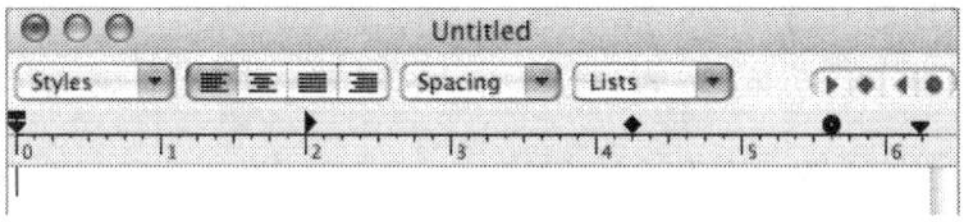

![Figure 34 ruler with tabs set]

**Figure 34** Start by setting tabs and positioning the insertion point at the beginning of the line.

![Figure 35 ruler with First Name]

First Name|

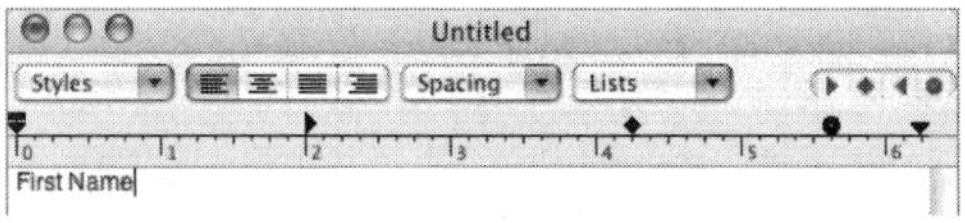

**Figure 35** If desired, enter text at the beginning of the line.

![Figure 36 ruler with First Name Last Name]

First Name          Last Name|

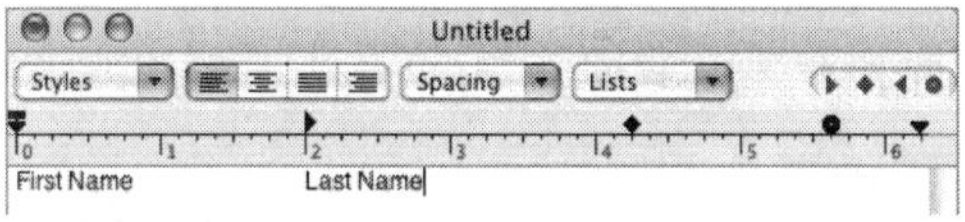

**Figure 36** Press Tab and enter text at the first tab stop.

![Figure 37 ruler with First Name Last Name Title Rate]

First Name          Last Name          Title     Rate|

**Figure 37** The first line of a table created with tabs.

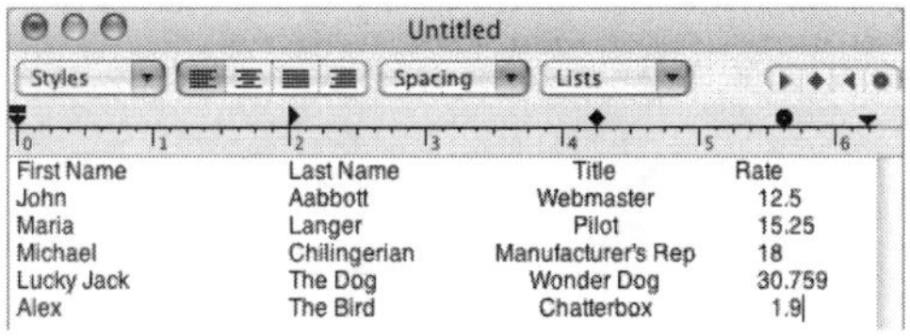

| First Name | Last Name | Title | Rate |
|---|---|---|---|
| John | Aabbott | Webmaster | 12.5 |
| Maria | Langer | Pilot | 15.25 |
| Michael | Chilingerian | Manufacturer's Rep | 18 |
| Lucky Jack | The Dog | Wonder Dog | 30.759 |
| Alex | The Bird | Chatterbox | 1.9| |

**Figure 38** A completed table. Note how the text lines up with each type of tab stop.

## To set tab stops

Add and remove tab stops from the bottom half of the ruler as follows:

◆ To remove a tab stop, drag it from the ruler into the document window (**Figure 32**). When you release the mouse button, the tab is removed.

◆ To add a tab stop, drag one of the tab icons on the ruler—left, center, right, or decimal—into position on the ruler (**Figure 33**). When you release the mouse button, the tab is placed.

## ✔ Tips

■ A tab stop is the position the insertion point moves to when you press Tab.

■ Tab settings affect entire paragraphs. When you press Return to begin a new paragraph, the tab stops you set for the current paragraph are carried forward.

## To use tab stops

1. Add and remove tab stops as instructed above.

2. Position the insertion point at the beginning of the paragraph for which tab stops are set (**Figure 34**).

3. If desired, enter text at the beginning of the line (**Figure 35**).

4. Press Tab.

5. Enter text at the tab stop (**Figure 36**).

6. Repeat steps 4 and 5 until you have entered text as desired at all tab stops. **Figure 37** shows an example.

7. Press Return.

8. Repeat steps 2 through 7 for each paragraph you want to use the tab stops for. **Figure 38** shows a completed table using tab stops.

## To set indentation

1. Select the paragraph(s) for which you want to set indentation (**Figure 39**).

2. Drag one of the icons on the end of the ruler (**Figure 40**) to the left or right:

   ▲ To set the first line indentation for a paragraph, drag the horizontal rectangle icon.

   ▲ To set the left indent, drag the downward-facing triangle on the left end of the ruler.

   ▲ To set the right indent, drag the downward-facing triangle on the right end of the ruler.

   As you drag, a yellow box with a measurement inside it indicates the exact position of the indent. When you release a marker, the text shifts accordingly (**Figure 41**).

## ✔ Tip

■ TextEdit Help refers to the left and right indents as *margins*. Technically speaking, this is incorrect terminology, since margins normally refer to the area between the printable area and edge of the paper.

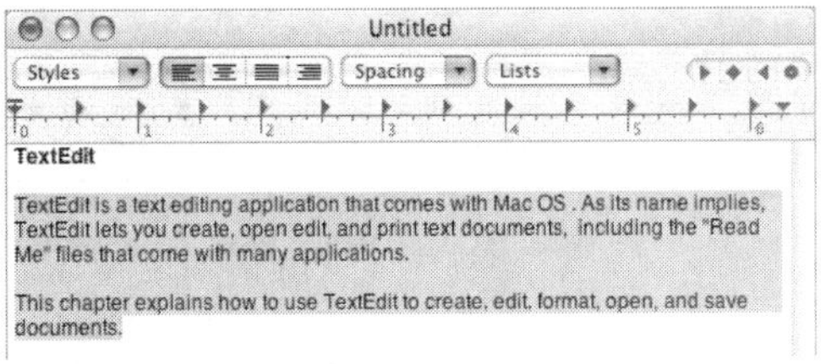

**Figure 39** Select the paragraphs you want to format.

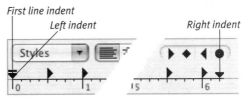

First line indent
Left indent
Right indent

**Figure 40** The indent markers on TextEdit's ruler.

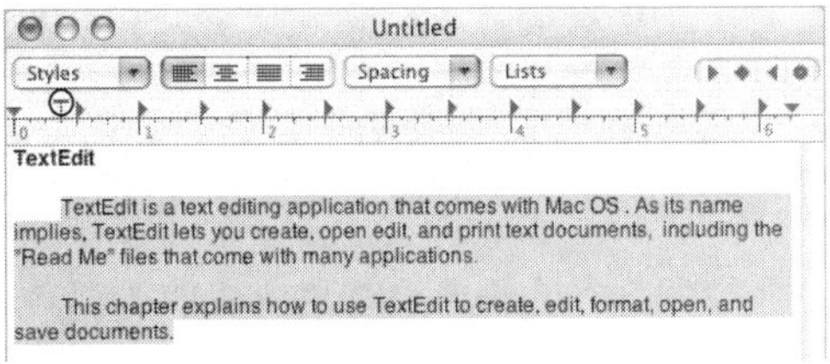

**Figure 41** In this example, the first line indent marker was shifted to the right, thus indenting just the first line of each paragraph.

| Edit | |
|---|---|
| Undo Set Font | ⌘Z |
| Redo Center | ⇧⌘Z |
| Cut | ⌘X |
| Copy | ⌘C |
| Paste | ⌘V |
| Paste and Match Style | ⌥⇧⌘V |
| Delete | |
| Complete | ⌥⎋ |
| Select All | ⌘A |
| Insert | ▶ |
| Find | ▶ |
| Spelling | ▶ |
| Speech | ▶ |
| Special Characters... | ⌥⌘T |

**Figure 42**
The Edit menu with Undo and Redo commands displayed. If one of these commands were not available, it would be gray.

# Undoing & Redoing Actions

The Undo command enables you to reverse your last action, thus offering an easy way to fix errors immediately after you make them. The Redo command, which is available only when your last action was to use the Undo command, reverses the undo action.

## ✔ Tips

- The Undo and Redo commands are available in most applications and can be found at the top of the Edit menu.

- TextEdit supports multiple levels of undo (and redo). That means you can undo (or redo) several actions, in the reverse order that they were performed (or undone).

- The exact wording of the Undo (and Redo) command depends on what was last done (or undone). For example, if the last thing you did was change the font for selected text, the Undo command will be Undo Set Font (**Figure 42**).

## To undo the last action

Choose Edit > Undo (**Figure 42**), or press ⌘Z. The last thing you did is undone.

## ✔ Tip

- To undo multiple actions, choose Edit > Undo repeatedly.

## To redo an action

After using the Undo command, choose Edit > Redo (**Figure 42**), or press Shift ⌘Z. The last thing you undid is redone.

## ✔ Tip

- To redo multiple actions, choose Edit > Redo repeatedly.

UNDOING & REDOING ACTIONS

# Copy, Cut, & Paste

The Copy, Cut, and Paste commands enable you to duplicate or move document contents. Text that is copied or cut is placed on the Clipboard, where it can be viewed if desired and pasted into a document.

## ✔ Tip

- Almost all Mac OS-compatible applications include the Copy, Cut, and Paste commands on the Edit menu. These commands work very much the same in all applications.

## To copy text

1. Select the text that you want to copy (**Figure 43**).

2. Choose Edit > Copy (**Figure 44**), or press ⌘ ⌘ C.

   The text is copied to the Clipboard so it can be pasted elsewhere. The original remains in the document.

## To cut text

1. Select the text that you want to cut (**Figure 43**).

2. Choose Edit > Cut (**Figure 44**), or press ⌘ ⌘ X.

   The text is copied to the Clipboard so it can be pasted elsewhere. The original is removed from the document.

## To paste Clipboard contents

1. Position the insertion point where you want the Clipboard contents to appear (**Figure 45**).

2. Choose Edit > Paste (**Figure 44**), or press ⌘ ⌘ V.

   The Clipboard's contents are pasted into the document (**Figure 46**).

**Figure 43** Select the text you want to copy or cut.

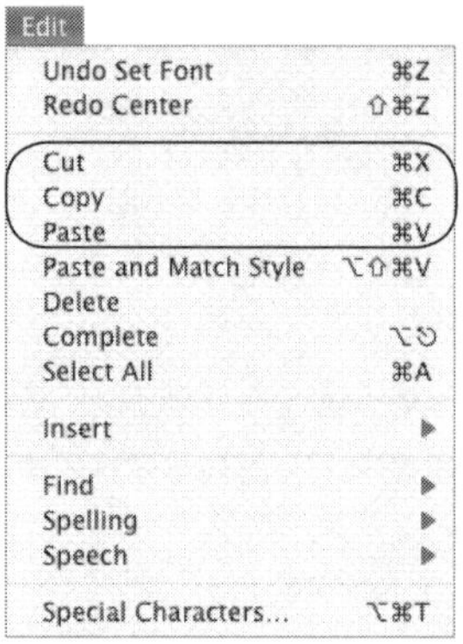

**Figure 44** The Copy, Cut, and Paste commands are all on the Edit menu.

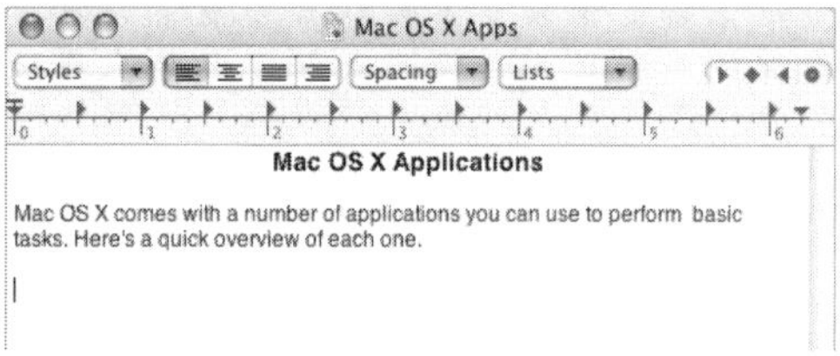

**Figure 45** Position the insertion point where you want the contents of the Clipboard to appear.

**Figure 46** The contents of the Clipboard are pasted into the document.

## ✔ Tip

- The Clipboard contains only the last item that was copied or cut. Using the Paste command, therefore, pastes in the most recently cut or copied selection.

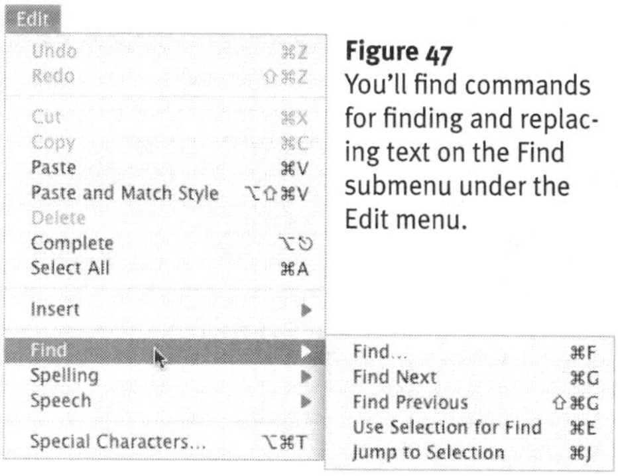

**Figure 47**
You'll find commands for finding and replacing text on the Find submenu under the Edit menu.

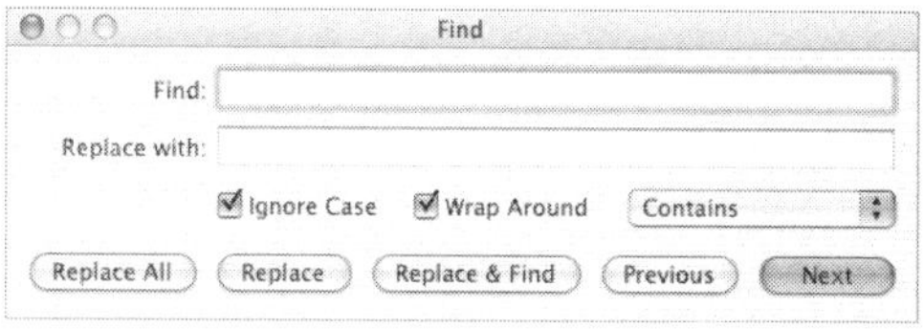

**Figure 48** The Find dialog.

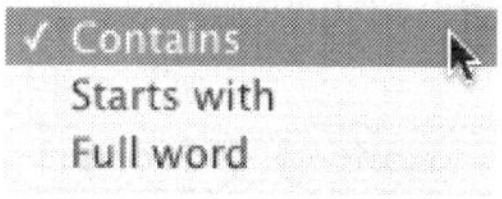

**Figure 49** Use this pop-up menu to indicate how TextEdit should match the Find text.

# Find & Replace

TextEdit's find and replace features enable you to quickly locate or replace occurrences of text strings in your document.

## ✔ Tip

- Most word processing and page layout applications include find and replace features. Although these features are somewhat limited in TextEdit, full-featured applications such as Microsoft Word and Adobe InDesign enable you to search for text, formatting, and other document elements as well as plain text.

## To find text

1. Choose Edit > Find > Find (**Figure 47**), or press ⌃ ⌘ F. The Find dialog appears (**Figure 48**).

2. Enter the text that you want to find in the Find field.

3. To find text from the insertion point forward (rather than the entire document), turn off the Wrap Around check box.

4. To perform a case-sensitive search, turn off the Ignore Case check box.

5. To indicate how TextEdit should match the Find text, select the appropriate option from the pop-up menu (**Figure 49**).

6. Click Next, or press Return or Enter. If the text you entered in the Find field is found, it is highlighted in the document.

## ✔ Tip

- To find subsequent or previous occurrences of the Find field entry, choose Edit > Find > Find Next or Edit > Find > Find Previous (**Figure 47**) or press ⌃ ⌘ G or Shift ⌃ ⌘ G.

**FINDING TEXT**

## To replace text

1. Choose Edit > Find > Find (**Figure 47**), or press ⌃⌘F. The Find dialog appears (**Figure 48**).

2. Enter the text that you want to replace in the Find field.

3. Enter the replacement text in the Replace with field (**Figure 50**).

4. To replace text from the insertion point forward (rather than the entire document), turn off the Wrap Around check box.

5. To perform a case-sensitive search, turn off the Ignore Case check box.

6. To indicate how TextEdit should match the Find text, select the appropriate option from the pop-up menu (**Figure 49**).

7. Click the buttons at the bottom of the Find dialog to find and replace text:

   ▲ **Replace All** replaces all occurrences of the Find word with the Replace word.

   ▲ **Replace** replaces the currently selected occurrence of the Find word with the Replace word.

   ▲ **Replace & Find** replaces the currently selected occurrence of the Find word with the Replace word and then selects the next occurrence of the Find word.

   ▲ **Previous** selects the previous occurrence of the Find word.

   ▲ **Next** selects the next occurrence of the Find word.

8. When you're finished replacing text, click the Find dialog's close button to dismiss it.

## ✖ Warning!

■ Use the Replace All button with care! It will not give you an opportunity to preview and approve any of the replacements it makes.

**Figure 50** You can set up the Find dialog to find and replace text.

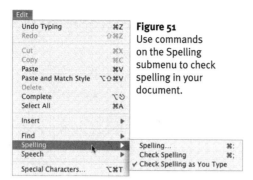

**Figure 51**
Use commands on the Spelling submenu to check spelling in your document.

TextEdit is a text editing application that comes with Mac OS. As its name implies, TextEdit lets you create, open edit, and print text documents, including the "Read Me" files that come with many applications.

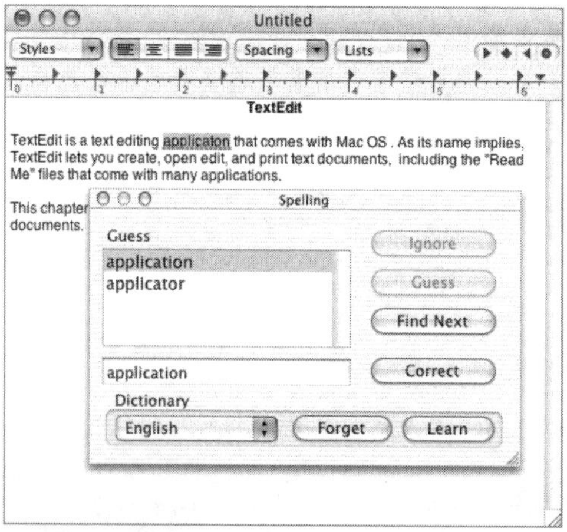

**Figure 52** Use the Spelling dialog to resolve possible misspelled words.

# Checking Spelling

TextEdit includes a spelling checker that you can use to manually or automatically check spelling in your document.

## To manually check spelling

1. Choose Edit > Spelling > Spelling (**Figure 51**) or press Shift ⌘ ; to display the Spelling dialog and start the spelling check.

   TextEdit selects and underlines the first possible misspelled word it finds. The word appears in a field in the Spelling dialog and any suggested corrections appear in the Guess list (**Figure 52**).

2. You have several options:
   - ▲ To replace the word with a guess, select the replacement word and click Correct.
   - ▲ To enter a new spelling for the word, enter it in the box where the incorrect spelling appears and click Correct.
   - ▲ To ignore the word, click Ignore.
   - ▲ To skip the word and continue checking, click Find Next.
   - ▲ To add the word to TextEdit's dictionary, click Learn. TextEdit will never stop at that word again in any document.

3. Repeat step 2 for each word that TextEdit identifies as a possible misspelling.

4. When you're finished checking spelling, click the Spelling dialog's close button to dismiss it.

## ✔ Tip

- ■ You can use the Forget button in the Spelling dialog (**Figure 51**) to remove a word that you previously added to the dictionary. Select the Word in the Guess list, then click the Forget button. The word is removed.

## To check spelling as you type

1. Choose Edit > Spelling > Check Spelling As You Type (**Figure 51**).

   As you enter text into the document, TextEdit checks the spelling of each word. It places a dashed red underline under each word that isn't in its dictionary. (**Figure 53**).

2. Manually correct a misspelled word using standard text editing techniques covered near the beginning of this chapter.

   *or*

   Hold down (Control) and click a misspelled word. Then choose a correct spelling from the contextual menu that appears (**Figure 54**). The misspelled word is replaced with the word you chose.

## ✔ Tips

- The Check Spelling As You Type option in TextEdit may automatically be enabled. To disable it, choose Edit > Spelling > Check Spelling As You Type.

- If you display a contextual menu as instructed in step 2 (**Figure 54**), you can also use the Ignore Spelling or Learn Spelling commands to ignore the underlined word or add it to the dictionary.

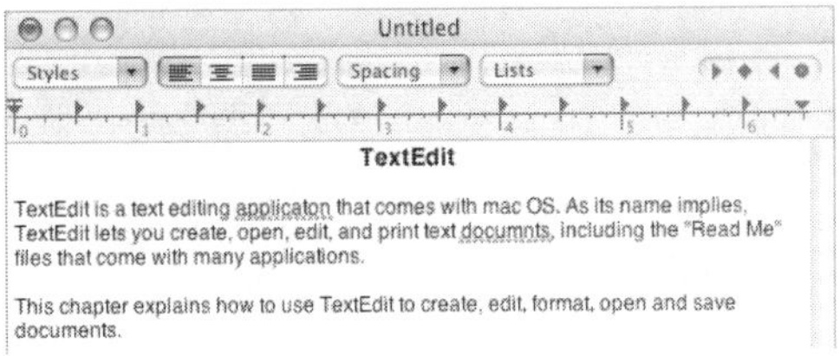

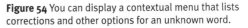

**Figure 53** With automatic spelling check enabled, TextEdit underlines possible misspelled words as you type.

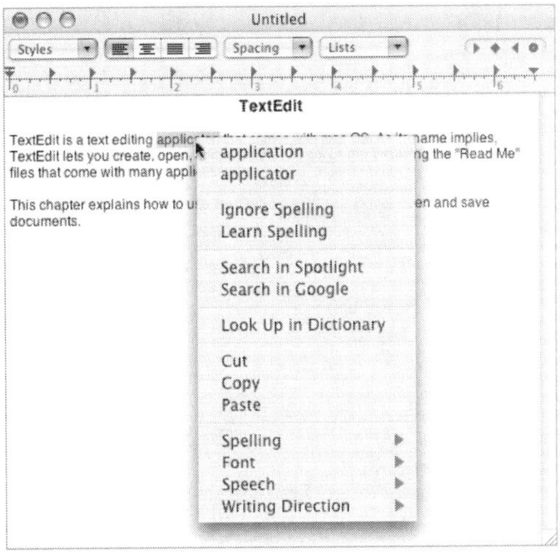

**Figure 54** You can display a contextual menu that lists corrections and other options for an unknown word.

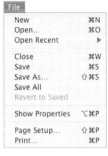

**Figure 55**
The File menu includes commands for working with files.

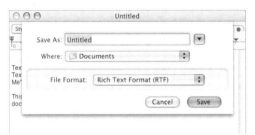

**Figure 56** Use the Save As dialog to enter a name and select a location for saving a file.

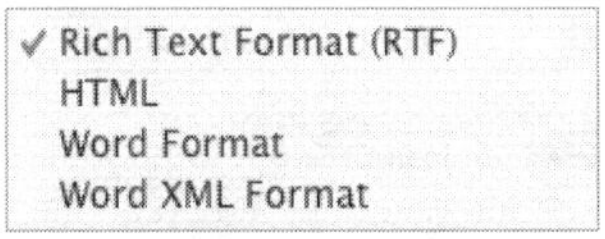

✓ Rich Text Format (RTF)
 HTML
 Word Format
 Word XML Format

**Figure 57** The Format pop-up menu enables you to save documents in four different formats.

**Figure 58** The name of a saved document appears in its title bar.

# Saving & Opening Files

When you're finished working with a Text-Edit document, you may want to save it. You can then open it another time to review, edit, or print it.

## To save a document for the first time

1. Choose File > Save (**Figure 55**), or press ⌘S.

   *or*

   Choose File > Save As (**Figure 55**), or press Shift ⌘S.

   The Save As dialog sheet appears (**Figure 56**).

2. Enter a name and select a location for the file.

3. Choose an option from the File Format pop-up menu (**Figure 57**):

   ▲ **Rich Text Format (RTF)** is a standard format that can be read by most word processing and page layout applications.

   ▲ **HTML** is HyperText Markup Language format, which is readable by Web browser software such as Safari.

   ▲ **Word Format** is Microsoft Word format, which can be opened and read by Microsoft Word or any other application capable of reading Word files.

   ▲ **Word XML Format** is Word Extensible Markup Language format.

4. Click Save, or press Return or Enter.

   The document is saved with the name you entered in the location you specified. The name of the document appears on the document's title bar (**Figure 58**).

*Continued on next page...*

SAVING DOCUMENTS

*Continued from previous page.*

## ✔ Tips

■ I explain how to use the Save As dialog in **Chapter 7**.

■ There's only one difference between the File menu's Save and Save As commands (**Figure 55**):

▲ The Save command opens the Save As dialog only if the document has never been saved.

▲ The Save As command *always* opens the Save As dialog.

■ By default, TextEdit creates Rich Text Format (RTF) files and appends the *.rtf* extension to the files it saves. This extension does not appear unless the Show all file extensions option is enabled in Finder Preferences. I discuss Finder preferences in **Chapter 6**.

■ To save a TextEdit document as a plain text document (with a *.txt* extension), choose Format > Make Plain Text (**Figure 59**) and click OK in the confirmation dialog that may appear. Then follow the steps on the previous page to save the document. As shown in **Figure 60**, the pop-up menu in the Save As dialog offers a variety of Plain Text Encoding options rather than Rich Text Format and Word Format. Keep in mind that if you save a document as a plain text document, any formatting applied to document text will be lost.

■ Generally speaking, plain text documents are more compatible than RFT or Word documents and RTF documents are more compatible than Word documents.

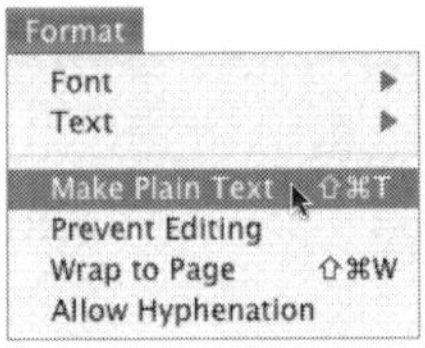

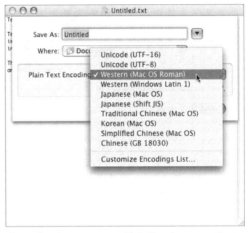

**Figure 59**
To save a document as a plain text document, begin by choosing Make Plain Text from the Format menu.

**Figure 60** When you save a Plain Text document, Text-Edit offers other formatting options. If you're not sure what to pick here, leave it set to the default setting.

**Figure 61** A bullet in the document window's close button...

| Window | |
|---|---|
| Minimize | ⌘M |
| Zoom | |
| Bring All to Front | |
| ✓ About TextEdit.txt | |
| • Mac OS X Apps | |

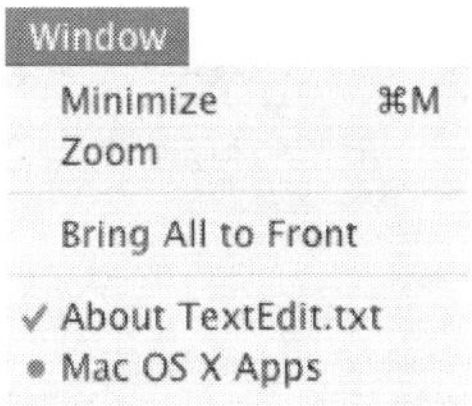

**Figure 62**
...or beside its name in the Window menu indicates that the document has unsaved changes.

## To save changes to an existing document

Choose File > Save (**Figure 55**), or press ⌃ ⌘ S.

The document is saved. No dialog appears.

## ✔ Tips

- TextEdit identifies a document with changes that have not been saved by displaying a bullet in the document window's close button (**Figure 61**) and to the left of the document's name in the Window menu (**Figure 62**).

- It's a good idea to save changes to a document frequently as you work with it. This helps prevent loss of data in the event of an application or system crash or power outage.

## To save an existing document with a new name or in a new location

1. Choose File > Save As (**Figure 55**).

2. Use the Save As dialog that appears (**Figure 56**) to enter a different name or select a different location (or both) for the file.

3. Click Save, or press Return or Enter.

   A copy of the document is saved with the name you entered in the location you specified. The new document name appears in the document's title bar. The original document remains untouched.

## ✔ Tip

- You can use the Save As command to create a new document based on an existing document—without overwriting the original document with your changes.

## To open a document

1. Choose File > Open (**Figure 55**), or press ⌃ ⌘O.

2. Use the Open dialog that appears (**Figure 63**) to locate and select the document that you want to open.

3. Click Open, or press Return or Enter.

## ✔ Tip

- I explain how to use the Open dialog in **Chapter 7**.

## To close a document

1. Choose File > Close (**Figure 55**), or press ⌃ ⌘W.

2. If the document contains unsaved changes, a Close dialog like the one in **Figure 6** appears.

   ▲ Click Don't Save to close the document without saving it.

   ▲ Click Cancel or press Esc to return to the document without closing it.

   ▲ Click Save or press Return or Enter to save the document.

   The document closes.

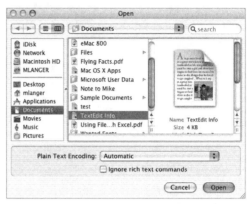

**Figure 63** Use the Open dialog to locate and open a file.

# Dashboard

**10**

## Dashboard & Widgets

*Dashboard*, a brand new feature of Mac OS X, gives you instant access to simple applications called *widgets*. Widgets work with other applications such as iTunes, iCal, and Address Book to provide you with quick access to the most commonly used features. They also work with the Internet to get up-to-date information such as stock quotes, weather, and Yellow Pages listings.

Mac OS X 10.4 comes with a bunch of widgets, all accessible from the new Widget Bar that you can display at the bottom of your screen. In this chapter, I explain how to use Dashboard to display the Widget Bar and widgets and how you can use each of the widgets that come with Mac OS X.

### ✔ Tips

- Apple is actively encouraging developers to build more widgets. If you like using widgets and want more, be sure to check out Apple's Dashboard Web page, www.apple.com/macos/dashboard/.

- Have you been using a Macintosh long enough to remember Desk Accessories? If so, widgets should seem pretty familiar— they're a new twist on an old idea.

**DASHBOARD & WIDGETS**

# Opening & Closing Dashboard

The main purpose of Dashboard is to make widgets easily accessible without interfering with your work. Apple achieves this by making Dashboard quick and easy to open and close.

## To open Dashboard

Click the Dashboard icon in the Dock.

*Or*

Press F12.

Your screen dims and the last widgets you accessed appear (**Figure 1**).

## To close Dashboard

Click anywhere on the screen other than on a widget.

*Or*

Press F12.

The widgets disappear and your screen returns to normal brightness.

**Figure 1** Dashboard with four widgets displayed: Calculator, World Clock, Calendar, and Weather.

**Figure 2** The Widget Bar appears at the bottom of your screen.

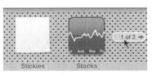

**Figure 3** Click one of the arrow buttons...

**Figure 4** ...to view other installed widgets.

# Working with the Widget Bar

The Widget Bar gives you access to all installed widgets.

## To display the Widget Bar

With Dashboard open, click the ✚ button in the lower-left corner of your screen (**Figure 2**).

Your screen's view slides up to make room for the Widget Bar at the bottom of your screen. Close buttons appear for each widget that is open.

## To see other widgets

Click the arrow button on the left or right end of the Widget Bar (**Figure 3**).

The Widget Bar scrolls to show more installed widgets (**Figure 4**).

## ✔ Tip

- Clicking the More Widgets button above the right end of the Widget Bar (**Figure 2**) launches your default Web browser and displays a Web page on Apple's Web site where you can download more widgets. I explain how to install widgets later in this chapter.

## To hide the Widget Bar

Click the ✖ button near the lower-left corner of your screen.

The Widget Bar disappears and your screen's view slides back down to display all of the screen's contents (**Figure 1**).

WORKING WITH THE WIDGET BAR

# Opening & Closing Widgets

To use a widget, you must open it. If you want it to appear every time you open Dashboard, you can leave it open when you close Dashboard. Otherwise, you can close the widget.

## To open a widget

1. Open Dashboard (**Figure 1**). If the widget you want to use is already displayed, you can skip the following steps; the widget is already open and ready to use.

2. If the widget you want to use is not already displayed, open the Widget Bar (**Figure 2**).

3. Click the icon for the widget you want to use (**Figure 5**).

   The widget you clicked appears onscreen and is ready to use (**Figure 6**).

## ✔ Tip

■ One of the cool thing about widgets is that you can open more than one copy of the same widget. So, for example, if you want to view the World Clock for Wickenburg, AZ, and Oshkosh, WI, you simply open the World Clock widget twice and configure each one for one of the cities.

## To close a widget

If the Widget Bar is displayed, an ✖ button should appear at the upper-left corner of the widget (**Figure 2**).

*Or*

If the Widget Bar is not displayed, hold down the [Option] key and point to the widget you want to close. An ✖ button appears at its upper-left corner (**Figure 7**).

Click the ✖ button. The widget closes.

**Figure 5** In the Widget Bar, click the icon for the widget you want to open.

**Figure 6** The widget you clicked appears among other open widgets.

**Figure 7** To display the close button for a widget, hold down [Option] and point to the widget.

Click to scroll
through the
record's contents

Enter a search
word or phrase

Click an arrow to
scroll through all
found records

Click to open the record in
Address Book

**Figure 8** The Address Book widget,
displaying one of my contacts.

# Address Book

The Address Book widget works with the
Address Book application to give you quick
access to your contacts.

## ✔ Tip

- I tell you how to use the Address Book
  application in **Chapter 8**.

## To use the Address Book widget

1. Open the Address Book widget.

2. Enter a search word or phrase in the box
   at the bottom-right corner of the window.
   Address Book quickly displays the first
   card that matches what you entered.

3. If necessary, click one of the arrow buttons to scroll through the contacts until
   you find the one you want (**Figure 8**).

## ✔ Tip

- You can click the red button in the bottom of the Address Book widget's window
  to open the currently displayed contact in
  the Address Book application.

# Calculator

The Calculator widget puts simple calculations at your fingertips.

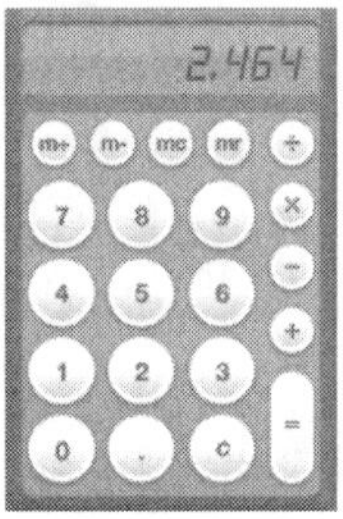

## To use the Calculator widget

1. Open the Calculator widget.

2. Use your keyboard to enter the formula you want to calculate.

   *or*

   Click the buttons on the Calculator's keypad to enter the formula you want to calculate.

   The results appear in the Calculator window (**Figure 9**).

## ✔ Tip

■ For more advanced calculations, be sure to check out the Calculator application, which I discuss in **Chapter 8**.

**Figure 9**
For simple calculations, you can't beat the handy Calculator widget.

**Figure 10**
The Calendar widget.

*Previous month* | *Next month*
*Today*

**Figure 11** Click the large date to collapse or expand the calendar display.

# Calendar

The Calendar widget gives you access to the events you manage with iCal.

## ✔ Tip

- I tell you about iCal in **Chapter 8**.

## To use the Calendar widget

1. Open the Calendar widget (**Figure 10**).

2. To view a specific month click the up and down arrows at the bottom of the calendar to scroll through the months.

## ✔ Tip

- Clicking the large date on the calendar collapses the calendar window to show just the current date (**Figure 11**).

# Dictionary

The Dictionary widget offers a quick way to look up the definitions, pronunciations, and synonyms for a word.

## ✔ Tip

■ You may also be interested in the Dictionary application, which I discuss in **Chapter 8**.

## To use the Dictionary widget

1. Open the Dictionary widget (**Figure 12**).

2. Enter a word in the box on the right end of the widget's window and press (Return). The window expands to show the word's definition (**Figure 13**).

3. Click the right pointing arrow at the top of the Dictionary window to display the Thesaurus entry for the word (**Figure 14**).

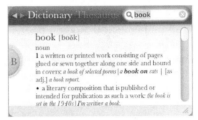

**Figure 12** The Dictionary widget looks like this when you first open it.

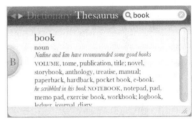

**Figure 13** The Dictionary can show you a word's definitions...

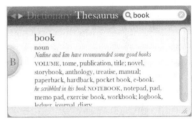

**Figure 14** ...or its synonyms.

**DICTIONARY**

**Figure 15** The Flight Tracker widget.

**Figure 16** Use the drop-down lists to set search criteria for airline, departure city, and arrival city.

**Figure 17** Flight Tracker displays search results.

**Figure 18** Clicking the Track Flight button displays flight status information.

# Flight Tracker

Flight Tracker can provide you with information about airline flights all over the world, including arrival and departure times, en route progress, and delays.

## ✔ Tips

■ Flight Tracker requires an Internet connection to gather information.

■ If you think Flight Tracker is useful, you might want to check out the Flights feature of Sherlock, which I discuss in **Chapter 15**.

## To use the Flight Tracker widget

1. Open the Flight Tracker widget (**Figure 15**).

2. Use the three drop-down lists on the left side of the widget window to choose an airline (**Figure 16**), departure city, and arrival city.

3. Click the Find Flights button. Flight Tracker lists all of the flights that match your criteria (**Figure 17**).

4. To check the status of an en route flight, select the flight and click the Track Flight button. Flight Tracker displays a graphic of the route with information about the plane's location and speed (**Figure 18**).

FLIGHT TRACKER

# iTunes

The iTunes widget gives you an alternate means to control iTunes playback. Once iTunes is running and playing a song, you can use the iTunes widget to stop or start play, change play volume, go to the previous or next song, or change the playlist.

## ✔ Tip

- I explain how to use iTunes in **Chapter 8**.

## To use the iTunes widget

1. If iTunes isn't already running, launch it.

2. Open the iTunes widget (**Figure 19**).

3. Use widget buttons and sliders to control iTunes play:

   ▲ Click the Stop/Start button to stop or start playing the current song.

   ▲ Click the Previous button once to go to the beginning of the current song; click it twice to go to the previous song.

   ▲ Click the Next button to go to the next song.

   ▲ Drag the volume dial around to change play volume.

4. To change the playlist, click the i button to flip over the widget (**Figure 20**), choose a different playlist from the pop-up menu, and click Done to return to the front side of the widget.

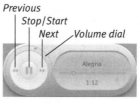

Previous
   Stop/Start
      Next    Volume dial

**Figure 19** The iTunes widget enables you to control iTunes play.

**Figure 20** The "back side" of the widget has a pop-up menu for selecting a playlist.

**Figure 21**
A blank Stickies window.

**Figure 22**
Type a note right into the window.

**Figure 23**
You have to point to where the i button should be to get it to appear.

**Figure 24**
The flip side of the Stickies window offers a few formatting options.

# Stickies

The Stickies widget enables you to create reminder notes that look a lot like the sticky notes you might already have all over your computer monitor—hopefully, on the plastic part around the glass.

## ✔ Tip

■ Mac OS X 10.4 also includes a more powerful Stickies application. I tell you about it in **Chapter 8**.

## To use the Stickies widget

1. Open the Stickies widget. A blank note window appears (**Figure 21**).

2. Click in the top of the window to position an insertion point and type your note (**Figure 22**).

3. To set Stickies formatting options, point to the lower-right corner of the Stickies window and click the i button that appears (**Figure 23**). The widget flips over so you can set paper color, font, and text size. Click Done to flip the note window back to the front.

## ✔ Tip

■ To create another sticky note, open the Stickies widget again.

STICKIES

# Stocks

The Stocks widget enables you to keep track of your favorite securities throughout the day.

## ✔ Tips

- The Stocks widget requires an Internet connection to download security price information.

- Stock quotes, which are provided by Quote.com, are delayed up to 20 minutes.

- If you like the Stocks widget, be sure to check out the Stocks feature of Sherlock, which I discuss in **Chapter 15**.

## To use the Stocks widget

1. Open the Stocks widget.

2. To see a chart for a security, click the symbol for the security in the list (**Figure 25**).

3. To change the chart period, click one of the buttons within the chart area.

4. To customize the list of securities, point to the bottom-right corner of the Stocks widget to display an i button (**Figure 26**) and click the button to flip the widget over (**Figure 27**). Then:

   - ▲ To add a security to the list, enter the company name or ticker symbol in the box at the top of the window and click the + button.

   - ▲ To remove a security from the list, select the security you want to remove and click the Remove button.

   - ▲ To display the daily value change as a percentage rather than a dollar value, turn on the Show change as a percentage check box.

   - ▲ To save your changes, click Done.

**Figure 25**
The Stocks widget with my favorite investment selected. (I bought at $13 per share and it has split twice since then. Apple does reward the faithful.)

**Figure 26**
Click the i button to access Stocks widget options.

**Figure 27**
Use the flip side of the Stocks widget window to add and remove securities from its list.

## ✔ Tip

- To view a Web page on the Quote.com Web site with information about the security, double-click the name of the security on the front side of the Stock widget window (**Figure 25**).

**Figure 28**
The Tile Game widget features —what else?— a tiger.

**Figure 29**
Shuffle the tiles before starting to play.

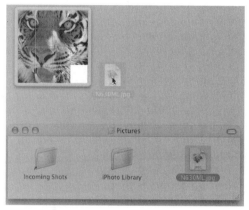

Figure 30 Drag the icon for an image file from the Finder onto the Tile Game widget window.

**Figure 31**
When you release the mouse button, the image appears in the game. How cool is that?

# Tile Game

Feel like a break? You can play the Tile Game to test your puzzle-solving skills.

## ✔ Tip

- If you've been using a Macintosh as long as I have, you may remember a tile game called Puzzle that was available as a Desk Accessory in System 7. That was a very long time ago.

## To use the Tile Game widget

1. Open the Tile Game widget (**Figure 28**).

2. To shuffle the tiles, click the picture.

3. To stop shuffling the tiles, click the picture again (**Figure 29**).

4. To slide a tile into the adjacent blank space, click the tile. Repeat this process until you have unshuffled all the tiles to re-form the picture.

## To customize the picture

1. If the Tile Game widget is not already open, open it (**Figure 28**).

2. Press F12 to close Dashboard.

3. In the Finder, locate the icon for the picture you want to use in the Tile Game and start dragging it out of the Finder window. Do not release the mouse button.

4. Press F12 again to open Dashboard (**Figure 30**).

5. Continue dragging the icon onto the Tile Game window.

6. Release the mouse button. The picture appears in the Tile Game widget (**Figure 31**).

TILE GAME

# Translation

The Translation widget can translate text on the fly from one language to another.

## ✔ Tips

- The Translation widget requires an Internet connection to work.

- Remember, the Translation widget generates a computer-based translation. Although it *should* make sense, it probably won't be perfect.

- If you like the Translation widget, you should like Sherlock's Translation feature, which I tell you about in **Chapter 15**.

## To use the Translation widget

1. Open the Translation widget.

2. Use the pop-up menus to choose the languages you want to translate from and to.

3. Type the text you want to convert in the top half of the window. The translation appears almost immediately in the bottom half of the window (**Figure 32**).

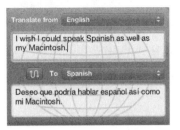

**Figure 32** The Translation widget can make you multilingual—at least while you're sitting at your computer.

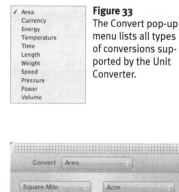

**Figure 33**
The Convert pop-up menu lists all types of conversions supported by the Unit Converter.

**Figure 34** Set all options and enter a value. Unit Converter performs the calculations instantly.

# Unit Converter

The Unit Converter widget enables you to convert from one unit of measurement to another.

## ✔ Tips

■ You can also find a conversion feature in the Calculator application, which I discuss in **Chapter 8**.

■ You must have an Internet connection to convert currency units.

## To use the Unit Converter widget

1. Open the Unit Converter widget.

2. Choose an option from the Convert pop-up menu (**Figure 33**).

3. Choose options from the two units pop-up menus. Make sure one unit is what you want to convert from and the other is what you want to convert to.

4. Enter a value in the box beneath the unit you want to convert from.

   The conversion appears in the other box (**Figure 34**).

# Weather

The Weather widget provides basic weather information for cities throughout the world.

## ✔ Tip

■ You must have an Internet connection to use the Weather widget.

## To use the Weather widget

1. Open the Weather widget. By default, the weather for Cupertino, CA, appears (**Figure 35**).

2. To view a six-day forecast (**Figure 36**), click the middle of the widget.

3. Click the i button in the lower-right corner of the widget (**Figure 37**) to flip the widget over (**Figure 38**).

4. Set options as necessary:

   ▲ **City, State, or ZIP Code** is the city and state or ZIP code of the city you want weather for.

   ▲ Degrees is the unit of measurement: °F or °C.

   ▲ Include lows in 6-day forecast includes low temperatures in the six-day forecast (**Figure 39**).

5. Click Done to save your settings and view the weather.

## ✔ Tip

■ Want to track weather in more than one city at a time? Just open another Weather widget window.

**Figure 35**
By default, the Weather widget displays current Cupertino weather.

**Figure 36**
Click the widget to view a six-day forecast.

**Figure 37** Click the i button in the corner of the widget.

**Figure 38**
You can set options on the flip side of the Weather widget.

**Figure 39**
Here's what I can look forward to this week, including the lows.

WEATHER

**Figure 40**
The World Clock displays "Apple Time."

**Figure 41** Click the i button to display options.

**Figure 42**
Choose a continent and city from these pop-up menus.

# World Clock

The World Clock widget enables you to check the time in any major city in the world.

## ✔ Tip

- For the World Clock's time to be accurate, the correct time must be set in the Date & Time preferences pane. I explain how to use the Date & Time preferences pane in **Chapter 21**.

## To use the World Clock widget

1. Open the World Clock widget. By default, it displays the current time in Cupertino, CA (**Figure 40**).

2. Click the i button in the lower-right corner of the widget (**Figure 41**) to flip it over (**Figure 42**).

3. Choose a continent and city from the pop-up menus.

4. Click Done. The clock displays the city you chose.

## ✔ Tip

- Want to see clocks for more than one city at a time? Just open another World Clock widget window.

**WORLD CLOCK**

# Phone Book

The Phone Book widget puts a yellow pages directory at your fingertips.

## ✔ Tips

■ The Phone Book widget requires an Internet connection to use.

■ You can also find a yellow pages search feature in Sherlock, which I discuss in **Chapter 15.**

## To use the Phone Book widget

1. Open the Phone Book widget (**Figure 43**).

2. Enter a business name in the edit box.

   *or*

   Choose a category from the drop-down list (**Figure 44**).

   When you press Return, the Phone Book widget searches for matching businesses and displays results in an expanded window (**Figure 45**).

3. To fine-tune search options, click the i button in the lower-right corner of the widget (**Figure 46**) to flip the widget over (**Figure 47**). Then set options with the text box and pop-up menus and click Done.

**Figure 43** The Phone Book widget starts out like this.

**Figure 44** You can choose a category from the drop-down list.

*Click to add the entry to your Address Book*   *Click to enlarge the phone number display*

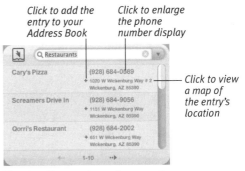

*Click to view a map of the entry's location*

**Figure 45** The search results appear in an expanded widget window. (If you're ever in Wickenburg, be sure to stop by Screamers for the best burger in town.)

**Figure 46** Click the i button in the widget's corner.

**Figure 47** Set options in the flip side window.

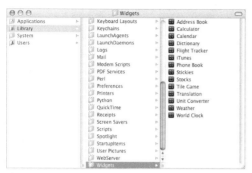

**Figure 48** You can find widgets installed in the Widgets folder inside the Library folder on your hard disk.

# Installing & Uninstalling Widgets

You can customize Dashboard by adding or removing widgets.

Additional widgets are available on Apple's Dashboard Web site, http://dashboard.apple.com. You may also be able to find widgets on shareware distribution Web sites and on Web sites for third-party vendors.

In many instances, the widget will come with its own installer, so all you have to do to install it is open the installer file. If the widget did not come with an installer, you can install it by dragging its widget file—which may display the *.wdgt* file extension— file into the Widgets folder in the Library folder on your hard disk (**Figure 48**). You should then be able to find the newly installed widget on the Widget Bar.

Uninstalling a widget is also simple. Just drag the widget out of the Widgets folder (**Figure 48**). The widget should not appear on the Widget Bar the next time you display it.

INSTALLING & UNINSTALLING WIDGETS

# Fonts

## Fonts & Font Formats

Fonts are typefaces that appear on screen and in printed documents. When they're properly installed, they appear on all Font menus and in font lists.

Mac OS X supports several types of fonts:

- ◆ **Data fork suitcase format** (.dfont) stores all information in the data fork of the file, including resources used by Mac OS drawing routines.

- ◆ **Microsoft Windows font formats** are Windows format font files. These include TrueType fonts (.ttf), TrueType collections (.ttc), and OpenType fonts (.otf).

- ◆ **PostScript fonts in Mac OS or Windows format** are used primarily for printing. These fonts must be accompanied by corresponding bitmapped font files.

- ◆ **Mac OS 9.x and earlier font formats** include Mac OS TrueType fonts and bitmapped fonts.

## ✔ Tips

- ■ Traditionally, Mac OS files could contain two parts, or *forks*: a *resource fork* and a *data fork*. This causes incompatibility problems with non-Mac OS systems, which do not support a file's resource fork. Data fork suitcase format fonts don't have resource forks, so they can work on a variety of computer platforms.

- ■ OpenType font technology was developed by Adobe Systems, Inc., and Microsoft Corporation. Designed to be cross-platform, the same font files work on both Mac OS and Windows computers.

- ■ PostScript font technology was developed by Adobe Systems, Inc.

# Font Locations

On a typical Mac OS X system, fonts can be installed in four or more places (**Table 1**). Where a font is installed determines who can use it.

◆ **User fonts** are installed in a user's Fonts folder (**Figure 1**). Each user can install, control, and access his or her own fonts. Fonts installed in a user's Fonts folder are available only to that user.

◆ **Local fonts** are installed in the Fonts folder for the startup disk (**Figure 2**). These fonts are accessible to all local users of the computer. Only an Admin user can modify the contents of this Fonts folder.

◆ **System fonts** are installed in the Fonts folder for the system (**Figure 3**). These fonts are installed by the Mac OS X installer and are used by the system. The contents of this Fonts folder should not be modified.

◆ **Classic fonts** are installed in the Fonts folder within the Mac OS 9.x System Folder (if Mac OS 9.x is installed). These are the only fonts accessible by the Classic environment, although Mac OS X can use these fonts, even when the Classic environment is not running.

◆ **Network fonts** are installed in the Fonts folder for the network. These fonts are accessible to all local area network users. This feature is normally used on network file servers, not the average user's computer. Only a network administrator can modify the contents of this Fonts folder.

**Table 1**

| Font Installation Locations | |
| --- | --- |
| **Font Use** | **Font Folder** |
| User | HD/Users/UserName/Library/Fonts/ |
| Local | HD/Library/Fonts/ |
| System | HD/System/Library/Fonts/ |
| Classic | HD/System Folder/Fonts |
| Network | Network/Library/Fonts/ |

**Figure 1** User fonts are installed in the Fonts folder within the user's Library folder.

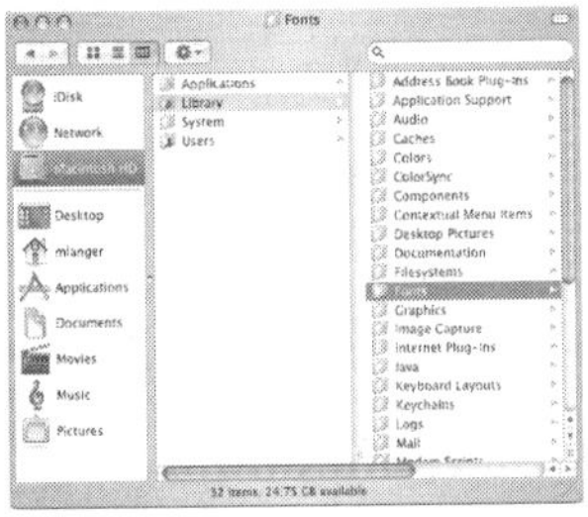

**Figure 2** Local fonts are installed in the Fonts folder within the startup disk's Library folder.

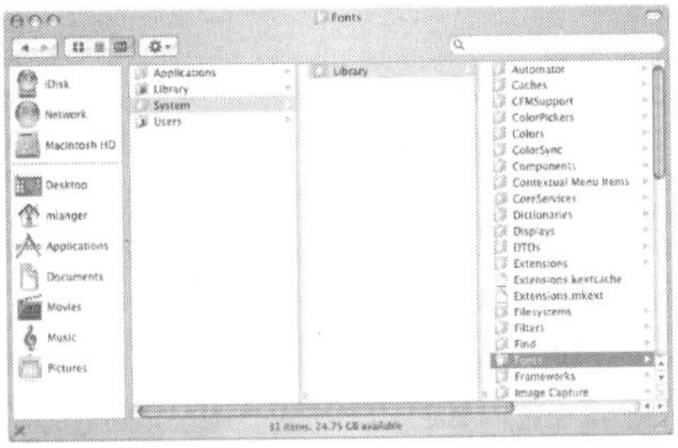

**Figure 3** System fonts are installed in the Fonts folder within the System's Library folder.

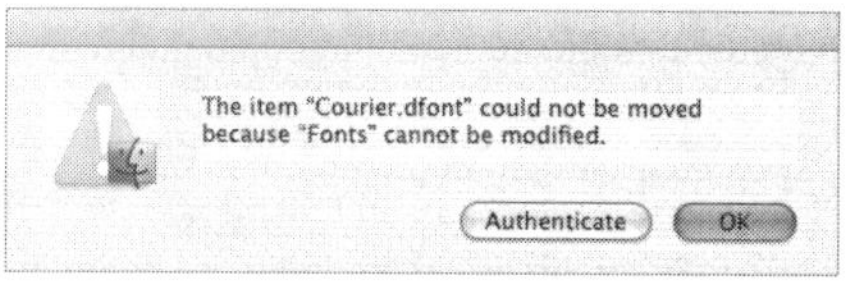

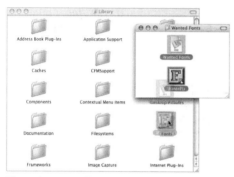

**Figure 4** A dialog like this appears if you try to change a Fonts folder and do not have enough privileges.

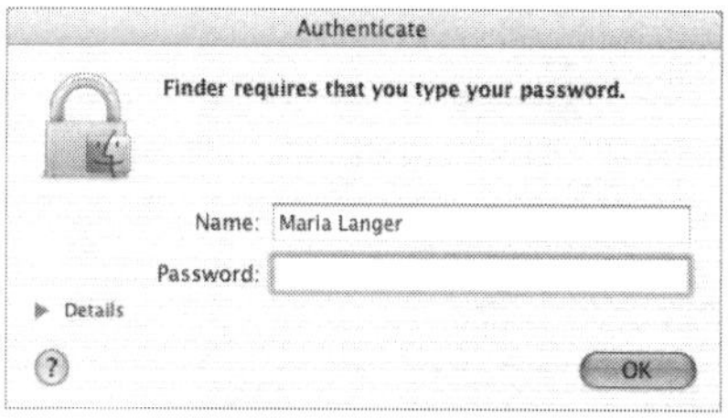

**Figure 5** If you have an Admin password, you can enter it in this dialog to complete the change.

**Figure 6** To manually install a font, drag it into (or onto) the appropriate Fonts folder. This illustration shows a PostScript font file with its accompanying bitmap font file being installed.

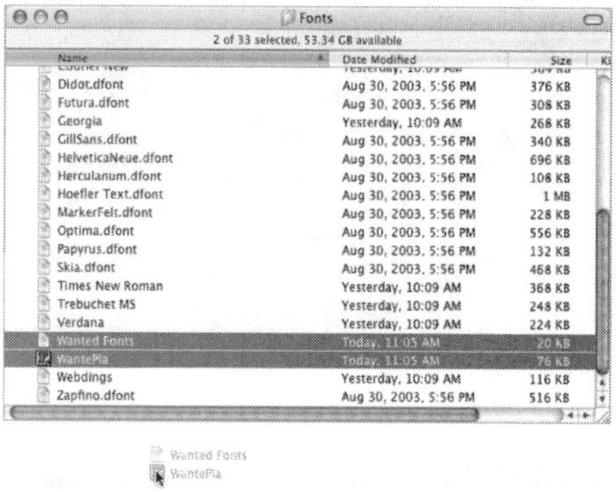

**Figure 7** To manually uninstall a font, drag it out of the Fonts folder. This illustration shows the font installed in **Figure 6** being uninstalled.

## ✔ Tips

- Duplicate fonts are resolved based on where they are installed, in the following order: User, Local, Network, System, and Classic. For example, if the same font existed as both a User and System font, the User font would be used.

- Changes to the Fonts folder take effect when an application is opened.

- If you do not have the correct privileges to change a Fonts folder, a dialog like the one in **Figure 4** will appear. If you have an Admin password, you can click the Authenticate button and enter the password in the dialog that appears (**Figure 5**) to complete the change. Otherwise, click OK and ask a user with Admin privileges to do it for you.

- I cover Mac OS 9.x and the Classic environment in **Chapter 18**.

- You can use Font Book to easily install or uninstall a font. I tell you about Font Book starting on the next page.

## To manually install a font

Drag all files that are part of the font into the appropriate Fonts folder (**Figure 6**).

## To manually uninstall a font

Drag all files that are part of the font out of the Fonts folder they were installed in (**Figure 7**).

# Font Book

Font Book is a Mac OS X utility that enables you to install, preview, search, activate, and deactivate fonts with an easy-to-use interface.

Font Book organizes all of your fonts into *libraries* and *collections*. Libraries, which appear above the split line in the Collection column, are groups of fonts organized by where they are installed. Collections, which appear below the split line, are groups of fonts organized to meet your needs. Font Book comes preconfigured with several libraries and collections, but you can add, remove, or modify others as desired.

Within each library or collection is one or more fonts, each of which may contain one or more typefaces. Each typeface is a slightly different version of the font—for example, bold, italic, or condensed.

Font Book makes it possible to turn fonts on or off. This helps keep your applications' font menus and lists neat by letting you display only those fonts that you want to display.

## ✔ Tips

- Font Book is integrated with the Font panel, which I discuss later in this chapter.

- With Font Book, you can create libraries of fonts insalled other than as discussed in the section titled "Font Locations" earlier in this chapter. This new feature offers more flexibility for managing fonts.

## To launch Font Book

Use one of the following techniques:

- ◆ Double-click the Font Book icon in the Applications folder (**Figure 8**).

- ◆ Choose Manage Fonts from the shortcut menu in the Font Panel (**Figure 44**).

Font Book's main window appears (**Figure 9**).

**Figure 8** You can find Font Book in the Applications folder.

**Figure 9** The main Font Book window lists libraries, collections, and fonts and displays a font preview.

**Figure 10** A folder containing the font files for a PostScript font, all ready to install.

## ✔ Tip

- Another way to launch Font Book is to double-click a font file's icon. Doing so displays a font preview window like the one in **Figure 11**.

**Figure 11**
Double-clicking a font file launches Font Book and opens a font preview window like this.

**Figure 12** The font is installed and appears in the main Font Book window.

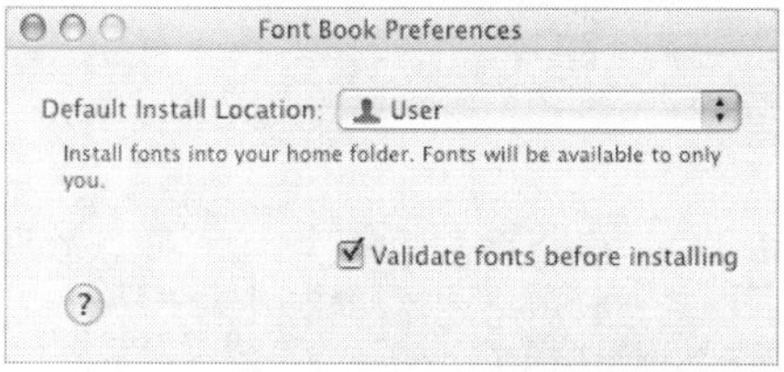

**Figure 13** The Preferences window enables you to specify a default location for installing font files.

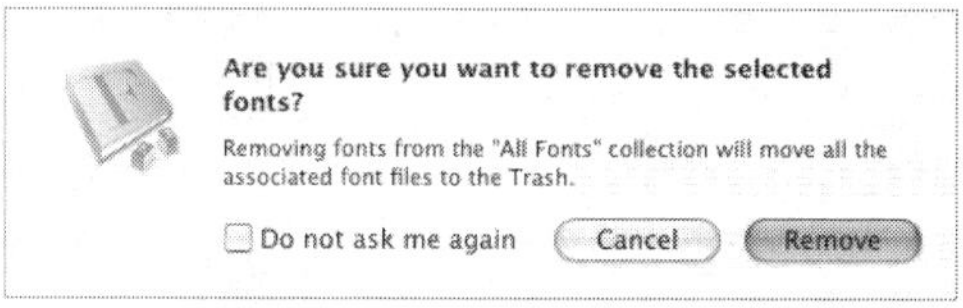

**Figure 14** A confirmation dialog like this one appears when you attempt to uninstall a font.

## To install a font

1. Insert the disc containing the font files you want to install or copy the font files to your hard disk.

2. Launch Font Book.

3. Double-click one of the Font files (**Figure 10**). A font window like the one in **Figure 11** appears.

4. Click the Install Font button.

   The font files are copied or moved to the Fonts folder inside the Library folder for your account, thus making it available to you only. The name of the Font appears selected in the main Font Book window (**Figure 12**).

## ✔ Tips

- You can change the default location for newly installed fonts. Choose Font Book > Preferences to display the Preferences window (**Figure 13**). Choose a library name from the Default Install Location pop-up menu and close the window to save your settings.

- You can also install a font by dragging the font's file icon(s) onto a collection name in the main Font Book window.

## To uninstall a font

1. Select the name of the font in the Font column of the main Font Book window (**Figure 11**).

2. Press (Delete).

3. A dialog sheet like the one in **Figure 14** appears. Click Remove.

   The font's files are moved to the Trash. Emptying the Trash removes them from your computer.

## To view fonts by library

In the Collections column of the Main Font Book window, select the name of the library you want to view.

The fonts in that library appear in the Font column (**Figure 15**).

## ✔ Tips

- There are two default libraries: User and Computer. I explain how to add a library later in this section.

- The User library is only enabled after at least one font has been installed in it.

- A font's library determines where the font is installed and how it can be accessed, as discussed near the beginning of this chapter.

- You can copy a font from one location to another by dragging it from the Font list to the name of another library. For example, to make a user font available to all users, select User in the Collection list and drag the font from the Font list to Computer in the Collection list (**Figure 16**).

## To view fonts by collection

In the Collection column of the main Font Book window, select the name of the collection you want to view.

The fonts in that collection appear in the Font column (**Figure 17**).

**Figure 15**
When you select a font location, the Font list displays all of the fonts installed in that location.

**Figure 16**
You can move a font from one location to another by dragging it within the Font Book window.

**Figure 17**
To see the fonts in a collection, select the name of the collection in the Collection list.

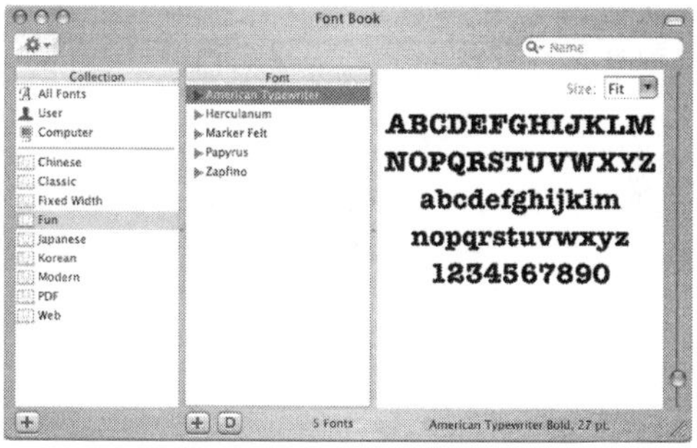

**Figure 18** Select the name of a font to view the typeface characters of that font.

**Figure 19** Select the name of a typeface to view that typeface's characters.

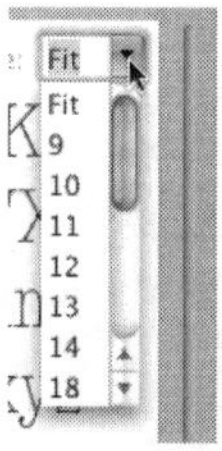

**Figure 20**
You can choose a font size from the Size drop-down list.

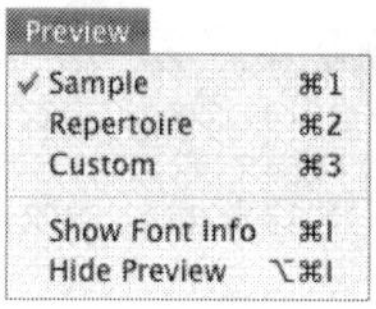

**Figure 21**
The Preview menu enables you to set preview area options.

## To preview font or typeface characters

1. In the Collection list of the main Font Book window, select All Fonts or the name of the collection that the font is part of (**Figure 17**).

2. In the Font list, select the name of the font you want to preview. The characters for the regular typeface of the font appear on the right side of the window (**Figure 18**).

3. To see a specific typeface for the font, click the triangle to the left of the font name to display all typefaces. Then click the name of the typeface you want to see. Its characters appear on the right side of the window (**Figure 19**).

## ✔ Tips

- To change the size of characters in the preview part of the window, enter a value in the Size box, choose a value from the Size drop-down list (**Figure 20**), or drag the slider on the far right side of the window.

- To change the text that appears in the preview part of the window, choose one of the first 21 options on the Preview menu (**Figure 22**):

  - ▲ **Sample** (⌘1) displays the characters shown throughout this chapter.

  - ▲ **Repertoire** (⌘2) displays all characters in ASCII order.

  - ▲ **Custom** (⌘3) enables you to specify your own sample text.

## To add a library

1. Choose File > New Library (**Figure 22**), or press Option ⌃ ⌘ N. An untitled library appears in the Collection list with its name selected (**Figure 23**).

2. Enter a new name for the collection and press Return (**Figure 24**).

## ✔ Tip

■ As shown in **Figures 23** and **24**, libraries appear above the split line in the Collection list.

## To add fonts to a library

1. In the Collection list, select the library you want to add fonts to (**Figure 24**).

2. Choose File > Add Fonts (**Figure 22**) or press ⌃ ⌘ O.

3. Use the Open dialog that appears (**Figure 25**) to locate and select the folder containing the font(s) you want to add.

4. Click Open.

   Font Book adds the fonts to the library (**Figure 26**).

## ✔ Tips

■ Adding fonts to a library you created does not copy or move the font from the folder you added it from. This makes it possible to use fonts stored in any folder on disk—even folders accessible via network.

■ I tell you more about using the Open dialog in **Chapter 7**.

**Figure 22** Font Book's File menu.

**Figure 23** An untitled library is added to the Collection list.

**Figure 24** Enter a name for the library and press Return.

**Figure 25** Use the Open dialog to locate and select a folder containing the fonts you want to add.

**Figure 26** The fonts in the folder you selected are added to the library.

**Figure 27**
An untitled collection appears in the Collection list with its name selected.

**Figure 28**
When you name the collection, it appears in alphabetical order in the Collection list.

**Figure 29**
Adding a font to a collection is a simple drag-and-drop operation.

## To add a collection

1. Click the Create a new collection (+) button at the bottom of the Collection list in the main Font Book window.

2. A new untitled collection appears with its name selected (**Figure 27**). Enter a name for the collection, and press ⌐Return⌐.

   The collection name appears in the list (**Figure 28**).

## To add a font to a collection

1. In the Collection list, select All Fonts (**Figure 12**) or the name of the library or collection that a font you want to add is part of (**Figure 17**).

2. Locate the font in the Font list.

3. Drag the font from the Font list onto the name of the collection you want to add it to (**Figure 29**). When you release the mouse button, the font is copied to that collection.

## ✔ Tip

- Dragging a font from one collection to another does not duplicate the font's files on your computer. It just adds a reference to the font to the collection.

**WORKING WITH COLLECTIONS**

## To remove a font from a library or collection

1. In the Collection list of the main Font Book window, select the name of the library or collection you want to modify.

2. In the Font list, select the font you want to remove.

3. Press ⌐Delete⌐. A dialog like the one in **Figure 30** or **31** appears. Click Remove.

### ✔ Tip

- Removing a font from a library removes the font from Font Book, thus making it unavailable for use in applications. Removing a font from a collection removes it from that collection but does not remove it from Font Book, so it is still available for use in applications.

## To remove a library or collection

1. In the Collection list, select the library or collection you want to remove (**Figure 24**).

2. Choose File > Delete *"Library Name"*.

3. Click Remove in the confirmation dialog that appears (**Figure 32**).

   The library or collection is removed.

### ✔ Tips

- Removing a library you created or a collection does not delete font files from disk.

- When you remove a library, its fonts are no longer available for use in applications. When you remove a collection, the collection name no longer appears in the Font panel, but the fonts it contains are still available for use in applications.

- You cannot remove the All Fonts, User, or Computer libraries.

**Figure 30** When you remove a font from a library, a confirmation dialog like this one appears.

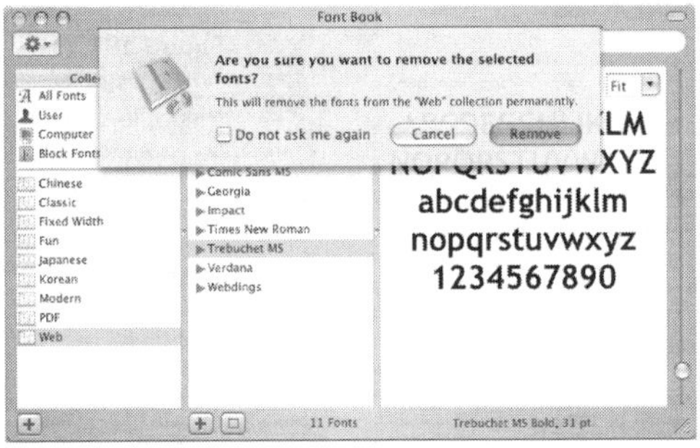

**Figure 31** When you remove a font from a collection, a confirmation dialog like this one appears.

**Figure 32** When you remove a library or collection, a confirmation dialog like this one appears.

REMOVING FONTS, LIBRARIES, & COLLECTIONS

Edit
Undo        ⌘Z
Redo        ⇧⌘Z
Cut         ⌘X
Copy        ⌘C
Paste       ⌘V
Delete      ⌘⌫
Select All  ⌘A
Disable "Comet" family   ⇧⌘D
Disable "Block Fonts"    ⇧⌘E
Resolve Duplicates
Find        ▶
Special Characters...    ⌥⌘T

**Figure 33**
Font Book's
Edit menu.

**Figure 34** The word *Off* appears beside a disabled library and all of its fonts.

*Enable button*

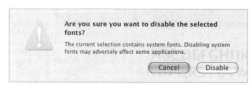

**Figure 35** This dialog appears when you disable a font within a collection.

**Figure 36** As this dialog warns, disabling a system font may adversely affect some applications.

## To disable a library or collection

1. In the Collection list, select the name of the library or collection you want to disable (**Figure 24**).

2. Choose Edit > Disable "*Collection Name*" (**Figure 33**) or press ⇧⌘E.

   The library or collection is disabled and the word *Off* appears beside it in the Collection column (**Figure 34**).

## ✔ Tips

- When you disable a library, you disable all of its fonts (**Figure 34**).

- A disabled collection will not appear in the Font panel.

- If a font appears in only one collection and that collection is disabled, the font is also disabled.

## To disable a font

1. In the Collection list, select the name of the library or collection containing the font you want to disable.

2. In the Font list, select the font you want to disable.

3. Choose Edit > Disable "*Font Name*" Family (**Figure 33**) or press ⇧⌘D.

4. In the confirmation dialog that appears (**Figure 35**), click Disable.

## ✔ Tips

- When you disable a font in a collection, that font will not appear in the Font panel when the collection is selected. When you disable a font in a library, that font is not available for use in any application.

- Font Book displays a dialog like the one in **Figure 36** when you try to disable a font that is used by the System.

## To enable a library or collection

1. In the Collection list, select the name of the disabled library or collection that you want to enable.

2. Choose Edit > Enable "Collection Name" (**Figure 37**).

   The library or collection is enabled.

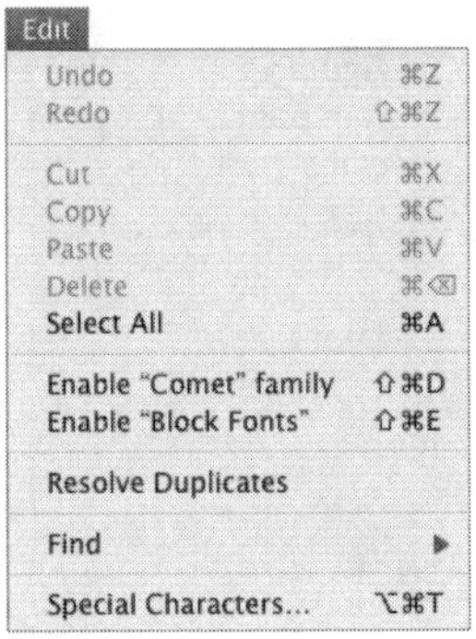

## To enable a font

1. If the font is disabled in a collection, in the Collection list, select the collection the font is part of.

   *or*

   If the font is disabled in a library, in the Collection list, select the library the font is part of.

2. In the Font list, select the font that is disabled.

3. Click the Enable button beneath the Font list (**Figure 34**). The font is enabled.

| Edit | |
| --- | --- |
| Undo | ⌘Z |
| Redo | ⇧⌘Z |
| Cut | ⌘X |
| Copy | ⌘C |
| Paste | ⌘V |
| Delete | ⌘⌫ |
| Select All | ⌘A |
| Enable "Comet" family | ⇧⌘D |
| Enable "Block Fonts" | ⇧⌘E |
| Resolve Duplicates | |
| Find | ▶ |
| Special Characters... | ⌥⌘T |

**Figure 37**
The Edit menu with a disabled library selected.

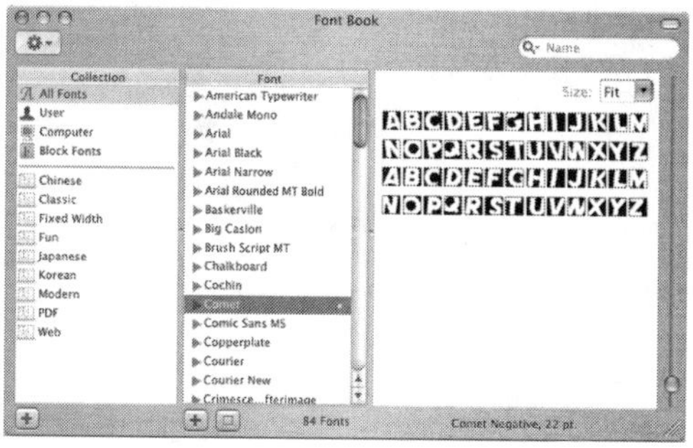

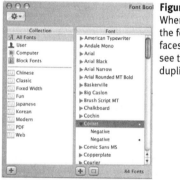

**Figure 38** A bullet beside a font name indicates that the font has a conflict.

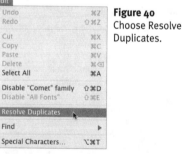

**Figure 39**
When you reveal the font's type-faces, you can see the problem: duplicates.

**Figure 40**
Choose Resolve Duplicates.

**Figure 41**
Font Book resolves the conflict by disabling one of the duplicate typefaces.

# To resolve font conflicts

1. In the Collection list, select All Fonts.

2. Locate and select a font with a bullet character to the right of its name (**Figure 38**).

3. If necessary, click the triangle to the left of the font name to display its typefaces. One or more of them should have bullet characters beside them (**Figure 39**).

4. Choose Edit > Resolve Duplicates (**Figure 40**).

   Font Book disables one of the conflicting typefaces (**Figure 41**).

## ✔ Tips

- Font conflicts like the one in **Figure 39** are often caused when multiple copies of a font or typeface are installed in the same computer but in different places. Disabling one of the copies stops the conflict.

- If you prefer (and have the correct privi-leges), you can delete a duplicate typeface. Follow steps 1 through 3 above, select one of the duplicate typefaces, and press (Delete). Then click Remove in the confir-mation dialog that appears.

- Keep in mind that if multiple users access your computer, disabling or deleting a conflicting font that is installed for the Computer (rather than for the User) may make that font unavailable for other users.

RESOLVING FONT CONFLICTS

# The Font Panel

The Font panel (**Figure 43**), which is fully integrated with Font Book, offers a standard interface for formatting font characters in a document.

In this part of the chapter, I explain how to use the Font panel to format text.

## ✔ Tips

- This chapter looks at the Font panel as it appears in TextEdit, the text editor that comes with Mac OS X. I discuss TextEdit in detail in **Chapter 9**.

- The Font panel is only available in Carbon and Cocoa applications—those written to take advantage of Apple-created libraries of code. That's why you'll find the Font panel in only some applications.

## To open TextEdit's Font panel

With TextEdit active, choose Format > Font > Show Fonts (**Figure 42**) or press ⌘ ⌘ T. The Font panel appears (**Figure 43**).

## ✔ Tips

- The command to open the Font panel in other applications that support it is similar.

- You can open Font Book from within the Font panel by choosing Manage Fonts from the shortcut menu (**Figure 44**).

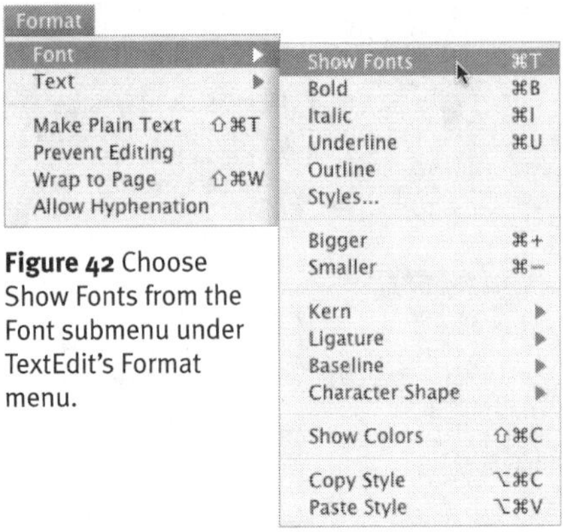

**Figure 42** Choose Show Fonts from the Font submenu under TextEdit's Format menu.

**Figure 43** TextEdit's Font panel.

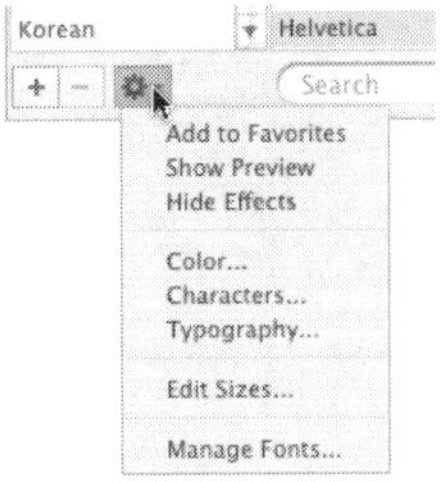

**Figure 44** The Font panel's shortcut menu.

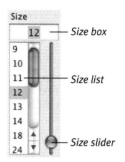

*Size box*

*Size list*

*Size slider*

**Figure 45** The Font panel offers three different ways to set the font size.

## To apply basic font formatting

1. Open the Font panel (**Figure 43**).

2. Select a collection from the Collections list.

3. Select a font family from the Family list.

4. Select a style from the Typeface list.

5. Set the font size by entering a value in the Size box, selecting a size from the Size list, or dragging the Size slider up or down (**Figure 45**).

   The changes you make are applied to selected text or to text typed at the insertion point.

## ✔ Tips

■ The styles that appear in the Typeface list vary depending on the font selected in the Family list. Some font families offer more styles than others.

■ *Oblique* is similar to italic. *Light, regular, medium, bold,* and *black* refer to font weights or boldness.

## To apply font effects

Use the effects controls at the top of the Font Panel window (**Figure 46**) to apply other font formatting options to selected text or start formatting at the insertion point:

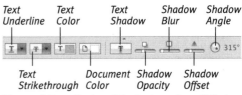

Figure 46 Along the top of the Font panel, you'll find a collection of effects menus, buttons, and controls.

◆ **Text Underline** offers four underline options: None, Single, Double, and Color. If you choose Color, you can use the Colors panel that appears (**Figure 47**) to set the underline color.

◆ **Text Strikethrough** offers four strike-through options: None, Single, Double, and Color. If you choose Color, you can use the Colors panel that appears (**Figure 47**) to set the strikethrough color.

◆ **Text Color** enables you to set the color of text. When you click this button, the Colors panel appears (**Figure 47**) so you can choose a color for text.

◆ **Document Color** enables you to set the color of the document background. When you click this button, the Colors panel appears (**Figure 47**) so you can choose a color for the entire document's background.

◆ **Text Shadow** adds a shadow to text characters (**Figure 48**).

◆ **Shadow Opacity** makes an applied shadow darker or lighter. Drag the slider to the right or left.

◆ **Shadow Blur** makes the shadow sharper or more blurry. Drag the slider to the right or left.

◆ **Shadow Offset** moves the shadow closer to or farther from the text. Drag the slider to the right or left.

◆ **Shadow Angle** changes the position of the shadow in relation to the text. (It's like moving the light source.) Drag the dial around to the desired angle.

Figure 47
The Colors panel enables you to select a color.

# The Shadow Knows...

Figure 48 It's easy to apply a shadow to text characters.

Figure 49
The Colors panel displaying the Color Sliders color model.

**Figure 50**
The Colors panel displaying the Color Palettes color model.

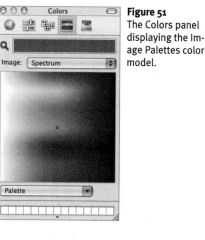

**Figure 51**
The Colors panel displaying the Image Palettes color model.

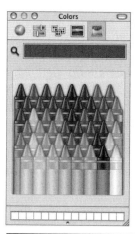

**Figure 52**
The Colors panel displaying my personal favorite color model: Crayons.

# To use the Colors panel

1. Click the icon along the top of the Colors panel to select one of the color models.

2. How you choose a color depends on the model you selected:

   ▲ **Color Wheel (Figure 47)** displays a circle of color. Click inside the circle to choose a color. You can drag the vertical slider up or down to change the brightness.

   ▲ **Color Sliders (Figure 49)** displays several sliders you can use to change color values. Start by selecting a slider group from the pop-up menu, then move the sliders to create a color.

   ▲ **Color Palettes (Figure 50)** displays clickable color samples. Choose a palette from the List pop-up menu, then click the color you want.

   ▲ **Image Palettes (Figure 51)** displays colors from an image. Click a color to select it.

   ▲ **Crayons (Figure 52)** displays different colored crayons. Click a crayon to choose its color.

   The color of the selected item changes immediately.

## ✔ Tip

■ You can use the color wells at the bottom of the Colors panel to store frequently used colors. Simply drag a color into an empty spot. Then, when you open the Colors panel, you can click a stored color to apply it.

USING THE COLORS PANEL

# The Character Palette

The Character Palette (**Figure 53**) enables you to type any character in any language for which a font is installed in your computer, including Asian and eastern European languages. It is especially useful for typing special characters, like mathematical symbols, arrows, and dingbats characters.

The Character Palette is available in some Mac OS X applications, including TextEdit. Once displayed, any character you click is inserted in the current document, at the insertion point.

**Figure 53**
In TextEdit, you can display the Character Palette by choosing Special Characters from the Edit menu.

## ✔ Tips

- Although you can enter foreign language characters into documents on your Macintosh, those characters may not appear properly when your documents are viewed on other computers.

- The Font panel is only available in Carbon and Cocoa applications—those written to take advantage of Apple-created libraries of code. That's why you'll find the Font panel in only some applications.

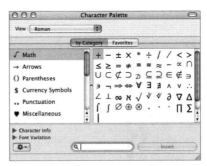

**Figure 54** The Character Palette, which displays characters viewed by category.

## To display the Character Palette

In TextEdit, choose Edit > Special Characters (**Figure 53**). The Character Palette appears (**Figure 54**).

## ✔ Tip

- You can also display the Character Palette by choosing Show Character Palette from the Input menu. I explain how to configure and use the Input menu in my discussion of the International preferences pane in **Chapter 21**.

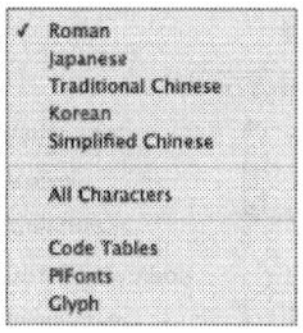

**Figure 55**
Use this pop-up menu to choose the characters to view.

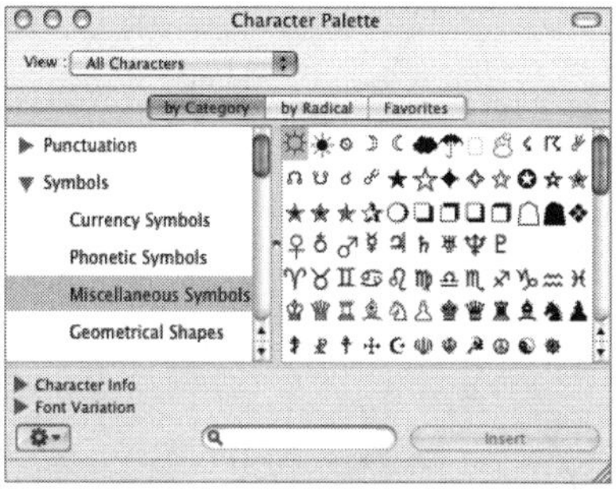

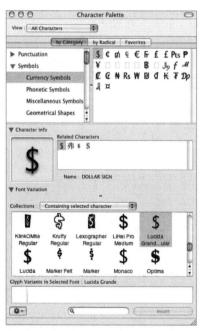

**Figure 56** When you choose an option from the View pop-up menu, the options in the Character Palette change.

**Figure 57** The Character Palette expanded to show Character Info and Font Variation.

## To insert a character with the Character Palette

1. In a document window, position the insertion point where you want the character to appear.

2. Display the Character Palette (**Figure 54**).

3. Choose a character group from the View pop-up menu (**Figure 55**). The window may change to offer different options (**Figure 56**).

4. Click a button above the scrolling lists to view characters in a specific order.

5. Select one of the options in the left scrolling list.

6. Select one of the characters in the right scrolling list.

7. Click Insert. The character is inserted at the insertion point in your document.

## ✔ Tips

- To display information about the selected character, click the triangle beside Character Info to reveal it (**Figure 57**).

- To specify a font for the character, click the triangle beside Font Variation to display the character in multiple fonts. You can then click the character in the font you want.

# Printing & Faxing

## Printing & Faxing

On a Mac OS system, printing and faxing is handled by the operating system rather than individual applications. You choose the Print command in the application that created the document you want to print. Mac OS steps in, displaying the Print dialog and telling the application how to send information to the printer or fax modem. There are two main benefits to this:

◆ If you can print documents created with one application, you can probably print documents created with any application.

◆ The Page Setup and Print dialogs look very much the same in every application.

This chapter covers most aspects of printing and faxing documents on a computer running Mac OS X.

## To print (an overview)

1. Add your printer to the Printer List.

2. Open the document that you want to print.

3. If desired, set options in the Page Setup dialog, and click OK.

4. Set options in the Print dialog, and click Print or Fax.

# Printer Drivers

A *printer driver* is software that Mac OS uses to communicate with a specific kind of printer. It contains information about the printer and instructions for using it. You can't open and read a printer driver, but your computer can.

There are basically two kinds of printers:

◆ A **PostScript** printer uses PostScript technology developed by Adobe Systems. Inside the printer is a *PostScript interpreter*, which can process PostScript language commands to print high-quality text and graphics. Examples of PostScript printers include most laser printers.

◆ A **non-PostScript** printer relies on the computer to send it all of the instructions it needs for printing text and graphics. It cannot process PostScript commands. Examples of non-PostScript printers include most inkjet or photo printers. Non-PostScript printers are generally more common for home and small business use, primarily because they are less expensive than PostScript printers. Their print quality is quite acceptable for most purposes.

A standard installation of Mac OS X installs many commonly used printer drivers. When you buy a printer, it should come with a CD that includes its printer driver software; if your computer does not recognize your printer, you'll need to install this software to use it.

## ✔ Tips

■ If you do not have a printer driver for your printer, you may not be able to print.

■ To install a printer driver, follow the instructions that came with its installer or installation disc.

■ If you need to install printer driver software for your printer, make sure it is Mac OS X compatible. If your printer did not come with Mac OS X compatible printer software, you may be able to get it from the printer manufacturer's Web site.

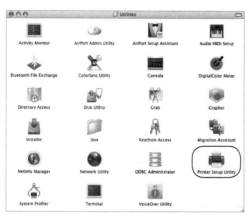

**Figure 1** Printer Setup Utility can be found in the Utilities folder inside the Applications folder.

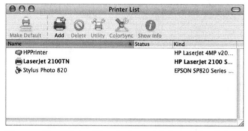

**Figure 2** The Printer List window with three printers.

# Printer Setup Utility

Printer Setup Utility (**Figure 1**) is an application that enables you to manage printers. With it, you can:

◆ Add printers and fax modems to the Printer List (**Figure 2**) that your computer consults when printing or faxing.

◆ Configure printers for printing.

◆ Create desktop printers for drag-and-drop printing.

◆ Create printer pools so your print jobs go to whatever networked printer is available when you're ready to print.

This part of the chapter looks at how you can use Printer Setup Utility to manage printers accessible to your computer.

## ✔ Tips

■ Mac OS X 10.4 is smart. If a USB printer is connected to your computer and turned on, Mac OS X automatically adds the printer to the printer list. No need to manually configure it!

■ You only have to add a printer if it does not already appear in the Printer List window (**Figure 2**). This needs to be done only once; Mac OS will remember all printers that you add.

PRINTER SETUP UTILITY

## To open Printer Setup Utility

1. Open the Utilities folder inside your Applications folder.

2. Double-click the Printer Setup Utility icon (**Figure 1**).

The Printer List window (**Figure 2**) should appear automatically. If it does not, follow the instructions on the next page to display it.

## ✔ Tips

- You can also open Printer Setup Utility by choosing Add Printer from the Printer pop-up menu (**Figure 37**) in the Print dialog.

- The first time you open Printer Setup Utility, it may display a dialog telling you that no printers are available (**Figure 3**). To add a printer, click the Add button and follow steps 2 and 3 in the section titled "To add a printer," beginning on the next page.

## To display the Printer List window

Choose View > Show Printer List (**Figure 4**), or press ⌘L.

The Printer List window appears (**Figure 2**).

## To add a printer listed in the Printer Browser

1. Choose Printers > Add Printer (**Figure 5**) or click the Add button in the Printer List window (**Figure 2**).

   The Printer Browser window appears (**Figure 6**). It lists all of the printers your computer "sees," by direct or network connection.

2. Select the name of the printer you want to add and click Add. The printer is added to the Printer List window (**Figure 2**).

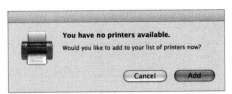

**Figure 3** This dialog appears when you open Printer Setup Utility and no printers have been added to the Printer List.

**Figure 4**
Use the View menu to show the Printer or Fax list.

**Figure 5**
The Printers menu includes commands for working with the Printer List and printers.

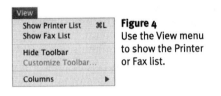

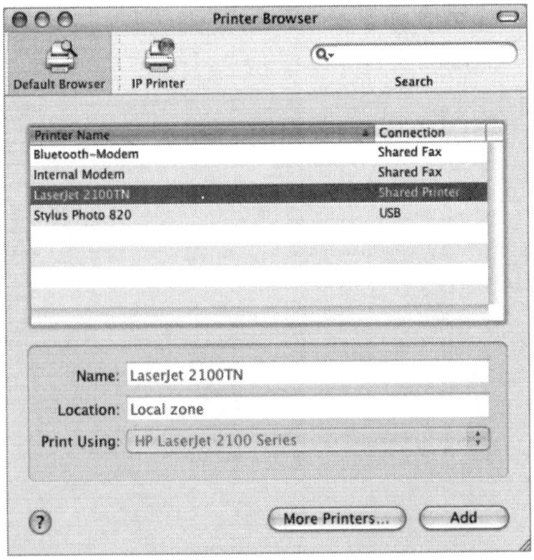

**Figure 6** The Printer Browser window lists all printers and fax modems your computer "sees."

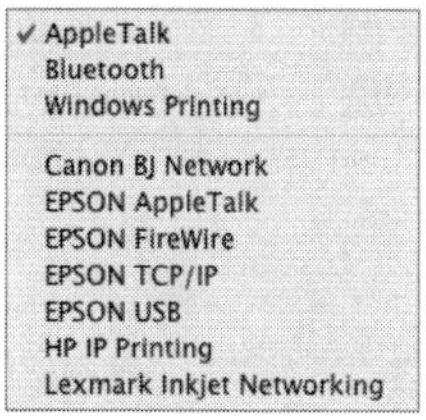

**Figure 7**
Use this pop-up menu to choose the type of printer connection.

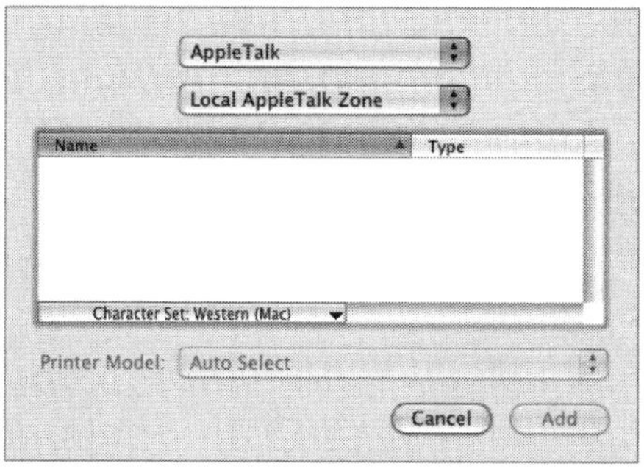

**Figure 8** Options for adding an AppleTalk printer,...

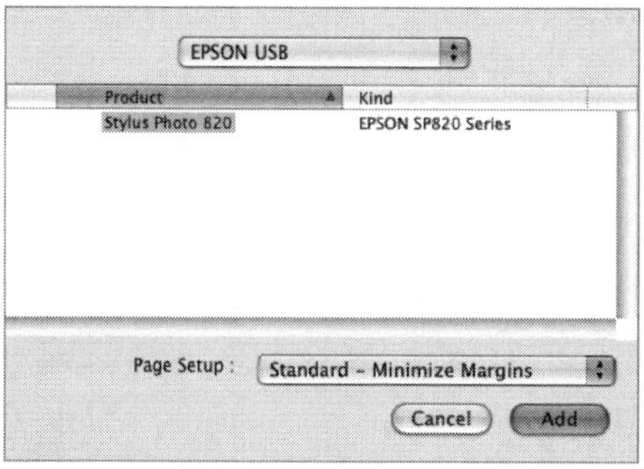

**Figure 9** ...an Epson USB printer,...

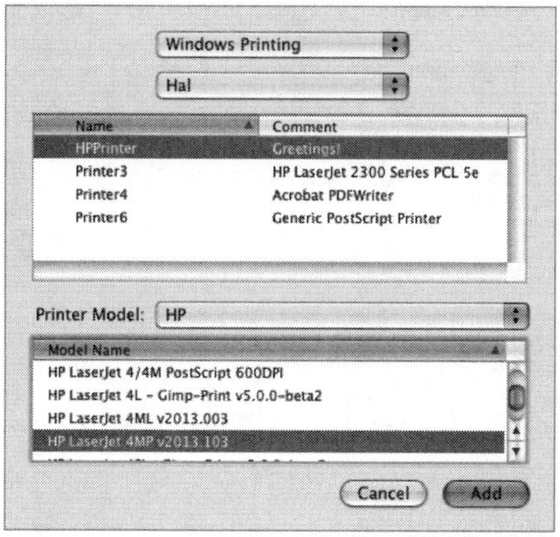

**Figure 10** ...and a printer connected to a Windows computer.

# To add a printer not listed in the Printer Browser

1. Choose Printers > Add Printer (**Figure 4**) or click the Add button in the Printer List window (**Figure 2**).

   The Printer Browser window appears (**Figure 6**).

2. Click the More Printers button.

3. A dialog sheet appears. Choose an option from the top pop-up menu (**Figure 7**) to indicate the type of printer connection. The dialog sheet changes to offer appropriate options; **Figures 8** through **10** show examples.

4. If you chose AppleTalk (**Figure 8**) or Epson AppleTalk, choose a network option from the second pop-up menu. Then wait while Printer Setup Utility looks for printers and displays a list of what it finds. Select the printer you want to add, and click Add.

   *or*

   If you chose Bluetooth, Canon BJ Network, Epson FireWire, Epson USB (**Figure 9**), or Lexmark Inket Network, Printer Setup Utility displays a list of printers it finds based on installed printer drivers. Select the printer you want to add, set other options if required, and click Add.

   *or*

   If you chose Windows Printing, choose a network option from the second pop-up menu, select a workgroup from the list, and click Choose. Select a computer in the workgroup, and click Choose again. Then log in to the computer, choose a printer in the list (**Figure 10**), and click Add.

*Continued on next page...*

**ADDING PRINTERS**

#### Chapter 12

*Continued from previous page.*

*or*

If you chose Epson TCP/IP, enter an IP address for the printer and click Verify. Then select the printer in the list and click Add.

*or*

If you chose HP IP Printing you can use two different techniques to add the printer:

▲ Click the Auto button, then click Discover, select a printer in the list, and click Add.

▲ Click the Manual button (**Figure 11**), enter the IP address for the printer, click Connect, and click Add.

The printer appears in the Printer List window (**Figure 2**).

## ✔ Tips

■ In step 4, if you're not sure what options to select or enter for a network printer, ask your network administrator.

■ If your printer is properly connected but it does not appear in step 4, you may have to install printer driver software for it. Printer drivers are discussed earlier in this chapter.

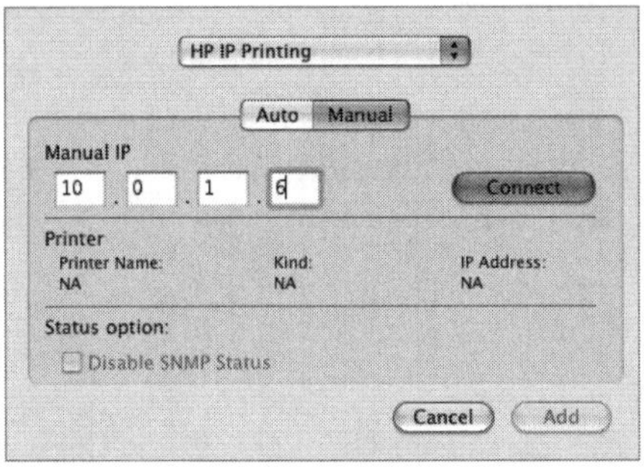

**Figure 11** The HP IP Printing option enables you to enter an IP address for the HP printer you want to add.

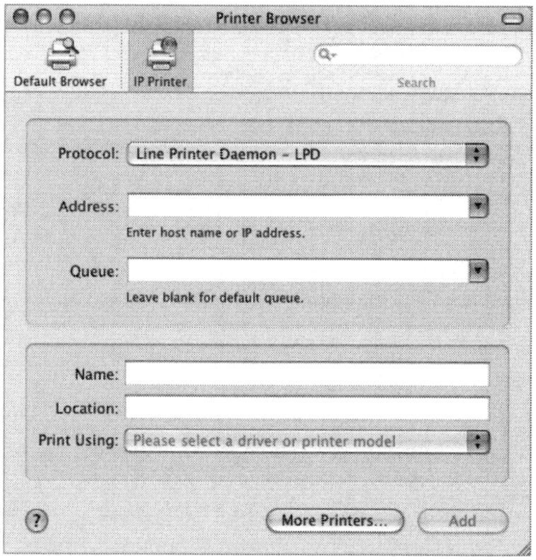

**Figure 12** The options for adding an IP Printer.

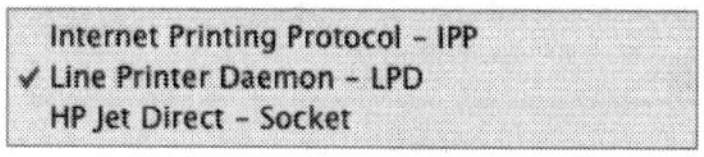

**Figure 13** The Protocol pop-up menu.

## To add an IP Printer

1. Choose Printers > Add Printer (**Figure 5**) or click the Add button in the Printer List window (**Figure 2**).

   The Printer Browser window appears (**Figure 6**).

2. Click the IP Printer button in the toolbar. The window changes to offer IP Printer options (**Figure 12**).

3. Set options in the dialog for the printer:

   ▲ **Protocol** (**Figure 13**) is the printer's connection protocol.

   ▲ **Address** is the IP address of the printer.

   ▲ **Queue** is the name of the print queue. This is an optional field.

   ▲ **Name** is the name of the printer.

   ▲ **Location** is the printer's location.

   ▲ **Print Using** enables you to select a printer driver for the printer so you can access printer-specific options.

4. Click Add. The printer is added to the Printer List window (**Figure 2**).

## ✔ Tip

■ In step 3, if you're not sure what options to select or enter for a network printer, ask your network administrator.

**ADDING PRINTERS**

## To delete a printer

1. In the Printer List window, select the printer you want to delete (**Figure 14**).

2. Click the Delete button in the Printer List window (**Figure 14**), choose Printers > Delete Selected Printers (**Figure 5**), or press ⌃ ⌘ Delete.

   The printer is removed from the list.

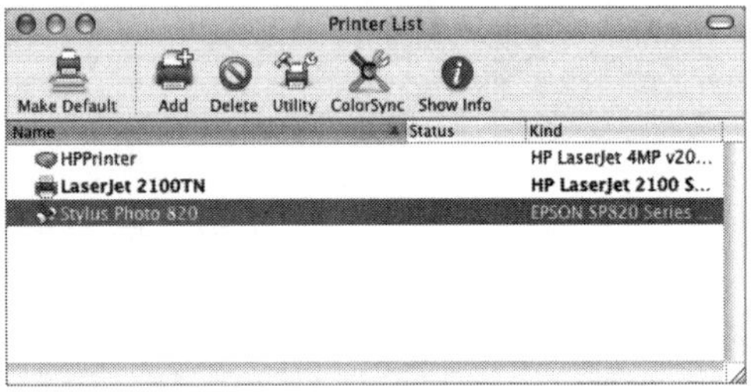

## To set the default printer

1. In the Printer list window, select the printer you want to set as the default (**Figure 14**).

2. Click the Make Default button in the Printer List window (**Figure 14**), choose Printers > Make Default (**Figure 5**), or press ⌃ ⌘ D.

   The name of the printer you selected becomes bold, indicating that it is the default printer.

## ✔ Tip

■ The default printer is the one that is automatically chosen when you open the Print dialog.

**Figure 14** Select the printer you want to work with.

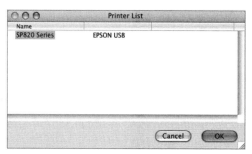

**Figure 15** If a list of printers appears, select the one you want to configure, and click OK.

![EPSON Printer Utility window]

SP820 Series (EPSON USB)

**EPSON StatusMonitor**
Use this utility to automatically check for errors and also check the level of ink remaining.

**Nozzle Check**
Use this utility if gaps or faint areas appear in your printout.

**Head Cleaning**
Use this utility if your print quality declines or the Nozzle Check indicates clogged nozzles.

**Print Head Alignment**
Use this utility if misaligned vertical lines appear in your printout.

**Figure 16** Here are the configuration options for an Epson Stylus Photo 820 printer. Configuration options for other printers will be different.

## To configure a printer

1. Select the printer you want to configure in the Printer List window (**Figure 14**).

2. Click the Utility button in the Printer List window (**Figure 14**) or choose Printers > Configure Printer (**Figure 5**).

   Printer Setup Utility launches the configuration software for your printer. In my case, it launches Epson Printer Utility.

3. If a list of printers appears (**Figure 15**), select the printer you want to configure, and click OK.

4. Follow the instructions that appear in the configuration window to configure or maintain your printer. **Figure 16** shows an example of the options available for an Epson Stylus Photo 820 printer in the Epson Printer Utility window.

5. When you are finished configuring the printer, close the configuration window.

## ✔ Tips

■ In step 2, if the Configure Printer command or Utility button in the Printer List window is gray or faded (**Figure 2**), the printer cannot be configured through Printer Setup Utility.

■ It's not possible to show all configuration options for all printers. The instructions and illustrations here should be enough to get you started with your printer. Consult the manual that came with your printer for more information.

**CONFIGURING PRINTERS**

## To view & change printer info

1. In the Printer List window, select the printer you want to view or change information for (**Figure 14**).

2. Choose Printers > Show Info (**Figure 5**), press ⌘⎵ⓘ, or click the Show Info button in the Printer List window (**Figure 14**). The Printer Info window for the printer appears (**Figure 17**).

3. Choose an option from the pop-up menu at the top of the dialog to view and set different options:

   ▲ **Name & Location** (**Figure 17**) enables you to view or change the name and location of the printer.

   ▲ **Printer Model** (**Figure 18**) enables you to set the brand and model for the printer.

   ▲ **Installable Options** (**Figure 19**) enables you to set preferences for options specific to your printer.

4. Click Apply Changes to save any changes you made.

5. Click the Printer Info window's close box to dismiss it.

## ✔ Tips

- ■ You can only change options for printers that are directly connected to your computer—not printers you access via printer sharing.

- ■ The options that appear in the Installable Options window (**Figure 19**) will vary from one printer to another.

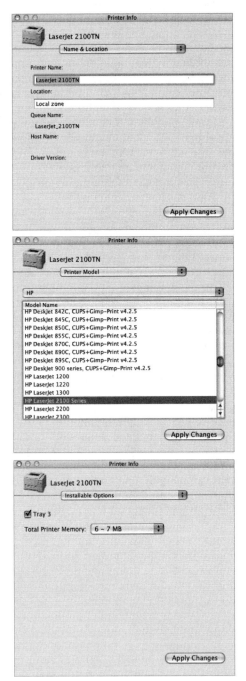

**Figures 17, 18, & 19** The three panes of the Printer Info window: Name & Location (top), Printer Model (middle), and Installable Options (bottom).

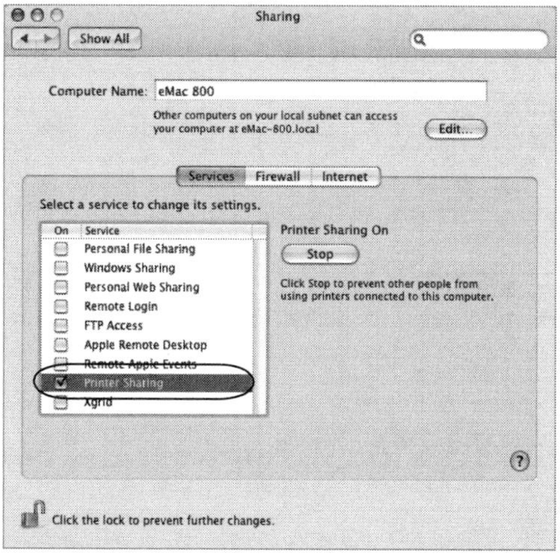

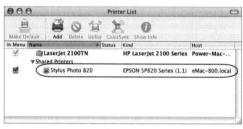

**Figure 20** Turn on the Printer Sharing check box in the Sharing preferences pane.

**Figure 21** Your printers appear in the Printer List on Mac OS X 10.3 computers...

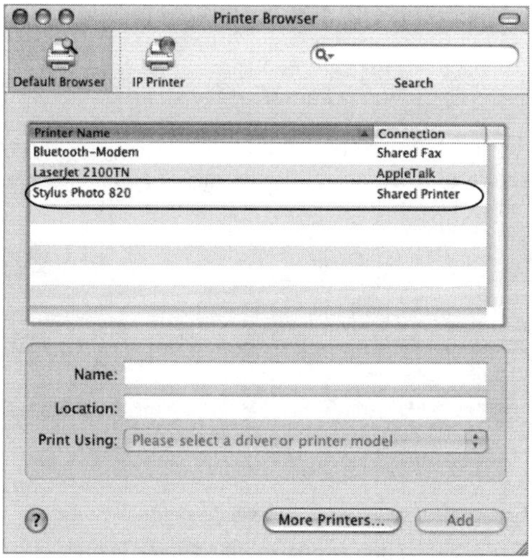

**Figure 22** ...and in the Printer Browser on Mac OS X 10.4 computers connected via network.

# To share a printer with other network users

1. Choose Apple > System Preferences, or click the System Preferences icon in the Dock.

2. In the System Preferences window that appears, click the Sharing icon.

3. If necessary, click the Services button to display its options (**Figure 20**).

4. Turn on the check box beside Printer Sharing in the Service list.

5. To share your printers with Windows users, turn on the Windows Sharing check box.

6. Choose System Preferences > Quit System Preferences or press ⌘Q to save your settings and dismiss System Preferences.

   The names of your shared printers appear in the Printers List in Printer Setup Utility for other computers on the network (**Figures 21** and **22**) and in the Printer pop-up menu in the Print dialog (**Figure 37**).

## ✔ Tip

- I tell you more about networking and the Sharing preferences pane in **Chapter 16**.

## To create a printer pool

1. In the Printer List window, select the printers you want to include in the printer pool (**Figure 23**). To select more than one printer at a time, hold down ⌘ ⌘ while clicking the name of each one.

2. Choose Printers > Pool Printers (**Figure 5**). A dialog sheet like the one in **Figure 24** appears.

3. Enter a name for the printer pool in the Printer Pool Name box.

4. To change the preferred printer order, drag the name of printer you want to use most often to the top of the list (**Figure 25**). When you release the mouse button, it moves into position (**Figure 26**).

5. Click the Create button.

   The name of the printer pool you created appears in the Printer List window (**Figure 27**) and in the Printer pop-up menu in Print dialogs (**Figure 37**).

## ✔ Tips

- The printer pool feature is brand new in Mac OS X 10.4.

- When you print to a printer pool, your computer automatically looks at each printer in the pool, in the order they are listed, and prints to the first one available.

**Figure 23** Select the printers you want to include in the pool.

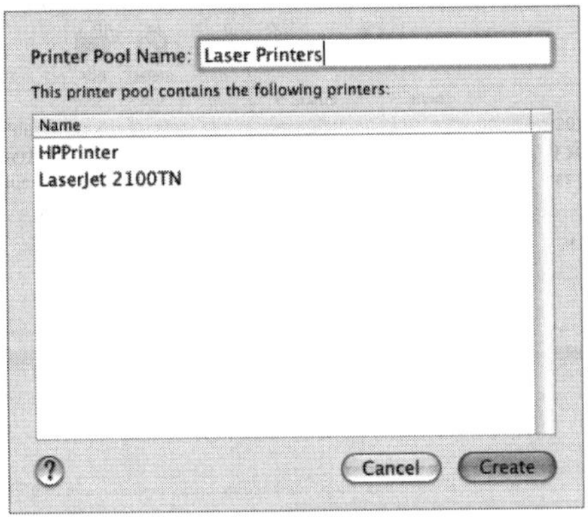

**Figure 24** Use this dialog to set options for the printer pool.

**Figure 25** Drag a printer to a new position in the list.

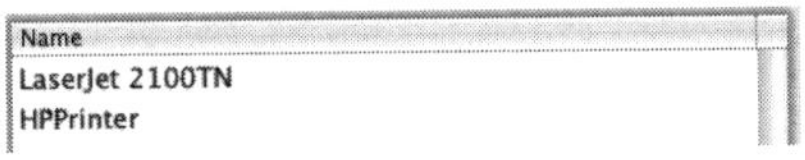

**Figure 26** When you release the mouse button, the printer moves.

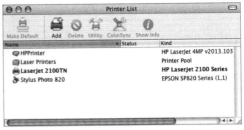

**Figure 27** The printer pool is added to the Printer List window.

**CREATING PRINTER POOLS**

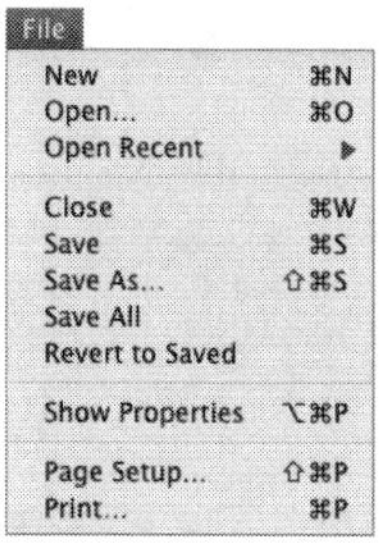

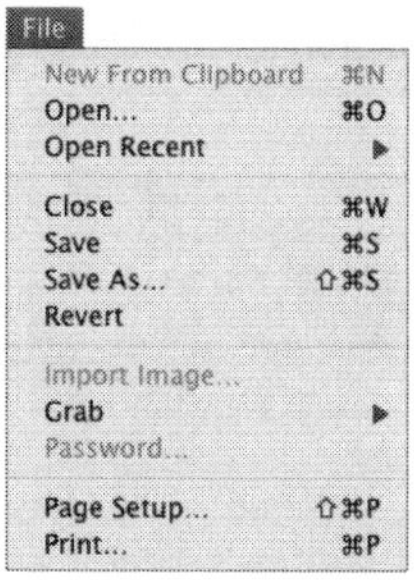

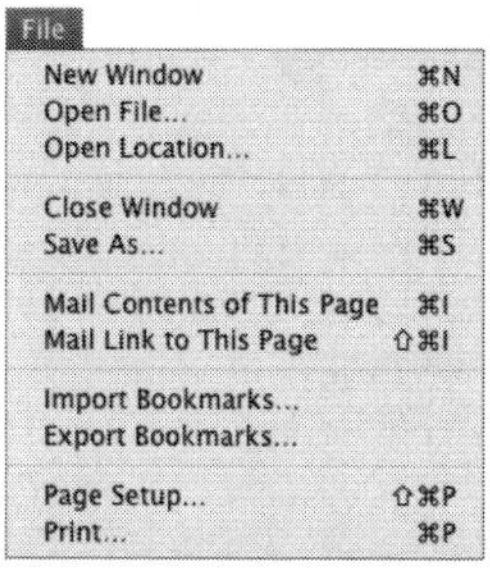

## The Page Setup Dialog

The Page Setup dialog (**Figure 29**) lets you set page options prior to printing, including the printer the document should be formatted for, paper size, orientation, and scale.

### To open the Page Setup dialog

Choose File > Page Setup (**Figures 28a, 28b, and 28c**). The Page Attributes options of the Page Setup dialog appears (**Figure 29**).

### To set Page Attributes

1. If necessary, choose Page Attributes from the Settings pop-up menu in the Page Setup dialog to display Page Attributes options (**Figure 29**).

2. Set options as desired:
   - ▲ To format the document for a specific printer, choose the printer from the Format for pop-up menu (**Figure 30**).
   - ▲ To change the paper size, choose an option from the Paper Size pop-up menu (**Figure 31**).
   - ▲ To change the page orientation, click the Orientation option you want.
   - ▲ To change the print scale, enter a scaling percentage in the Scale box.

3. Click OK to save your settings and dismiss the Page Setup dialog.

### ✔ Tips

■ The Format for pop-up menu (**Figure 30**) should list all of the printers that appear in Printer Setup Utility's Printer List window (**Figure 2**).

■ Options in step 2 vary depending on the printer selected from the Format for pop-up menu (**Figure 30**). Additional options may be available for your printer; check your printer's documentation for details.

**Figures 28a, 28b, & 28c**
The Page Setup and Print commands appear on most File menus, including TextEdit (top left), Preview (top right), and Safari (bottom left).

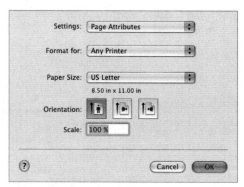

**Figure 29** The Page Setup dialog.

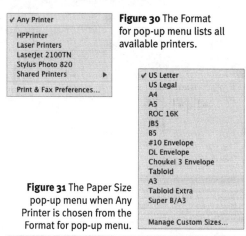

**Figure 30** The Format for pop-up menu lists all available printers.

**Figure 31** The Paper Size pop-up menu when Any Printer is chosen from the Format for pop-up menu.

## To add a custom paper size

1. Choose Manage Custom Sizes from the Paper Size pop-up menu (**Figure 31**) in the Page Setup dialog. The Custom Page Sizes dialog appears (**Figure 32**).

2. Click the + button. An untitled paper size appears in the list window (**Figure 33**).

3. Double-click the name of the paper size to select it and type a name.

4. Enter paper size and printer margin measurements in the appropriate boxes. **Figure 34** shows what the dialog might look like with sizes set for a custom postcard.

5. Repeat Steps 2 through 4 for each custom paper size you want to create.

6. Click OK to save your settings.

## ✔ Tips

- Custom paper sizes appear near the bottom of the Paper Size pop-up menu (**Figure 35**).

- To delete a custom paper size, select it in the Custom Page Sizes dialog (**Figure 34**), click the – button, and click OK.

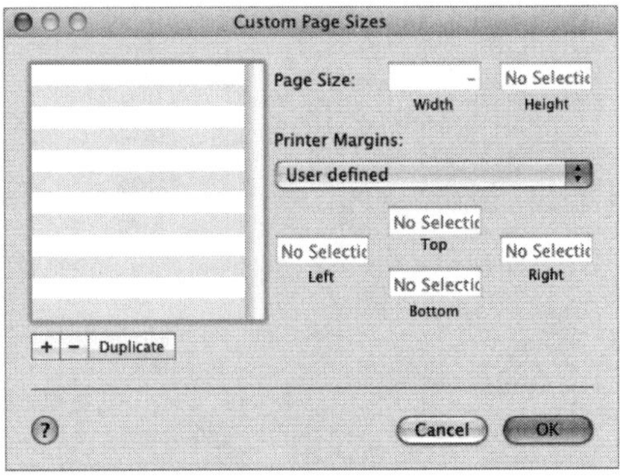

**Figure 32** The Custom Page Sizes dialog.

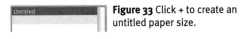

**Figure 33** Click + to create an untitled paper size.

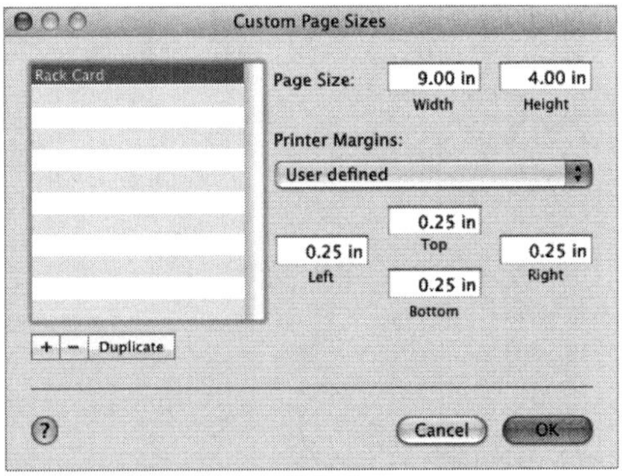

**Figure 34** An example of a custom paper size.

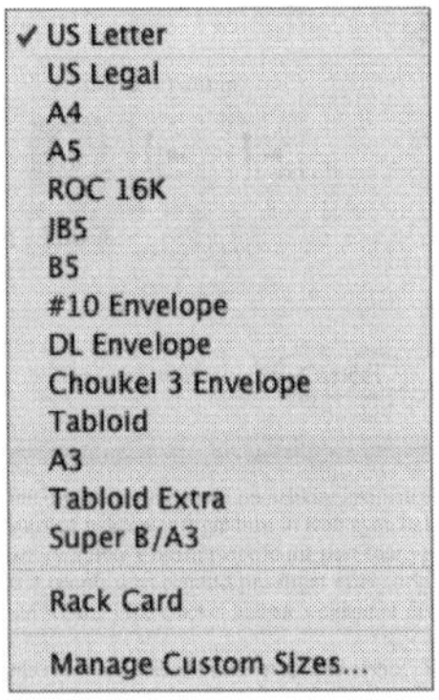

**Figure 35** Custom paper sizes appear near the bottom of the Paper Size pop-up menu.

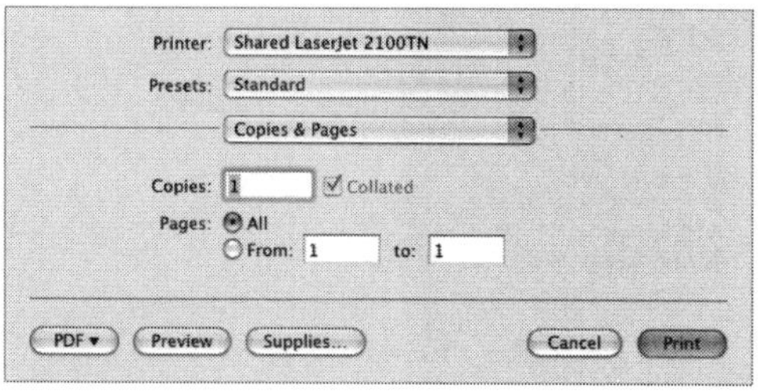

**Figure 36** The Copies & Pages pane of the Print dialog.

# Setting Options in the Print Dialog

The Print dialog (**Figure 36**)enables you to set printing options and send the print job to the printer. Like the Page Setup dialog, the Print dialog is a standard dialog, but two things can cause its appearance and options to vary:

◆ Print options vary depending on the selected printer.

◆ Additional options may be offered by specific applications.

This section explains how to set the options available for most printers and applications.

## ✔ Tips

■ If your Print dialog includes options that are not covered here, consult the documentation that came with your printer.

■ For information about using Print options specific to an application, consult the documentation that came with the application.

■ If an application offers application-specific print options, the application name will appear on the third pop-up menu (**Figures 38a** and **38b**) in the print dialog. For example, a Microsoft Word option on that menu would enable you to set Word-specific options.

## To open the Print dialog

Choose File > Print (**Figures 28a, 28b**, and **28c**), or press ⌃ ⌘ P. The Copies & Pages pane of the Print dialog appears (**Figure 36**).

## To select a printer

In the Print dialog (**Figure 36**), choose a printer from the Printer pop-up menu (**Figure 37**).

## ✔ Tips

- The Printer pop-up menu (**Figure 37**) should list all of the printers that appear in the Printer Setup Utility's Printer List window (**Figure 2**).

- Choosing Add Printer List from the Printer pop-up menu (**Figure 37**) opens Printer Setup Utility's Printer Browser window (**Figure 6**), which is discussed earlier in this chapter.

## To set Copies & Pages options

1. In the Print dialog, choose Copies & Pages from the third pop-up menu (**Figure 38a** or **38b**) to display Copies & Pages options (**Figure 36**).

2. In the Copies field, enter the number of copies of the document to print.

3. To collate multiple copies, turn on the Collated check box.

4. In the Pages area, select either the All radio button to print all pages or select the From radio button and enter values in the From and to fields to print specific pages.

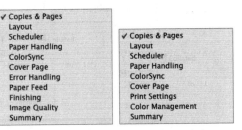

**Figure 37**
The Printer pop-up menu.

**Figures 38a & 38b** The pop-up menu beneath the Presets pop-up menu offers different options depending on the printer that is selected. The menu on the left is for a Hewlett-Packard LaserJet printer connected via network and the menu on the right is for an Epson Stylus Color printer connected directly to the computer via USB.

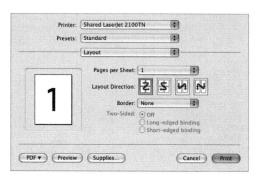

**Figure 39** The Layout pane of the Print dialog.

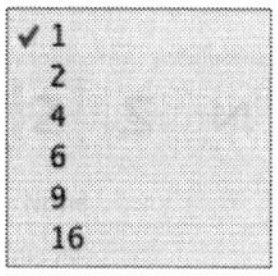

**Figure 40**
The Pages per Sheet
pop-up menu.

**Figure 41**
The Preview area indicates
the number of pages to be
printed per sheet, as well
as the page order.

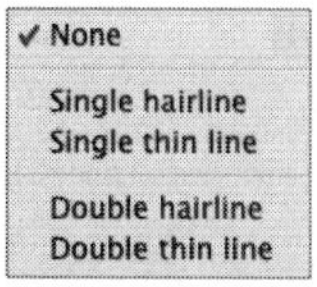

**Figure 42**
The Border
pop-up menu.

## To set Layout options

1. In the Print dialog, choose Layout from the third pop-up menu (**Figure 38a** or **38b**) to display Layout options (**Figure 39**).

2. To set the number of pages that should appear on each sheet of paper, choose an option from the Pages per Sheet pop-up menu (**Figure 40**). The preview area of the dialog changes accordingly (**Figure 41**).

3. To indicate the order in which multiple pages should print on each sheet of paper, select a Layout Direction option. The preview area of the dialog changes accordingly.

4. To place a border around each page, choose an option from the Border pop-up menu (**Figure 42**).

SETTING LAYOUT OPTIONS

## To schedule a print job

1. In the Print dialog, choose Scheduler from the third pop-up menu (**Figure 38a** or **38b**) to display the Scheduler pane (**Figure 43**).

2. Select one of the Print Document options:

   ▲ **Now** prints the document immediately.

   ▲ **At** enables you to specify a time at which the job should be printed. Be sure to enter a time in the box beside this option.

   ▲ **On Hold** sends the document to the print queue on hold. You must manually release the document for printing for it to print.

3. Choose one of the options from the Priority pop-up menu (**Figure 44**).

## ✔ Tips

- The Priority option in step 3 determines when your print job will print when you send it to a printer that already has print jobs waiting in the queue.

- If you're one of many people printing to a shared network printer, don't abuse the Priority feature by setting the highest priority for all of your documents. Believe it or not, other people print important stuff, too!

- I tell you about print queues, including how to work with print jobs that are on hold, later in this chapter.

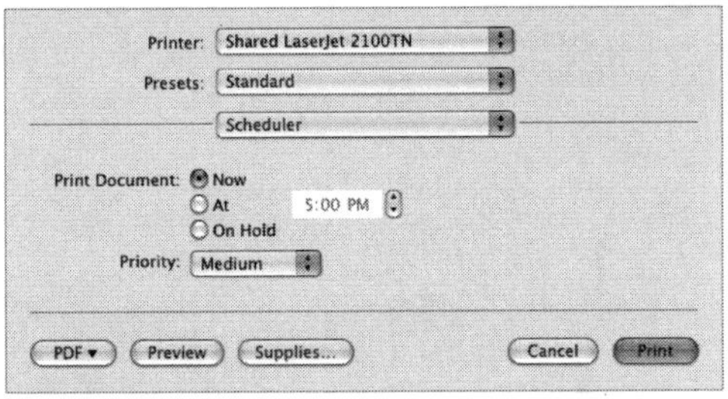

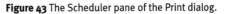

**Figure 43** The Scheduler pane of the Print dialog.

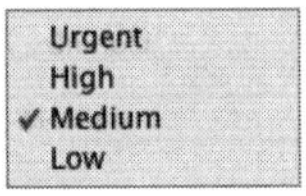

**Figure 44**
Use the Priority pop-up menu to tell the printer how important your print job is.

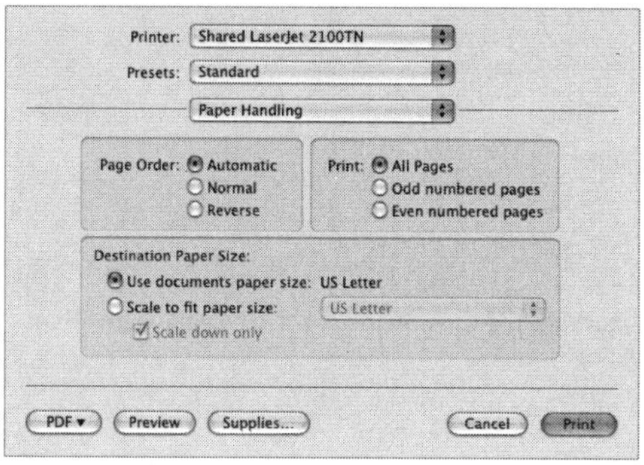

**Figure 45** The Paper Handling pane of the Print dialog.

## To set Paper Handling options

1. In the Print dialog, choose Paper Handling from the third pop-up menu (**Figure 38a** or **38b**) to display the Paper Handling pane (**Figure 45**).

2. Select a Page Order option:

   ▲ **Automatic** prints pages in the order determined by the software. This is normally first to last.

   ▲ **Normal** prints pages in the order of first to last.

   ▲ **Reverse** prints pages in the order of last to first.

3. Select a Print option:

   ▲ **All Pages** prints all pages.

   ▲ **Odd numbered pages** prints only odd numbered pages.

   ▲ **Even numbered pages** prints only even numbered pages.

4. Select a Destination Paper Size option:

   ▲ **Use document's paper size** uses the size selected in the Page Setup dialog (**Figure 29**).

   ▲ **Scale to fit paper size** enables you to choose a specific paper size from the pop-up menu. The menu includes all paper sizes supported by the selected printer. Turn on the Scale down only check box to allow the document to be reduced but not enlarged to fit.

## ✔ Tips

■ The Reverse page order option is useful if your printer places documents face up in the printer tray when printed. If your printer does this, however, the Automatic option may ensure that pages print in the right order. Experiment with a short document and see for yourself!

■ Some paper handling options may also be offered in application-specific print settings. For example, Microsoft Word enables you to print just odd or just even pages in its application-specific options.

## To set ColorSync options

1. In the Print dialog, choose ColorSync from the third pop-up menu (**Figure 38a** or **38b**) to display the ColorSync pane (**Figure 46**).

2. Choose an option from the Color Conversion pop-up menu (**Figure 47**):

   ▲ **Standard** tells the application you're using to control the color.

   ▲ **In Printer** tells the printer to control the color.

3. If desired, choose an option from the Quartz Filter pop-up menu (**Figure 48**).

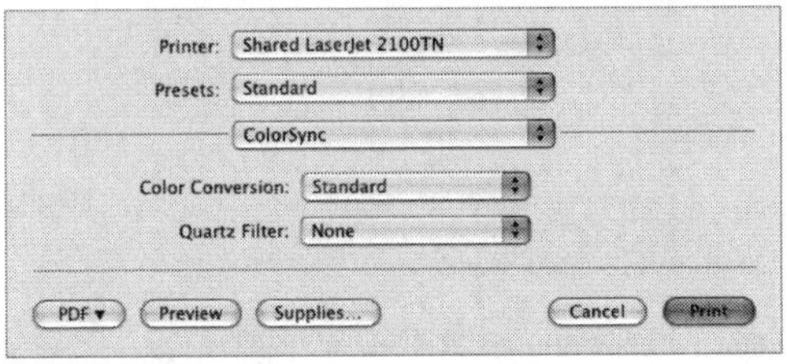

## ✔ Tips

■ ColorSync is a color matching technology that enables you to see accurate color on screen for documents that you print.

■ Quartz filters can modify printer output by adjusting color, adding visual effects, or changing resolution.

■ I discuss ColorSync and the ColorSync Utility briefly in **Chapter 22**.

■ To learn more about ColorSync, visit www.apple.com/colorsync/.

**Figure 46** The ColorSync preferences pane in the Print dialog.

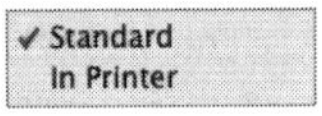

**Figure 47** The Color Conversion pop-up menu.

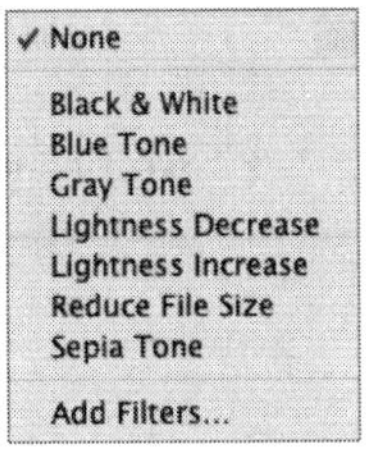

**Figure 48** The Quartz Filter pop-up menu.

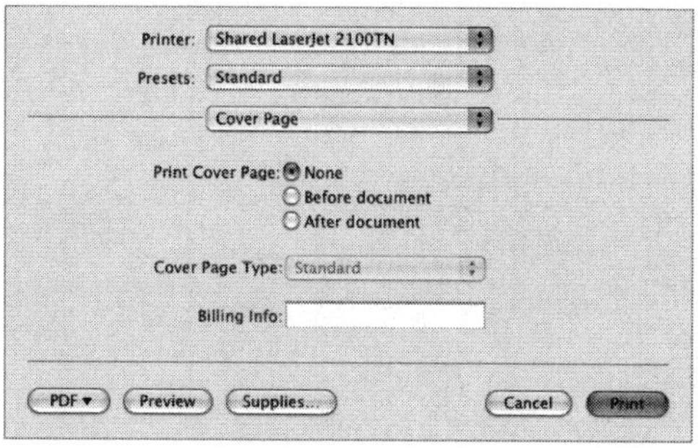

**Figure 49** The Cover Page pane of the Print dialog.

**Figure 50**
If you indicate that you want to print a cover page, you can choose from several formats.

## To set Cover Page options

1.  In the Print dialog, choose Cover Page from the third pop-up menu (**Figures 38a** and **38b**) to display Cover Page options (**Figure 49**).

2.  Select one of the Print Cover Page options:

    ▲ **None** does not print a cover page. If you select this option, you can skip the remaining steps.

    ▲ **Before document** prints a cover page at the beginning of the document.

    ▲ **After document** prints a cover page at the end of the document.

3.  Choose an option from the Cover Page Type pop-up menu (**Figure 50**).

4.  If desired, enter information in the Billing Info box. Whatever you enter will print on the cover page.

## ✔ Tips

■ A cover page is a single sheet of information about the print job that can be printed at the beginning or end of the job.

■ Cover pages waste paper! If you don't need a cover page, don't print one!

**SETTING COVER PAGE OPTIONS**

**299**

## To set Error Handling options

1. In the Print dialog, choose Error Handling from the third pop-up menu (**Figure 38a**) to display Error Handling options (**Figure 51**).

2. To specify how the printer should report PostScript errors, select one of the PostScript Errors options.

3. To specify how the printer should handle an out-of-paper situation for a multiple-tray printer, select one of the Tray Switching options.

## ✔ Tips

- These options are only available for PostScript printers.

- Tray switching options are only available for printers with multiple paper trays.

## To set Paper Feed options

1. In the Print dialog, choose Paper Feed from the third pop-up menu (**Figure 38a**) to display Paper Feed options (**Figure 52**).

2. To specify how paper trays should be used for paper feed, select one of the radio buttons.

3. To specify which paper tray(s) should be used for paper feed, choose options from the pop-up menu(s).

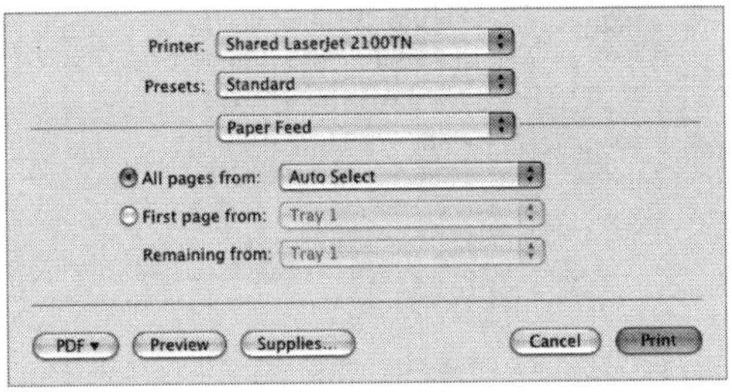

## ✔ Tip

- The options offered in the Paper Feed pane of the Print dialog (**Figure 52**) vary depending on your printer. The options here are for an HP LaserJet 2100TN.

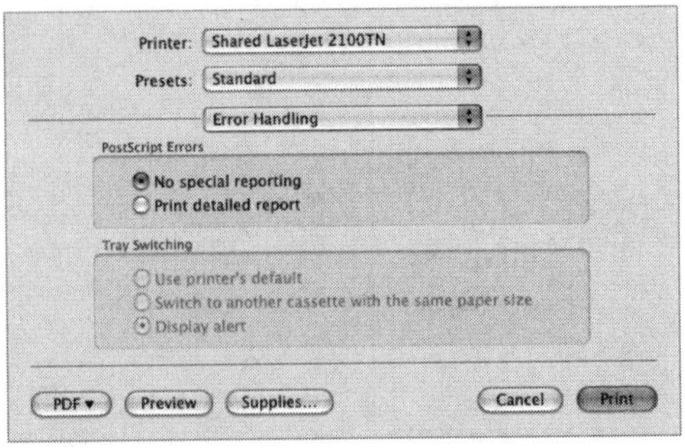

**Figure 51** The Error Handling pane of the Print dialog.

**Figure 52** The Paper Feed pane of the Print dialog.

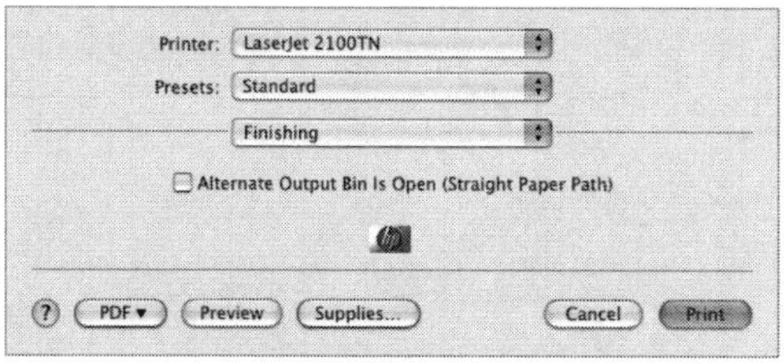

**Figure 53** The Finishing pane of the Print dialog for an HP LaserJet 2100TN printer.

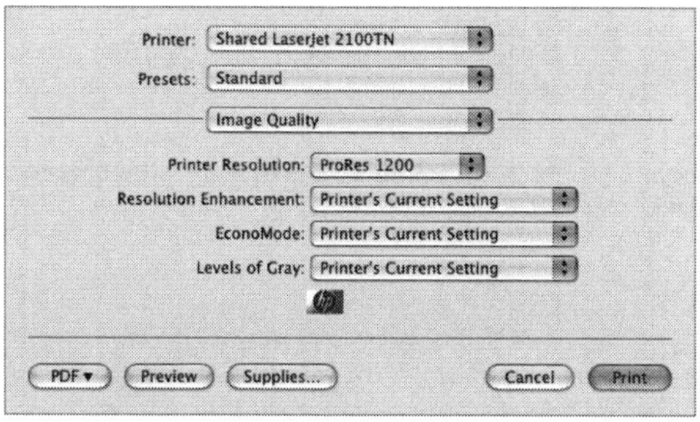

**Figure 54** The Image Quality pane of the Print dialog for an HP LaserJet 2100TN printer.

## To set Finishing options

1. In the Print dialog, choose Finishing from the third pop-up menu (**Figure 38a**) to display Finishing options (**Figure 53**).

2. Set options as desired.

## ✔ Tip

- Finishing options (**Figure 53**) vary from printer to printer —if they are offered at all. The options here are for an HP LaserJet 2100TN.

- For more information about finishing options offered by your printer, consult the manual that came with your printer.

## To set Image Quality options

1. In the Print dialog, choose Image Quality from the third pop-up menu (**Figure 38a**) to display Image Quality options (**Figure 54**).

2. Use the pop-up menus to set image quality options.

## ✔ Tips

- The options offered in the Image Quality pane of the Print dialog (**Figure 54**) vary depending on your printer. The options here are for an HP LaserJet 2100TN.

- For more information about image quality options offered by your printer, consult the manual that came with your printer.

SETTING FINISHING & QUALITY OPTIONS

## To set Print Settings options

1. In the Print dialog, choose Print Settings from the third pop-up menu (**Figure 38b**) to display the Print Settings pane (**Figure 55**).

2. Select the type of paper you will print on from the Media Type pop-up menu (**Figure 56**).

3. For a color printer, select an Ink option.

4. Set Mode options as desired. These options vary from printer to printer; check the documentation that came with your printer for details.

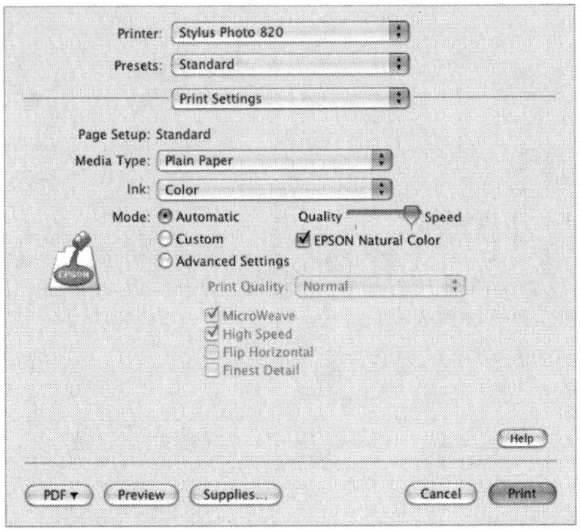

## To set Color Management options

1. In the Print dialog, choose Color Management from the third pop-up menu (**Figure 38b**) to display Color Management options (**Figure 57**).

2. To indicate the color management method, select one of the radio buttons near the top of the pane.

3. If you selected Color Controls, set options in the dialog as desired.

## ✔ Tips

■ Color management methods and options are far beyond the scope of this book.

■ ColorSync is discussed in **Chapter 22**.

## To view a summary of settings

1. In the Print dialog, choose Summary from the third pop-up menu (**Figures 38a** and **38b**).

   A summary of options in each settings category appears.

2. Click the triangle to the left of a settings category to view its settings (**Figure 58**).

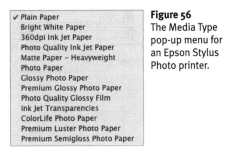

**Figure 55** The Print Settings pane of the Print dialog for an Epson Stylus Photo printer.

**Figure 56**
The Media Type pop-up menu for an Epson Stylus Photo printer.

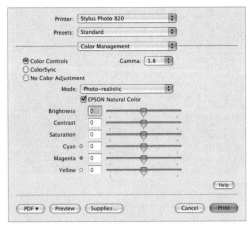

**Figure 57** The Color Management pane of the Print dialog with Color Controls selected.

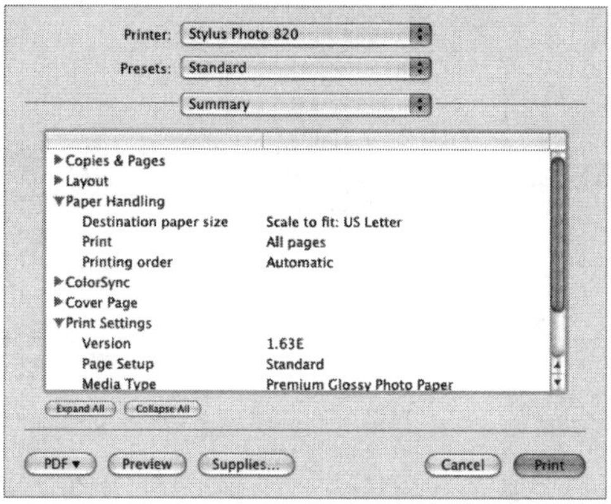

**Figure 58** The Summary pane of the Print dialog with two categories of settings displayed.

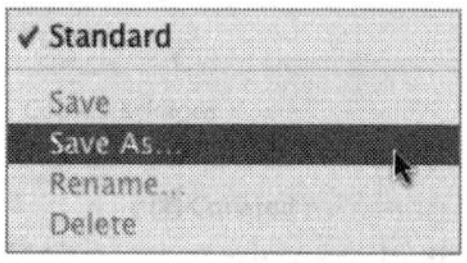

**Figure 59** Choose Save As from the Presets pop-up menu.

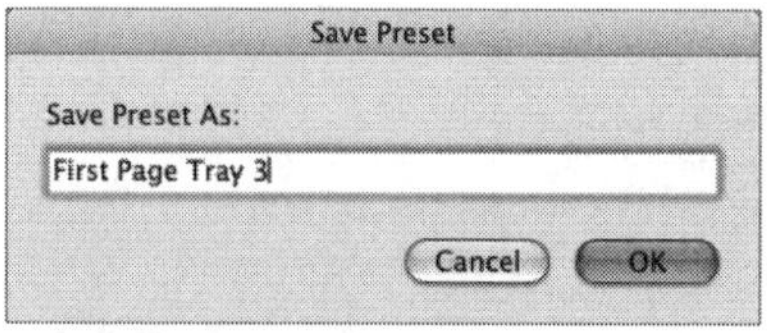

**Figure 60** The Save Preset dialog.

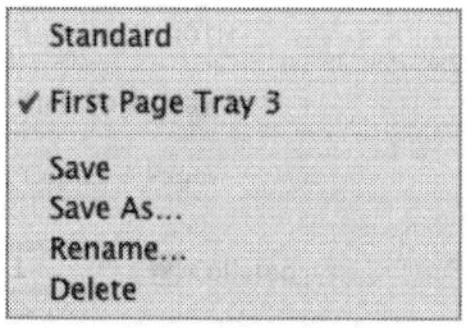

**Figure 61** The preset is added to the menu and chosen as the current preset.

**Figure 62** The Preset pop-up menu with several presets added.

# To save settings as a preset

1. In the Print dialog (**Figure 36**), choose Save As from the Presets pop-up menu (**Figure 59**).

2. Enter a name for the settings in the Save Preset dialog that appears (**Figure 60**).

3. Click OK.

   The name you entered is added to the Presets pop-up menu and chosen (**Figure 61**).

# ✔ Tip

- It's a good idea to save settings if you often have to change the Print dialog's settings. This can save time when you need to print.

# To save changes to preset settings

In the Print dialog (**Figure 36**), choose Save from the Presets pop-up menu (**Figure 61**). Your changes to the preset settings are saved.

# To use preset settings

In the Print dialog (**Figure 36**), choose the name of the preset settings you want to use from the Presets pop-up menu (**Figure 62**).

All Print dialog settings are set according to the saved settings.

# To delete a preset setting

1. In the Print dialog (**Figures 36**), choose the name of the preset settings you want to delete from the Presets pop-up menu (**Figure 61**).

2. Choose Delete from the Presets pop-up menu (**Figure 61**).

   The preset setting is deleted.

# Previewing Documents

The Print dialog enables you to create and view previews of your documents. You might want to use this feature to check the appearance of a document before printing it.

## To preview a document

1. Set options as desired in the Print dialog's panes.

2. In any pane of the Print dialog (**Figure 36**), click the Preview button. The Print dialog disappears and Mac OS opens Preview. A moment later, the document appears in a Preview window (**Figure 63**).

3. When you're finished previewing the document, you have three options:

   ▲ Choose File > Print, press ⌘ P, or click the Print button at the bottom of the Preview window (**Figure 63**) to display the Print dialog and print the document from Preview.

   ▲ Choose File > Save As or press Shift ⌘ S to display a Save dialog (**Figure 64**) and save the document as a PDF or graphic format file from within Preview.

   ▲ Choose Preview > Quit Preview or press ⌘ Q to quit Preview and return to the original document.

## ✔ Tips

- Preview is covered in **Chapter 8**. The Save dialog is covered in **Chapter 7**.

- Some applications, such as Microsoft Word, include a Print Preview command on their File menu. This displays a preview of the document from within the application and does not use Preview.

**Figure 63** The Preview button displays the document in a Preview window. You can use controls in the window's toolbar or commands in the View menu to scroll through document contents.

**Figure 64** Use a standard Save Location dialog to save the document as a PDF file.

**Figure 65** The PDF button is a menu in disguise.

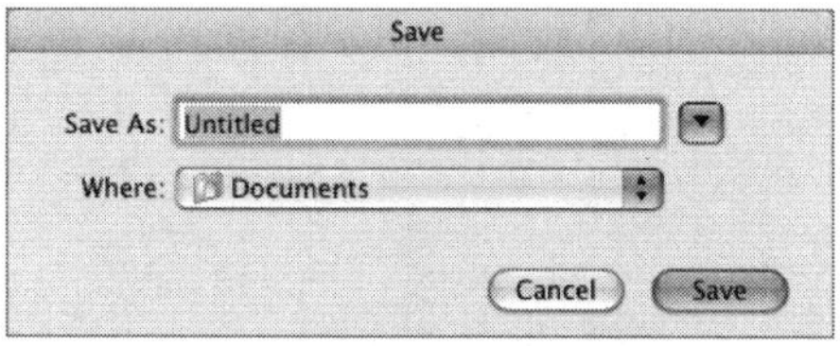

**Figure 66** Use this dialog to enter a name, select a location, and Save a document as a file.

# Saving Documents as PDF Files

PDF, which stands for Portable Document Format, is a standard file format that can be opened and read by Preview and Adobe Reader. PDF is a good format for distributing a formatted document when you're not sure what software the document's recipient has. Most computer users have some kind of PDF reader software; if they don't, they can download Adobe Reader for free.

The Print dialog offers two methods for saving a document as a PDF file: the quick way and the almost-as-quick way.

## ✔ Tip

- The commands below the split line on the PDF menu (**Figure 65**) are PDF workflows created with AppleScript or Automator. I tell you more about Mac OS X's automation tools in **Chapter 20**.

## To save a document as a PDF file

1. Set options as desired in the Print dialog's panes.

2. In any pane of the Print dialog (**Figure 36**), choose Save as PDF from the PDF button's menu (**Figure 65**).

3. Use the Save that appears (**Figure 66**) to enter a name and select a disk location for the PDF file.

4. Click Save.

## ✔ Tips

- The Save dialog is covered in**Chapter 7**.

- The Save as PDF command creates a high-resolution PDF file that may be quite large. To create a smaller PDF file suitable for onscreen viewing and e-mail, choose Compress PDF in step 2.

- Choosing Save PDF as PostScript from the PDF button's menu (**Figure 65**) saves the document as a PostScript file. It can then be printed by PostScript printers or imagesetters. This is an advanced feature that most users will never need to use.

# Faxing Documents

You can fax documents from within the Print dialog. All you need is a computer with a fax modem connected to a telephone line.

## To fax a document

1. Set options as desired in the Print dialog's panes.

2. In any pane of the Print dialog (**Figure 36**), choose Fax PDF from the PDF button's menu (**Figure 65**). The Print dialog changes to offer options for faxing the document (**Figure 67**).

3. Enter the name of the person you are faxing the document to in the To box. As you type, your computer attempts to match what you're typing to entries in your Address Book file (**Figure 68**). If you prefer, you can click the Addresses button to display a searchable Addresses window (**Figure 69**); double-click a fax number to enter it in the window.

4. If you need to dial a number to get a dial tone (like in an office or hotel) or a 1 for long distance, enter these numbers in the Dialing Prefix box.

5. If you have multiple fax modems, choose one from the Modem pop-up menu.

6. To include a fax cover page, turn on the Use Cover Page check box, type a subject in the Subject box, and type a message in the Message box.

7. Click Fax. A Print status dialog (**Figure 70**) appears briefly as the document is spooled to the fax modem's queue. A moment later, the computer dials and sends the fax.

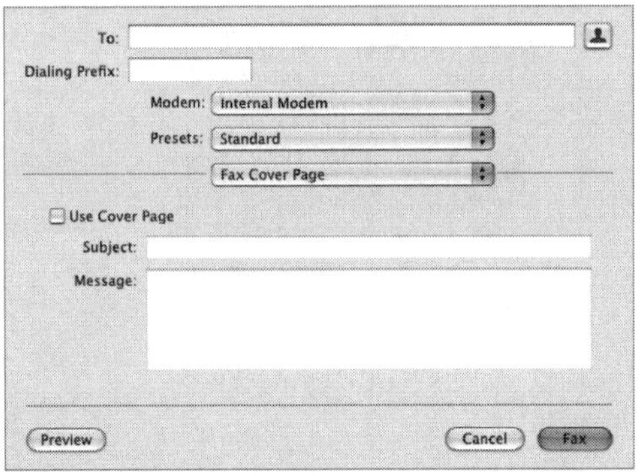

**Figure 67** Use this dialog sheet to set options for faxing a document from within the Print dialog.

**Figure 68** As you enter a recipient's name, your computer attempts to match it to Address Book entries.

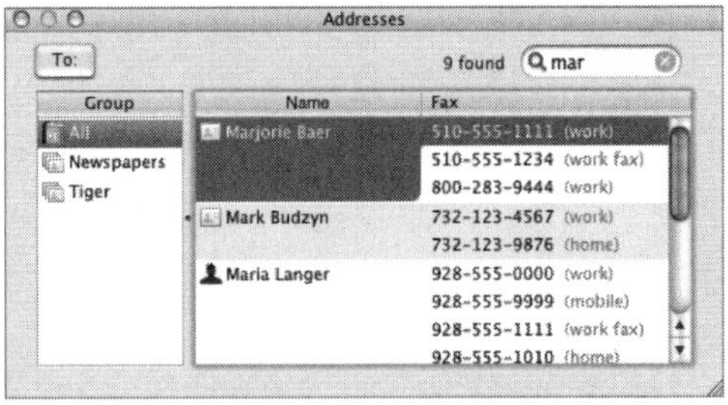

**Figure 69** Another way to add a recipient is to use the searchable Addresses window. This is especially useful when a recipient has more than one fax number; double-click the one you want.

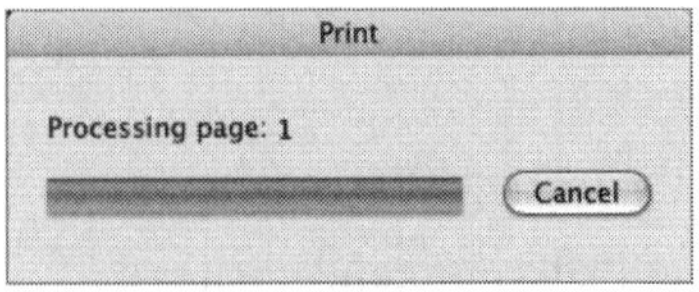

**Figure 70** A progress window like this appears as a print job is spooled to a fax or print queue.

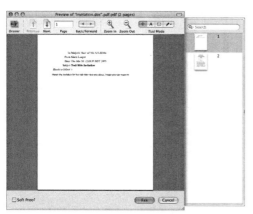

**Figure 71** You can click the Preview button to display a preview of your fax, including the cover page.

## ✔ Tips

■ In step 3, you don't have to enter a name. Instead, just enter a fax phone number. You might find this quicker when sending a one-time fax to someone whose fax number is not in your Address Book.

■ In step 3, you can enter multiple recipients in the To box. Separate each one with a comma (,).

■ Before step 7, you can click the Preview button to see what your fax will look like in Preview (**Figure 71**). Clicking the Fax button in the Preview window sends the fax.

■ The header on each page of the faxes you send includes the date, time, and page number.

# Printing Documents

The Print dialog also enables you to send a document to a printer to be printed.

## To print a document

1. Set options as desired in the Print dialog's panes.

2. In any pane of the Print dialog (**Figure 36**), click Print.

   The print job is sent to the print queue, where it waits for its turn to be printed. A progress window like the one in **Figure 70** appears as it is sent or *spooled*.

## ✔ Tips

- You can normally cancel a print job as it is being spooled to the print queue or printer by pressing ⌘.. Any pages spooled *before* you press ⌘., however, may be printed anyway.

- Canceling a print job that has already been spooled to a print queue is discussed later in this chapter.

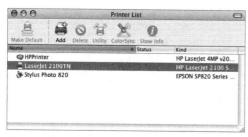

**Figure 72** Select the printer you want to create an icon for in the Printer List window.

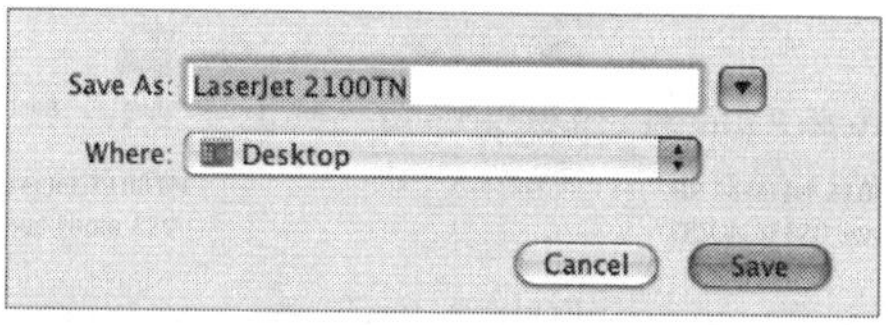

**Figure 73** Use this dialog to name and save the printer icon.

**Figure 74** Here's an example of a printer icon on the desktop.

**Figure 75** To print, simply drag the document icon onto the printer icon.

# Desktop Printers

Mac OS X's desktop printers feature enables you to create an icon for a printer you use frequently. Then, when you want to print a document on that printer, simply drag the document icon onto the printer icon.

## To create a desktop icon for a printer

1. Open Printer Setup Utility and display the Printer list.

2. Select the printer you want to create a desktop printer icon for (**Figure 72**).

3. Choose Printers > Create Desktop Printer (**Figure 5**), or press Shift ⌃ ⌘ D.

4. Use the Save As dialog that appears (**Figure 73**) to enter a name and choose a location for the desktop printer icon.

5. Click Save. An alias for the printer appears in the location you specified (**Figure 74**).

## ✔ Tip

■ Although Desktop is the default location in the Save As dialog (**Figure 73**), you can save a desktop printer anywhere on disk.

## To print with a desktop printer

1. Drag the icon for the document you want to print onto the printer icon (**Figure 75**).

2. When you release the mouse button, the document is sent to the print queue and prints.

## ✔ Tip

■ You can drag any number of document icons onto the printer icon. They will all be spooled to the printer.

USING DESKTOP PRINTERS

# Print Queues

A *print queue* is a list of documents or *print jobs* waiting to be printed. When you click the Print button to send a document to a printer, you're really sending it to the printer's queue, where it waits its turn to be printed.

You can open a printer's queue window to check the progress of print jobs that are printing; to stop printing; and to hold, resume, or cancel a specific print job.

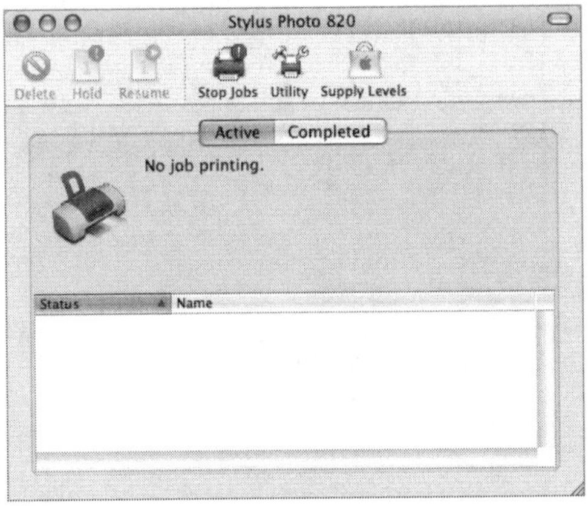

## ✔ Tip

■ Although this section discusses printer queues, your fax modem also has a queue that works exactly the same way.

## To open a printer's queue window

1. Open Printer Setup Utility and display the Printer List window (**Figure 2**).

2. Double-click the name of the printer for which you want to open the queue.

   *or*

   Select the name of the printer for which you want to open the queue, and choose Printers > Show Jobs (**Figure 5**) or press ⌘⌥O.

   *Or*

   Double-click the desktop icon for a printer (**Figure 74**).

The printer's queue window appears (**Figure 76 or 77**).

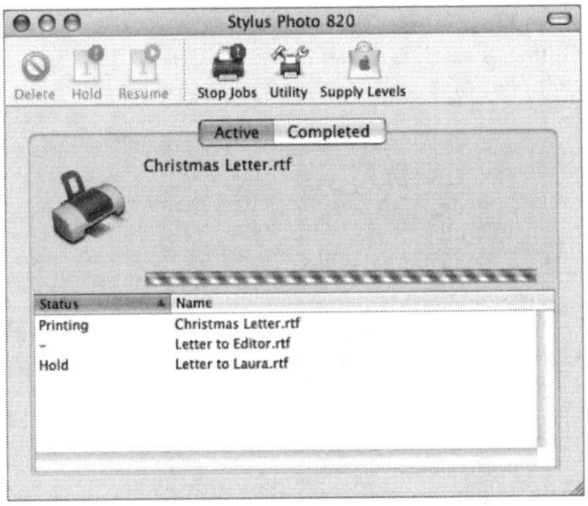

## ✔ Tips

■ When a document is in a print queue, the icon for the Printer that will print it appears in the Dock (**Figure 78**). Click the icon to view the printer's print queue.

**Figure 76** A printer's queue window, with no documents in the queue...

**Figure 77** ...and the same printer's queue window with three documents in the queue: one printing, one waiting to be printed, and one on hold.

**Figure 78** When print jobs are in a printer's queue, an icon for the printer appears in the Dock.

■ In Mac OS X 10.4, the printer's queue window has two panes: Active and Completed. Be sure to click the Active button to view the list of documents waiting to be printed (**Figures 76 and 77**).

**Figure 79** The queue status appears in the queue window.

**Figure 80** When you select a print job that is not on hold, the Delete and Hold buttons become active.

**Figure 81** When you select a print job that is on hold, the Resume button becomes active.

## To cancel a specific print job

1. In the printer's queue window (**Figure 77**), select the print job you want to cancel.

2. Click the Delete button (**Figure 80** or **81**)

   The job is removed from the print queue. If it was printing, printing stops.

## To stop all print jobs

Click the Stop Jobs button in the Print Queue window (**Figures 76** and **77**).

Any printing stops and the words *Jobs Stopped* appear in the print queue window (**Figure 79**).

## To restart print jobs

Click the Start Jobs button in the Print Queue window (**Figure 79**).

The next print job starts printing.

## To hold a specific print job

1. In the printer's queue window (**Figure 77**), select the print job you want to hold.

2. Click the Hold button (**Figure 80**).

   The word *Hold* appears in the Status column beside the job name in the queue window (**Figure 77**). If the job was printing, printing stops and another job in the queue begins to print.

## To resume a specific print job

1. In the printer's queue window (**Figure 77**), select the print job you want to resume.

2. Click the Resume button (**Figure 81**).

   The word *Hold* disappears from the Status column beside the job name in the queue window. If no other jobs are printing, the job begins to print.

## ✔ Tip

- You can also use this technique to start printing a job that you put on hold or scheduled for a later time using the Scheduler options in the Print dialog (**Figure 43**).

MANAGING THE PRINT QUEUE & PRINT JOBS

# The Finder's Print Command

Mac OS X 10.4 added a Print command to the Finder's File menu (**Figure 82**). This is a quick-and-dirty command for sending a selected document to the default printer, without even displaying the Print dialog.

## ✔ Tips

■ A Print command was available in Mac OS 9.x and earlier. Mac OS X 10.4 marks the return of this command.

■ The Finder's Print command works very much like the Print One command available in some applications.

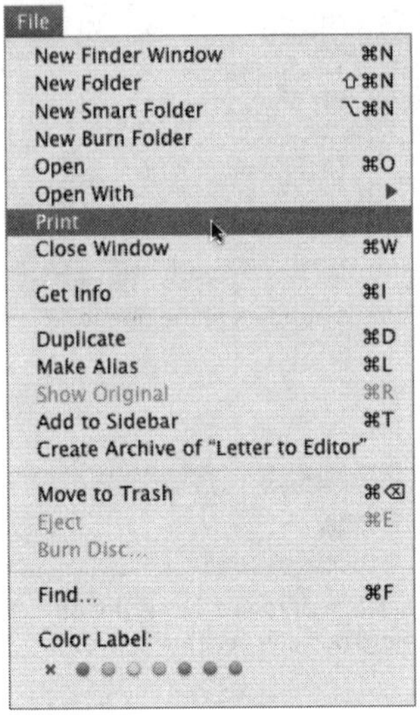

## To use the Finder's Print command

1. In a Finder window, select the document(s) you want to print.

2. Choose File > Print (**Figure 82**).

   If necessary, the application that created the document opens. The document is sent to the default printer and prints.

**Figure 82**
The Finder's Print command sends any selected document(s) to the default printer.

# Connecting to the Internet

## Connecting to the Internet

The *Internet* is a vast, worldwide network of computers that offers information, communication, online shopping, and entertainment for the whole family.

There are two ways to connect to the Internet:

◆ In a *direct* or *network connection*, your computer has a live network connection to the Internet all the time. This is relatively common for workplace computers on companywide networks. For home use, *cable modems* and *DSL*, which work like direct connections, are becoming quite popular.

◆ In a *modem* or *dial-up connection*, your computer uses its modem to dial in to a server at an *Internet Service Provider* (*ISP*), which gives it access to the Internet. Access speed is limited by the speed of your modem.

This chapter explains how to configure your system for an Internet connection, connect to the Internet, and use the Internet applications and utilities included with Mac OS X.

### ✔ Tips

■ An ISP is a business that provides access to the Internet for a fee.

■ The *World Wide Web* is part of the Internet. The Web and the *Web browser* software you use to access it are covered later in this chapter.

# TCP/IP, PPP, & Internet Connect

Your computer accesses the Internet via a TCP/IP connection. *TCP/IP* is a standard Internet *protocol*, or set of rules, for exchanging information.

A TCP/IP connection works like a pipeline. Once established, Internet applications—such as your Web browser and e-mail program—reach through the TCP/IP pipeline to get the information they need. When the information has been sent or received, it stops flowing through the pipeline. But the pipeline is not disconnected.

If you have a direct or network connection to the Internet, the Internet is accessible all the time. But if you connect via modem, you need to use Internet Connect software. This software, which comes with Mac OS, uses PPP to connect to TCP/IP networks via modem. *PPP* is a standard protocol for connecting to networks.

When you connect via modem using Internet Connect, you set up a temporary TCP/IP pipeline. Internet applications are smart enough to automatically use Internet Connect to connect to the Internet when necessary. When you're finished accessing Internet services you should tell Internet Connect to disconnect.

TCP/IP, PPP, & INTERNET CONNECT

# Using the Network Setup Assistant

The Network Setup Assistant is an application that steps you through the process of setting up an Internet connection using a telephone modem, cable modem, DSL modem, Airport wireless network, or local area network with Ethernet connection.

The Network Setup Assistant is easy to use. Just get it started and provide basic information about your Internet connection. It automatically sets options in the Network preferences pane for your connection.

In this part of the chapter, I explain how to use the Network Setup Assistant to set up an Internet connection.

## ✔ Tips

- If you set up your Internet connection as part of the setup process discussed in **Chapter 1**, your computer should be ready to connect to the Internet and you can skip ahead to the sections that discuss Internet connection software. But if you didn't set up your connection or your Internet connection information has changed since setup, the Network Setup Assistant is a good way to configure your computer to connect to the Internet.

- The Network Setup Assistant groups all settings for a connection as a *location*. If your computer has more than one way to connect to the Internet, you can create a location for each method.

- Before you use the Network Setup Assistant to configure your computer for an Internet connection, make sure you have all the information you need to properly configure the options. You can get all of the information you need from your ISP or network administrator.

## To launch the Network Setup Assistant

1. Choose Apple > System Preferences (**Figure 1**) or click the System Preferences icon in the Dock.

2. In the System Preferences window that appears, click the Network icon. Network preferences appears, displaying Network Status information (**Figure 2**).

3. Click the Assist me button at the bottom of the window.

4. A dialog like the one in **Figure 3** appears. Click the Assistant button.

   The Introduction screen of the Network Setup Assistant appears (**Figure 4**).

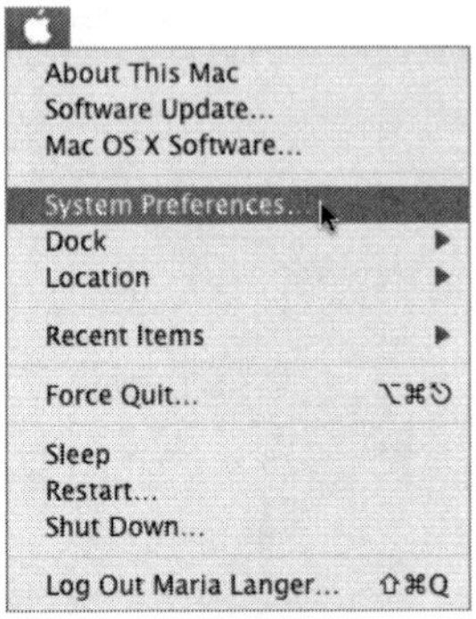

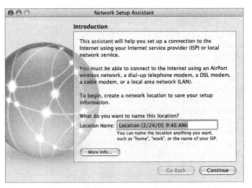

**Figure 1**
Choose System Preferences from the Apple menu.

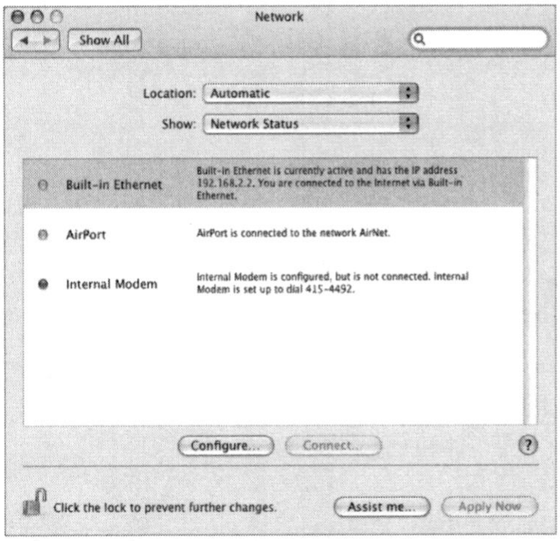

**Figure 2** Network Status information in the Network preferences pane. In this example, I have an active Internet connection via Ethernet, but I also have an AirPort connection and can dial into the Internet via an Internal modem.

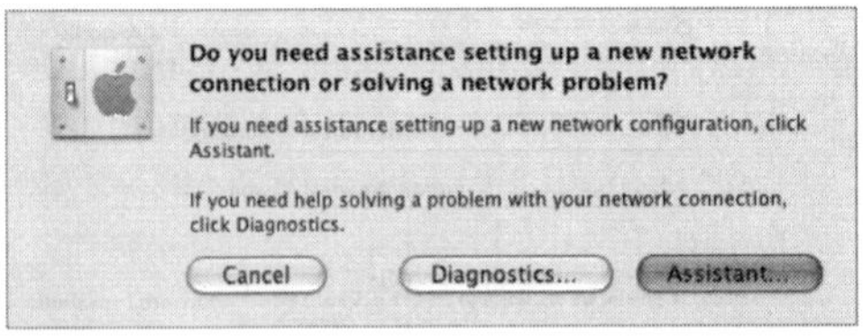

**Figure 3** This dialog appears when you click the Assist me button.

**Figure 4** The Introduction screen of the Network Setup Assistant.

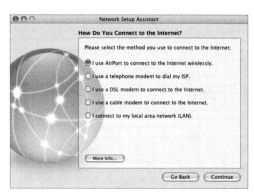

**Figure 5** Use this screen to indicate the type of connection you want to set up.

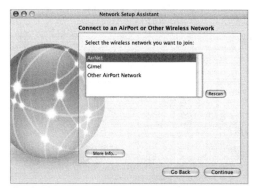

**Figure 6** Select the wireless network you want to connect to.

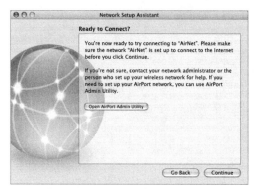

**Figure 7** Click Continue in this screen to connect.

# To set up an AirPort connection

1. In the Introduction screen of the Network Setup Assistant (**Figure 4**), enter a name for the connection in the Location Name box and click Continue.

2. In the How Do You Connect to the Internet? screen that appears next (**Figure 5**), select the I use AirPort to connect to the Internet wirelessly radio button. Click Continue.

3. In the Connect to an AirPort or Other Wireless Network screen (**Figure 6**), select the name of the wireless network you want to join. Click Continue.

4. In the Ready to Connect? screen (**Figure 7**), click Continue.

5. Wait while the Network Setup Assistant configures your connection. When it's finished, it displays a Congratulations! screen like the one in **Figure 8**. Click Done.

*Continued on next page...*

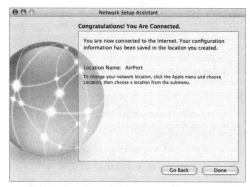

**Figure 8** This screen confirms that you have successfully configured the connection.

SETTING UP AN AIRPORT CONNECTION

*Continued from previous page.*

## ✔ Tips

- In step 3, if your wireless network does not appear, you can click the Rescan button to scan for available networks. If it still doesn't appear, check the configuration of your wireless network and its range to your computer. I tell you more about configuring an AirPort base station in **Chapter 16**.

- In step 3, if you want to connect to an existing wireless network that is not listed, select Other AirPort Network. Then enter the name of the network and your password in the boxes that appear (**Figure 9**) and click Continue.

- In step 4, you can click the Open AirPort Admin Utility button to check your AirPort base station configuration settings. I tell you about the AirPort Admin Utility application in **Chapter 16**.

## To set up a modem connection

1. In the Introduction screen of the Network Setup Assistant (**Figure 4**), enter a name for the connection in the Location Name box and click Continue.

2. In the How Do You Connect to the Internet? screen that appears next (**Figure 5**), select the I use a telephone modem to dial my ISP radio button. Click Continue.

3. In the Setting Up a Telephone Modem Connection screen (**Figure 10**), enter information about your connection:
   - ▲ **Account Name** is your user ID or account name on the ISP's system.
   - ▲ **Password** and **Password (Verify)** is your password on the ISP's system.
   - ▲ **ISP Phone Number** is the dial-up phone number for your ISP.

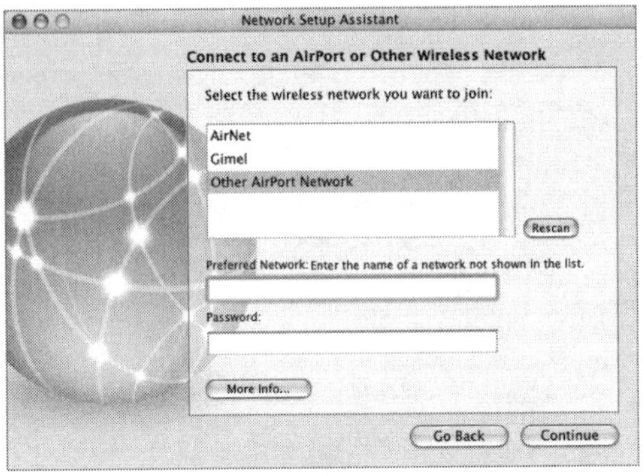

**Figure 9** If you want to connect to a network that is within range but not listed because of security settings, you can enter the network name and your password in this screen.

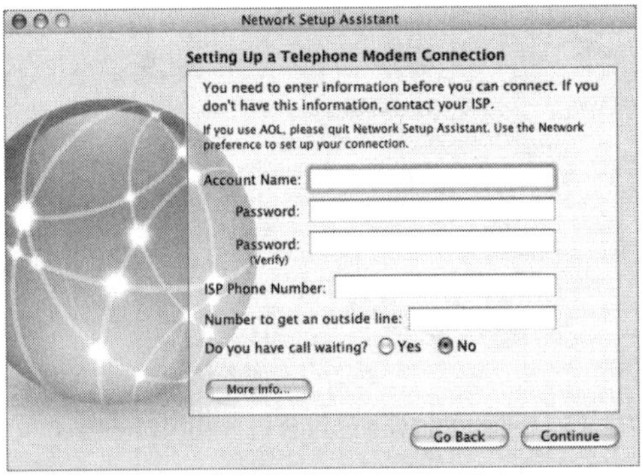

**Figure 10** Enter connection information from your ISP in this screen.

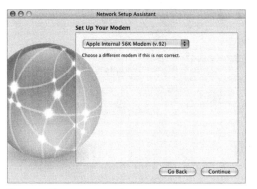

**Figure 11** Choose your modem.

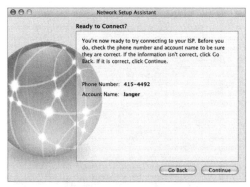

**Figure 12** Click Continue when you're finished setting options.

**Figure 13** Internet Connect automatically launches when you connect to the Internet via modem. Click Disconnect in this window when you're finished working online to free up your phone line.

▲ **Number to get an outside line** is the digit(s) you need to dial to get a regular dial tone. This usually only applies in offices or hotels.

▲ **Do you have call waiting?** enables you to indicate whether you have call waiting. If you do and select Yes, your computer will automatically disable it when you connect to the Internet.

4. Click Continue.

5. In the Set Up Your Modem screen (**Figure 11**), choose your modem from the pop-up menu. Click Continue.

6. In the Ready to Connect? screen (**Figure 12**), click Continue.

7. Wait while the Network Setup Assistant configures your connection and dials your ISP using Internet Connect. When it's finished, it displays a Congratulations! screen similar to the one in **Figure 8**. Click Done in that screen.

8. If you don't need to access the Internet now, click Disconnect in the Internal Modem window of Internet Connect (**Figure 14**). You can then choose Internet Connect > Quit Internet Connect.

## ✔ Tip

■ Your computer is pretty smart. If you have an internal modem, it will figure out what kind it is and automatically select it in step 5.

## To set up a DSL or cable modem connection

1. In the Introduction screen of the Network Setup Assistant (**Figure 4**), enter a name for the connection in the Location Name box and click Continue.

2. In the How Do You Connect to the Internet? screen that appears next (**Figure 5**), select the I use a DSL modem to connect to the Internet or the I use a cable modem to connect to the Internet radio button. Click Continue.

3. In the Ready to Connect? screen (**Figure 14**), click Continue.

4. If you are unable to connect automatically, a screen like the one in **Figure 15** appears. Select the appropriate radio button and provide the required information. Click Continue.

5. A Congratulations! screen like the one in **Figure 8** appears. Click Done.

## ✔ Tip

■ You may need to consult your ISP to get the information required to complete step 4. In most instances, however, you can skip that step because you'll be able to connect automatically.

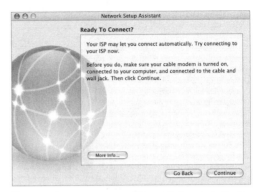

**Figure 14** In most cases, you'll be able to automatically connect via DSL or cable modem.

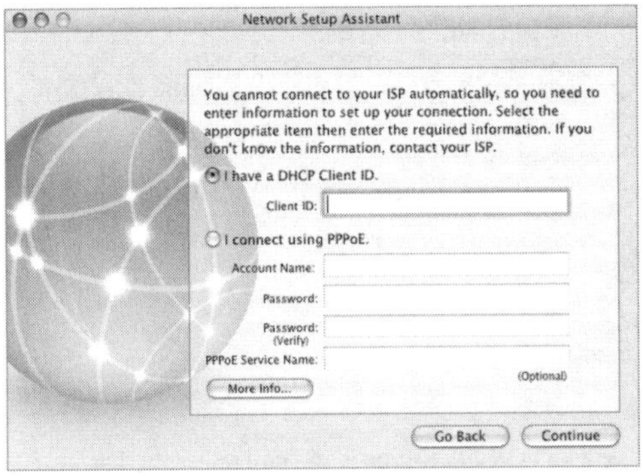

**Figure 15** If you can't automatically connect, this screen appears so you can enter connection information provided by your ISP.

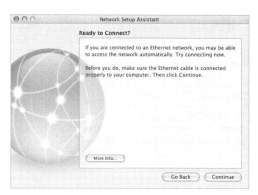

**Figure 16** Click the Continue button to try to connect automatically.

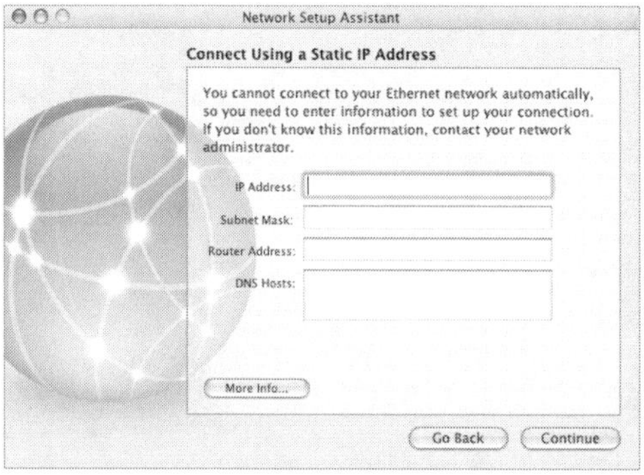

**Figure 17** If you have a static IP address, you can enter IP information in this screen.

## To set up a LAN connection

1. In the Introduction screen of the Network Setup Assistant (**Figure 4**), enter a name for the connection in the Location Name box and click Continue.

2. In the How Do You Connect to the Internet? screen that appears next (**Figure 5**), select the I connect to my local area network (LAN) radio button. Click Continue.

3. In the Ready to Connect? screen (**Figure 16**), click Continue.

4. If you are unable to connect automatically, a screen like the one in **Figure 17** appears. Enter IP information for your connection and Click Continue.

5. A Congratulations! screen like the one in **Figure 8** appears. Click Done.

## ✔ Tip

■ You may need to consult your network administrator or ISP to get the information required to complete step 4. In most instances, however, you can skip that step because you'll be able to connect automatically.

# Working with Locations

If you've used the Network Setup Assistant to create one or more location settings, you can choose the one you want to use to connect to the Internet. You can also rename and remove locations. You do all this in the Network Preferences pane.

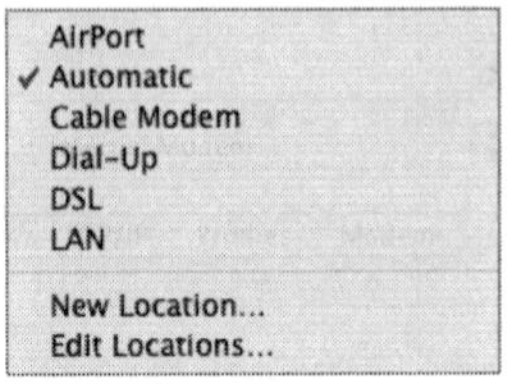

AirPort
✓ Automatic
Cable Modem
Dial-Up
DSL
LAN

New Location...
Edit Locations...

**Figure 18** The Location pop-up menu with a bunch of locations added. (It's unlikely that you'll have this many location settings!)

## To choose a location

1. Choose Apple > System Preferences (**Figure 1**) or click the System Preferences icon in the Dock.

2. In the System Preferences window that appears, click the Network icon. Network preferences appears, displaying Network Status information (**Figure 2**).

3. Choose the location you want to use from the Location pop-up menu (**Figure 18**).

4. Click Apply Now. Network Status (**Figure 2**) changes to reflect your settings.

## ✔ Tip

■ *Automatic* (**Figure 18**) is the default location setting. It senses the best connection option and chooses it for you.

CHOOSING A LOCATION

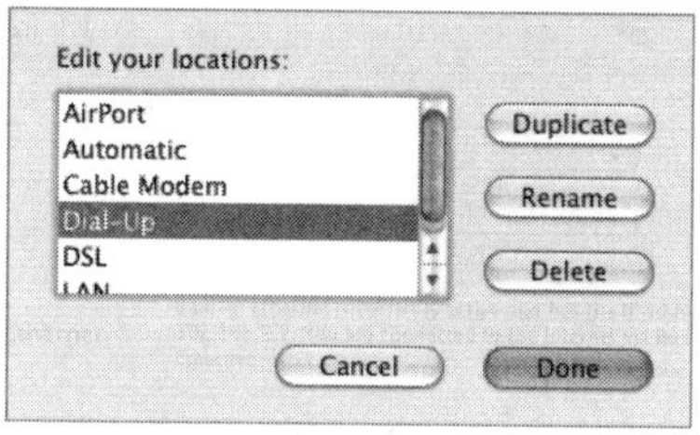

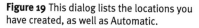

**Figure 19** This dialog lists the locations you have created, as well as Automatic.

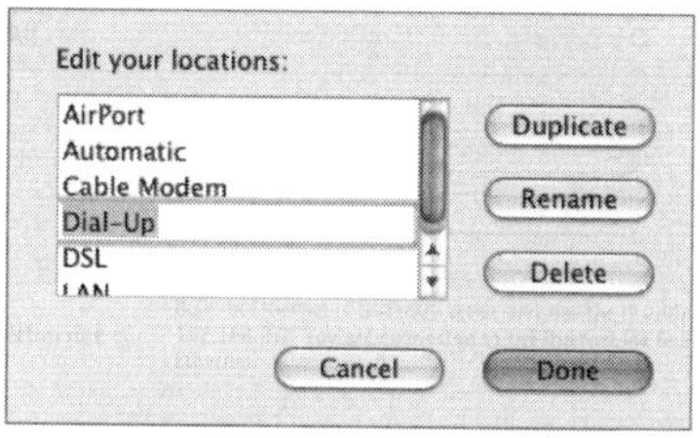

**Figure 20** When you click the Rename button, it places an edit box around the selected location's name so you can rename it.

## To edit locations

1. In the Network preferences pane, choose Edit Locations from the Location pop-up menu (**Figure 18**). A dialog like the one in **Figure 19** appears. It lists all locations.

2. Select the location you want to work with.

3. Click one of the three buttons beside the location list:

   ▲ **Duplicate** makes a copy of the location and adds it to the list. You can rename the location, click Done, and then modify settings in the Network Preferences pane to configure the new location based on settings for the one you duplicated.

   ▲ **Rename** puts an edit box around the location name (**Figure 20**) so you can rename it.

   ▲ **Delete** deletes the location settings.

4. When you are finished working with locations, click Done.

## To change a location's settings

1. In the Network preferences pane, choose the location you want to modify from the Location pop-up menu (**Figure 18**).

2. Make changes in the Network preferences pane as discussed in the section titled "Setting Internet Options in Network Preferences" starting on the next page.

3. Click Apply.

4. Choose System Preferences > Quit System Preferences or press ⌃ ⌘ Q.

**EDITING LOCATIONS**

# Setting Internet Options in Network Preferences

The Network pane of System Preferences displays information about your Internet connection (**Figure 2**) and enables you to manually configure your Internet connection:

- For **dial-up** or **direct connections**, you can set options to configure your TCP/IP address and proxy information.

- For **dial-up connections only**, you can set options for your PPP connection to the Internet and your modem.

- For **direct connections only**, you can set options for your PPPoE connection.

This part of the chapter explains how you can manually set Internet options in the Network preferences pane.

## ✔ Tips

- If all of this sounds confusing to you, don't mess with it. Instead, use the Network Setup Assistant, which I discuss earlier in this chapter, to set up a new connection with the correct settings.

- If your Internet configuration is working fine, don't change it! Internet connections follow one of the golden rules of computing: *If it ain't broke, don't fix it.*

- *PPPoE*, which stands for *Point to Point Protocol over Ethernet*, is a connection method used by some cable and DSL ISPs.

- Before you set Network preferences, make sure you have all the information you need to properly configure the options. You can get all of the information you need from your ISP or network administrator.

- I tell you more about networking in **Chapter 16**.

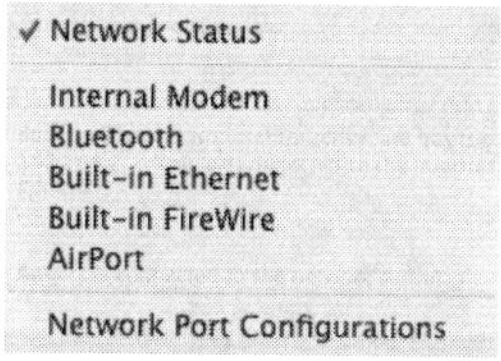

✓ Network Status

Internal Modem
Bluetooth
Built-in Ethernet
Built-in FireWire
AirPort

Network Port Configurations

**Figure 21**
Use this pop-up menu
to choose the type of
connection you want
to set up.

## To open Network preferences

1. Choose Apple > System Preferences
   (**Figure 1**) or click the System Preferences
   icon on the Dock.

2. In the System Preferences window that
   appears, click the Network icon to display
   the Network pane (**Figure 2**).

3. Choose an option from the Show pop-up
   menu (**Figure 21**) to view and modify
   connection details.

   ▲ **Network Status** shows a summary of
   your network connections and their
   status (**Figure 2**).

   ▲ **Internal Modem** shows the settings
   for an internal modem.

   ▲ **Bluetooth** shows settings for a Bluetooth mobile phone.

   ▲ **Built-In Ethernet** shows the settings
   for the built-in Ethernet port.

   ▲ **Built-in FireWire** shows settings for a
   FireWire connection to another
   computer.

   ▲ **Network Port Configurations** is an
   advanced option that enables you to
   add, enable, configure, and disable
   other network ports.

## ✔ Tips

■ The options that appear on the Show
  pop-up menu (**Figure 21**) vary depending
  on your computer model and its features.

■ You can also view the details for a specific
  type of connection by double-clicking it
  in the Network Status pane of Network
  preferences (**Figure 2**).

OPENING NETWORK PREFERENCES

## To set PPP options for a dial-up connection

1. In the Network pane of System Preferences (**Figure 2**), choose Internal Modem (or Modem) from the Show pop-up (**Figure 21**).

2. Click the PPP button to display PPP options (**Figure 22**).

3. Enter the dialup information provided by your ISP:

   ▲ **Service Provider** is the name of your ISP.

   ▲ **Account Name** is your user ID on your ISP's system.

   ▲ **Password** is your password on your ISP's system.

   ▲ **Telephone Number** and **Alternate Number** are the primary and alternate phone numbers you dial to connect to your ISP.

4. To save your account password, turn on the Save password check box.

5. Click Apply Now.

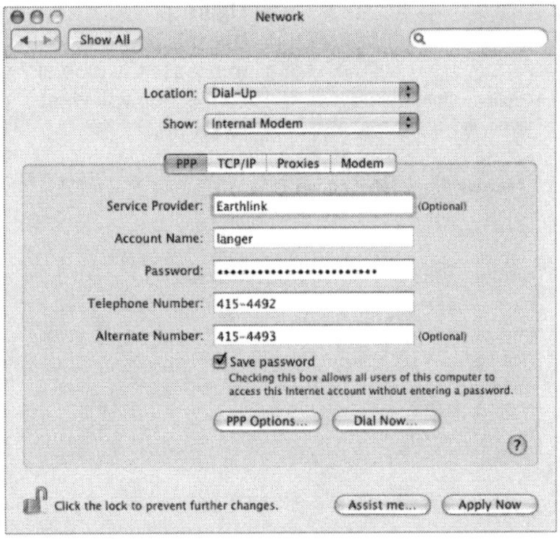

## ✔ Tips

- If you dial into the Internet via AOL, don't follow the steps here. Instead, follow the instructions in the section titled "To set TCP/IP options" later in this section. Be sure to choose AOL Dialup from the Configure IPv4 pop-up menu (**Figure 27**).

- Do not use the settings illustrated in **Figure 22**. Use the settings provided by your ISP.

**Figure 22** The PPP pane of Network preferences for a modem connection should include all of the information your computer needs to dial in and log on to the ISP's server. (The information here is not real.)

- In step 4, if you turn on the Save password check box, you won't have to enter your password when you connect to the Internet. Be aware, however, that anyone who accesses your computer will be able to connect to the Internet with your account.

- Clicking the PPP Options button displays a dialog sheet with advanced options for configuring your PPP connection.

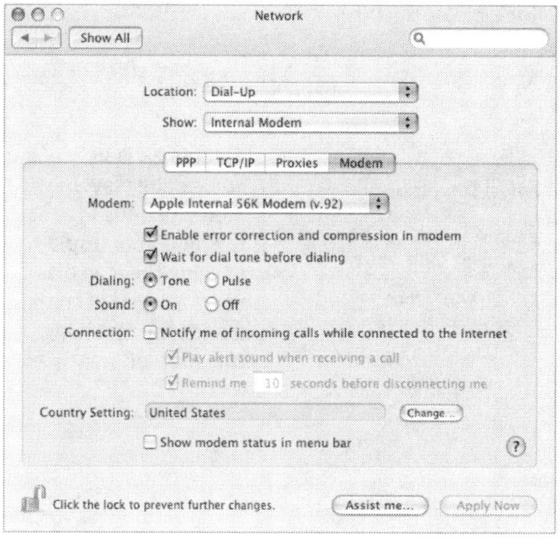

**Figure 23** Modem options for a dial-up connection.

## To set Modem options for a dial-up connection

1. In the Network pane of System Preferences (**Figure 2**), choose Internal Modem (or Modem) from the Show pop-up (**Figure 21**).

2. Click the Modem button to display Modem options (**Figure 23**).

3. Choose your modem type from the Modem pop-up menu.

4. To minimize errors and speed up data transfer, turn on the Enable error correction and compression in modem check box.

5. To instruct your computer to wait until it "hears" a dial tone before it dials, turn on the Wait for dial tone before dialing check box.

6. Select a dialing radio button:
   - ▲ **Tone** enables you to dial with touch-tone dialing.
   - ▲ **Pulse** enables you to dial with pulse dialing. Select this option only if touchtone dialing is not available on your telephone line.

7. Select a Sound radio button:
   - ▲ **On** plays dialing and connection sounds through the modem or computer speaker.
   - ▲ **Off** dials and connects silently.

8. If you have call waiting and want to be alerted for incoming calls, turn on the Notify me of incoming calls while connected to the Internet check box. You can then toggle settings two options:

*Continued on next page...*

SETTING MODEM OPTIONS

*Continued from previous page.*

▲ **Play alert sound when receiving a call** plays an audible alert when an incoming call is detected while you're connected to the Internet.

▲ **Remind me** *n* **seconds before disconnecting me** displays a reminder dialog the number of seconds you specify before disconnecting you from the Internet to answer the incoming call.

9. To change the Country Setting for your location, click the Change button beside Country Setting. This displays the Date & Time preferences pane so you can set country options.

10. To include a modem status icon and menu in the menu bar (**Figures 24** and **25**), turn on the Show modem status in menu bar check box.

11. Click Apply Now.

## ✔ Tips

■ The Modem menu in step 3 includes dozens of modems, so yours should be listed. If it isn't, choose another model from the same manufacturer.

■ The Enable error correction and compression in modem option in step 4 is not available for all modems.

■ In step 7, you may want to keep modem sounds on until you're sure you can connect. This enables you to hear telephone company error recordings that can help you troubleshoot connection problems. You can always turn sound off later.

■ If you do not have call waiting or don't want to be bothered by incoming calls if you do, keep the Notify me check box turned off in step 8.

*Modem status icon*

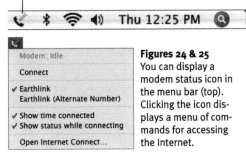

**Figures 24 & 25**
You can display a modem status icon in the menu bar (top). Clicking the icon displays a menu of commands for accessing the Internet.

**SETTING MODEM OPTIONS**

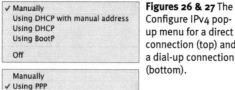

**Figures 26 & 27** The Configure IPv4 pop-up menu for a direct connection (top) and a dial-up connection (bottom).

# To set TCP/IP options

1. In the Network pane of System Preferences (**Figure 2**), choose your type of connection from the Show pop-up (**Figure 21**).

2. If necessary, click the TCP/IP button to display TCP/IP options.

3. Choose one of the options from the Configure IPv4 pop-up menu (**Figures 26 and 27**). The option you select determines the appearance of the rest of the screen. **Figures 28** through **34** show examples.

4. If necessary, enter the appropriate IP addresses and domain names in the fields.

5. Click Apply Now.

*Continued on next page...*

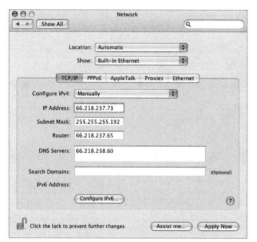

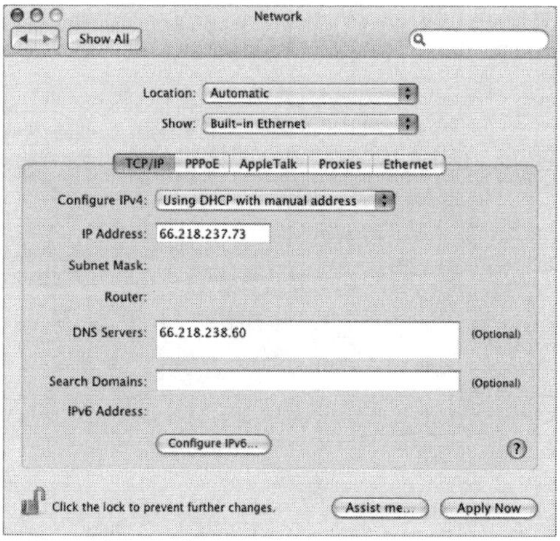

**Figure 28** This example shows a manual TCP/IP configuration for an Ethernet (direct) connection. You'd use this for a static IP address.

**Figure 29** This example combines a manually entered static IP address with DHCP addressing.

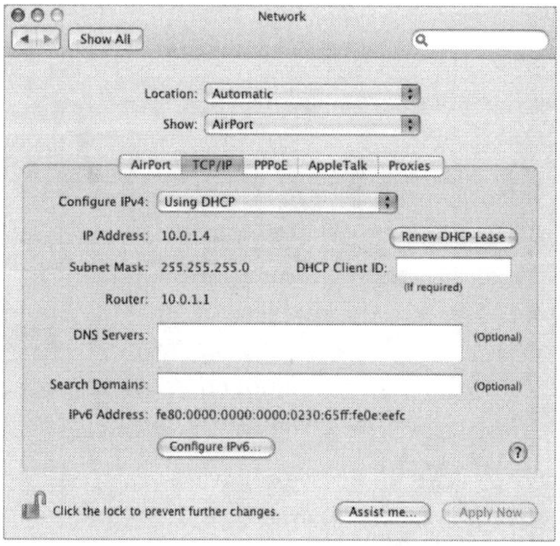

**Figure 30** This is the most commonly used option: using DHCP to obtain a dynamically assigned IP address.

*Continued from previous page.*

## ✔ Tips

- Do not use the settings illustrated here. Use the settings provided by your ISP or network administrator.

- DHCP is a type of network addressing system.

- If you're not sure which option to choose in step 4, ask your network administrator.

- In step 5, if you turn on the Save password check box, you won't have to enter your password when you connect to the Internet. Be aware, however, that anyone who accesses your computer with your login will also be able to connect to the Internet with your account.

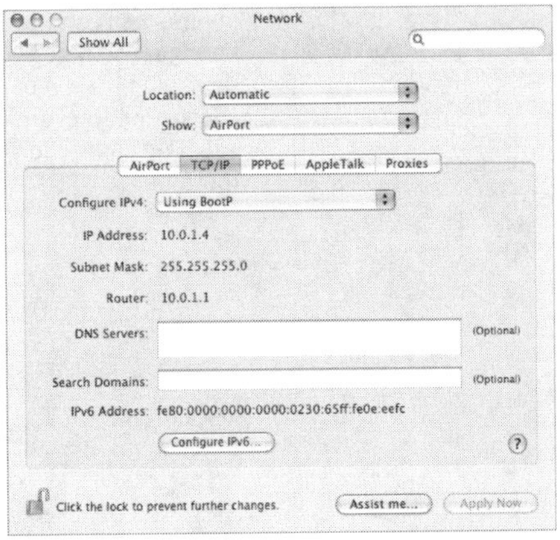

**Figure 31** Here's a BootP setup for a direct connection.

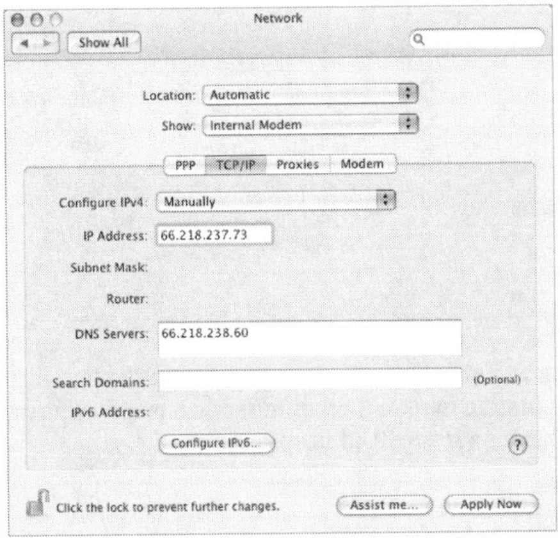

**Figure 32** On rare occasions, you may have a dial-up connection with a static IP address.

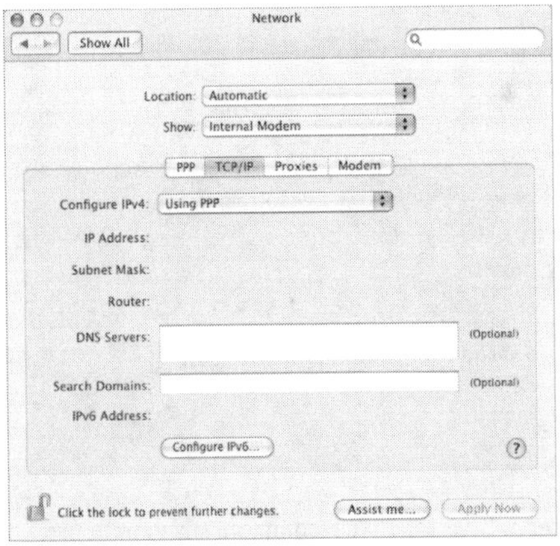

**Figure 33** Most dial-up connections use PPP.

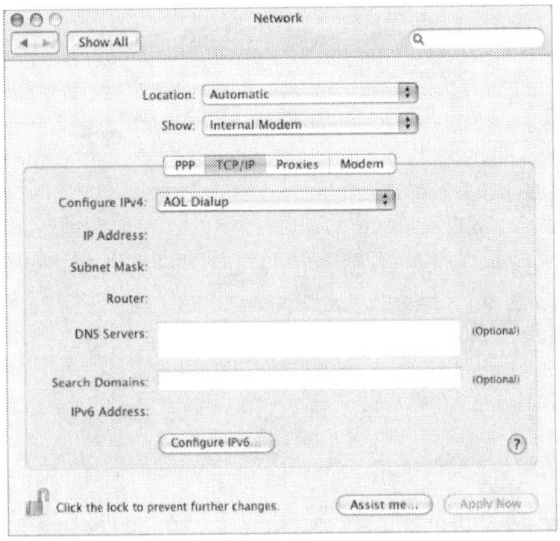

**Figure 34** If you connect via AOL, be sure to choose AOL Dialup.

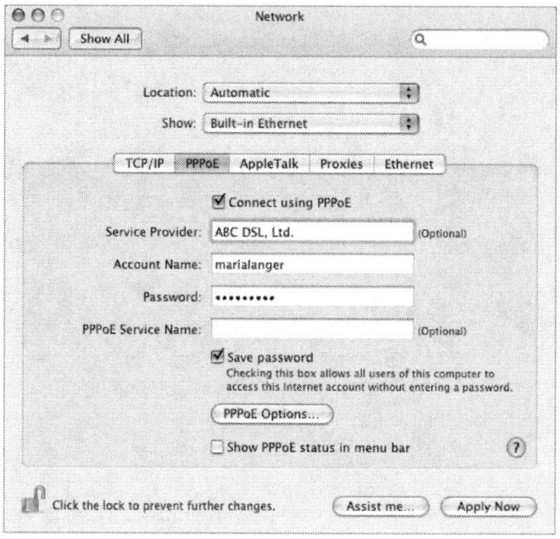

**Figure 35** You can use the PPPoE tab to set up a PPPoE connection to a DSL server.

## To set PPPoE options

1. In the Network pane of System Preferences (**Figure 2**), choose your type of connection from the Show pop-up (**Figure 21**).

2. If necessary, click the PPPoE button to display PPPoE options (**Figure 35**).

3. Turn on the Connect using PPPoE check box and enter the connection information provided by your ISP. **Figure 35** shows an example.

4. Click Apply Now.

## ✔ Tips

- PPPoE is sometimes used for DSL connections to the Internet.

- If your ISP does not instruct you to configure for a PPPoE connection, do not follow these instructions. A PPPoE configuration is seldom needed for an Internet connection.

- Clicking the PPPoE Options button displays a dialog sheet with advanced options for configuring PPPoE.

## To set proxy options

1. In the Network pane of System Preferences (**Figure 2**), choose your type of connection from the Show pop-up (**Figure 21**).

2. If necessary, click the Proxies button to display Proxies options (**Figure 36**).

3. Turn on the check box beside each proxy option you need to set up. Then enter appropriate information for each one.

4. Click Apply Now to save your changes to Network preferences.

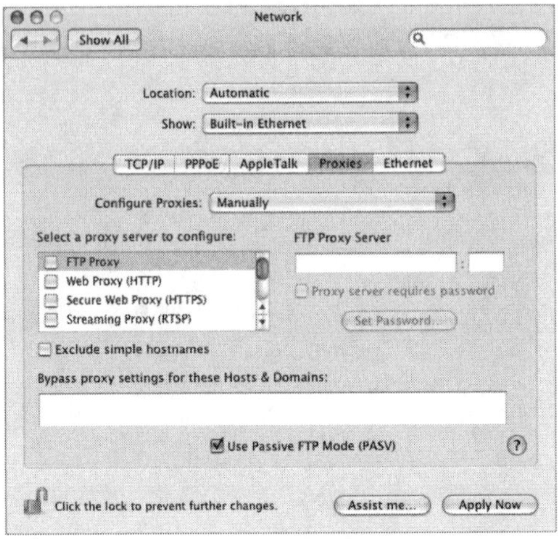

## ✖ Warning!

- Do not change settings in the Proxies tab of Network preferences unless instructed by your ISP or network administrator. Setting invalid values may prevent you from connecting to the Internet.

## ✔ Tips

- Proxies options are the same for dial-up connections as they are for direct connections.

- Proxies are most often required for network connections; they are seldom required for dial-up connections.

- Proxies enable your Internet connection to work with security setups such as firewalls that protect network computers from hackers. For more information about proxy settings on your network, consult your network administrator.

**Figure 36** The Proxies options of the Network preferences pane.

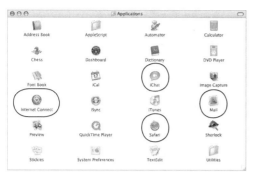

**Figure 37** The Applications folder includes a number of applications for accessing the Internet.

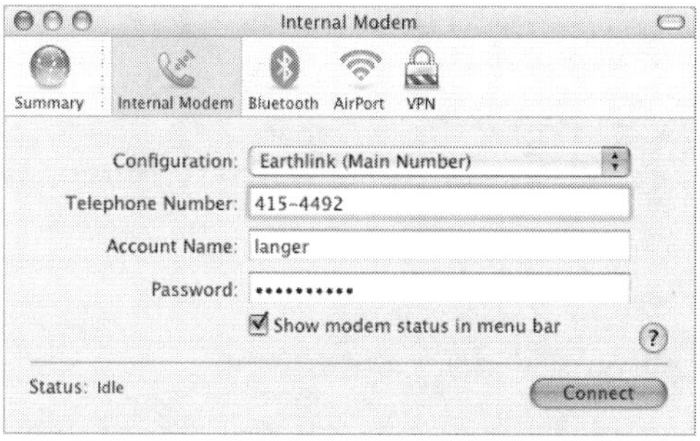

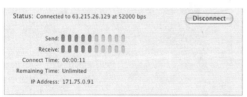

**Figure 38** Internet Connect's Internal Modem pane.

Status: Contacting PPP Server...    [ Cancel ]

**Figure 39** The Status area displays connection status information while you are connecting...

Status: Connected to 63.215.26.129 at 52000 bps    [ Disconnect ]

Send: ▌▌▌▌▌▌▌▌▌▌▌
Receive: ▌▌▌▌▌▌▌▌▌▌▌
Connect Time: 00:00:11
Remaining Time: Unlimited
IP Address: 171.75.0.91

**Figure 40** ...and after you have connected.

# Connecting to an ISP

You can establish a PPP connection to your ISP by using Internet Connect to dial in.

## ✔ Tip

■ If you have a network connection to the Internet—including a cable modem or DSL connection—you are always connected and can skip this section.

## To connect to an ISP

1. Open the Internet Connect icon in the Applications folder (**Figure 37**).

2. If necessary, click the Internal Modem button to display its settings (**Figure 38**).

3. Check the settings and make changes as necessary.

4. Click the Connect button. Internet Connect dials your modem. It displays the connection status in its Status area (**Figure 39**).

   When Internet Connect has successfully connected, the Connect button turns into a Disconnect button and the Status area fills with connection information (**Figures 13** and **40**).

## ✔ Tips

■ The settings in Internet Connect (**Figure 38**) come from the PPP pane of Network preferences for a modem connection (**Figure 22**).

■ Internet Connect does not have to be open while you are connected to the Internet.

## To disconnect from an ISP

1. Open or switch to Internet Connect.

2. Click the Disconnect button (**Figures 13** and **40**). The connection is terminated.

# Internet Applications

Mac OS X includes three applications for accessing the Internet:

**Figure 41** You can open Safari, Mail, and iChat by clicking their icons in the Dock.

- ◆ **Mail** is an Apple program that enables you to send and receive e-mail messages.

- ◆ **iChat** is an Apple program that enables you to exchange instant messages and conduct audio or video conferences with .Mac, AIM (AOL Instant Messenger), and Jabber users.

- ◆ **Safari** is an Apple program that enables you to browse Web sites and download files from FTP sites.

This section provides brief instructions for using these three programs—just enough to get you started. You can explore the other features of these programs on your own.

## ✔ Tips

- ■ Mail and Safari are set as the default e-mail and Web browser programs.

- ■ Internet Explorer is a Microsoft program that enables you to browse Web sites and download files from FTP sites. Although Internet Explorer does not come with Mac OS X 10.4, it's quite popular. It can be downloaded from Microsoft's Mactopia Web site, www.mactopia.com.

## To open an Internet application

Use one of the following techniques:

- ◆ Open the icon for the application in the Applications folder (**Figure 37**).

- ◆ Click the icon for the application in the Dock (**Figure 41**).

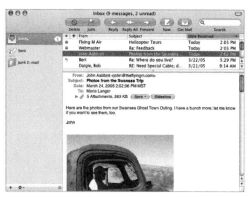

**Figure 42** The Mail main window with an incoming message displayed.

# Mail

Mail (**Figure 42**) is an e-mail application. It enables you to send and receive e-mail messages using your Internet e-mail account.

Here's how it works. Imagine having a mailbox at the post office. As mail comes in, the postmaster sorts it into the boxes—including yours. To get your mail, you need to go to the post office to pick it up. While you're there, you're likely to drop off any letters you need to send.

E-mail works the same way. Your e-mail is delivered to your e-mail server—like the post office where your mailbox is. The server software (like the postmaster) sorts the mail into mailboxes. When your e-mail client software (Mail, in this case) connects to the server via the Internet, it picks up your incoming mail and sends any outgoing messages it has to send.

If you set up your Internet connection and provided e-mail information when you first configured Mac OS X, that information is automatically stored in Mail so it's ready to use. Just open Mail and it automatically makes that virtual trip to the post office to get and send messages.

In this part of the chapter, I explain how to set up an e-mail account with Mail, just in case you need to add an account. I also explain how to compose, send, read, and retrieve e-mail messages.

## ✔ Tip

- The first time you open Mail, a dialog appears, asking if you want to import e-mail addresses from another e-mail program. If you do, click Yes and follow the instructions that appear onscreen to perform the import.

# To set up an e-mail account

1. Choose Mail > Preferences, or press ⌘ ⌘ ,.

2. In the Mail Preferences window that appears, click the Accounts button to display its options (**Figure 43**).

3. Click the + button beneath the list of accounts.

4. A dialog sheet like the one in **Figure 44** appears. Enter information for the account:

   ▲ **Account Type** is the type of e-mail account. Your options are .Mac, POP, IMAP, or Exchange.

   ▲ **Account Description** is a name to distinguish this account from other accounts.

   ▲ **Full Name** is your full name.

   ▲ **User Name** (for .Mac accounts only) is your .Mac user name.

   ▲ **Email Address** (for all account types other than .Mac) is your e-mail address.

   ▲ **Password** (for .Mac accounts only) is your .Mac account password.

5. Click Continue. If you created a .Mac account, skip ahead to step 8.

6. In the Incoming Mail Server dialog (**Figure 45**), enter information for your incoming mail server and click Continue.

   ▲ **Incoming Mail Server** is the domain name or IP address of your incoming mail server.

   ▲ **User Name** is your user ID on the mail server.

   ▲ **Password** is your password on the mail server.

**Figure 43** The Accounts pane of Mail Preferences.

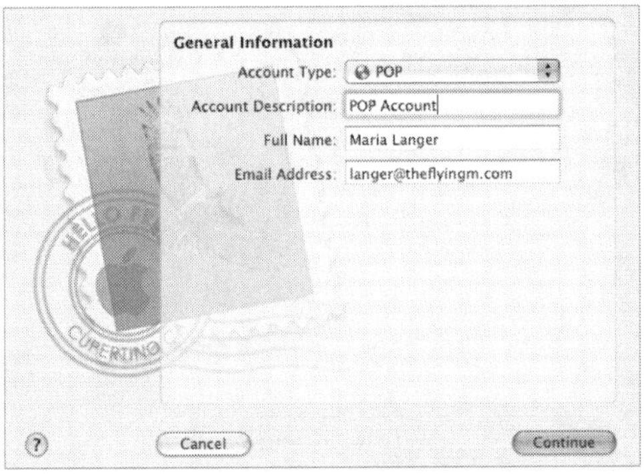

**Figure 44** Start by providing general information about the account.

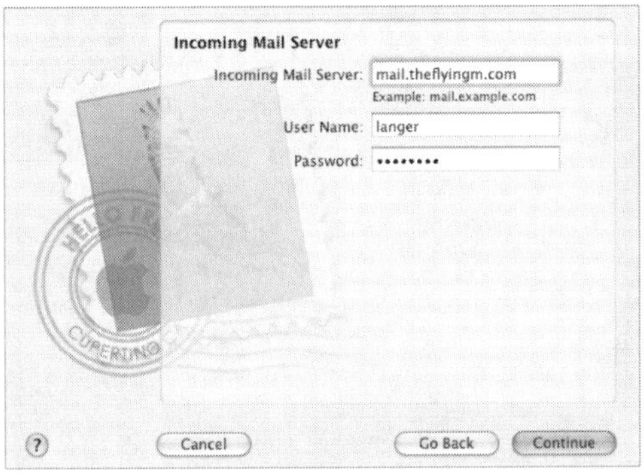

**Figure 45** For most account types, you'll have to enter information about your incoming mail server.

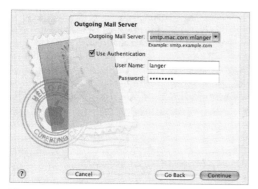

**Figure 46** For most types of e-mail accounts, you'll also have to provide outgoing mail server info.

**Figure 47** Mail displays a summary of the account information it has confirmed.

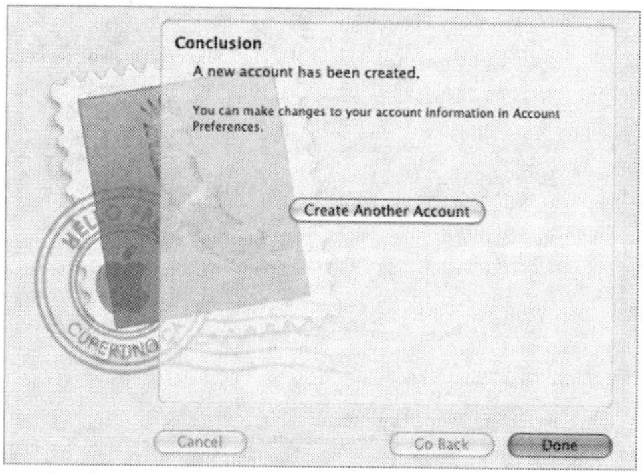

**Figure 48** When you're finished, you have two options: create another account or close the dialog and get back to work.

▲ **Outlook Web Access Server** (for Exchange accounts only) is the domain name or IP address of the Outlook server for Web access to e-mail.

7. In the Outgoing Mail Server dialog (**Figure 46**), enter information for your outgoing mail server and click Continue.

▲ **Outgoing Mail Server** is the domain name or IP address of your outgoing mail server. You can choose a server from the drop-down list or enter information for a different server.

▲ **Use Authentication** tells Mail to send your user name and password when sending mail. This is required by most mail servers. If you turn on this check box, be sure to enter your account user name and password in the boxes below it.

8. When Mail has verified all information you entered, it displays the results in an Account Summary window (**Figure 47**). Click Continue.

9. The Conclusion window appears (**Figure 48**). You have two options:

▲ **Create Another Account** enables you to repeat steps 4 through 9 to create another e-mail account.

▲ **Done** dismisses the dialog sheet so you can continue working with Mail.

10. The new account is added to the Accounts list (**Figure 49**). Click the window's close button to close the Accounts window.

*Continued on next page...*

**SETTING UP E-MAIL ACCOUNTS**

*Continued from previous page.*

## ✔ Tips

- Another way to set up a new e-mail account is to choose File > Add Account. Then follow steps 4 through 9 on the previous two pages.

- You only have to set up an e-mail account once. Mail will remember all of your settings.

- Your ISP or network administrator can provide all of the important information you need to set up an e-mail account, including the account name, password, and mail servers.

- If you have a .Mac account and want to set up another account, you must enter a domain name or IP address for a different outgoing mail server (**Figure 46**) for that account. The .Mac outgoing mail server will only send e-mail messages for a .Mac account. Outgoing or SMTP server information should be provided by your ISP.

- You can set other options for an account by clicking the Mailbox Behaviors and Advanced buttons in the Accounts pane (**Figure 43**). Explore these options on your own.

**Figure 49**
The new account is added to the Accounts list.

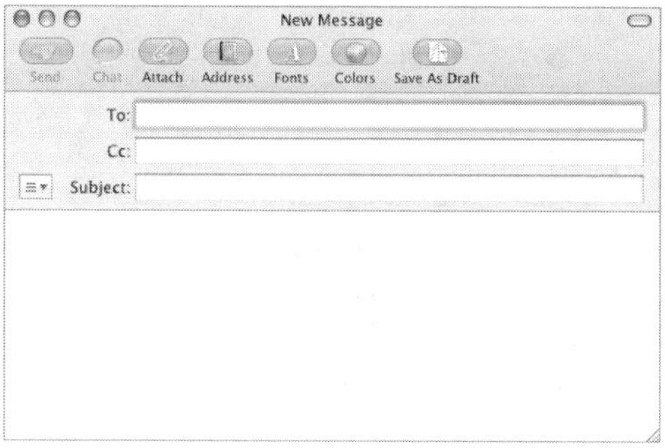

**Figure 50** Clicking the New button opens a New Message window like this one.

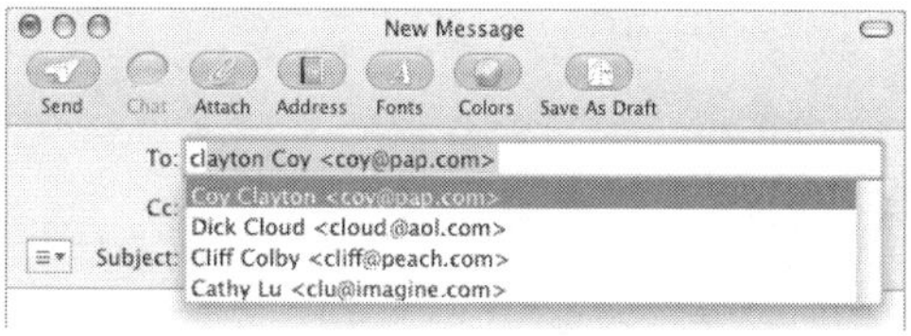

**Figure 51** When you begin to type in a name, Mail tries to match it to entries in Address Book.

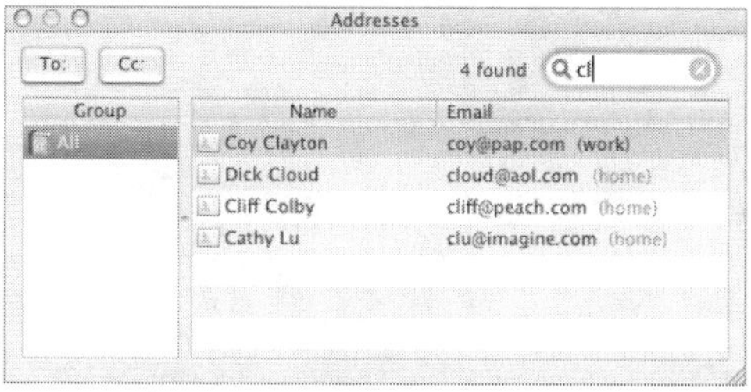

**Figure 52** You can also use an Addresses window to enter a recipient's e-mail address.

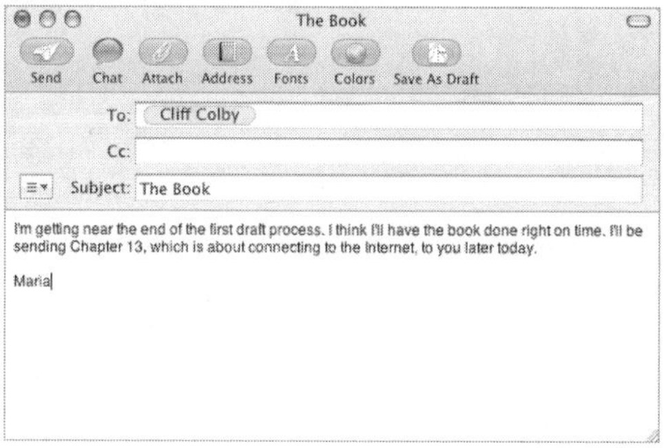

**Figure 53** Here's a short message ready to be sent.

# To create & send a message

1. Click the New button at the top of the main Mail window (**Figure 42**). The New Message window appears (**Figure 50**).

2. Use one of the following techniques to enter the recipient's address in the To box:
   ▲ Type the recipient's e-mail address.
   ▲ If the recipient is someone in your Address Book file or someone you have received an e-mail message from in the past, enter the person's name. As you type, Mail attempts to match the name (**Figure 51**). Click the correct entry.
   ▲ Click the Address button. Use the searchable Addresses window that appears (**Figure 52**) to locate the recipient's name and double-click it.

3. Repeat step 2 to add additional names. When you are finished, click Tab twice.

4. Enter a subject for the message in the Subject field, and press Tab.

5. Type your message in the large box at the bottom of the window. When you are finished, the window might look like the one in **Figure 53**.

6. Click the Send button. The message window closes and Mail sends the message.

# ✔ Tips

■ Address Book is covered in **Chapter 8**.

■ To add a file as an attachment to the message, drag the file's icon from a Finder window into the message body.

■ If you have a modem connection to the Internet, you must connect before you can send a message.

## To retrieve e-mail messages

1. Click the Get Mail button at the top of the main window (**Figure 42**).

2. Mail accesses the Internet, then connects to your e-mail server and downloads messages waiting for you. Incoming messages appear in a list when you select the Inbox in the Mailboxes column (**Figure 42**).

## ✔ Tips

- A blue bullet character appears beside each unread e-mail message (**Figure 42**).

- Messages that Mail thinks are junk mail are colored brown. You can set junk mail filtering options in the Junk Mail preferences window (**Figure 54**). Choose Mail > Preferences and click the Junk Mail button to get started. You'll find that Mail's junk mail filter can weed out at least 75% of the junk mail that you get.

- You can configure Mail to have multiple mailboxes to organize your incoming e-mail more effectively. Use commands under the Mailbox menu to create and customize mailboxes.

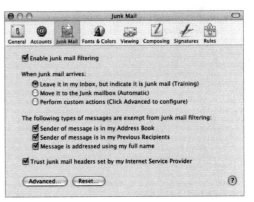

**Figure 54** The Junk Mail preferences window enables you to set options that weed out junk mail messages.

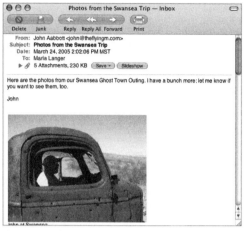

**Figure 55** Double-click a message to open it in its own window.

**Figure 56** Clicking the Attachments triangle displays icons for attachments. In this example, five JPEG image files are attached..

**Figure 57** The Save menu enables you to save all attachments or a specific attachment. If the attachment is a photo, you can even save it directly to iPhoto (if installed).

## To read a message

1. Click the message that you want to read. It appears in the bottom half of the main Mail window (**Figure 42**).

2. Read the message.

## ✔ Tips

■ You can also double-click a message to display it in its own message window (**Figure 55**).

■ To view a list of message attachments (when present), click the triangle beside the paper clip icon in the message header. The header expands to show icons for each attachment (**Figure 56**). To save attachments, click the Save button to display a menu (**Figure 57**) and choose the desired option. A Save As dialog appears so you select a location to save the file(s).

■ If a message includes photos, you can click the Slideshow button to display a slide show of all photos, one at a time (**Figure 58**). This is a new feature in Mac OS X 10.4.

**Figure 58** You can display photo attachments as a slide show, right from within Mail.

## To reply to a message

1. Click the Reply or Reply All button at the top of the window. A preaddressed message window with the entire message quoted appears (**Figure 59**).

2. Type your reply, in the message body.

3. Click Send.

## ✔ Tip

- The Reply button addresses the reply to the person who sent you the message. The Reply All button addresses the reply to the person who sent you the message and sends a copy of the message to all other recipients.

## To forward a message

1. Click the Forward button at the top of the window. A copy of the message appears in a new message form (**Figure 60**).

2. Enter the e-mail address of the person you want to forward the message to in the To box.

3. If desired, enter a message at the top of the message body.

4. Click Send.

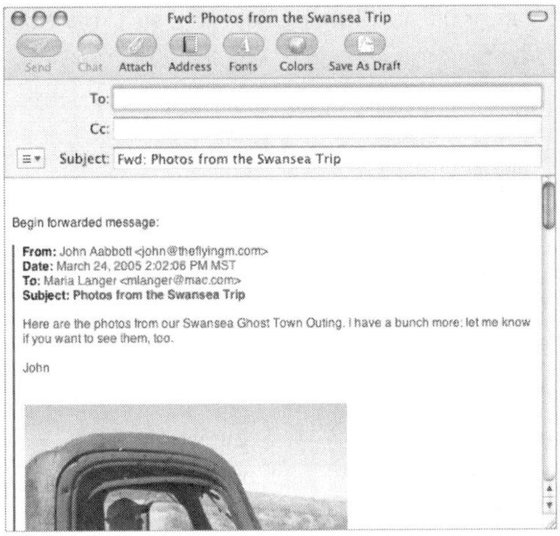

## To add a message's sender to the Address Book

1. Select (**Figure 42**) or open (**Figure 55**) the message sent by the sender you want to add.

2. Choose Message > Add Sender to Address Book or press ⌃ ⌘ Y.

   Mail automatically adds the person's name and e-mail address to Address Book's entries. You can open Address Book and add additional information for the record as desired.

**Figure 59** When you click the Reply button, a pre-addressed message window appears.

**Figure 60** A forwarded message includes the entire message and any attachments.

# iChat

iChat enables you to conduct live chats or audio or video conferences with .Mac, AIM (AOL Instant Messenger), and Jabber users.

Here's how it works. The first time you open iChat, you configure it with your .Mac or AIM account information, as well as the information for your buddies who use iChat or AIM. Then, while you're connected to the Internet with iChat running, iChat does two things:

◆ It tells iChat and AIM users that you're available to receive instant messages and participate in chats.

◆ It tells you when your buddies are connected via iChat or AIM and available to receive instant messages and participate in chats.

When a buddy is available, sending him an instant message is as easy as clicking a button and typing what you want to say. If more than one buddy is available, you can open a chat window and invite them to participate together.

iChat also includes AV (audio and video conferencing) features. If you have a microphone or a compatible video camera (including Apple's iSight camera), you can have live audio or video chats with your buddies.

In this part of the chapter, I explain how to configure iChat for your account, set up an iChat buddy list, invite a buddy to a chat, and participate in text or video chats.

## ✔ Tips

■ To use iChat, you must have a .Mac or AIM account. To use the AV features, you must have a microphone (for audio only) or compatible video camera (for audio and video) and a fast Internet connection.

■ To learn more about iChat, visit www. apple.com/ichat/. To learn more about the iSight camera, check out www.apple.com/ isight/.

iCHAT

## To set up iChat

1. Open iChat as discussed earlier in this chapter.

2. Read the information in the Welcome to iChat AV dialog that appears (**Figure 61**) and click Continue.

3. In the Set up iChat Instant Messaging dialog (**Figure 62**), enter your name and .Mac or AIM account information. Be sure to select the correct option from the Account Type pop-up menu (**Figure 63**). Then click Continue.

4. The Set up Jabber Instant Messaging dialog appears next (**Figure 64**).

   If you're on a network that supports the Jabber instant messaging protocol, turn on the check box and enter your Jabber account name and password in the boxes and click Continue.

   *or*

   If you will not be using Jabber instant messaging, just click Continue.

5. The Set up Bonjour Messaging dialog appears next (**Figure 65**).

   If you're on a Bonjour network and want to exchange instant messages with people on your network, turn on the Use Bonjour Messaging check box and click Continue.

   *or*

   If you will not be using Bonjour messaging, just click Continue.

**Figure 61** The Welcome to iChat AV window tells you a little about iChat AV.

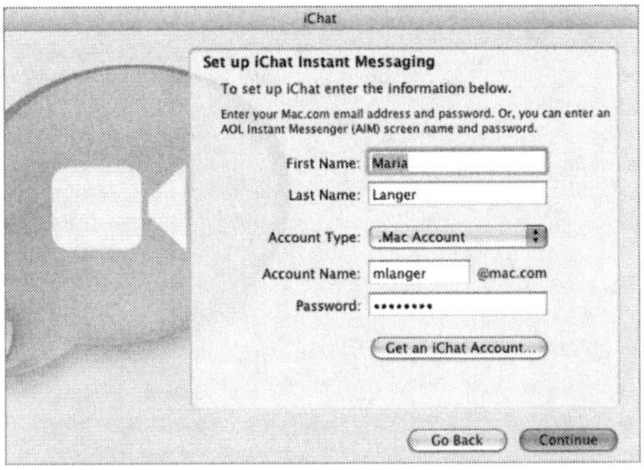

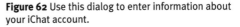

**Figure 62** Use this dialog to enter information about your iChat account.

**Figure 63**
The Account Type pop-up menu.

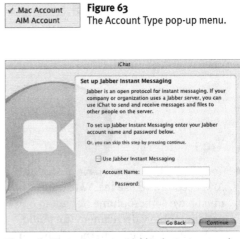

**Figure 64** iChat now support Jabber instant messaging.

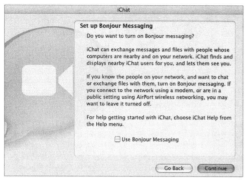

**Figure 65** A dialog like this asks whether you want to enable Bonjour messaging.

**Figure 66** If you have a compatible video camera attached, you'll see what it sees in this dialog. (Hmm. I look better this year than last year. Must be clean living.)

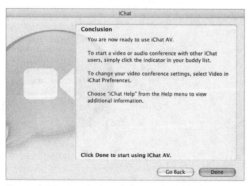

**Figure 67** The Conclusion dialog at the end of the iChat setup process.

6. The Set up iChat AV dialog appears next. If you have a compatible video camera attached to your computer and turned on, you'll see an image (**Figure 66**). Otherwise, a message will say that there is no camera attached to the computer. If you have a microphone, you'll also see a sound level indicator that moves as you make noise. Click Continue.

7. Read the information in the Conclusion dialog (**Figure 67**). and click Done.

8. A Buddy List window with a "Connecting" message appears next. Wait while iChat connects to the chat servers. The Buddy List expands to list your buddies and their online status (**Figure 68**).

*Continued on next page...*

**Figure 68**
Your Buddy list window shows all of your buddies and their status.

#### Chapter 13

*Continued from previous page.*

## ✔ Tips

- In step 3, if you don't have a .Mac account or AIM account, click the Get an iChat Account button. This launches your Web browser and connects you to the Internet so you can sign up for a free .Mac iChat screen name.

- In step 6, if a message appears stating that your camera is in use by another application, disconnect the camera, wait a moment, and reconnect it. This usually solves this problem with my iChat and iSight setup; it should work for you, too.

- Bonjour (formerly known as Rendezvous) is a type of networking that's part of Mac OS X. You can learn more about networking in **Chapter 16**.

- If you have enabled Bonjour messaging, two windows appear—a Buddy List window (**Figure 68**) and a Bonjour window that looks just like it (**Figure 69**). The instructions in this chapter should help you get started using iChat with Bonjour, too.

- If you set a picture for yourself in Address Book, that picture automatically appears for you in iChat (**Figures 68** and **69**). I explain how to use Address Book in **Chapter 8**.

- If you have used any version of iChat before—even if you used it on another computer—iChat retrieves your previous buddy list from the Internet and displays it in the Buddy List window (**Figure 68**).

**Figure 69**
If you've enabled Bonjour messaging, a Bonjour window opens, too.

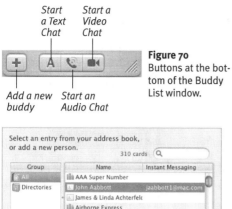

Start a Text Chat · Start a Video Chat

Add a new buddy · Start an Audio Chat

**Figure 70**
Buttons at the bottom of the Buddy List window.

Select an entry from your address book,
or add a new person.

310 cards

| Group | Name | Instant Messaging |
|---|---|---|
| All | AAA Super Number | |
| Directories | John Aabbott | jaabbott1@mac.com |
| | James & Linda Achterfeld | |
| | Airborne Express | |
| | Harry Allen | |
| | David Allred | |
| | Paul Alukonis | |

New Person · Cancel · Select Buddy

**Figure 71** To add a person from your Address Book to your Buddy List, select his or her record and click Select Buddy.

Enter the buddy's AIM screen name or Mac.com account:

Account Type: .Mac

Account Name: jackthedog  @mac.com

Address Book Information (optional):

Buddy Icon

First Name: Jack
Last Name: Dog
Email: jackthedog@mac.com

Cancel · Add

**Figure 72** To add a new person (or my dog, in this example) to your Buddy List, fill in this form.

**Figure 73**
Buddies who are available appear in black type with a color-coded bullet beside their names. Buddies who are offline appear in gray type. A telephone or camera icon beside a buddy name indicates audio or video capabilities.

## To add a buddy

1. Click the Add a new buddy button at the bottom of the Buddy List window (**Figure 70**).

   *or*

   Choose Buddies > Add Buddy, or press [Shift][⌘][A].

2. A dialog sheet like the one in **Figure 71** appears. You have two choices:

   ▲ To add a person in your Address Book to your Buddy List, select a name in the dialog and click Select Buddy.

   ▲ To add a person not in your Address Book to your Buddy List, click the New Person button. Then fill out the form that appears by entering information about the person you want to add (**Figure 72**). Click Add.

## ✔ Tips

■ You can add as many .Mac and AIM accounts as you like to your buddy list.

■ A buddy's online status and audio or video capabilities is indicated in the buddy list with a color-coded bullet and phone or camera icons. **Figure 73** shows some examples.

■ If your Buddy List remains empty after adding buddies, you may have the list configured to show only available buddies. Choose View > Show Offline Buddies to display all buddies in the list, regardless of availability.

## To remove a buddy

1. Select the name of the buddy you want to remove.

2. Press [Delete].

3. Click OK in the confirmation dialog that appears.

## To conduct a text chat

1. In the Buddy List, select the name of a buddy who is available for chatting (**Figure 74**).

2. Click the Start a Text Chat button at the bottom of the Buddy List window (**Figure 70**). A window like the one in **Figure 75** appears.

3. Enter your message in the box at the bottom of the window. As you type, a "cloud" appears beside your icon to indicate that you're writing something (**Figure 76**).

4. Press Return. The comment appears in the top half of the window beside your icon (**Figure 77**).

5. Wait for your buddy to answer. Her comments appear in the top half of the window beside her icon (**Figure 78**). If your buddy starts typing again, a "cloud" appears beside her icon (**Figure 79**).

6. Repeat steps 3 through 5 to continue your instant message conversation in the window. **Figure 80** shows an example of the start of a conversation between a freelance writer and one of her editors.

**Figure 74**
Select a buddy who is available for chatting. If the buddy has a custom icon, it appears when she becomes available. From that point forward, it is saved in iChat.

**Figure 75**
As you begin to type, a "cloud" appears beside your icon.

**Figure 76**
Type your message in the box.

**Figure 77** When you press Return, your message appears in the top half of the window.

**Figure 78** When your buddy responds, her message appears beside her icon.

**Figure 79** A "cloud" appears beside your buddy's icon as she types.

**Figure 80**
The start of a conversation.

CONDUCTING TEXT CHATS

**Figure 81**
Select a buddy who is available for video chatting.

**Figure 82** Try to be patient while you wait for the buddy to respond. (I look pretty dazed here, don't I?)

**Figure 83** When the buddy appears, start talking! (This is Lars from Tucson, who is getting ready to start medical school. He's getting to be a regular in my Mac OS books!)

## To conduct a video chat

1. In the Buddy List, select the name of a buddy who is available for video chatting (**Figure 81**).

2. Click the Start a Video Chat button at the bottom of the Buddy List window (**Figure 70**). A window like the one in **Figure 82** appears.

3. Wait until your buddy responds. When he accepts the chat, the window changes to show his live image, with yours in a small box (**Figure 83**).

4. Talk!

## ✔ Tips

- To conduct a video chat, both you and your buddy must have video capabilities. Look for a camera icon beside a buddy's name (**Figure 81**).

- Video chats work best when both parties are accessing the Internet at speeds of 256Kbps or faster. You will notice an annoying time delay if you access at slow speed.

## To end a chat

Click the close button in the chat window (**Figures 80** and **83**). Be sure to say "Bye" first!

## To respond to a text chat invitation

1. When another iChat user invites you to a text chat, his message appears in a window on your desktop (**Figure 84**). Click the window to display an Instant Message window (**Figure 85**).

2. To accept the invitation, enter a message in the box at the bottom of the window (**Figure 86**) and click Accept or press Return. The message appears in the main window, which expands to display the chat (**Figure 87**).

   *or*

   To decline the invitation, click the Decline button or click the window's close button. The Instant Message window disappears.

   *or*

   To prevent the person from ever bothering you again with an invitation, click the Block button. Then click Block in the confirmation dialog that appears (**Figure 88**). The Instant Message window disappears.

**Figure 84** A chat invitation appears in a little window like this.

**Figure 85** Click the window to expand it.

**Figure 86** Enter your message in the bottom of the window.

**Figure 87** When you accept a chat, the window expands so you can read and write messages.

**Figure 88** Click Block in this dialog to prevent an annoying person from bothering you.

**Figure 89** When you get a video chat invitation, you'll hear the sound of a ringing phone and a dialog like this appears.

**Figure 90** Use one of the buttons at the bottom of the window to respond to the invitation. (Boy, do I look spaced out here!)

**Figure 91** When you accept an invitation, the caller's smiling face appears and you can start talking. (This is Lincoln and Ben Colby, who talked to me from California.)

# To respond to a video chat invitation

1.  When another iChat user invites you to a video chat, an invitation window like the one in **Figure 89** appears and iChat makes a phone ringing sound. Click the window to display a Video Chat window (**Figure 90**).

2.  To accept the invitation, click Accept or press Return. iChat establishes a connection with the caller and the window changes to show his live image, with yours in a small box (**Figure 91**). Start talking!

    *or*

    To decline the invitation, click the Decline button or click the window's close button. The Video Chat window disappears.

# Safari

Safari is a Web browser application. It enables you to view, or *browse,* pages on the World Wide Web.

A Web *page* is a window full of formatted text and graphics (**Figures 92** and **93**). You move from page to page by clicking text or graphic links or by opening *URLs* (*uniform resource locators*) for specific Web pages. These two methods of navigating the World Wide Web can open a whole universe of useful or interesting information.

## ✔ Tips

- Safari now supports *RSS* (Really Simple Syndication) feeds. RSS makes it possible to scan articles from several Web sites in one browser window, be notified when a Web site has new articles, and search specific Web sites for terms. I tell you how to get started using RSS later in this section.

- You can easily identify a link by pointing to it; the mouse pointer turns into a pointing finger (**Figure 92**).

- You can change the default home page by specifying a different page's URL in Safari's General preferences (**Figure 94**). Choose Safari > Preferences and click the General button to get started.

## To follow a link

1. Position the mouse pointer on a text or graphic link. The mouse pointer turns into a pointing finger (**Figure 92**).

2. Click. After a moment, the page or other location for the link you clicked will appear (**Figure 93**).

Mouse pointer when pointing to a clickable link    RSS feed button

**Figure 92** When you launch Safari, it displays the default home page.

**Figure 93** Clicking the link in **Figure 92** displays this page.

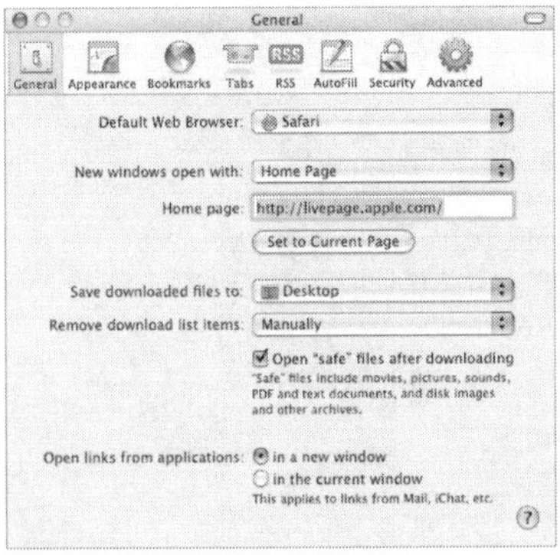

**Figure 94** You can change the default Home page and other settings in Safari's preferences window.

SAFARI, FOLLOWING LINKS

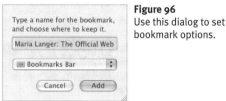

*Previous page*, *Reload page*, *Next page*, *Add bookmark for page*, *Address field*

**Figure 95** Enter the URL in the Address field at the top of the Safari window, and press (Return).

**Figure 96**
Use this dialog to set bookmark options.

Type a name for the bookmark, and choose where to keep it.

Maria Langer: The Official Web

Bookmarks Bar

Cancel    Add

**Figure 97**
This pop-up menu offers a variety of locations in which to save a bookmark.

✓ 🖥 Bookmarks Bar
 📄 Apple
 📄 News
 📄 Bookmarks Menu
 📄 News
  📄 US
  📄 Business
  📄 Technology
 📄 Mac
 📄 Kids
 📄 Sports
 📄 Entertainment
  📄 Movies & DVDs
  📄 iTunes
 📄 Shopping
 📄 Travel
 📄 Tools and Reference
 📄 Other...
 📄 Imported IE Favorites
  📄 Toolbar Favorites
  📄 Apple
  📄 Apple Education
  📄 Where to Buy Macintosh Products
  📄 Macintosh Publications
  📄 QuickTime

## To view a specific URL

Enter the URL in the address field near the top of the Safari window (**Figure 95**), and press (Return) or (Enter).

## To bookmark a page

1. Display the Web page that you want to create a bookmark for.

2. Click the Add bookmark for page button (**Figure 95**), choose Bookmarks > Add Bookmark, or press (⌘ D).

3. A dialog sheet like the one in **Figure 96** appears. Enter a name for the bookmark in the box, then choose a location for it from the pop-up menu (**Figure 97**) and click Add.

   The name you specified is added in the location you specified—either the bookmarks bar (**Figure 98**) or the Bookmarks menu (**Figure 99**).

## ✔ Tips

- Once a page has been added to the Bookmarks menu, you can display it by selecting its name from the menu.

- The synchronization feature of .Mac, which I discuss in **Chapter 14**, can automatically synchronize Safari bookmarks between computers.

Maria Langer: The Official Web Site*
http://www.marialanger.com/
Maria Langer   Apple (26)▾   Amazon   eBay   Yahoo!   News (76)▾

**Figure 98** In this example, I added a bookmark for my Home page to the bookmarks bar.

Bookmarks
Hide All Bookmarks          ⌥⌘B
Add Bookmark...             ⌘D
Add Bookmark Folder        ⇧⌘N
🖥 Bookmarks Bar       ▶       🌐 Maria Langer    ⌘1
                              📄 Apple (26)      ▶
                              🌐 Amazon          ⌘2
                              🌐 eBay            ⌘3
                              🌐 Yahoo!          ⌘4
                              📄 News (76)       ▶
                              View All RSS Articles

**Figure 99** This bookmark also appears on the Bookmarks Bar submenu under the Bookmarks menu.

## To access an RSS feed

Click the RSS button that appears in the address bar (**Figure 92**).

*Or*

Enter the URL for an RSS feed in the address bar and press [Return].

*Or*

On a Web page, click the link for an RSS feed.

The page changes to RSS feed format (**Figures 100** and **101**).

## ✔ Tips

- RSS feeds are sometimes referred to as XML feeds.

- If Safari can find an RSS feed for a site you are viewing, it automatically displays an RSS button in the address bar (**Figure 92**).

- You can find RSS feeds by choosing Bookmarks > Bookmarks Bar > View All RSS Articles (**Figure 99**). **Figure 102** shows what the feed page looked like today when I tried it.

- You can return to the regular Web page view for an RSS feed by clicking the RSS button in the address bar again.

**Figure 100** The RSS feed for the page in **Figure 92**.

**Figure 101** The RSS feed for my personal blogs. I use iBlog software, which automatically creates an RSS feed per my specifications.

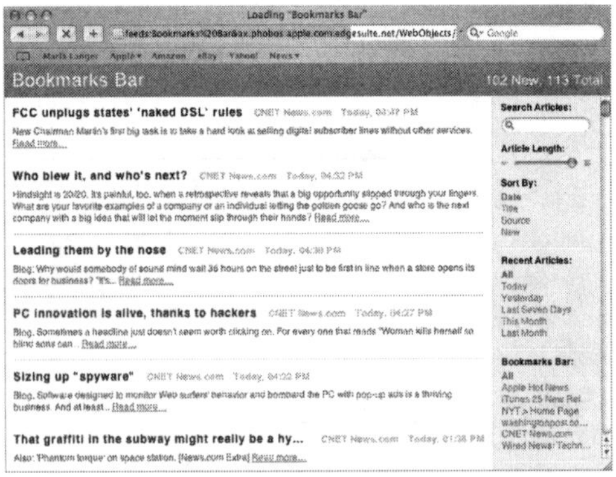

**Figure 102** Choosing View All RSS Articles from the Bookmarks Bar submenu displayed this page on March 25, 2005.

# .Mac

**Figure 1** The .Mac home page explains what .Mac is all about and enables you to get more information about its features.

## .Mac

Apple has embraced the Internet revolution and encourages Mac OS users to get connected to the Internet. One of the ways it does this is with .Mac (pronounced *dot Mac*).

.Mac, which can be found on the Mac.com part of Apple's Web site (**Figure 1**), offers a wide range of features for Macintosh users, including:

◆ **Mail** gives you an e-mail address in the .mac domain that can be accessed via Apple's Mail software, any other e-mail client software, or a Web browser.

◆ **Address Book** puts all your Address Book entries on your .Mac account, where you can access them from any computer.

◆ **Bookmarks** puts all of your Safari bookmarks on your .Mac account, where you can access and use them from any computer.

◆ **HomePage** lets you create and publish a custom Web site hosted on Apple's Web server, using easy-to-use, online Web authoring tools.

◆ **iDisk** gives you hard disk space on Apple's server for saving or sharing files.

◆ **iCards** lets you send custom greeting cards to anyone with an e-mail address.

*Continued on next page...*

*Continued from previous page.*

◆ **Backup** enables you to perform manual or automatic backups to iDisk, CD, or DVD.

◆ **Virex** is McAfee Virex software, which protects your computer from viruses, "Trojan horses," worms, and other computer infections.

◆ **iCal** enables you to publish your iCal calendars on the .Mac Web site so they can be viewed by others. I explain how to publish iCal calendars on the Web in **Chapter 8**.

◆ **Learning Center** enables you to access a variety of Web-based tutorials to help you get the most out of .Mac and your Mac.

A .Mac account also enables you to synchronized data between multiple Macs and to use iChat for chatting with other .Mac and AIM members.

There are two levels of .Mac membership:

◆ **Trial Membership** lets you work with .Mac features for 60 days. Not all features are available to trial members, but the price is right: it's free!

◆ **Full Membership** gives you full access to all .Mac features. When this book went to press, the annual fee was $99.95 per year.

Although this chapter explains how to sign up for and use the Full Membership features of a .Mac account, it provides enough information for you to explore a Trial Membership.

## ✔ Tips

■ To use .Mac, you must have an Internet connection. I explain how to connect to the Internet in **Chapter 13**.

■ You can learn more about .Mac at www.mac.com (**Figure 1**).

■ I explain how to use iChat in **Chapter 13**.

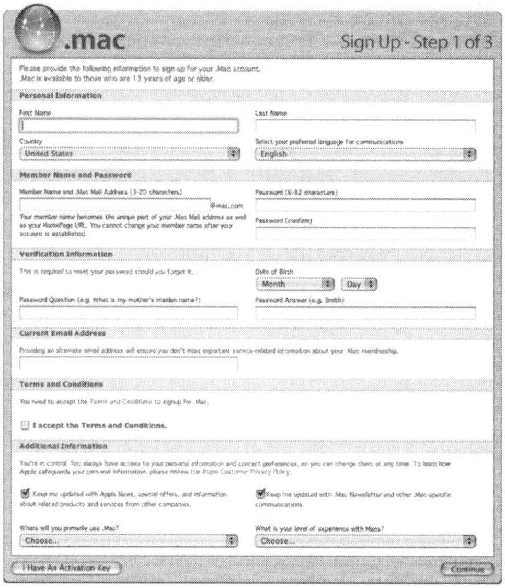

**Figure 2** To join .Mac, start by filling out the Sign Up form.

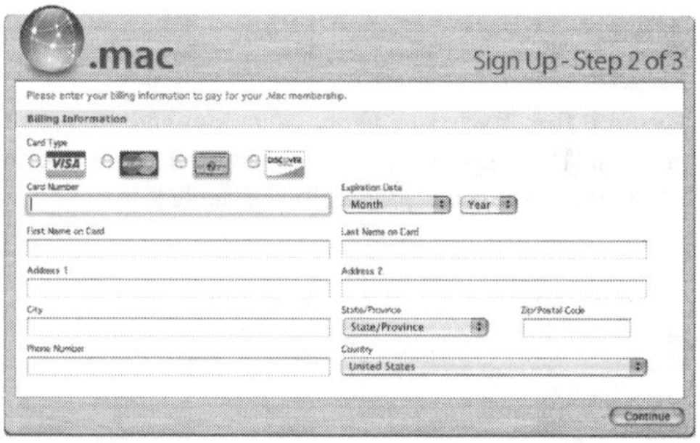

**Figure 3** Use the Billing Information form to enter credit card information to pay for your membership.

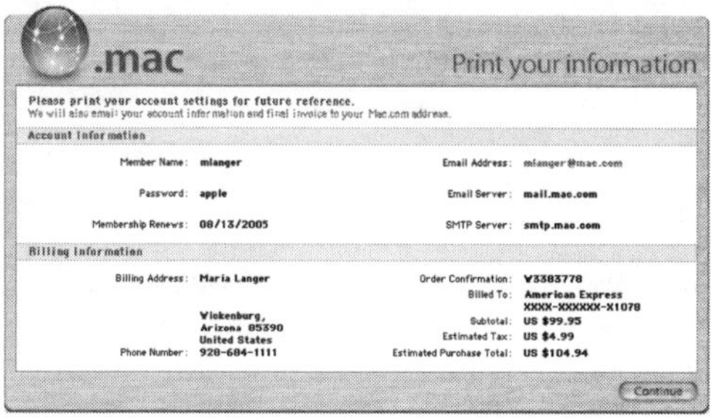

**Figure 4** When your membership has been processed, all of your membership information appears on a page like this.

# Joining & Accessing .Mac

In order to use .Mac features, you must become either a Trial or Full member. These instructions explain how to join .Mac with a full membership.

## ✔ Tips

■ You must be 13 years of age or older to join .Mac.

■ If you are already a member of .Mac, you can skip this section.

## To join .Mac

1. Use your Web browser to view the .Mac Home page at www.mac.com (**Figure 1**).

2. Click the Join Now button.

3. Fill in the Sign Up form that appears in your Web browser window (**Figure 2**).

4. Click the Continue button at the bottom of the form.

5. Fill in the Billing Information form that appears (**Figure 3**).

6. Click the Continue button at the bottom of the form.

7. When your account has been set up, a Print your information page like the one in **Figure 4** appears. Use your browser's Print command to print the information for future reference.

8. Click Continue.

9. A Thank You page appears next. It summarizes the features of .Mac. Click the Start Using .Mac button at the bottom of the page to go to the .Mac Home page, where you're already logged in (**Figure 5**).

Continued on next page...

*Continued from previous page.*

## ✔ Tips

- After step 6, if the Member name you selected is already in use, you'll be prompted to enter a different member name. Follow the instructions that appear to continue.

- You'll need the e-mail address and server information that appears in the Print your information window to set up your .Mac e-mail account in an e-mail client application other than Mail.

## To log in to .Mac

1. Use your Web browser to view the .Mac Home page at www.mac.com (**Figure 1**).

2. Click the Log In link.

3. Enter your member name and password in the appropriate boxes of the log in form (**Figure 6**) and click Enter. The .Mac Home page appears (**Figure 5**).

## ✔ Tip

- Your member name may automatically be entered in the Log In form (**Figure 6**).

## To log out

Click the Log Out link on the .Mac Home page (**Figure 5**) or the Log Out button at the top of any .Mac page.

## ✔ Tip

- If you do not log out of .Mac, anyone using your computer will have access to your .Mac account. It's a good idea to log out after using .Mac when you're working on a shared computer.

**Figure 5** The .Mac page when you're logged in to your account. The page changes daily (if not more often), so what you see probably won't look exactly like this.

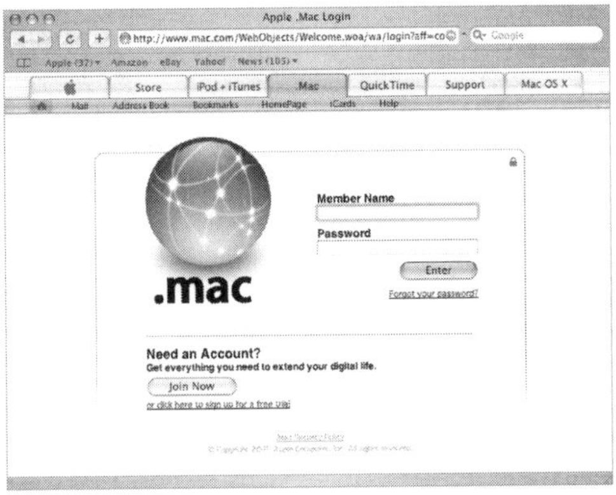

**Figure 6** Use this log-in form to log in to your .Mac account.

```
  About This Mac
  Software Update...
  Mac OS X Software...

  System Preferences...
  Dock                      ▶
  Location                  ▶

  Recent Items              ▶

  Force Quit...            ⌥⌘⌦

  Sleep
  Restart...
  Shut Down...

  Log Out Maria Langer...   ⇧⌘Q
```

**Figure 7**
Choose System Preferences from the Apple menu.

# Configuring .Mac Preferences

.Mac has several features that work directly with your Macintosh:

◆ **Sync** enables you to synchronize data on your computer with your .Mac account and other Macintoshes. This is extremely useful if you have more than one Macintosh or often access your data on the .Mac Web site.

◆ **iDisk** disk space can be synchronized to match an iDisk folder on your computer. Your iDisk's Public folder can be accessed by others, making it easy to share files with friends or associates.

◆ **Backup** uses the Backup application to automatically back the files you select to your iDisk disk space.

To take advantage of these features, you need to provide configuration information on your Macintosh so it can communicate with .Mac. You do this with the .Mac preferences pane.

## ✔ Tip

■ I explain how to set .Mac preferences for iDisk later in this chapter.

## To open the .Mac preferences pane

1. Choose Apple > System Preferences (**Figure 7**), or click the System Preferences icon in the Dock.

2. In the System Preferences window that appears, click the .Mac icon to display the .Mac preferences pane.

## To set .Mac Account preferences

1. In the .Mac preferences pane, click the Account button to display its options (**Figure 8**).

2. Enter your .Mac member name and password in the appropriate boxes.

   Your computer goes online to validate your password. If your account information has been correctly entered, a message like the one in **Figure 9** confirms that your password is valid.

## ✔ Tips

- ■ If you created a .Mac account when you registered Mac OS X, .Mac preferences (**Figure 9**) should already contain your .Mac login information.

- ■ Clicking the Account Info button in the .Mac preferences pane (**Figure 9**) launches your default Web browser so you can log into your .Mac account. It then displays the Account Settings page (**Figure 10**), with basic information about your account.

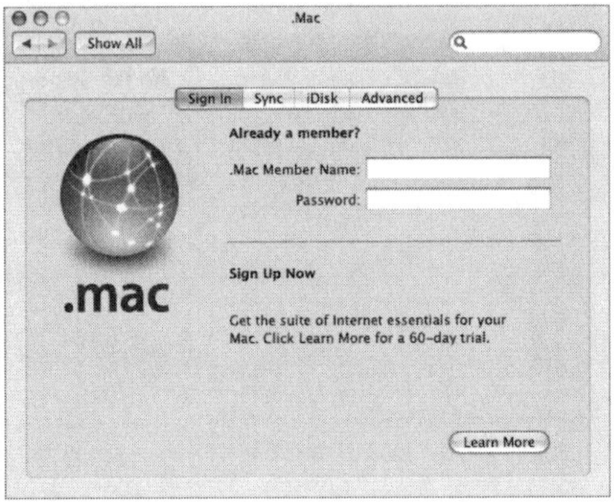

**Figure 8** Enter .Mac log in information in the .Mac preferences pane.

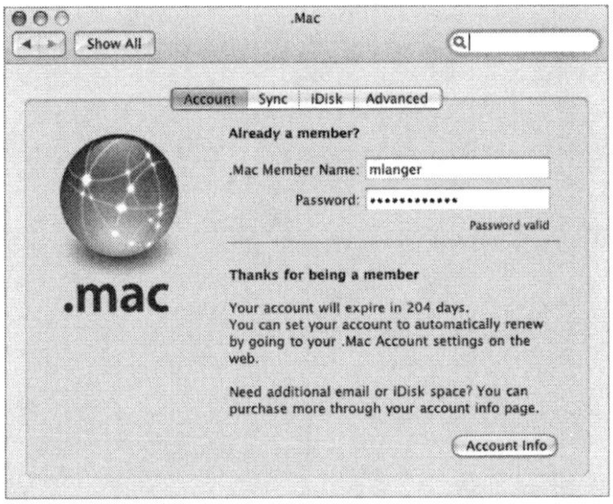

**Figure 9** When Mac OS X has verified your .Mac account, it tells you.

**Figure 10** Clicking the Account Info button displays the Account Settings page on the .Mac Web site.

**Figure 11** The Sync options of the .Mac preferences pane.

Last .Mac Sync: Today at 12:53 PM
Sync Now
Open .Mac Sync Preferences...

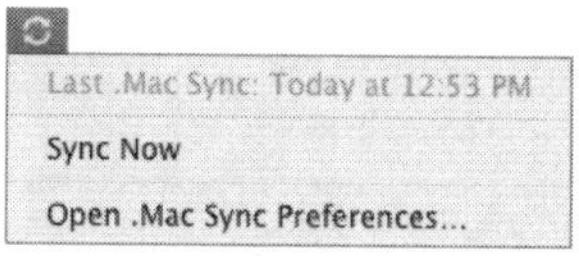

**Figure 12** You can add a Sync menu like this one to your menu bar.

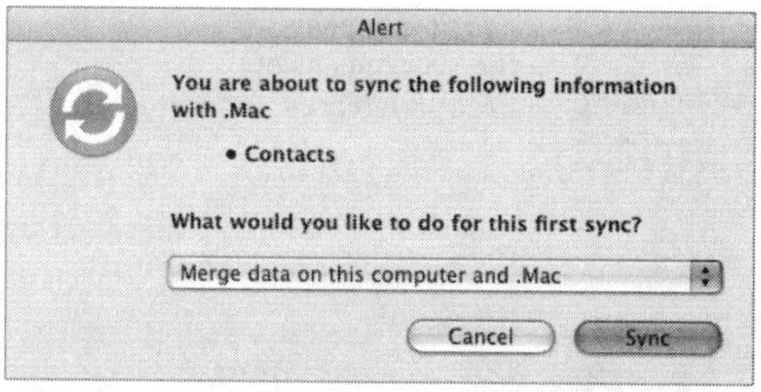

**Alert**

You are about to sync the following information with .Mac

• Contacts

What would you like to do for this first sync?

Merge data on this computer and .Mac

Cancel    Sync

**Figure 13** A dialog like this might appear at least once the first time you perform a synchronization.

## To synchronize data with .Mac & other Macs

1. In the .Mac preferences pane, click the Sync button to display its options (**Figure 11**).

2. Turn on the Synchronize with .Mac check box.

3. Choose an option from the pop-up menu:
   ▲ **Automatically** synchronizes when the data has changed.
   ▲ **Every Hour, Every Day,** or **Every Week** synchronizes periodically.
   ▲ **Manually** requires that you initiate a synchronization.

4. Turn on the check box beside each item you want to synchronize with .Mac.

5. To add a Sync menu to the menu bar (**Figure 12**) turn on the Show status in menu bar check box.

6. Click the Sync Now button.

7. A dialog like the one in **Figure 13** may appear. Choose an option from the pop-up menu and click Sync:
   ▲ **Merge data on this computer and .Mac** merges whatever data is on your computer with whatever data is stored on your .Mac account.
   ▲ **Replace data on .Mac** replaces whatever data is stored on your .Mac account with the data on your computer.
   ▲ **Replace data on this computer** replaces the data on your computer with whatever data is stored on your .Mac account.

*Continued on next page...*

Synchronizing with .Mac & Other Macs

*Continued from previous page.*

8. If a dialog like the one in **Figure 14** appears, click Review now. Then use the dialog that appears (**Figure 15**) to select the correct entry for each conflict and click Done.

9. Wait while all data is synchronized. When synchronization is complete, the sync date appears in the Sync options of the .Mac preferences pane (**Figure 16**). You can close the .Mac preferences window.

## ✔ Tips

■ Enabling this feature by following step 2 automatically registers your computer with the .Mac server. If you have more than one computer, you can see a list of registered computers by clicking the Advanced tab in the .Mac preferences pane (**Figure 17**). The computers in this list are the ones that will be synchronized with .Mac.

■ If you choose Manual in step 3, you must click the Sync Now button in the Sync options of the .Mac preferences pane (**Figure 11**) or choose Sync Now from the Sync menu (**Figure 12**) every time you want to synchronize data.

■ In step 7, the dialog in **Figure 13** may appear more than once the first time you perform a synchronization.

## To disable .Mac synchronization

1. In the .Mac preferences pane, click the Sync button to display its options (**Figure 11**).

2. Turn off the Synchronize with .Mac check box.

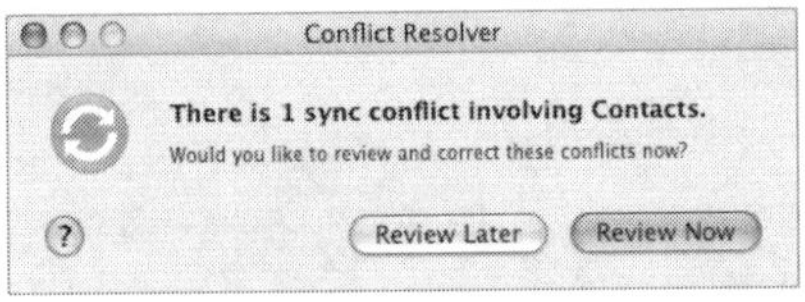

**Figure 14** Merging your computer's data with .Mac data may result in conflicts.

**Figure 15** In this example, there's a duplicate record. Choose the one you want to keep by clicking it and then click Done.

**Figure 16**
The last sync date and time appears in the Sync options of .Mac preferences.

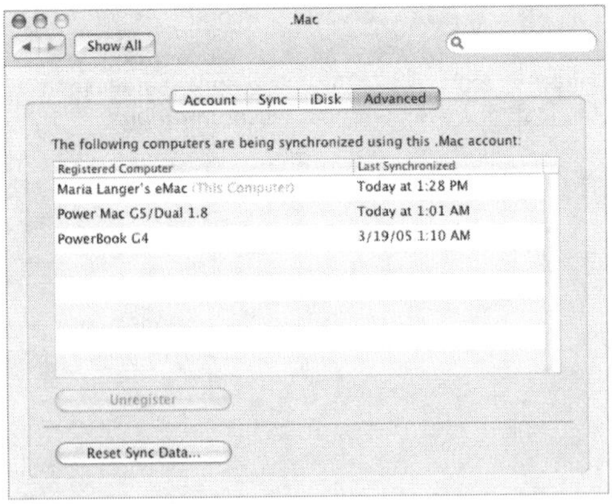

**Figure 17** The Advanced options of the .Mac preferences pane lists all computers that will be synchronized with .Mac.

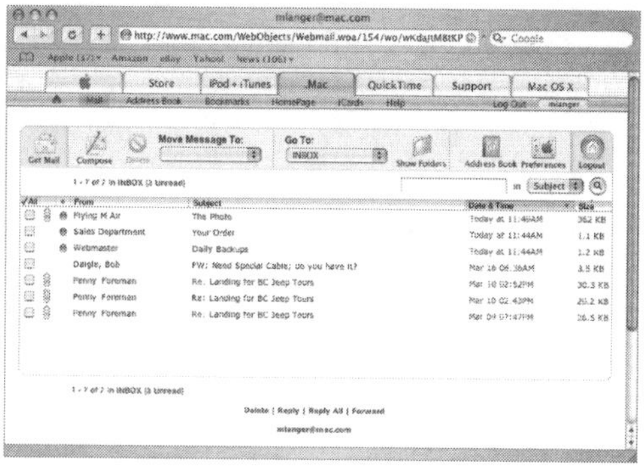

**Figure 18** A Mail Inbox with messages.

# Mail

*Mail* is .Mac's e-mail feature. When you set up a .Mac account, you automatically get an e-mail account in the mac.com domain name. For example, if your member name is *johnjones*, your email account would be *johnjones@mac.com*.

Your .Mac e-mail account can be accessed with Mac OS X's Mail application or any other e-mail client software—such as Entourage or Eudora. Simply set it up as a IMAP account using the following information:

**User Name:** *your .Mac member name*
**Password:** *your password*
**Incoming Mail Server:** mail.mac.com
**Outgoing Mail Server:** smtp.mac.com

Your .Mac e-mail account can also be accessed via the Web on the .Mac Web site. This feature enables you to read and reply to your e-mail from any computer with a connection to the Internet.

This part of the chapter explains the basics of reading and sending e-mail messages using Mail on the .Mac Web site.

## ✔ Tip

- I explain how to use the Mail application in **Chapter 13**.

## To access your Mail account

1. Log in to your .Mac account on the .Mac Web site.

2. Click the Mail button on the .Mac home page (**Figure 5**).

3. If a log in form appears (**Figure 6**), enter your password and click Enter.

   Your Mail Inbox window appears (**Figure 18**).

## To read & work with messages

1. Click the subject of the message you want to read. The message appears in the Web browser window (**Figure 19**).

2. To read the next or previous message, click the up or down arrow beneath the toolbar.

   *or*

   To return to the folder you were viewing, click the blue link for the folder name beneath the toolbar.

   *or*

   Click one of the buttons in the toolbar to work with the message:

   ▲ **Delete** deletes the message.

   ▲ **Reply** opens a reply form (**Figure 25**) and addresses it to the message sender.

   ▲ **Reply All** opens a reply form (**Figure 25**) and addresses it to the sender and anyone else the message was originally addressed to.

   ▲ **Forward** opens a message forwarding form with the body of the original message copied to the body of the form.

   ▲ **Add Sender** adds the sender's name and e-mail address to your .Mac Address Book.

   ▲ **Print Ready** opens a new window that includes only the message and its headers (**Figure 21**). You can print this window using the File menu's Print command.

   *or*

   To move the message to a specific folder, choose the folder name from the Move Message To pop-up menu (**Figure 20**)

**Figure 19** When you click a message subject, the message appears in a Web browser window.

**Figure 20**
Use this pop-up menu to move a message to a different folder.

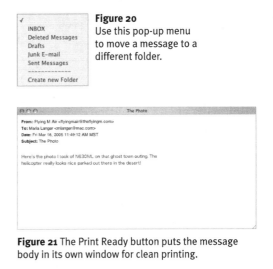

**Figure 21** The Print Ready button puts the message body in its own window for clean printing.

## ✔ Tips

■ A blue bullet beside the From column in the message list indicates that that message has not yet been read.

■ If a message includes an attachment (**Figure 19**), you can click the Download button to download the attachment to your hard disk.

■ I tell you about the .Mac Address Book feature later in this chapter.

Figure 22

**Figure 22**
Use this pop-up menu to display the contents of a specific folder.

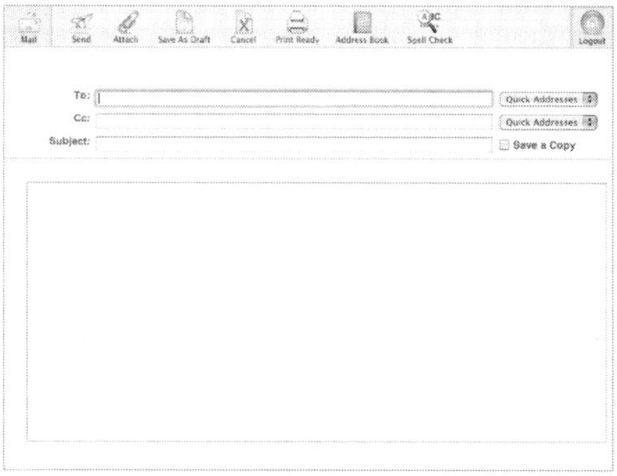

**Figure 23** A new message form, all ready to be filled in.

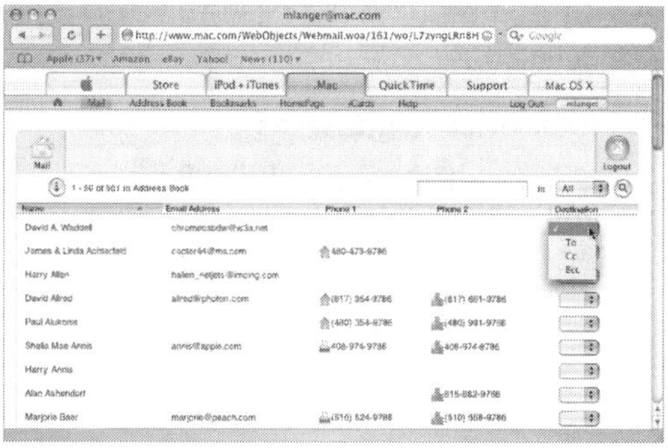

**Figure 24** You can use the Address Book to address a message.

# To update the Inbox

Click the Get Mail button (**Figure 18**). The Inbox is updated to include any new messages that have been received since the Inbox's contents were last displayed.

# To view a specific folder

Choose the folder name from the Go To pop-up menu (**Figure 22**) in any folder list window (**Figure 18**).

# To delete messages in a folder

1. Turn on the check box beside the message(s) you want to delete.

2. Click the Delete button in the toolbar. The message(s) is deleted and the window reappears with the message(s) gone.

# To send a message

1. Click the Compose button in the toolbar to display a new message form (**Figure 23**).

2. Fill in the To, Cc (if desired), and Subject fields in the form.

3. To save a copy of the form in the Sent Messages folder, turn on the Save a Copy check box.

4. Enter the body of the message in the large box at the bottom of the form.

5. Click Send. The message is sent.

# ✔ Tips

- To look up and insert e-mail addresses from Address Book, click the Address Book button, use the pop-up menus beside a person's name to specify a message form field (**Figure 24**), and click Apply.

- To include more than one e-mail address in the To or Cc field, separate each address with a comma.

**Figure 25** A message reply form already has the To and Subject fields filled in.

## To reply to a message

1. With the message you want to reply to displayed (**Figure 19**), click the Reply or Reply All button.

2. A message reply form appears (**Figure 25**). Its To and Cc fields are already filled in with the appropriate e-mail addresses.

3. If desired, change the contents of the Subject field.

4. To save a copy of the form in the Sent Messages folder, turn on the Save a Copy check box.

5. Insert your reply in the large text field at the bottom of the form.

6. Click Send. The message is sent.

## ✔ Tips

- By default, the body of the original message is quoted in the reply. You can edit or delete this text if desired.

- If the original message was very long, it may be included with the reply as an attachment.

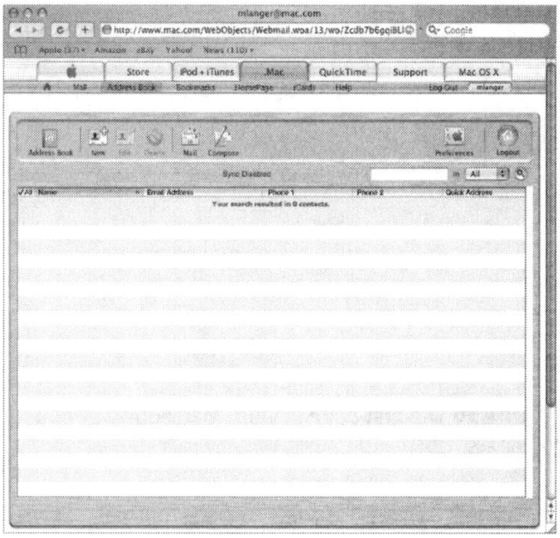

Figure 26 Your address book is empty before you add records or synchronize it.

Figure 27 Address Book preferences for your .Mac account.

**Sync in progress...**

Please wait while your .Mac Address Book is being synchronized.

Figure 28 A progress message appears while the Address Book data is synchronized for the first time.

# Address Book

Address Book enables you to maintain a list of contacts on the Web in your .Mac account. By synchronizing your computer's Address Book with your .Mac account Address Book, you can automatically duplicate your computer's address book on the Web so you can access its information from any computer with an Internet connection.

## ✔ Tips

- Like all information for your .Mac account, your Address Book is accessible only to you—you must log in to .Mac to view it.

- The instructions in this section assume you are using .Mac's sync feature to synchronize Contacts on your computer to your .Mac account. Consult the section titled "To synchronize data with .Mac & other Macs" earlier in this chapter for details.

## To set up .Mac Address Book synchronization

1. On the .Mac Home page (**Figure 5**), click the Address Book link.

2. A list of contacts appears. If you have not entered any contacts, it will be empty (**Figure 26**).

3. Click the Preferences button. A page like the one in **Figure 27** appears.

4. Turn on the check box under Syncing and click Save.

   A "Sync in progress" message appears (**Figure 28**) while the address book information from your computer that is stored on your .Mac account is synchronized with your .Mac address book. When it's finished, the entries appear (**Figure 29**).

*Continued on next page...*

SETTING UP .MAC ADDRESS BOOK SYNC

*Continued from previous page.*

## ✔ Tips

■ As you can see, it's a two step process to get your computer's contacts into your .Mac address book. The first step is to sync your computer with .Mac to get the information onto the .Mac server. This step is covered in the section titled "To synchronize data with .Mac & other Macs" earlier in this chapter. The second step, covered here, is to sync the address book feature of the .Mac Web site with the data already stored there. Fortunately, you only have to set these two syncs up once; your Mac and .Mac will do everything else for you from that point forward.

■ Once Address Book syncing has been set up as instructed here, the Address Books will automatically be synced each time your computer syncs with .Mac.

■ With syncing set up, any changes you make to your .Mac address book on the .Mac Web site will automatically be saved to all computers registered for syncing with your .Mac account.

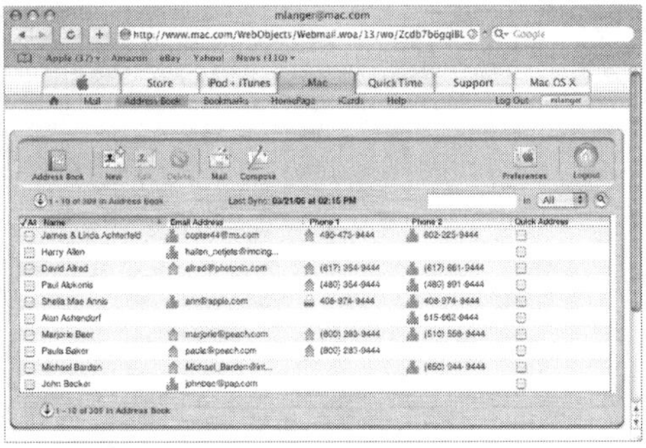

**Figure 29** The first page of your .Mac Address Book appears.

**SETTING UP .MAC ADDRESS BOOK SYNC**

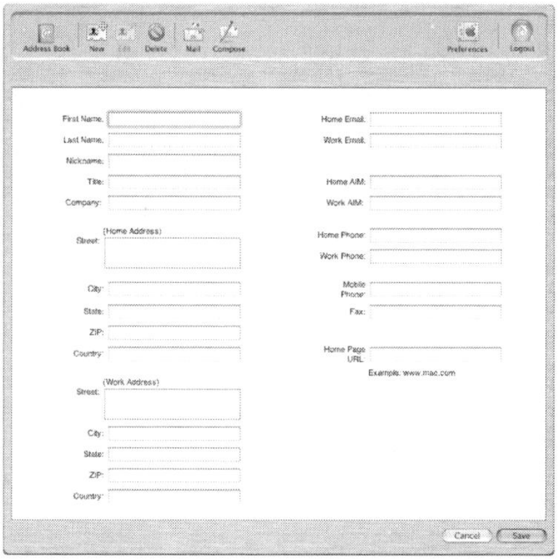

**Figure 30** Fill in this form to create a new entry.

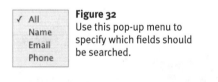

**Figure 31** A confirmation page appears when you try to delete Address Book entries.

✓ All
Name
Email
Phone

**Figure 32**
Use this pop-up menu to specify which fields should be searched.

**Figure 33** Details for an entry appear in a page like this.

# To work with the Address Book list

Use buttons, check boxes, and other elements in the Address Book list (**Figure 18**) to work with entries:

◆ To add an Address Book entry, click the New button. Then fill out the form that appears (**Figure 30**) and click Save.

◆ To edit an entry, turn on the check box to the left of the entry name and click Edit. A form similar to the one in **Figure 30** appears, with some fields already filled in. Make changes as necessary and click Save.

◆ To delete one or more entries, turn on the check box to the left of entry names and click the Delete button. A confirmation window like the one in **Figure 31** appears. Click Yes to delete the entries. If syncing is turned on, the entries will also be deleted from that Address Book data on your computer when you sync.

◆ To access Mail, click the Mail button (to display your Inbox; **Figure 18**) or the Compose button (to display a new message form; **Figure 23**).

◆ To search for an entry, enter search criteria in the text box and choose a field from the pop-up menu (**Figure 32**). Then click the magnifying glass button. A list of matches appears.

◆ To see all details for an entry, click the entry name. A page with all recorded information for the entry appears (**Figure 33**).

◆ To set Address Book preferences, click the Preferences button and set options on the page that appears (**Figure 27**).

**WORKING WITH THE ADDRESS BOOK LIST**

# Bookmarks

.Mac's Bookmarks feature enables you to synchronize your Safari bookmarks between your computer and your .Mac account. Once the bookmarks are stored on .Mac, you can access them from any computer with an Internet connection, making it easy to surf your favorite Web sites, even when you're away from your computer.

## To set up Bookmarks synchronization

1. On the .Mac Home page (**Figure 5**), click the Bookmarks link.

2. A Welcome screen appears (**Figure 34**). Click the Open Bookmarks button. A small, narrow Bookmarks window appears (**Figure 35**).

3. Click the Preferences button at the bottom of the window (**Figure 35**). .Mac Bookmarks preferences appear in the window (**Figure 36**).

4. Click to check the Turn on .Mac Bookmarks Synchronization check box.

5. Click Save.

   A "Sync in progress" message appears (**Figure 37**) while your computer synchronizes the bookmarks stored in your .Mac account with .Mac's Bookmarks. When it's finished, the .Mac bookmarks page reappears (**Figure 35**).

**Figure 34** Clicking the Bookmarks button displays this screen.

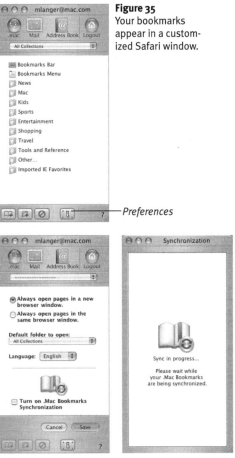

**Figure 35** Your bookmarks appear in a customized Safari window.

*Preferences*

**Figure 36** Set preferences for .Mac Bookmarks in this window.

**Figure 37** This message appears while bookmarks are being synchronized.

BOOKMARKS

**Figure 38**
You can use this pop-up menu to select one of your bookmark collections.

**Figure 39**
Bookmarks within a collection or folder appear in this window.

*Add Bookmark*    *Add Folder*    *Delete*

**Figure 40** Enter information and click Add to create a new bookmark.

**Figure 41** Click an X button to delete a bookmark or folder.

## To open .Mac Bookmarks

1. Click the Bookmarks link on the .Mac Home page (**Figure 5**).

2. An introductory page like the one in **Figure 34** appears. Click the Open Bookmarks button.

   A Safari window like the one in **Figure 35** appears. It lists all bookmark collections.

## To work with the Bookmarks list

Use buttons and menus within the Bookmarks list window (**Figure 35**) to work with your bookmarks:

◆ To open a collection, choose its name from the pop-up menu (**Figure 38**) or double-click its folder in the list. A list of bookmarks and folders within that collection appears (**Figure 39**).

◆ To open a bookmarked page, click the bookmark's icon or name. The page opens in a new Safari window.

◆ To add a new bookmark, click the Add Bookmark button (**Figure 39**). Enter bookmark information in the fields that appear (**Figure 40**) and click Add.

◆ To add a new bookmark folder, click the Add Folder button (**Figure 39**). Enter folder information in the fields that appear and click Add.

◆ To delete a bookmark or folder, display it in the bookmarks list, click the Delete button (**Figure 39**), and then click the X beside the item you want to delete (**Figure 41**). Click the Delete button that appears to confirm the deletion.

◆ To set Bookmarks preferences, click the Preferences button (**Figure 35**), set options in the window that appears (**Figure 36**), and click Save.

# HomePage

*HomePage* is a Web-based authoring tool that you can access from the .Mac Web site. With it, you can create Web pages for a variety of purposes, all without knowing a single tag of HTML.

This part of the chapter explains how you can use the templates included in HomePage to create a Web page or site and announce it to your friends and family members.

## ✔ Tip

- HomePage uses images and other media already saved in your iDisk storage space. For that reason, it's a good idea to copy the images, movies, and other media you want to appear on your Web pages to appropriate locations on iDisk *before* creating a page. I tell you about iDisk later in this chapter.

## To create a Web page or site

1. Click the HomePage button on the .Mac home page (**Figure 5**).

2. In the HomePage main window (**Figure 42**), select one of the themes listed in tabs along the left side of the window. The template previews change to show templates for that page.

3. Click the template preview you want to use.

4. HomePage begins by displaying a series of pages that prompt you for information, such as a folder in your iDisk storage space that contains images or text that you want to appear on the page. Follow the instructions that appear onscreen to replace placeholder text with your own text and choose pictures. You can click the Preview button to see the results of your edits. **Figures 43** through **45** show

**Figure 42** The HomePage main window, showing the Photo Album templates.

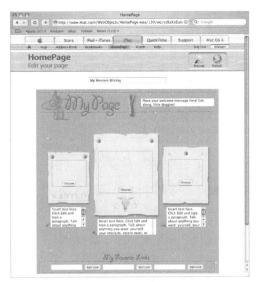

**Figure 43** A template includes blank spaces for pictures, placeholder text, and boxes to enter links.

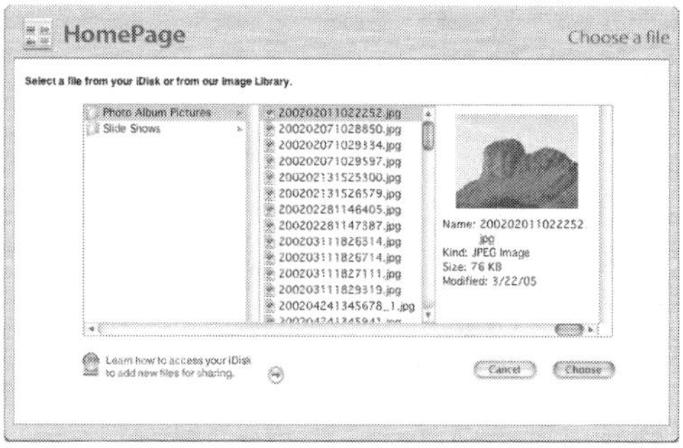

**Figure 44** You can add photos from your iDisk.

**Figure 45** Here's a preview of the completed page before it has been published.

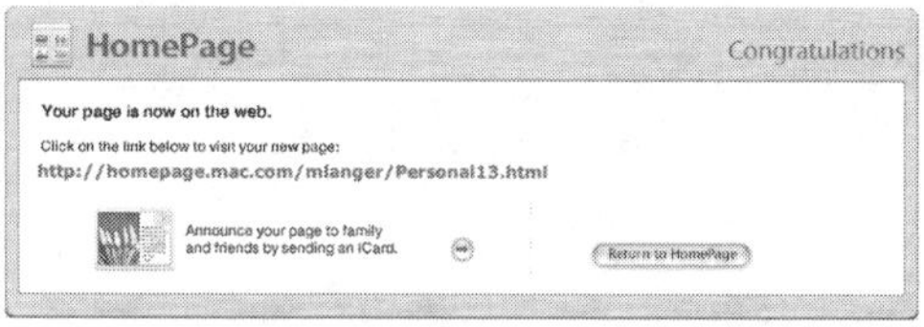

**Figure 46** HomePage confirms that your page has been published and provides its URL. It also offers a link you can click to announce the page with an iCard.

some of the screens for creating a page using the Western Writing template.

5. When you're satisfied with your finished page or site, click the Publish button. HomePage saves its Web page files to your iDisk storage space and displays a Congratulations screen, which includes the URL for the site (**Figure 46**).

6. To announce your page or site to your friends or family members, click the iCard link. Then select an image, fill out the form, and click Send iCard in the page that appears (**Figure 47**).

## ✔ Tips

- It's impossible for me to cover every single instruction for creating every single type of Web page. The information presented here should be enough to get you started creating any type of Web page. Don't be afraid to experiment!

- I provide more information about using iCards next.

- Once a page has been created, it will be listed near the top of the HomePage main page. You use buttons beneath the list to add, delete, or edit pages.

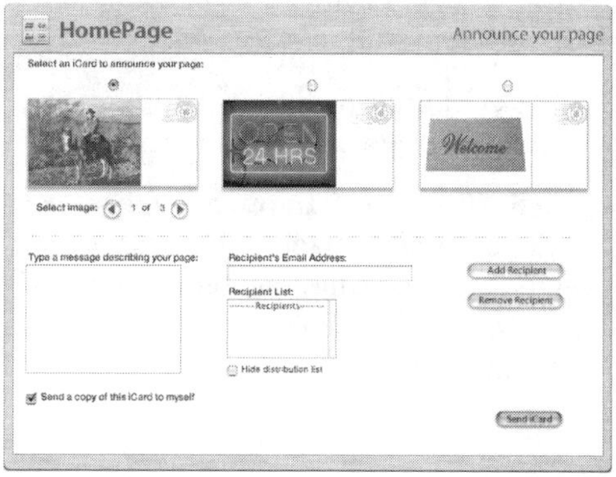

**Figure 47** Fill out a form like this to send an iCard announcing the Web page to your family and friends.

# iCards

*iCards* is a .Mac feature that enables you to send postcard-like e-mail messages to anyone with an e-mail address. The cards you send can use one of many photos available within iCards or a photo or other image from your iDisk storage space.

## ✔ Tips

- You do not need to be a member of .Mac to send or receive iCards. However, only .Mac members can send custom iCards that utilize their own images.

- The announcement feature of HomePage (**Figure 47**) utilizes iCards to tell people about the Web sites you publish with HomePage.

## To send an iCard

1. Click the iCards button on the .Mac home page (**Figure 5**).

2. In the iCards main window (**Figure 48**), click one of the category links.

3. On the Select Card page (**Figure 49**), click to select one of the stock images.

4. On the Compose/Edit page (**Figure 50**), enter a message in the box near the top of the window. Then select a radio button for the font you want applied.

5. Click Continue to display the addressing window (**Figure 51**).

6. In the Enter emails box, enter the e-mail addresses of the people you want to send the postcard to. If you enter more than one address, separate each address with a comma.

7. Click Send Card.

**Figure 48** iCards' main page on the .Mac Web site.

**Figure 49** Choose the image that you want to appear on your card.

Figure 50 Use this page to enter a message and select a font for your iCard.

Figure 51 Finally, use this page to enter the e-mail addresses of card recipients.

8. The You're Done! page appears, confirming that your card has been sent. Buttons on the page enable you to return to the iCards main page (**Figure 48**), return to the category you just viewed (**Figure 49**), or send the same card to someone else (**Figure 51**).

## ✔ Tips

■ If you click the Create Your Own category in step 2, a Select Image page that enables you to browse through pictures in your iDisk storage space appears (**Figure 52**). Use the file list to locate and preview the image you want to use. Click the Select this Image button to use the currently displayed image on your iCard. Then follow steps 4 though 8 to complete and send your card.

■ In step 6, you can click the Address Book button to select recipients from your .Mac Address Book. I discuss the .Mac address book earlier in this chapter.

Figure 52 Use a page like this to locate and select an image from your iDisk storage space.

# iDisk

*iDisk* is 250 MB of private hard disk space on an Apple Internet server that you can use to store files and publish a Web site. But rather than deal with complex FTP software to access your iDisk space, Apple gives you access from within the Finder's Sidebar (**Figure 53**) and within Open and Save dialogs (**Figures 68 and 67**). Best of all, you manage files in your iDisk storage space just like you manage files on any other mounted volume.

**Figure 53** The contents of your iDisk home folder.

Your iDisk storage space (**Figure 53**) is preorganized into folders, just like your Mac OS X Home folder:

◆ **Documents** is for storing documents. This folder is completely private; only you have access to it.

◆ **Music**, **Pictures**, and **Movies** are for storing various types of media. By storing multimedia files in these folder, they're available to other .Mac programs, including iCard and HomePage.

◆ **Public** is for storing files you want to share with others. This folder can only be opened by a .Mac member who knows your member name.

◆ **Sites** is for storing Web pages that you want to publish on the World Wide Web. HomePage, a .Mac feature I discuss earlier in this chapter, automatically stores Web pages here. You can also create Web pages with another authoring tool and publish them by placing them in this folder.

◆ **Backup** is for data files that have been backed up using the Backup feature of .Mac, which I discuss later in this chapter. It is a read-only folder, so you cannot manually add anything to it. This folder may not appear until you use the Backup feature.

iDisk

◆ **Software** is a read-only folder maintained by Apple Computer. It contains Apple software updates and other download-able third-party applications that might interest you. The contents of this folder do not count toward the 250 MB of disk space iDisk allows you—which is a good thing, because many of these files are very large!

◆ **Library** is for storing support files used by .Mac features. Normally, you would not change the contents of this folder.

This part of the chapter tells you how you can access your iDisk storage space from your computer.

## ✔ Tips

■ iDisk is a great place to store secondary backups of important files. Your iDisk storage space is an excellent off-premises backup for added protection against data loss. As a .Mac member, you can automate this process with the Backup feature of .Mac, which I discuss later in this chapter.

■ You can purchase additional iDisk space from Apple if you need it. I explain how on the next page.

■ Technically, the 250 MB of disk space that comes with a .Mac account is split between Mail and iDisk. That's why the capacity shown in **Figure 54** is 235 MB. You can set the amount of space allocated to each feature by logging into the .Mac Web site and setting preferences there.

■ I cover file management operations such as copying and deleting files in **Chapters 2 through 4.**

■ Your iDisk home folder (**Figure 53**) also includes a text file called About your iDisk, which has more information about iDisk. You can open this file with TextEdit.

iDisk

## To set iDisk preferences

1. Choose Apple > System Preferences (**Figure 7**), or click the System Preferences icon in the Dock.

2. In the System Preferences window that appears, click the .Mac icon to display the .Mac preferences pane.

3. Click the iDisk button. Your computer connects to the Internet to retrieve iDisk information. When it's finished, your iDisk settings appear (**Figure 54**).

4. To buy more iDisk storage space, click the Buy More button. Your computer's default Web browser opens and displays a log in page for the .Mac Web site. Follow the instructions that appear onscreen to complete the transaction. The storage space is made available to you almost immediately.

5. To copy the contents of your iDisk storage space to your computer's hard disk, click the Start button. You can then choose one of the Synchronize options:

   ▲ **Automatically** automatically syncs your iDisk and its local copy when you connect to the Internet.

   ▲ **Manually** requires you to initiate a synchronization.

6. Set options to control Public folder access:

   ▲ **Allow others to** enables you to specify whether other users can only read the contents of your Public folder or both read and save files to your Public folder.

   ▲ **Password protect your Public Folder** enables you to set a password that users must enter to access your Public folder. When you turn on this option, a password dialog sheet appears (**Figure 55**). Enter the same password twice and click OK.

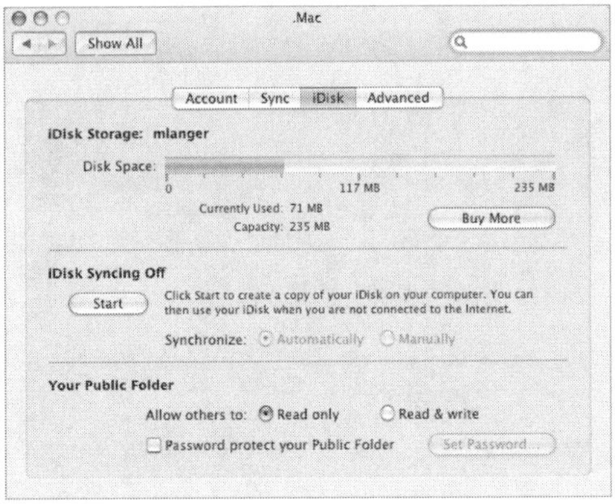

**Figure 54** The iDisk options of the .Mac preferences pane.

**Figure 55** Use this dialog to set a password to protect your Public folder on iDisk.

**Figure 56** The iDisk window after synchronization is enabled.

**Figure 57** You can see sync status in iDisk's Finder window.

**Figure 58** Use the Actions pop-up menu to manually initiate a sync.

7. Choose System Preferences > Quit System Preferences or press ⌘Q to save your changes.

## ✔ Tips

■ Creating a copy of your iDisk on your computer is a great way to quickly access most iDisk items, even when you're not connected to the Internet.

■ When your iDisk is being synchronized, spinning arrows appear beside the iDisk icon in the Sidebar and a progress bar appears at the bottom of the window (**Figure 56**). When syncing is complete, a dialog tells you, the icon stops spinning and a bullet appears inside it, and the sync status appears in the status bar (**Figure 57**).

■ The first time your computer syncs with iDisk can take some time. You can continue working with your computer while the sync is in progress.

■ When you create a copy of your iDisk, your entire iDisk is not copied to your computer. Instead, your computer makes aliases to the Backup, Library, and Software folders (**Figure 57**), which can be rather large and which cannot be modified by you anyway.

■ To manually sync your iDisk, choose Sync Now from the Actions pop-up menu (**Figure 58**) when iDisk is selected in the Sidebar.

■ You can change the password you set up in step 6 by clicking the Set Password button (**Figure 54**).

## To open your iDisk storage space from the Finder

Click the iDisk icon in the Sidebar (**Figure 53 or 57**).

*or*

Choose Go > iDisk > My iDisk (**Figure 39**) or press [Shift] [⌘] [I].

A Finder window with your iDisk contents appears (**Figure 53 or 57**) and an iDisk icon appears on the desktop (**Figure 60**).

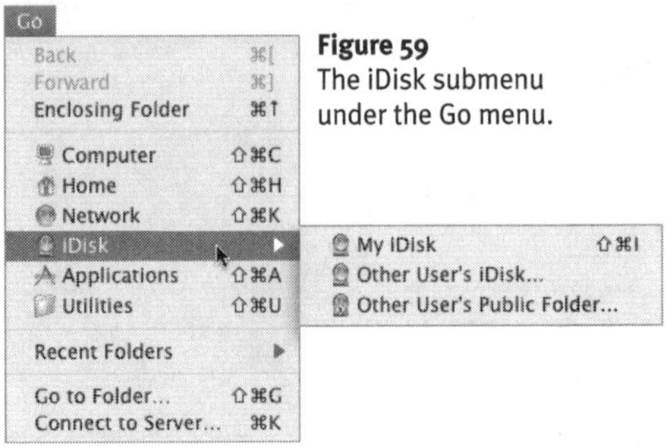

**Figure 59**
The iDisk submenu under the Go menu.

## ✔ Tip

■ The status bar of the Finder window (**Figure 53 or 57**) tells you how much space is left in your iDisk storage space. To display the status bar, make sure the window is active and then choose View > Show Status Bar.

**Figure 60**
Volume icons representing iDisk storage space appear on your desktop when you access iDisk.

## To open another user's iDisk

1. Choose Go > iDisk > Other User's iDisk (**Figure 59**).

2. In the Connect To iDisk dialog that appears (**Figure 61**), enter the user's .Mac member name and password to open the iDisk. Then click Connect.

A window displaying the contents of the user's iDisk appears (**Figure 62**) and an icon for that iDisk appears on the desktop (**Figure 60**).

**Figure 61** Use this dialog to enter the user's member name and password.

**Figure 62** A window displaying the contents of the user's iDisk appears.

**Figure 63** Use this dialog to enter the member's name.

**Figure 64** If a Public folder is password-protected, a dialog like this appears.

## To open a user's Public folder

1. Choose Go > iDisk > Other User's Public Folder (**Figure 59**).

2. In the Connect To iDisk Public Folder dialog that appears (**Figure 63**), enter the .Mac member name and click Connect.

3. If the Public folder is password-protected, a WebDAV File System Authentication dialog like the one in **Figure 64** appears. Enter the password to access the folder and click OK.

A window displaying the contents of the user's Public folder appears (**Figure 65**) and an icon for that folder appears on the desktop (**Figure 60**).

**Figure 65** A window containing the contents of the user's Public folder appears.

## To save a file to iDisk from within an application

1. Choose File > Save As (**Figure 66**) to display the Save dialog.

2. If necessary, click the triangle beside the Save As box to display the Sidebar and file locations (**Figure 67**).

3. In the Sidebar, click iDisk and choose a location on iDisk in which to save the file.

4. Enter a name for the file in the Save As box.

5. Click Save. The file is saved to the folder you selected in your iDisk storage space.

## To open a file on iDisk from within an application

1. Choose File > Open (**Figure 66**) to display the Open dialog.

2. In the Sidebar, click iDisk (**Figure 68**) and choose the folder in which the file you want to open resides.

3. In the list of files, select the file you want to open.

4. Click Open. The file is opened in a document window.

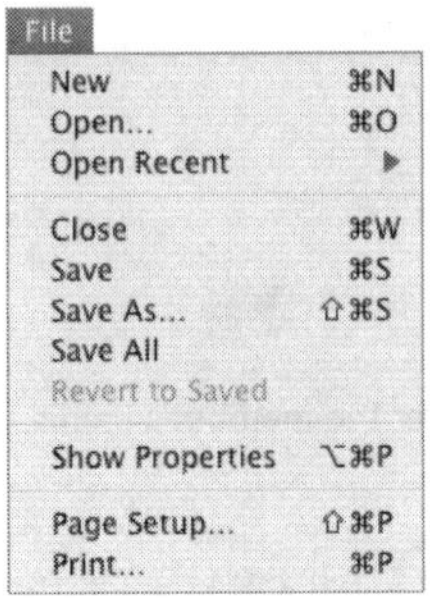

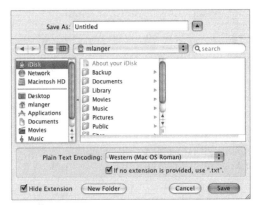

**Figure 66**
Like most other applications, TextEdit's File menu includes commands for saving and opening files.

**Figure 67** Click iDisk in the Save dialog's Sidebar to open the iDisk folder.

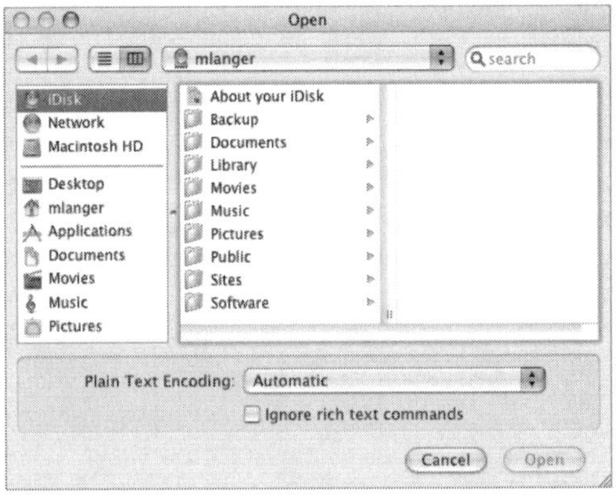

**Figure 68** Click iDisk in the Open dialog's Sidebar to access folders and files stored on your iDisk.

SAVING & OPENING iDISK FILES

**Figure 69** Backup's download page on the .Mac Web site.

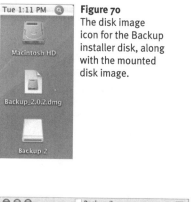

**Figure 70**
The disk image icon for the Backup installer disk, along with the mounted disk image.

**Figure 71** The contents of the Backup installer disk.

# Backup

*Backup* is an application that works with a .Mac account. It enables you to back up all or part of your hard disk to CD, DVD, or your iDisk storage space.

To use Backup, you must download and install the Backup software. You can get it from the Backup main page on the .Mac Web site. Once installed, you set options to determine what should be backed up and where it should be backed up to.

## To download & install Backup

1. Click the Backup button on the .Mac Web site to display the Backup main page.

2. Click the Download Backup 2 button.

3. On the Download Backup page that appears (**Figure 69**), click the link for Backup 2.0.2 (or later, if a later version is available).

4. Wait while Backup downloads. If you display the Downloads window of Safari, you can see its progress.

5. If necessary, double-click the Backup disk image file icon to mount the installer disk (**Figure 70**). It should appear on your desktop, unless you changed your browser's default download location.

6. If necessary, double-click the Backup disk to open its window (**Figure 71**).

7. Double-click the Backup.pkg icon to launch the Installer.

8. If a dialog appears, asking if the Installer package can run a program, click Continue.

*Continued on next page...*

**DOWNLOADING & INSTALLING BACKUP**

*Continued from previous page.*

9. Follow the instructions that appear in installer windows (**Figure 72**) to install the software on your hard disk. Along the way, an Authenticate dialog like the one in **Figure 73** may appear. Enter an administrator's name and password and click OK.

10. Click the Close button in the final Installer window to quit the installer.

11. Drag the Backup installer disk to the Trash to unmount it.

## ✔ Tips

- In step 4, if a dialog appears, asking you if you're sure you want to continue downloading the file, click Continue.

- Backup is installed in your Applications folder (**Figure 74**).

- After installing Backup, you can delete the Backup installer disk image file. Personally, I like to archive software like this on CD in case I ever need to reinstall it from scratch.

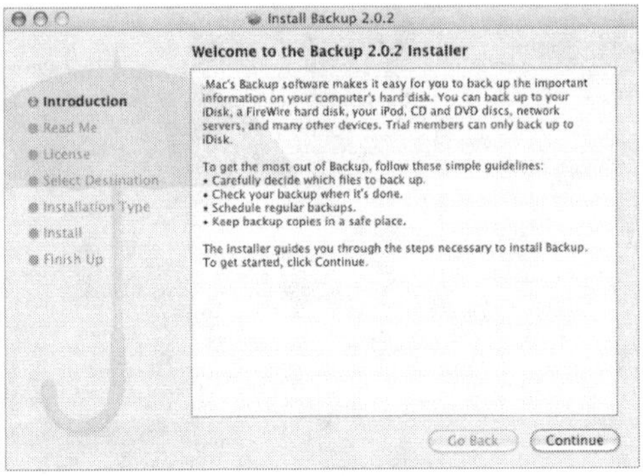

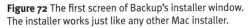

**Figure 72** The first screen of Backup's installer window. The installer works just like any other Mac installer.

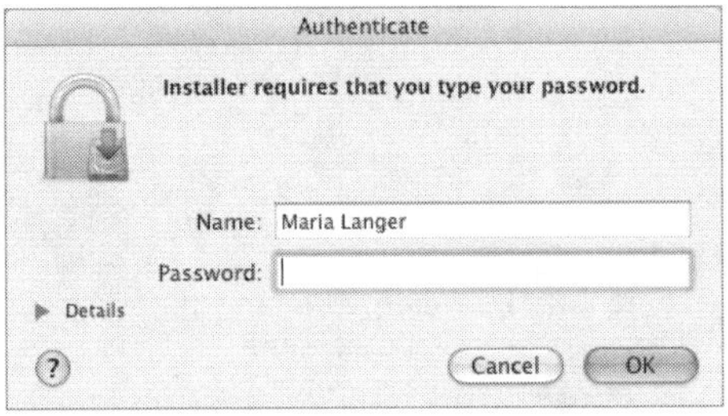

**Figure 73** Before you can install Backup, you may need to prove that you have administrator privileges.

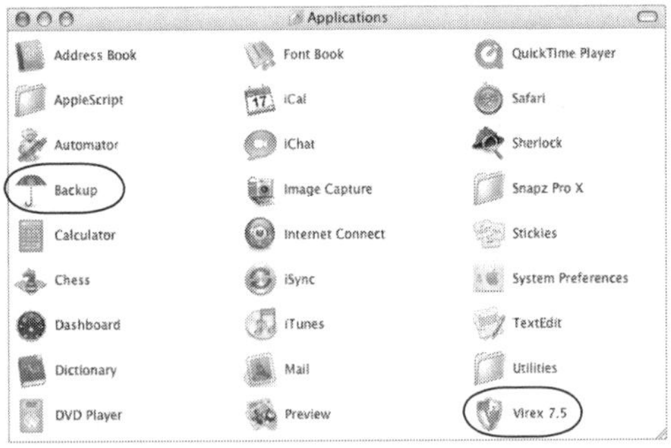

**Figure 74** Backup and Virex are installed in your Applications folder.

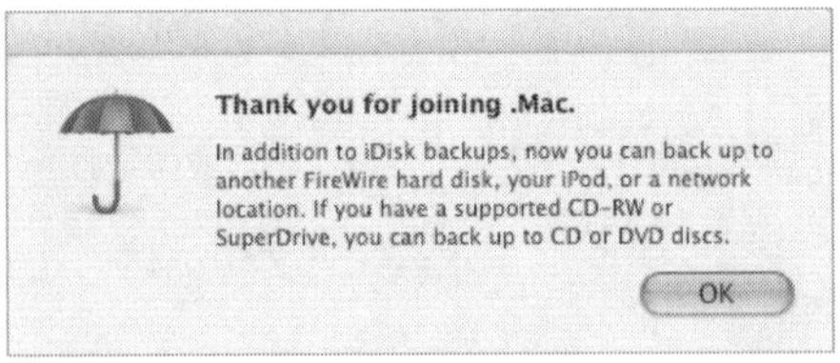

**Figure 75** The first time you run Backup, it may display a dialog thanking you for joining .Mac.

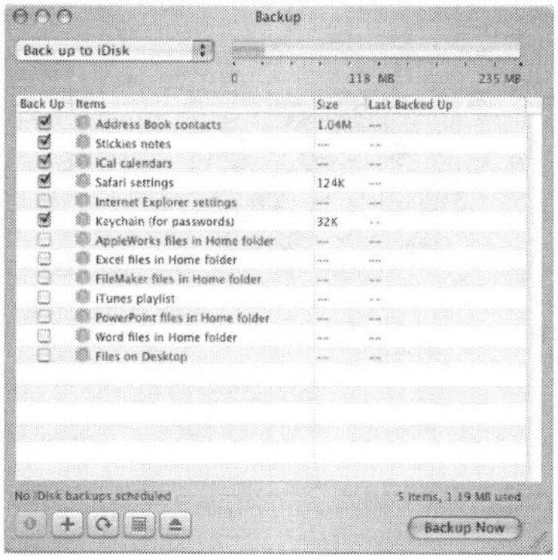

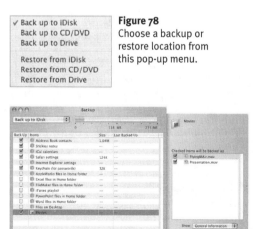

**Figure 76** Backup's main window.

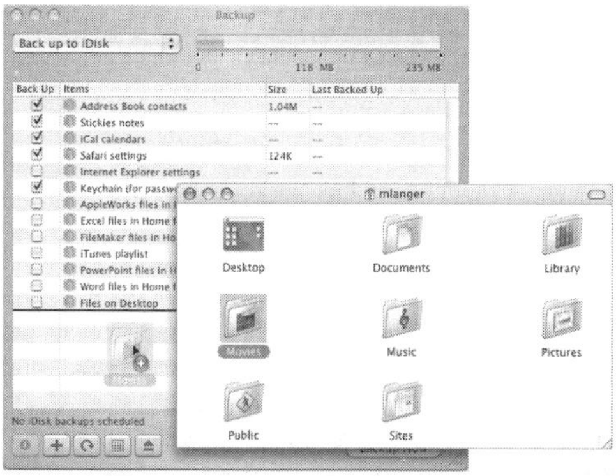

**Figure 77** To add an item to the Backup list, simply drag its icon into the Backup window.

✓ Back up to iDisk
  Back up to CD/DVD
  Back up to Drive

  Restore from iDisk
  Restore from CD/DVD
  Restore from Drive

**Figure 78** Choose a backup or restore location from this pop-up menu.

**Figure 79** Double-clicking an item in Backup's window displays a drawer that itemizes contents.

## To configure Backup

1. Double-click the Backup icon in the Applications folder (**Figure 74**).

2. Backup connects to the Internet and confirms that you have a valid .Mac account. When it's finished, it may display a dialog like the one in **Figure 75**. Click OK to dismiss it.

3. The main Backup window appears (**Figure 76**). It lists all the predefined items that Backup can recognize. Modify the item list as follows:

   ▲ To indicate whether a listed item should be backed up, toggle the Back Up check box beside it.

   ▲ To add an item to be backed up, drag the icon for the item from a Finder window into the Backup window (**Figure 77**).

   ▲ To remove an item from the list, select it and press Delete.

4. Choose a backup location from the pop-up menu at the top of the window (**Figure 78**).

## ✔ Tips

- You must have your .Mac account information properly entered in the .Mac preferences pane (**Figure 9**) for Backup to complete step 2.

- List items with tiny package icons (**Figure 76**) are called *QuickPicks*. They make it possible to quickly locate and back up specific types of files, no matter where they are located in your Home folder.

- If you double-click an item in the list, a drawer slides out and displays a list of files that will be backed up (**Figure 79**).

## To schedule backups to iDisk

1. In the main Backup window (**Figure 76**), make sure Back up to iDisk is chosen from the pop-up menu (**Figure 78**).

2. Click the Schedule automatic backups to your iDisk button, which looks like a calendar, at the bottom of the window.

3. Set options in the dialog sheet that appears (**Figure 80**) to set the frequency and time of the Backup.

4. Click OK.

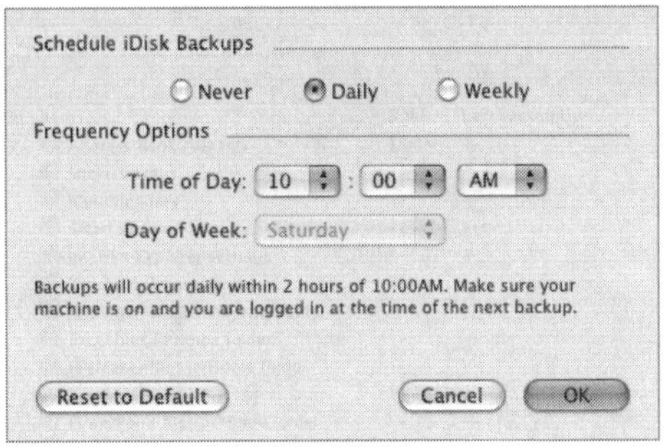

### ✔ Tips

- Although you can set automatic backups to any location on the pop-up menu in **Figure 78**, that location must be available at the time of backup for the backup to occur.

- For a scheduled backup to occur:
    - ▲ Your computer must be turned on and not set to sleep.
    - ▲ You must be logged in to the computer. You can use Fast User Switching, as discussed in **Chapter 16** so others can log in without logging you out.
    - ▲ The Backup application cannot be running.

- Scheduled backups are completed in the background as you work and do not disrupt your normal work session.

- I've been using the automatic backup feature of Backup for over two years now and I love it! It takes care of backing up the little files I'd normally neglect, like my Address Book and iCal calendars, as well as folders full of important documents I wouldn't want to lose.

Schedule iDisk Backups
○ Never  ⊙ Daily  ○ Weekly
Frequency Options
Time of Day: 10 : 00 AM
Day of Week: Saturday

Backups will occur daily within 2 hours of 10:00AM. Make sure your machine is on and you are logged in at the time of the next backup.

Reset to Default    Cancel    OK

**Figure 80** Use this dialog to schedule automatic backups to iDisk.

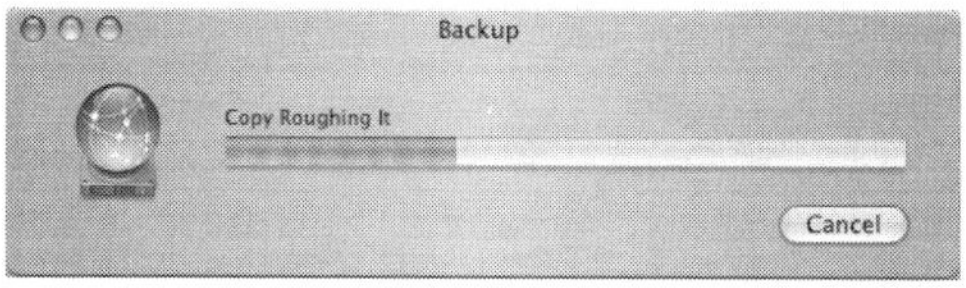

**Figure 81** A window like this appears as Backup works.

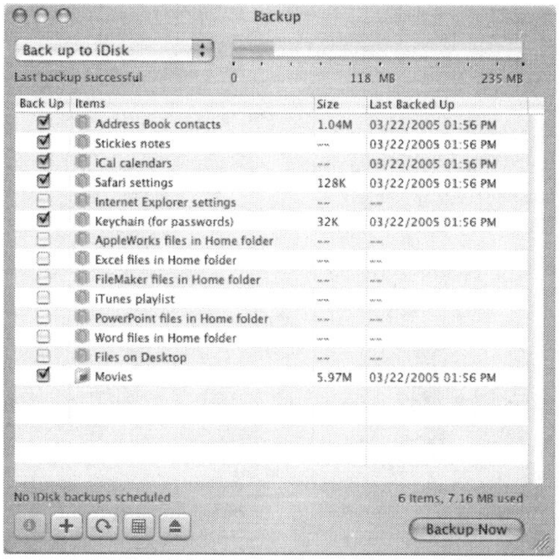

**Figure 82** The main backup window indicates the status of the previous backup.

# To manually back up to iDisk

1. In the main Backup window (**Figure** 76), make sure Back up to iDisk is chosen from the pop-up menu (**Figure** 78).

2. Click the Backup Now button.

   A backup window like the one in **Figure 81** appears to indicate the progress of the backup. When it's finished, Backup's main window reappears, indicating the last backup date for all of the backed up files (**Figure 82**).

## To manually back up to CD or DVD

1. In the main Backup window (**Figure 76**), choose Back up to CD/DVD from the pop-up menu (**Figure 78**).

2. If necessary, select the items you want to back up as discussed earlier in this section.

3. Click the Backup Now button.

4. A dialog like the one in **Figure 83** appears. Enter a name for the backup and click Begin Backup.

5. The Burn Disc dialog appears and the CD/DVD drive opens. Insert a blank CD or DVD and close the drive.

6. Click Burn in the Burn Disc dialog (**Figure 84**).

7. A backup window like the one in **Figure 85** appears to indicate the progress of the backup, CD or DVD burn, and verification. When Backup is finished, the CD/DVD drive opens and a dialog like the one in **Figure 86** appears. Remove the CD or DVD from the drive and Click OK to dismiss the dialog.

## ✔ Tips

- Backing up to CD or DVD rather than iDisk makes it possible to restore damaged files from backups when an Internet connection is not available.

- If a backup requires more than one CD or DVD, Backup will prompt you to insert them.

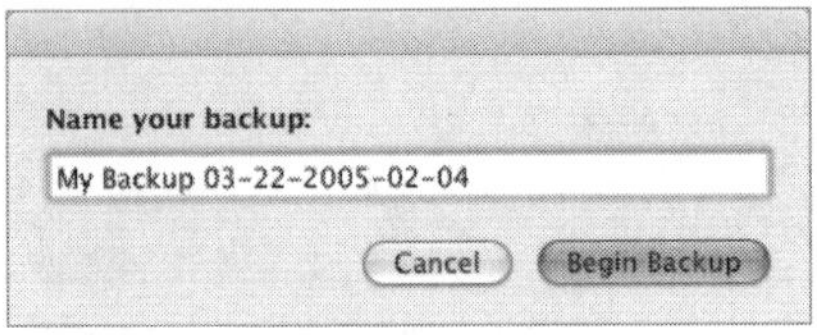

**Name your backup:**

My Backup 03-22-2005-02-04

Cancel | Begin Backup

**Figure 83** Use this dialog to specify a name for the backup disc.

Burn Disc

Burn Disc In:   PIONEER DVD-RW DVR-104

Ready to burn.

Eject | Cancel | Burn

**Figure 84** The Burn Disc dialog after a disc has been inserted.

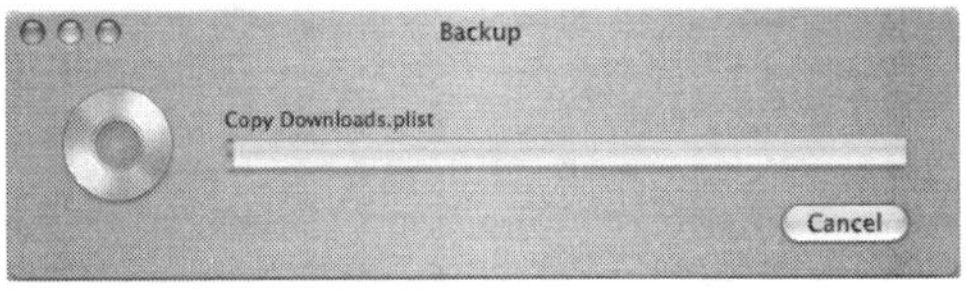

Backup

Copy Downloads.plist

Cancel

**Figure 85** Backup shows the backup progress.

**Your backup has been completed successfully.**

Your final disc has been named "My Backup 03-22-2005-02-04 Master". You should label the disc with the same name. For additional details see Log.

Your backup used 1 disc.

OK

**Figure 86** A dialog like this one confirms that the backup was successful.

MANUALLY BACKING UP TO CD OR DVD

**Figure 87** When you choose Back up to Drive, a Set button appears at the top of the Backup window.

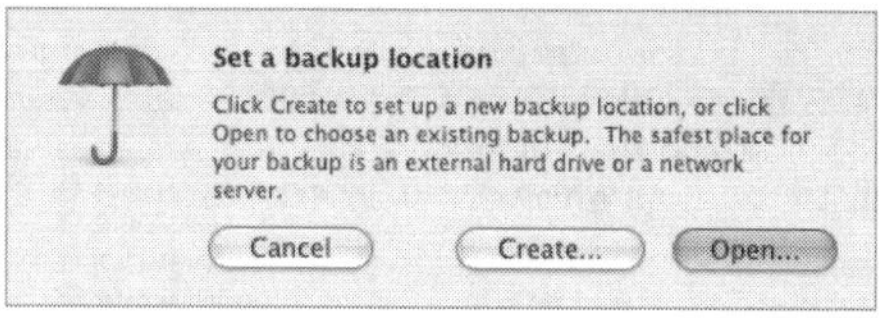

**Figure 88** You have two choices for the backup location.

Save As: Untitled

**Figure 89** Use this Save As dialog to specify a name and location for the backup file.

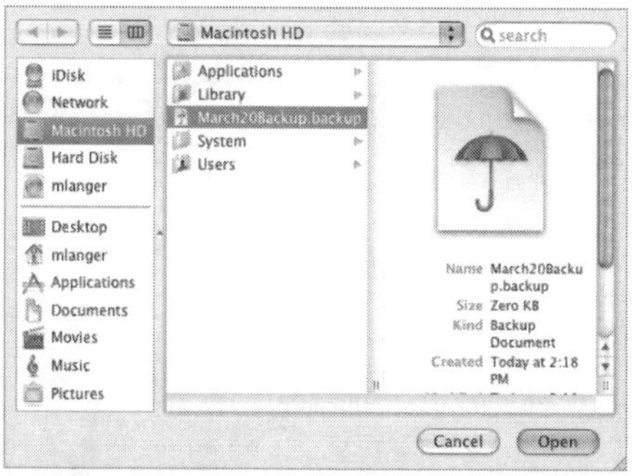

**Figure 90** Or use this Open dialog to select an existing backup file.

**Figure 91** The name of the backup file appears at the top of the main Backup window.

**Figure 92** A disk icon appears in the Backup window when it backs up to a disk.

# To manually back up to another drive

1. In the main Backup window (**Figure 76**), choose Back up to Drive from the pop-up menu (**Figure 78**).

2. Click the Set button (**Figure 87**).

3. A dialog like the one in **Figure 88** appears. You have two choices:

   ▲ Create enables you to create a new backup file. If you click Create, use a Save As dialog like the one in **Figure 89** to enter a name, choose a disk location, and click Create.

   ▲ Open enables you to back up to an existing file. If you click Open, use an Open dialog like the one in **Figure 90** to locate the backup file, select it, and click Open.

   The name of the backup file appears beside the Set button in the main Backup window (**Figure 91**).

4. If necessary, select the items you want to back up as discussed earlier in this section.

5. Click the Backup Now button.

   A backup window like the one in **Figure 92** appears to indicate the progress of the backup. When Backup is finished, the main Backup window reappears.

## ✔ Tip

■ Although you can back up to the same disk on which the files reside, that backup won't do you much good if the disk crashes. It's always a good idea to back up to a separate disk—and the farther away from your computer, the better!

## To restore files

1. In the main Backup window (**Figure 76**), choose a Restore option from the pop-up menu (**Figure 78**).

2. If you chose Restore from CD/DVD, a dialog like the one in **Figure 93** appears. Click the eject button to open the CD or DVD drive. Insert the CD or DVD containing the backup you want to restore from and close the drive.

3. In the main Backup window, click to place a check box beside each item you want to restore (**Figure 94**).

4. Click the Restore Now button.

5. If the file you are restoring already exists, a dialog like the one in **Figure 95** appears. Click Replace or Skip to either replace the existing copy with the backup or keep the existing copy. Repeat this step each time the dialog appears.

   A restore progress dialog like the one in **Figure 96** appears. When it disappears, the restore is finished.

## ✔ Tip

- In step 5, you can turn on the Apply to All check box (**Figure 95**) to either skip or replace all duplicate files.

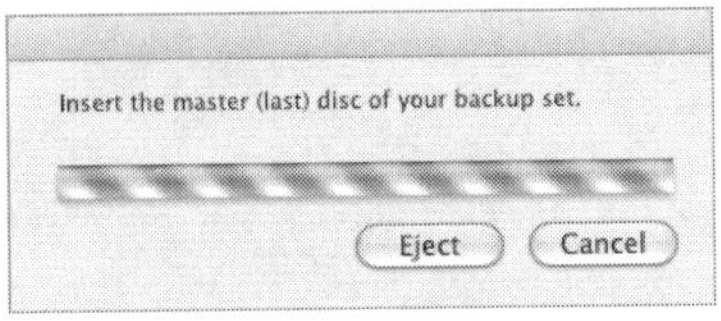

**Figure 93** When you restore from a CD or DVD, Backup displays a dialog like this one with instructions on which disc to insert.

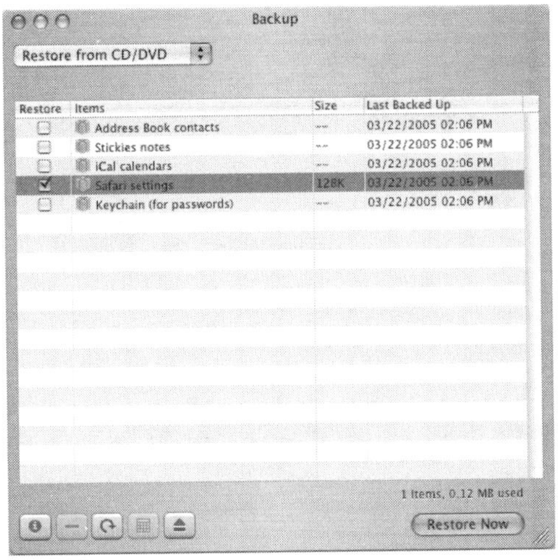

**Figure 94** Turn on the check boxes beside each item you want to restore.

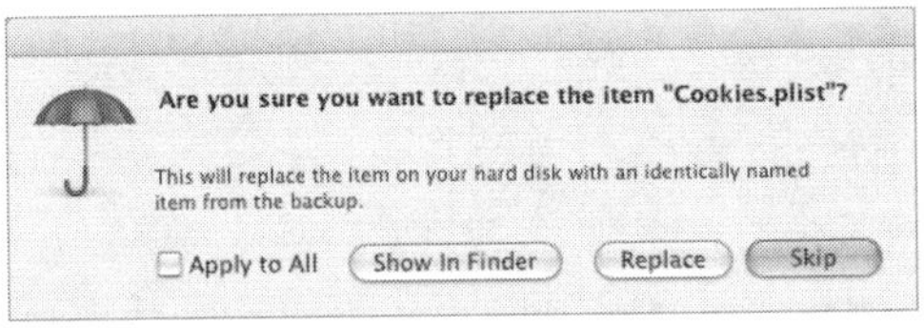

**Figure 95** Backup asks whether you want to overwrite existing files with the backup copies.

**Figure 96** A progress dialog like this one appears as the files are restored.

RESTORING FILES

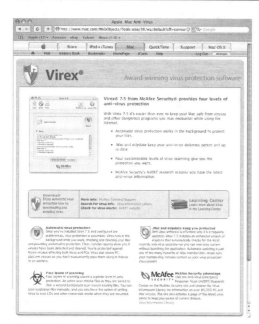

**Figure 97** The Virex main page on .Mac.

# Virex

*Virex* (**Figure 97**) gives .Mac members access to McAfee Virex virus protection software, Virex updates, and other virus protection resources. This .Mac feature can prevent a lot of headaches if used correctly.

In this part of the chapter, I explain how to download, install, configure, use, and update Virex software.

## ✔ Tips

- Virus protection software is only good if you keep it updated and use it regularly.

- You can help prevent viruses from harming your computer with a little common sense. Since most viruses are transmitted by opening files, don't open files that you receive via e-mail from strangers—and be thoughtful about opening files from folks you do know. This simple safeguard can protect your computer and help prevent the further spread of viruses.

- When it comes to viruses, Mac OS users are lucky. There are far fewer viruses that affect Macintosh computers than Wintel systems.

## To download & install Virex

1. Click the Virex button on the .Mac home page (**Figure 5**) to display the Virex main page (**Figure 97**).

2. Click the Download link.

3. On the Download Virex page that appears, click the link for Virex 7.5.1 (or a later version if one is available).

4. Wait while Virex downloads. If you display the Downloads window of Safari, you can see its progress.

5. If necessary, double-click the Virex disk image file icon to mount the installer disk (**Figure 98**). (It should appear on your desktop, unless you changed your browser's default download location.)

6. If necessary, double-click the Virex 7.5.1 GM disk to open its window (**Figure 99**).

7. Double-click the Virex 7.5.pkg icon to launch the Installer.

8. If a dialog appears, asking if the package can run a program, click Continue.

9. Follow the instructions that appear in installer windows (**Figure 100**) to install the software on your hard disk. If an Authenticate dialog appears (**Figure 73**), enter an administrator name and password and click OK.

10. Click the Restart button in the final Installer window to quit the installer and restart your computer.

### ✔ Tips

- In step 4, if a dialog appears, asking you if you're sure you want to continue downloading the file, click Continue.

- Virex is installed in your Applications folder (**Figure 74**).

- After installing Virex, you can delete the Virex installer disk image file.

**Figure 98**
The Virex installer disk image and mounted disk on the Desktop.

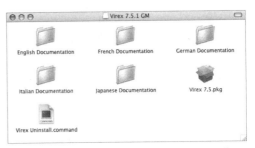

**Figure 99** The contents of the Virex 7.5.1 GM installer disk.

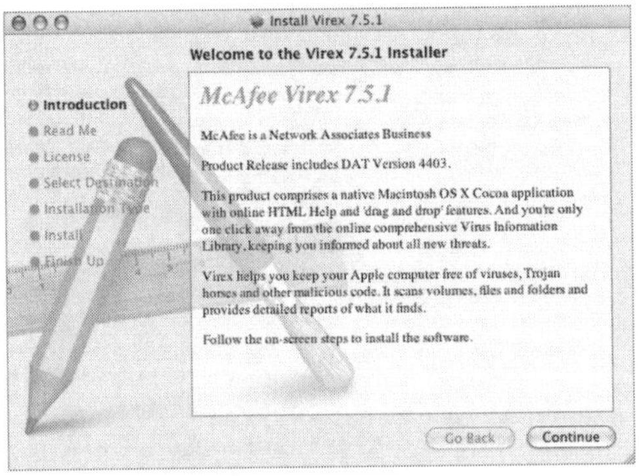

**Figure 100** The Virex Installer's first screen.

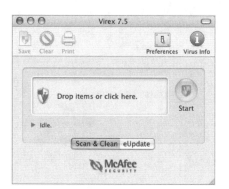

**Figure 101** The Virex main window.

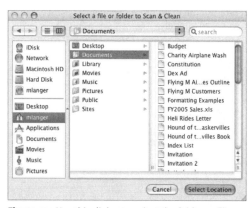

**Figure 102** Use this dialog to select the folder or file you want to scan for viruses.

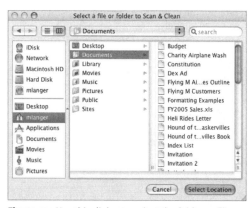

**Figure 103** As Virex scans, it displays its progress.

## To scan for viruses

1. Open the Virex 7.5 icon in the Applications folder (**Figure 74**).

2. Virex may display a dialog requesting an administrator's password. Enter the password and click OK. Virex uses its eUpdate feature to connect to the Internet and check for virus updates. If it finds any, it automatically installs them.

3. In the main Virex window (**Figure 101**), click the Virex icon to display a dialog like the one in **Figure 102**.

4. Select the folder or file you want to scan.

5. Click Select Location. The name of the folder or file you selected appears in the main Virex window.

6. Click Start.

7. Wait while Virex scans for viruses. It displays its progress in its main window as it works; you can click the triangle to expand the window and display details (**Figure 103**).

## ✔ Tips

- You can manually initiate an eUpdate by clicking the eUpdate button in Virex's main window (**Figure 101**) and then clicking the Start button.

- In step 3, you can simply drag a file or folder onto the Virex icon in the main Virex window (**Figure 101**) to select it. You can then skip steps 4 and 5.

- The more you scan, the longer the scan will take. For example, scanning your hard disk will take far longer than scanning just your Home folder.

- You can continue using your computer while Virex scans.

# Learning Center

Learning Center is a collection of Web-based tutorials to help you learn more about .Mac, your computer, and Apple software. Learning Center contents are always changing, but as this book went to press, they included tutorials for .Mac, Mac OS X, iLife '05, iPod, and older versions of Keynote and iLife.

## To access Learning Center

1. On the .Mac home page, click the Learning Center link to display the Learning Center's main page.

2. Select an item in the Category column. The middle column is populated with tutorial topic names.

3. Select a tutorial in the middle column. Information about the tutorial appears in the right column (**Figure 104**).

4. To begin the tutorial, click the Start Learning button.

   *or*

   To see individual topics within the tutorial, click the Topics button (**Figure 105**). You can then click a topic to go right to that part of the tutorial.

**Figure 104** The Learning Center offers a number of Web-based tutorials.

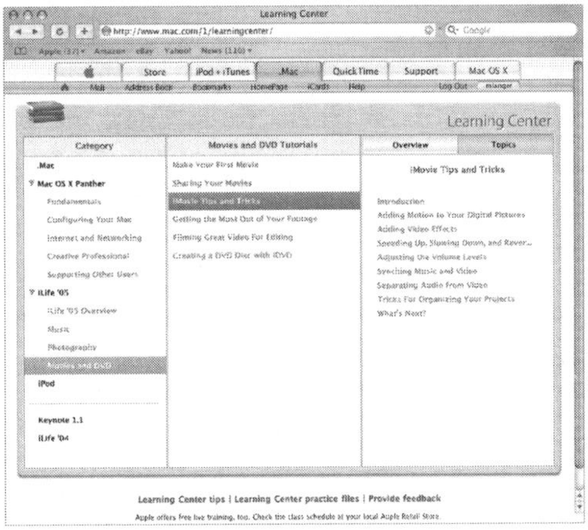

**Figure 105** If you don't want to go through all parts of a tutorial, you can view a list of topics within the tutorial and select the topic that interests you.

# Using
# Sherlock

**Figure 1** Sherlock's Channels window.

**Figure 2** You can launch Sherlock by opening its icon in the Applications folder.

## Sherlock

Sherlock (**Figure 1**) is Apple's Internet search utility. It enables you to search for information found on Web sites all over the world, including stock quotes and news, business listings, movie show times in your area, and flight information.

This chapter explain show to use Sherlock's search features to search the Internet.

### ✔ Tip

- To use Sherlock, your computer must have access to the Internet. **Chapter 13** covers accessing the Internet.

## To launch Sherlock

Open the Sherlock icon in the Applications folder (**Figure 2**).

Sherlock opens and displays a list of channels in its Toolbar collection (**Figure 1**).

# Channels & Collections

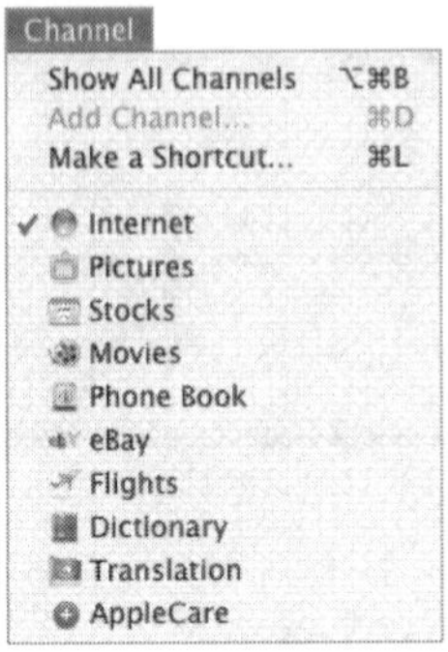

Sherlock's interface (**Figure 1**) includes a feature called *channels*, which enables you to organize search sites based on the types of information they can find for you. Sherlock comes preconfigured with ten primary Apple-provided channels:

◆ **Internet** lets you search the Internet for general information.

◆ **Pictures** enables you to search for pictures of people, places, and things.

◆ **Stocks** enables you to track prices and get news about stocks in your portfolio.

◆ **Movies** enables you to get information about movie locations and show times, as well as watch movie trailers.

◆ **Phone Book** enables you to search for businesses and get driving directions.

◆ **eBay** lets you participate in online auctions on eBay.

◆ **Flights** enables you to get information about flight arrivals.

◆ **Dictionary** lets you look up words and acronyms to get their meanings and synonyms.

◆ **Translation** enables you to translate words and phrases between several languages.

◆ **AppleCare** lets you search for Macintosh products and technical information.

Channels are organized by *collection*. A collection is a group of channels. Sherlock comes preconfigured with several collections:

◆ **Toolbar** includes channels that appear on Sherlock's toolbar. When you customize the toolbar, the list changes accordingly.

**Figure 3**
You can open a channel by choosing its name from the Channel menu.

**Figure 4** The Apple Channels collection lists channels provided by Apple.

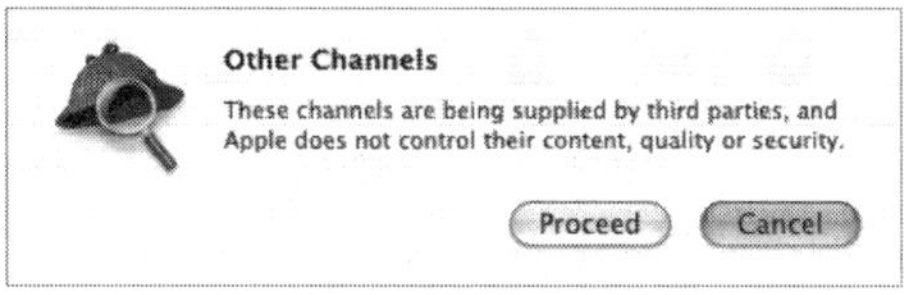

**Figure 5** The first time you try to view the Other Channels collection, a dialog like this may appear.

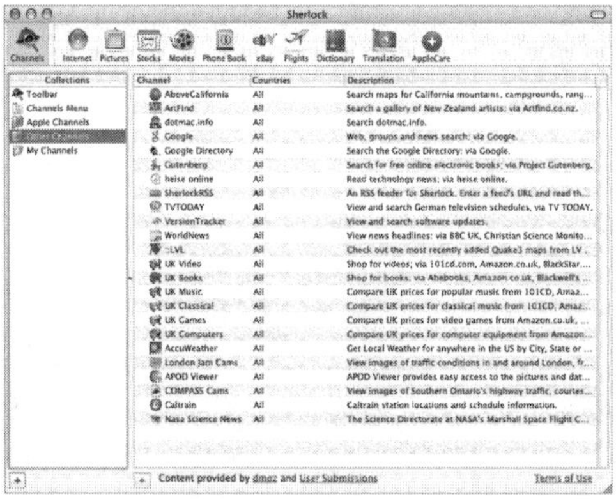

**Figure 6** Here's an example of what the Other Channels collection might look like.

♦ **Channels Menu** includes channels that appear on the Channels menu (**Figure 3**). When you add a shortcut to the Channels menu, the list changes accordingly.

♦ **Apple Channels** includes channels provided by Apple Computer, Inc.

♦ **Other Channels** includes channels from third-party providers.

♦ **My Channels** is a user-customizable list of channels where you can store your favorite channels.

## ✔ Tip

■ I explain how to customize Sherlock by adding channels, collections, and Channels menu shortcuts near the end of this chapter.

## To view a collection

Click the name of the collection in the Collections list. A list of the channels in that collection appears in the main part of the window (**Figures 1** and **4**).

## ✔ Tip

■ When you select the Other Channels collection for the first time, a dialog like the one in **Figure 5** appears. Click Proceed to view the collection contents (**Figure 6**).

## To open a channel

Use one of the following techniques:

♦ Double-click the name of the channel in the channels list (**Figures 1, 4**, and **6**).

♦ Click the icon for the channel in the toolbar at the top of any Sherlock window (**Figures 1, 4**, and **6**).

♦ Choose the name of the channel from the Channel menu (**Figure 3**).

# The Internet Channel

You can use Sherlock to search the Internet for Web sites with information about topics that interest you. Unlike most other Internet search engines, Sherlock can search multiple directories (or *search sites*) at once. Best of all, you don't need to know special search syntax. Just enter a search word or phrase in plain English, select the search sites you want to use, and put Sherlock to work. It displays matches in order of relevance, so the most likely matches appear first.

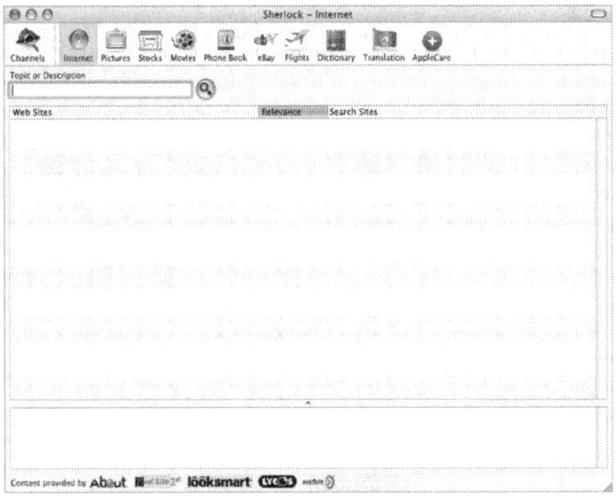

**Figure 7** Use Sherlock's Internet channel to search the Internet for general information.

## ✔ Tip

- Sherlock utilizes the search sites that are listed at the bottom of the Internet window (**Figure 7**). These sites may change.

**Figure 8** Enter a search word or phrase in the box.

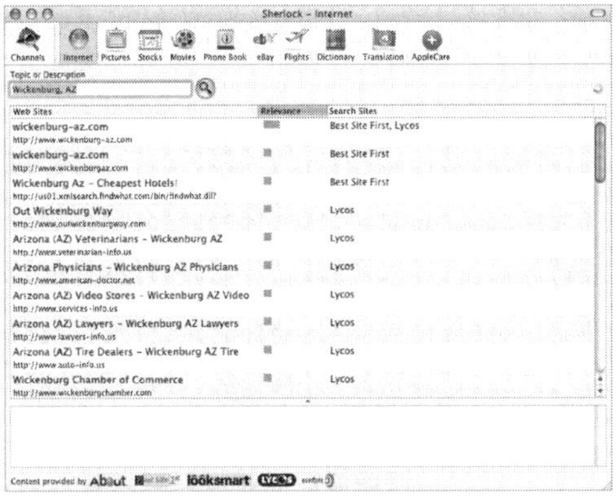

## To search for Web content

1. Open the Internet channel (**Figure 7**).

2. Enter a search word or phrase in the Topic or Description box near the top of the window (**Figure 8**).

3. Click the magnifying glass button to begin the search.

4. After a moment, the matches begin to appear. You can begin working with matches immediately or wait until Sherlock has finished searching (**Figure 9**).

## ✔ Tips

- When entering words in step 2, enter at least two or three words you expect to find in documents about the topic you are searching for. This helps narrow down the search, resulting in more useful matches.

- To perform a new search, follow steps 2 and 3. A new results list replaces the original list.

**Figure 9** Sherlock displays matches, in order of relevance, in its window.

Figure 10 Double-clicking the name of a Web page displays the page in your Web browser window. Here's my favorite Web site for my favorite western town.

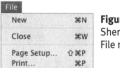

**Figure 11**
Sherlock's
File menu.

## To work with found sites

1. Scroll through the list of items found (**Figure 9**) to locate an item that interests you.

2. To open an item's Web page, double-click it. Your Web browser launches and displays the page in its window (**Figure 10**).

## ✔ Tips

■ You can sort the items found list in the Sherlock window (**Figure 9**) by clicking one of its column headings. To reverse the sort order, just click the same column heading again.

■ To open a separate Sherlock window to perform a new search (without disturbing the items found list), choose File > New (**Figure 11**) or press ⌘N.

# The Pictures Channel

Sherlock's Pictures channel enables you to search for pictures of people, places, and things. You can use these pictures for a variety of things, such as writing school reports, building Web pages,or creating advertising campaigns.

## ✦ Note

- As this book went to press, Sherlock's Pictures channel was still unavailable. As a result, the information on these two pages is based on the Pictures Channel as it worked with Sherlock in Mac OS X 10.3 Panther. The revised versions of these pages will be available for download on this book's companion Web site, www.langerbooks.com/macosquickstart/ when they can be written.

## ✔ Tip

- Most of the photos that Sherlock finds are stock photography images that are protected by U.S. copyright law. These images must be licensed or purchased before they can be used.

## To search for pictures

1. Open the Pictures channel (**Figure 12**).

2. Enter a search word or phrase in the Picture Topic or Description box near the top of the window.

3. Click the magnifying glass button to begin the search.

4. After a moment, the matches begin to appear as thumbnail images. You can begin working with matches immediately or wait until Sherlock has finished searching (**Figure 13**).

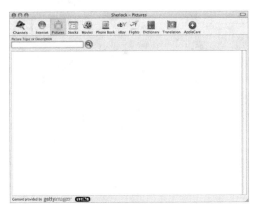

**Figure 12** Sherlock's Pictures channel.

**Figure 13** A search using the word *cowboy* results in pictures of cowboys (of all ages).

## ✔ Tip

- To perform a new search, follow steps 2 and 3. A new results list replaces the original list.

**Figure 14** When you select a photo's thumbnail, the URL for its location on the Web appears in the bottom of the Sherlock window.

**Figure 15** Double-clicking a thumbnail image displays a Web page with more information about the photo, including licensing information.

## To work with found photos

1. Scroll through the thumbnail images found (**Figure 13**) to locate a photo that interests you.

2. Click the photo to select it. The URL for the photo's location on the Web appears in the bottom of the Sherlock window (**Figure 14**).

3. To open a photo Web page, double-click it. Your Web browser launches and displays the page in its window (**Figure 15**). The page will include licensing information if it applies.

## ✔ Tip

- To open a separate Sherlock window to perform a new search (without disturbing the items found list), choose File > New (**Figure 11**) or press ⌃⌘N.

# The Stocks Channel

Sherlock's Stocks channel lets you get stock quotes, news headlines and stories, and charts for stocks. You enter the company name or ticker symbol and put Sherlock to work. It retrieves the information and displays it in the Stocks window.

## ✔ Tip

■ Although the stock quotes are delayed 15 minutes, they are constantly updated as long as the Stocks window is open.

## To look up stock information for a company

1. Open the Stocks channel. Sherlock connects to the Internet and retrieves information about the last companies you looked up, which it displays in its window (**Figure 16**).

2. Enter the name or ticker symbol for a company in the Company Name or Ticker Symbol box near the top of the window (**Figure 17**).

3. Click the magnifying glass button to begin the search.

   The company name and information is added to the list and appears in the window (**Figure 18**).

## ✔ Tips

■ In step 1, the first time you open the Stocks channel, it displays information for Apple Computer, Inc.

■ After step 3, if you entered a company name or ticker symbol that Sherlock does not recognize, it displays a "Company name or ticker symbol not found" message beside the magnifying glass icon. Repeat steps 2 and 3 to try again.

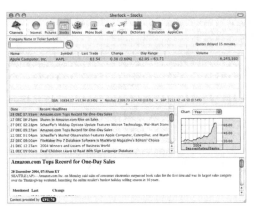

**Figure 16** Sherlock's Stocks channel.

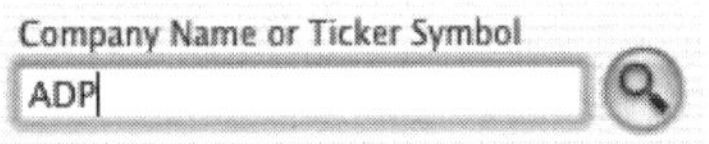

**Figure 17** Enter a ticker symbol (like this) or a company name.

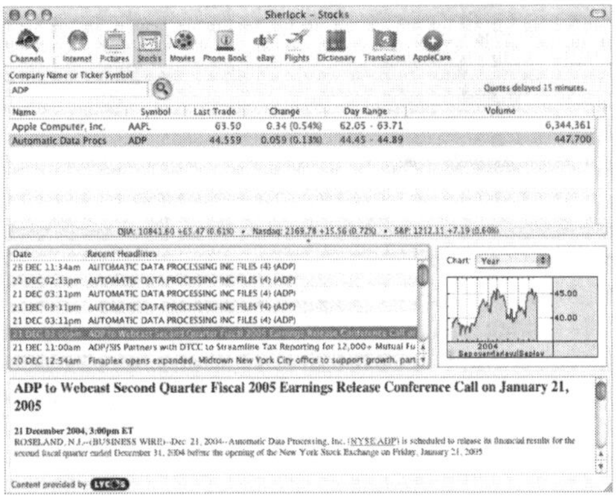

**Figure 18** The company you added appears in the window.

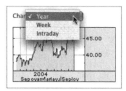

**Figure 19** A news story viewed in a Web browser window.

**Figure 20** The Chart menu offers three charting options.

## To view news stories

Click a headline in the Stocks window. The story appears in the bottom of the window (**Figure 18**).

*Or*

1. Click a headline in the Stocks window. A link to a story appears in the bottom of the window.

2. Click the link. Sherlock launches your Web browser to display the article on the Web (**Figure 19**).

## To view a different chart

Choose an option from the Chart pop-up menu (**Figure 20**). The chart changes accordingly.

## To remove a company from the list

1. Select the company you want to remove from the list.

2. Press Delete. The company disappears.

## ✔ Tip

- The fewer companies in the list, the quicker Sherlock can display and update information. This also speeds up the Stocks channel's loading time.

# The Movies Channel

Sherlock's Movies channel (**Figures 21** and 24) offers a great way to get local movie listings and show times, without picking up the phone.

## To search for movie show times

1. Open the Movies channel.

2. Choose a recent entry from the Find Near drop-down list.

   *or*

   Enter an Address Book entry name or city and state in the Find Near box.

3. If necessary, click the Movies button on the far left side of the window. After a moment, a list of current movies appears in the leftmost list (**Figure 21**).

4. Select the name of a movie that you'd like to see. A list of theaters showing the movie appears in the middle list and information about the movie, including a movie poster and QuickTime movie trailer, appears in the bottom of the window (**Figure 22**).

5. Select the name of the theater where you'd like to see the movie. A list of showtimes appears in the rightmost list and the theater location appears in the bottom of the window (**Figure 23**).

6. Repeat steps 4 and 5 to find other show-times for movies.

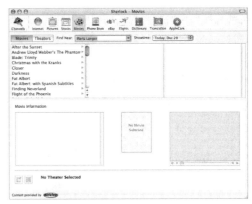

**Figure 21** The Movies channel with the Movies option selected.

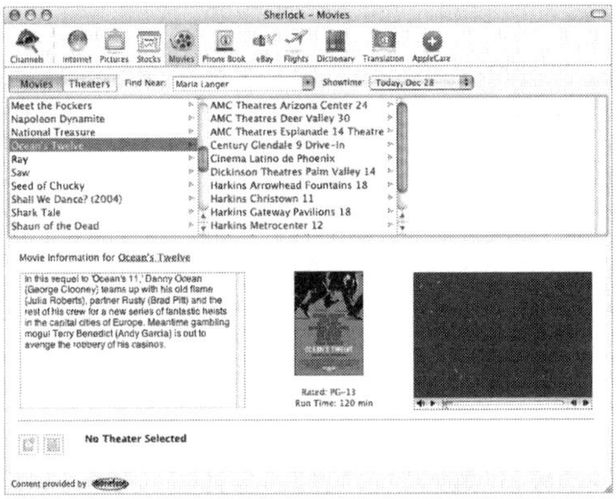

**Figure 22** When you select a movie, a list of nearby theaters appears, along with movie info.

**Figure 23** When you select a theater, a list of show-times and theater location information appears.

**SEARCHING FOR MOVIE SHOWTIMES**

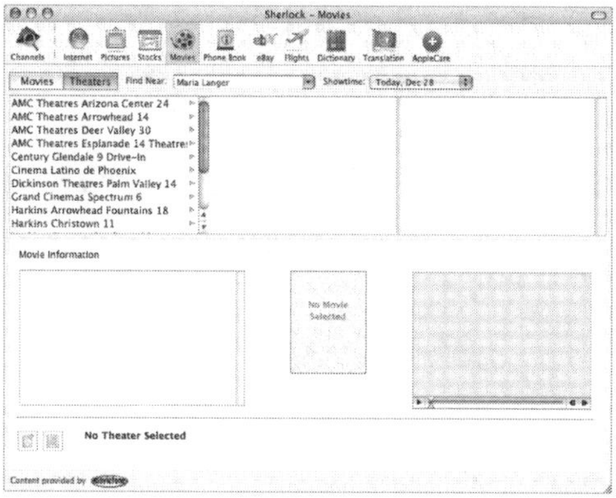

# To search theater schedules

1. Open the Movies channel.

2. Choose a recent entry from the Find Near drop-down list.

   *or*

   Enter an Address Book entry name or city and state in the Find Near box.

3. If necessary, click the Theaters button on the far left side of the window. After a moment, a list of nearby theaters appears in the leftmost list (**Figure** 24).

4. Select the name of a theater you'd like to see the schedule for. A list of movies playing at that theater appears in the middle list and additional information about the theater appears in the bottom of the window (**Figure 25**).

5. Select the name of the movie you'd like to see. A list of showtimes appears in the rightmost list and information about the movie, including a QuickTime movie trailer, appears in the bottom right of the window (**Figure 26**).

6. Repeat steps 4 and 5 to find other theater schedules.

**Figure 24** The Movies channel with the Theaters option selected.

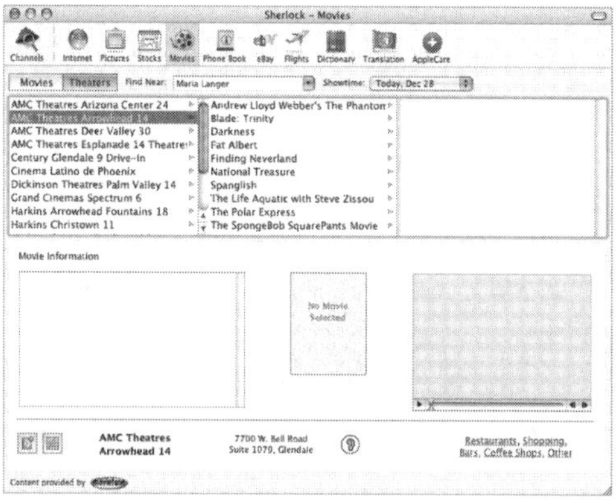

**Figure 25** Select a theater to display a list of what's playing there.

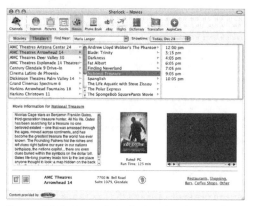

**Figure 26** Select a movie to display showtimes and movie information.

# To work with the results window

1. Follow the instructions on one of the previous two pages to view movie listings and showtimes (**Figures 23** and **26**).

2. Perform any of the following tasks:

   ▲ To play the movie trailer, click the play button when the movie is finished downloading from the Internet. I explain how to play QuickTime movies in **Chapter 8**.

   ▲ To see theater show times for a different day, choose the date from the Showtime pop-up menu near the top of Sherlock's window.

   ▲ To add the theater to Address Book, click the Add this theater to your Address Book button on the lower left corner of the window.

   ▲ To get a map and driving directions to the theater, click the See a map with driving directions to this theater button in the lower left corner of the window. Sherlock switches to the Phone Book channel to get the information for you. (I tell you about the Phone Book channel next.)

   ▲ To learn about restaurants, shopping, bars, coffee shops, and other businesses in the area, click one of the blue underlined links in the lower right corner of the window. Sherlock switches to the Phone Book channel to get the information for you (**Figure 27**).

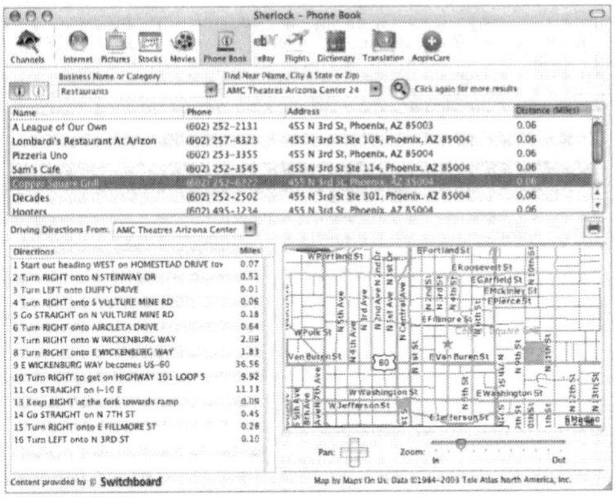

**Figure 27** Clicking the restaurants link in **Figure 26** displays a list of restaurants near the theater. Selecting one of the restaurants displays directions and a map.

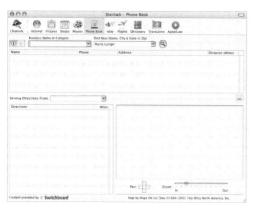

**Figure 28** Sherlock's Phone Book channel.

**Figure 29**
The Business Name
or Category drop-
down list includes
standard categories,
as well as recently
accessed business
names.

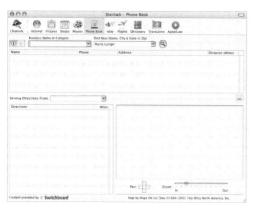

**Figure 30** Select a business to display driving directions
and a map.

# The Phone Book Channel

The Phone Book channel (**Figure 28**) is a
great way to find local businesses and get the
directions you need to find them.

## ✔ Tip

- The Phone Book channel was known as
  the Yellow Pages channel in previous
  versions of Sherlock.

## To search for a business listing

1. Open the Phone Book channel (**Figure 28**).

2. Choose a recent entry from the Find Near
   drop-down list.

   *or*

   Enter an Address Book entry name or city
   and state in the Find Near box.

3. Enter a business name or category in the
   Business Name or Category box.

   *or*

   Choose a category or recent business
   name from the Business Name or Category drop-down list (**Figure 29**).

4. Click the magnifying glass button to begin
   the search.

5. After a moment, search results begin to
   appear. Select a listing to view driving
   directions and a map in the bottom half
   of the window (**Figure 30**)

## ✔ Tip

- In many instances, driving directions are
  for the shortest route, which may not be
  the quickest or most convenient. If I
  followed the driving directions in **Figure
  30**, for example, I'd hit at least 50 traffic
  lights; I know a slightly longer but quicker
  route with only four traffic lights. Which
  do you think I'd take?

# The eBay Channel

The eBay channel (**Figure 31**) enables you to search for items available for sale on eBay, an online auction Web site. You enter search criteria, and Sherlock retrieves a list of found items from eBay. You can then track the auction within Sherlock or visit the auction's Web page, where you can bid on it.

## To search for items on eBay

1. Open the eBay channel and make sure the Search button is selected (**Figure 31**).

2. Enter search criteria in the top part of the window, right beneath the toolbar.

3. Click the magnifying glass button to start the search.

4. After a moment, search results begin to appear. The first item is selected and information about it appears in the bottom half of the window (**Figure 32**).

5. To see information about another item in the list, click it to select it.

6. To get more information about an item, double-click it. Your Web browser launches and displays the item's page on eBay (**Figure 33**).

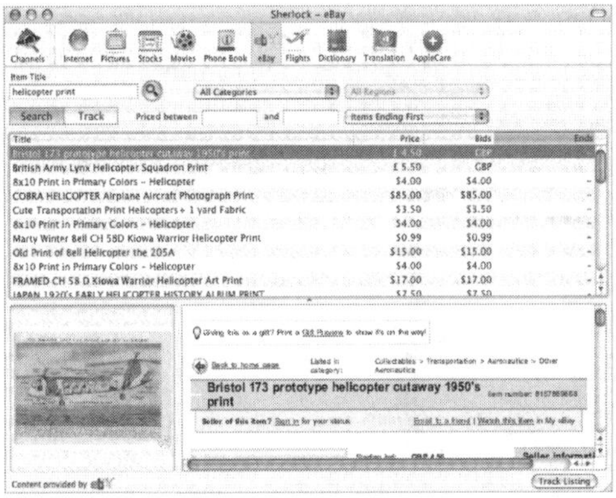

## ✔ Tip

- Use search criteria to narrow down the search. The more entries you make in the search criteria area, the fewer matches will appear in the list of matches.

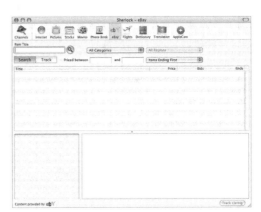

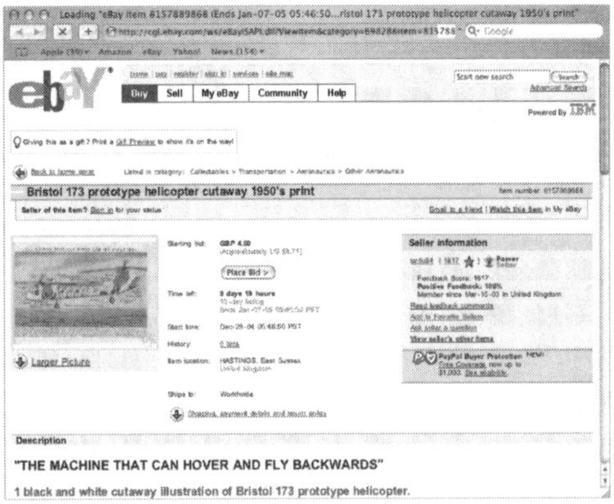

**Figure 31** Sherlock's eBay channel.

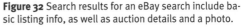

**Figure 32** Search results for an eBay search include basic listing info, as well as auction details and a photo.

**Figure 33** Double-clicking an item in Sherlock's window displays its Web page on eBay.

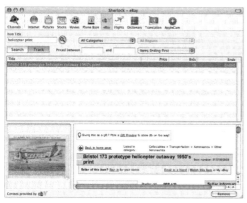

**Figure 34** Clicking the Track button at the top of Sherlock's eBay channel displays a list of the auctions you are tracking.

## To track an eBay auction item

1. Select the item you want to track in the list of found items (**Figure 32**).

2. Click the Track Listing button at the bottom of the Sherlock window.

3. The item is added to the Track list in the eBay channel; click the Track button near the top of the window to see it (**Figure 34**).

## ✔ Tip

- Items you track on eBay remain in the Track list (**Figure 34**) until the auction is over.

## To bid on an eBay item

1. Double-click the item you want to bid on in the list of found items (**Figure 32**) or the list of items you are tracking (**Figure 34**) to display its Web page (**Figure 33**).

2. Read the information on the page carefully.

3. Enter your bid in the form near the bottom of the page.

## ✔ Tip

- You must have an account on eBay to bid on items. Setting up an account is free. Follow the instructions on the eBay Web site to learn more.

TRACKING & BIDDING ON EBAY ITEMS

# The Flights Channel

The Flights channel (**Figure 35**) enables you to get departure and arrival information for airline flights. Enter search criteria in the top of the window and Sherlock displays results from a database of flights. This is handy for checking the status of a flight you think might be delayed—it could prevent you from waiting longer than you need to at the airport!

## ✔ Tip

■ The Flights channel provides information about current day flights only.

## To search for flight information

1. Open the Flights channel (**Figure 35**).

2. Enter search criteria in the top part of the window, right beneath the toolbar.

3. Click the magnifying glass button to start the search.

4. After a moment, search results begin to appear. Click a flight to get information about it (**Figure 36**).

## ✔ Tip

■ In step 4, if a check mark appears in the Chart column for a flight, a graphic of the flight's position and weather appears in the bottom right of the window (**Figure 36**). Is this cool or what?

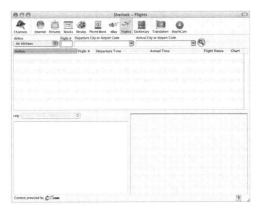

**Figure 35** Sherlock's Flights channel.

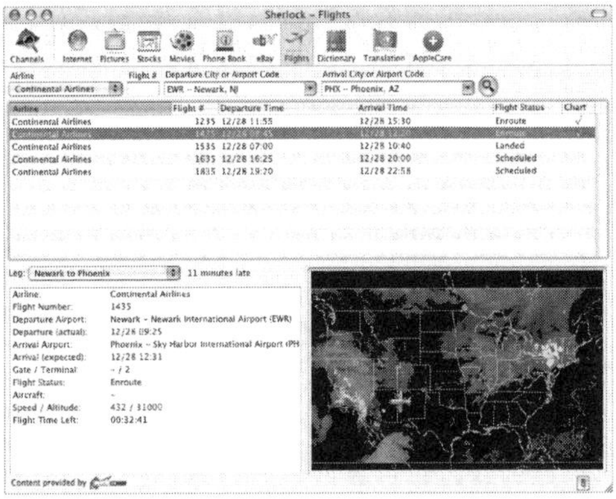

**Figure 36** Sherlock displays information about a flight when you select it.

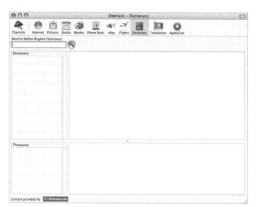

**Figure 37** Sherlock's Dictionary channel.

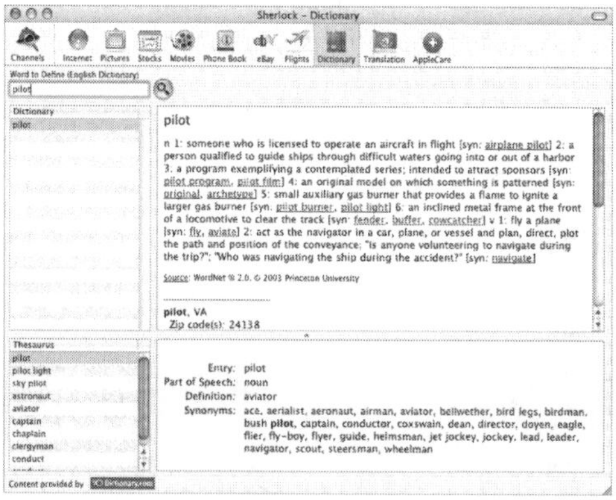

**Figure 38** Sherlock looks up a word and displays its definition and synonyms.

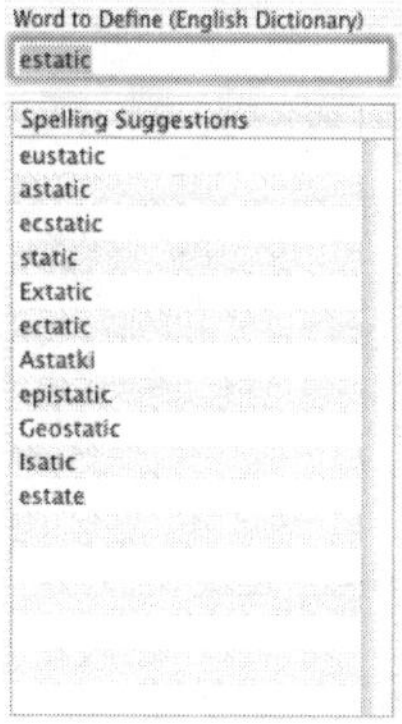

**Figure 39**
Can't spell? Not a problem. Sherlock displays a list of words it thinks you might have been trying to spell.

# The Dictionary Channel

The Dictionary channel (**Figure 37**) enables you to get definitions and synonyms for words and acronyms. Enter the word you want to learn about and let Sherlock look it up on Dictionary.com.

## To define a word

1. Open the Dictionary channel (**Figure 37**).

2. Enter the word or acronym you want to define in the Word to Define box.

3. Click the magnifying glass button to look up the word.

4. Wait while Sherlock looks up the word. After a moment, search results appear in the window (**Figure 38**):

   ▲ The Dictionary list displays words that either exactly match what you entered or are related to what you entered. Select the word to see a definition in the box beside it.

   ▲ The Thesaurus list displays synonyms for the word you selected in the list above it. Select a synonym to see more information and synonyms.

## ✔ Tips

■ To look up one of the words in the Dictionary or Thesaurus list, double-click it.

■ If Sherlock can't find the word because you misspelled it (heck, I did it twice while experimenting!), the Spelling Suggestions list appears in place of the Dictionary list (**Figure 39**). Double-click a word in the list to look it up.

**DEFINING WORDS**

# The Translation Channel

Sherlock's Translation channel (**Figure 40**) uses online software tools to translate words and phrases between several languages, including: English, Chinese (Simplified and Traditional), Dutch, French, German, Greek, Italian, Japanese, Korean, Portuguese, Russian, and Spanish. Type in what you want to translate, click a button, and let Sherlock do the rest.

## ✔ Tip

■ Because translations are handled by software tools and not by human translators, they should not be relied upon for complete accuracy.

## To translate a word or phrase

1. Open the Translation channel (**Figure 40**).

2. Enter the word or phrase you want to translate in the Original Text box.

3. Select a translation option from the pop-up menu (**Figure 41**).

4. Click the Translate button between the top and bottom halves of the Translation window. The translation and a fine-print disclaimer appear in the bottom half of the window (**Figure 42**).

**Figure 40** Sherlock's Translation channel.

**Figure 41**
The pop-up menu offers quite a few translation options.

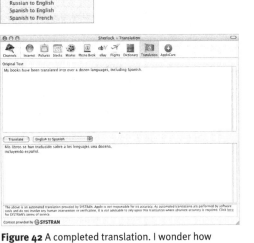

**Figure 42** A completed translation. I wonder how accurate this is?

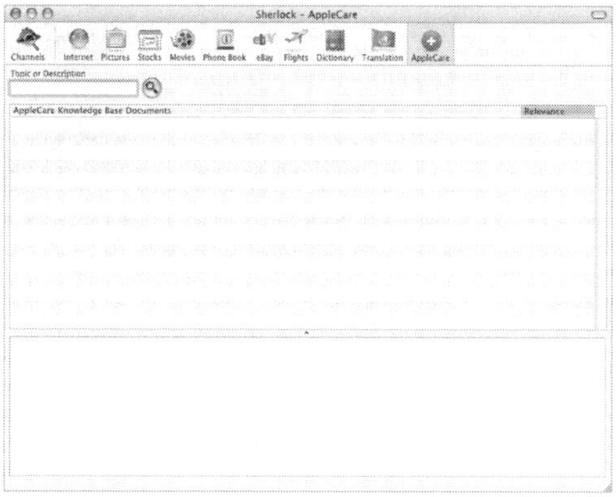

**Figure 43** Sherlock's AppleCare channel.

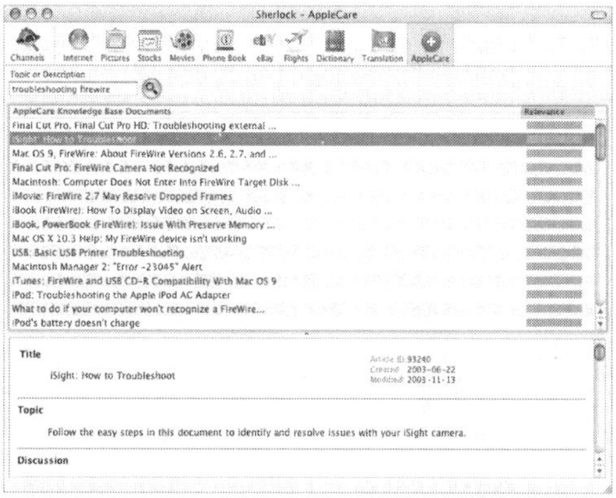

**Figure 44** Sherlock displays a list of Knowledge Base documents in the window. Click a document name to display it in the bottom half of the window.

# The AppleCare Channel

Sherlock's AppleCare channel (**Figure 43**) is your direct connection to Apple's Knowledge Base of information about Macintosh computers and software. It's a great place to learn more about your hardware and the Mac OS.

## To search the AppleCare Knowledge Base

1. Open the AppleCare channel (**Figure 43**).

2. Enter a search word or phrase in the Topic or Description box near the top of the window.

3. Click the magnifying glass button to start the search.

4. After a moment, search results begin to appear. Click an item in the list to display its document in the bottom half of the window (**Figure 44**).

# Customizing Sherlock

There are a number of ways you can customize Sherlock so it works the way you want it to. Make your own collections of channels, customize the toolbar, and add channels to the Channels menu. This part of the chapter explains how.

## ✔ Tip

- You cannot modify the Apple Channels or Other Channels collections.

## To move or copy a channel from one collection to another

1. Display the collection in which the channel you want to move or copy appears.

2. Drag the channel name from the channel list to the name of the collection you want to move or copy it to (**Figure 45**). The channel appears in that collection list.

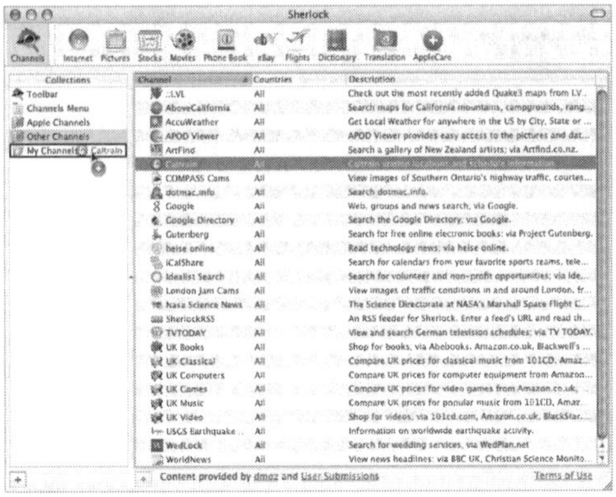

## ✔ Tips

- Dragging a channel from the Apple Channels or Other Channels collection copies the channel. Dragging a channel from any other collection list moves the channel.

- You can force a channel to be copied (rather than moved) by holding down Option while dragging it to the destination collection.

- Modifying the Toolbar or Channels Menu collection automatically modifies the toolbar or Channels menu.

**Figure 45** Drag a channel from one collection to another to move or copy it.

**MOVING & COPYING CHANNELS**

Figure 46 Sherlock's View menu.

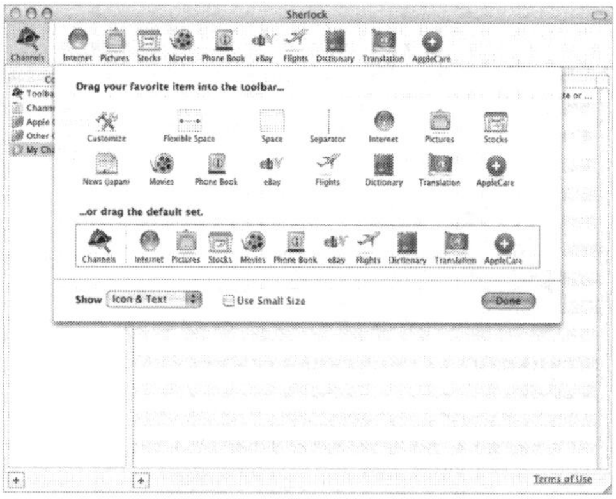

Figure 47 The Customize Toolbar dialog sheet.

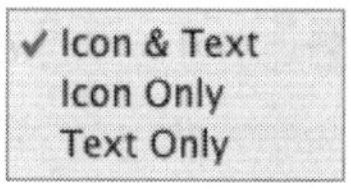

Figure 48
The Show pop-up menu lets you specify how the toolbar should appear.

## To remove a channel from a collection

1. Display the collection you want to modify.

2. Select the channel you want to remove.

3. Press Delete. The channel is removed from the collection.

## To customize the toolbar

Follow the instructions on the previous page and this page to add or remove channels in the Toolbar collection.

*Or*

1. Choose View > Customize Toolbar (**Figure 46**). A dialog sheet like the one in **Figure 47** appears.

2. To change toolbar icons, use any combination of the following techniques:

   ▲ To add a button to the toolbar, drag its icon from the dialog to the toolbar.

   ▲ To remove a button, drag it off the toolbar.

   ▲ To restore the toolbar to the default buttons, drag the default set of buttons to the toolbar.

3. To change the way icons are displayed on the toolbar, choose an option from the Show pop-up menu (**Figure 48**).

4. To display smaller icons, turn on the Use Small Size check box.

5. When you're finished making changes, click Done.

## ✔ Tip

■ It is not necessary to display the Customize Toolbar dialog sheet (**Figure 47**) to add channel buttons to the toolbar. Simply drag a channel from any list to the toolbar to add an icon for it.

**REMOVING CHANNELS, CUSTOMIZING TOOLBAR**

## To create a shortcut for a channel

1. Open the channel you want to create a shortcut for.

2. Choose Channel > Make a Shortcut (**Figure 3**), or press ⌃ ⌘ L.

3. A dialog like the one in **Figure 49** appears. Enter a name and choose a disk location for the shortcut file.

4. Click Make. A shortcut file is saved in the location you specified with the name you entered (**Figure 50**).

## ✔ Tips

■ Sherlock shortcuts offer a quick way to open a specific Sherlock channel. Simply double-click the file's icon to launch Sherlock and display the channel.

■ I explain how to use a Save As dialog in **Chapter 7**.

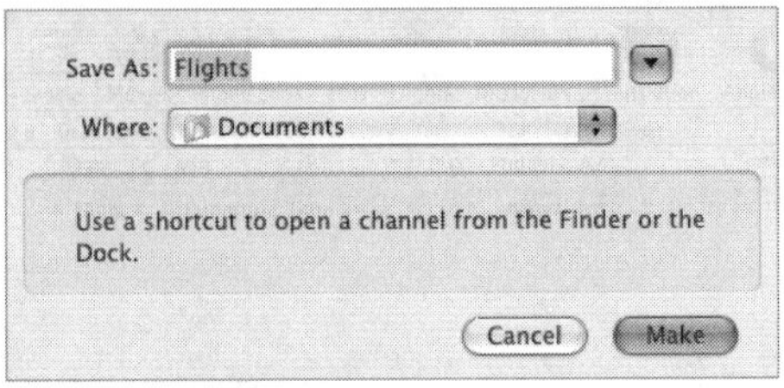

Save As: Flights

Where: Documents

Use a shortcut to open a channel from the Finder or the Dock.

Cancel    Make

**Figure 49** Use a dialog like this one to name and save a channel shortcut.

**Figure 50**
Here's what a shortcut for the Flights channel looks like.

Flights

CREATING CHANNEL SHORTCUTS

# Networking

## Networking

*Networking* uses direct connections and network protocols to connect your computer to others on a network. Once connected, you can share files, access e-mail, and run special network applications on server computers.

This chapter looks at *peer-to-peer networking*, which uses the built-in features of Mac OS X to connect to other computers for file and application sharing. It also covers some of the advanced network configuration tools available as Mac OS X utilities.

## ✔ Tips

- If you use your computer at work, you may be connected to a companywide network; if so, you'll find the networking part of this chapter very helpful. But if you use your computer at home and have only one computer, you won't have much need for the networking information here.

- A discussion of Mac OS X Server, which is designed to meet the demands of large workgroups and corporate intranets, is beyond the scope of this book.

- This chapter touches only briefly on using networks to connect to the Internet. Connecting to the Internet is discussed in detail in **Chapter 13**.

# Basic Networking Terms

Before I explain how to use your Mac on a network, let me take a moment or two to introduce and define some of the networking terminology used throughout this chapter. You'll find these words used again and again whenever you deal with networking features.

## AppleTalk

*AppleTalk* is a networking protocol used by Macintosh computers to communicate over a network. It's the software that makes networking work. Fortunately, it's not something extra you have to buy—it's part of Mac OS X.

## TCP/IP

*TCP/IP* is a networking protocol that is used for connecting to the Internet. Mac OS X computers can use both AppleTalk to communicate with local networks and TCP/IP to communicate with the Internet.

## Bonjour

*Bonjour* (formerly *Rendezvous*) is a networking technology introduced by Apple with Mac OS X 10.2. It simplifies network setup by enabling your computer to automatically recognize other Bonjour-compatible network devices. Bonjour works over both Ethernet and AirPort.

## ✔ Tip

■ Bonjour can be used with iChat to initiate live chats with other Mac OS X users on your network. I cover iChat in **Chapter 11**.

## AirPort

*AirPort* is the name for Apple's wireless networking technology. (It is also called *WiFi*.) Through AirPort, your Mac can join wireless networks. AirPort networks can operate as fast as 54 megabits per second.

## Ethernet

*Ethernet* is a network connection method that is built in to all Mac OS X-compatible computers. It uses Ethernet cables that connect to the Ethernet ports or network interface cards of computers and network printers. Additional hardware such as *routers* and *hubs* may be needed, depending on the network setup and device.

Ethernet comes in three speeds: 10, 100 (also called *Fast Ethernet*), and 1000 (also called *Gigabit Ethernet*) megabits per second. The maximum speed of the computer's communication with the rest of the network is limited by the maximum speed of the cable, hub, and other network devices.

## ✔ Tips

■ Network hardware configuration details are far beyond the scope of this book. The information here is provided primarily to introduce some of the network terms you might encounter when working with your computer and other documentation.

■ *LocalTalk* is an older Mac OS-compatible network method. Slow and supported only by older Macintosh models with serial ports, it is rarely used in today's networks and is not covered in this book.

**Figure 1** You configure sharing with two System Preferences panes: Network and Sharing.

# Setting Up Network Sharing

To share files, applications, and printers with other network users, you must set options in two System Preferences panes (**Figure 1**):

◆ **Network** allows you to enable AppleTalk and choose your AppleTalk zone and configuration.

◆ **Sharing** allows you to name your computer, enable types of sharing and access, and control how other users can run applications on your computer.

This part of the chapter explains how to set up sharing via an AirPort or Ethernet connection. It also explains how to share files once the configuration is complete.

## ✔ Tips

■ Although file sharing is possible with other protocols and types of connections, it is impossible for me to cover all configuration options here. If you're using a different type of network and don't have instructions for using it with Mac OS X, read through the instructions here. Much of what you read may apply to your setup.

■ If your computer is on a large network, consult the system administrator before changing any network configuration options.

**SHARING FILES & APPLICATIONS**

## To view network status

1. Choose Apple > System Preferences (**Figure** 2), or click the System Preferences icon in the Dock.

2. In the System Preferences window that appears (**Figure** 1), click the Network icon.

   An overview of your network status appears (**Figure** 3).

## ✔ Tips

- If the Network preferences pane does not list network connections as shown in **Figure** 3, choose Network Status from the Show menu (**Figure** 4).

- Network Status on your computer may not exactly match what is shown in **Figure** 3. For example, on my computer, I have both AirPort and Ethernet for network connections; if you have one or the other (but not both) only the one you have will appear in the list.

- As shown in **Figure** 3, Network Status will clearly indicate which network connection is used for Internet communications.

- I tell you more about connecting to the Internet in **Chapter 13**.

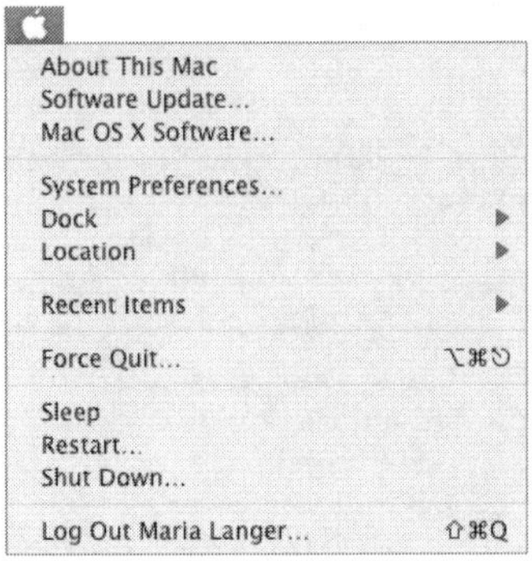

**Figure 2**
The Apple menu.

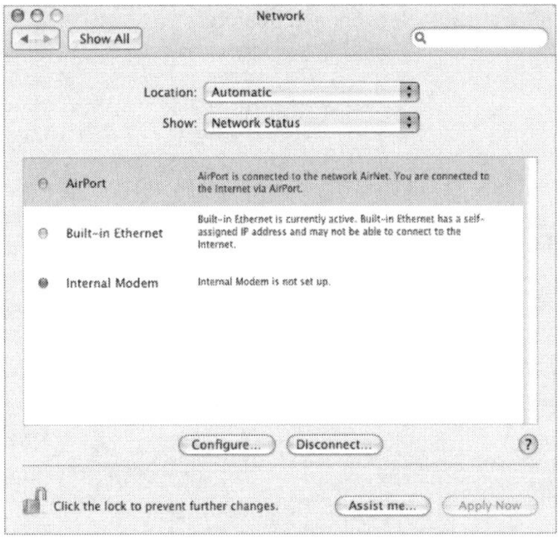

**Figure 3** As shown here, my computer gets its Internet connection via AirPort, but is also connected to an Ethernet network via its built-in Ethernet port. It has an Internal modem, but it hasn't been configured.

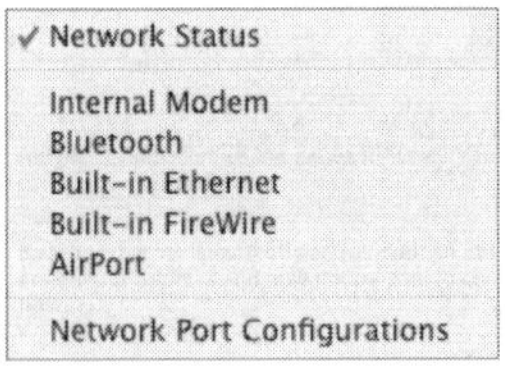

**Figure 4**
The Show pop-up menu.

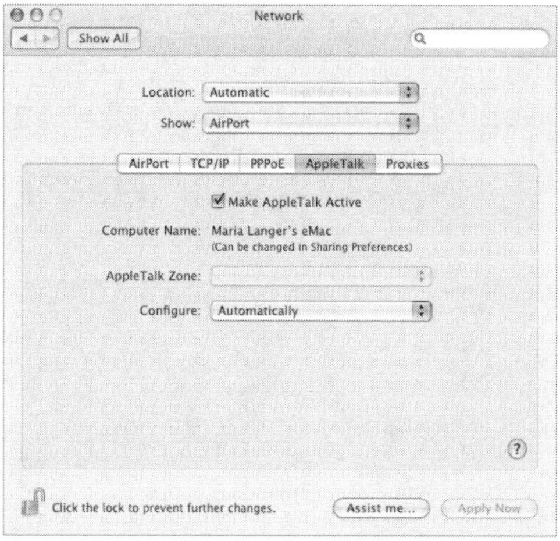

**Figure 5** The AppleTalk options in the Network preferences pane.

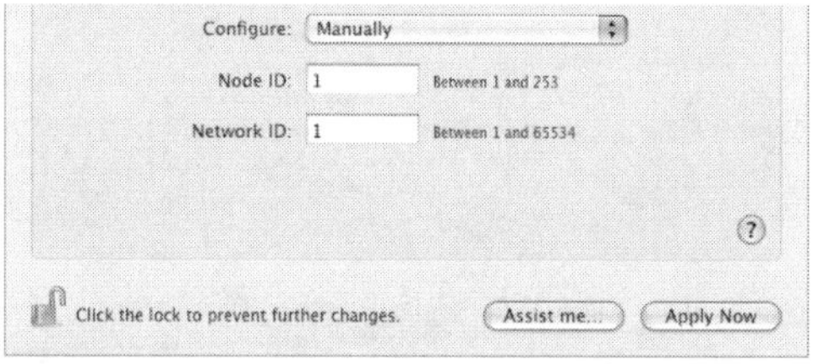

**Figure 6** If you choose Manually, you have to enter correct network identification information.

## To set AppleTalk Network preferences

1. Follow the steps on the previous page to open the Network Preferences pane and view Network Status (**Figure 3**).

2. Choose the network connection you want to set AppleTalk preferences for from the Show pop-up menu (**Figure 4**).

   *or*

   Double-click the connection you want to set AppleTalk preferences for in the list of connections (**Figure 3**).

3. Click the AppleTalk button to display AppleTalk options (**Figure 6**).

4. Turn on the Make AppleTalk Active check box.

5. Click Apply Now.

6. If necessary, choose a zone from the AppleTalk Zone pop-up menu.

7. Choose an option from the Configure pop-up menu:

   ▲ **Automatically** automatically configures your computer with the correct network identification information.

   ▲ **Manually** displays Node ID and Network ID boxes for you to enter network identification information (**Figure 6**).

8. If you made changes in step 6 or 7, click Apply Now again.

## ✔ Tips

- AppleTalk zones are normally only present in large networks.

- In step 7, if you choose Manually, you must enter the correct information for AppleTalk to work.

## To set the computer's identity

1. Choose Apple > System Preferences (**Figure 2**), or click the System Preferences icon in the Dock.

2. In the System Preferences window that appears (**Figure 1**), click the Sharing icon to display the Sharing preferences pane (**Figure 7**).

3. Enter a name in the Computer Name box (**Figure 8**).

4. To change the identifier for your computer on the local subnet, click the Edit button to display a dialog like the one in **Figure 9**. Enter a new name in the Local Hostname box; the name you enter must end in *.local*, which cannot be changed. Click OK.

## ✔ Tips

- By default, the local subnet identifier is the computer name with dashes substituted for spaces, followed by *.local*.

- Your computer name is not the same as your hard disk name.

- If your computer is on a large network, give your computer a name that can easily distinguish it from others on the network. Ask your system administrator; there may be organization-wide computer naming conventions that you need to follow.

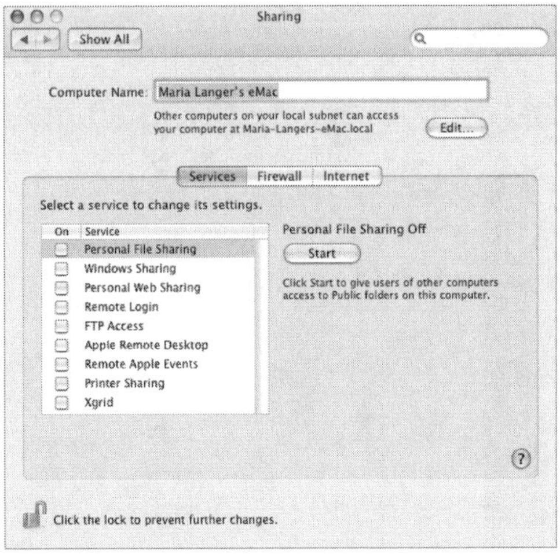

**Figure 7** The Services options in the Sharing preferences pane.

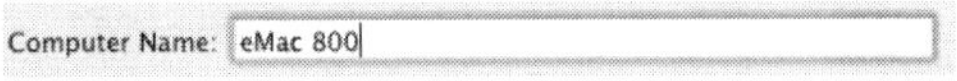

**Figure 8** Enter a new name for your computer.

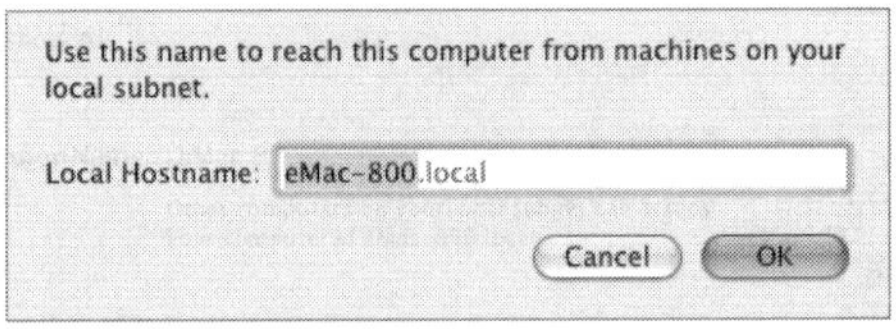

**Figure 9** Use this dialog to change the identifier of your computer on the local subnet.

## To enable sharing services

1. Choose Apple > System Preferences (**Figure 2**), or click the System Preferences icon in the Dock.

2. In the System Preferences window that appears (**Figure 1**), click the Sharing icon in the Internet & Network row to display the Sharing preferences pane.

3. If necessary, click the Services button to display its options (**Figure 7**).

4. Turn on the check box beside each sharing service you want to enable:

   ▲ **Personal File Sharing** lets Macintosh users access Public folders on your computer.

   ▲ **Windows Sharing** lets Windows users access shared folders using SMB, a Windows file sharing technology.

   ▲ **Personal Web Sharing** enables others to view Web pages in your Sites folder.

   ▲ **Remote Login** lets others access your computer using Secure Shell (SSH) client software, such as Terminal.

   ▲ **FTP Access** enables others to exchange files with your computer using FTP client software.

   ▲ **Apple Remote Desktop** enables others to access the computer using Apple Remote Desktop software, a program that makes it possible to run one computer from another.

   ▲ **Remote Apple Events** lets applications on other Mac OS computers send Apple Events to your computer.

   ▲ **Printer Sharing** enables others to use printers connected to your computer.

   ▲ **Xgrid** enables Xgrid controllers on your network to distribute tasks to your computer to perform.

*Continued on next page...*

ENABLING SHARING SERVICES

*Continued from previous page.*

## ✔ Tips

- In step 4, turning on the check box beside an item is the same as selecting the item and clicking the Start button that appears beside it. Likewise, turning off an item's check box is the same as selecting it and clicking the Stop button.

- When you select a service that is turned on, a note beneath the list of services explains how your computer can be accessed by that service. **Figures 10**, **11**, and **12** show examples.

- With Personal Web Sharing enabled, the contents of the Sites folder within your Home folder are published as Personal Web Sharing Web sites. To access a user's Web site, use the following URL: http://*IPaddress*/~*username*/ where *IPaddress* is the IP address or domain name of the computer and *username* is the name of the user on that computer.

- When a user accesses your computer via Remote Login, he accesses the Unix shell underlying Mac OS X. Keep in mind that turning on this option can open your computer to hackers who can use the Unix command-line interface to modify your system setup. Unix is covered in **Chapter 19**.

- Apple Remote Desktop and Xgrid are not part of Mac OS X and are not covered in this book. You can learn more about Apple Remote Desktop at www.apple.com/remotedesktop/ and Xgrid at www.apple.com/acg/xgrid/.

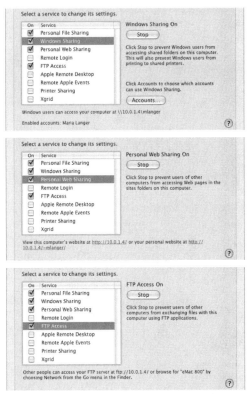

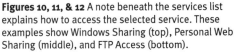

**Figures 10, 11, & 12** A note beneath the services list explains how to access the selected service. These examples show Windows Sharing (top), Personal Web Sharing (middle), and FTP Access (bottom).

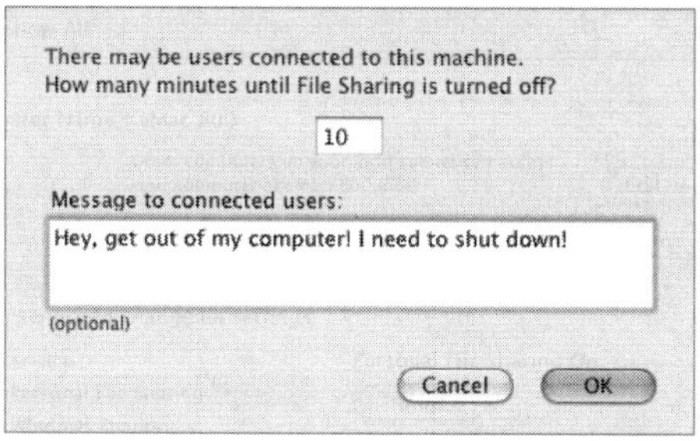

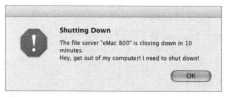

**Figure 13** You can use a dialog like this to specify how long before sharing shuts down and include a personal message.

**Figure 14** Here's what a connected user sees when you shut down file sharing, using the settings shown in **Figure 13**.

## To disable sharing services

1. Choose Apple > System Preferences (**Figure 2**), or click the System Preferences icon in the Dock.

2. In the System Preferences window that appears (**Figure 1**), click the Sharing icon to display the Sharing preferences pane.

3. If necessary, click the Services tab to display its options (**Figure 7**).

4. Turn off the check box beside the sharing service you want to disable.

5. If a dialog sheet like the one in **Figure 13** appears, enter the number of minutes in which sharing will be disabled in the top box and click OK.

## ✔ Tips

- In step 5, the value you enter determines how long before sharing is disabled. If you're in a hurry, enter a smaller value than the default value, which is 10.

- When you disable file sharing, a dialog like the one in **Figure 14** appears on the screen of each connected user, warning them that the server (your computer) will be shutting down.

- In step 5, you can also enter a message in the bottom box to send to connected users. **Figures 13** and **14** show examples.

# To set firewall options

1. Choose Apple > System Preferences (**Figure 2**), or click the System Preferences icon in the Dock.

2. In the System Preferences window that appears (**Figure 1**), click the Sharing icon to display the Sharing preferences pane.

3. If necessary, click the Firewall button to display Firewall options (**Figure 15**).

4. To start firewall protection, click Start.

5. Turn on the check box beside each type of sharing you want to *exclude* from firewall protection. The options are the same as those discussed in the section titled "To enable sharing services" earlier in this chapter, plus:

   ▲ **iChat Bonjour** enables network users to conduct chats with you.

   ▲ **iTunes Music Sharing** enables network users to listen to your iTunes playlists.

   ▲ **iPhoto Bonjour Sharing** enables network users to see your iPhoto albums. (This requires iPhoto, which is not part of Mac OS X and not covered in this book.)

   ▲ **Network Time** enables your computer to update its internal clock via network time server.

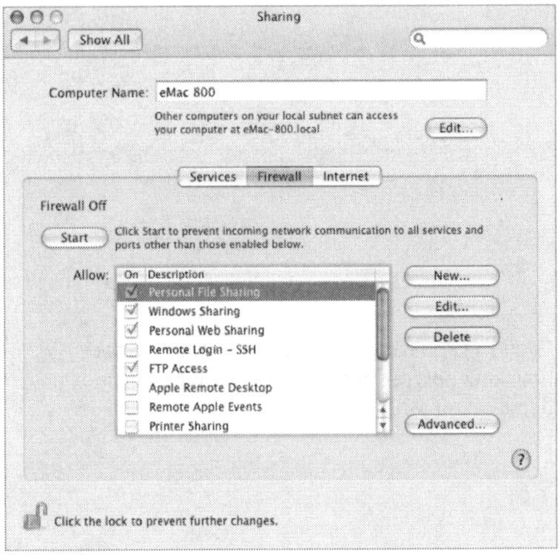

**Figure 15** The Firewall tab of the Sharing preferences pane lets you configure and enable Mac OS X's built-in firewall.

Specify a port on which you would like to receive networking traffic. Other ports can be specified by selecting 'Other' in the Port Name popup. Then enter a the port name and a number (or a range or series of port numbers) along with a description.

Port Name: CVS

TCP Port Number(s): 2401

UDP Port Number(s):

Cancel     OK

**Figure 16** Use a dialog like this to add a port to the Firewall tab's list.

✓ CVS
ICQ
IRC
MSN Messenger
QuickTime
Retrospect
SMB (without netbios)
Timbuktu
VNC
WBEM
WebSTAR Admin
Xcode distributed build

Other

**Figure 17**
Mac OS X comes preconfigured with many commonly used ports.

You can use these advanced firewall settings to further refine the security of your computer.

☐ Block UDP Traffic
Prevents UDP communications from accessing resources on your computer.

☐ Enable Firewall Logging
Provides information about firewall activity, such as blocked sources, blocked destinations, and blocked attempts.     Open Log...

☑ Enable Stealth Mode
Ensures that any uninvited traffic receives no response — not even an acknowledgement that your computer exists.

(?)     Cancel     OK

**Figure 18** Mac OS X 10.4 includes advanced options to fine-tune a firewall setup.

## ✔ Tips

- A *firewall* is security software that prevents incoming network access to your computer.

- In step 5, each type of sharing corresponds to one or more network ports.

- To add a port to the Description (Ports) list, click the New button. In the dialog that appears (**Figure 16**), choose an option from the Port Name pop-up menu (**Figure 17**), enter port numbers in the boxes beneath it, and click OK. The port is added to the list.

- Clicking the Advanced button in the Firewall options of the Sharing preferences pane (**Figure 15**) displays more setup options, as shown in **Figure 18**. You can use these options to fine-tune the way the firewall feature works.

- To stop firewall protection, click Stop in step 4 and skip step 5. (The Stop button appears in place of the Start button when the firewall is enabled.)

**SETTING FIREWALL OPTIONS**

## To share an Internet connection with other network users

1. Choose Apple > System Preferences (**Figure 2**), or click the System Preferences icon in the Dock.

2. In the System Preferences window that appears (**Figure 1**), click the Sharing icon to display the Sharing preferences pane.

3. If necessary, click the Internet button to display Internet sharing options (**Figure 19**).

4. Choose an option from the Share your connection from pop-up menu (**Figure 20**) to specify which Internet connection you want to share.

5. Turn on the check box(es) to indicate how the computers you are sharing the Internet connection with are connected to your computer.

6. Click Start.

7. A dialog like the one in **Figure 21** may appear. If you're sure you want to share the connection, click OK.

## ✔ Tips

■ When you share an Internet connection, the total connection speed is divided among the active connections. So, for example, if two computers are actively sharing a 256 Kbps cable modem connection with you, the speed of each connection will only be about 85 Kbps.

■ To stop sharing an Internet connection with other network users, follow steps 1 through 3 above, then click the Stop button.

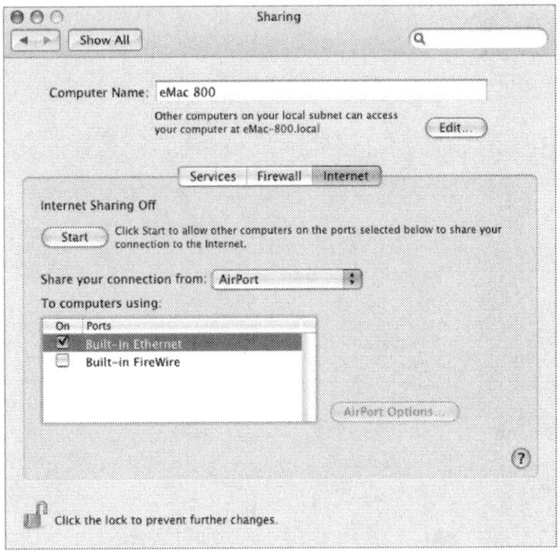

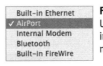

**Figure 19** Internet sharing options make it possible to share an Internet connection with other computers on a network.

**Figure 20** Use this pop-up menu to indicate which Internet connection you want to share.

**Figure 21** A dialog like this may appear when you start sharing an Internet connection.

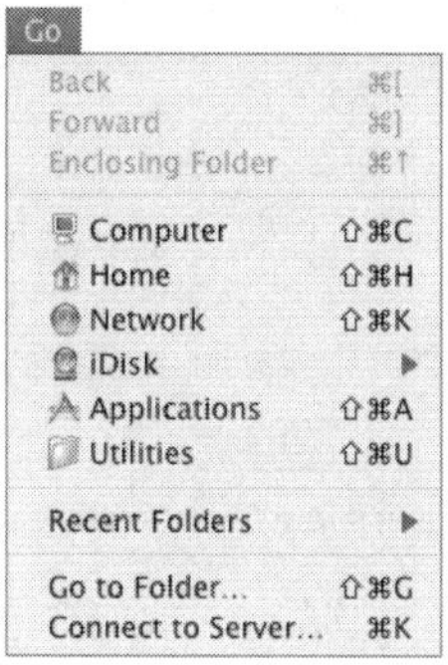

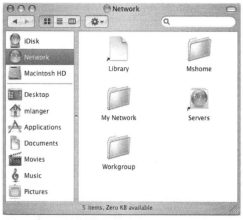

**Figure 22**
The Go menu.

**Figure 23** Clicking the Network icon in the Sidebar displays the network browser.

# Connecting to Another Computer for File Sharing

Once network and sharing options have been set up for sharing, you can connect to another computer and access its files. Mac OS X offers two ways to do this:

◆ The Go menu's Connect to Server command (**Figure 22**) prompts you to enter the address of the server you want to connect to. You enter a user name and password to connect, choose the volume you want to access, and display its contents in Finder windows.

◆ The network browser enables you to browse the computers on the network—from the Finder (**Figure 23**) and from within Open and Save dialogs. You open an alias for another computer and you're prompted for a user name and password. Enter login information, choose a volume, and work with the files just as if they were on your computer.

The main difference between these two methods is that the Connect to Server command makes it possible to connect to servers that are not listed in the network browser.

The next few pages provide instructions for connecting to other computers using both methods, along with some tips for speeding up the process in the future.

## ✔ Tips

■ I tell you about mounting volumes in **Chapter 3**.

■ Mac OS X's networking features refer to network-accessible computers as *servers*.

■ The access privileges you have for network volumes varies depending on the privileges set for that volume or folder. I tell you about privileges later in this chapter.

## To use the network browser

1. Choose Go > Network (**Figure 18**), press ⇧⌘K, or click the Network icon in the Sidebar. The Network window opens (**Figure 23**).

2. To see servers in your local network or subnet, open the My Network folder (**Figure 24**).

   *or*

   To see servers in a specific network area or workgroup, click the folder for that area or workgroup (**Figure 25**).

3. To open a server, double-click its alias icon.

4. A dialog like the one in **Figure 26** appears. Enter a user name and password that is recognized by the server and click Connect.

5. A dialog displays the volumes available for access (**Figure 27**). Double-click the volume you want to mount.

   An icon for the mounted volume appears on your desktop and in the top half of the Sidebar. You can open the volume like any other disk to work with its contents (**Figure 28**).

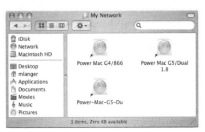

**Figure 24** The servers on my local subnet.

**Figure 25** The Mshome workgroup on my network includes my significant other's Sony laptop.

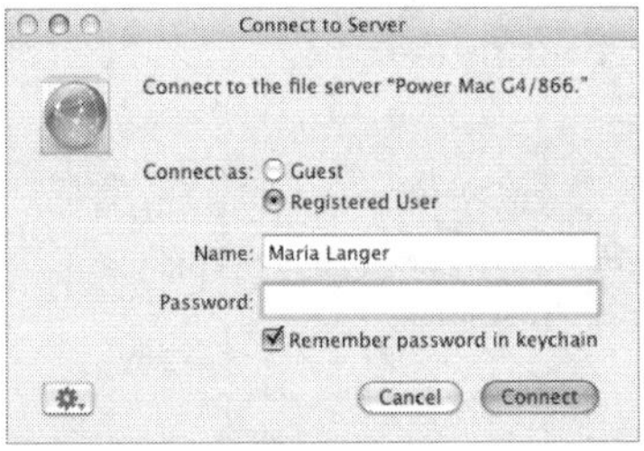

**Figure 26** Use a dialog like this to log in to the server.

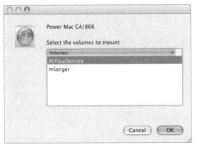

**Figure 27** Choose the volume you want to mount.

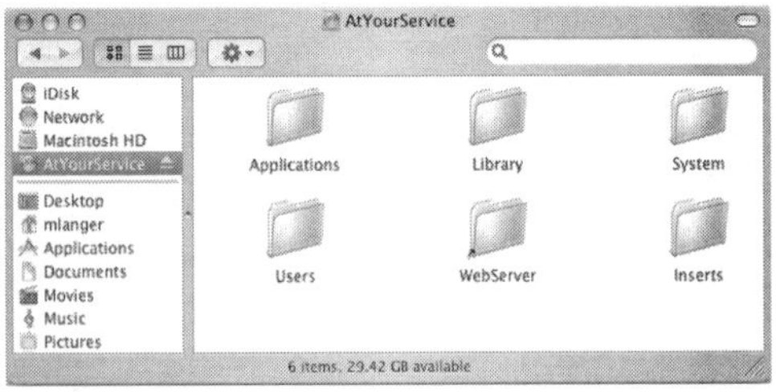

**Figure 28** Opening the volume displays its contents.

USING THE NETWORK BROWSER

Connect to Server
Server Address:
afp://10.0.1.5
Favorite Servers:
http://idisk.mac.com/cliff/Public
afp://10.0.1.2
Remove
Browse
Connect

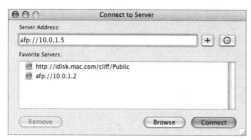

**Figure 29** The Connect to Server dialog.

Recent Servers
afp://10.0.1.2
afp://10.0.1.5
ftp://66.218.237.73/
http://idisk.mac.com/cliff/Public
afp://Power-Mac-G5-Dual.local
Clear Recent Servers...

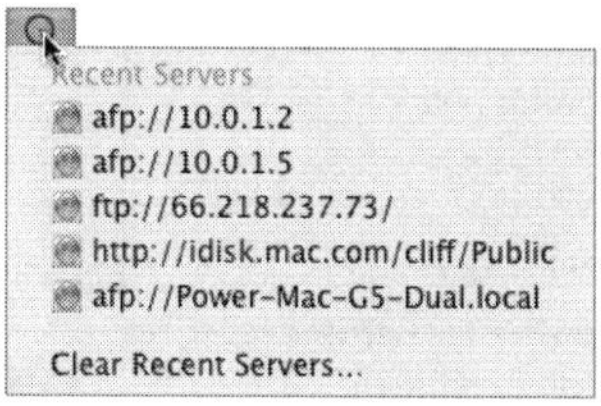

**Figure 30** Use this pop-up menu to choose a recently opened server.

## To use the Connect to Server command

1. In the Finder, choose Go > Connect to Server (**Figure 22**), or press [⌘ ⌘][K].
2. In the Connect To Server dialog that appears (**Figure 29**), enter the network address of the server you want to connect to.
3. Click Connect.
4. A dialog like the one in **Figure 26** appears. Enter a user name and password that is recognized by the server and click Connect.
5. A dialog displays the volumes available for access (**Figure 27**). Double-click the volume you want to mount.
6. Click OK.

   An icon for the mounted volume appears on your desktop and in the top half of the Sidebar. You can open the volume like any other disk to work with its contents (**Figure 28**).

### ✔ Tips

- After step 2, you can click the + button to add the server address to the Favorite Servers list in the Connect to Server dialog (**Figure 29**). You can then access a favorite server by double-clicking its address in the list.
- In step 2, to open a recently opened server, choose its address from the Recent Servers pop-up menu (**Figure 30**).

## To set login options as a registered user

1. Follow the steps on one of the previous two pages to display a login dialog like the one in **Figure 26**.

2. Select the Registered User radio button and enter your login information in the appropriate boxes.

3. Choose Options from the shortcut menu in the bottom left corner of the dialog (**Figure 31**) to display login options (**Figure 32**).

4. Toggle check boxes as desired and click the OK button:

   ▲ **Allow sending password in clear text** sends your password over the network without encryption.

   ▲ **Warn when sending password in clear text** warns you before sending your password without encryption.

   ▲ **Allow secure connections using SSH** enables you to establish a secure connection when using a Secure Shell client such as Terminal.

   ▲ **Warn when connection does not support SSH** warns you when the connection you are trying to make does not support SSH. This option can only be enabled if the option above it is enabled.

5. Follow the remaining steps on one of the previous two pages to complete the login process.

## ✔ Tip

■ Turning on the Remember password in keychain check box in the login dialog (**Figure 26**) saves your password so you won't be prompted to enter it again the next time you connect to that server. I tell you about Keychain Access in **Chapter 17**.

**Figure 31** Commands on the login window's shortcut menu make it possible to change your password on the server or set connection options.

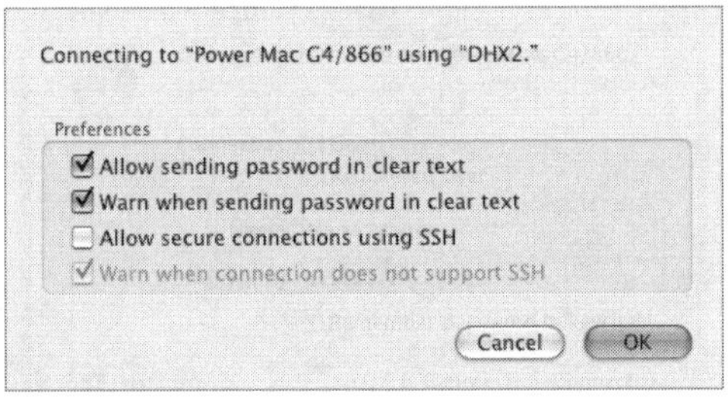

**Figure 32** You can set login options in a dialog like this one.

**SETTING LOGIN OPTIONS**

Change password for "Maria Langer" on "Power Mac G4/866."

Old password: [                    ]

New password: [                    ]

Verify: [                    ]

( Cancel )  ( OK )

**Figure 33** Use this dialog to change your password on the server.

## To change your password on the server

1. Follow the steps earlier in this section to display a login dialog like the one in **Figure 26**.

2. Select the Registered User radio button and enter your user name in the Name box.

3. Choose Change password from the shortcut menu in the bottom left corner of the dialog (**Figure 31**) to display a dialog like the one in **Figure 33**.

4. Enter your current password in the Old password box.

5. Enter a new password in the New password and Verify boxes.

6. Click OK.

7. In the login window, enter your new password in the Password box and click Connect.

8. Follow the steps earlier in this section to mount and open the server volume you want to use.

CHANGING YOUR PASSWORD

# Users, Groups, & Privileges

Network file and application sharing access is determined by the users and groups set up for the computer, as well as the privileges settings for each file or its enclosing folder.

## Users & Groups

Each person who connects to a computer (other than with Guest access) is considered a *user*. Each user has his own user name or ID and a password. User names are set up by the computer's system administrator, using the Accounts preferences pane. The password is also assigned by the system administrator, but in most cases, it can be changed by the user in the Accounts preferences pane when logged in to his account. This enhances security.

Each user can belong to one or more groups. A *group* is one or more users who have the same privileges. Some groups are set up automatically by Mac OS X when you install it and add users with the Users preferences pane. Other groups can be set up by the system administrator using a program such as NetInfo Manager.

## ✔ Tips

- Setting up users and using the Accounts preferences pane is discussed in detail in **Chapter 17**. Setting up groups is an advanced network administration task that is beyond the scope of this book.

- I discuss NetInfo Manager briefly near the end of this chapter.

**Figures 34, 35, & 36**
Privileges settings for the Applications folder (top), Public folder (middle), and Drop Box folder inside my public folder (bottom).

# Privileges

Each file or folder can be assigned a set of privileges. Privileges determine who has access to a file and how it can be accessed.

There are four possible privileges settings:

◆ **Read & Write** privileges allow the user to open and save files.

◆ **Read only** privileges allow the user to open files but not save files.

◆ **Write only (Drop Box)** privileges allow the user to save files but not open them.

◆ **No Access** means the user can neither open nor save files.

Privileges can be set for three categories of users:

◆ **Owner** is the user or group who can access and set access privileges for the item. In Mac OS X, the owner can be you (if it's your computer and you set it up), system, or admin.

◆ **Group** is the group that has access to the item.

◆ **Others** is everyone else on the network, including users logged in as Guest.

## ✔ Tips

■ In previous versions of Mac OS, which were not designed as multiuser systems, you were the owner of most (if not all) items on your computer.

■ You can check or set an item's privileges in the Ownership & Permissions area of the Info window for the item (**Figures 34, 35,** and **36**).

## To set an item's owner, group, & privileges

1. Select the icon for the item for which you want to change privileges.

2. Choose File > Get Info (**Figure 37**), or press ⌘⌥⌘①.

3. In the Info window that appears, click the triangle beside Ownership & Permissions to expand the window and display permissions information (**Figures 34, 35, and 36**).

4. To change the owner and group for an item, choose an option from the Owner (**Figure 38**) or Group (**Figure 39**) pop-up menu. You may need to click the lock icon beside an item to unlock it or enter an administrative password before the change can be made.

5. To change the privileges for an item, choose options from the Access and Others pop-up menus (**Figure 40**).

6. If the item is a folder, to apply the settings to all folders within it, click the Apply to enclosed items button.

7. Close the Info window to save your changes.

## ✔ Tips

- You cannot change privileges for an item if you are not the owner (**Figure 34**) unless you have an administrator password.

- The Write only (Drop Box) privilege is only available for folders and disks.

- The privileges you assign to one category of users will affect which privileges can be assigned to another category of user. For example, if you make a folder Read only for Everyone, you can only make the same folder Read & Write or Read only for the Group and Owner.

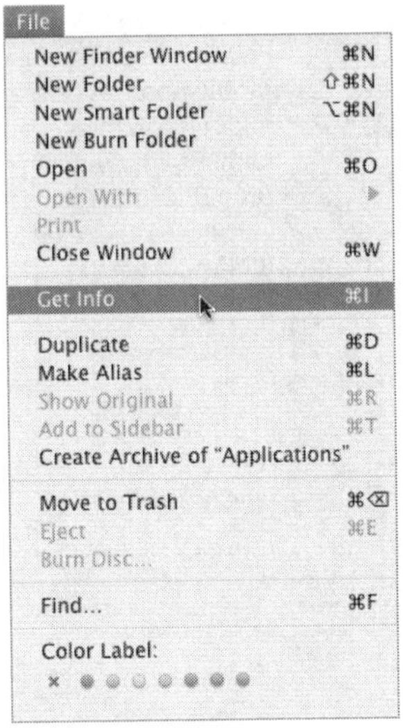

**Figure 37**
Choose Get Info from the File menu.

**Figure 38**
The Owner pop-up menu includes users I created (at the top of the list) and those created by Mac OS X.

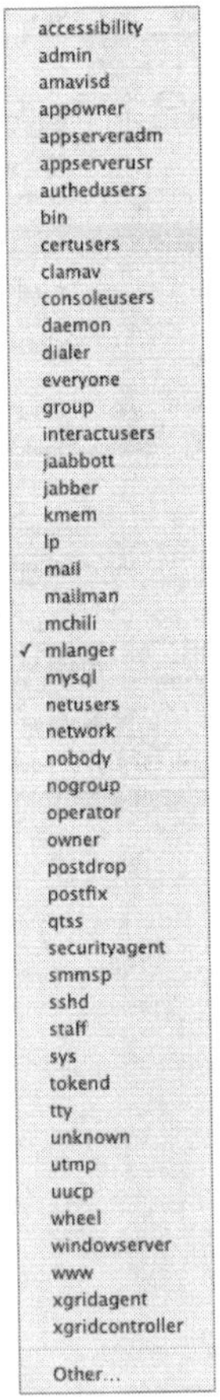

**Figure 39**
When I installed Mac OS X 10.4, it created all of these groups.

**Figure 40** Use this pop-up menu to set privileges for each category of user.

# AirPort

AirPort is Apple's wireless local area network technology. It enables your computer to connect to a network or the Internet via radio waves instead of wires.

Apple offers three types of AirPort devices:

◆ **AirPort Base Station** is an external device that can connect to a network via Ethernet cable or can act as a modem for connecting to the Internet via phone lines.

◆ **AirPort Express** is an external device that can connect to a network via Ethernet or can extend the range of an existing AirPort network. It also has the ability to receive data from iTunes on an AirPort-equipped Mac or PC to play music on your stereo.

◆ **AirPort card** is a networking card inside your computer that enables your computer to communicate with a base station or another AirPort-equipped computer.

There are two ways to use AirPort for wireless networking:

◆ Use an AirPort-equipped computer to connect to other AirPort-equipped computers.

◆ Use an AirPort Extreme base station or AirPort Express to link an AirPort-equipped computer to the Internet or to other computers on a network. This makes it possible for a computer with an AirPort card to communicate with computers without AirPort cards.

**AIRPORT**

*Continued on next page...*

*Continued from previous page.*

Mac OS X includes two programs for setting up an AirPort network (**Figure 41**):

◆ **AirPort Setup Assistant** offers an easy, step-by-step approach for configuring a base station. In most cases, this is the only tool you'll need to set up a base station.

◆ **AirPort Admin Utility** enables you to set advanced options that cannot be set with the AirPort Setup Assistant.

This part of the chapter explains how to configure an AirPort base station and connect to an AirPort network with an AirPort-equipped computer.

## ✔ Tips

■ AirPort is especially useful for PowerBook and iBook users who may work at various locations within range of a base station.

■ An AirPort network can include multiple base stations and AirPort-equipped computers.

■ You can learn more about AirPort devices and networking at Apple's AirPort home pages, www.apple.com/airportextreme/ and www.apple.com/airportexpress/.

■ The current versions AirPort Extreme and AirPort Express hardware are fully compatible with the original version of AirPort hardware.

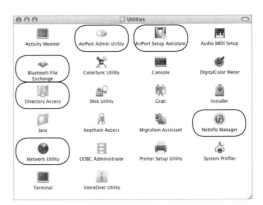

**Figure 41** The Utilities folder includes a number of applications for working with networks.

**AIRPORT**

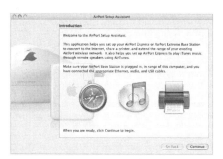

**Figure 42** The first screen of the AirPort Setup Assistant explains what it does.

**Figure 43** Use this screen to indicate that you want to set up a new base station.

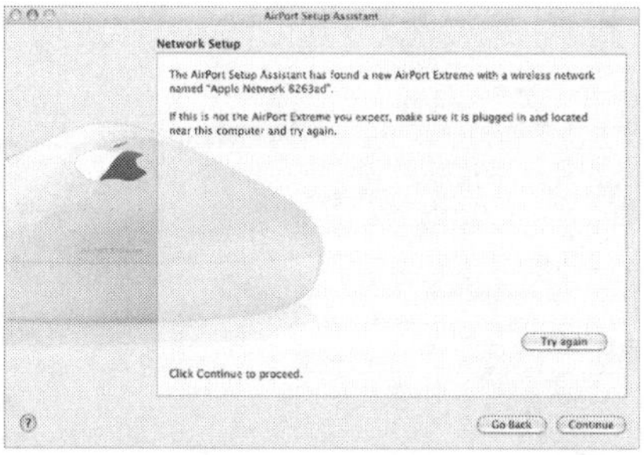

![AirPort Setup Assistant Network Setup screen]

**Figure 44** AirPort Setup Assistant scans for new base stations within range and displays information about the base station it found.

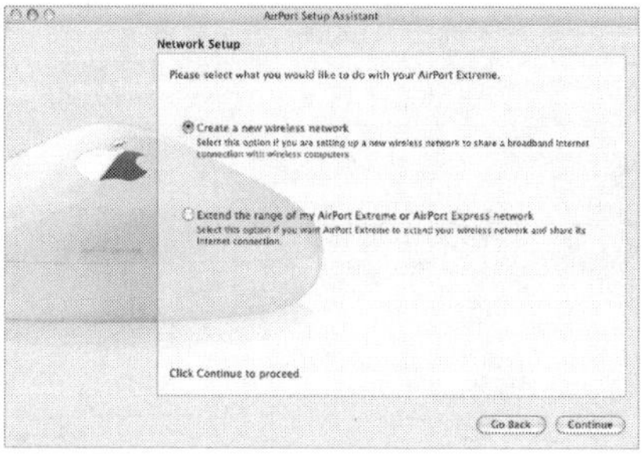

![AirPort Setup Assistant Create new wireless network screen]

**Figure 45** Use this screen to indicate that you want to set up a new network.

## To set up an AirPort base station

1. Open the AirPort Setup Assistant icon in the Utilities folder (**Figure 41**) inside the Applications folder.

2. Read the information in the Introduction window that appears (**Figure 42**) and click Continue.

3. In the next screen (**Figure 43**), choose Set up a new AirPort Base Station and click Continue.

4. The AirPort Setup Assistant uses the computer's AirPort card to scan for base stations. It then displays the Network Setup window with the name of the base station it has found (**Figure 44**). Click Continue.

5. In the next screen (**Figure 45**), select Create a new wireless network and click Continue.

6. In the next screen (**Figure 46**), enter personalization information and click Continue:

   ▲ **Wireless Network Name** is the name of the network.

   ▲ **AirPort Extreme Name** is the name of the AirPort base station.

*Continued on next page...*

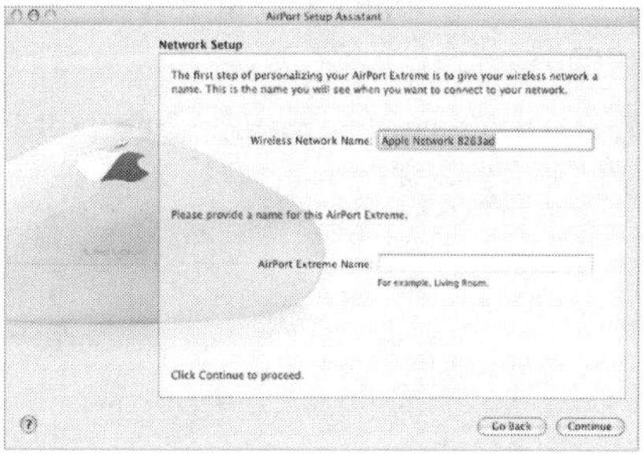

![AirPort Setup Assistant Network Setup personalization screen]

**Figure 46** Use this screen to name the network and the base station.

*Continued from previous page.*

7. In the next screen (**Figure 47**), select a security option and click Continue:

   ▲ **128-bit WEP** is a more compatible security method. If you choose this option, enter a password of exactly 13 characters in both text boxes to ensure compatibility with non-Macintosh computers on the network.

   ▲ **WPA Personal** is a more secure security method that only works with WPA-compatible computers. If you choose this option, enter a password of 8 to 63 characters in both text boxes.

   ▲ **No security** does not secure the network at all. Anyone within range can connect.

8. The first Internet Setup screen appears next. It displays the configuration information the base station has already sensed (**Figure 48**). If necessary, enter connection information in the boxes. Then click Continue.

9. In the next screen (**Figure 49**), enter a password in both boxes to protect the base station settings and click Continue.

10. In the Summary window that appears (**Figure 50**), click the Update button.

11. Wait while the AirPort Setup Assistant updates and restarts the base station. A progress dialog appears while it restarts (**Figure 51**).

12. In the final screen (**Figure 52**), click Quit.

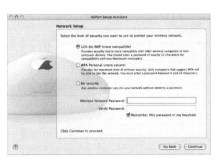

**Figure 47** Choose a security option and, if necessary, enter a password to secure the network.

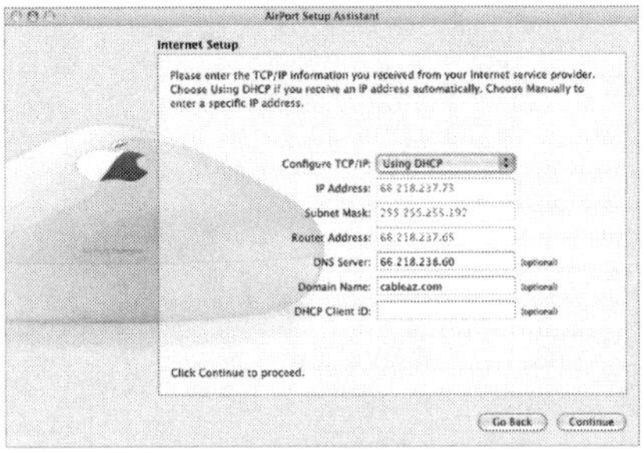

**Figure 48** The AirPort base station may be able to sense how it is connected to the Internet. If so, the first Internet Setup screen will be filled out for you.

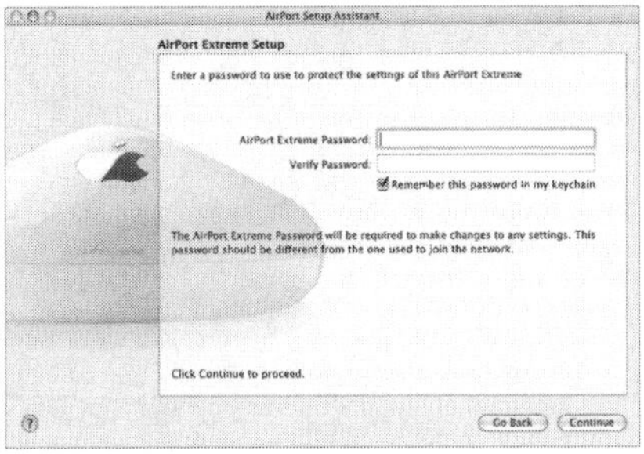

**Figure 49** Enter a password to protect the base station settings from unauthorized changes.

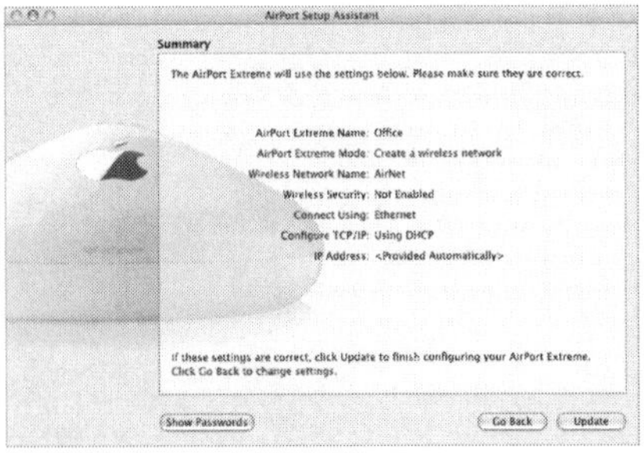

**Figure 50** AirPort Setup Assistant summarizes the setup information.

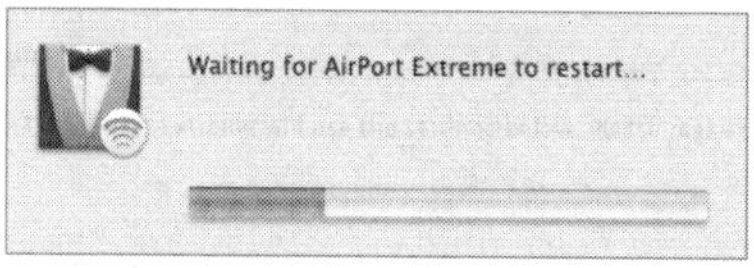

**Figure 51** Wait while the base station restarts.

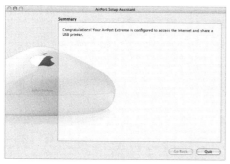

**Figure 52** The final screen confirms that the base station has been configured.

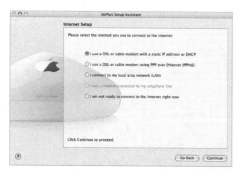

**Figure 53** This dialog appears if your base station's firmware needs to be updated.

## ✔ Tips

■ You can only use the AirPort Setup Assistant on a computer with an AirPort card installed. If a card is not installed, the Assistant will tell you.

■ If your base station has already been configured, in step 3 (**Figure 43**), you must select the Change settings on an existing AirPort Base Station option. Most of these steps will not apply and your setup options will be limited.

■ If your Airport Base Station was used with a previous version of Mac OS, a dialog sheet may appear after step 4, telling you that its firmware must be updated (**Figure 53**). Click Update to update the firmware.

■ In step 8, if the Internet connection method that appears (**Figure 48**) is incorrect, click the Go Back button. You can then choose a different type of connection in the screen that appears (**Figure 54**). When you click Continue, follow the onscreen prompts to enter details about the connection.

■ If you are the only user of your AirPort network, it's okay to have the same password for the network as the base station. But if multiple users will be using the network, you should assign a different password to the base station to prevent other users from changing base station settings.

**Figure 54** If the connection information in **Figure 48** is wrong, click Go Back to set the correct option in this screen.

**S**ETTING **U**P **A**IRPORT **B**ASE **S**TATIONS

## To view & modify AirPort base station settings

1. Open the AirPort Admin Utility icon in the Utilities folder (**Figure 41**) inside the Applications folder.

2. The AirPort Admin Utility uses the computer's AirPort card to scan for base stations. It then displays the Select Base Station window (**Figure 55**). Select the base station you want to work with and click Configure.

3. In the password dialog that appears (**Figure 56**), enter the base station's password and click OK.

4. The AirPort pane for the base station appears (**Figure 57**). Click buttons to view and modify setup information:

   ▲ **AirPort** (**Figure 57**) displays general base station and network information and enables you to change the base station password and network security options.

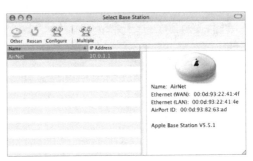

**Figure 55** Use this dialog to select the base station you want to work with.

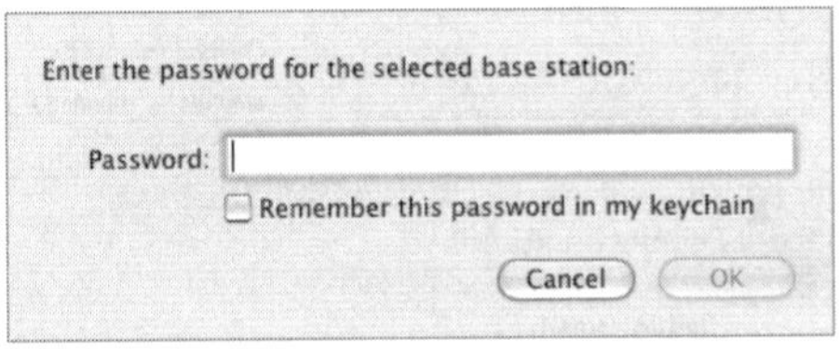

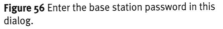

**Figure 56** Enter the base station password in this dialog.

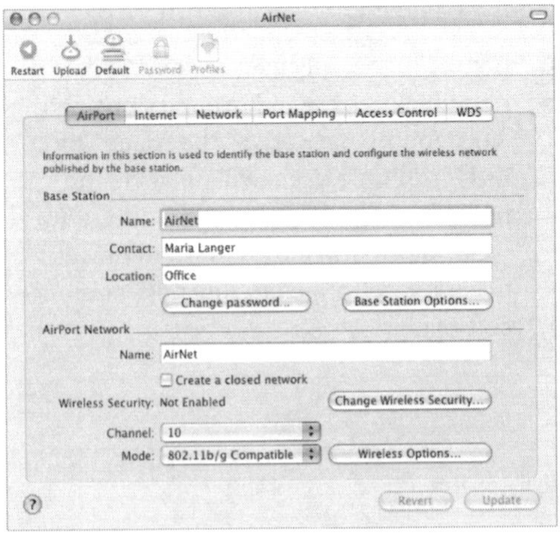

**Figure 57** The AirPort pane of the AirPort Admin Utility includes many basic configuration options.

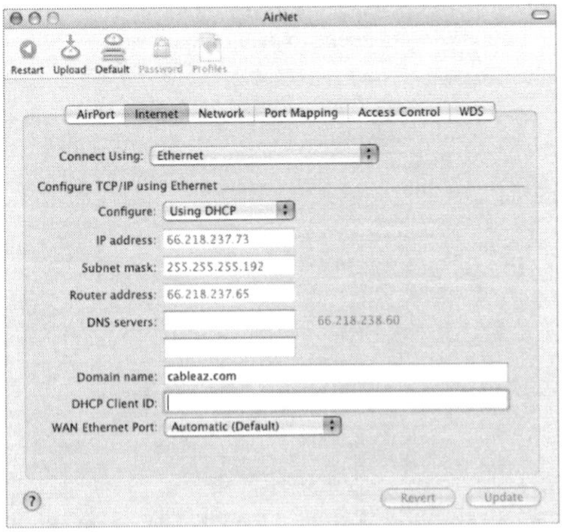

**Figure 58** The Internet pane of the AirPort Admin Utility displays Internet connection configuration information.

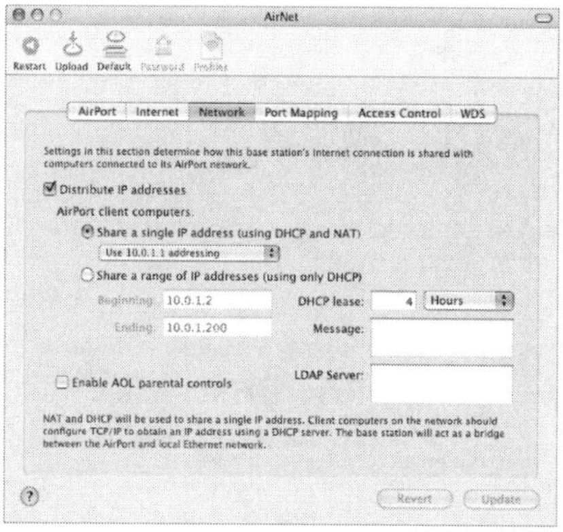

**Figure 59** The Network pane includes options for distributing IP addresses.

**Figure 60** The Port Mapping pane let's you tap into an advanced feature to map TCP/IP ports to computers.

**Figure 61** The Access Control pane enables you to restrict access by AirPort ID.

▲ **Internet** (**Figure 58**) displays information about the Internet connection.

▲ **Network** (**Figure 59**) displays options for distributing IP addresses to the computers that access the AirPort network.

▲ **Port Mapping** (**Figure 60**) enables you to map TCP/IP ports to specific IP addresses on the network.

▲ **Access Control** (**Figure 61**) enables you to restrict access based on a computer's AirPort ID.

▲ **WDS** (**Figure 62**) enables you to use the base station with other base stations to expand the range of the wireless network.

5. If you make changes in step 4, click the Update button to send changes to the base station. A status window like the one in **Figure 63** appears while it works.

6. When you're finished viewing and modifying settings, choose AirPort Admin Utility > Quit AirPort Admin Utility or press ⌘Q.

*Continued on next page...*

**Figure 62** The WDS pane enables you to configure the base station to expand the network range.

VIEWING BASE STATION SETTINGS

*Continued from previous page.*

## ✔ Tips

- The AirPort Admin Utility can also be used to configure a base station from scratch. But I think you'll find it much easier to use the AirPort Setup Utility as instructed earlier in this section. I know I do!

- In step 3, if a keychain item exists for your base station, a dialog like the one in **Figure 64** may appear instead of the one in **Figure 56**. Click Allow. I tell you about Keychain Access in **Chapter 17**.

- I tell you more about connecting to the Internet in **Chapter 13**.

- As shown in **Figures 59** through **62**, some of the configuration options offered by AirPort Admin Utility are advanced and powerful. Do not make changes to these options unless you know what you're doing!

- Want more advanced information about setting up an AirPort network? Consult the document I turn to when fine-tuning mine: Designing AirPort Networks. This PDF manual, which was written by Apple, can be downloaded from http://manuals.info.apple.com/en/airport/DesigningAirPortNetworks0190271.pdf.

- Setting up AirPort Express should run along a similar path to setting up AirPort Extreme, especially if you aren't using it to play music on a stereo.

**Figure 63** When you click Update, the configuration information is uploaded to the base station.

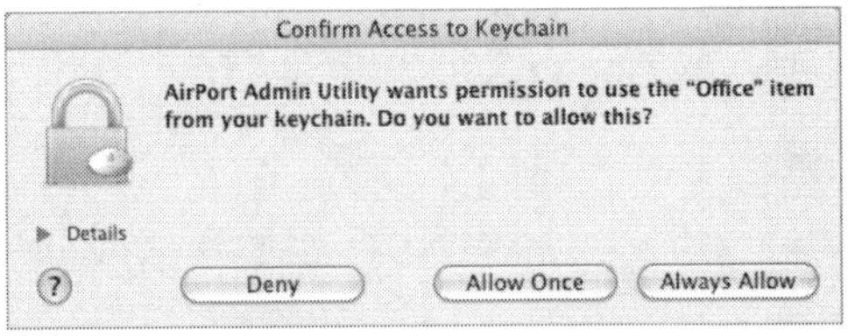

**Figure 64** If a keychain item exists for your base station, a dialog like this may appear instead of the password dialog.

**Figure 65**
The AirPort status menu shows signal strength (in the menu bar icon) and offers options for working with AirPort networks.

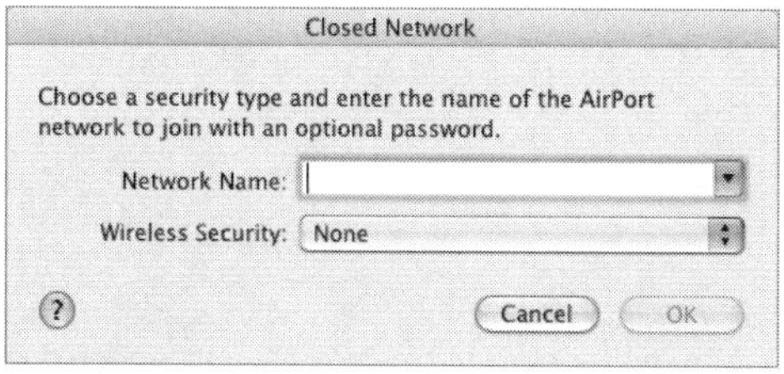

**Figure 66** Use the Closed Network dialog to connect to an AirPort network that does not appear on the AirPort Status menu.

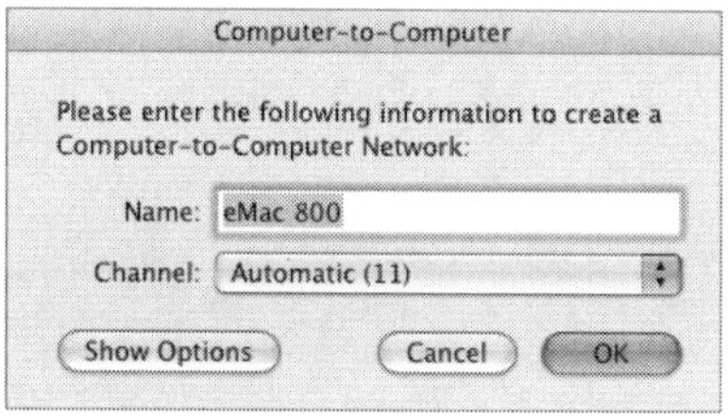

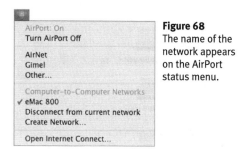

**Figure 67** Use this dialog to create a computer-to-computer network.

**Figure 68**
The name of the network appears on the AirPort status menu.

## To use the AirPort status menu

Choose commands on the AirPort status menu (**Figure 65**) to perform the following tasks:

◆ **Turn AirPort Off** disables AirPort on your computer.

◆ *Network Name* connects you to that network. If multiple networks are within range, all of them will appear on the menu.

◆ **Other** displays the Closed Network dialog (**Figure 66**), which you can use to join a network that doesn't appear on the AirPort Status menu. Enter the name of the network and its password (if necessary) and click OK.

◆ **Create Network** displays the Computer-to-Computer dialog (**Figure 67**), which you can use to create a network between your computer and another AirPort-equipped computer. When you click OK in this dialog, the new network appears on the menu (**Figure 68**) on your computer, as well as on other computers in range. Choose the new network on both computers to connect. When you're finished using the network, choose Disconnect from current network.

◆ **Open Internet Connect** opens the Internet Connect application, which I discuss in **Chapter 13**.

## ✔ Tips

■ The number of curves in the AirPort status menu's icon indicates the signal strength. The more curves, the stronger the signal.

■ If the base station has a dial-up connection to the Internet, a Connect command will also appear on this menu. Use this command to connect to the Internet.

# Bluetooth

Bluetooth is a very short-range—30 feet or less—wireless networking technology. It enables you to connect Bluetooth-enabled computers, personal digital assistants (PDAs), and mobile phones to each other and to the Internet. It also lets you connect Bluetooth-enabled input devices, such as a mouse or keyboard, to your Mac.

Mac OS X 10.4 includes two tools for working with Bluetooth:

◆ The **Bluetooth preferences pane**, which is available if your computer is Bluetooth enabled, allows you to configure Bluetooth and set up Bluetooth devices with the Bluetooth Setup Assistant.

◆ **Bluetooth File Exchange** enables you to send files from one Bluetooth device to another or browse files on another Bluetooth-enabled computer.

This part of the chapter explains how to configure and use Bluetooth to exchange files between two computers. Although this chapter does not go into specifics about using other devices, it should be enough to get you started using your Bluetooth device with Mac OS X.

## ✔ Tips

■ Don't confuse Bluetooth with AirPort. These are two similar yet different technologies. AirPort enables an AirPort-enabled computer to connect to and exchange information with computers and devices on an entire network. Bluetooth, however, enables your computer to connect to and exchange information with a single Bluetooth-enabled device.

■ To use Bluetooth with Mac OS X, your computer must have built-in Bluetooth or a Bluetooth adapter. Bluetooth adapters are available from the Apple Store (www.apple.com/store/) and other sources. You must also have a Bluetooth-enabled device to connect to.

■ You can find a complete list of currently available devices on the official Bluetooth Web site, www.bluetooth.com.

■ For detailed information about using your Bluetooth-enabled device with Mac OS X, consult the documentation that came with the device or its manufacturer's Web site.

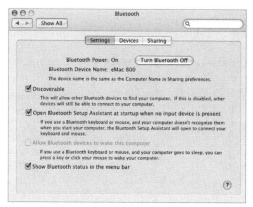

**Figure 69** The Settings pane of the Bluetooth preferences pane.

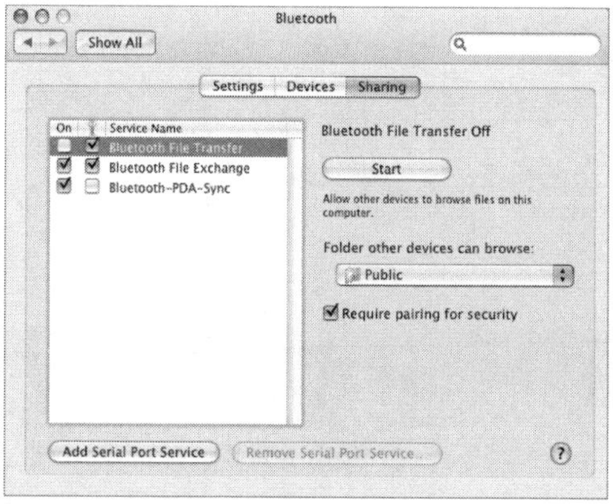

**Figure 70** Options for configuring the Bluetooth File Transfer service.

# To set Bluetooth preferences

1. Choose Apple > System Preferences (**Figure 2**), or click the System Preferences icon in the Dock.

2. In the System Preferences window that appears (**Figure 1**), click the Bluetooth icon.

3. Click the Settings button in the Bluetooth preferences pane that appears (**Figure 69**) and set options as desired:

   ▲ **Discoverable** enables other Bluetooth devices to easily find your computer.

   ▲ **Open Bluetooth Setup Assistant at startup when no input device is present** tells your computer to launch the Bluetooth Setup Assistant if no keyboard or mouse is connected; this assumes that you're going to set up a Bluetooth input device.

   ▲ **Allow Bluetooth devices to wake this computer** makes it possible for a Bluetooth device to wake the computer. This option is not supported by all computer models.

   ▲ **Show Bluetooth status in the menu bar** displays the Bluetooth status menu (**Figure 86**).

4. Click the sharing button (**Figure 70**) and set options to enable and configure Bluetooth services:

   ▲ **Bluetooth File Transfer** (**Figure 70**) enables other Bluetooth devices to browse files on your computer. With this service enabled, you can use the pop-up menu to choose a folder that can be browsed.

*Continued on next page...*

*Continued from previous page.*

▲ **Bluetooth File Exchange (Figure 71)** enables you to send and receive files via Bluetooth. With this service enabled, you can use the pop-up menus to set configuration options.

▲ **Bluetooth-PDA-Sync (Figure 72)** enables you to use Bluetooth to sync a Bluetooth-enabled PDA with your computer. With this service enabled, you can set configuration options for the PDA.

5. Click the Devices button to view a list of Bluetooth devices you have set up. Select one of the devices in the list to learn about it (**Figure 82**). Use buttons on the right side of the window to work with the list.

6. Choose System Preferences > Quit System Preferences or press ⌃⌘Q.

## ✔ Tips

■ The Bluetooth icon only appears in System Preferences if a Bluetooth adapter is connected to your computer.

■ In step 4, if you turn on the Require pairing for security check box for any service, the other device must be added to your list of paired device before communication between the two devices can take place.

■ I explain how to set up paired devices on the next page.

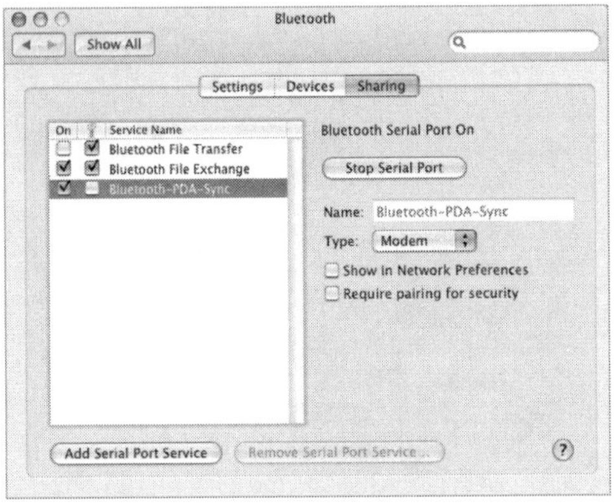

**Figure 72** Options for configuring the Bluetooth-PDA-Sync service.

**Figure 71** Options for configuring the Bluetooth File Exchange service.

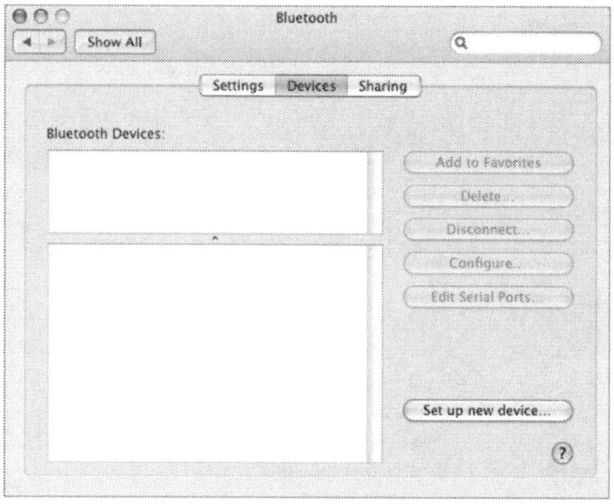

**Figure 73** The Devices pane of the Bluetooth preferences pane before any devices have been paired.

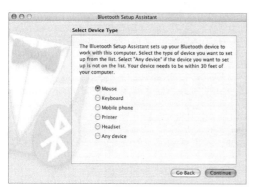

**Figure 74** The Introduction screen for the Bluetooth Setup Assistant.

# To pair devices with the Bluetooth Setup Assistant

1. Choose Apple > System Preferences (**Figure 2**), or click the System Preferences icon in the Dock.

2. In the System Preferences window that appears (**Figure 1**), click the Bluetooth icon.

3. Click the Devices button to display its options (**Figure 73**).

4. Click the Set up new device button.

5. The Bluetooth Setup Assistant Introduction screen appears (**Figure 74**). Click Continue.

6. In the Select Device Type screen (**Figure 75**), select the type of device you will be using and click Continue.

7. The Bluetooth Device Set Up screen appears next. The Assistant locates all Bluetooth devices within range and displays them in a list (**Figure 76**). Select the device you want to work with and click Continue.

*Continued on next page...*

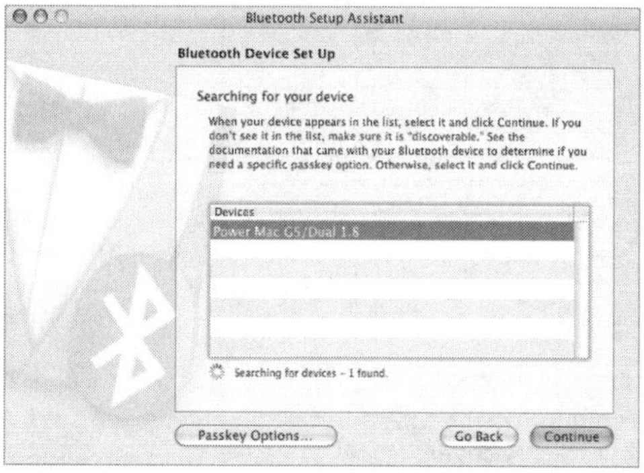

**Figure 75** Select the device you want to set up.

**Figure 76** The Bluetooth Setup Assistant prompts you to select a type of device.

*Continued from previous page.*

8. The next screen displays a random pass-key and provides instructions (**Figure 77**). Look at the device you want to configure. It should display a message prompting you to enter the passkey (**Figure 78**). Enter the passkey and click Pair.

9. A Conclusion screen appears next (**Figure 79**). To set up another device, click the Set up another device button and follow steps 6 though 9 above. Otherwise, click Quit.

The paired device appears in the Devices list in the Bluetooth preferences pane (**Figure 80**).

## ✔ Tips

- This process may differ, depending on the device you want to configure. But the Assistant makes the process easy to complete, so you should be able to figure it out.

- You can modify or delete device pairings in the Devices pane of the Bluetooth preferences pane (**Figure 80**).

**Figure 77** Your computer displays a passkey in big numbers (so you can see it from 30 feet away, I guess).

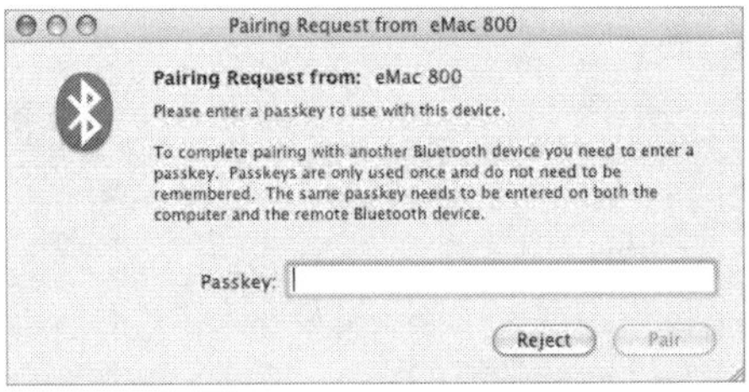

**Figure 78** On the device, you'll see a prompt like this one. In this example, I'm setting up my eMac to exchange files via Bluetooth with my G5. This is what I see on the G5.

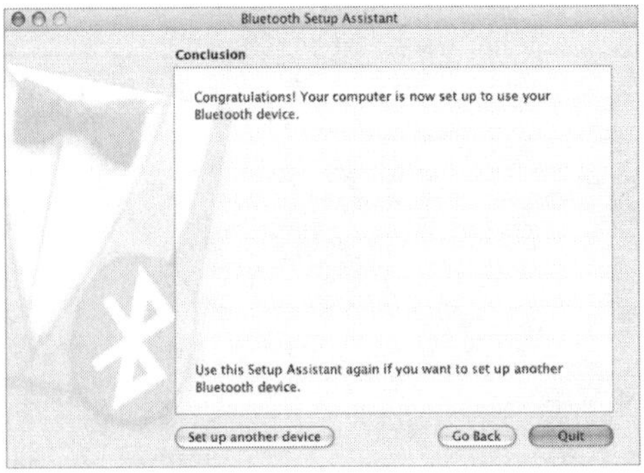

**Figure 79** When you've successfully entered the pass-key, the devices are paired.

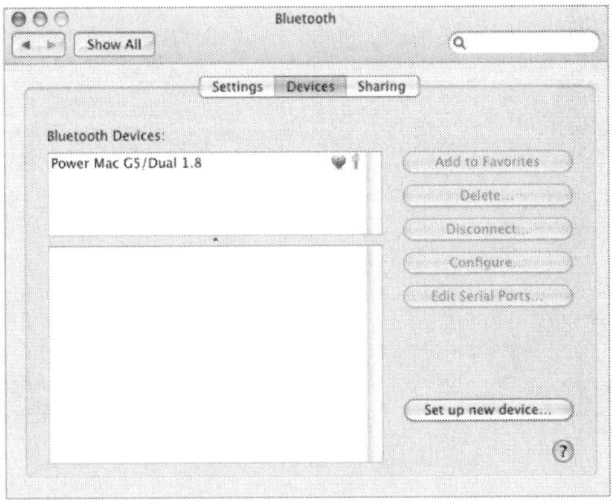

**Figure 80** The device appears in the Devices list.

USING THE BLUETOOTH SETUP ASSISTANT

**Figure 81** Use this dialog to select the file you want to send.

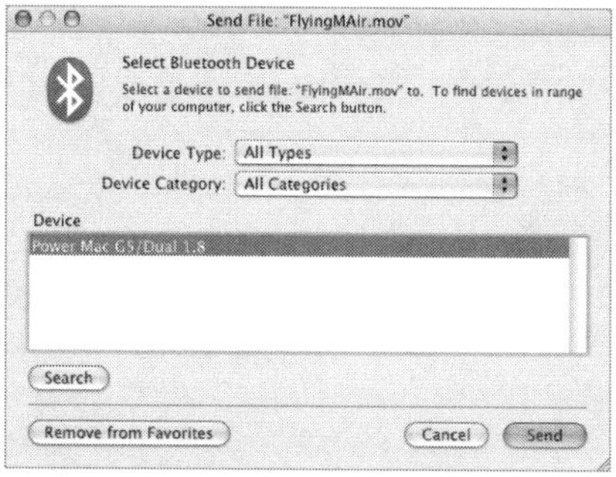

**Figure 82** Select the device you want to send the file to.

**Figure 83** Your computer waits for a response.

**Figure 84** Tell the device to accept the file.

**Figure 85** The device displays information about the received file.

## To send a file from one Bluetooth device to another

1. Open the Bluetooth File Exchange icon in the Utilities folder (**Figure 41**) inside the Applications folder.

2. If necessary, choose File > Send File to display the Select File to Send dialog (**Figure 81**).

3. Locate and select the file you want to send. Then click Send.

4. A Send File dialog appears (**Figure 82**). In the Device list, select the device you want to send the file to and click Send.

5. A dialog like the one in **Figure 83** appears while your computer waits for the device to accept the file. On the device, you'll see an Incoming File Transfer message (**Figure 84**). Click Accept.

   When the file has been transferred, the device displays a dialog with information about it (**Figure 85**).

## ✔ Tips

- In step 3, you can select multiple files by holding down ⌘ while clicking each one.

- In step 4, you can narrow down the list of devices in the Device list (**Figure 82**) by choosing options from the Device Type and Device Category pop-up menus.

- In step 5, you can turn on the Accept all without warning check box to receive all files without giving you an opportunity to accept or decline.

- You can click the magnifying glass button in the Incoming File Transfer window (**Figure 85**) to open the folder where the file has been saved.

## To use the Bluetooth status menu

Choose commands on the Bluetooth status menu (**Figure 86**) to perform the following tasks:

◆ **Turn Bluetooth Off** disables Bluetooth on your computer.

◆ **Discoverable** enables other Bluetooth devices to easily find your computer.

◆ **Set up Bluetooth Device** launches the Bluetooth Setup Assistant, which I discuss earlier in this section, so you can set up a Bluetooth Device.

◆ **Send File** launches Bluetooth File Exchange, which I discuss earlier in this section, so you can send a file to a Bluetooth device.

◆ **Browse Device** launches Bluetooth File Exchange so you can browse the contents of a Bluetooth device.

◆ **Open Bluetooth Preferences** opens the Bluetooth preferences pane (**Figure 69**).

**Figure 86**
The Bluetooth status menu offers commands for working with Bluetooth devices.

## ✔ Tip

■ The Bluetooth status menu only appears if the Show Bluetooth status in the menu bar option is turned on in the Settings pane of Bluetooth preferences (**Figure 69**).

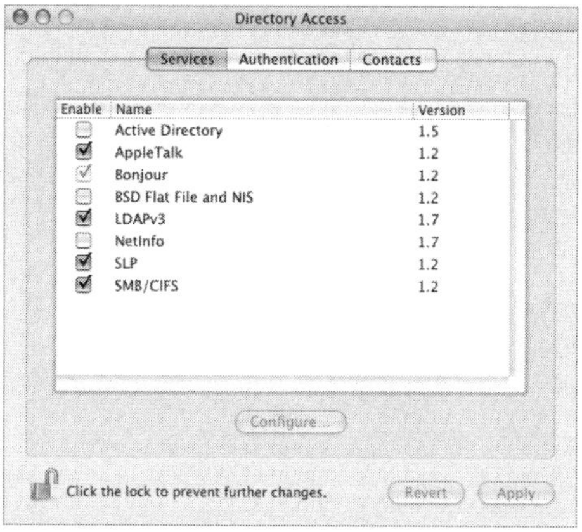

**Figure 87** The Services options of Directory Access.

**Figure 88** The Authentication options of Directory Access.

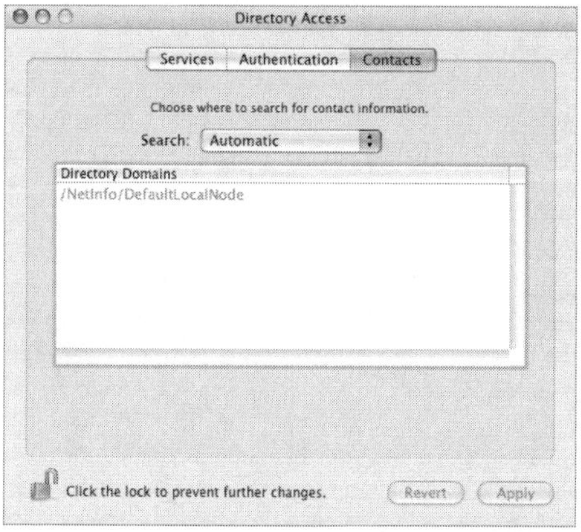

**Figure 89** The Contacts options of Directory Access.

# Advanced Network Administration Tools

The Utilities folder (**Figure 41**) inside the Applications folder includes three powerful utilities you can use to modify and monitor a network: Directory Access, NetInfo Manager, and Network Utility. Although a complete discussion of these utilities is beyond the scope of this book, here's an overview so you know what they do.

## Directory Access

Directory Access enables you to select the directory services your computer can access and configure how it connects to them.

Directory Access has three panes of options:

- ◆ **Services** (**Figure 87**) are the types of directory services your computer can access. Toggle a check box to turn access on or off.

- ◆ **Authentication** (**Figure 88**) enables you to specify where your computer should look for administrator user name and password information.

- ◆ **Contacts** (**Figure 89**) enables you to specify where your computer should look for contact information, including names and addresses.

## ✔ Tips

- ■ Don't understand what all this is about? Then don't change the settings in Directory Access! This is an administrative tool that, if misused, can mess up your computer.

- ■ When you open Directory Access, it is locked. You must click the lock button at the bottom of the window and enter an administrator's name and password to make any changes.

DIRECTORY ACCESS

# NetInfo Manager

NetInfo Manager (**Figure 90**) enables you to explore and, if you have administrative access, modify the network setup of your computer. With it, you can create and modify network users, groups, and domains and manage other network resources.

NetInfo Manager works by opening the NetInfo data hidden away within Mac OS X's configuration files. Although these files can also be explored and modified with command-line interface tools, NetInfo Manager's interface is a bit easier to use.

NetInfo Manager is a network administrator tool that requires advanced knowledge of the inner workings of Mac OS X networks.

## ✖ Caution!

- Making changes with NetInfo Manager when you don't know what you're doing is a good way to damage NetInfo data files. If you do enough damage, you could make it impossible to use your computer.

## ✔ Tips

- When you open NetInfo Manager, it is locked. You must click the lock button at the bottom of the window and enter an administrator's name and password to make any changes.

- If you want to learn more about NetInfo data and NetInfo Manager, look for the document titled "Using NetInfo," which is available on Apple's Mac OS X Server resources page, www.apple.com/server/resources.html.

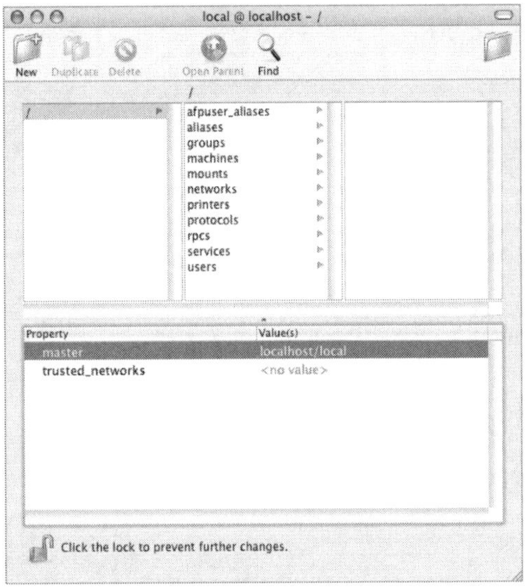

**Figure 90** NetInfo Manager's main window.

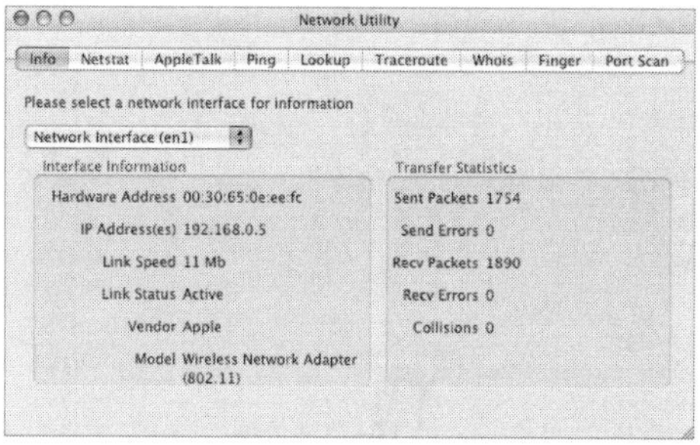

**Figure 91** Use the Info button to get information about a network interface.

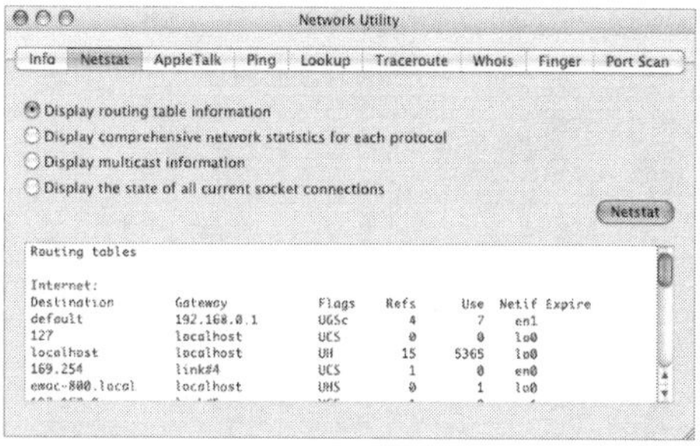

**Figure 92** Use the Netstat button to get network performance statistics.

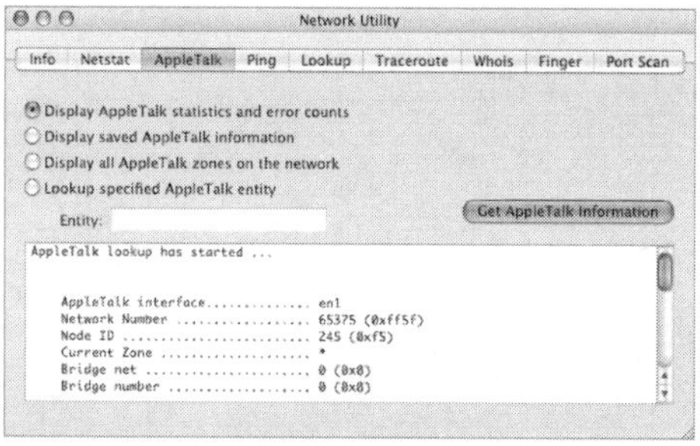

**Figure 93** Use AppleTalk button to get information about AppleTalk on your network.

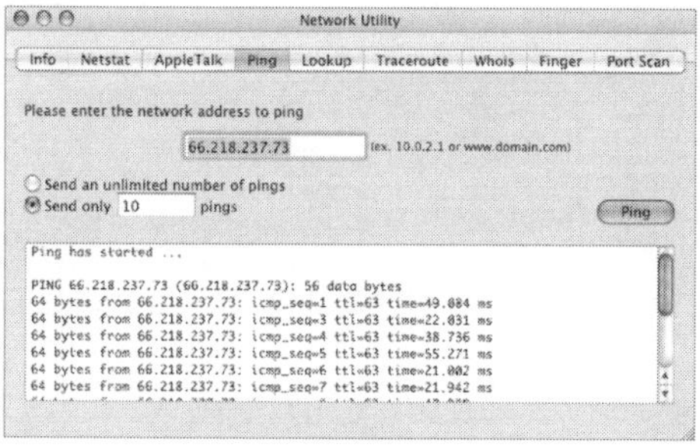

**Figure 94** Use the Ping button to "ping" another computer on the network or Internet.

# Network Utility

Network Utility is an information-gathering tool to help you learn more about and troubleshoot a network. Its features are made available in eight tabs:

◆ **Info** (**Figure 91**) provides general information about the network interfaces.

◆ **Netstat** (**Figure 92**) enables you to review network performance statistics.

◆ **AppleTalk** (**Figure 93**) provides information about your AppleTalk network.

◆ **Ping** (**Figure 94**) enables you to test your computer's access to specific domains or IP addresses.

◆ **Lookup** (**Figure 95**) uses a domain name server to convert between IP addresses and domain names.

◆ **Traceroute** (**Figure 96**) traces the route from your computer to another IP address or domain.

◆ **Whois** (**Figure 97**) uses a whois server to get information about the owner and IP address of a specific domain name.

◆ **Finger** (**Figure 98**) gets information about a person based on his e-mail address.

◆ **Port Scan** (**Figure 99**) scans a specific IP address for active ports.

Continued on next page...

**NETWORK UTILITY**

*Continued from previous page.*

## ✔ Tips

- The tools within Network Utility are used primarily for troubleshooting network problems and getting information about specific users or systems.

- Many of these utilities are designed to work with the Internet and require Internet access.

- In this day and age of increased privacy and security, you'll find that the Finger utility (**Figure 98**) is seldom successful in getting information about a person. (Heck, I couldn't even get information out of my own server!)

**Figure 95** Use the Lookup button to get the IP address for a specific domain name.

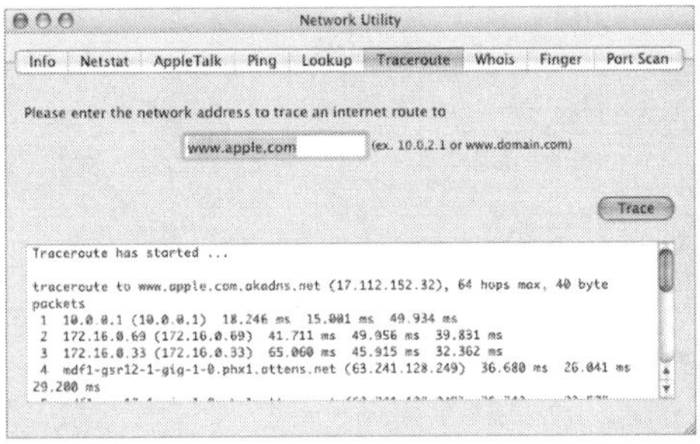

**Figure 96** Use the Traceroute button to trace the routing between your computer another IP address.

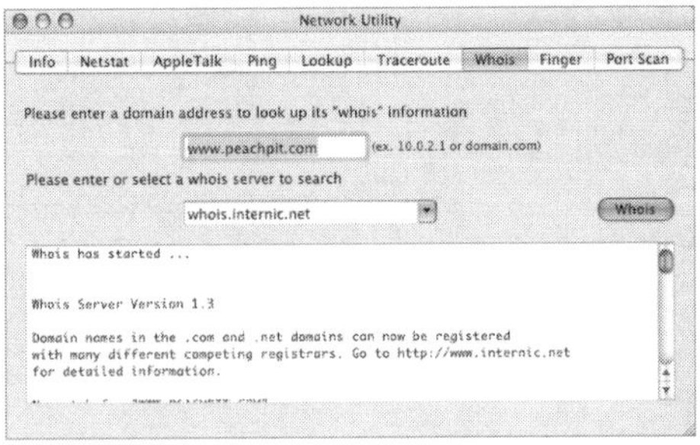

**Figure 97** Use the Whois button to look up information about a domain name.

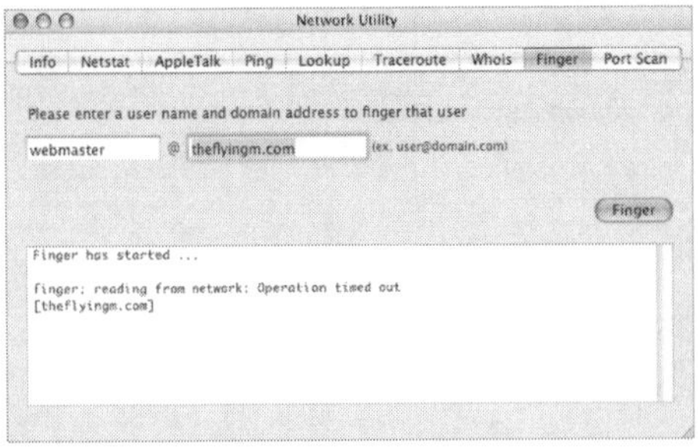

**Figure 98** Use the Finger button to look up information about a person based on his e-mail address.

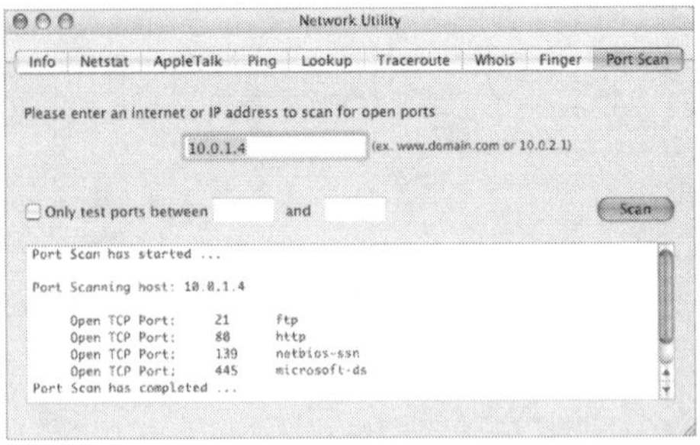

**Figure 99** Use the Port Scan button to check for active ports on another IP address or domain name.

NETWORK UTILITY

# Multiple Users & Security

## Multiple Users & Security

Mac OS X is designed to be a multiple-user system. This means that different individuals can log in and use a Mac OS X computer. Each user can install his own applications, configure his own desktop, and save his own documents. User files and setup is kept private. When each user logs in to the computer with his account, he can access only the files that belong to him or are shared.

In addition to login passwords to protect each user's private files, each user can take advantage of the keychain access feature, which enables him or her to store passwords for accessing data online or on a network. And for those users who are serious about security, Mac OS X's FileVault feature enables them to encrypt their Home folders, thus making it virtually impossible for anyone to hack in and read their files.

In this chapter, I discuss the multiple user and security features of Mac OS X.

## ✔ Tips

- Using a multiple-user operating system doesn't mean that you can't keep your computer all to yourself. You can set up just one user—you.

- **Chapters 3** and **19** provide some additional information about how Mac OS X's directory structure is set up to account for multiple users.

# Configuring Mac OS X for Multiple Users

In order to take advantage of the multiple users feature of Mac OS X, you need to set up user accounts.

The Mac OS X Setup Assistant, which I discuss in **Chapter 1**, does part of the setup for you. Immediately after you install Mac OS X, the Setup Assistant prompts you for information to set up the Admin user. If you are your computer's only user, you're finished setting up users. But if additional people—coworkers, friends, or family—will be using your computer, it's in your best interest to set up a separate user account for each one, then specify what each user is allowed to do on the computer. You do all this with the Accounts preferences pane (**Figure 2**).

In this section, I explain how to add, modify, set capabilities for, and delete user accounts.

## ✔ Tips

- I tell you more about accessing another user's folders and files later in this chapter.

- You also use the Accounts preferences pane to modify settings for your own account and to set up Login Options and Login Items, as I discuss later in this chapter.

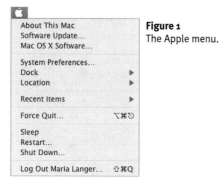

**Figure 1**
The Apple menu.

## To open the Accounts preferences pane

1. Choose Apple > System Preferences (**Figure 1**) or click the System Preferences icon on the Dock.

2. In the System Preferences window that appears, click the Accounts icon (in the System area) to display the Accounts preferences pane (**Figure 2**).

## ✔ Tip

- When you first access the Accounts preferences pane, its options may be locked. If so, you will not be able to make changes. If the padlock icon at the bottom of the preferences pane looks locked, click it to display an authenticate dialog like the one in **Figure 3**. Enter an administrator name (if one isn't already there) and password in the text boxes and click OK. The padlock will unlock so it looks like the one in **Figure 2**. You can now make changes as discussed throughout this chapter. I tell you more about locking and unlocking preferences in **Chapter 21**.

**Figure 2** The Accounts preferences pane with the Admin user selected.

**Figure 3** Use the Authenticate dialog to unlock Accounts preferences, if necessary.

**OPENING THE ACCOUNTS PREFERENCES PANE**

## To add a new user

1. In the Accounts preferences pane (**Figure 2**), click the + button at the bottom of the accounts list to display a blank new user dialog sheet **Figure 4**.

2. Enter the name of the user in the Name box.

3. Enter an abbreviated name for the user in the Short Name box. This name should be in lowercase characters and should not include spaces.

4. Enter a password for the user in the Password and Verify boxes. The password should be at least six characters long.

5. If desired, enter a hint for the password in the Password Hint box.

6. If the user should be given administrator privileges, turn on the Allow user to administer this computer check box.

7. Click Create Account. The new account appears in the list of accounts on the left side of the Accounts preferences pane (**Figure 5**).

8. Click the System Preferences window's close button to save your settings and quit System Preferences.

A folder for the new user appears in the Users folder.

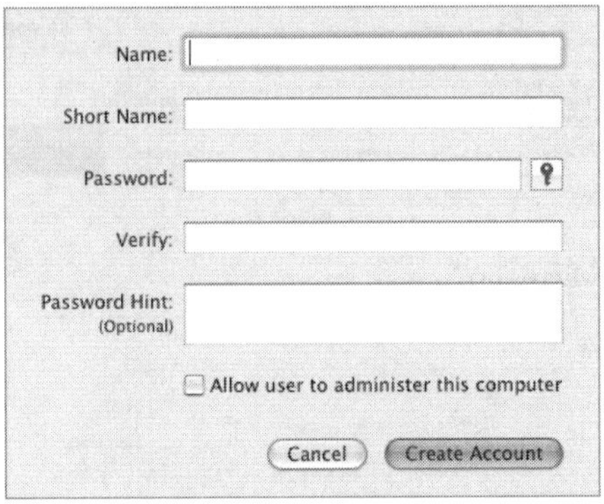

**Figure 4** Creating a new user account is as simple as filling in a form.

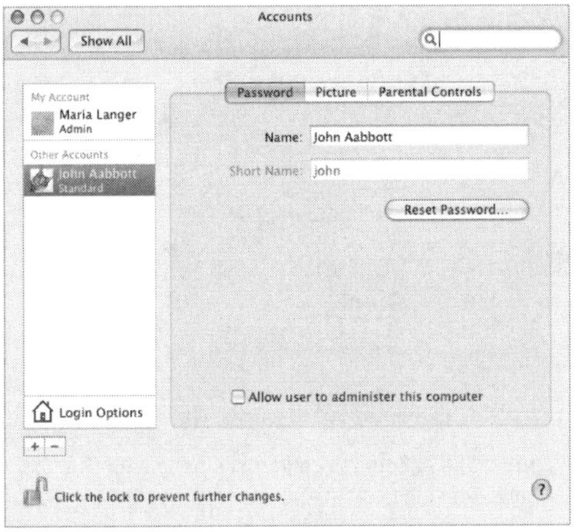

**Figure 5** The new account appears in the accounts list.

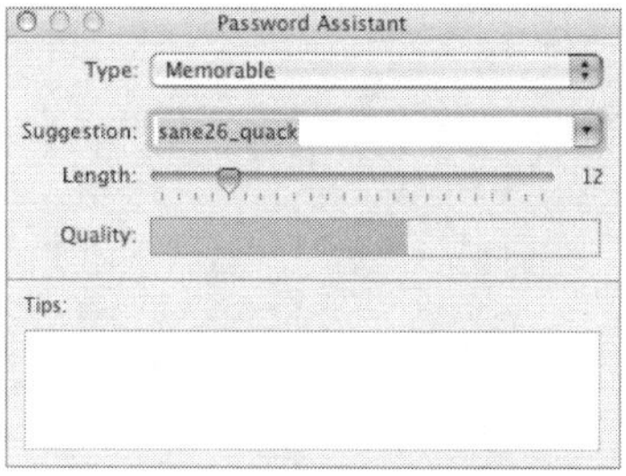


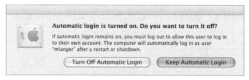

**Figure 6** Mac OS X 10.4's new Password Assistant helps you come up with a secure password that you might even be able to remember.

**Figure 7** If automatic login is turned on when you create a new user, a dialog like this appears so you can turn if off, if you like.

## ✔ Tips

- In step 4, you can use the Password Assistant to generate a random password. Click the Key button beside the Password box to display the Password Assistant (**Figure 6**), choose an option from the Type pop-up menu, drag the slider to modify the password length, and consider the password that appears in the Suggestion box. This feature is brand new in Mac OS X 10.4.
- After step 7, a dialog like the one in **Figure 7** may appear, asking if you want to turn off automatic login. Click the button for the option you prefer; I tell you about automatic login later in this chapter.

## To modify an existing user's settings

1. Display the Accounts preferences pane (**Figure 4**).
2. In the accounts list, select the name of the account you want to modify.
3. Make changes as desired in each pane of the Accounts preferences pane for the user.

Adding New Users, Modifying Users

## To give a user Administrator privileges

1. In the Accounts preferences pane, click to select the name of the user you want to give Administrator privileges to (**Figure 5**).

2. If necessary, click the Password button to display Password options (**Figure 5**).

3. Turn on the check box labeled Allow user to administer this computer. The word *Admin* appears under the user name in the account list (**Figure 8**).

## ✖ Warning!

- Only give Administrator privileges to individuals you trust and who have a good understanding of how Mac OS X works. An Administrator has access to the entire computer and can make changes that lock you out or prevent the computer from working properly.

## To change a user's password

1. In the Accounts preferences pane, click to select the name of the user you want to change the password for (**Figure 5**).

2. If necessary, click the Password button to display Password options (**Figure 5**).

3. Click the Change Password or Reset Password button.

4. A dialog like the one in **Figure 9** or **10** appears, depending on whether you are changing your password (**Figure 9**) or resetting someone else's password (**Figure 10**). Enter the appropriate password information in each box.

5. Click Change Password (**Figure 9**) or Reset Password (**Figure 10**) to save your changes.

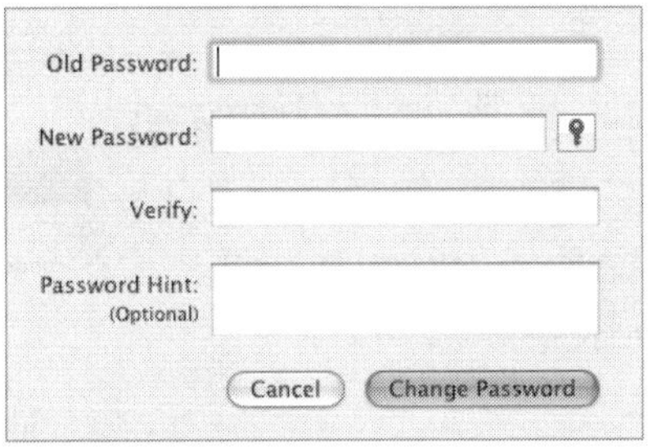

**Figure 8** When you enable Administrator privileges for a user, the word *Admin* appears under his name.

**Figures 9 & 10** Use a dialog like one of these to change your own password (above) or, if you have administrator privileges, to change someone else's password (below).

GIVING PRIVILEGES, CHANGING PASSWORDS

Figure 11 The Picture options of the Accounts preferences dialog.

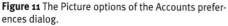

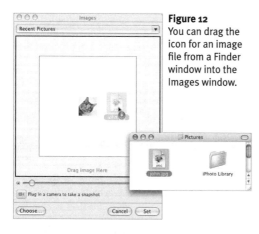

**Figure 12**
You can drag the icon for an image file from a Finder window into the Images window.

**Figure 13**
When the image appears in the window, you can drag it into position and use the slider to adjust the cropping box.

# To change a user's picture

1. In the Accounts preferences pane, click to select the name of the user you want to change the picture for (**Figure 5**).

2. Click the Picture button to display Picture options (**Figure 11**).

3. Scroll through the pictures on the right side of the window to find one you like and click it to select it.

   *or*

   Click the Edit button to display the Images dialog. Then drag the icon for an image from a Finder window into the image area of the Images dialog (**Figure 12**) so the image appears in the window (**Figure 13**). You can drag the image into position and drag the slider to change the cropping frame for the image. Then click Set.

4. The picture changes to the image you selected or inserted (**Figure 14**).

# ✔ Tip

■ A user's picture appears in his Address Book card, the Login screen, and as his default iChat picture.

Figure 14 The image appears as the user's picture.

## To specify login items

1. In the Accounts preferences pane, click to select the name of the account you logged in with (**Figure 2**). Normally, this will be your account, but if you want to set login items for another user, you must log in with that user's account.

2. Click the Login Items button to display its options (**Figure 15**).

3. To add a startup item, drag its icon into the list (**Figure 16**) or click the + button at the bottom of the list and use the dialog sheet that appears (**Figure 17**) to locate, select, and open the item. The item you dragged or selected appears in the list.

   *or*

   To remove an item from the list, click to select it and then click the – button at the bottom of the list. The item disappears from the list.

4. To automatically hide an item when it launches, turn on the Hide check box beside it.

## ✔ Tips

■ *Login items*, which were referred to as *startup items* in Mac OS X 10.3, are applications, documents, folders, or other items that are automatically opened when you log in or start up the computer.

■ You can set the order in which items open by dragging them up or down in the list.

**Figure 15** Login items in the Accounts preferences pane.

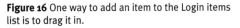

**Figure 16** One way to add an item to the Login items list is to drag it in.

**Figure 17** You can use a dialog sheet like this one to locate, select, and open the item you want to add as a startup item.

**SPECIFYING LOGIN ITEMS**

**Figure 18** Parental Controls options enable you to control how your children—or other users—can access the computer.

**Figure 19** Use this dialog to list the e-mail addresses of people who can send e-mail to the user.

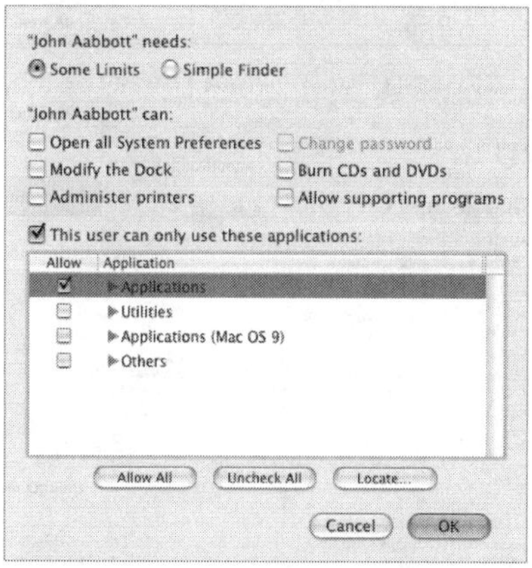

**Figure 20** The Some Limits enables you to specify what a user can do and which programs he can access.

# To set parental controls or limit a user's access

1. In the Accounts preferences pane, click to select the name of the user you want to set access limitations for (**Figure 5**).

2. Click the Parental Controls button to display Parental Controls options (**Figure 18**).

3. To prevent the user from getting e-mail from e-mail addresses other than the ones you specify, turn on the Mail check box and, if necessary, click the Configure button to set options (**Figure 19**). Click the + button beneath the Person list and enter the complete e-mail address for a person you want to add to the list. If you turn on the Send permission e-mails to check box, e-mail from anyone who isn't included on the Person list will automatically be forwarded to the e-mail address you enter; this makes it possible to see who is trying to send e-mail to the user and what that e-mail contains.

4. To prevent the user from modifying important Finder and System settings and limit access to specific applications, turn on the Finder & System check box. Then click the Configure button to set options (**Figure 20**). Select the Some Limits radio button, then toggle check boxes to set limits and click OK.
   - ▲ **Open all System Preferences** enables the user to open and make changes in all System Preferences.
   - ▲ **Modify the Dock** enables the user to add or remove Dock items. (This only affects the Dock as it appears for the user's account.)

Continued on next page...

LIMITING A USER'S ACCESS

▲ **Administer printers** enables the user to access Printer Setup Utility and use it to change the computer's printer setup.

▲ **Change password** lets the user change his password. To enable this option, you must turn on the Open all System Preferences check box.

▲ **Burn CDs and DVDs** enables the user to burn CDs and DVDs.

▲ **Allow supporting programs** enables applications that are not specifically listed in the dialog to open.

▲ **This user can only use these applications** enables you to specify exactly which applications the user can access. To allow the user to access all applications within a folder, turn on the check box beside the folder name. (*Others* refers to applications that are not in any of the other folders.) To allow the user to access some of the applications within a specific folder, click the triangle beside the folder name to display a list of all applications within the folder (**Figure 21**). Then turn on the check box beside each application the user can access.

5. To limit who the user can chat with using iChat, turn on the iChat check box and click the Configure button to set options (**Figure 22**). Click the + icon to display a list of Buddies from the Address Book (**Figure 23**), select name, and click Select Buddy. Repeat this process for each buddy you want to allow and click OK.

6. To limit the Web sites that the user can access, turn on the Safari check box. You must then log in as the user, open Safari, and add bookmarks for domain names you want to allow. You'll have to enter an administrator name and password to make changes to the bookmarks bar.

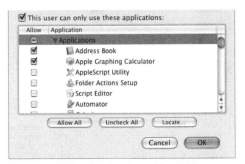

**Figure 21** Clicking the triangle beside a folder name displays a list of all the applications within that folder. You can then enable or disable specific applications.

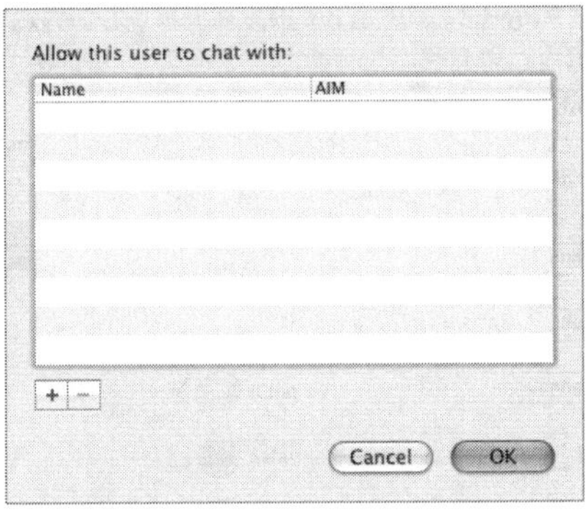

**Figure 22** Use this dialog to list the buddies the user can chat with.

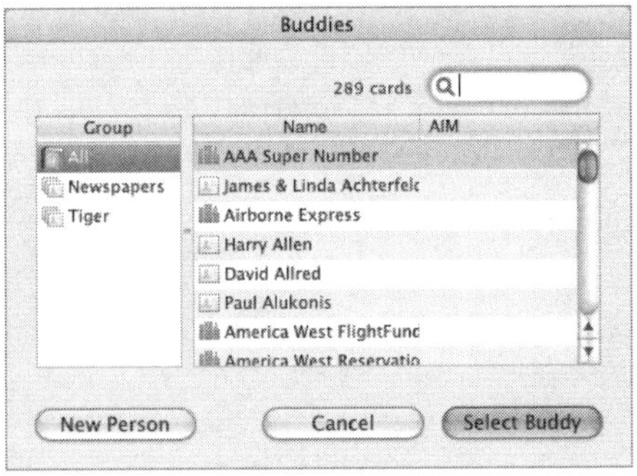

**Figure 23** Select a name and click the Select Buddy button.

7. To prevent the user from viewing profanity in the Dictionary application, turn on the Dictionary check box.

## ✔ Tips

■ You cannot set Parental Controls options for an administrator.

■ Parental Controls for Mail and iChat are a good way to prevent your children from getting e-mail from or chatting with people you don't know.

■ Parental Controls for Safari are a good way to limit the Web sites your children access.

■ Keep in mind that Parental Controls only work with the applications listed in the Parental Controls options of the Accounts preferences pane. To truly limit control, you must think through your control strategy and close up all loopholes. For example, if both Safari and Internet Explorer are installed on the computer, and you set up allowed sites on Safari for your children, you must disable Internet Explorer for their accounts to prevent them from using that to access other sites. Kids are smart. They'll find any loophole you leave them.

■ I tell you about Mail, iChat, and Safari in **Chapter 13**, System Preferences in **Chapter 21** and elsewhere throughout the book, and Dictionary in **Chapter 8**.

LIMITING A USER'S ACCESS

## To enable Simple Finder for a user

1. In the Accounts preferences pane, select the name of the user you want to enable Simple Finder for (**Figure 5**).

2. Click the Parental Controls button to display Parental Controls options.

3. Turn on the Finder & System check box and click the Configure button beside it.

4. Select the Simple Finder radio button to display Simple Finder options (**Figure 24**).

5. Specify which applications a user is allowed to work with:

   ▲ To allow the user to access all applications within a folder, turn on the check box beside the folder name. (*Others* refers to applications that are not in any of the other folders.)

   ▲ To allow the user to access some of the applications within a specific folder, click the triangle beside the folder name to display a list of all applications within the folder (**Figure 21**). Then turn on the check box beside each application the user can access.

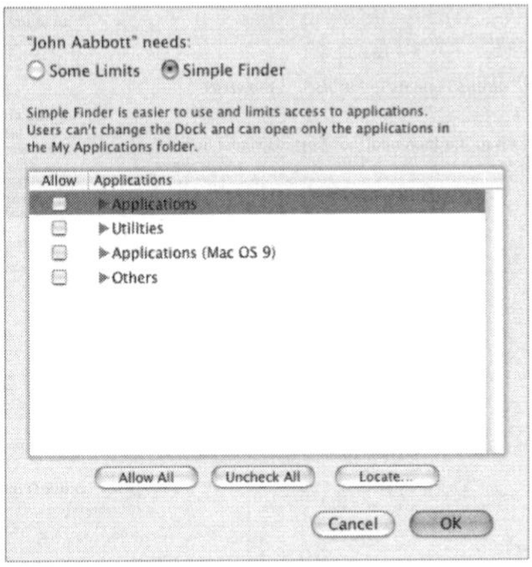

## ✔ Tip

■ Simple Finder (**Figure 25**), as the name suggests, is a highly simplified version of the Finder. Designed for users with little or no knowledge of computers, it offers a safe, highly controlled environment for kids and novices. If you want to try Simple Finder, create a new user with Simple Finder enabled, then log in as that user. If you've been using a Mac for more than a few years, I guarantee you'll go nuts in about five minutes. (I didn't even last two.)

**Figure 24** Simple Finder options for a user account.

**Figure 25** Simple Finder is an extremely simple version of the Finder.

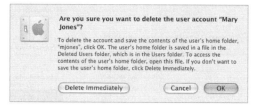

**Figure 26** Mac OS X confirms that you really do want to delete the user and offers two options for doing it.

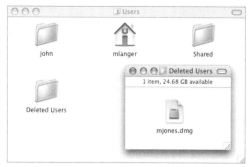

**Figure 27** The Users folder contains Home folders for each current user and a Shared folder that all users can access. If any users have been deleted, you may also find a Deleted Users folder which contains disk images of deleted users' Home folders.

## To delete a user account

1. In the Accounts preferences pane, select the name of the user you want to delete.

2. Click the – button at the bottom of the accounts list.

3. A dialog sheet like the one in **Figure 26** appears. You have two options to delete the user:

   ▲ **Delete Immediately** removes all traces of the user from the computer.

   ▲ **OK** removes the user from the Account list and saves the contents of the user's Home folder as a file in the Deleted Users folder inside the Users folder (**Figure 27**).

## ✔ Tip

■ When you delete a user's account, he can no longer log in to the computer and access his files.

## To set log in options

1. In the Accounts preferences pane, click the Login Options button at the bottom of the accounts list (**Figure 28**).

2. To prevent the Login window from appearing at startup, turn on the Automatically log in as check box and choose a user from the pop-up menu. If you choose a user other than the name already selected, a dialog sheet like the one in **Figure 29** appears. Enter the user's password and click OK.

3. Select a Display login window as option:

    ▲ **List of users** displays the name of each user. Click a name to display a password box for the user and log in.

    ▲ **Name and password** displays boxes for the user name and password. Enter the user name and password to log in.

4. Toggle check boxes to enable other options:

    ▲ **Show the Restart, Sleep, and Shut Down buttons** shows these buttons in the login window.

    ▲ **Show Input menu in login window** displays the Input menu in the login window so a user can enter special characters during login.

    ▲ **Use VoiceOver at login window** enables the VoiceOver feature to provide voice prompts for the login window.

    ▲ **Show password hints** displays the password hint for an account after the user has tried entering his password three times without success. Turning this option on also displays a Forgot Password button in the login window; you can click this button to display an account's password hint.

**Figure 28** The Login options in the Accounts preferences pane.

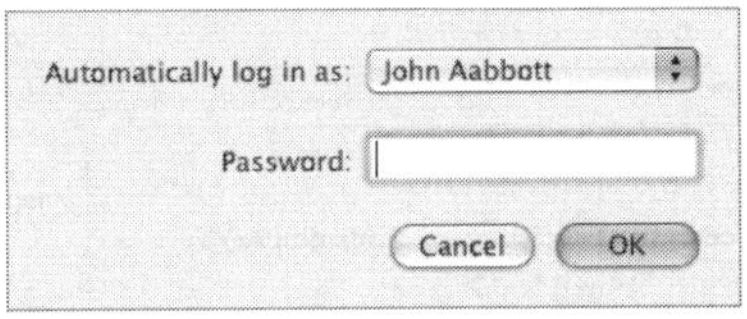

**Figure 29** Enter the user's password in this dialog sheet.

**Figure 30** This Warning dialog tells you a little about the fast user switching feature.

▲ **Enable fast user switching** makes it possible for a user to log in without logging out another user. When you turn on the Enable fast user switching check box a Warning dialog like the one in **Figure 30** appears. If you trust other computer users, click OK.

## ✔ Tips

- Automatically logging in is especially useful if you're the only person who uses your computer and it's in a secure location.

- With the automatically log in feature enabled, the log in window only appears when you log out or purposely display it via the fast user switching option.

- Although I consider myself somewhat of a screenshot expert (there are over 2,000 shots in this book alone), I could not figure out a way to take a screenshot of a Login window in Mac OS X 10.4. Sorry!

- I explain how to log in and out of a Mac OS X computer in **Chapter 2**.

- The Name and Password option in step 2 is more secure, since it requires users to know user names to log in.

- I tell you about the Input menu in **Chapter 21**, VoiceOver in **Chapter 22**, and fast user switching later in this chapter.

# Fast User Switching

*Fast user switching* is a Mac OS X feature that enables one user to log in and use the computer without another user logging out.

**Figure 31**
Fast user switching puts a menu like this one on the far right end of the menu bar.

The main benefit to this is that it's fast (hence the name). You don't need to close all open documents and quit all applications for another user to access his account. That means you don't have to reopen all those documents and applications when he's done and you can continue using the machine.

## ✔ Tip

- Before you can use fast user switching, you must enable it. You can learn how in the section titled "To set login options" on the previous two pages.

## To use fast user switching

1. With the computer turned on and a user already logged in, choose a user account from the menu at the far right end of the menu bar (**Figure 31**).

2. In the Login window that appears, enter the account password and click Log In.

   The screen changes (using a cool graphic effect) to the account you logged in to.

## ✔ Tips

- The user menu (**Figure 31**) indicates each user's status:
  - ▲ A user name that cannot be selected (Maria Langer in **Figure 31**) is the active user.
  - ▲ A white check mark in an orange circle appears beside the name of any user who is logged in.

- You must always enter a password to switch to another account, even if that account is already logged in.

FAST USER SWITCHING

**Figure 32** Each user's Home folder is preconfigured with folders for storing documents and settings files.

**Figure 33** The Home folder in **Figure 31** when viewed by another user.

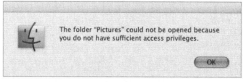

**Figure 34** A dialog like this one appears if you try to open another user's private folder.

# The Home Folder

Mac OS X creates a Home folder for each user account in the Users folder (**Figure 27**), with the user's short name as the folder name. The icon for the folder appears as a house for the user who is currently logged in and as a regular folder for all other users. Each user's Home folder contains folders for storing his files (**Figure 32**):

◆ **Desktop** contains all items (other than mounted disks) on the user's desktop.

◆ **Documents** is the default file location for document files.

◆ **Movies**, **Music**, and **Pictures** are for storing video, audio, and image files.

◆ **Sites** is for the user's Web site, which can be put online with the Personal Web Sharing feature.

◆ **Library** is for storing various preferences files, as well as fonts.

◆ **Public** is for storing shared files.

◆ **Applications**, when present, is for storing applications installed by the user for his private use.

## ✔ Tips

■ You can quickly open your Home folder by clicking the name of your Home folder in the Sidebar.

■ Personal Web Sharing is discussed in **Chapter 16** and fonts are covered in **Chapter 11**.

■ Although a user can open another user's Home folder, he can only open the Public and Sites folders within that user's Home folder; all other folders are locked (**Figure 33**). A dialog like the one in **Figure 34** appears if you attempt to open a locked folder.

# Sharing Files with Other Users

Mac OS X offers several ways for multiple users of the same computer to share files with each other:

**Figure 35** Each user's Public folder contains a Drop Box folder for accepting incoming files.

◆ The **Shared** folder in the Users folder (**Figure 27**) offers read/write access to all users.

◆ The **Public** folder in each user's Home folder (**Figure 32**) offers read access to all users.

◆ The **Drop Box** folder in each user's Public folder (**Figure 35**) offers write access to all users.

## ✔ Tips

■ *Read* access for a folder enables users to open files in that folder. *Write* access for a folder enables users to save files into that folder.

■ File sharing over a network is covered in **Chapter 16**.

## To make a file accessible to all other users

Place the file in the Shared folder in the Users folder (**Figure 27**).

*Or*

Place the file in the Public folder in your Home folder (**Figure 32**).

## ✔ Tip

■ If your computer is managed by a system administrator, check to see where the administrator prefers public files to be stored.

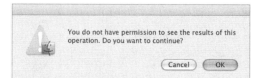

**Figure 36** When you drag a file into a Drop Box folder, a dialog like this appears.

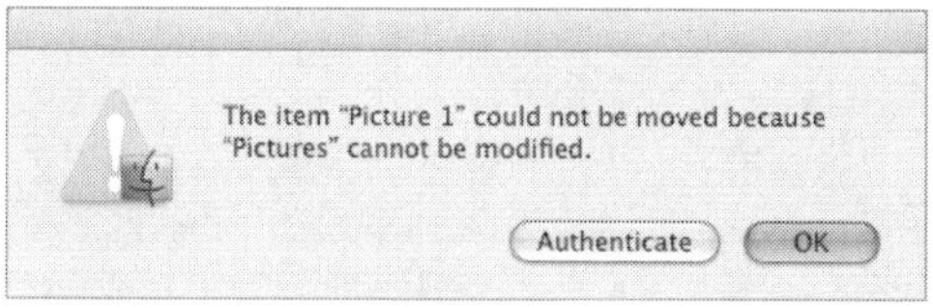

**Figure 37** You can't place files into another user's Public folder or any other locked folder...

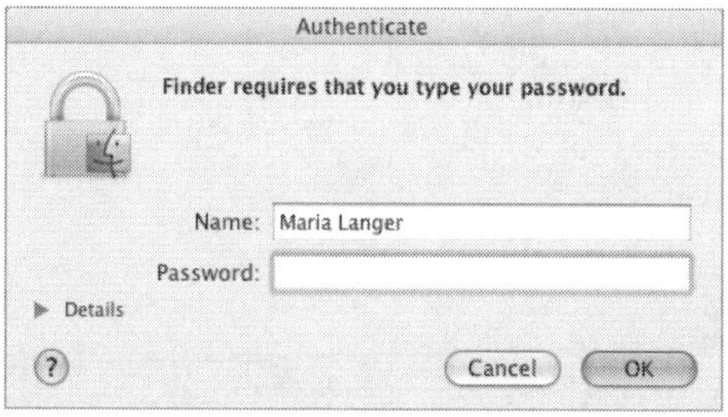

**Figure 38** ...unless you can prove you're an administrator.

## To make a file accessible to a specific user

1. Drag the file's icon onto the Drop Box folder icon inside the Public folder in the user's Home folder (**Figure 35**).

2. A dialog like the one in **Figure 36** appears. Click OK. The file moves into the Public folder.

## ✔ Tips

■ When you drag a file into a Drop Box folder, the file is moved—not copied—there. You cannot open a Drop Box folder to remove its contents. If you need to keep a copy of the file, hold down Option while dragging the file into the Drop Box folder to place a copy of the file there. You can then continue working with the original.

■ To use the Drop Box, be sure to drag the file icon onto the Drop Box folder icon. If you drag an icon into the Public folder, a dialog like the one in **Figure 37** appears, telling you that you can't modify the Public folder. You can click the Authenticate button and enter an administrator password in the Authenticate dialog (**Figure 38**) to override this warning and put the file there anyway.

# Keychain Access

The Keychain Access feature offers users a way to store passwords for accessing password-protected applications, servers, and Internet locations. Each user's keychain is automatically unlocked when he logs in to the computer, so the passwords it contains are automatically available when they are needed to access secured files and sites.

## ✔ Tips

- Mac OS X automatically creates a keychain for each user. This is the default, or *login*, keychain.

- Keychain Access only works with applications that are keychain-aware.

- You can also use your keychain to store other private information, such as credit card numbers and bank personal identification numbers (PINs).

## To open Keychain Access

Open the Keychain Access icon in the Utilities folder inside the Applications folder (**Figure 39**).

The keychain window for your default keychain appears (**Figure 40**). It lists all of the items in your keychain.

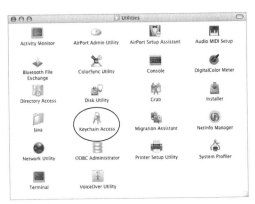

**Figure 39** You can find Keychain Access in the Utilities folder inside the Applications folder.

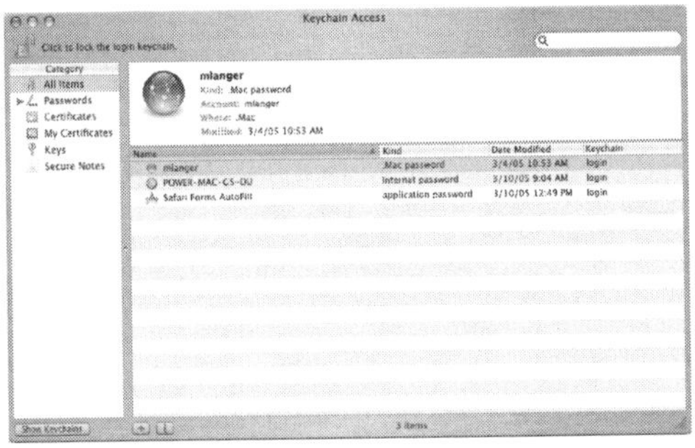

**Figure 40** The Keychain window for a default keychain.

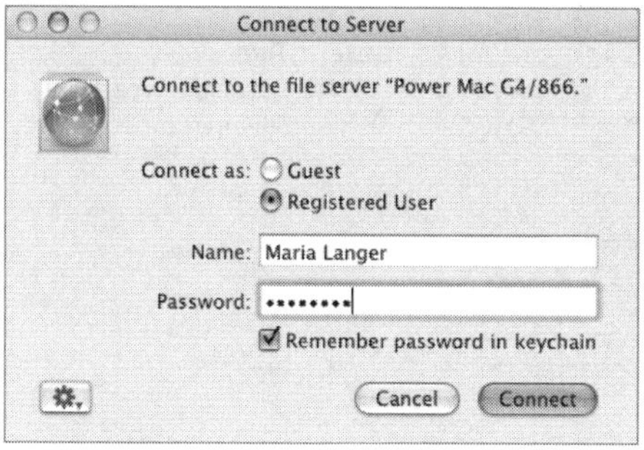

**Figure 41** This example shows the login dialog for accessing another computer on the network.

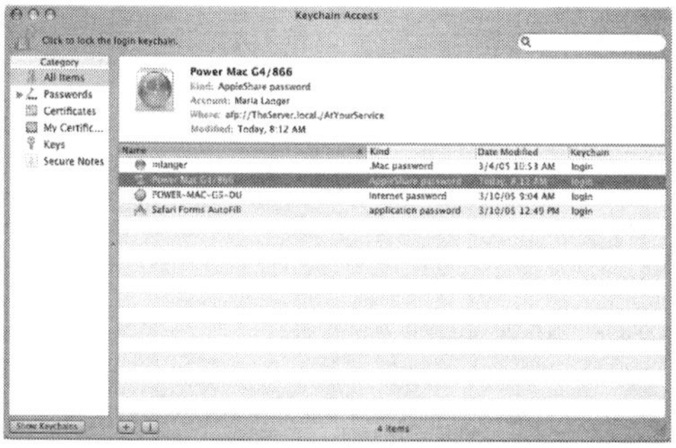

**Figure 42** The item is added to your keychain.

## To add a keychain item when accessing a secure application, server, or Internet location

1. Follow your normal procedure for accessing the secure item.

2. Enter your password when prompted (**Figure 41**).

3. Turn on the Remember password in keychain check box (**Figure 41**). (In some applications, you may have to click an Options button to see it.)

4. Finish accessing the secure item. When you open Keychain Access, you'll see that the password has been added to your keychain (**Figure 42**).

## ✔ Tip

■ The exact steps for adding a keychain when accessing a secure item vary based on the item you are accessing and the software you are using to access it.

## To add a password item manually

1. Open Keychain Access (**Figure 42**).

2. Click the + button beneath the list of keychain items, choose File > New Password Item (**Figure 43**), or press ⌘ N to display the New Keychain Item dialog (**Figure 44**).

3. Enter an identifying name or Internet URL for the item in the Keychain Item Name box.

4. Enter the user ID or account name or number for the item in the Account Name box.

5. Enter the password for the item in the Password box.

6. Click Add. The new item is added to your keychain.

## ✔ Tip

■ If you turn on the Show Typing check box in the New Password Item dialog (**Figure 43**), the password you enter will appear as text rather than as bullets. You may want to use this option to be sure that you're typing the password correctly, since you only enter it once.

**Figure 43**
Keychain Access's File menu.

| File | |
|------|------|
| New Password Item... | ⌘N |
| New Secure Note Item... | ⇧⌘N |
| New Keychain... | ⌥⌘N |
| Import... | ⇧⌘I |
| Export... | ⇧⌘E |
| Delete Keychain "login" | |
| Close | ⌘W |
| Lock Keychain "login" | ⌘L |
| Lock All Keychains | |
| Make Keychain "login" Default | |

Keychain Item Name:

Enter a name for this keychain item. If you are adding an Internet password item, enter its URL (for example: http://www.apple.com)

Account Name:

Enter the account name associated with this keychain item.

Password:

Enter the password to be stored in the keychain.
☐ Show Typing

Cancel    Add

**Figure 44** Use this dialog to manually enter password item information.

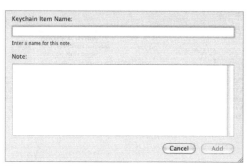

**Figure 45** Use this dialog to enter other private information that you want to keep handy but secure.

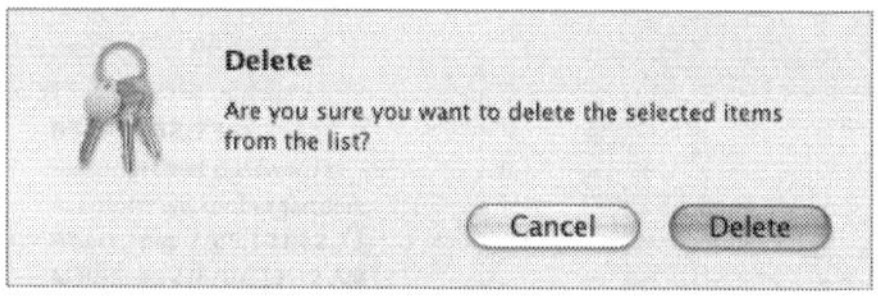

**Figure 46** A dialog like this appears when you delete a keychain item.

## To add a secure note

1. Open Keychain Access (**Figure 42**).

2. Choose File > New Secure Note Item (**Figure 43**) or press (Shift)(⇧)(⌘)(N) to display the New Secure Note Item dialog (**Figure 45**).

3. Enter an identifying name for the note in the Keychain Item Name box.

4. Enter the note in the Note box.

5. Click Add. The new item is added to your keychain.

## To delete a keychain item

1. Open Keychain Access (**Figure 42**).

2. Select the keychain item you want to remove.

3. Press (Delete).

4. A dialog like the one in **Figure 46** appears. Click Delete.

   The item is removed from the keychain.

## ✔ Tip

■ Removing a keychain item does not prevent you from accessing an item. It just prevents you from accessing it without entering a password.

**ADDING NOTES, DELETING KEYCHAIN ITEMS**

## To get general information about a keychain item

1. Open Keychain Access.

2. Select the keychain item you want to learn about.

3. Click the i button at the bottom of the keychain item list. A window with information about the keychain item appears.

4. If necessary, click the Attributes button to show general information about the item (**Figures 47** and **48**).

5. To see the item password, turn on the Show password check box (**Figure 47**).

   *or*

   To see a note, turn on the Show note check box (**Figure 48**).

6. When you are finished working with keychain information, click the window's close box to dismiss it.

## ✔ Tip

■ In step 5, if you turn on the Show password (**Figure 47**) or Show note (**Figure 48**) check box, a dialog like the one in **Figure 49** may appear. To see the password or note, you must enter the keychain password (your user password, for the default keychain) and click the Allow Once or Always Allow button. I tell you more about this dialog later in this chapter.

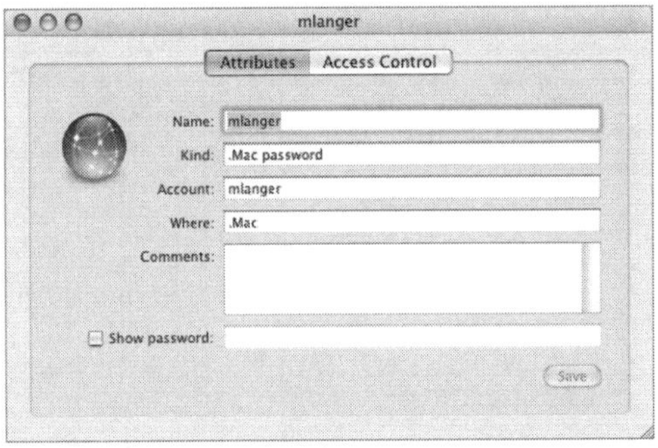

**Figure 47** The Attributes pane of the Keychain Access window for a keychain with a note selected.

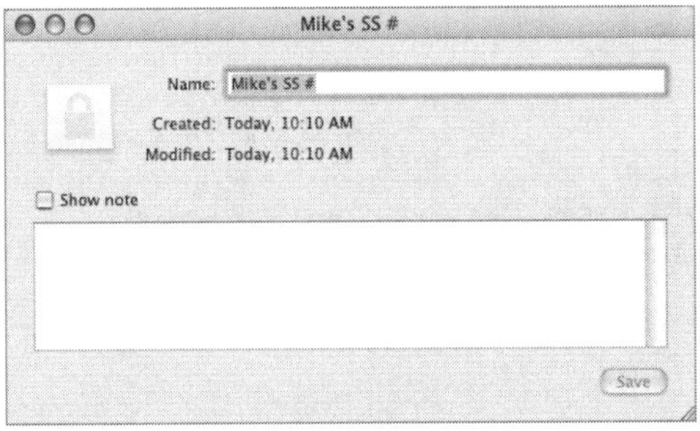

**Figure 48** General information for a note.

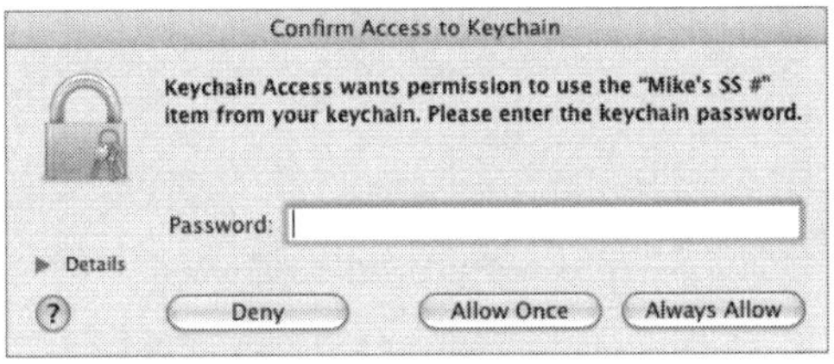

**Figure 49** This dialog appears when you try to view the password or note in a keychain item.

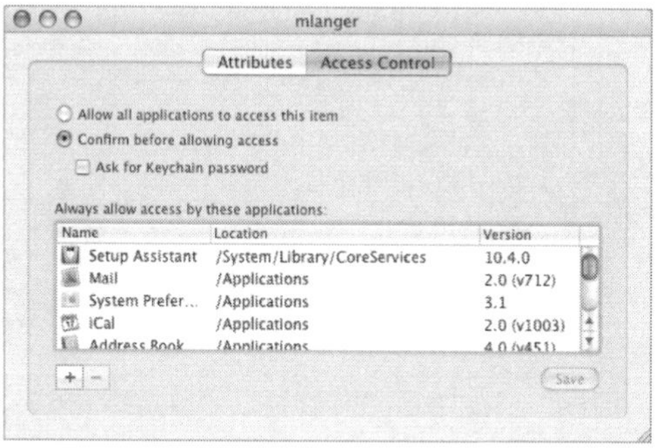

**Figure 50** Access Control information for a keychain item.

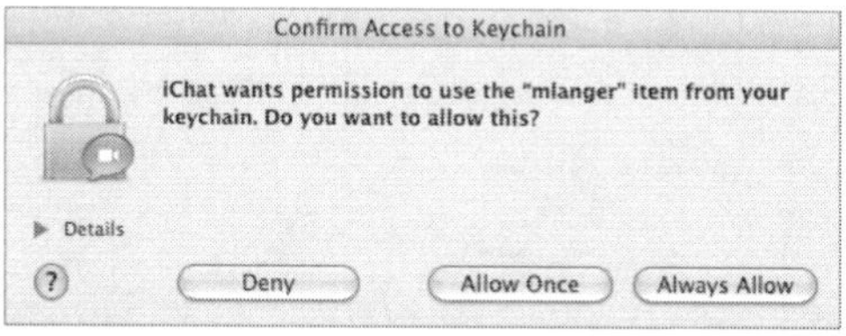

**Figure 51** When an application that does not have permission to use a keychain item wants to use it, it displays a dialog like this.

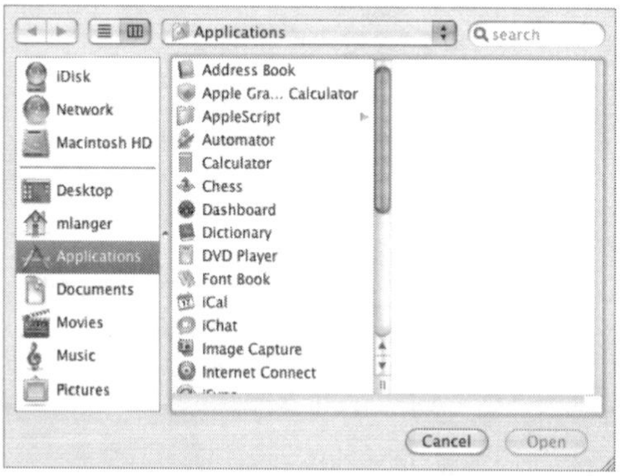

**Figure 52** Use a standard Open dialog like this one to add applications to the list of allowed applications.

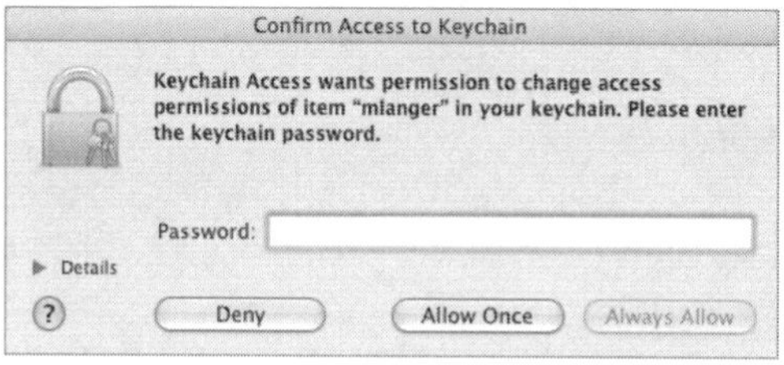

**Figure 53** You must enter a password in this dialog to change Access Control settings.

# To set Access Control options

1. Open Keychain Access.

2. Select the keychain item you want to set Access Control options for.

3. Click the i button at the bottom of the keychain item list. A dialog with information about the keychain item appears.

4. Click the Access Control button (**Figure 50**).

5. Select an access option:

   ▲ **Allow all applications to access this item** enables any application to access the item, without displaying a confirmation dialog. If you choose this option, skip ahead to step 7.

   ▲ **Confirm before allowing access** displays a confirmation dialog for each application that attempts to access the item (**Figure 51**). To specify whether the dialog should include a password prompt (**Figure 49**), toggle the Ask for Keychain password check box.

6. If desired, use the + and – buttons in the window to modify the list of applications that can access the item without displaying the confirmation dialog:

   ▲ + displays a dialog sheet like the one in **Figure 52**, which you can use to locate and choose an application to add to the list.

   ▲ – removes a selected application from the list.

7. Click Save.

8. A dialog like the one in **Figure 53** appears. Enter the keychain password in the box and click Allow Once to save the change.

9. Click the window's close box to dismiss it.

**481**

## To use a keychain item

1. Follow your normal procedure for accessing the secure item.

2. If Access Control settings are set up to allow access to the item without confirmation, the item opens without displaying any dialog.

   *or*

   If Access Control settings are set up to require a confirmation, a dialog like the one in **Figure 49** or **51** appears. Enter a password (if necessary; **Figure 51**) and click a button:

   ▲ **Deny** prevents use of the keychain item. You will have to manually enter a password to access the secure item.

   ▲ **Allow Once** enables the keychain to open the item this time.

   ▲ **Always Allow** enables the keychain to open the item and adds the item to the Access Control application list so the dialog does not appear again.

## ✔ Tips

■ The only reason I can think of for denying access with a keychain is if you have another user name and password you want to use.

■ If a keychain item does not exist for the secure item, you'll have to go through the usual procedure for accessing the item.

**Figure 54** Use this dialog to name and save a new keychain.

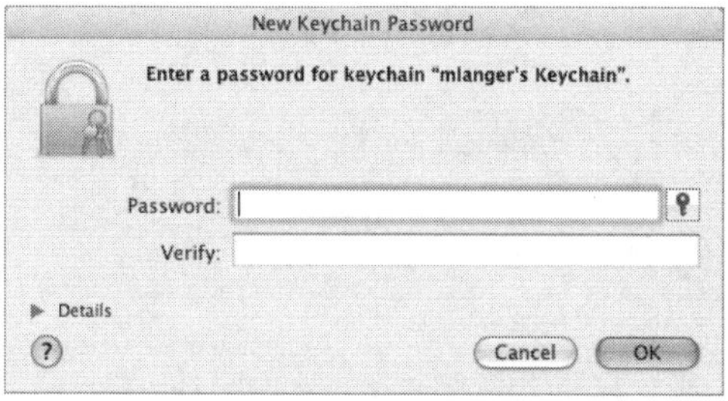

**Figure 55** Set the keychain's password by entering the same password or phrase in both edit boxes.

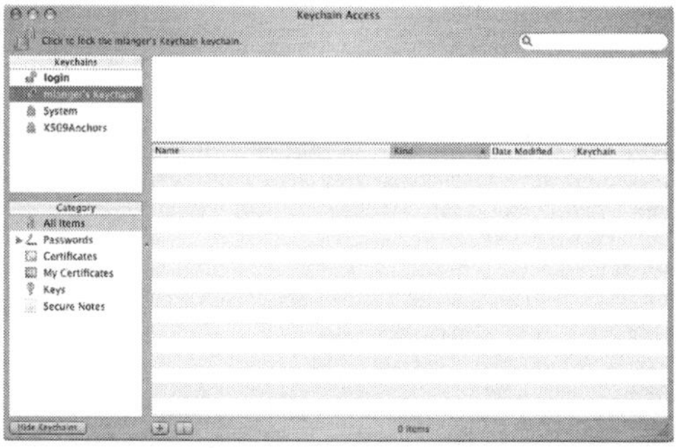

**Figure 56** Clicking the Show Keychains button displays a list of all keychains.

## To create a new keychain

1. Open Keychain Access (**Figure 42**).

2. Choose File > New Keychain (**Figure 43**) or press Option ⌃ ⌘ N.

3. Enter a name for the keychain in the New Keychain dialog that appears (**Figure 54**) and click Create.

4. The New Keychain Password dialog appears (**Figure 55**). Enter the same password in each box and click OK.

## ✔ Tips

- If you're an organization nut, you may want to use multiple keychains to organize passwords for different purposes. Otherwise, one keychain should be enough for you. (It is for me.)

- In step 3, although you can specify a different location to save the new keychain, it's a good idea to save it in the default location, the Keychains folder.

- In step 4, you can click the key button to use the Password Assistant (**Figure 6**) to help you come up with a secure password. I tell you briefly about the Password Assistant earlier in this chapter.

## To view a different keychain

1. Open Keychain Access (**Figure 42**).

2. If necessary, click the Show Keychains button at the bottom of the Category list to display the Keychains list (**Figure 56**).

3. Select the keychain you want to view (**Figure 56**).

## ✔ Tip

- As shown in **Figure 56**, your computer creates and maintains other keychains which are used by the system.

## To unlock a keychain

1. Open Keychain Access and click the Show Keychains button to display the Keychain list (**Figure 56**).

2. Select the keychain you want to unlock.

3. Click the padlock button at the top of the Keychain Access window.

4. The Authenticate dialog appears (**Figure 57**). Enter the password for the keychain and click OK. The icon beside the keychain name changes so it looks unlocked.

## ✔ Tips

- The password for the login keychain Mac OS X automatically creates for you is the same as your login password.

- By unlocking a keychain, you make its passwords available for use by applications as set in the keychain's access controls.

## To lock a keychain

1. Open Keychain Access and click the Show Keychains button to display the Keychain list (**Figure 56**).

2. Select the keychain you want to lock.

3. Click the padlock button at the top of the Keychain Access window. The icon beside the keychain name changes so it looks locked.

## ✔ Tips

- When a keychain is locked, if you try to open a secure item for which you have a keychain item, the Unlock Keychain dialog appears (**Figure 58**). You must enter your keychain password and click OK to unlock the keychain before the keychain item can be used.

**Figure 57** The Authenticate dialog appears when you use Keychain Access to unlock a keychain.

**Figure 58** The Unlock Keychain dialog appears when you attempt to open an item for which a keychain item exists but the keychain is locked.

- To quickly lock all keychains, choose File > Lock All Keychains (**Figure 43**).

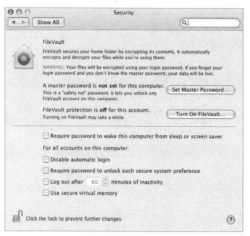

**Figure 59** The Security preferences pane.

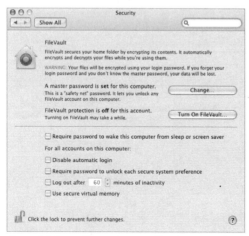

**Figure 60** Use this dialog to set up a master password for the entire computer.

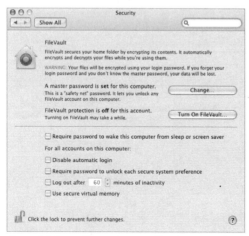

**Figure 61** When a Master Password has been set, the Security preferences pane tells you.

# FileVault

FileVault enables you to encrypt your Home folder using Advanced Encryption Standard 128-bit (AES-128) encryption. This makes it virtually impossible for any hacker to access the files in your Home folder. Best of all, it's all done quickly and transparently—files are decrypted automatically when you log in and encrypted again when you log out.

## ✔ Tips

- I say "virtually impossible" above because I don't believe that anything is really *impossible*. But this comes pretty close—certainly close enough for most people!

- If you're worried about someone recovering one of your deleted files, use the Secure Empty Trash command when you empty the Trash. I tell you more about deleting files in **Chapter 3**.

## To enable FileVault for the computer

1. Make sure all other users are logged off.

2. Log in with an administrator account.

3. Choose Apple > System Preferences (**Figure 1**) or click the System Preferences icon in the Dock.

4. Click the Security button to display the Security preferences pane (**Figure 59**).

5. Click Set Master Password.

6. In the dialog sheet that appears (**Figure 60**), enter the same password in the top two boxes. Then enter a password hint in the bottom box and click OK.

   The Security preferences pane indicates that a master password has been set (**Figure 61**).

*Continued on next page...*

**FILEVAULT, SETTING MASTER PASSWORD**

*Continued from previous page.*

## ✔ Tips

- By setting a master password, you make it possible for users to use the FileVault feature. You do not, however, enable it for any particular account.

- The master password is used as a "safety net" to help users who have forgotten their account password. After trying unsuccessfully to log in three times, you can click the Forgot Password button and enter the master password when prompted to reaccess your account.

- In step 7, don't forget to enter a password hint that'll help you remember the master password. If you forget the master password, you or other users could be locked out of your Home folder forever.

- To change the Master Password, follow steps 1 through 4, then click Change in the Security preferences pane (**Figure 61**) to display the Change Master Password dialog (**Figure 62**). Enter the current password in the top box and the new password and hint in the next three boxes. Click OK.

- Once you enter a master password, you cannot remove it.

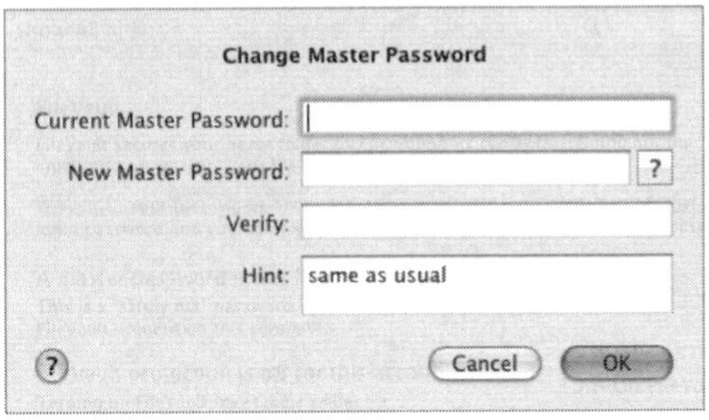

**Figure 62** Use this dialog to change the master password.

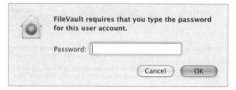

**Figure 63** To turn on FileVault, enter your password in this dialog.

You are now ready to turn on FileVault protection.

WARNING: Your files will be encrypted using your login password. If you forget your login password and you don't know the master password, your information will be lost.

Once you turn on FileVault, you will be logged out and FileVault will encrypt your entire home folder. Depending on how much information you have, this could take a while. You will not be able to log in or use this computer until the initial setup is completed.

You can't log in to this account from another computer to use it for Windows file or printer sharing.

☐ Use secure erase    Cancel    Turn On FileVault

**Figure 64** A dialog like this explains what happens when you turn on FileVault.

## ✔ Tips

■ In step 6, if you turn on the Use secure erase check box (**Figure 64**), your computer will automatically use the Secure Empty Trash feature each time you delete a file and empty the Trash. I tell you more about this feature in **Chapter 3**.

## To protect your Home folder with FileVault

1. Log in to your account.

2. Choose Apple > System Preferences (**Figure 1**) or click the System Preferences icon in the Dock.

3. Click the Security button to display the Security preferences pane (**Figure 61**).

4. Click Turn On FileVault.

5. A dialog like the one in **Figure 63** appears. Enter your account password and click OK.

6. A dialog like the one in **Figure 64** appears next. Read it carefully! Then click the Turn On FileVault button.

   You are logged out and a FileVault window appears. It shows encryption progress and may display an estimate of how long it will take to finish.

7. When the encryption process is done, a Login window appears. Log in to your account.

   From that point forward, every time you open a file in your Home folder, your computer decrypts it before displaying it. When you close a file, your computer encrypts it.

■ The initial encryption process can be time consuming, depending on how many files are in your Home folder.

■ You cannot use the automatic login feature to log in a user with FileVault enabled. I tell you about the automatic log in feature earlier in this chapter.

PROTECTING YOUR HOME FOLDER

## To turn off FileVault

1.  Log in to your account.

2.  Choose Apple > System Preferences
    (**Figure 1**) or click the System Preferences
    icon in the Dock.

3.  Click the Security button to display the
    Security preferences pane, which indicates
    that FileVault is turned on (**Figure 65**).

4.  Click Turn Off FileVault.

5.  A dialog like the one in **Figure 63** appears.
    Enter your account password and click OK.

6.  A dialog like the one in **Figure 66** appears
    next. Click the Turn Off FileVault button.

    You are logged out and a FileVault window
    appears. It shows decryption progress
    and may display an estimate of how long
    it will take to finish.

7.  When the decryption process is done, a
    Login window appears. Log in to your
    account.

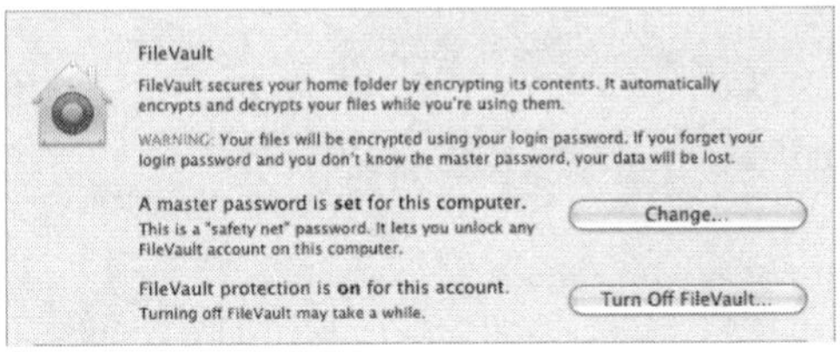

**Figure 65** You can tell that FileVault is enabled by looking in the Security preferences pane.

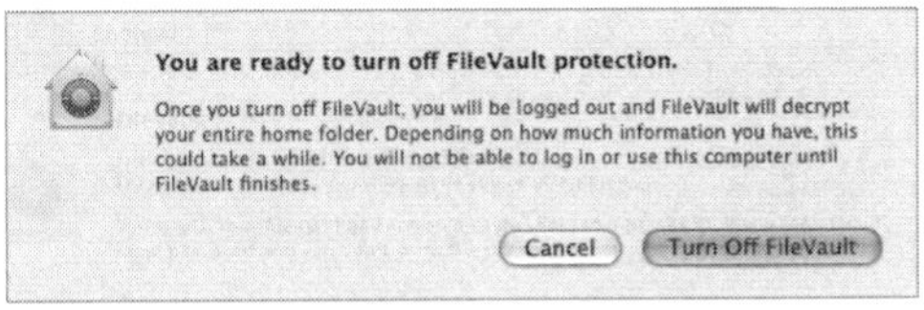

**Figure 66** This dialog appears when you turn off
FileVault.

# Enhancing System Security

The Security preferences pane (**Figures 59** and **61**) offers additional options for enhancing security on your computer. Here's how you can use them to make your computer more secure.

## ✔ Tip

- You must be logged in as an administrator to change Security preferences pane settings.

## To set system security options

1. Choose Apple > System Preferences (**Figure 1**) or click the System Preferences icon in the Dock.

2. Click the Security button to display the Security preferences pane (**Figure 59** or **61**).

3. Set options in the bottom half of the window as desired:

   ▲ **Require password to wake this computer from sleep or screen saver** displays an Authenticate dialog when you wake your computer or deactivate the screen saver.

   ▲ **Disable automatic login** turns off the automatic login feature.

   ▲ **Require password to unlock each secure system preference** displays an Authenticate dialog when a user opens a System preferences pane that requires administrative privileges.

   ▲ **Log out after $n$ minutes of inactivity** automatically logs out a user when he has been inactive for the number of minutes you specify.

   ▲ **Use secure virtual memory** encrypts the invisible virtual memory file your computer maintains while running.

## ✔ Tip

- I tell you about the automatic login feature earlier in this chapter and about System preferences in **Chapter 21**.

# The Classic Environment 18

## The Classic Environment

One of the goals of the Mac OS X development team was to build an operating system that would allow for compatibility with most existing Mac application software. After all, who would buy Mac OS X if they couldn't use their favorite applications with it?

The developer's strategy was to make it possible for Mac OS 9.1 or later to run as a process within Mac OS X. Users could then run applications that had not yet been updated for Mac OS X within the Mac OS 9.x process, which is called the *Classic environment*.

The Classic environment utilizes a complete Mac OS 9.x System Folder that contains just about all the components you'd find on a computer that doesn't have Mac OS X installed. This System Folder is so complete, you may even be able to start your computer from it—that means you can choose whether to boot from Mac OS 9.x or Mac OS X.

This chapter provides an overview of the Mac OS 9.x installation and configuration process, then explains how you can use the Classic environment and Mac OS 9.x to work with applications that aren't ready for Mac OS X.

### ✔ Tip

■ In 2003, Apple began selling Macs that won't start from Mac OS 9.x. The Classic environment, however, is still available to run pre-Mac OS X applications.

# Installing Mac OS 9.x

In order to use Mac OS 9.x and the Classic environment, you must install it. How you do this depends on how Mac OS X was installed on your computer:

◆ If you updated your computer from Mac OS 9.2 or later to Mac OS X and did not initialize your hard disk as part of the installation process, Mac OS 9.x is still installed on your computer, so you probably won't need to do a thing.

◆ If you updated your computer from Mac OS 9.0 or earlier to Mac OS X, you'll need to update the existing version of Mac OS to 9.1 or later.

◆ If you erased or initialized your hard disk when you installed or upgraded to Mac OS X, then only Mac OS X is installed. You'll need to install Mac OS 9.2 or later.

◆ If you purchased a new computer with both Mac OS X and Mac OS 9.2 or later preinstalled, you're all set and probably don't need to do a thing.

This section explains how to install or update to Mac OS 9.2.

## ✔ Tip

■ Although you can use Mac OS 9.1 with Mac OS X 10.4, the first time you start the Classic environment, Mac OS X displays a dialog like the one in **Figure 1**. If you have a Mac OS 9.2 updater disc, follow the instructions in the dialog to update to Mac OS 9.2. If you don't plan to update to Mac OS 9.2, you can turn on the Don't show again check box so the dialog doesn't bother you every time you launch the Classic environment.

**Figure 1** This dialog may appear the first time you run the Mac OS 9.1 Classic environment under Mac OS X 10.4.

**Figure 2**
The Mac OS
Install icon.

**Figure 3** The Welcome window appears when you launch the Mac OS 9.2 installer.

**Figure 4** Use this window to select a destination location. The currently installed version of the System software is identified here.

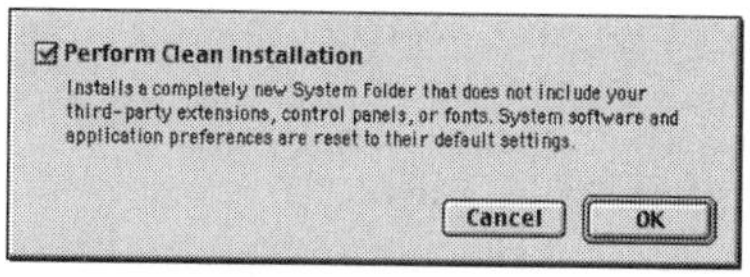

**Figure 5** Be sure to perform a clean installation if you're installing Mac OS 9.2 on a system that only has Mac OS X installed.

**Figure 6** Read this information before you continue the installation.

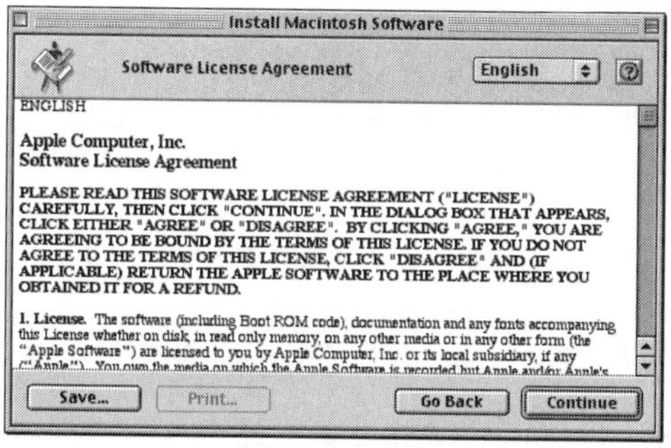

**Figure 7** The Software License Agreement window.

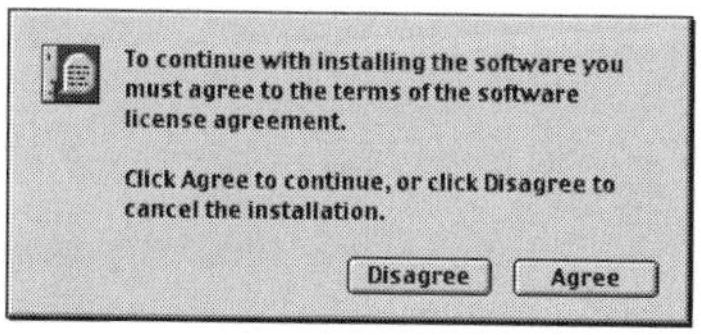

**Figure 8** You must click Agree in this dialog to complete the installation.

## To install Mac OS 9.2 from an Install CD

1. Start your computer from the Mac OS 9.2 installation disc. The easiest way to do this is to insert the installation disc, then hold down C while restarting your computer.

2. If necessary, open the icon for the Install disc to display disc contents.

3. Double-click the Mac OS Install icon (**Figure 2**) to launch the installer.

4. In the Welcome window (**Figure 3**), click Continue.

5. In the Select Destination window (**Figure 4**), use the Destination Disk pop-up menu to select the disk on which you want to install Mac OS 9.2. Then:

   ▲ If Mac OS 9.0 or earlier is already installed on the disk, click Select. This tells the installer to update that version of Mac OS.

   ▲ If Mac OS X is the only system software installed on the disk, click the Options button, turn on the check box beside Perform Clean Installation (**Figure 5**), and click OK. Then click Select. This tells the installer to add a new System Folder for Mac OS 9.2.

6. Read the contents of the Important Information window (**Figure 6**), and click Continue.

7. Read the contents of the Software License Agreement window (**Figure 7**), and click Continue.

8. Click Agree in the dialog that appears (**Figure 8**).

9. Click Start in the Install Software window (**Figure 9**) to start the installation.

*Continued on next page...*

INSTALLING MAC OS 9.2

*Continued from previous page.*

10. When the installation is complete, click Quit in the dialog that appears.

11. Choose Special > Restart to restart your computer with Mac OS 9.2.

12. The Mac OS Setup Assistant Introduction window appears (**Figure 52**). Follow the instructions later in this chapter to configure Mac OS 9.2.

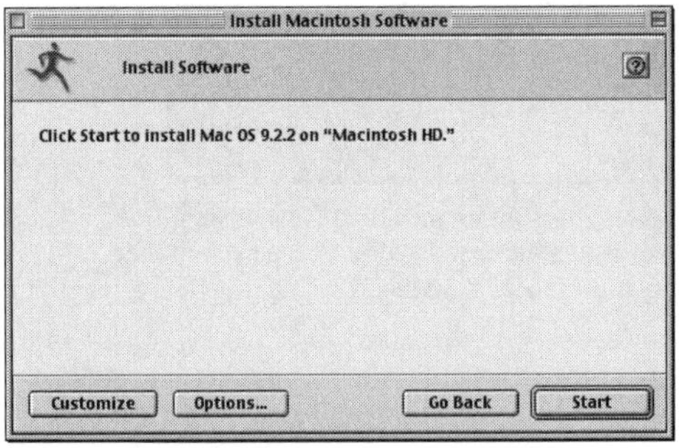

## ✔ Tips

- If the computer was started with Mac OS X and holding down Ⓒ won't start from the installer disc, follow these steps:

  1. Choose Apple > System Preferences.

  2. In the System Preferences window that appears, click the Startup Disk icon.

  3. In the Startup Disk preferences pane, select the folder icon for the Mac OS 9.2 installer disc (**Figure 10**).

  4. Click Restart.

  5. If a dialog sheet like the one in **Figure 11** appears, click Restart.

- If you cannot start your computer with the Mac OS 9 Install disc or, after step 3, if a message appears telling you that the application cannot run on your computer, you'll have to use the Restore CDs that came with your computer to install Mac OS 9.x. I explain how on the next page.

- These instructions assume that you don't want to customize the installation.

- I provide detailed instructions on how to install Mac OS 9.1 in *Mac OS 9.1: Visual QuickStart Guide*. That book's instructions also apply to installing Mac OS 9.2. The information provided here, however, should be enough to install Mac OS 9.2 for use with Mac OS X.

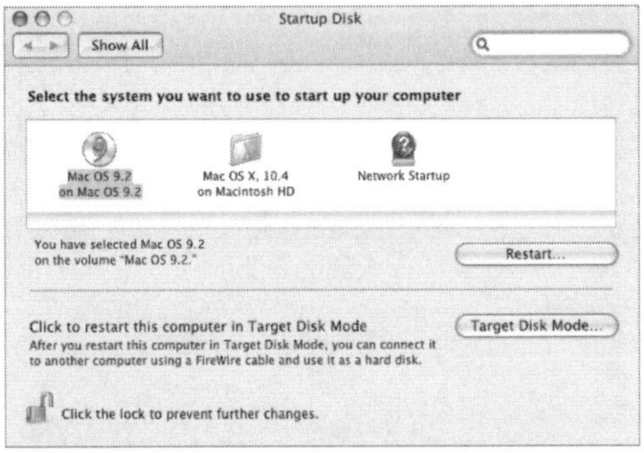

**Figure 9** Click Start to begin the installation.

**Figure 10** Use the Startup Disk preferences pane to select the Mac OS 9.2 installer disc.

**Figure 11** If this dialog appears, click Restart.

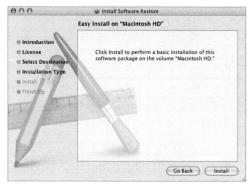

**Figure 12**
The contents of the first Restore CD for my "test mule," an eMac with SuperDrive.

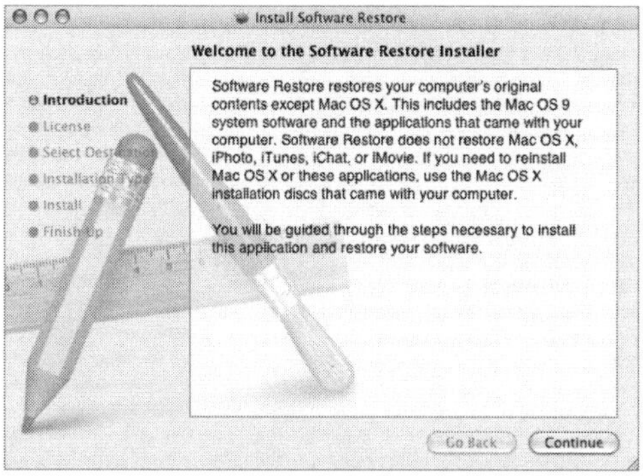

**Figure 13** The first screen of the Restore Installer.

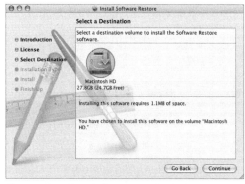

**Figure 14** Use this window to specify which disk the installer should be installed on.

**Figure 15** The last window before the Restore Installer is installed.

# To install Mac OS 9.2 from Software Restore CDs

1. Insert the first Software Restore CD.

2. If necessary, open the icon for the Restore disc to display disc contents (**Figure 12**).

3. Double-click the SoftwareRestore.pkg icon to launch the installer.

4. If a dialog appears, telling you that the installer needs to run a program, click Continue.

5. In the Introduction window (**Figure 13**), click Continue.

6. Read the contents of the License window, and click Continue.

7. Click Agree in the dialog sheet that appears.

8. In the Select Destination window (**Figure 14**), click to select the icon for the disk on which you want to install Mac OS 9.2. Then click Continue.

9. In the Installation Type window (**Figure 15**), click Install.

10. An Authenticate dialog like the one in **Figure 16** appears. Enter an administrator's name and password and click OK.

11. Wait while the Restore Installer is installed. When a dialog appears, telling you it is finished, click Close.

12. The Restore Installer's main window appears (**Figure 17**). Click Continue.

13. An Authenticate dialog like the one in **Figure 16** appears again. Enter an administrator's name and password and click OK.

14. The installer may prompt you to insert a specific restore disc. Follow the instructions that appear onscreen.

*Continued on next page...*

*Continued from previous page.*

15. In the Restore Software window that appears, turn off all of the check boxes except the one marked Mac OS 9 (**Figure 18**). (You'll have to turn off the Restore All check box first.) Then click Continue.

16. Wait while Mac OS 9.2 is installed. As the installer works, it may eject discs and request different discs to be inserted. Follow all instructions that appear onscreen.

17. When the Restore Complete window appears (**Figure 19**), click Quit.

## ✔ Tips

- ■ If you read these instructions carefully, you'll note that it's a two-step process. The first step is to install the Restore Installer. The second step is to use the Restore Installer to install Mac OS 9.2.

- ■ This is the only way you can install Mac OS 9.2 on computers that won't start from Mac OS 9.x.

- ■ You cannot start your computer from a Software Restore disc. You must start in Mac OS 10.2 or later.

- ■ It is not necessary to erase your hard disk to install Mac OS 9 with the Restore discs. If the only option is to erase your hard disk, you're probably using the wrong restore disc.

- ■ When the installation process is finished, you should see two additional folders on your hard disk: System Folder and Applications (Mac OS 9).

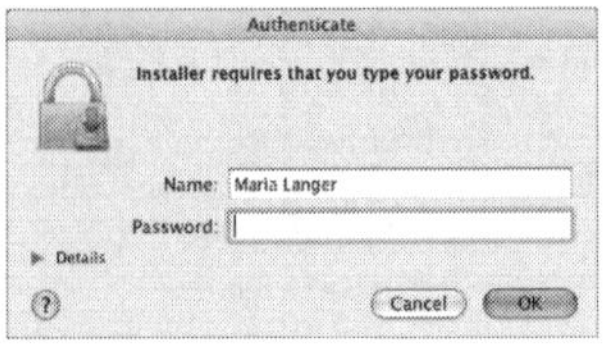

**Figure 16**
Mac OS X requires that you prove you have administrative privileges before installing any software.

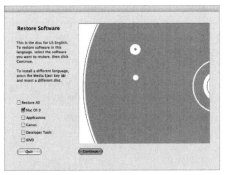

**Figure 17** The first screen of the Restore Installer.

**Figure 18** Use this window to specify what you want to install.

**Figure 19** When the installation is complete, the Installer tells you.

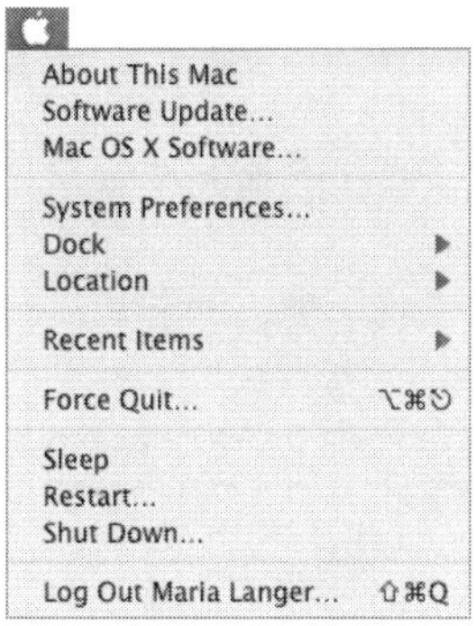

**About This Mac**
**Software Update...**
**Mac OS X Software...**

**System Preferences...**
**Dock** ▶
**Location** ▶

**Recent Items** ▶

**Force Quit...** ⌥⌘⊗

**Sleep**
**Restart...**
**Shut Down...**

**Log Out Maria Langer...** ⇧⌘Q

**Figure 20**
The Apple menu.

**Figure 21** You can also open System Preferences by clicking its icon on the Dock.

# Using the Classic Preferences Pane

In Mac OS X, you set options for the Classic environment with the Classic preferences pane. This pane offers options in three areas:

◆ **Start/Stop** (**Figure 22**) enables you to launch the Classic environment within Mac OS X, or to restart or force quit the Classic environment once it is running.

◆ **Advanced** (**Figure 31**) enables you to set Startup and sleep options for the Classic environment and to rebuild the desktop files used by the Classic environment.

◆ **Memory/Versions** (**Figure 36**) displays information about Mac OS 9 processes currently running in the Classic environment.

This section explains how to use the Classic preferences pane.

## To open the Classic preferences pane

1. Choose Apple > System Preferences (**Figure 20**), or click the System Preferences icon in the Dock (**Figure 21**).

2. In the System Preferences window that appears, click the Classic icon in the System row. The Classic preferences pane appears (**Figure 22**).

USING THE CLASSIC PREFERENCES PANE

## To select a startup volume for Classic

1. Open the Classic preferences pane.

2. Click the Start/Stop button to display its options (**Figure 22**).

3. Select the name of the disk or volume containing the Mac OS 9.x System Folder you want to use for the Classic environment.

## ✔ Tip

- In most cases, only one option will appear in the list of startup volumes. In that case, the volume that appears will automatically be selected and you can skip this procedure.

## To manually start the Classic environment

1. Open the Classic preferences pane.

2. Click the Start/Stop button to display its options (**Figure 22**).

3. Click the Start button.

4. A dialog with a progress bar appears (**Figure 23**). A Classic icon appears in the Dock and turns orange, from bottom to top, as Classic loads (**Figure 24**).

   When Classic is finished starting, the progress bar and Dock icon disappear. In the Start/Stop tab of the Classic preferences pane (**Figure 25**), the words "Classic is running" appear and the Stop, Restart, and Force Quit buttons become active.

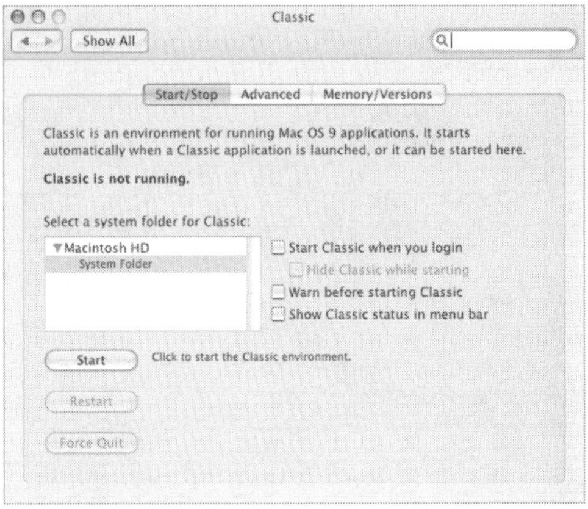

**Figure 22** The Start/Stop options of the Classic preferences pane.

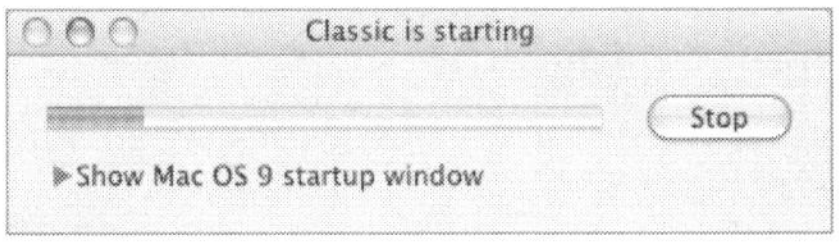

**Figure 23** This progress bar...

**Figure 24** ...and Dock icon appear when the Classic environment starts up.

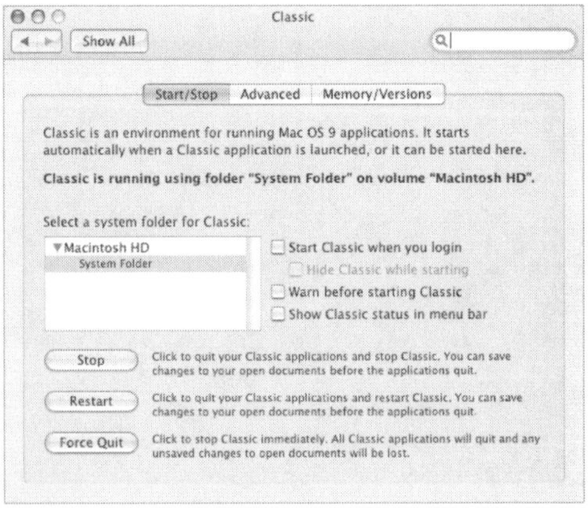

**Figure 25** The Start/Stop options indicate that Classic is running and offers options to stop it.

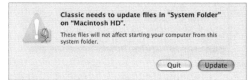

**Figure 26** If this dialog appears, click Update.

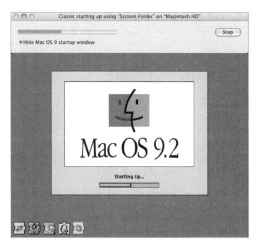

**Figure 27** You can expand the progress window to show the Mac OS 9.x startup screen. (For some people, it's like taking a trip down Macintosh Memory Lane.)

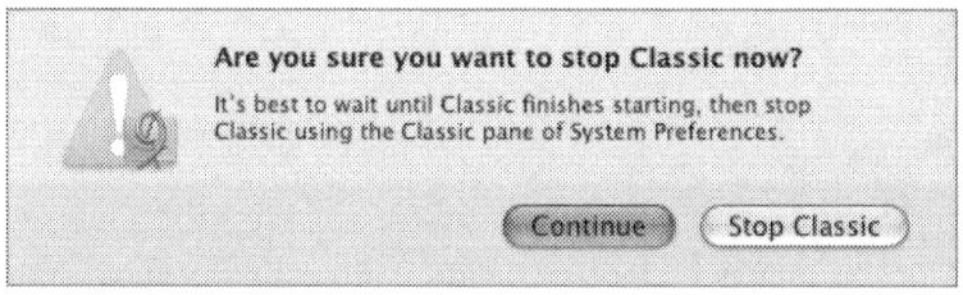

**Figure 28** Although you can stop Classic while it's starting, it's best to wait until it's finished.

## ✔ Tips

- If a dialog appears, telling you that you need to upgrade QuickTime, click Continue. I explain how to update software for Mac OS 9 later in this chapter.

- If a dialog appears, telling you that you need to update files (**Figure 26**), click Update. This dialog should only appear the first time you launch the Classic environment after installing or updating your system software.

- If you click the triangle beside Show Mac OS 9 desktop window in the Classic is starting window (**Figure 23**), the window expands to show the Mac OS 9.x startup screen (**Figure 27**).

- If you change your mind while Classic is starting, you can click the Stop button beside the progress bar (**Figure 23**) to stop it. As the dialog that appears warns (**Figure 28**), it's better to let Classic finish starting up before you stop it.

- Remember, the Classic environment starts automatically when you launch a Classic application, so it isn't necessary to manually start it when you want to run a classic application.

*STARTING CLASSIC*

## To automatically start the Classic environment when you log in to Mac OS X

1. Open the Classic preferences pane.

2. Click the Start/Stop button to display its options (**Figure 22**).

3. Turn on the Start Classic when you login check box.

4. If you don't want to see the Classic progress bar (**Figure 23**) or startup window (**Figure 27**), turn on the Hide Classic while starting check box.

### ✔ Tip

■ You may want to use this feature if you use Classic applications often. This makes Classic ready anytime you want to use it, so you don't have to wait for Classic to start up when you open a Classic application.

## To be warned each time the Classic environment automatically starts

1. Open the Classic preferences pane.

2. Click the Start/Stop button (**Figure 22**).

3. Turn on the Warn before starting Classic check box.

### ✔ Tip

■ With this feature enabled, each time you attempt to open a Classic application when the Classic environment is not already running, a dialog like the one in **Figure 29** appears.

**Figure 29** A dialog like this appears when you set the Warn before starting Classic option and start a Mac OS 9 application when the Classic environment isn't already running.

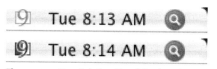

**Figures 30a & 30b** A tiny Mac OS 9 icon indicates when the Classic environment is not running (top) and when it is (bottom).

## To monitor Classic status in the menu bar

1. Open the Classic preferences pane.

2. Click the Start/Stop button (**Figure 22**).

3. Turn on the Show Classic status in menu bar check box.

### ✔ Tip

- With this option enabled, a tiny Mac OS 9 icon appears in the menu bar. The icon is gray if the Classic environment is not running (**Figure 30a**) and black with a half filled-in background if it is running (**Figure 30b**). The icon also blinks as Classic starts.

## To stop the Classic environment

1. Open the Classic preferences pane.

2. Click the Start/Stop button (**Figure 25**).

3. Click the Stop button.

4. If Classic applications with unsaved documents are open, your computer switches to the open applications, one at a time, and offers you an opportunity to save the unsaved documents. Save changes as desired.

   Your computer quits all open Classic applications and stops the Classic environment.

### ✔ Tip

- If you're having trouble with the Classic environment and the Stop command won't work, you can click the Force Quit button in the Start/Stop tab to stop Classic. Doing so, however, quits all Classic applications without giving you an opportunity to save changes to documents. Only click Force Quit if you cannot stop Classic any other way.

**MONITORING STATUS, STOPPING CLASSIC**

## To restart the Classic environment

1. Open the Classic preferences pane.

2. Click the Start/Stop button to display its options (**Figure 25**).

3. Click the Restart button.

4. If Classic applications with unsaved documents are open, your computer switches to the open applications, one at a time, and offers you an opportunity to save the unsaved documents. Save changes as desired.

   Your computer quits all open Classic applications and restarts the Classic environment.

## ✔ Tip

■ Use the Restart button if a Classic application unexpectedly quits. This flushes out memory allocated to the Classic environment and can prevent other Classic applications from having related problems.

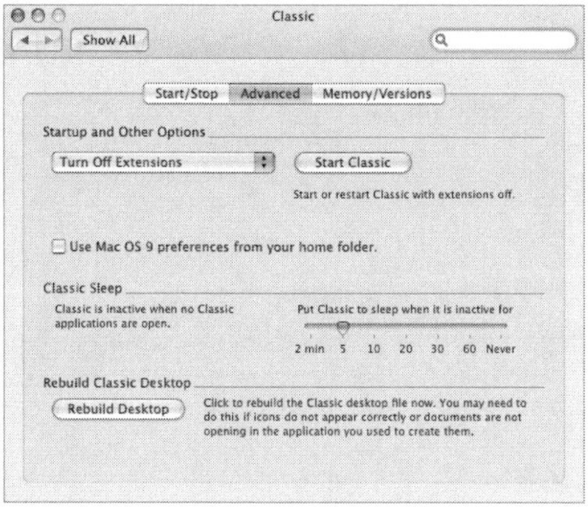

**Figure 31** The Advanced tab of the Classic preferences pane.

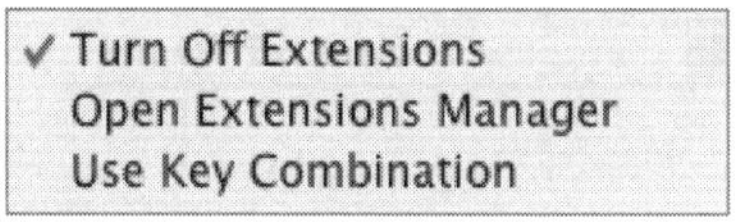

**Figure 32** Use this pop-up menu to set startup options.

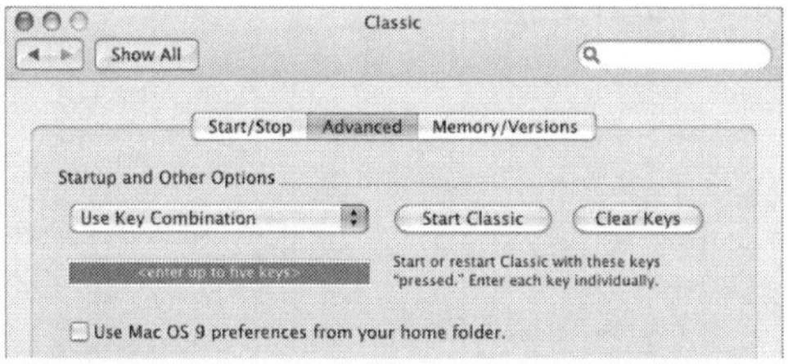

**Figure 33** When you choose Use Key Combination, the dialog changes to display a box for entering your keystrokes.

# To set Classic Startup options

1. Open the Classic preferences pane.

2. Click the Advanced button to display its options (**Figure 31**).

3. Choose an option from the pop-up menu in the Startup Options area (**Figure 32**):

   ▲ **Turn Off Extensions** turns off all Mac OS 9.x extensions when Classic starts or restarts. (This is the same as holding down (Shift) when starting from Mac OS 9.x.)

   ▲ **Open Extensions Manager** automatically opens Extensions Manager when Classic starts or restarts. (This is the same as holding down (Spacebar) when starting from Mac OS 9.x.)

   ▲ **Use Key Combination** enables you to enter up to five keys to start or restart Classic. If you choose this option, the window changes to display a box for your keystrokes and instructions (**Figure 33**). Press the keys, one at a time, to enter them in the box.

4. To use preference settings from your Home folder rather than the System Folder selected in the Start/Stop tab (**Figure 22**), turn on the Use Mac OS 9 preferences from your home folder check box.

5. Click Start Classic (**Figure 31**) or Restart Classic (if Classic is already running) to start or restart Classic with your startup option set.

## ✔ Tip

■ The option you select in Step 3 only applies when Classic is started or restarted from the Advanced tab of the Classic preferences pane (**Figure 31**).

## To set Classic sleep options

1. Open the Classic preferences pane.

2. Click the Advanced button to display its options (**Figure 31**).

3. Use the slider to specify how long Classic should be inactive before it sleeps.

## ✔ Tips

- The Classic environment is said to be *inactive* when no Classic applications are running.

- When the Classic environment is sleeping, it uses fewer system resources. This can increase performance on an older computer, especially one with a slow CPU or the minimum required amount of RAM.

- If you launch a Classic application while the Classic environment is sleeping, it may take a moment or two for Classic to wake and the application to appear. This is still quicker than starting Classic.

## To rebuild the Classic desktop

1. Open the Classic preferences pane.

2. Click the Advanced button to display its options (**Figure 31**).

3. Click Rebuild Desktop.

4. A dialog sheet like the one in **Figure 34** appears. Select the names of the disks you want to rebuild the desktop file for and click Rebuild.

   A status bar appears in the bottom half of the Advanced area (**Figure 35**). When it disappears, the process is complete.

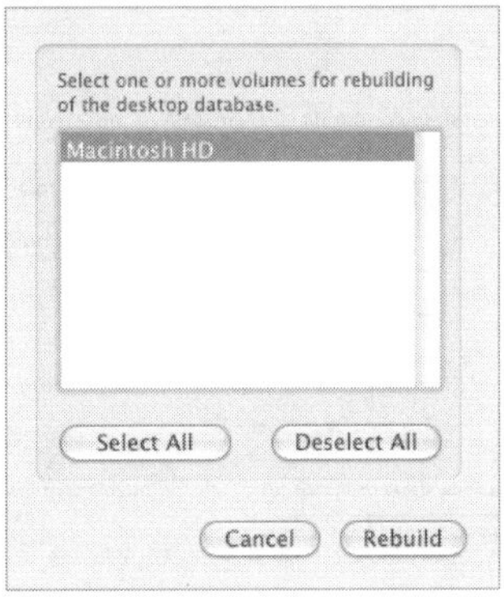

**Figure 34** Use this dialog sheet to choose the disks you want to rebuild the desktop for.

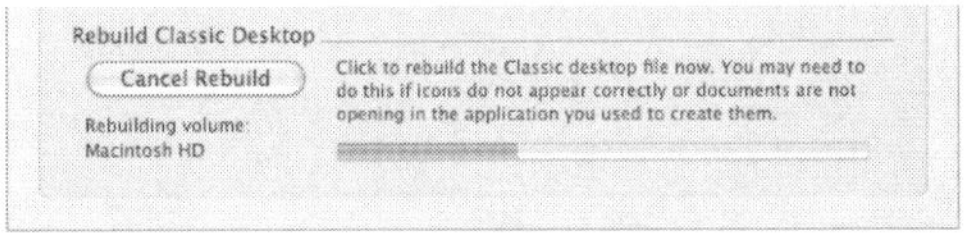

**Figure 35** A progress bar appears in the Advanced tab of the Classic preferences pane when you rebuild the Mac OS 9.x desktop.

## ✔ Tips

- You may want to rebuild the Mac OS 9.x desktop if icons are not properly displayed in the Classic environment or when starting your computer from Mac OS 9.x.

- You can use the Rebuild Desktop feature to rebuild the Mac OS 9.x desktop even if the Classic environment is not running.

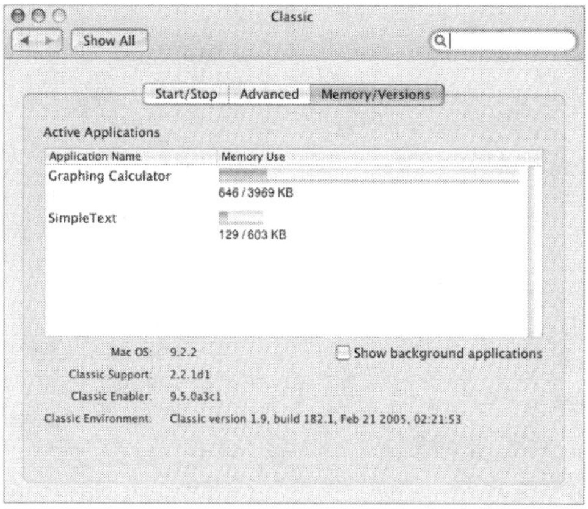

**Figure 36** The Memory/Versions area of the Classic preferences pane, with two applications running.

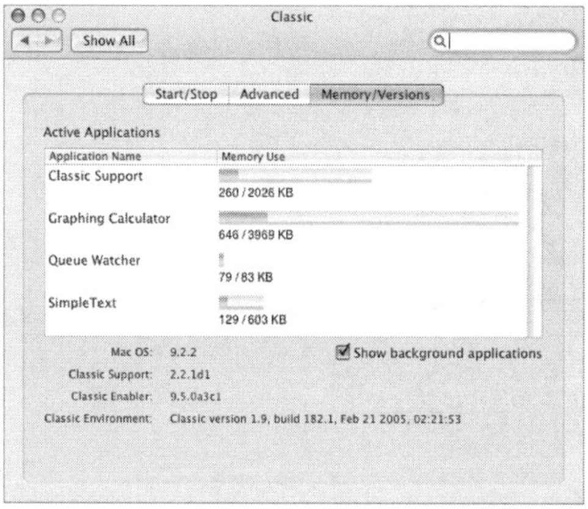

**Figure 37** You can include background applications in the list of active applications.

## To check Classic application memory usage & versions

1. Open the Classic preferences pane.

2. Click the Memory/Versions button. The window displays a list of all active Classic applications, as well as Mac OS and Classic version information (**Figure 36**).

3. To include background applications in the list (**Figure 37**), turn on the Show background applications check box.

## ✔ Tip

- If you have Mac OS 9.x experience, this window's list should look familiar—it's very much like the list that appears in the About this Mac window of a Macintosh running Mac OS 9.

# Using Classic Applications

When you open an icon for a Classic application or a document created with a Classic application, Mac OS X automatically starts the Classic environment and opens the application within it (**Figure 38**). The Mac OS X Aqua appearance disappears, replaced with the more sedate appearance of Mac OS 9.x.

While the Classic environment is in use, certain operations work differently than they do in Mac OS X:

◆ The Classic Apple (**Figure 39**) and File (**Figure 40**) menus contain different commands than they do in Mac OS X. In addition, Classic applications do not include a menu named after the application; the commands normally under that menu can be found on the File and Window (if available) menus.

◆ To print from the Classic environment, you must select and set up a printer with the Chooser (**Figure 41**). To open the Chooser, choose Apple > Chooser (**Figure 39**). The Print dialog (**Figure 42**) offers different options than those in Mac OS X.

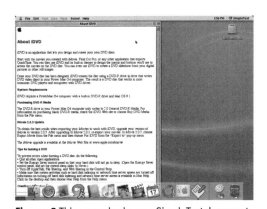

**Figure 38** This example shows a SimpleText document open in the Classic environment on a Mac OS X system.

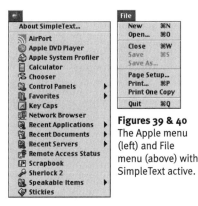

**Figures 39 & 40** The Apple menu (left) and File menu (above) with SimpleText active.

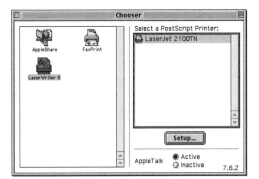

**Figure 41** Use the Chooser to set up and select a printer for printing documents from Classic applications.

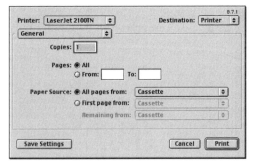

**Figure 42** The Classic Print dialog offers different options than the one for Mac OS X.

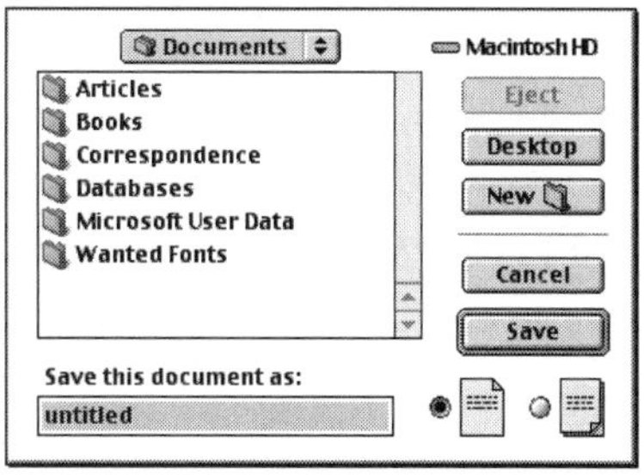

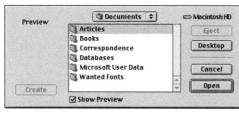

**Figure 43** The Classic Save As ...

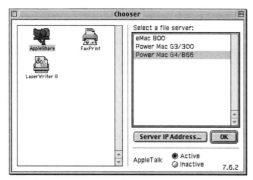

**Figure 44** ...and Open dialogs look and work a little differently than in Mac OS X.

◆ Although you use a Save As dialog (**Figure 43**) to save a document and an Open dialog (**Figure 44**) to open a file, the dialogs look and work differently than in Mac OS X.

◆ To connect to a networked computer from the Classic environment, you must open one of its disks with the Chooser (**Figure 45**). To open the Chooser, choose Apple > Chooser (**Figure 39**).

◆ System preferences can be set with control panels (**Figure 46**).

These are just a few differences between Mac OS X and the Classic environment. As you work with Classic applications, you're likely to find more.

*Continued on next page...*

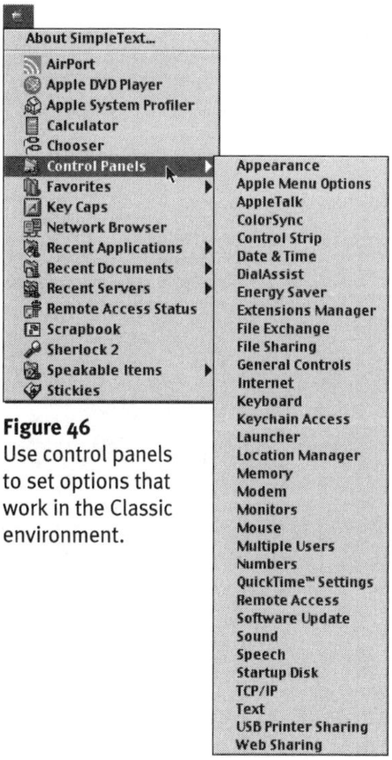

**Figure 45** You also use the Chooser to open other disks available via a network.

**Figure 46**
Use control panels to set options that work in the Classic environment.

**USING CLASSIC APPLICATIONS**

## ✔ Tips

■ Not all applications are supported by the Classic environment. If you try to open an application that was not written for Mac OS X and a dialog like the one in **Figure 47** appears, you'll have to restart your computer with Mac OS 9.x to use it.

■ You cannot access the Classic Finder from within Mac OS X. To use the Classic Finder, you must restart your computer from Mac OS 9.x, as instructed later in this chapter.

■ Unfortunately, it is impossible to explore all differences between Mac OS 9 and Mac OS X without going into a complete discussion of Mac OS 9.x. If you feel that you need more Mac OS 9.x information, consider picking up a copy of *Mac OS 9.1: Visual QuickStart Guide*, which covers Mac OS 9.1 in detail. Mac OS 9.2 is very similar.

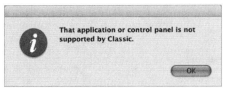

**Figure 47** If an application cannot be opened in the Classic environment, Mac OS X tells you.

# Starting Your Computer with Mac OS 9.x

If you plan to do a lot of work with Classic applications, you may want to start your computer with Mac OS 9.x and work without using Mac OS X at all. You can do this by selecting your Mac OS 9.x System Folder as the startup disk and restarting your computer.

## ✔ Tips

- Not all Macintosh models can start from Mac OS 9.x. If you bought your computer in 2003 or later, it probably can't. You can, however, run Mac OS 9 applications in the Classic environment.

- You may find that some large and complex Classic applications work a bit better on an older Macintosh model when you start with Mac OS 9.x.

- If you start your computer from Mac OS 9.x, you cannot use Mac OS X features and applications. You must restart with Mac OS X to use Mac OS X.

- All the differences discussed on the previous three pages apply when you start your computer from Mac OS 9.x *except* compatibility issues—all Mac OS 9.x applications will work when you start with Mac OS 9.x, even those that are not compatible with the Classic environment.

## To restart with Mac OS 9.x

1. Choose Apple > System Preferences (**Figure 20**), or click the System Preferences icon in the Dock (**Figure 21**).

2. In the System Preferences window that appears, click the Startup Disk icon.

3. In the Startup Disk preferences pane, select the folder icon for the Mac OS 9.x System Folder (**Figure 48**).

4. Click Restart.

5. If a dialog sheet like the one in **Figure 49** appears, click Save and Restart.

   Your computer restarts from the Mac OS 9.x System Folder (**Figure 50**).

## ✔ Tip

■ If a Mac OS 9.x System Folder does not appear in step 3, your computer cannot start from Mac OS 9.

## To restart with Mac OS X

1. Choose Apple > Control Panels > Startup Disk (**Figure 46**).

2. In the Startup Disk control panel, select the folder icon for the Mac OS X System folder (**Figure 51**).

3. Click Restart.

   Your computer restarts from the Mac OS X System folder.

## ✔ Tip

■ In step 2, you may have to click the triangle beside the name of your hard disk to display the System folders inside it (**Figure 51**).

**Figure 48** Mac OS X's Startup Disk preferences pane.

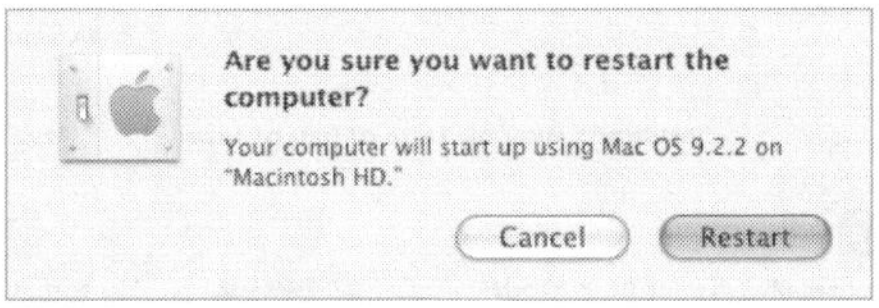

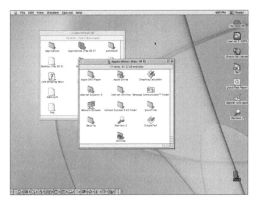

**Figure 49** If this dialog appears, click Save and Restart.

**Figure 50** The Mac OS 9.2.2 Finder.

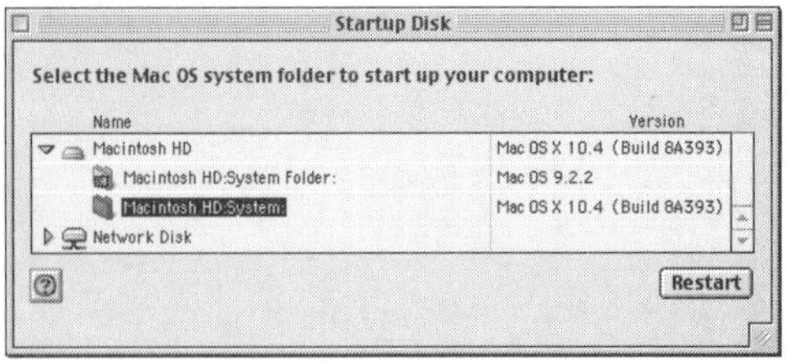

**Figure 51** Mac OS 9.2.2's Startup Disk control panel.

**Figure 52** The Introduction window for the Mac OS Setup Assistant.

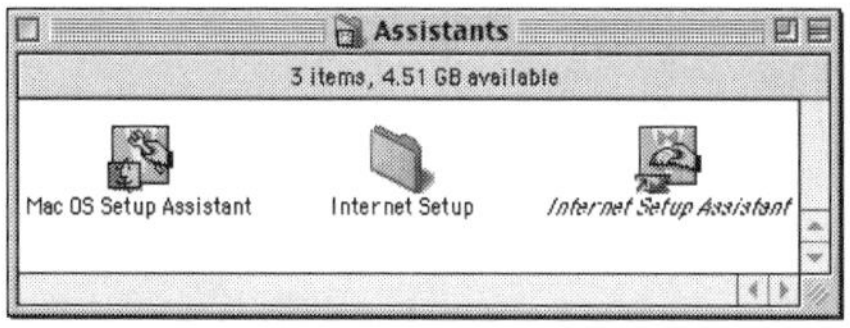

**Figure 53** If, for some reason, the Mac OS Setup Assistant doesn't launch automatically, you can open its icon to launch it.

# Configuring Mac OS 9.2

When you start your computer for the first time with Mac OS 9.2, the Mac OS Setup Assistant may automatically launch (**Figure 52**). This program steps you through the process of configuring Mac OS 9.2.

## ✔ Tip

- Use the Mac OS Setup Assistant to configure Mac OS 9.2, even if you are an experienced Mac OS user. The Setup Assistant can properly set all configuration options in Mac OS 9.2 control panels; setting control panels manually may interfere with the operation of Mac OS X.

## To use the Mac OS Setup Assistant

1. If the Mac OS Setup Assistant does not automatically appear when you first restart your computer with Mac OS 9.x, open its icon. You can find it in *Hard Disk Name*: Applications (Mac OS 9):Utilities: Assistants (**Figure 53**).

2. Read the instructions that appear in each screen of the Mac OS Setup Assistant and enter information when prompted. Click the right-pointing triangle button to move from one screen to the next.

## ✔ Tip

- If you need step-by-step instructions for configuring Mac OS 9.x with the Mac OS Setup Assistant, you can find it in *Mac OS 9.1: Visual QuickStart Guide* or online, on the companion Web site for *Mac OS X 10.4 Tiger: Visual QuickStart Guide*, www.langerbooks.com/macosquickstart/.

# Unix Basics for Mac OS X 19

## Unix & Mac OS X

In 1996, Apple affirmed the power of the Unix operating system and decided on a radical strategy for its new operating system: Apple would built Mac OS on top of Unix. The result of the decision, Mac OS X, was a complete overhaul of the old Macintosh system software, from the ground up.

What does that mean to you? It means that lurking beneath Mac OS X's attractive graphic user interface is a classic, popular command line interface. And, if you like typing commands and seeing text results in a little window onscreen, you can roll up your sleeves and give Unix a try, right on your Macintosh.

If you don't know any Unix commands, don't panic! Fortunately, you don't have to know a single keystroke of Unix to get the most out of your Macintosh. In a way, using Mac OS X is like driving your car: you don't need to know how to adjust your valves or rebuild your transmission to drive, do you? Likewise, you don't need to know any Unix commands to use your Mac, even though Unix is purring happily "under the hood."

This chapter gives you a glimpse of the world of Unix. It's not by any means a complete discussion, but it should get you familiar enough with Unix so you can enter Unix commands, when instructed, without fear.

It may also open a whole new world for you: a world of geeky command line instructions.

### ✔ Tip

■ Looking for more information about Unix than what you can find here? Check out *Unix: Visual QuickStart Guide, 2nd Edition* by Deborah Ray and Eric Ray, *Unix Advanced: Visual QuickPro Guide* by Chris Herborth, and *Unix for Mac OS X 10.4 Tiger: Visual QuickPro Guide* by Matisse Enzer.

# Unix Directories & Files

Before I start my discussion of Unix commands, let's take a look at the structure of the Unix file system.

## The directory system

Like the Macintosh file system, the Unix file system starts at the top level with a *root* directory, which can contain files and *subdirectories*. The root directory in Mac OS 9 and earlier is named after your hard disk. The root directory in Unix is named / (a slash without any other characters following it). Subdirectories below the root directory are indicated by listing them after the root slash. Each subdirectory is separated from the subdirectory it resides within by a slash.

For example, a home directory could be /Users/ronh. That means that in the root directory, /, is a subdirectory called *Users*, inside of which is a subdirectory called *ronh*.

## ✔ Tips

- On Mac OS, subdirectories are also known as *folders*.

- Unix uses a forward slash (/) to separate subdirectories, not a backslash (\) as in Windows or MS-DOS.

- I discuss the home directory later in this chapter. It is also covered in more detail in **Chapter 3**.

## File names

There are two things about Unix file names that you should be aware of.

First, although Unix file names are normally case-sensitive, in the Mac OS Extended file system (HFS+), file names are not case-sensitive. What does this mean to you? Just that you need to be aware of the case of file names, especially if you move files to another Unix

machine—for example, to a Unix Web server. Remember, on every other Unix machine in the known universe, upper- and lowercase are different. It's a good idea to pretend that this is the case on your Mac OS X machine, too.

Second, Unix file names do not normally include space characters. Although the Mac OS X Finder has no problem with spaces in file names, the underlying Unix uses spaces to separate commands, options, and operands. Spaces in Unix file names will cause you no end of grief because Unix will misinterpret them as operand separators in the commands you enter and your commands will perform unpredictably. If you need to enter a command that includes a file name with space characters, enclose the file name in single quotation marks so the system recognizes it as a single entity in the command.

## Invisible files

File names that begin with a dot (.) are *hidden*. Programs such as the shell, mail, and editors use these files to store preferences and other data.

Note that Unix has two unusually named subdirectories, one with a single dot (.) and another with double dots (..). These are shorthand ways for Unix to refer to "the current directory" and "the directory above this one" (also called the *parent directory*). The Unix operating system gives these plain files special treatment, as you'll learn later in this chapter in the discussion of the cd command.

## ✔ Tip

- I explain how to include invisible files in a file list later in this chapter.

# Terminal, the Shell, & Console

In the Utilities folder (**Figure 1**) inside the Applications folder is a utility called *Terminal* (**Figure 2**). This application is your window into the Unix world lurking deep inside Mac OS X. If you're old enough, you may remember using big, clunky video terminals to communicate with large mainframes. Terminal mimics the operation of those CRT terminals, but it uses your computer's screen, keyboard, and CPU instead of dumb-terminal hardware.

When you run Terminal, it connects to a communication process inside your Mac called a *shell*. The shell is a program that interprets human actions such as the typing of commands and the starting and stopping of jobs. It passes these requests to the computer and is responsible for sending the results of your actions to the Terminal window.

Each shell has its own set of features. The default shell that Mac OS X assigns to new accounts is called *bash*, which stands for Bourne-Again SHell (don't ask; there are far too many Unix in-jokes to deal with in this book). This is a change from Mac OS X 10.2 (Jaguar), which assigned *tcsh* (pronounced "t-shell") as the default shell.

Religious wars have been fought over which shell is best and the debate is certainly beyond the scope of this book. bash is a derivative of the *bourne* shell and tcsh is a derivative of the *csh* (c-shell). The bash shell is a powerful shell that includes many enhancements, some of which were borrowed from csh, such as a command line editor, file-name completion, and a command history. bash also contains a script command processor that allows you to build interactive programs and preprogrammed command series, similar to what you can do with AppleScript.

The Terminal application and the shell work together, allowing you to communicate with and control your computer. But they are separate entities. Terminal is responsible for accepting commands and displaying results, and the shell is responsible for interpreting and executing commands. You can use Terminal to talk to a variety of shells. You can open as many Terminal windows as you need—they each work independently.

Mac OS X also includes a utility called *Console* (**Figure 3**), which is an application that displays system messages. Keeping the console.log window open and watching it can tell you a lot about what's happening on your system.

## ✔ Tips

- bash is an extended version of the standard *sh*, or "bourne-shell," that's part of Unix. You can get more information about bash by typing man bash at the shell prompt. (More on the man command later.)

- If you are debugging programs, use Console to view error messages.

# To launch Terminal

Double-click the Terminal icon in the Utilities folder (**Figure 1**) inside the Applications folder. A Terminal window with a shell prompt appears (**Figure 2**).

## ✔ Tip

- The shell prompt shown in **Figure 2** ([eMac:~] ronh$) includes the following components:

  ▲ *Computer name* is the name of the computer you're logged into.

  ▲ *Directory* is the current directory. ~ (the tilde character) is Unix shorthand for your home directory.

  ▲ *User name* is your user name, which, in this example, is ronh.

# To launch Console

Double-click the Console icon in the Utilities folder (**Figure 1**) inside the Applications folder. The console.log window appears (**Figure 3**).

## ✔ Tip

- Console is discussed in a bit more detail in **Chapter 22**.

**Figure 1** The contents of the Utilities folder includes applications for working with Unix.

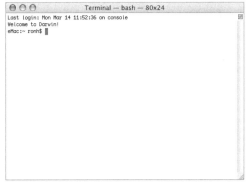

**Figure 2** A Terminal window with a shell prompt.

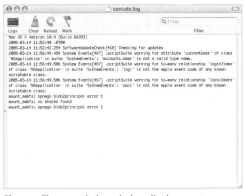

**Figure 3** The console.log window displays system messages.

# Unix Command Basics

You work with Unix by typing commands in a Terminal window at the shell prompt. Press [Return] after each command to enter it. The results of the command entry appear in the Terminal window, followed by a new shell prompt.

Most Unix commands can be used with options that make them do slightly different things. For instance, the ls command has 35 options in Mac OS X. To include an option with a command, enter the command followed by a space, a hyphen, and the option. For example, to use the l option with the ls command, you'd enter ls -l.

You can use more than one option at a time by stringing them together. Some commands, such as ls, let you put all the options together after a single hyphen. Other commands require that you use a separate hyphen for each option.

## ✔ Tips

- Typing commands in a command-line interface (CLI) offers advantages beyond what is possible with a graphical user interface (GUI) such as the Finder.

- If, while working with Unix commands in the Terminal window, you are either flooded with output that you'd like to stop or faced with a command that seems stuck, try pressing [Control][C] to break the current command. If that doesn't work, close the Terminal window and open a new one.

- Throughout this chapter, an ellipsis (...) in command syntax means that you can repeat the previous operand as many times as you wish. For instance, rather than saying cp *source-file1 source-file2 source-fileN target-directory*, I'll say cp *source-file ... target-directory*, meaning that you can include as many source files as you like in the command.

# Listing Directory Contents with the ls Command

ls is one of the most basic Unix commands. It enables you to list the contents of a directory.

## ✔ Tip

- ■ The commands in this section assume that the shell prompt is displaying your home directory (~).

## To list the contents of your home directory

Type ls and press [Return].

A list of the contents of your home directory appears (**Figure 4**).

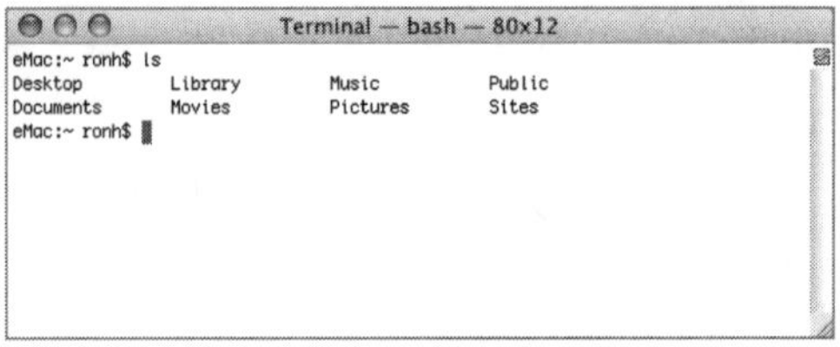

## To list the contents of a subdirectory

Type ls followed by the subdirectory name (for example, ls Library) and press [Return].

A list of the contents of the subdirectory you typed appears (**Figure 5**).

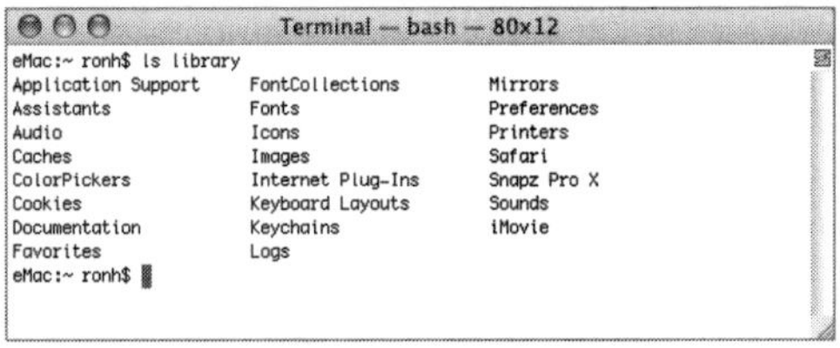

## To view a long directory listing

Type ls -l and press [Return].

A list of the contents of your home directory, including permissions, owner, size, and modification date information, appears (**Figure 6**).

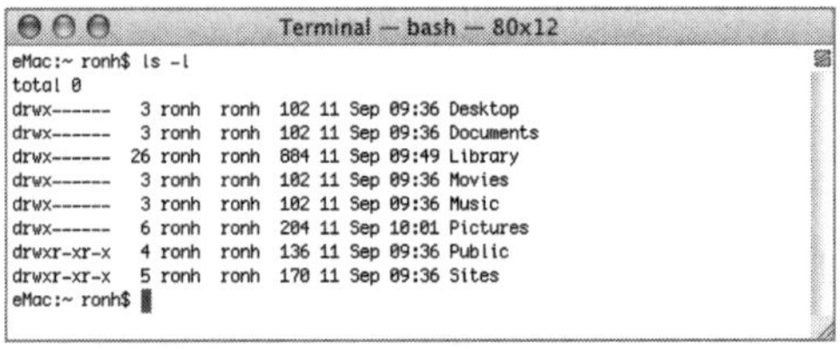

## ✔ Tip

- ■ I tell you more about permissions later in this chapter.

## To include invisible items in a directory listing

Type ls -a and press [Return].

A list of the contents of your home directory, including invisible items, appears (**Figure 7**).

**Figure 4** A simple directory listing using the **ls** command.

**Figure 5** A listing for the library subdirectory.

**Figure 6** The long version of a directory listing includes permission, owner, file size, and modification date information.

**Figure 7** A directory listing that includes invisible subdirectories.

**Table 1**

| man pages Sections | |
| --- | --- |
| Section | Type of Command or File |
| 1 | User commands |
| 2 | System calls |
| 3 | Library routines |
| 4 | I/O and special files |
| 5 | Administrative files |
| 6 | Games |
| 7 | Miscellaneous |
| 8 | Administrative and maintenance commands |

# Viewing man pages

One important Unix command tells you everything you ever wanted to know about Unix commands and files: the man command. It displays information about commands and files documented in the on-line manual pages. These *man pages* are included with every version of Unix.

The man pages present information about a command one page at a time. You can use keystrokes to advance to the next line or page of the man pages. You must quit the man pages feature to enter other Unix commands.

Like a book, man pages are broken into chapters called *sections* (**Table 1**). Each section is designed for a specific type of user. For example, a programmer will be interested in different man pages than a user or a system administrator. There are some man pages that document identical sounding items yet are intended for different users.

## ✔ Tip

■ The man pages for commands and files can be lengthy and complex. Don't worry if you don't understand everything on a man page. Just take what you need. As you understand more about Unix, more will make sense.

VIEWING MAN PAGES

## To view man pages for a command

Type man followed by the name of the command (for example, man ls), and press [Return].

The first page of the reference manual for the command appears (**Figure 8**).

## To view the next line of a man page

Press [Return].

The manual advances one line.

## To view the next page

Press [Spacebar].

The manual advances one page (**Figure 9**).

## To quit man pages

Press [Q].

Terminal returns you to the shell prompt.

## To get man pages for man

Type man man and press [Return].

The first page of the reference manual for the online manual appears (**Figure 10**).

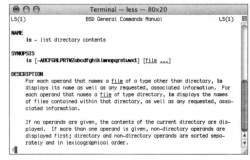

**Figure 8** The first man page for the **ls** command.

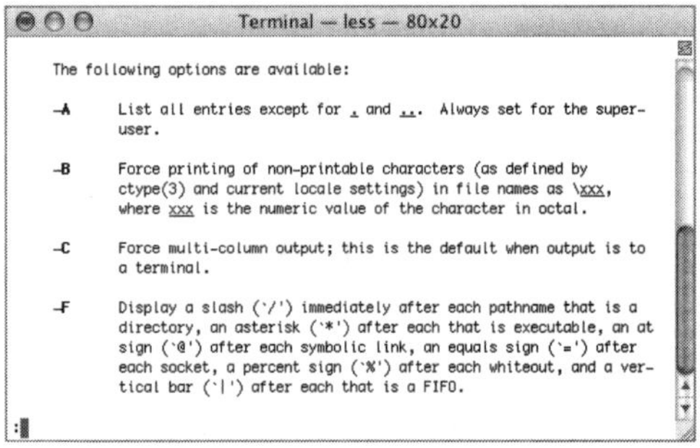

**Figure 9** The second page for the **ls** command.

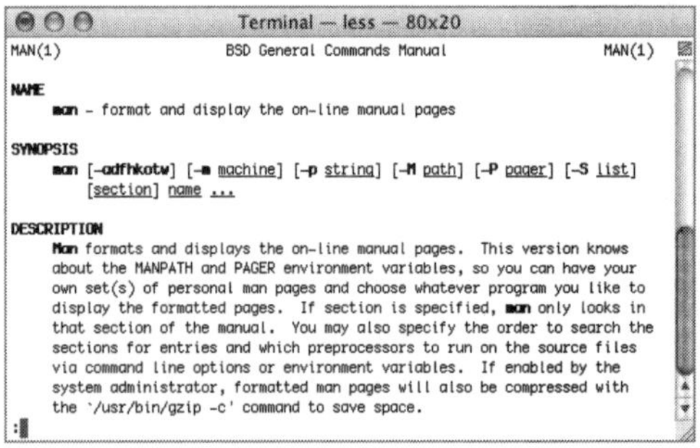

**Figure 10** The first man page for **man**.

# Moving Around with the cd Command

Up to now, you haven't moved around in the directory tree. You've been fixed in place in your home directory. Changing directories is easy—just use the cd (change directory) command, followed by the destination you want to move to.

You have two ways to indicate a destination: with an *absolute path* or a *relative path*.

◆ An absolute path specifies the location of a file or subdirectory, starting at the root directory and working downward.

◆ A relative path specifies the location of a file or subdirectory starting at your present location.

Let's look at an example. Suppose I'm currently in my home directory (/Users/ronh) and I want to move to the /usr/bin directory. I could specify the destination with its absolute path: /usr/bin. Or I could use the relative path to go up two directories to the root and then down two directories to the one I want. This is where the special "double-dot" (..) directory name that I discussed earlier comes into play; it indicates the directory above the current one. So the relative path from my home directory to /usr/bin would be ../../usr/bin.

## ✔ Tips

■ The cd command does not have any options and has no man page of its own because it's built in to the shell. You can find out more about the shell by using the man pages; enter man bash and press ⌐Return⌐.

■ Absolute paths, which always start with a forward slash (/), work no matter where you are located in the Unix file system because they start from the root directory.

■ Relative paths are especially useful if you are deep inside the directory structure and want to access a file or subdirectory just one level up. For example, it's a lot easier to type ../images/flower.jpg than /Users/ronh/Documents/ClipArt/Plants/Color/images/flower.jpg—and it's a lot easier to remember, too!

## To change directories using an absolute path

Type cd followed by the absolute path to the directory you want (for example, cd /usr/bin) and press Return.

The current directory changes and the path to the directory appears in the shell prompt (**Figure 11**).

## To change directories using a relative path

Type cd followed by the relative path to the directory you want (for example, from your home directory, type cd ../../usr/bin) and press Return.

The current directory changes and the path to the directory appears in the shell prompt (**Figure 12**).

## To move to a subdirectory using an absolute path

Type cd followed by the absolute path to the subdirectory (for example, cd /Users/ronh/Sites) and press Return.

The current directory changes and the path to the directory appears in the shell prompt (**Figure 13**).

## To move to a subdirectory using a relative path

Type cd followed by the relative path to the subdirectory (for example, from your home directory, type cd Sites) and press Return.

The current directory changes and the path to the directory appears in the shell prompt (**Figure 14**).

```
eMac:~ ronh$ cd /usr/bin
eMac:/usr/bin ronh$
```

**Figure 11** Here's how you can change the current directory to /usr/bin using an absolute path...

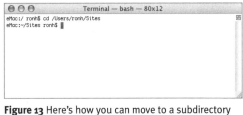

```
eMac:/ ronh$ cd ../../usr/bin
eMac:/usr/bin ronh$
```

**Figure 12** ...or a relative path from your home directory.

```
eMac:~ ronh$ cd /Users/ronh/Sites
eMac:~/Sites ronh$
```

**Figure 13** Here's how you can move to a subdirectory using an absolute path...

```
eMac:~ ronh$ cd Sites
eMac:~/Sites ronh$
```

**Figure 14** ...or with a relative reference.

## ✔ Tip

- Do not include a forward slash (/) before a subdirectory name. Doing so tells Unix to start at the root directory (as if you were entering an absolute path) and could result in an error message (**Figure 15**).

THE cd COMMAND

Terminal — bash — 80x12
eMac:~ ronh$ cd /Sites
-bash: cd: /Sites: No such file or directory
eMac:~ ronh$

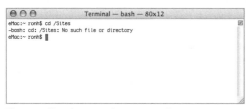

**Figure 15** If you enter an incorrect path, an error message appears.

Terminal — bash — 80x12
eMac:~ ronh$ cd Sites
eMac:~/Sites ronh$ ls
images index.html
eMac:~/Sites ronh$

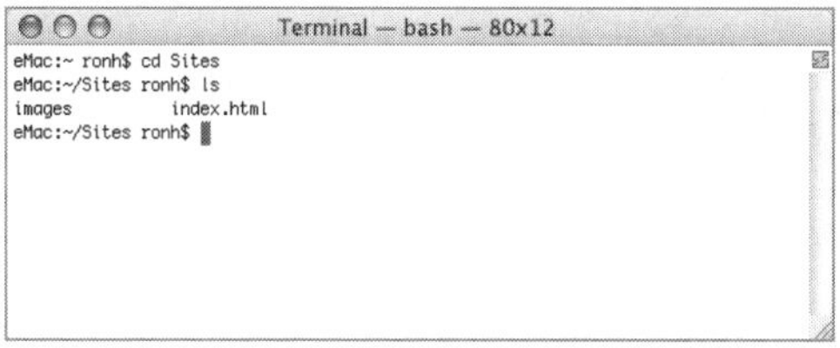

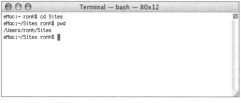

**Figure 16** Once you're in a directory, using the **ls** command by itself displays the contents of that directory.

Terminal — bash — 80x12
eMac:~ ronh$ cd Sites
eMac:~/Sites ronh$ pwd
/Users/ronh/Sites
eMac:~/Sites ronh$

**Figure 17** The **pwd** command displays the complete path to the current directory.

### To list the contents of the current directory

Type ls and press Return.

The contents of the directory appear in the Terminal window (**Figure 16**).

### To return to your home directory

Type cd (without any arguments) and press Return.

The current directory changes to your home directory and the tilde (~) character appears in the shell prompt.

#### ✔ Tip

- The tilde character is Unix shorthand for "home directory." So, for example, if you wanted to change to the home directory for user name rosef, you could type cd ~rosef.

## Getting the Directory Location with the pwd Command

You might be wondering how to find out exactly where you are after doing many cd commands. Unix has a spiffy little command just for this: pwd (present working directory).

### To learn the current directory

Type pwd and press Return.

The complete path to the current directory appears, followed by the shell prompt (**Figure 17**).

# Wildcards in File Names & Directories

One frustrating activity in Mac OS 9.x and earlier was working with a group of files. Other than Shift-clicking or dragging to select the group, you had no good way to select group items by name—for example, to select all files that started with the characters *file* and ended with the characters *.doc*.

Unix, however, makes this easy by enabling you to use three special characters as wildcards:

◆ **Asterisk** (*), which is referred to as star, is a wildcard for zero or more characters—any character!

◆ **Question mark** (?) is a wildcard for any single character.

◆ **Brackets** ([ and ]) around one or more characters act as a wildcard for any of the enclosed characters.

You can place the wildcard wherever you want in the name you are searching for. As you can imagine, wildcards are powerful tools for selecting or listing files or subdirectories.

## ✔ Tip

■ The brackets wildcard can include individual characters, such as [ABCD] or character ranges, such as [A-G] or [1-6].

## Using wildcards

The best way to explain how you can use wildcards is to show you some examples.

Suppose your Documents subdirectory contained the following subdirectories and files:

| | | |
|---|---|---|
| dir1 | file03.doc | file12.txt |
| dir2 | file04.doc | file20.txt |
| dir30 | file05.doc | file21.txt |
| file01.doc | file10.txt | file38.txt |
| file02.doc | file11.txt | file39.txt |

```
● ● ●              Terminal — bash — 80x12
eMac:~/Documents ronh$ ls file*
file01.doc    file04.doc    file11.txt    file21.txt
file02.doc    file05.doc    file12.txt    file38.txt
file03.doc    file10.txt    file20.txt    file39.txt
eMac:~/Documents ronh$ ls file*doc
file01.doc    file02.doc    file03.doc    file04.doc    file05.doc
eMac:~/Documents ronh$ ls *txt
file10.txt    file12.txt    file21.txt    file39.txt
file11.txt    file20.txt    file38.txt
eMac:~/Documents ronh$ ▌
```

**Figure 18** These examples show how you can use the asterisk wildcard to list specific files in a directory.

```
● ● ●              Terminal — bash — 80x12
eMac:~/Documents ronh$ ls file1?.txt
file10.txt    file11.txt    file12.txt
eMac:~/Documents ronh$ ls file?0.txt
file10.txt    file20.txt
eMac:~/Documents ronh$ ls dir?
dir1:

dir2:
eMac:~/Documents ronh$ ls file?1.*
file01.doc    file11.txt    file21.txt
eMac:~/Documents ronh$ ▌
```

**Figure 19** These examples show the question mark wildcard in action. (Both dir1 and dir2 are empty directories; that's why no files are listed for them.)

```
● ● ●              Terminal — bash — 80x12
eMac:~/Documents ronh$ ls file1[12].txt
file11.txt    file12.txt
eMac:~/Documents ronh$ ls file[01][02].*
file02.doc    file10.txt    file12.txt
eMac:~/Documents ronh$ ▌
```

**Figure 20** Here are two examples for the bracket wildcard.

Here are some examples to illustrate the asterisk wildcard (**Figure 18**):

◆ To work with all the files that start with the characters *file*, you enter file*.

◆ To work with all the files that begin with the characters *file* and end with the characters *doc*, you enter file*doc.

◆ To work with all the files that end with the characters *txt*, you enter *txt.

These examples illustrate the question mark wildcard (**Figure 19**):

◆ To work with files named *file10.txt*, *file11.txt*, and *file12.txt*, you enter file1?.txt.

◆ To work with files named *file10.txt* and *file20.txt*, you enter file?0.txt.

◆ To work with subdirectories named *dir1* and *dir2*, you enter dir?.

◆ To work with files named *file01.doc*, *file11.txt*, and *file21.txt*, you enter file?1.*. (Okay, so that one uses two wildcards.)

And these examples illustrate the brackets wildcard in action (**Figure 20**):

◆ To work with files named *file11.txt* and *file12.txt* (but not *file10.txt*), you enter file1[12].txt.

◆ To work with files named *file01.doc*, *file10.txt*, and *file11.txt*, you enter file[01][01].*. (Yes, that's another one with multiple wildcard characters.)

## To view a directory list using a wildcard

Type ls followed by the search string for the files or directories you want to display (see previous examples) and press [Return].

A list containing only the files and directories that match the search string appear (**Figures 18**, **19**, and **20**).

WILDCARDS IN FILE NAMES & DIRECTORIES

# Copying & Moving Files

Unix also includes commands for copying and moving files: cp and mv. These commands enable you to copy or move one or more source files to a target file or directory.

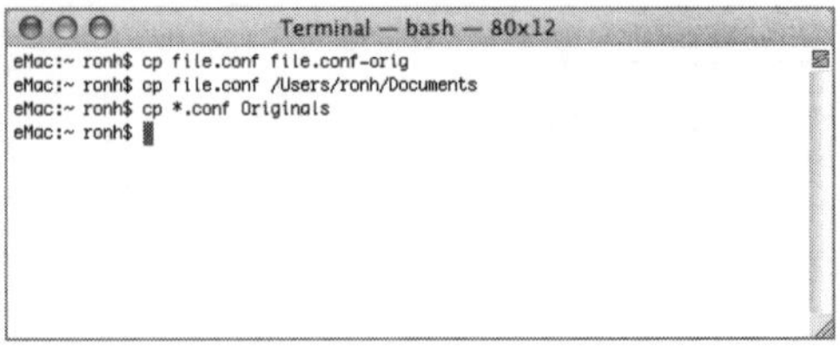

Figure 21 Here's the cp command in action.

## ✔ Tips

- Why copy a file? Usually, to make a backup. For instance, before you edit a configuration file, you should create a backup copy of the original. This way you can revert back to the original if your edits "break" something in the file.

- The mv command can also be used to rename a file.

- The cp and mv commands support several options. You can learn more about them in the man pages for these commands. Type man cp or man mv and press (Return) to view each command's man pages.

- Unix does not confirm that a file has been copied or moved when you correctly enter a command (**Figures 21** and **22**). To check to see if a file has been copied or moved to the correct destination, you can use the ls command to get a listing for the target directory. The ls command is covered earlier in this chapter.

## To copy a file to the same directory

Type cp *source-file target-file* and press (Return) (**Figure 21**).

For example, cp file.conf file.conf-orig would duplicate the file named *file.conf* and assign the name *file.conf-orig* to the duplicate copy.

## ✔ Tips

- The *source-file* and *target-file* names must be different.

- The *source-file* operand can be a file or a directory.

```
●  ●  ●           Terminal — bash — 80x12
eMac:~ ronh$ mv file.conf file.conf-backup
eMac:~ ronh$ mv file.conf-backup Documents
eMac:~ ronh$ mv file.conf-orig Documents/file.conf-backup2
eMac:~ ronh$ █
```

**Figure 22** Here's the **mv** command in use.

## To copy files to another directory

Type cp *source-file ... target-directory* and press
Return (**Figure 21**).

For example, cp file.conf /Users/ronh/Documents
would copy the file named *file.conf* in the
current directory to the directory named
*Documents* in my home folder.

## To copy files using a wildcard

Type cp followed by the wildcard search
string for the source file and the name of the
target directory and press Return (**Figure 21**).

For example, cp *.conf Originals would copy all
files ending with *.conf* in the current directory
to the subdirectory named *Originals*.

## To rename a file

Type mv *source target* and press Return
(**Figure 22**).

For example, mv file.conf file.conf-backup
would rename *file.conf* as *file.conf-backup*.

## To move files to another directory

Type mv *source ... directory* and press Return
(**Figure 22**).

For example, mv file.conf Documents
would move the file named *file.conf* in
the current directory to the subdirectory
named *Documents*.

## To move a file to another directory & rename it

Type mv *source directory/filename* and press
Return (**Figure 22**).

For example, mv file.conf-orig Documents/
file.conf-backup2 would move the file named
*file.conf-orig* in the current directory to the
subdirectory named *Documents* and name
it *file.conf-backup2* in its new location.

COPYING & MOVING FILES

# Making Symbolic Links with ln

Mac OS enables you to make aliases to files. It should come as no surprise that Unix does, too. But in Unix, aliases are called *symbolic links*. And rather than use a menu command or shortcut key to create them, you use the ln (make links) command with its -s option.

**Figure 23** These examples show the commands for creating symbolic links to a file and a directory.

## ✔ Tips

■ Mac OS aliases and Unix symbolic links make it convenient to access deeply buried files or to organize files differently than the way the operating system organizes them.

■ If you omit the -s option, the ln command creates a hard link. Hard links can't cross file systems (or partitions) and can't normally refer to directories.

■ Unix does not tell you if the source file to which you want to create a symbolic link does not exist. As a result, it's possible to create an alias that doesn't point to anything.

■ You can learn more about other options for the ln command in its man pages. Type man ln and press Return to display them.

## To make a link to a file

Type ln -s *source-file target-file* and press Return (**Figure 23**).

For example, ln -s file1 alias1 creates an alias called *alias1* that points to the file called *file1*. In this example, both files (the source and the target) are in the current directory.

## To make a link to a directory

Type ln -s *source-directory target-file* and press Return (**Figure 23**).

For example, ln -s ~ronh/Library/Favorites ./Favs creates a alias called *Favs* in the current directory (./) that points to the directory called *Favorites*, which is in the directory called *Library*, inside the home directory (~) of the user ronh.

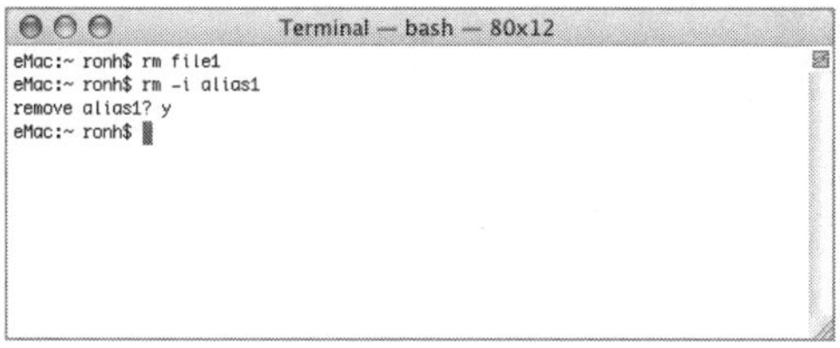

**Figure 24** The **rm** command in action, with and without the **-i** option.

# Removing Files & Directories with rm & rmdir

Unix includes two commands that you can use to delete files and directories: rm (remove) and rmdir (remove directory).

## ✖ Warning!

■ rm may be the most dangerous command in Unix. Because Unix doesn't have a Trash that lets you recover mistakenly deleted files, when you delete a file, it's gone forever.

## ✔ Tips

■ There are two options that you may want to use with the rm command:

▲ -i tells the rm command to ask permission before deleting each file (**Figure 24**). You must press Y and then Return at each prompt to delete the file. This is especially useful when using the rm command with wildcard characters, since it can help prevent files from being accidentally deleted.

▲ -R, which stands for *recursively*, tells the rm command to delete everything within a directory, including its sub-directories and their contents. The -R option can be very dangerous; you may want to use it in conjunction with the -i option to confirm each deletion.

■ The rm command's *file* operand can be a file or a directory name. If you are deleting a non-empty directory, you must use the -R (recursive) option.

■ You can learn more about the rm and rmdir commands and their options on their man pages. Type man rm or man rmdir and press Return to view each command's man pages.

USING rm & rmdir

## To remove a file

Type rm *file* ... and press Return. For example, rm file1 removes the file named *file1* from the current directory (**Figure 24**).

## To remove files using a wildcard character

Type rm followed by the wildcard search string and press Return. For example, rm *.bak removes all files ending with *.bak* from the current directory.

## To remove all files in a directory

Type rm * and press Return (**Figure 25**).

### ✔ Tips

- You may want to include the -i option (for example, rm -i *) to confirm each deletion so you do not delete files by mistake.

- Since the rm command cannot remove directories without the -R option, an error message may appear when you use the rm * command string in a directory that contains subdirectories (**Figure 25**).

## To remove all files & subdirectories in a directory

Type rm -R * and press Return (**Figure 25**).

### ✖ Warning!

- This is the most dangerous command in all of Unix. If you enter this command in the root directory (/), you will erase the entire disk (if you have permission). Use this command with care!

### ✔ Tip

- You may want to include the -i option (for example, rm -Ri *; **Figure 25**) to confirm each deletion so you do not delete files or subdirectories by mistake.

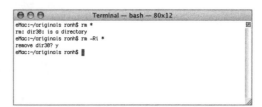

**Figure 25** Two more examples of the **rm** command. In the first, the **rm \*** command string deletes all files in the directory, but not the subdirectory named dir30. In the second, the **-Ri** options delete all contents with confirmation; the only item still in the directory is the subdirectory named dir30.

**Figure 26** This example shows two attempts to delete a subdirectory. The first, using the **rmdir** command, is not successful because the directory is not empty. The second, using the **rm -R** command string, does the job.

**Figure 27** In this example, the **mkdir** command is used to create three new subdirectories.

## To remove an empty directory

Type rmdir *directory* ... and press ⌨Return. For example, rmdir Originals removes the subdirectory named *Originals* in the current directory (**Figure 26**).

## ✔ Tip

- The rmdir command will result in an error message if the directory you are trying to remove is not empty (**Figure 26**).

## To remove a directory & its contents

Type rm -R *directory* and press ⌨Return. For example, rm -R Originals removes the directory named *Originals* even if it is not empty (**Figure 26**).

# Creating a New Directory with mkdir

You can also create new directories. You'll do this with the mkdir command.

## ✔ Tip

- You can learn more about the mkdir command and its options on its man pages. Type man mkdir and press ⌨Return to view the command's man pages.

## To create a new directory

Type mkdir *directory-name* ... and press ⌨Return. For example, mkdir Project1 Project2 Project3 makes three new subdirectories in the current directory: *Project1*, *Project2*, and *Project3* (**Figure 27**).

# Viewing File Contents

Unix offers a few tools for examining the contents of files:

- ◆ cat (concatenate) lists one or more files to the Terminal window.

- ◆ less outputs files in page-size chunks, enabling you to view the contents of large files one screen at a time.

- ◆ head displays the first lines of a file.

- ◆ tail displays the last lines of a file.

- ◆ wc displays a count of the number of lines, words, and characters in a file.

## ✔ Tip

- ■ To learn more about these commands, check out their man pages. Type man cat, man less, man head, man tail, or man wc and press ⌈Return⌋ to display the command's man page.

## To list a file's contents

Type cat *file* ... (for example, cat example.rtf) and press ⌈Return⌋. cat lists the entire file in the Terminal window without stopping (**Figure 28**).

## ✔ Tips

- ■ Do not use cat to list binary executable files (that is, any non-text file, such as an application). Because they contain many nonprintable characters, they could cause Terminal to act strangely. If this happens, close the Terminal window and open a new one.

- ■ If you specify more than one file, cat lists them one after another without any indication that it has finished one file and started another one.

**Figure 28** In this example, the **cat** command is used to view the contents of an RTF file. The first few lines of the file—which you wouldn't see when viewing the file with an RTF-compatible word processor (such as TextEdit)—are formatting codes.

- ■ I explain how to use the cat command and output redirection to combine multiple files and output them to a new file later in this chapter.

- ■ If you use cat to list a long file, Terminal may not be able to store all of the lines. You may prefer to use the more command to output the file in page-sized chunks. You can learn more about the more command by typing man more.

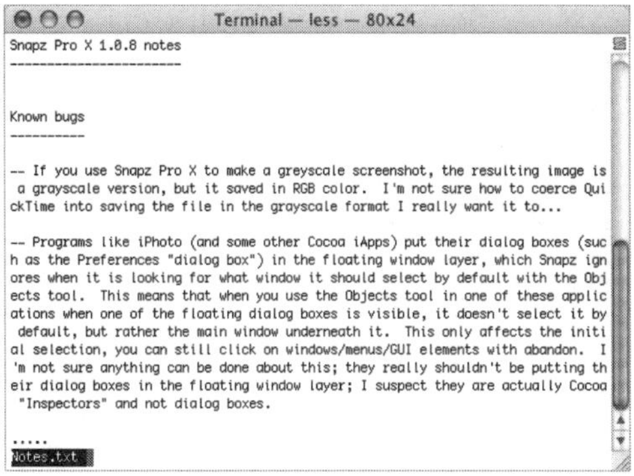

**Figure 29** The **less** command in action.

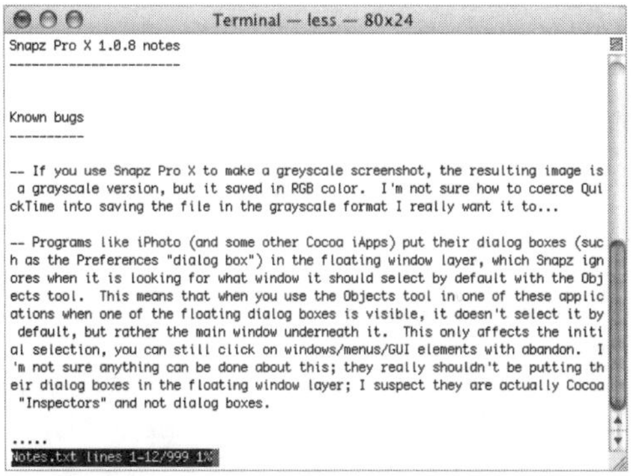

**Figure 30** In this example, the **-m** option was used with the **less** command. See how the prompt at the bottom of the page changes?

## To page through the contents of a file

1. Type less *file* (for example, less Notes.txt) and press Return. The first page of the file appears in the Terminal window (**Figure 29**). The last line tells you the name of the file.

2. Use one of the following keystrokes:
   ▲ Press Spacebar to advance one screen.
   ▲ Press Return to advance one line.
   ▲ Press D to advance one half screen.

3. Repeat step 2 to view the entire file.

   *or*

   Press Q to return to the shell prompt.

## ✔ Tips

- When you reach the end of the file, you must press Q to return to the shell prompt.

- You can use the -m option to display a more instructive prompt at the bottom of the screen (**Figure 30**).

- You can also use wildcard characters to specify multiple files. When you reach the end of each file, tell less to proceed to the next file by typing :n. Less will display the file names at the start of each file.

- Like the man command discussed earlier in this chapter, the less command is a *pager*. A pager displays information one screen at a time, enabling you to page through it.

USING less

## To show the first lines of a file

Type head [-n *count*] *file* ... and press Return, where *count* is the number of lines at the beginning of the file that you want to display. For example, head -n 15 sample.txt displays the first 15 lines of the file named *sample.txt* (**Figure 31**).

### ✔ Tips

- If you omit the -n *count* operand, head displays the first ten lines of the file.

- You can specify multiple files. If you do, head displays the file names at the start of each file.

## To show the last lines of a file

Type tail [-n *count*] *file* ... and press Return, where *count* is the number of lines at the end of the file that you want to display. For example, tail -n 15 sample.txt displays the last 15 lines of the file named *sample.txt* (**Figure 32**).

### ✔ Tips

- If you omit the -n *count* operand, tail displays the last ten lines of the file.

- You can specify multiple files. If you do, tail displays the file names at the start of each file.

- The -f option (for example tail -f log.txt) displays the last lines of the file but prevents the tail command from terminating. Instead, tail waits for the file to grow. As new lines are added to the file, tail immediately displays them. You may find this useful if you want to watch a log file grow and see the latest entries as they are added. You may also use it to watch an error log file when you are debugging a program. You cannot use the -f option if you specify multiple files; to monitor multiple files with the tail command, open multiple Terminal windows.

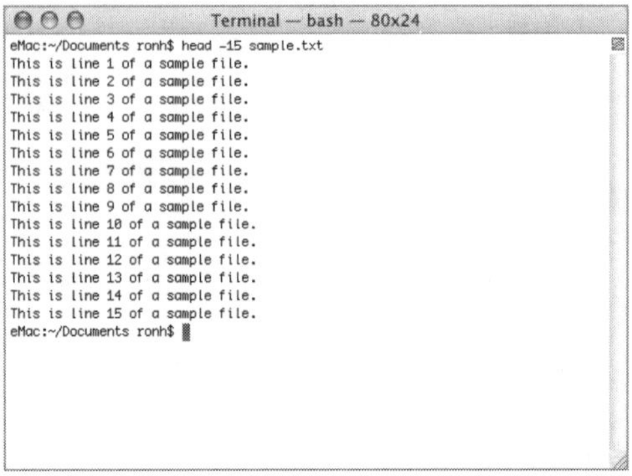

**Figure 31** The **head** command displays the first bunch of lines in a file...

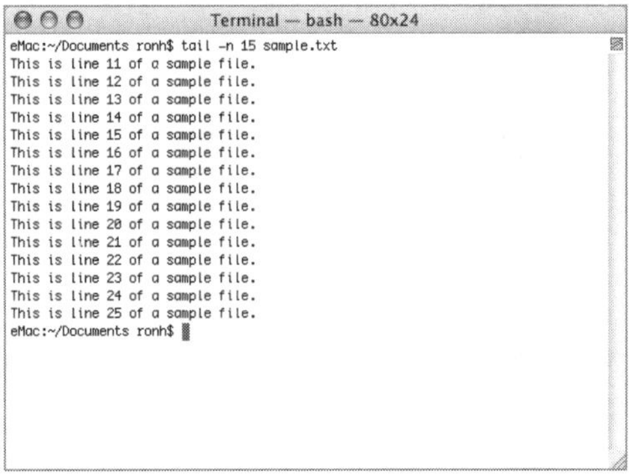

**Figure 32** ...and the **tail** command displays the last bunch.

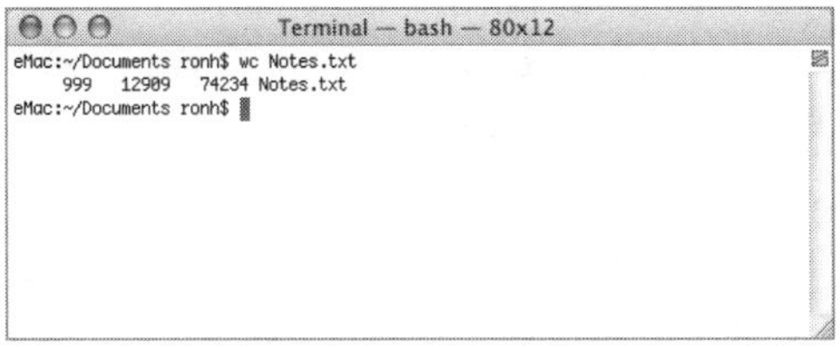

**Figure 33** The **wc** command shows the number of lines, words, and characters in a file.

## To count the lines, words, & characters in a file

Type wc *file* ... (for example, wc Notes.txt), and press (Return). The number of lines, words, and characters (or bytes) in the file you specified is displayed in the Terminal window (**Figure 33**).

## ✔ Tip

- You can use any combination of options for the wc command:

  -c displays the number of characters

  -w displays the number of words

  -l displays the number of lines

  With no options, wc displays all three pieces of information in this order: lines, words, characters, file name (**Figure 33**).

USING WC

# Creating & Editing Files with pico

Although it's easy to use a GUI text editor in Mac OS X, it's a good idea to know a little about Unix text editors and how they work. This way, if you ever find yourself sitting in front of a Unix system, you'll have a chance at making it usable.

Unix offers a number of text editors: the easy-to-use pico, the ever-present vi, and the geek-favorite emacs. Which one you use is a personal decision: Each has strengths and weaknesses. It is far beyond the scope of this chapter (or book) to help you master any one of these, let alone all three. Because pico is the easiest Unix text editor to use, I'll introduce it here.

## ✔ Tips

- The emacs and vi text editors are so powerful and complex that entire books have been written about them. You can learn a little more about them in their somewhat inadequate man pages; type man emacs or man vi and press Return to view them.

- pico is normally a piece of the pine email package, but Apple did not make pine part of the standard Mac OS X Unix installation. You can download the entire pine-pico package for Mac OS X from www.osxgnu.org/software/Email/pine/.

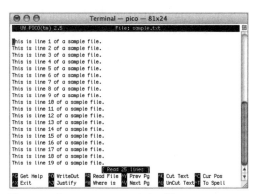

**Figure 34 pico** can open an existing file...

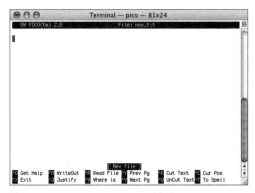

**Figure 35** ...or create a new one with the name you specify.

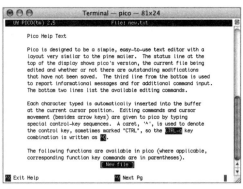

**Figure 36** The beginning of **pico's** onscreen help.

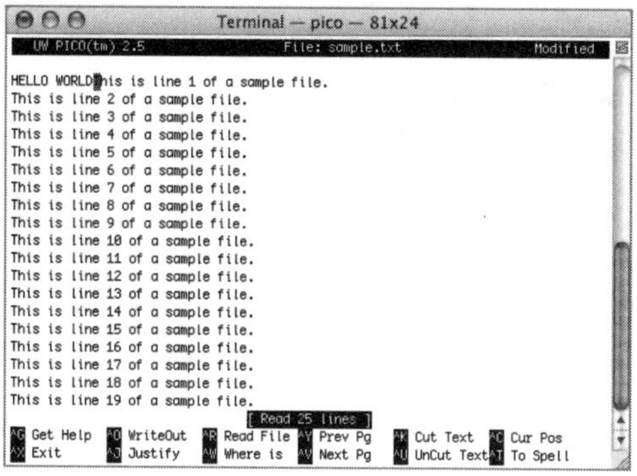

**Figure 37** Text is inserted at the cursor.

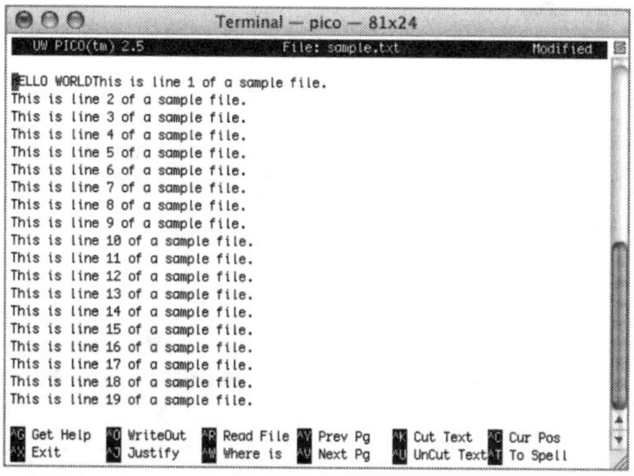

**Figure 38** Position the cursor on the character you want to delete.

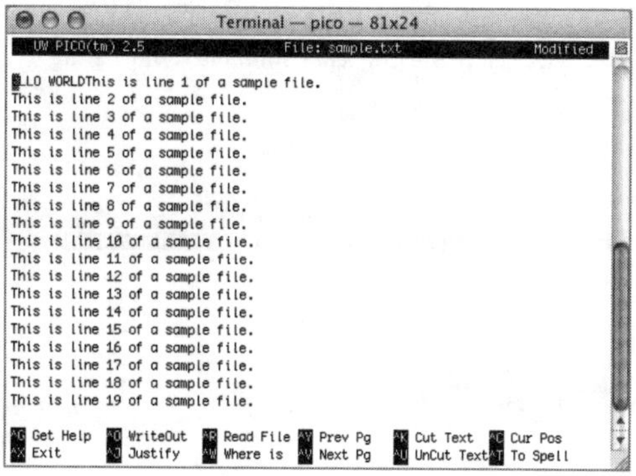

**Figure 39** Text at the cursor is deleted.

## To open a file with pico

Type pico *file* (for example, pico sample.txt) and press [Return].

pico starts up in the Terminal window. If you entered the name of an existing file, the first 25 lines of the file appear (**Figure 34**). If you entered the name of a file that does not already exist, pico creates a new file for you (**Figure 35**). Either way, the pico menu appears at the bottom of the window. The cursor appears as a gray box at the beginning of the file.

## To use pico menu commands

Press the keystroke for the command you want. Each command includes [Control] (indicated by ^). For example, you can view onscreen help by pressing [Control][G] (**Figure 36**).

## To navigate through text

To move one character in any direction, press the corresponding arrow key.

*Or*

To move to the previous or next page, press [Control][Y] or [Control][V].

## To insert text

1.  Position the cursor where you want to insert character(s) (**Figure 34**).

2.  Type the character(s) you want to insert. The new text is inserted (**Figure 37**).

## To delete text

1.  Position the cursor on the character you want to delete (**Figure 38**).

2.  Press [Control][D]. The character disappears (**Figure 39**).

**USING pico**

537

## To cut & paste text

1. Use the arrow keys to position the cursor at the beginning of the text you want to cut (**Figure 34**).

2. Press [Control][Shift][^]. *[Mark Set]* appears near the bottom of the window (**Figure 40**).

3. Use the arrow keys to position the cursor at the end of the block you want to cut. Text between the starting point and cursor turns black (**Figure 41**).

4. Press [Control][K] (Cut Text). The selected text disappears (**Figure 42**).

5. Position the cursor where you want to paste the text (**Figure 43**).

6. Press [Control][U] (Uncut Text). The cut text appears at the cursor (**Figure 44**).

## ✔ Tip

■ *[Mark Set]* (**Figure 40**) indicates that you have marked the beginning of a text selection.

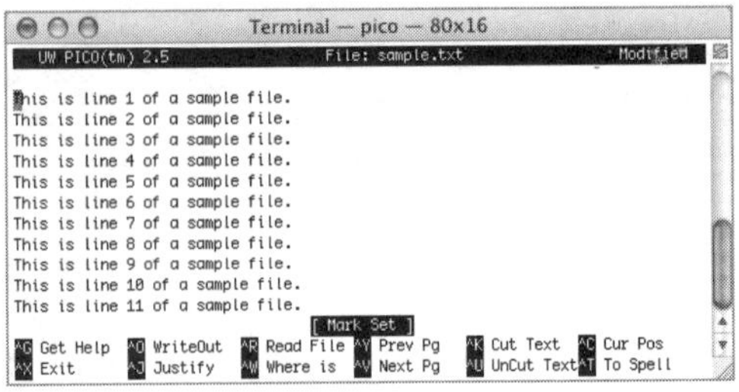

**Figure 40** *[Mark Set]* appears in the window.

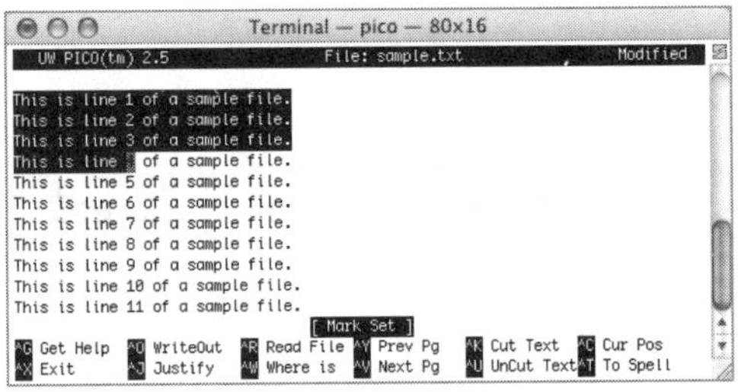

**Figure 41** Use the arrow keys to select text.

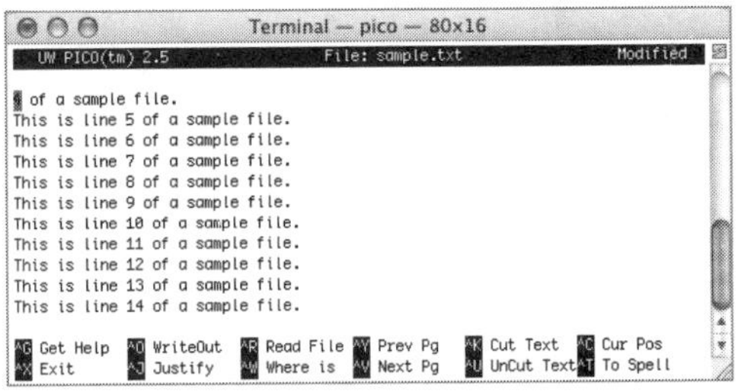

**Figure 42** Using the Cut Text command removes the selected text.

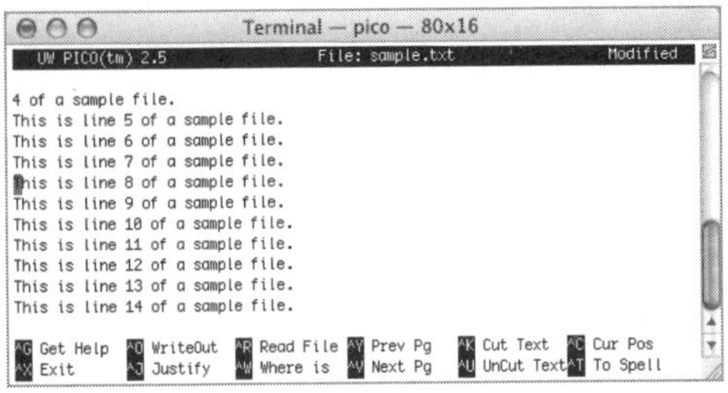

**Figure 43** Position the cursor where you want to paste the text.

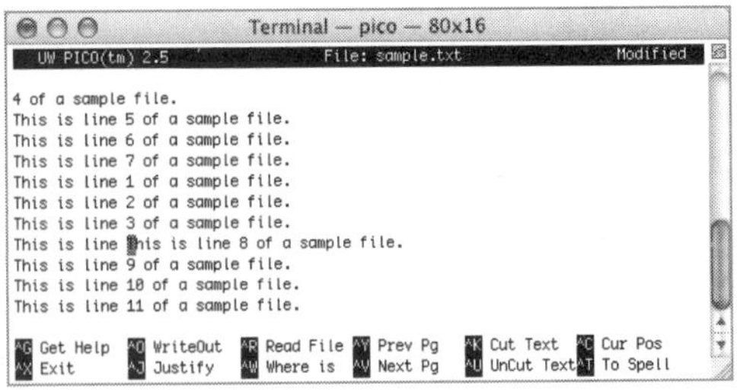

**Figure 44** Using the Uncut Text command pastes the text back into the document.

USING PICO

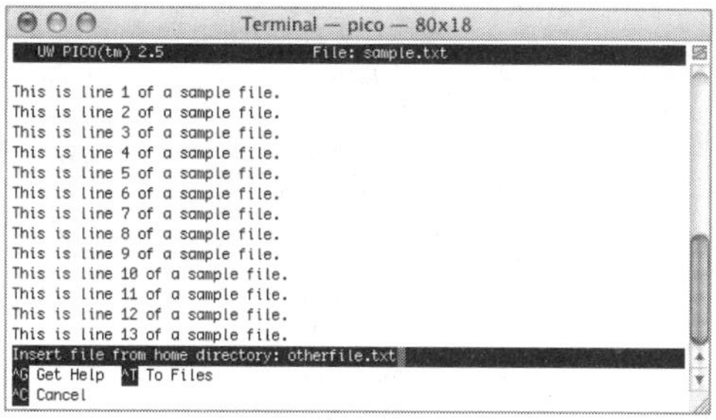

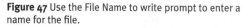

**Figure 45** Enter the name of the file you want to insert at the Insert file prompt.

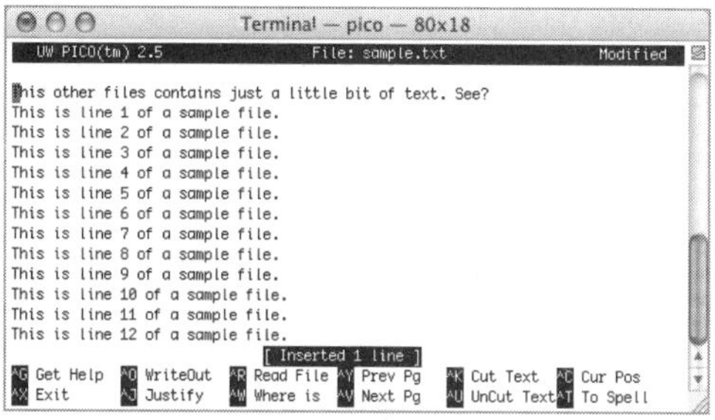

**Figure 46** The file is inserted at the cursor.

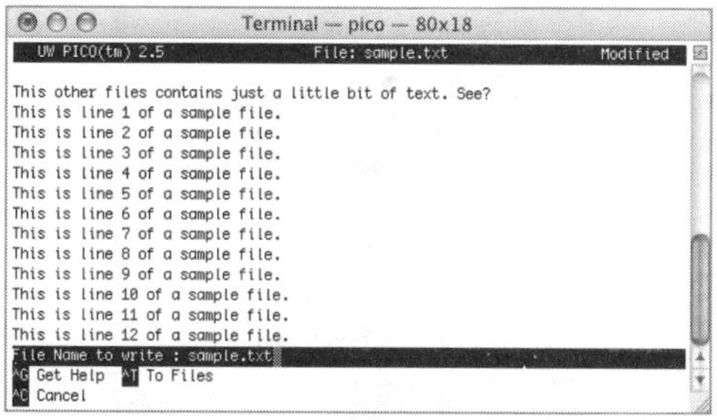

**Figure 47** Use the File Name to write prompt to enter a name for the file.

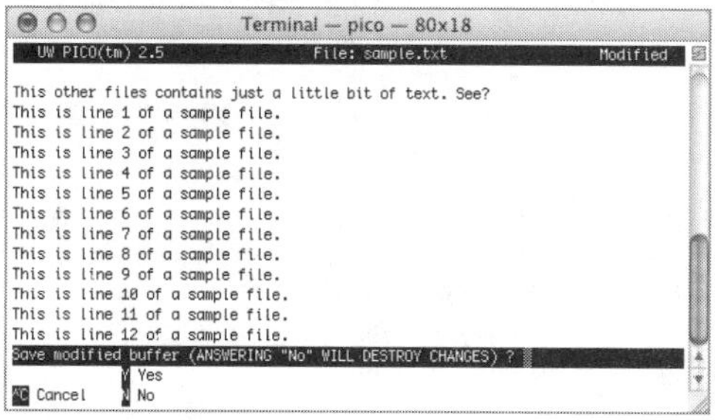

**Figure 48** The Save modified buffer prompt enables you to save changes to the file before you exit pico.

## To insert an existing file

1. Position the cursor where you want to insert the file (**Figure 34**).

2. Press (Control)(R) (Read File).

3. The Insert file prompt appears at the bottom of the window. Enter the path name for the file you want to insert (**Figure 45**) and press (Return). The contents of the file appear at the cursor (**Figure 46**).

## To save changes to a file

1. Press (Control)(O) (WriteOut). The File Name to write prompt appears at the bottom of the window, along with the name of the file you originally opened (**Figure 47**).

2. To save the file with the same name, press (Return).

   *or*

   To save the file with a different name, use (Delete) to remove the existing file name, enter a new file name, and press (Return). The file is saved.

## To exit pico

1. Press (Control)(X) (Exit).

2. If you have made changes to the file since opening it, the Save modified buffer prompt appears at the bottom of the window (**Figure 48**).

   ▲ Press (Y) and then (Return) to save changes to the file and exit pico.

   ▲ Press (N) and then (Return) to exit pico without saving changes to the file.

**USING pico**

# Output Redirection

In all of the Unix commands up to this point that produced output—such as man and ls—the command output appears in the Terminal window. This is called the *standard output device* of Unix.

But the shell can also redirect the output of a command to a file instead of to the screen. This *output redirection* enables you to create files by writing command output to a file.

Output redirection uses the greater-than character (>) to tell the shell to place the output of a command into a file rather than listing it to the screen. If the output file already exists, it is overwritten with the new information.

Similarly, a pair of greater-than signs (>>) tells the shell to append the output of a command to the end of a file rather than erasing the file and starting from the beginning. If the output file does not already exist, the shell creates a new file with the name you specified.

This section offers some examples of output redirection.

## To sort a file & output it to another file

Type sort *file* > *output-file* and press ⟨Return⟩.

For example, sort sample.txt > alpha.txt would sort the lines in the file named *sample.txt* and write them to a file named *alpha.txt*.

## To save a directory listing as a file

Type ls > *output-file* and press ⟨Return⟩.

For example, ls -la > list.txt creates a file named *list.txt* that contains a complete directory listing in the long format (**Figure 49**).

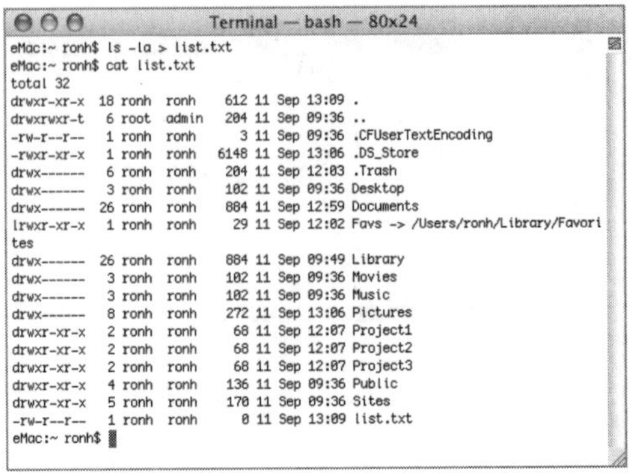

**Figure 49** This example shows how the **ls** command can be used to save a directory listing as a text file. The **cat** command was used in the illustration to display the contents of the new file.

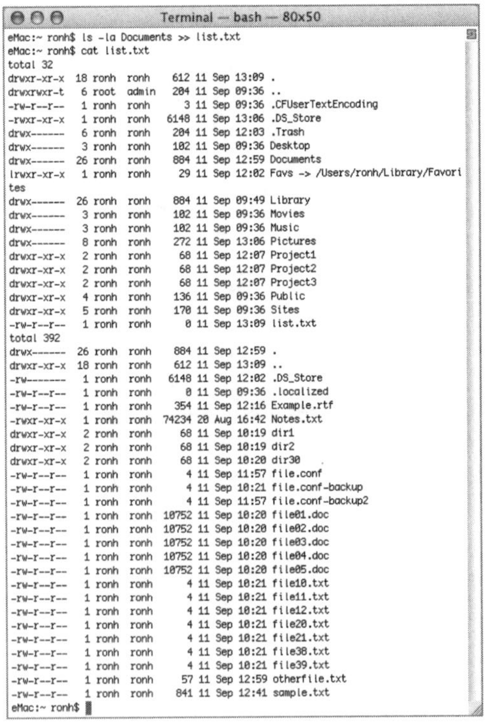

**Figure 50** This example uses >> to append another directory to the one in **Figure 49** and display the combined files with the **cat** command.

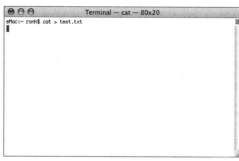

**Figure 51** Using the **cat** command with an output file name starts **cat** and waits for text entry.

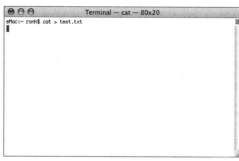

**Figure 52** Enter the text you want to include in the file.

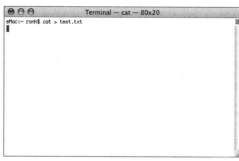

**Figure 53** Press [Control] [D] to save the file.

## To append output to an existing file

Type *command* >> *output-file* and press [Return].

For example, ls -la Documents >> list.txt would append a directory listing for the Documents subdirectory to the list.txt file (**Figure 50**).

## To create a text file with cat

1. Type cat > *output-file* (for example, cat > test.txt) and press [Return]. The cat command starts and waits for you to type text (**Figure 51**).

2. Enter the text you want to include in the file. You can press [Return] to start a new line if desired (**Figure 52**).

3. When you're finished entering text, press [Control] [D] (**Figure 53**). ([Control] [D] is the ASCII "End Of Transmission" character.)

   The new file is saved with the name you specified.

## ✔ Tip

■ Normally, the cat command uses a source-file argument; that is, you normally tell cat to list a specific file to the screen. If you do not specify a source-file for cat, it takes source data from the *standard input device*, which is usually the keyboard, and redirects it to the output-file.

## To combine files with cat

Type cat *file1* ... > *output-file* and press [Return].

For example, cat firstfile.txt secondfile.txt thirdfile.txt > combinedfile.txt combines the files named *firstfile.txt*, *secondfile.txt*, and *thirdfile.txt*, in that order, and saves them as a file named *combinedfile.txt*.

# Unix Passwords & Security

You may think, "I don't care if someone reads my mail" or "I don't store important files in my directory, so who needs a good password?"

This is exactly what *crackers* count on. Many times, these crackers don't want to read your mail or erase your files; they want to install their own programs that take up your computer time and Internet bandwidth. They steal resources from you and slow down your computer and Internet response time. They also install *Trojan horse* programs that allow them to break into your computer at a future date. These Trojan horses are designed to look and act exactly like other normal programs you expect to see on the machine.

When a cracker breaks into your computer system, your only course of action is to take the machine off the network and rebuild the operating system from scratch. It's virtually impossible to detect Trojan horses, which is why you must rebuild your system. The rebuild process can take days, and you lose communication during that time. Scared? Good. Your first line of defense is to use good passwords.

The object when choosing a password is to pick a password that is easy for you to remember but difficult for someone else to guess. This leaves the cracker no alternative but a brute-force search, trying every possible combination of letters, numbers, and punctuation. A search of this sort, even conducted on a machine that could try one million passwords per second (most machines can try less than one hundred per second), would require, on average, over one hundred years to complete. With this as your goal, here are some guidelines you should follow for password selection.

## Dos

◆ Do use a password with nonalphabetic characters: digits or punctuation mixed into the middle of the password. For example, *ronh3;cat*.

◆ Do use a password that contains mixed-case letters, such as *ROnHCAt*.

◆ Do pick a password that is easy to remember, so you don't have to write it down. (And *never* write it on a sticky note and stick it on your monitor.)

◆ Do use a password that you can quickly type, without having to look at the keyboard. This makes it harder for someone watching over your shoulder to steal your password. If someone is watching, ask them to turn their head.

## Don'ts

- Don't use your login name in any form—for example, as it is, reversed, capitalized, or doubled.

- Don't use your first name, last name, or initials in any form.

- Don't use your spouse's, child's, or pet's name.

- Don't use other information that is easily obtained about you. This includes license plate numbers, addresses, telephone numbers, social security numbers, the brand of your automobile, and the name of the street you live on.

- Don't use a password that consists of all digits or all the same letter. This significantly decreases the search time for a cracker.

- Don't use a word contained in dictionaries (either English or foreign language), spelling lists, or other lists of words (for example, the Star Trek series, movie titles, Shakespeare plays, cartoon characters, Monty Python episodes, the *Hitchhiker's Guide* series, myths or legends, place names, sports words, and colleges). These are all part of the standard dictionaries that come with cracking software, and the crackers can always add their own dictionaries.

- Don't use a word simply prefixed or suffixed with a number or a punctuation mark.

- Don't substitute a zero for the letter O or substitute a numeral one for the letter L or I.

- Don't use a password shorter than six characters.

## Password ideas

Although these password rules may seem extreme, you have several methods for choosing secure, easy-to-remember passwords that also obey the rules. For example:

- Choose a line or two from a song or poem and then use the first letter of each word. For example, if you pick, "In Xanadu did Kubla Kahn a stately pleasure dome decree," you would have *IXdKKaspdd*. "Ding dong the Witch is dead" becomes *DdtWid*.

- Create a password by alternating between one consonant and one or two vowels, as long as eight characters. This provides nonsense words that are usually pronounceable and thus easily remembered. For example, *moatdup* and *jountee*.

- Choose two short words and concatenate them with a punctuation character. For example: *dog:rain* or *ray/gun* or *kid?goat*.

## To change your password

1. In the Terminal window, type passwd and press [Return].

2. The shell prompts you to enter your old password (**Figure 54**). Enter it and press [Return].

3. The shell prompts you to enter your new password (**Figure 55**). Enter it, and press [Return].

4. The shell prompts you to enter your new password again (**Figure 56**). Enter it and press [Return].

## ✔ Tips

■ When you enter your old and new password, the cursor in the Terminal window does not move. This is an added security feature; someone looking over your shoulder as you type can't even see how many characters you typed.

■ The new password you select must be at least five characters in length.

■ You can also change your password in the Accounts preferences pane. I explain how in **Chapter 17**.

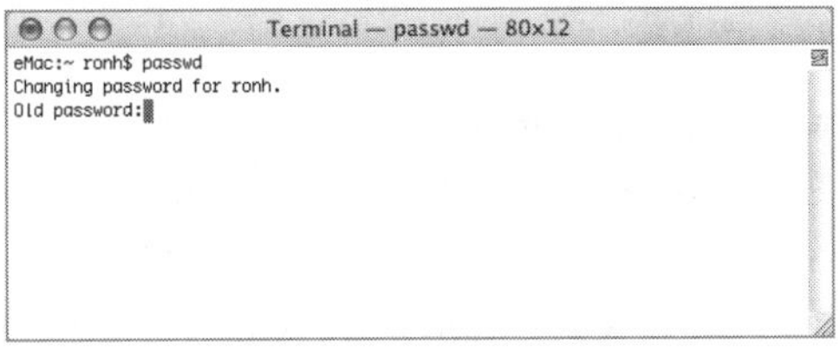

**Figure 54** First, the shell prompts you for your current password.

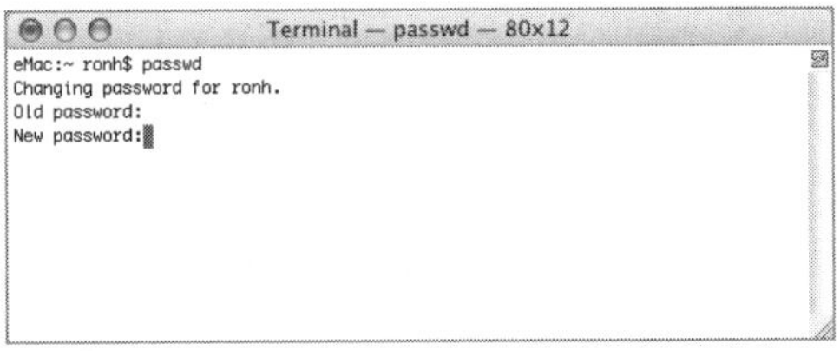

**Figure 55** Next, it prompts you to enter your new password.

**Figure 56** Finally, it prompts you to re-enter your new password.

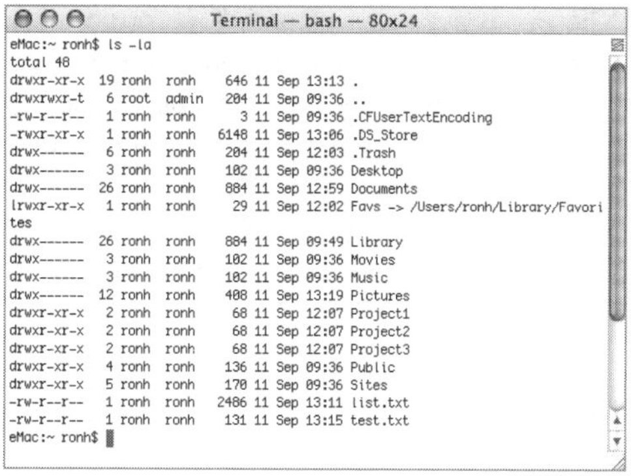

**Figure 57** A directory listing including permissions and other information for files.

# File & Directory Permissions & Ownership

If you've ever used file sharing on your Mac, you probably noticed that you can set permissions for folders and files, giving certain users, groups of users, or everyone read-only, read-write, or no access. (This is covered in **Chapter 4**.) Unix has almost the same system with users, groups, and public permissions.

Through the ls command, which I cover earlier in this chapter, you can learn quite a bit more about the ownership and permissions of files on your system. For example, take a look at the ls -la listing for a home directory, in **Figure 57**. There's lots of useful information on each line.

The first line (starting with the word *total*) is the number of 512-byte blocks used by the files in the directories that follow. Below that, each line contains seven columns of information about each subdirectory and file.

## Permissions

The group of characters at the beginning of the line (for example, drwxr-xr-x in the first entry) indicates the entry's type and permissions.

The first character indicates the type of entry:

◆ d indicates a directory.

◆ – indicates a file.

◆ l indicates a link to another file.

The next nine characters of the permissions can be broken into three sets of three characters each. The first set of three is permissions for the owner of the file, the second set is permissions for the group owner, and the third set is permissions for everyone else who has access to the entry.

*Continued on next page...*

FILE & DIRECTORY PERMISSIONS

*Continued from previous page.*

♦ r indicates read permissions. This permission enables the user to open and read the file or directory contents.

♦ w indicates write permissions. This permission enables the user to make changes to the file or directory contents, including delete it.

♦ x indicates execute permissions. For an executable program file, this permission enables the user to run the program. For a directory, this permission enables the user to open the directory.

♦ – indicates no permission.

For example, the file named *example.rtf* in **Figure 57** can be written to and read by the owner (ronh) and can only be read by the group (staff) and everyone else.

## Links

The next column shows the number of links. This is a count of the files and directories contained within a directory entry. It's set to 1 for normal files.

## Owner

The third column is the owner of the file or directory. Normally this will be the name of your account. Sometimes, the system creates files for you, and you may see another owner. For example, the .. directory in **Figure 57** was created by the system, which gave ownership to root, the superuser.

## Group

The group is listed next. Just as in file sharing in Mac OS 9.x and earlier, you can create groups of users that have separate permissions. To find out what group you are a member of, type groups and press Return.

When your account is created, a group is also created with the same name as your short name, with you as the sole member of the group. If you want special groups for people (for example, marketing, staff, sysadmins), you can set these up using NetInfo Manager if you are an administrator of the system.

## File size

The number in the fifth column gives the size of the entry in bytes.

## Modification date

The sixth column shows the date and time that the file or directory was last modified. A directory is modified whenever any of its contents are modified.

## Filename

Last, you see the name of the file or directory.

# More about File & Directory Ownership

Normally when you create a new file, you are given ownership of that file and it is assigned to your default group. Your default group is assigned to you by Mac OS X when you are given your user account by the system administrator. You can belong to multiple groups. Unless the system administrator specifically assigns you to a different group, in Mac OS X, the default group is a unique group with the same name as your short name and with you as the sole member.

## ✔ Tip

■ The admin user can use the chown and chgrp commands to change the ownership of a file or directory. You can learn more about these commands by viewing their man pages. In the Terminal window, type man chown or man chgrp and press Return to view the command's man pages.

# Changing Permissions for a File or Directory

Unix includes a command for setting file or directory permissions: chmod. Although this command can be a bit complicated, it is important. The security of your files and subdirectories depends on its proper usage.

The chmod command uses the following syntax:

chmod *mode file* ...

The complex part of the chmod command is understanding what can go in the mode operand. This is where you specify the owner (also called user), group, and other (everyone else) permissions. You have two ways to do this: numerically and symbolically.

## ✔ Tip

- You can learn more about the chmod command by viewing its man pages. In the Terminal window, type man chmod and press ⎸Return⎹.

## Numeric permission modes

Numeric permission modes uses numbers to represent permissions options. The best way to explain this is to provide an example. Remember, the nine characters of the permissions coding in a directory listing can be broken down into three sets of three:

```
rwx      rwx      rwx
user     group    other
```

Each character can  be represented with an octal digit (a number between 0 and 7) by assigning values to the r, w, and x characters, like this:

```
421      421      421
rwx      rwx      rwx
user     group    other
```

So, if you want to give read and write permission for a file called *file1* to the owner, that would be a 4 (read) plus a 2 (write), which adds up to to a 6. You could then give read only permission to the group and others by assigning the value 4 (read). The command to do all this is chmod 644 file1. (The 644 permission is one you'll see often on text files that are readable by everyone. A permission of 600 would make a file private.)

## Symbolic permission modes

Symbolic permission modes enables you to add or remove privileges using symbols. For example, to remove write permission from the group and others, type chmod go-w file1. This translates to "take away write permissions from the group and others."

The ownership symbols you use for this are:

u   user (owner) of the file or directory

g   group owner of the file or directory

o   others (everyone)

a   all three (user, group, and others)

The symbols for the permissions you can add or take away are:

r   read

w   write

x   execute

Finally, the operations you can perform are:

+   add the permission

–   remove the permission

=   set (add) the following permissions

You can combine more than one symbol in a mode and more than one "equation" if you separate them with commas. For example, chmod a+rwx,o-w file1 gives universal read, write, and execute access to all and then takes away write permission from others to file1. (The equivalent numerical permission would be 775.)

## To change the permissions for a file or directory

In the Terminal window, type chmod *mode file* ... (for example, chmod 644 file1) and press Return.

## ✖ Warning!

■ Do not change the ownership and permissions of files on your computer without reason or if you're not sure what you're doing. The operating system assumes that certain files belong to certain users and have specific privileges. If you change the ownership or permissions on some system files, you may render your computer unusable! It's usually safe to modify your own files—those that you create—but unless you know what you are doing, stay away from other files.

## ✔ Tip

■ If you include the -R option in the command (for example, chmod -R 644 folder1), the change is made recursively down through the directory tree. In other words, the change is made to the folder and every file and folder within it.

# Learning What's Happening on Your System

A few Unix commands can provide you with answers to questions about your system: "Who is logged in?" "What are they doing?" "What jobs are taking up all my CPU cycles?" "How long has my system been up?"

◆ uptime tells you how long it has been since you last restarted and what your workload is.

◆ who tells you who is logged in to your system, where they're logged in from, and when they logged in.

◆ w tells you who is online and what they are doing.

◆ last tells you who has logged into your computer.

◆ ps and top tell you what jobs are running on your computer.

This section explains how to use each of these commands and shows simulated output so you know what you might expect to learn.

## ✔ Tip

■ You can learn more about these commands by viewing their man pages. In the Terminal window, type man uptime, man who, man w, man last, man ps, or man top and press (Return) to view the command's man pages.

# To learn your workload & how long since you last restarted

In the Terminal window, type uptime and press (Return).

The results might look something like what you see in **Code 1**. You see the current time, the time since the last restart, or boot (7 days, 17 hours, and 48 minutes), and load averages of how many active jobs were in the queue during the last 1, 5, and 15 minutes. The load shown here is high because my system is running the SETI@home screensaver. Normally these numbers will be less than 1.

# To learn who is on your system

In the Terminal window, type who and press (Return).

The results might look something like what you see in **Code 2**. In this example, I'm logged in remotely twice from the machine with the IP address 192.168.2.1, once as root and once as myself. I'm also logged in from a remote location (isaac.exploratorium.edu) and at the system console.

# To learn who is online & what they are doing

In the Terminal window, type w and press (Return).

The command's output looks something like **Code 3**. The w command first does an uptime command. Then it gives you information about each user, when they logged in, and how long it's been since they've done anything.

**Code 1** The results of the **uptime** command.

```
Terminal — bash — 80x24
7:21PM  up 7 days, 17:48, 5 users, load
averages: 1.87, 1.80, 1.67
```

**Code 2** The results of the **who** command.

```
Terminal — bash — 80x24
ronh    console   Sep 2 01:35
ronh    typ1      Sep 9 19:13   (192.168.1.2)
root    ttyp3     Sep 9 19:13   (192.168.1.2)
ronh    ttyp4     Sep 9 19:16   (isaac.explorator)
```

**Code 3** The results of the **w** command.

```
Terminal — bash — 80x24
7:28PM  up 7 days, 17:55, 5 users, load averages: 1.90,
1.80, 1.67
USER  TTY FROM             LOGIN@   IDLE   WHAT
ronh  co  -                02Sep01  7days  -
ronh  p1  192.168.1.2      7:13PM   0      -
ronh  p2  -                Thu01AM  13     -
root  p3  192.168.1.2      7:13PM   0      -
ronh  p4  isaac.explorator 7:16PM   0      -
```

## To learn who has logged in to your machine recently

In the Terminal window, type last and press ⌐Return⌐.

The output should look similar to **Code 4**. The last command spews out a list of everyone who has logged in to your machine, when and from where they logged in, how long they stayed, and when you last shut down or restarted your machine.

*Or*

In the Terminal window, type last *user* (where *user* is the user name of a specific user) and press ⌐Return⌐.

If you specify a user, last will show only the logins for that user.

**USING LAST**

**Code 4** The results of the **last** command.

| | | | Terminal — bash — 80x24 | | |
|---|---|---|---|---|---|
| ronh | ttyp4 | isaac.explorator | Sun Sep 9 | 19:16 | still logged in |
| root | ttyp3 | 192.168.1.2 | Sun Sep 9 | 19:13 | still logged in |
| ronh | ttyp1 | 192.168.1.2 | Sun Sep 9 | 19:13 | still logged in |
| ronh | ttyp1 | 192.168.1.2 | Sat Sep 8 | 23:20 - 00:07 | (00:46) |
| ronh | ttyp1 | sodium.explorato | Sat Sep 8 | 16:05 - 16:13 | (00:08) |
| ronh | ttyp1 | 192.168.1.2 | Sat Sep 8 | 00:03 - 00:40 | (00:36) |
| ronh | ttyp3 | 192.168.1.2 | Thu Sep 6 | 22:19 - 00:01 | (01:41) |
| ronh | ttyp1 | 192.168.1.2 | Thu Sep 6 | 22:01 - 00:01 | (02:00) |
| ronh | ttyp1 | 192.168.1.2 | Thu Sep 6 | 10:13 - 10:37 | (00:23) |
| ronh | ttyp2 | | Thu Sep 6 | 01:17 | still logged in |
| ronh | ttyp1 | 192.168.1.2 | Thu Sep 6 | 00:56 - 02:06 | (01:09) |
| ronh | ttyp1 | 192.168.1.2 | Mon Sep 3 | 23:47 - 01:51 | (02:04) |
| ronh | ttyp1 | 192.168.1.2 | Mon Sep 3 | 14:12 - 23:19 | (09:06) |
| ronh | console | localhost | Sun Sep 2 | 01:35 | still logged in |
| reboot | ~ | | Sun Sep 2 | 01:35 | |
| shutdown | ~ | | Sun Sep 2 | 01:33 | |
| ronh | ttyp2 | 192.168.1.2 | Sun Sep 2 | 00:53 - 01:23 | (00:30) |

## To learn what jobs are running

In the Terminal window, type ps and press [Return].

The ps command tells you what you are running at the instant you run the command.

*Or*

In the Terminal window, type top and press [Return].

The top command gives you a running commentary of the top ten jobs. If you expand the size of the Terminal window, top shows more than the top ten jobs. Press [Q] to quit top.

## ✔ Tip

■ You may find Activity Monitor (in the Utilities folder) a more useful utility to see the processes that are running. Activity Monitor is covered in **Chapter 22**.

# Archive & Compression Utilities

Long before utilities such as StuffIt and Zip existed—long before the Mac existed, in fact!—Unix users could group files together into *archives* and compress the archives to take up less disk space, which was vastly more expensive then. Unix offers several archiving and compression tools:

◆ tar (short for *t*ape *ar*chive) was originally used to combine a collection of files into a single file, which was written to tape. But you don't have to write the file to tape; you can write it to any device your Unix system knows about: disks, tapes, CD-Rs, even Terminal.

◆ compress and uncompress do what you probably expect them to: compress and expand files. Text files are very compressible, sometimes 10 to 1. Files that have already been compressed such as JPEG and MPEG files and QuickTime movies, however, can actually become larger.

◆ gzip is a newer set of utilities that are like compress and uncompress on steroids. gzip includes more options and offers better compression ratios.

## ✔ Tips

■ You can learn more about these commands by viewing their man pages. In the Terminal window, type man tar, man compress, man uncompress, or man gzip and press [Return] to view the command's man pages.

■ It's useful to know something about these tools because you will encounter them if you download software from Internet archives.

## To create an archive from an entire directory tree

Type tar [-cxtvpf] [-C *directory*] *archive file* ... and press Return. (Consult **Table 2** for tar options.)

Here are some examples using the tar command:

◆ tar -cf archive.tar file1 directory1 file2 creates and then writes to the archive named *archive.tar*: *file1*, *directory1* and all its contents, and *file2* in that order.

◆ tar -tvf old-archive.tar displays everything in the archive called *old-archive.tar* but does not extract anything. The t option just prints the contents of a tar archive.

◆ tar -xpvf old-archive.tar extracts the files and directories in the archive file called *old-archive.tar* and puts the resulting files in the current directory. The v option reports progress and the p option preserves the ownerships and modification dates of the original files. (The tar file is unaffected and remains on the disk.)

◆ tar -xpvf old-archive.tar -C /usr/local/src extracts the files and directories in the archive file called *old-archive.tar* and puts the resulting files in the directory */usr/local/src*.

## ✔ Tip

■ It's a standard procedure to end archive names with a .tar suffix, and you should honor this standard to keep evil spirits out of your computer.

**Table 2**

### tar Options

| Option | Description |
|--------|-------------|
| -c | Creates a new archive |
| -x | Extracts files from the named archive |
| -t | Displays a list of files and directories in the named archive |
| -v | Verbose mode: Tells you everything tar is doing |
| -p | Preserves permissions, owners, and modification dates if possible |
| -f | Archives files to the following filename or extracts files from the following archive name |
| -C | Puts extracted files in the specified location |

## To compress & decompress with compress & uncompress

Type compress *file* ... (for example, compress file.txt), and press [Return].

*Or*

Type uncompress *file* ... (for example, uncompress file.z), and press [Return].

### ✔ Tips

■ Your original file is removed if either of the commands successfully complete the compression or decompression.

■ By convention, compressed files should have a .Z extension. The compress command will automatically append this extension to the filename.

## To compress or decompress with gzip & gunzip

Type gzip *file* ... and press [Return]. This compresses the files, adds the .gz suffix to their names, and removes the original files.

*Or*

Type gunzip *file* ... and press [Return]. This uncompresses the files and removes the original archive.

### ✔ Tips

■ The gzip command has several options. The r option, for recursive, goes into specified subdirectories and compresses or uncompresses the files. The v option, for verbose, tells the command to report its progress.

■ zcat file lists the contents of a compressed file to Terminal (or pipes the content to another command) without altering the original archive.

# Automation Tools

**Figure 1** The Applications folder includes two tools to automate tasks: AppleScript and Automator.

## Automation Tools

Computers are supposed to make our lives easier, right? They can—if we "teach" them to perform repetitive tasks automatically.

For example, when I start work in the morning, I start my computer and launch the applications I use every day: Mail, iCal, iTunes, InDesign, and Photoshop. I check my e-mail, delete the junk mail, and start playing one of my iTunes playlists. Then I open the folders and documents I'm working on: book chapters and the folder in which I store the chapter's files. When I'm done with a book's chapter, I save it as a PDF file, create an archive of the chapter's folder, and upload it all to my publisher's FTP site. There's a lot of repetitive tasks here—tasks my computer has been trained to do automatically at my request. This saves me time—let's face it: my Mac can do things a lot faster than I can.

Mac OS X includes two tools for automating repetitive tasks:

- ◆ **Automator**, which is brand new in Mac OS X 10.4, enables you to build workflows that automate tasks in multiple applications—all without knowing a single line of programming code.

- ◆ **AppleScript** is a scripting language that enables you to automate tasks and extend the functionality of Mac OS.

This chapter takes a closer look at these two automation tools.

# Automator

Automator is a brand new Mac OS X application. With it, you can automate tasks with drag-and-drop simplicity.

Here's how it works. You use Automator to create a *workflow*. A workflow is a series of steps, called *actions*, each of which work with a specific application. For example, a Finder action might connect to a server or create an archive. A Mail action might check for new mail or send messages. You drag actions from a list to a workflow window, where you can set options, if necessary.

There are two related concepts you must keep in mind when working with actions:

◆ **Input** is information required for an action to complete. Input can be something you provide, such as a selection of items in a window, or it can be the result of another action. Not all actions require input.

◆ **Result** is the outcome of an action. In many cases, it can be used by another action. Not all actions have results.

For example, iCal's New iCal Events action takes Address Book groups from a previous action and uses them for an iCal event that includes group members as attendees. For this action to work properly, the previous action must result in Address Book groups. The next action can use the resulting iCal events, if necessary.

When all necessary actions have been added to your workflow, you save the workflow so you can use it again and again. Each time you use it, it performs the steps or actions it includes, thus automating the task.

This part of the chapter tells you how you can get started using Automator to build workflows and automate your tasks.

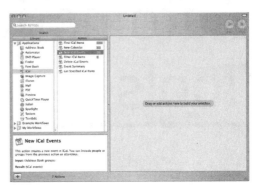

**Figure 2** An untitled workflow window.

## ✔ Tips

■ Automator includes dozens of actions that work with the applications that come with Mac OS X. More actions will be available as the technology catches on and developers create actions for their applications.

■ You can learn more about Automator and download additional actions at Apple's Automator Web site, www.apple.com/automator/.

■ If this introduction to Automator isn't enough for you, be sure to check out Ethan Wilde's *Automator for Mac OS X: Visual QuickStart Guide*.

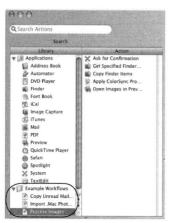

**Figure 3** Automator comes with example workflows you can try.

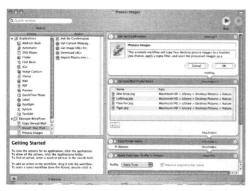

**Figure 4** Here's the workflow window for the Process Images example workflow. I won't tell you what it does—try it for yourself!

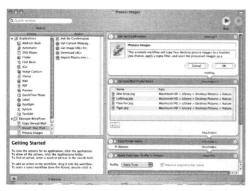

**Figure 5** Automator's File menu.

## To launch Automator

Open the Automator icon in the Applications folder (**Figure 1**).

An untitled workflow window appears (**Figure 2**).

## To try the example workflows

1. In the Library column of the workflow window, click the triangle beside Example Workflows. Workflows within the folder appear (**Figure 3**).

2. Double-click the workflow you want to try. It appears in its own workflow window (**Figure 4**).

3. Click the Run button.

## ✔ Tips

■ Don't try the Import .Mac Photo Album into iPhoto workflow unless you have iPhoto installed. Doing so will result in an error message in a pesky dialog that's not easy to get rid of.

■ You can review the actions for a workflow by examining contents of the Action column and the workflow area on the right side of the workflow window (**Figure 4**). This is a great way to learn more about how actions work together in workflows.

## To create a new workflow

Choose File > New (**Figure 5**), or press ⌘N.

An untitled workflow window appears (**Figure 2**).

LAUNCHING AUTOMATOR, TRYING EXAMPLES

## To create a workflow

1. Plan the steps of your workflow. The best way to do this is to manually perform the actions and make notes.

2. In the Library column, select the application that will perform an action for the workflow. A list of installed actions appears in the Action column (**Figure 6**).

3. Drag the action you want from the Action list to the workflow area on the right side of the window (**Figure 7**). When you release the mouse button, the action's options appear (**Figure 8**).

4. Set options in the action. How you do this varies depending on the action. The action in **Figure 8**, for example, requires me to enter a URL. I'd click the + button to add a new URL to the list, then double-click the URL to display an edit box around it (**Figure 9**), type a URL, and press ⟨Return⟩. Then I'd select the Apple URL in the list and click the – button to delete it.

5. Repeat steps 2 through 4 for each action you want to add. Be sure to drag them into the workflow area in the order in which you want them to run. **Figure 10** shows an example with a bunch of actions added.

6. Use the pop-up menu for the input item at the top of an action (**Figure 11**) to indicate whether the input should come from the results of the previous action. Do this for each action as necessary.

**Figure 6**
When you select a library, a list of installed actions for that library appears in the Action column.

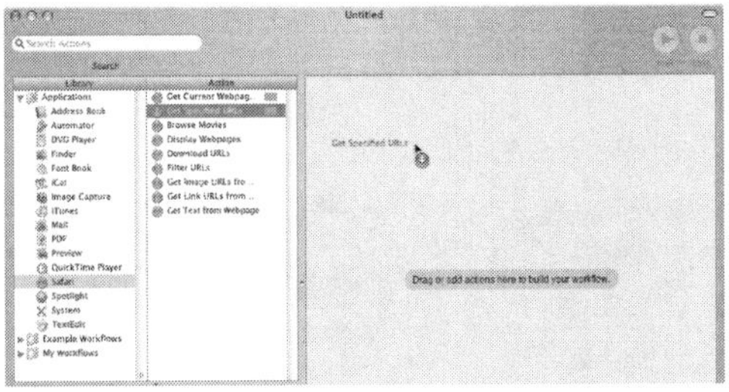

**Figure 7** Drag an action to the workflow area.

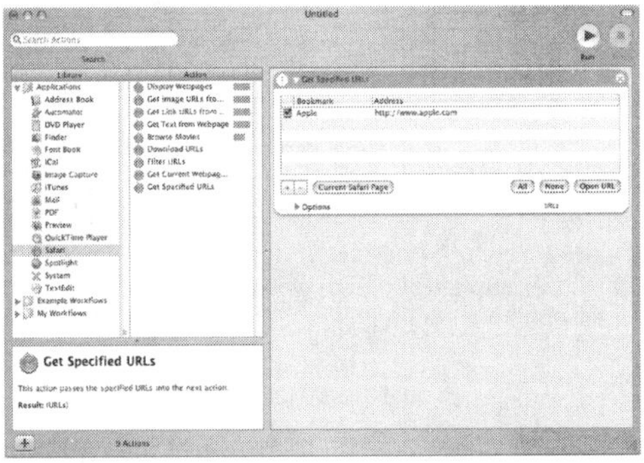

**Figure 8** The action appears in the workflow area, where you can set its options.

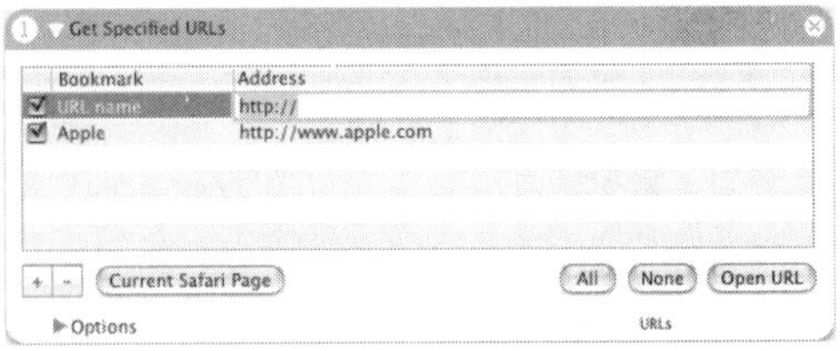

**Figure 9** In this example, I'm preparing to enter a new URL.

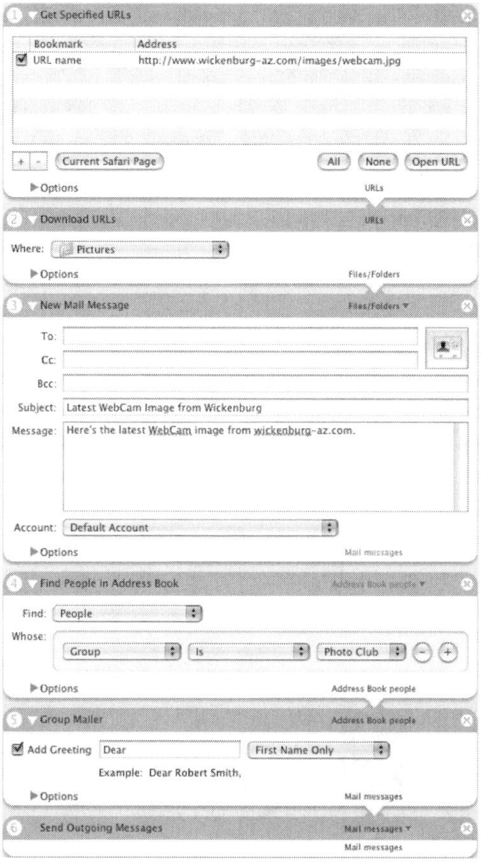

**Figure 10** Here are the actions for a workflow I dreamed up. The workflow downloads the latest Webcam image from a Web site I manage, then sends it via e-mail to all members of a group set up in Address Book.

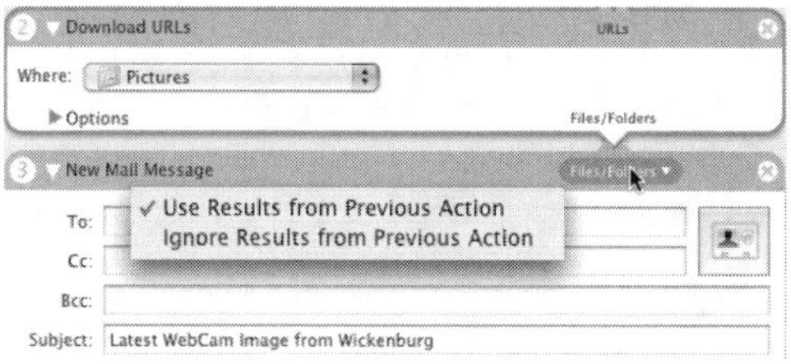

**Figure 11** Use a pop-up menu like this one to indicate whether an action's input should come from the previous action.

## ✔ Tips

■ You can change the order of actions in the workflow area by dragging them up or down in the list.

■ Automator visually indicates whether an action gets its input from a previous action, as shown in **Figures 12** and **13**.

■ Clicking the triangle beside Options in an action's configuration window displays additional options. Normally, this includes just the Show Action When Run check box (**Figure 14**), which, when turned on, instructs Automator to display each action when it runs as part of the workflow. You might find this useful for debugging the workflow, but in most cases, you'll want to keep this check box turned off.

■ You should be able to duplicate the workflow shown in **Figure 10** and run it on your computer. Before you do, create an Address Book group with a few people you think might want to see the view out my window and select that group in workflow step 4.

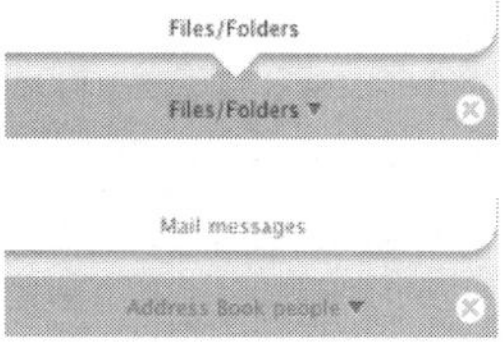

**Figures 12 & 13** If an action uses the previous action's results for input, the action boxes connect (top). If an action doesn't use the previous action's results, the boxes do not connect.

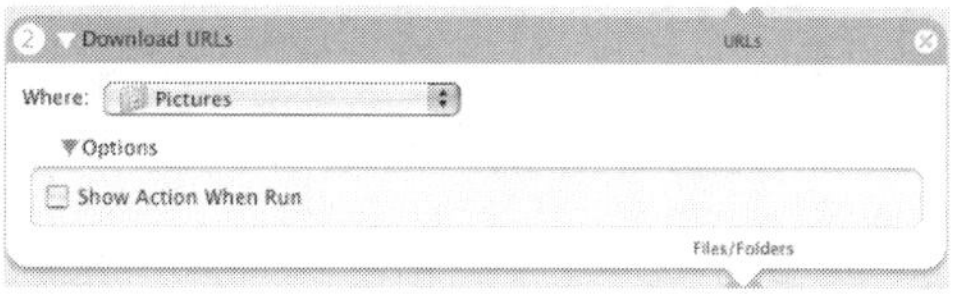

**Figure 14** The Show Action When Run check box can help you debug a workflow.

## To save a workflow

1. Choose File > Save As (**Figure 5**).

2. Use the Save Location dialog that appears (**Figure 15**) to enter a name and choose a location to save the file.

3. Choose an option from the File Format pop-up menu:

   ▲ **Workflow** saves the file as an Automator workflow document. Opening a workflow document opens Automator so you can run or modify the workflow.

   ▲ **Application** saves the file as an application. Opening the application runs it without opening Automator.

4. Click Save.

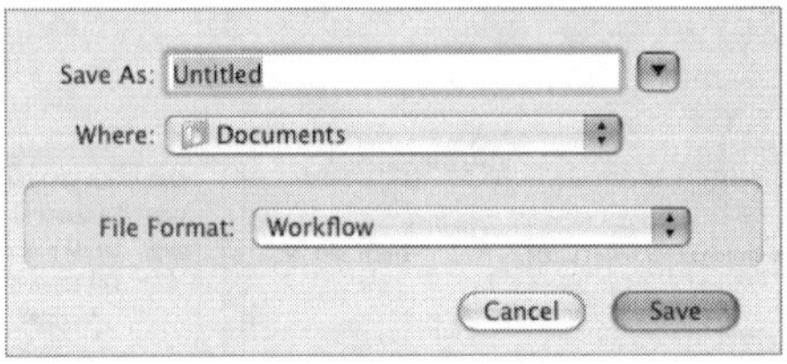

## ✔ Tips

■ If you save a workflow as a workflow format file in your Documents folder, it automatically appears in the My Workflows folder in the Library column of the workflow window (**Figure 16**).

■ You can share saved workflow files with other Macintosh users so they can use them on their computers.

**Figure 15** Use a standard Save Location dialog to save your workflows.

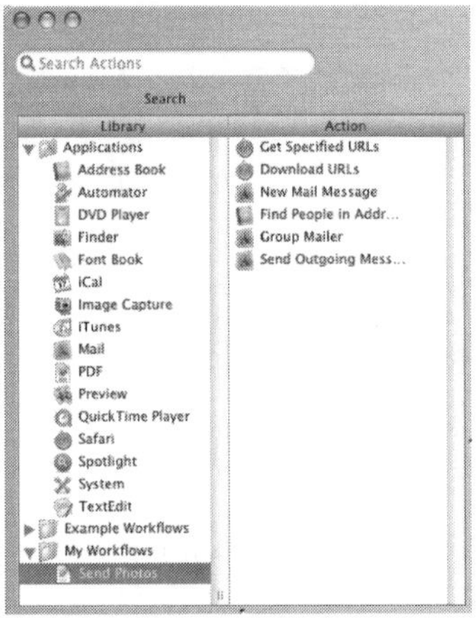

**Figure 16** A saved workflow appears in the My Workflows folder in the Library column.

Send Photos    Send Photos

**Figures 17 & 18** Finder icons for an Automator workflow document (left) and an Automator workflow application (right).

## To open a workflow

In the Finder, double-click the workflow icon. One of two things happens:

◆ If the workflow is a workflow document (**Figure 17**), it opens in Automator.

◆ If the workflow was saved as an application (**Figure 18**), it runs.

*Or*

In Automator, double-click the workflow in the My Workflows folder of the Library column (**Figure 16**). The workflow opens in Automator.

## To modify a workflow

1. Open the workflow in Automator.

2. Modify the contents of the workflow area as desired:

   ▲ To remove an action, click the X button, at the top of the action's configuration window.

   ▲ To add an action, drag it from the Action column to the workflow area.

   ▲ To change the order of actions, drag them up or down in the workflow area.

3. Choose File > Save (**Figure 5**) to save your changes.

## ✔ Tip

■ You can modify a workflow that was saved as an application by dragging its icon onto the Automator icon to open it in Automator.

# AppleScript Basics

AppleScript (**Figure 19**) is the scripting language that comes with Mac OS. It enables you to automate tasks and extend the functionality of Mac OS X.

You use AppleScript's Script Editor application to write small programs or *scripts* that include specially worded *statements*. AppleScript statements are converted by Mac OS into *Apple events*—messages that can be understood by the operating system and applications. When you run a script, the script can send instructions to the operating system or applications and receive messages in return.

For example, say that at the end of each working day, you back up the contents of a specific folder to a network disk before you shut down your computer. The folder is large and the network is slow, so you often have to wait ten minutes or more to shut down the computer when the backup is finished. You can write a script that mounts the network drive, backs up the folder, and shuts down your computer automatically. You simply run the script, turn out the lights, and go home. AppleScript does the rest.

In this part of the chapter, I introduce AppleScript's components to give you an idea of how it works and what you can do with it.

**Figure 19** The contents of the AppleScript folder inside the Applications folder.

## ✔ Tip

- You can find a lot more information about AppleScript, including tutorials, sample scripts, and a reference manual, at Apple's AppleScript Web site, www. apple.com/applescript/.

**Figure 20** The three basic file formats for an Apple-Script: a script (left), an application (middle), and a text file (right). Note the file name extensions for these formats.

**Figure 21** The Script Editor window with a very simple script. Note how Script Editor formats the script for easy reading.

# AppleScript Files

There are three main types of AppleScript files (**Figure 20**):

◆ **Scripts** (formerly *compiled scripts*) are completed scripts that can be launched from an application's script menu or the Script Menu. Double-clicking a compiled script icon launches Script Editor.

◆ **Applications** (or *applets*) are full-fledged applications that can be launched by double-clicking their icons.

◆ **Text files** are plain text files containing AppleScript statements. They can be opened with Script Editor or any text editor and can be run from within Script Editor. Double-clicking a script text file icon launches the application in which it was written.

# Script Editor

Script Editor is an application you can use to write AppleScript scripts. It has a number of features that make it an extremely useful tool for script writing:

◆ The Script Editor window (**Figure 21**) can automatically format script statements so they're easy to read.

◆ The syntax checker can examine your script statements and identify any syntax errors that would prevent the script from running or compiling.

◆ The Open Dictionary command makes it possible to view an application's diction-ary of AppleScript commands and classes (**Figure 22**).

◆ The record script feature can record actions as script steps.

◆ The Save and Save As commands enable you to save scripts in a variety of formats.

**APPLESCRIPT BASICS**

# AppleScript Dictionaries

Scriptable applications include *AppleScript dictionaries*, which list and provide syntax information for valid AppleScript commands and classes. These dictionaries are a valuable reference for anyone who wants to write scripts.

An AppleScript dictionary is organized into *suites*. Each suite includes a number of related *commands* and *objects*. Commands are like verbs—they tell an application to do something. *Objects*, which include *classes* and *elements*, are what a command can be performed on. For example, in TextEdit's Standard Suite, *close* is a command that can be performed on an object such as *window*. *Properties* help distinguish objects; for example, the *file type* property can help distinguish one *file* object from another.

**Figures 22** and **23** show examples of AppleScript Dictionaries for two applications: Finder and TextEdit. If you've worked with previous versions of Script Editor, you may notice that the Dictionary window has been reworked for Mac OS X 10.4 to better organize information. Colored symbols help visually distinguish between suites, commands, classes, elements, and properties. You can click an item in one of the top three columns or a link in the bottom half of the window to instantly display related information in the bottom half of the window.

## ✔ Tip

- ■ Although dictionaries are helpful for learning valid AppleScript commands, they are not sufficient for teaching a beginner how to write scripts.

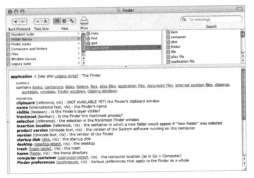

**Figure 22** The Standard Suite of Finder's AppleScript dictionary.

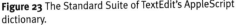

**Figure 23** The Standard Suite of TextEdit's AppleScript dictionary.

APPLESCRIPT BASICS

## AppleScript Utility

AppleScript Utility, which is new in Mac OS X 10.4, enables you to set various scripting options, such as the default script editing application, and install or remove a Script Menu. When installed, the Script Menu adds a menu full of example scripts to the menu bar. You can modify this menu by removing scripts you don't use or adding your own custom scripts.

## ✔ Tip

- AppleScript Utility replaces Install Script Menu and Remove Script Menu, two utilities that appeared in the Mac OS X 10.3 version of AppleScript.

## Folder Actions

Folder Actions is a feature of Mac OS X that works with AppleScript. You create a script that performs a specific task, then attach that script to a folder. When the folder is modified in a predefined way—for example, when it is opened or a file is added to it—the script activates and performs its task.

How can Folder Actions help you? Here's an example. Suppose you're writing a book and every time you finish a chapter, you need to upload a copy of it to an FTP site so your editors can download and review it. You can write a script that uploads any new file added to a folder to the FTP site. Attach that script to a folder and *voilà*! Every time you save a copy of a chapter to the folder, it is automatically sent for review.

## ✔ Tip

- To learn more about writing scripts for Folder Actions, visit www.apple.com/applescript/folder_actions/.

**APPLESCRIPT BASICS**

# Using AppleScript

As with most programming languages, AppleScript can be extremely complex—far too complex to fully cover in this book. On the following pages, I explain how you can get started using AppleScript. This introduction should be enough to help you decide whether you want to fully explore the world of AppleScript programming.

## ✔ Tip

- When you're ready for more how-to information for using AppleScript, I highly recommend Sal Soghioian's excellent book, *AppleScript 1-2-3*, published by Peachpit Press.

## To launch Script Editor

Open the Script Editor icon in the Apple-Script folder in your Applications folder (**Figure 19**). An untitled Script Editor window appears (**Figure 24**).

*Or*

Open the icon for a script (**Figure 20**, left). The script appears in a Script Editor window (**Figure 21**).

## To write a script

1. If necessary, choose File > New (**Figure 25**) or press ⌘ ⌘ N to open an empty Script Editor window (**Figure 24**).

2. If desired, click the Description button at the bottom of the window and type a description for the script in the pane above it.

3. Type the script steps in the top half of the window. Text appears in purple as you type. Be sure to press Return after each line. **Figure 26** shows an example of another simple script.

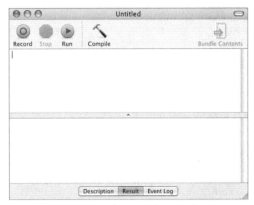

**Figure 24** A new untitled Script Editor window.

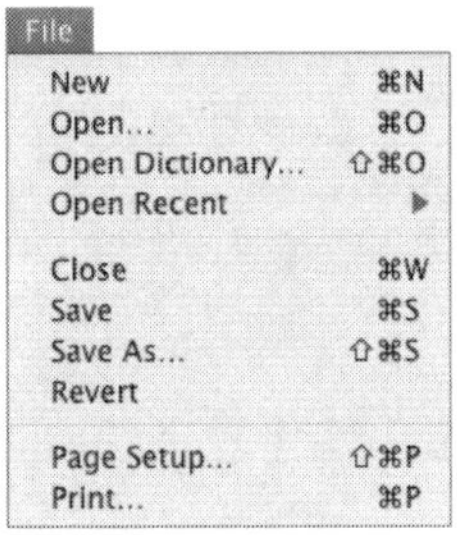

**Figure 25** Script Editor's File menu.

**Figure 26** A painfully simple script.

**LAUNCHING SCRIPT EDITOR, WRITING SCRIPTS**

Figure 27 The script from **Figure 26** after it has been compiled.

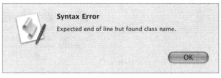

Figure 28 If the script contains an error, you'll see a dialog sheet like this one when you attempt to compile it.

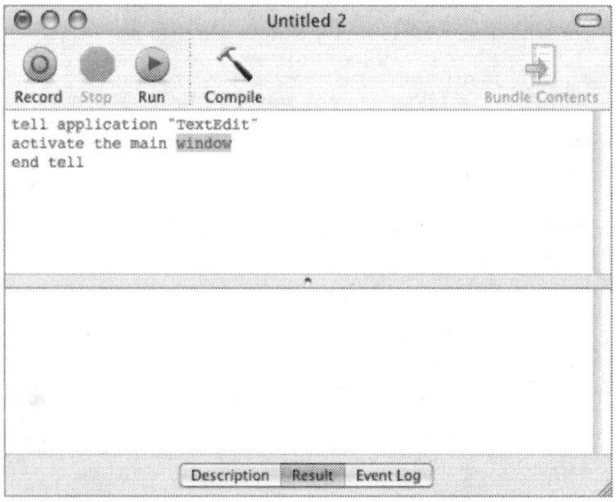

![Script Editor window showing Untitled 2](tell application "TextEdit" / activate the main window / end tell)

Figure 29 Script Editor helps you debug a script by highlighting problems.

# To check the syntax for a script

Click the Compile button in the script window (**Figure 26**).

If your script's syntax is error-free, Script Editor formats and color-codes your statements (**Figure 27**).

*Or*

If Script Editor finds a problem with your script, it displays a dialog that describes the problem (**Figure 28**) and indicates where it is in the script by selecting it (**Figure 29**). Click OK to dismiss the dialog and fix the problem.

## ✔ Tips

■ The syntax checker uses AppleScript's *compiler* to translates the script into *code* that can be read and understood by your computer. (Compiled code does not appear on screen.) If the script cannot be compiled, a syntax error results.

■ Unfortunately, even if you write a script without any syntax errors, the script is not guaranteed to work. The only way to make sure a script works is to run it.

**CHECKING SYNTAX**

## To record a script

1. If necessary, choose File > New Script (**Figure 25**) or press ⌘ ⌘ N to open an empty Script Editor window (**Figure 24**).

2. If desired, click the Description button at the bottom of the window and type a description for the script in the pane above it.

3. Click the Record button.

4. Perform the steps you want Script Editor to record. As you work, Script Editor writes AppleScript instructions in the Script Editor window (**Figure 30**).

5. When you are finished recording steps, switch to the Script Editor window and click the Stop button. Script Editor writes the last instruction for the script (**Figure 31**).

## ✔ Tips

- Unfortunately, Script Editor's recorder does not work with all applications. If you attempt to record a task and Script Editor does not write any instructions, the application you are using is not recordable.

- Before you record a script, it's a good idea to know exactly what you want to do. This will prevent errors—which will also be recorded by Script Editor's recorder!

- Once you have a script recorded by Script Editor, you can edit it as necessary to customize it.

**Figure 30** Script Editor records the steps as you complete them.

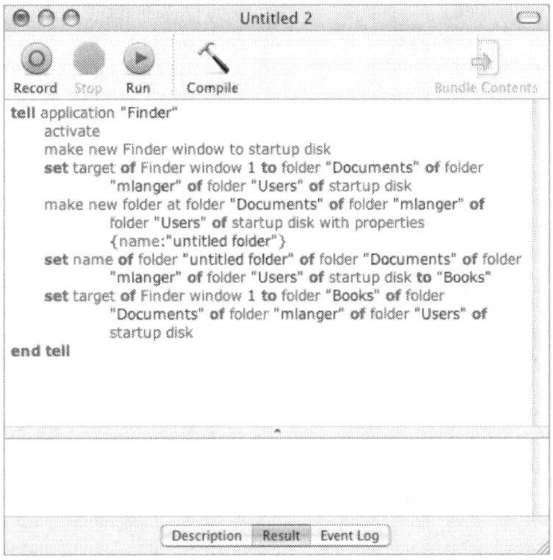

**Figure 31** When you click the Stop button, Script Editor writes the last step.

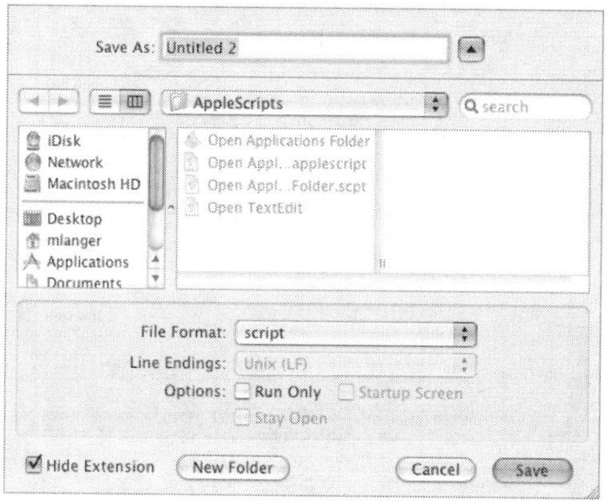

**Figure 32** Script Editor's Save Location dialog.

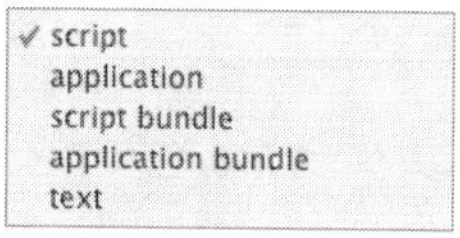

✓ script
application
script bundle
application bundle
text

**Figure 33**
The File Format
pop-up menu.

**Figure 34** A script's name appears in the Script Editor window's title bar.

## To save a script

1. Choose File > Save (**Figure 25**) or press
   ⌃ ⌘ S to display the Save Location dialog
   (**Figure 32**).

2. Enter a script name in the Save As box.

3. Choose a file format from the File Format
   pop-up menu (**Figure 33**).

4. Use the Where part of the dialog to select
   a location in which to save the file.

5. Click Save.

   The file is saved on disk. The script name
   appears in the title bar of the Script
   Editor window (**Figure 34**).

## ✔ Tips

- You cannot save a script if it will not
  compile. Check the script syntax before
  attempting to save the file; I explain how
  earlier in this section.

- If you're not sure what to choose in step
  3, choose script.

- It's a good idea to save a script before
  trying to run it for the first time.

- Using the Save Location dialog is covered
  in **Chapter 7**.

## To run a script

Do one of the following:

◆ To run a compiled script from within Script Editor, click the Run button in the Script Editor window (**Figure 31**).

◆ To run an application from the Finder, double-click the icon for the applet (**Figure 20**, middle).

If the script is valid, it performs all script commands.

*Or*

If the script is not valid, an error message appears (**Figure 35**). Click OK.

## ✔ Tip

■ If a script has been saved as an application, opening it from the Finder automatically runs it.

## To open an application's AppleScript dictionary

1. Choose File > Open Dictionary (**Figure 25**) or press ⌘Shift⌘O.

2. In the Open Dictionary dialog that appears (**Figure 36**), select a dictionary and click Open. The dictionary opens in its own window (**Figures 22 and 23**).

3. Click the name of a suite, command, or class to display its information in the right side of the window.

**Figure 35** When you run a script that contains an error, AppleScript displays an error message like this one.

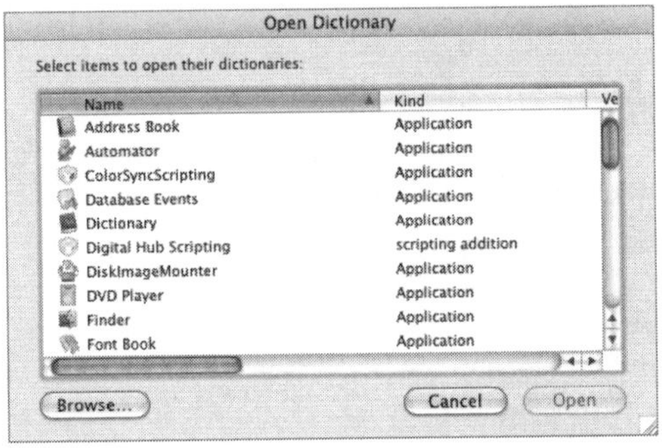

**Figure 36** Use the Open Dictionary dialog to open the AppleScript dictionary for a scriptable application.

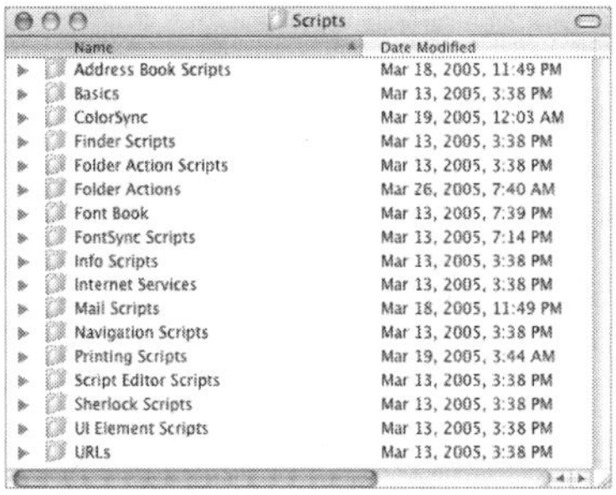

**Figure 37** AppleScript comes with dozens of sample scripts to perform a wide variety of tasks.

**Figure 38** Some scripts can be complex, like this one, which accesses the Internet to get the current temperature at your location. (A thermometer outside your window would be simpler.)

## To examine an example script

1. Double-click the Example Scripts alias icon in the AppleScript folder (**Figure 19**) to open the Scripts folder (**Figure 37**).

2. Open the folder containing the script you want to examine.

3. Double-click the example script file's icon to open it in Script Editor (**Figures 38 and 39**).

## ✔ Tips

- You can modify and experiment with these example scripts as desired.

- If you make changes to an example script, I highly recommend that you use the Save As command to save the revised script with a different name or in a different location. Doing so will keep the original example intact, in case you want to consult it again.

- You can download additional sample scripts from Apple's AppleScript Web site, www.apple.com/applescript/.

**Figure 39** Other scripts can be very simple, like this one-liner to open the AppleScript Web site's home page.

## To enable Script Menu

1. Open the AppleScript Utility in the Apple-Script folder (**Figure 19**).

2. In the AppleScript Utility window that appears (**Figure 40**), turn on the Show Script Menu in menu bar check box. The Script Menu immediately appears in the menu bar (**Figure 41**).

3. Choose AppleScript Utility > Quit Apple-Script Utility, or press ⌃ ⌘ Q.

## ✔ Tip

■ You can remove the Script Menu by turning off the Show Script Menu in menu bar check box (**Figure 40**).

## To run a script with Script Menu

Choose the script you want to run from one of the submenus under the Script menu (**Figure 42**).

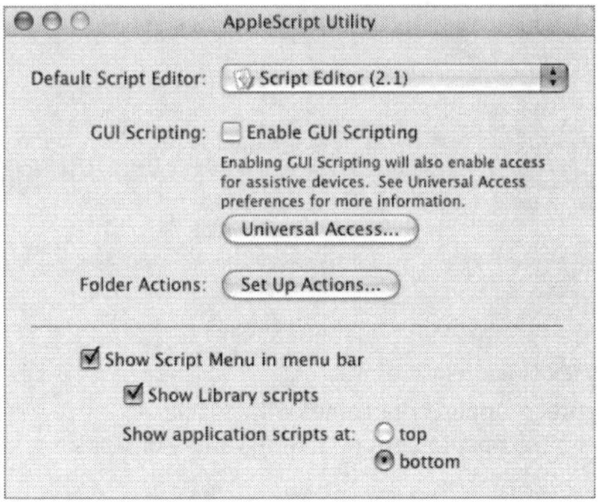

**Figure 40** AppleScript Utility's window.

**Figure 41** The Script menu icon appears near the right end of the menu bar.

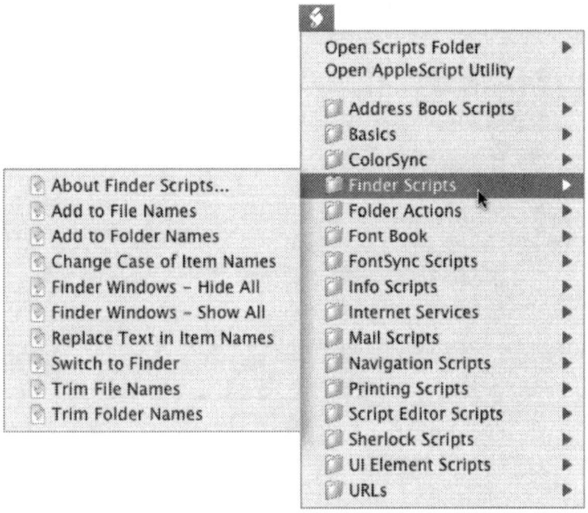

**Figure 42** Script Menu's submenus correspond to the folders in the Scripts folder shown in **Figure 37**.

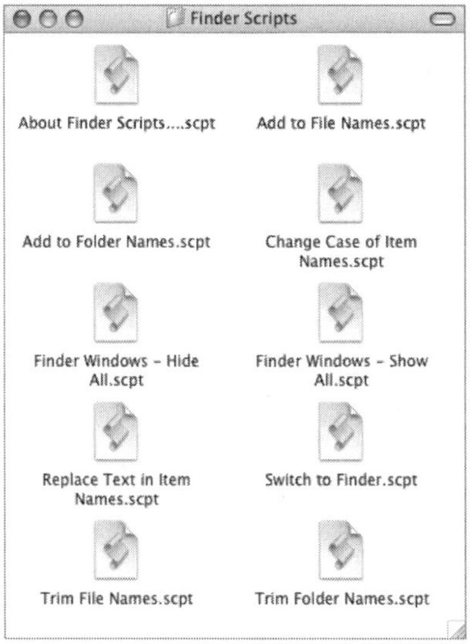

**Figure 43** The contents of the folders inside the Scripts folder correspond to the items on the folder's submenu, as you can see by comparing this folder's contents to the submenu in **Figure 42**.

## To remove a Script Menu script

1. Double-click the Example Scripts alias icon in the AppleScript folder (**Figure 19**) to open the Scripts folder (**Figure 37**).

2. Open the folder that contains the script you want to remove (**Figure 43**).

3. Drag the script out of the folder.

## ✔ Tip

- To move a script from one Script menu submenu to another, drag it from the folder in which it is stored to the folder corresponding to the submenu you want it to appear on.

## To add a Script Menu script

1. Write or record an AppleScript and save it as a script.

2. Double-click the Example Scripts alias icon in the AppleScript folder (**Figure 19**) to open the Scripts folder (**Figure 37**).

3. Drag the icon for the script you want to add into the folder corresponding to the submenu you want the script to appear on.

# System Preferences 21

**Figure 1** The System Preferences window, with icons for all panes displayed.

## System Preferences

One of the great things about Mac OS is the way it can be customized to look and work the way you want it to. Many customization options can be set within the System Preferences application (**Figure 1**). That's where you'll find a variety of preferences panes, each containing settings for a part of Mac OS.

System Preferences panes are organized into four categories:

◆ **Personal** preferences panes enable you to set options to customize various Mac OS X appearance and operation options for personal tastes. This chapter covers Appearance, Dashboard & Exposé, Desktop & Screen Saver, Dock, International, and Spotlight.

◆ **Hardware** preferences panes control settings for various hardware devices. This chapter covers CDs & DVDs, Displays, Energy Saver, Keyboard & Mouse, Print & Fax, and Sound.

◆ **Internet & Network** preferences panes enable you to set options related to Internet and network connections. This chapter covers QuickTime.

◆ **System** preferences panes control various aspects of your computer's operation. This chapter covers Date & Time, Software Update, Speech, Startup Disk, and Universal Access.

## ✔ Tip

■ Other Preferences panes are covered elsewhere in this book:

▲ .Mac, in **Chapter 14**.

▲ Accounts and Security, in **Chapter 17**.

▲ Bluetooth (which only appears if a Bluetooth adapter is installed) and Sharing, in **Chapter 16**.

▲ Classic (which only appears if Mac OS 9.x is installed), in **Chapter 18**.

▲ Network, in **Chapters 13** and **16**.

## To open System Preferences

Choose Apple > System Preferences (**Figure 2**).

*Or*

Click the System Preferences icon in the Dock (**Figure 3**).

The System Preferences window appears (**Figure 1**).

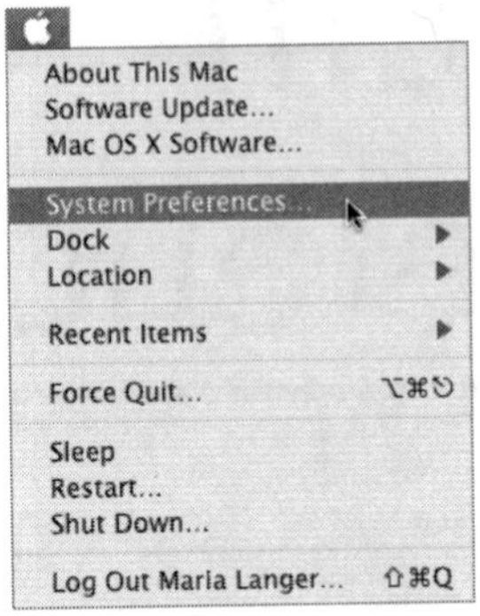

## To open a preferences pane

Click the icon for the pane you want to display.

*Or*

Choose the name of the pane you want to display from the View menu (**Figure 4**).

## To show all preferences pane icons

Choose a command from the System Preferences' View menu (**Figure 4**):

◆ **Organize by Categories** ($\boxed{\circ}$ $\mathbb{H}$ $\boxed{L}$) displays all icons organized by category (**Figure 1**).

◆ **Organize Alphabetically** displays all icons organized alphabetically by name (**Figure 5**).

*Or*

Click the Show All button in the toolbar of the System Preferences window (**Figures 1 and 5**). This displays all icons in the last view used—by category or alphabetically.

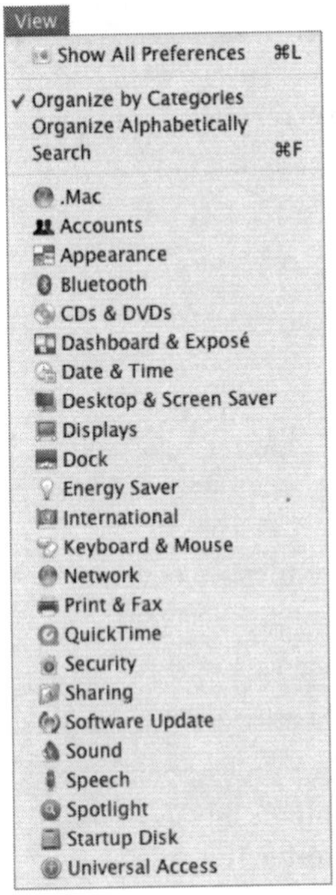

**Figure 2**
To open System Preferences, choose System Preferences from the Apple menu...

**Figure 3** ...or click the System Preferences icon in the Dock.

**Figure 4**
The View menu lists all of the System Preferences panes.

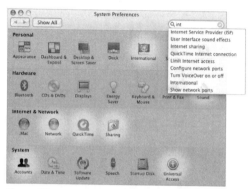

**Figure 5** System Preferences pane icons can also be displayed alphabetically.

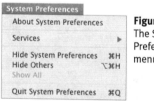

**Figure 6** You can now search system preferences to find the preference pane you need to perform a task.

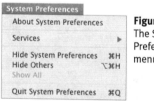

**Figure 7**
The System
Preferences
menu.

## To find a preference pane by task or topic

1.  Enter a search word or phrase in the search box in the upper-right corner of the System Preferences window. Three things happen (**Figure 6**):

    ▲ The window gets dark.

    ▲ Icons for related preference panes are highlighted.

    ▲ A menu of possible topics appears.

2.  Select a topic from the menu.

    *or*

    Click a highlighted icon.

    The appropriate preference pane opens.

## ✔ Tip

■ The ability to search system preferences is brand new in Mac OS X 10.4.

## To quit System Preferences

Use one of the following techniques:

◆ Choose System Preferences > Quit System Preferences (**Figure 7**).

◆ Press ⌃⌘Q.

◆ Click the System Preferences window's close button.

# Appearance

The Appearance preferences pane (**Figure 8**) enables you to set options for color, scroll bar functionality, recent items, and text smoothing.

## To set Appearance preferences

In the Appearance preferences pane (**Figure 8**), set options as desired:

◆ **Appearance** sets the color for buttons, menus, and windows throughout Mac OS X and Mac OS X applications.

◆ **Highlight Color** sets the highlight color for text in documents, fields, and lists.

◆ **Place scroll arrows** determines where scroll arrows should appear in windows and scrolling lists:

▲ **At top and bottom** places a scroll arrow at each end of the scroll bar (**Figure 9**).

▲ **Together** places both scroll arrows together at the bottom or right end of the scroll bar (**Figure 10**).

◆ **Click in the scroll bar to** determines what happens when you click in the scroll track of a scroll bar.

▲ **Jump to the next page** scrolls to the next window or page of the document.

▲ **Scroll to here** scrolls to the relative location in the document. For example, if you click in the scroll track two-thirds of the way between the top and bottom, you'll scroll two-thirds of the way through the document. This is the same as dragging the scroller to that position.

▲ **Use smooth scrolling** scrolls the contents of a window smoothly, without jumping.

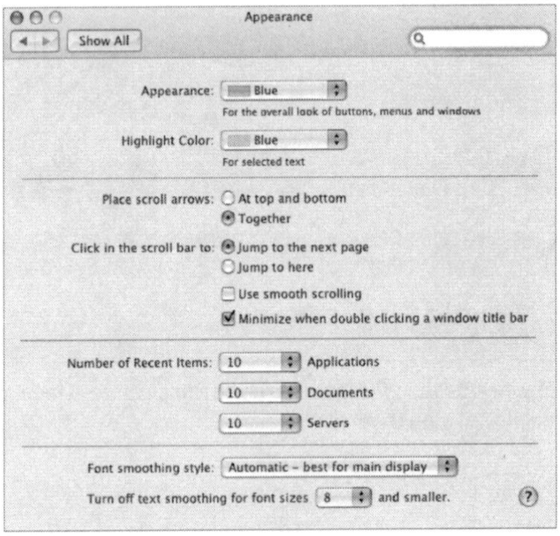

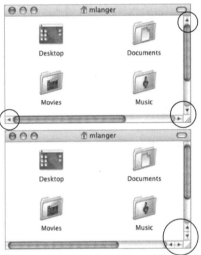

**Figure 8** The Appearance preferences pane.

**Figures 9 & 10** A window with scroll bars at top and bottom (top) and the same window with scroll bars together (bottom).

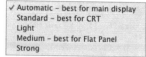

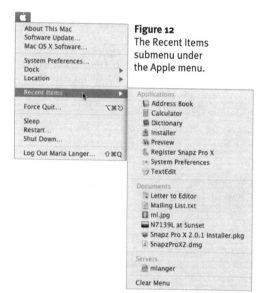

**Figure 11** The Font smoothing style pop-up menu.

**Figure 12**
The Recent Items submenu under the Apple menu.

12-point text with text smoothing turned on.

12-point text with text smoothing turned off.

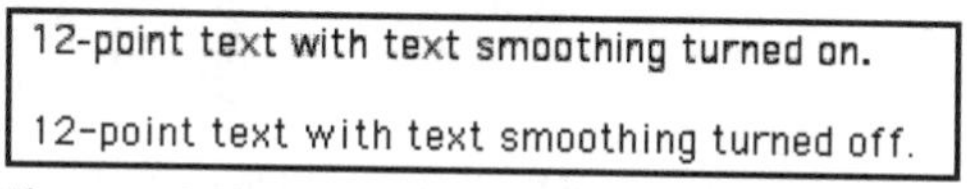

**Figure 13** As these example show, text smoothing can change the appearance of text on screen.

▲ **Minimize when double clicking a window title bar** minimizes a window to the Dock when you double-click its title bar.

◆ **Applications, Documents,** and **Servers** enables you to choose the number of items you want Mac OS X to consider "recent" when displaying recent applications, documents, and servers. Options range from None to 50.

◆ **Font smoothing style (Figure 11)** determines how Mac OS X smooths text onscreen.

◆ **Turn off text smoothing for font sizes** enables you to choose a minimum font size for text smoothing. Text in the font size you set and smaller will not be smoothed. Your options range from 4 to 12.

## ✔ Tips

■ I tell you about minimizing windows in **Chapter 2**.

■ Recent items appear on the Recent Items submenu under the Apple menu **(Figure 12)**.

■ You can clear the Recent Items submenu by choosing Apple > Recent Items > Clear Menu **(Figure 12)**.

■ Font or text smoothing uses a process called *antialiasing* to make text more legible onscreen. Antialiasing creates gray pixels between black ones and white ones to eliminate sharp edges. **Figure 13** shows what text looks like with text smoothing turned on and off.

# CDs & DVDs

The CDs & DVDs preferences pane lets you specify what should happen when you insert a CD or DVD. The options that appear vary depending on your computer's CD and DVD capabilities. **Figure 14** shows how this preferences pane appears for an eMac with a SuperDrive, which is capable of reading and writing both CDs and DVDs.

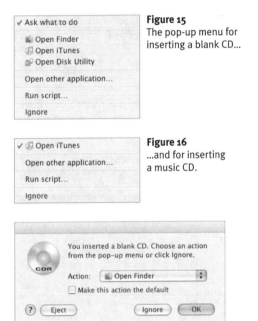

**Figure 14** The CDs & DVDs preferences pane on an iMac with a SuperDrive.

## To specify what should happen when you insert a CD or DVD

Choose an option from the pop-up menu beside the event that you want to set. The menus are basically the same; **Figures 15** and **16** shows an example for inserting a blank CD and a music CD. Your options are:

◆ **Ask what to do** displays a dialog like the one in **Figure 17**, which enables you to tell your computer what to do each time you insert that type of disc. If you turn on the Make this action the default check box in the dialog, you will change the setting for that type of disc in the CDs & DVDs preferences pane.

◆ **Open** *application name* opens the specified application. Use this option if you always want to open a specific application when you insert that type of disc.

◆ **Open other application** displays a dialog like the one in **Figure 18**. Use it to select and open the application that should open when you insert that type of disc.

◆ **Run script** displays a dialog like the one in **Figure 18**. Use it to select and open an AppleScript applet that should open when you insert that type of disc. (I discuss AppleScript in **Chapter 20**.)

◆ **Ignore** tells your computer not to do anything when you insert that type of disc.

**Figure 15**
The pop-up menu for inserting a blank CD...

**Figure 16**
...and for inserting a music CD.

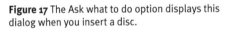

**Figure 17** The Ask what to do option displays this dialog when you insert a disc.

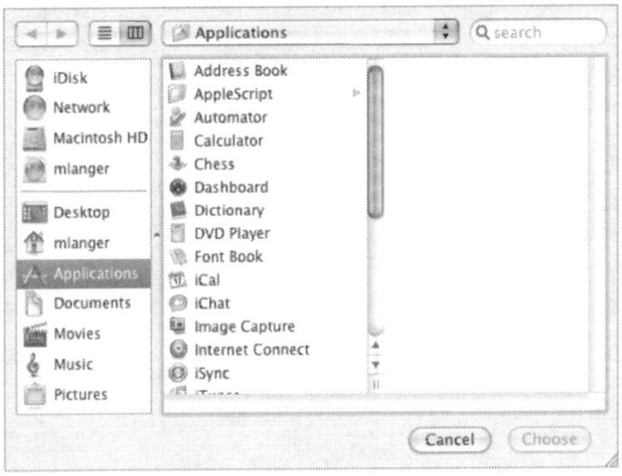

**Figure 18** Use this dialog to select an application or script to run when you insert a disc.

**SETTING CD & DVD OPTIONS**

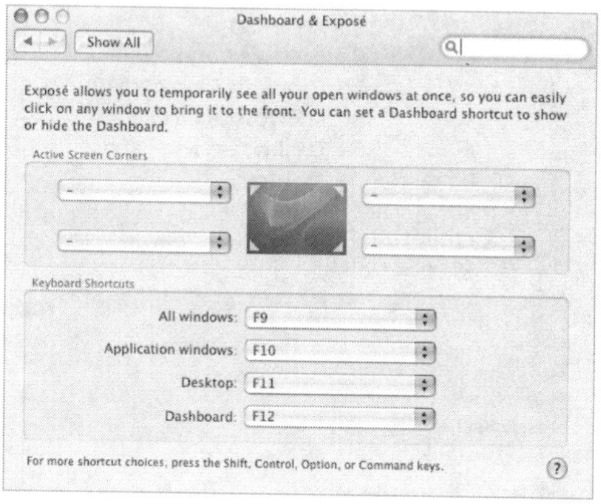

**Figure 19** Default settings in the Dashboard & Exposé preferences pane.

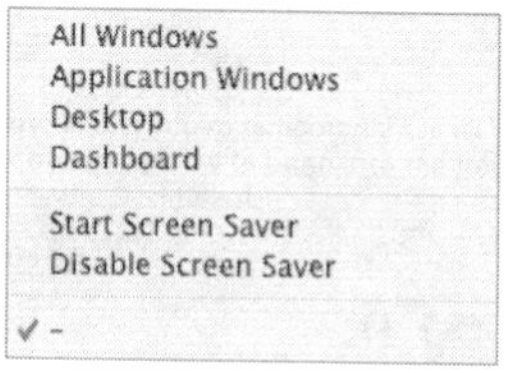

**Figure 20**
Use this pop-up menu to configure hot corners.

# Dashboard & Exposé

Dashboard & Exposé preferences enable you to customize the way the Dashboard and Exposé features work and to set "hot corners" that activate or prevent the activation of the screen saver feature.

## ✔ Tip

■ I explain how to use Dashboard in **Chapter 10**, Exposé in **Chapter 4**, and Mac OS X's built-in screen saver later in this chapter.

## To set hot corners

In the Dashboard & Exposé preferences pane (**Figure 19**), choose an option from the pop-up menu (**Figure 20**) for the screen corner you want to configure. The option you choose determines what happens when you move your mouse pointer to that corner of the screen:

◆ **All Windows** uses Exposé to display all open window. This is the same as pressing F9 with default Exposé settings.

◆ **Application Windows** uses Exposé to display all windows for the active application. This is the same as pressing F10 with default Exposé settings.

◆ **Desktop** uses Exposé to move all windows aside so you can see the Desktop. This is the same as pressing F11 with default Exposé settings.

◆ **Dashboard** displays Dashboard's widgets This is the same as pressing F12 with default Dashboard settings..

◆ **Start Screen Saver** immediately displays the screen saver.

◆ **Disable Screen Saver** prevents the screen saver from automatically starting.

◆ – does nothing.

**583**

## To set Dashboard and Exposé keyboard shortcuts

In the Dashboard & Exposé preferences pane (**Figure 19**), choose an option from the Keyboard Shortcuts pop-up menu for the feature you want to configure (**Figure 21**).

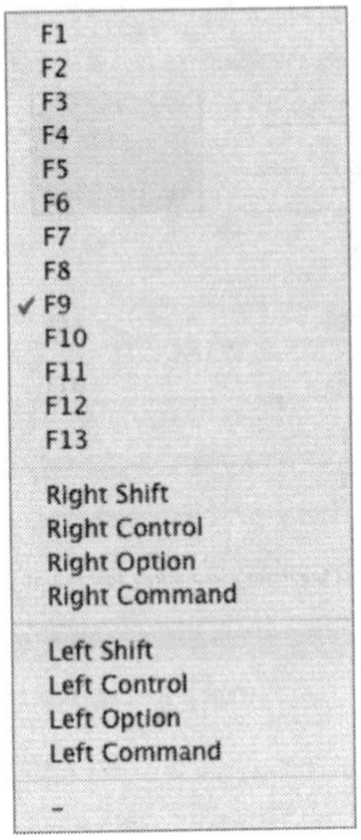

### ✔ Tips

■ Right and Left on the Keyboard Shortcuts pop-up menu (**Figure 21**) refer to the →  and ← keys.

■ Shift, Control, Option, and Command on the Keyboard Shortcuts pop-up menu (**Figure 21**) refer to the Shift, Control, Option, and ⌘ keys.

```
F1
F2
F3
F4
F5
F6
F7
F8
✓ F9
F10
F11
F12
F13

Right Shift
Right Control
Right Option
Right Command

Left Shift
Left Control
Left Option
Left Command

–
```

**Figure 21**
Use this pop-up menu to set the keyboard shortcut to invoke Dashboard and Exposé features.

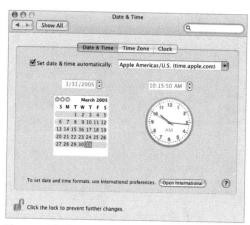

**Figure 22** The Date & Time pane of the Date & Time preferences pane.

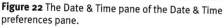

**Figure 23** Click the part of the date that you want to change, then use the arrow buttons to change the value.

# Date & Time

The Date & Time preferences pane includes three panes for setting the system time and clock options:

◆ **Date & Time (Figure 22)** enables you to manually set the date and time.

◆ **Time Zone (Figure 25)** enables you to set your time zone.

◆ **Clock (Figure 27)** enables you to set options for the appearance of the clock.

## To manually set the date & time

1. In the Date & Time preferences pane, click the Date & Time button (**Figure 22**).

2. If necessary, turn off the Set date & time automatically check box.

3. To change the date, click the part of the date you want to change (**Figure 23**), then type a new value or use the tiny arrow buttons beside the date to change the value.

4. To change the time, click the part of the time that you want to change and type a new value or use the tiny arrow buttons beside the time to change the value.

5. Click Save.

## ✔ Tips

■ You can't manually change the date or time if you have enabled the network time server feature; I tell you more about that on the next page.

■ Another way to change the time in step 4 is to drag the hands of the analog clock so they display the correct time.

**SETTING THE DATE & TIME**

## To automatically set the date & time

1. In the Date & Time preferences pane, click the Date & Time button (**Figure 22**).

2. Turn on the Set date & time automatically check box.

3. Choose the closest time server from the drop-down list (**Figure 24**).

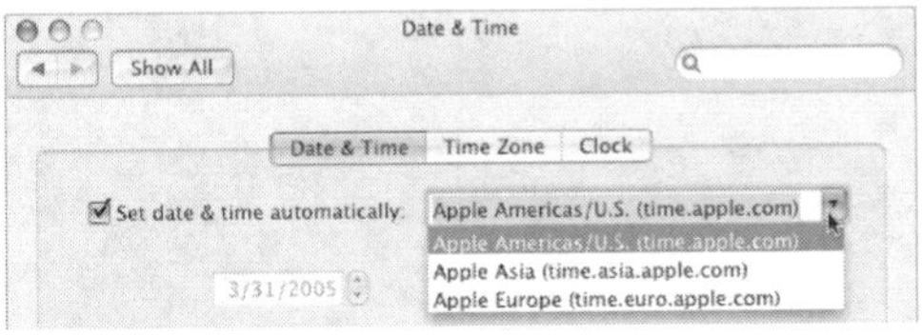

### ✔ Tip

■ With the network time server feature enabled, your computer will use its Internet connection to periodically get the date and time from a time server and update the system clock automatically. This ensures that your computer's clock is always correct.

## To set the time zone

1. In the Date & Time preferences pane, click the Time Zone button (**Figure 25**).

2. Click your approximate location on the map. A white bar indicates the time zone area (**Figure 25**).

3. If necessary, choose the name of your time zone from the Closest City drop-down list beneath the map (**Figure 26**).

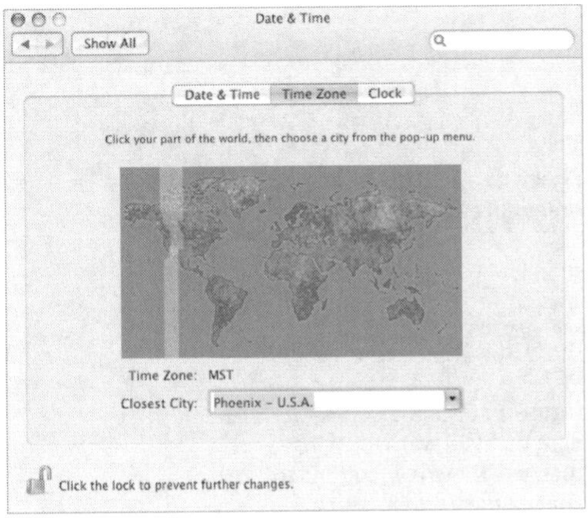

### ✔ Tips

■ In step 3, only those time zones within the white bar on the map are listed in the drop-down list (**Figure 26**). If your time zone does not appear, make sure you clicked the correct area in the map in step 2.

■ It's a good idea to choose the correct time zone, since Mac OS uses this information with the network time server (if utilized) and to properly change the clock for daylight saving time.

**Figure 24** The drop-down list includes time servers all over the world.

**Figure 25** The Time Zone pane of the Date & Time preferences pane, with a time zone selected.

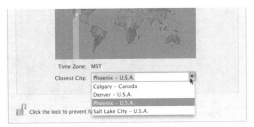

**Figure 26** The Closest City drop-down list only displays cities in the currently selected time zone.

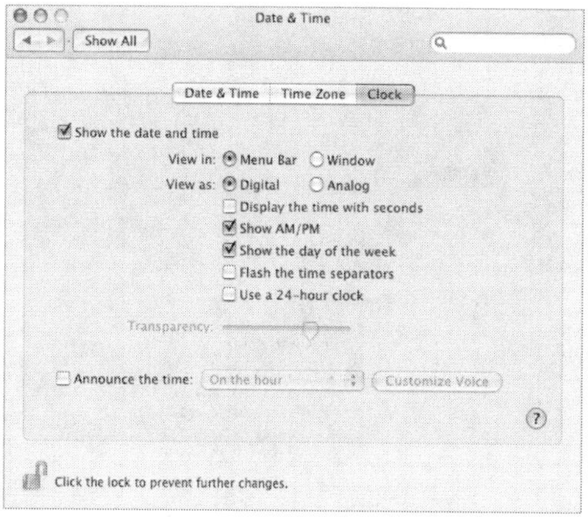

Figure 27 The Clock pane of the Date & Time preferences pane.

**Figure 28**
You can display the clock in a floating window. This example shows a digital clock.

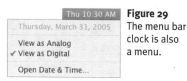

**Figure 29**
The menu bar clock is also a menu.

## ✔ Tip

■ The menu bar clock is also a menu that displays the full date and time and offers options for changing the clock display (**Figure 29**).

## To set clock options

1. In the Date & Time preferences pane, click the Clock button (**Figure 27**).

2. To enable the clock, turn on the Show the date and time check box.

3. Select a View in radio button:
   ▲ **Menu Bar** puts the clock in the menu bar, which is the default location.
   ▲ **Window** puts the clock in a floating window (**Figure 28**).

4. Select a View as radio button:
   ▲ **Digital** displays the date and time with letters and numbers.
   ▲ **Analog** displays the time on an analog clock. If you select this option, you cannot set options in step 5.

5. Toggle check boxes to customize the clock's appearance:
   ▲ **Display the time with seconds** displays the seconds as part of the time.
   ▲ **Show AM/PM** displays AM or PM after the time.
   ▲ **Show the day of the week** displays the three-letter abbreviation for the day of the week before the time.
   ▲ **Flash the time separators** blinks the colon(s) in the time every second.
   ▲ **Use a 24-hour clock** displays the time as a 24-hour (rather than 12-hour) clock.

6. If you selected Window in step 3, you can use the Transparency slider to set the transparency of the clock window.

7. To instruct your computer to vocally announce the time periodically, turn on the Announce the time check box and choose a frequency option from the pop-up menu.

**SETTING CLOCK OPTIONS**

# Desktop & Screen Saver

The Desktop & Screen Saver preferences pane (**Figures 30 and 35**) enables you to set the background picture for the Mac OS X desktop and configure a screen saver that appears when your computer is idle.

## ✔ Tips

- Mac OS X's built-in screen saver doesn't really "save" anything. All it does is cover the normal screen display with graphics, providing an interesting visual when your computer is inactive.

- The Energy Saver preferences pane offers more protection for LCD displays than Screen Saver. Energy Saver is covered later in this chapter.

## To set the desktop picture

1. In the Desktop & Screen Saver preferences pane, click the Desktop button to display Desktop options (**Figure 30**).

2. In the list on the left side of the window, select an image collection or folder. The images in the collection appear on the right side of the window.

3. Click to select the image you want. It appears in the image well above the collection list and the desktop's background picture changes (**Figure 31**).

4. If the picture's dimensions are not the same as the screen resolution, choose an option from the pop-up menu beside the image preview (**Figure 32**) to indicate how it should appear.

5. To change the picture periodically, turn on the Change picture check box and select a frequency option from the pop-up menu (**Figure 33**). Turning on the Random order check box beside this displays the images in random order.

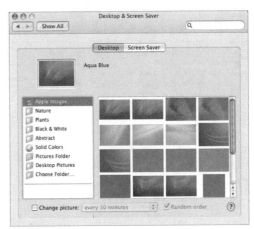

**Figure 30** The Desktop pane of the Desktop & Screen Saver preferences pane.

**Figure 31** In this example, I've selected a photo of the Grand Canyon from my Pictures folder.

| ✔ Fill screen | **Figure 32** |
|---|---|
| Stretch to fill screen | Choose an option to indicate |
| Center | how the picture should appear |
| Tile | onscreen. |

| when logging in | **Figure 33** |
|---|---|
| when waking from sleep | Use this pop-up menu |
|  | to set the picture |
| every 5 seconds | changing frequency. |
| every minute |  |
| every 5 minutes |  |
| every 15 minutes |  |
| ✔ every 30 minutes |  |
| every hour |  |
| every day |  |

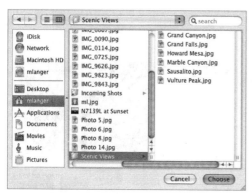

**Figure 34** Use this dialog to locate, select, and choose a folder containing pictures.

## ✔ Tips

- For best results, use pictures that are the same size or larger than your screen resolution. For example, if your screen resolution is set to 1024 x 768, the image should be at least this size. You can check or change your screen resolution in the Displays preferences pane, which I discuss later in this chapter.

- The image collection list on the left side of the Desktop pane (**Figures 30 and 31**) include predefined collections installed with Mac OS X, as well as access to your Pictures folder, your iPhoto library (if iPhoto is installed), and any iPhoto albums you may have set up.

- In step 2, if you select Choose Folder, you can use a dialog like the one in **Figure 34** to locate, select, and open another folder that contains images.

- In step 5, you can only turn on the Change picture check box if you selected a collection above the divider line in the collection list in step 2—in other words, any image except an iPhoto library image.

- Although you can have your desktop display a virtual slide show by setting the picture changing frequency in step 5 to a low value like 5 seconds, you may find it distracting—and nonproductive—to have the background change that often. I know I would!

**SETTING THE DESKTOP PICTURE**

# To configure the screen saver

1. In the Desktop & Screen Saver preferences pane, click the Screen Saver button to display Screen Saver options (**Figure 35**).

2. In the Screen Savers list, select a screen saver module. The preview area changes accordingly.

3. To set options for the screen saver, click Options. Not all screen savers can be configured and the options that are available vary depending on the screen saver you selected in Step 2. **Figures 36** and **37** show two examples.

4. To see what the screen effect looks like on your screen, click Test. The screen goes black and the screen effect kicks in. To go back to work, move your mouse.

5. To have the screen saver start automatically after a certain amount of idle time, drag the Start screen saver slider to the desired value.

6. To set "hot corners" that activate or deactivate the screen saver, click the Hot Corners button to display the Active Screen Corners dialog (**Figure 38**). Choose an option from each pop-up menu (**Figure 39**) to specify what should happen when you position the mouse pointer in the corresponding corner. When you're finished, click OK to save your settings.

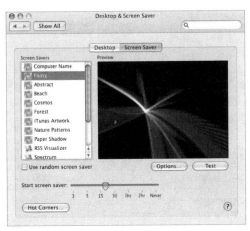

**Figure 35** The Screen Saver pane of the Desktop & Screen Saver preferences pane.

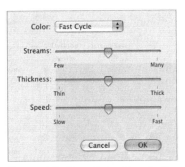

**Figure 36** Configuration options for the Flurry screen saver.

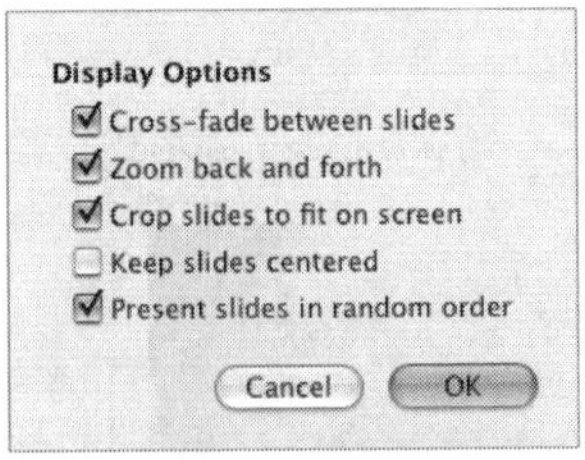

**Display Options**
- ☑ Cross-fade between slides
- ☑ Zoom back and forth
- ☑ Crop slides to fit on screen
- ☐ Keep slides centered
- ☑ Present slides in random order

Cancel   OK

**Figure 37** Configuration options for slide show screen savers.

**Figure 38** Use this dialog to set hot corners for activating or deactivating the screen saver. In this example, it's set so that if I put my mouse pointer in the upper-left corner of the screen, the screen saver never goes on, and if I put my mouse pointer in the lower-right corner of the screen, the screen saver goes on immediately.

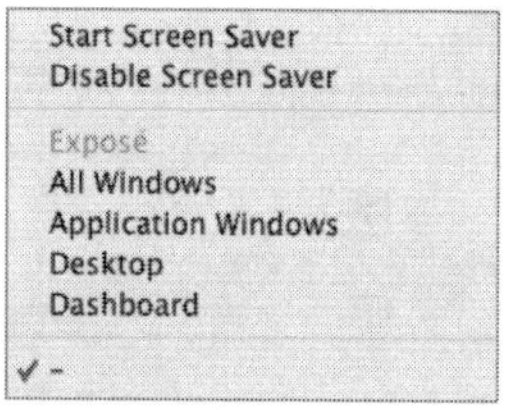

Start Screen Saver
Disable Screen Saver

Exposé
All Windows
Application Windows
Desktop
Dashboard

✓ –

**Figure 39**
This pop-up menu includes Screen Saver, Exposé, and Dashboard options.

## ✔ Tips

- If you're not picky about what screen saver appears, you can turn on the Use random screen saver check box after step 1 and skip steps 2 through 4.

- In step 2, if you select Choose Folder, you can use a dialog like the one in **Figure 34** to locate, select, and open another folder that contains images.

- The .Mac screen effects module enables you to display slides published on a .Mac member's iDisk with iPhoto. This requires a connection to the Internet. To publish your slides on iDisk, you must have a .Mac member account and iPhoto. I cover .Mac in **Chapter 11**; a discussion of iPhoto, which is part of Apple's iLife suite of software, is beyond the scope of this book.

- As shown in **Figure 39**, you can use the Active Screen Corners dialog to set up hot corners for Exposé and Dashboard, too.

- In step 6, you can configure the hot corners any way you like. For example, you can set it up so every corner starts the screen saver.

CONFIGURING THE SCREEN SAVER

**591**

# Displays

The Displays preferences pane enables you to set the resolution, geometry, colors, and other settings for your monitor. Settings are organized into panes; this section covers the Display (**Figure 40**) and Color (**Figure 44**) panes.

## ✔ Tip

- The options that are available in the Displays preferences pane vary depending on your computer and monitor. The options shown in this chapter are for an eMac.

## To set basic display options

1. In the Displays preferences pane, click the Display button (**Figure 40**).

2. Set options as desired:

   ▲ **Resolutions** control the number of pixels that appear on screen. The higher the resolution, the more pixels appear on screen. This makes the screen contents smaller, but shows more onscreen, as shown in **Figures 41** and **42**.

   ▲ **Colors** controls the number of colors that appear on screen. The more colors, the better the screen image appears.

   ▲ **Refresh Rate** controls the screen refresh rate, in hertz. The higher the number, the steadier the image.

   ▲ **Show displays in menu bar** displays a menu of recently used display settings in the menu bar (**Figure 43**). You can use the pop-up menu beneath this option to specify how many recent settings should appear in the menu.

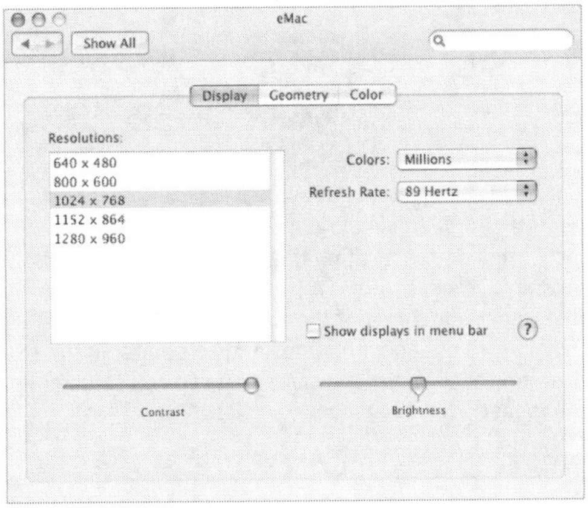

**Figure 40** The Display pane of the Displays preferences pane for an eMac.

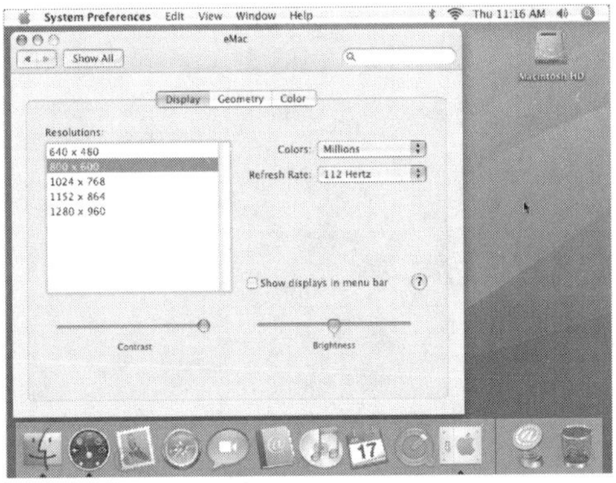

**Figure 41** An eMac display set to 800 x 600 resolution...

**Figure 42** ...and the same display set to 1280 x 960 resolution.

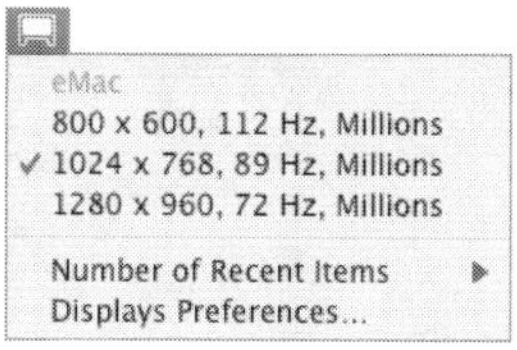

**Figure 43**
The Displays menu in the menu bar.

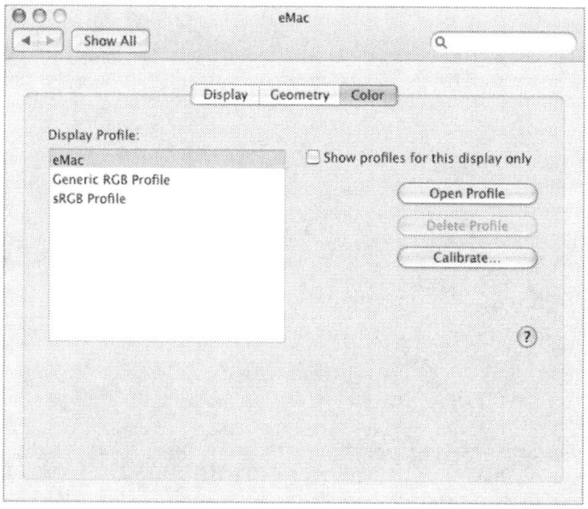

**Figure 44** The Color pane of the Displays preferences pane for an eMac.

▲ **Contrast** and **Brightness** enable you to adjust the display's contrast and brightness by dragging the sliders.

## To set display color profile

1. In the Displays preferences pane, click the Color button (**Figure 44**).

2. Select one of the Display Profiles.

## ✔ Tips

■ Color profiles is an advanced feature of Mac OS that enables you to display colors onscreen as they will appear when printed.

■ Clicking the Calibrate button in the Color tab of the Displays preferences pane opens the Display Calibrator Assistant, which I discuss in **Chapter 22**.

**SETTING DISPLAY COLOR OPTIONS**

# Dock

The Dock preferences pane (**Figure 45**) offers several options for customizing the Dock's appearance and functionality.

## To customize the Dock

In the Dock preferences pane (**Figure 45**), set options as desired:

◆ To set the size of the Dock and its icons, drag the Dock Size slider to the left or right.

◆ To enable Dock icon magnification (**Figure 46**), turn on the Magnification check box. Then drag the slider to the left or right to specify how large the magnified icons should become when you point to them.

◆ To change the Dock's position on the screen, select one of the Position on screen options: Left (**Figure 47**), Bottom (**the default**), or Right.

◆ To set the special effect Mac OS X uses to minimize a window to an icon in the Dock and maximize an icon from the Dock to a window, choose an option from the Minimize using pop-up menu:

▲ **Genie Effect**, the default option, shrinks the window into the Dock like a genie slipping into a magic lamp. (Well, how else could you describe it?)

▲ **Scale Effect** simply shrinks the icon into the Dock.

◆ To display the "bouncing icon" animation while a program is launching, turn on the Animate opening applications check box.

◆ To hide the Dock until you need it, turn on the Automatically hide and show the Dock check box. With this feature enabled, the Dock disappears until you move the mouse pointer to the edge of the screen where the Dock is positioned.

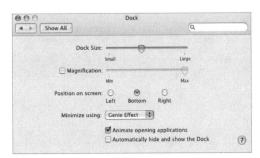

**Figure 45** The Dock preferences pane.

**Figure 46** With magnification enabled, when you point to an icon in the Dock, it grows so you can see it better.

**Figure 47** When you set the Dock's position to Left, it appears as a vertical bar of icons on the left side of the screen, below the Apple menu.

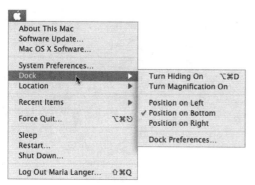

**Figure 48** Use the Dock submenu under the Apple menu to set some Dock options.

## ✔ Tips

- You can use the Dock submenu under the Apple menu (**Figure 48**) to set some Dock options without opening the Dock preferences pane. (You can also use this submenu to open the Dock preferences pane.)

- If you think the Dock takes up too much valuable real estate on your screen, try one of these options:

  ▲ Set the Dock size smaller, then enable magnification so the icons enlarge when you point to them.

  ▲ Position the Dock on the right. In most cases, document and Finder windows won't need to cover that area of the screen.

  ▲ Turn on the Automatically hide and show the Dock check box. (This is what I do and it works like a charm.)

- You can add, remove, or rearrange icons on the Dock by dragging them, as discussed in **Chapter 6**.

CUSTOMIZING THE DOCK

# Energy Saver

The Energy Saver preference pane (**Figures 49** and **52**) enables you to specify settings for automatic system, display, and hard disk sleep. These settings can reduce the amount of power your computer uses when idle.

## ✔ Tips

■ Energy Saver settings are especially important for PowerBook and iBook users running on battery power.

■ To wake a sleeping display, press any key. A sleeping hard disk wakes automatically when it needs to.

■ Display sleep is a better way to protect flat panel displays and displays on Power-Books and iBooks than a screen saver. Mac OS X's built-in screen saver is covered earlier in this chapter.

## To set Energy Saver sleep options

1. In the Energy Saver preferences pane, click the Sleep button to display its options (**Figure 49**).

2. Set options as desired:

   ▲ To set the computer sleep timing, drag the top slider to the left or right.

   ▲ To set different display sleep timing, drag the second slider to the left or right. (You cannot set display sleep for longer than computer sleep.)

   ▲ To tell your computer to put the hard disk to sleep when it isn't needed, turn on the check box.

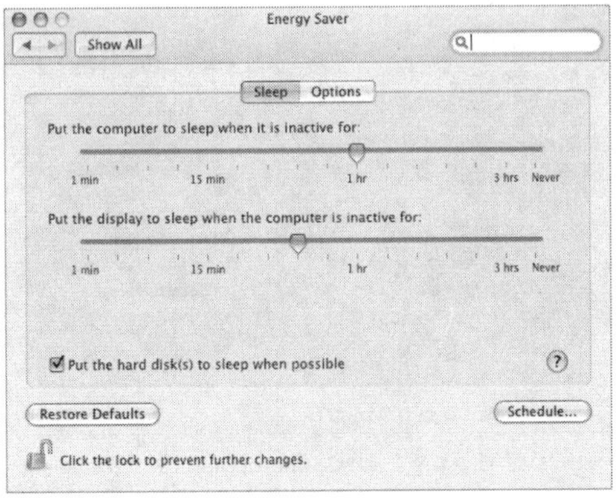

**Figure 49** The Sleep pane of the Energy Saver preferences pane.

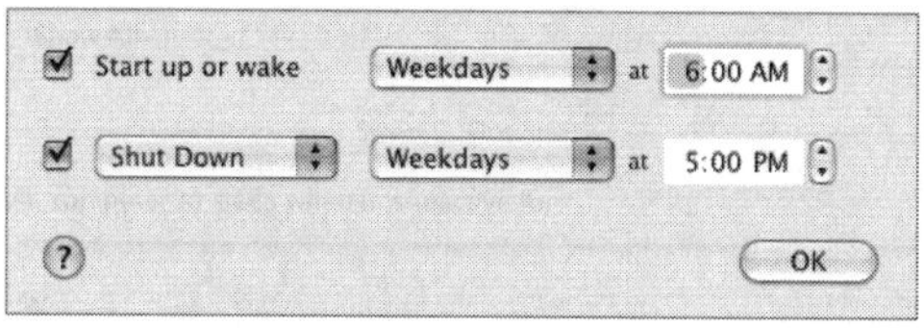

**Figure 50** The Schedule options for the Energy Saver preferences pane.

Weekdays
Weekends
✓ Every Day

Monday
Tuesday
Wednesday
Thursday
Friday
Saturday
Sunday

**Figure 51**
Use this pop-up menu to specify the days you want to start up or shut down the computer automatically.

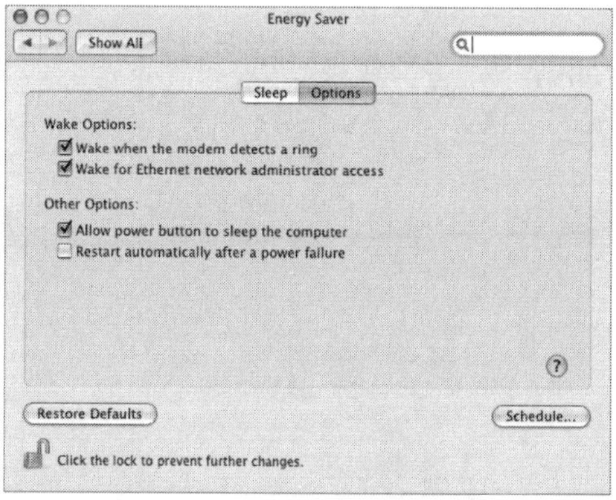

**Figure 52** The Options pane of the Energy Saver preferences pane.

## ✔ Tip

- If your computer is being used as a server, it's important to turn on the Restart automatically check box. This ensures that the computer is running whenever possible.

## To schedule start up & shut down

1. In the Energy Saver preferences pane, click the Schedule button to display its options (**Figure 50**).

2. To start the computer automatically, turn on the top check box. Then choose an option from the pop-up menu (**Figure 51**) and enter a time beside it.

3. To shut down the computer automatically, turn on the second check box, choose an option from the second pop-up menu in that line (**Figure 51**), and enter a time beside it.

## ✔ Tip

- To set the computer to sleep rather than shut down, after step 3, choose Sleep from the first pop-up menu in the second line.

## To set Energy Saver waking & restarting options

1. In the Energy Saver preferences pane, click the Options button (**Figure 52**).

2. Set wake and other options as desired:

   - ▲ **Wake when the modem detects a ring** wakes the computer from System sleep when the modem detects an incoming call.

   - ▲ **Wake for Ethernet network administrator access** wakes the computer from computer sleep when it detects a Wake-on-LAN packet.

   - ▲ **Allow power button to sleep the computer** puts the computer to sleep when you press the power button. This option does not appear for all computers.

   - ▲ **Restart automatically after a power failure** automatically restarts the computer when power is restored after a power failure.

**SETTING OTHER ENERGY SAVER OPTIONS**

# International

The International preferences pane enables you to set options that control how Mac OS X works in an environment where U.S. English is not the primary language or multiple languages are used.

International preferences are broken down into three different categories: Language (**Figure 53**), Formats (**Figure 57**), and Input Menu (**Figure 60**).

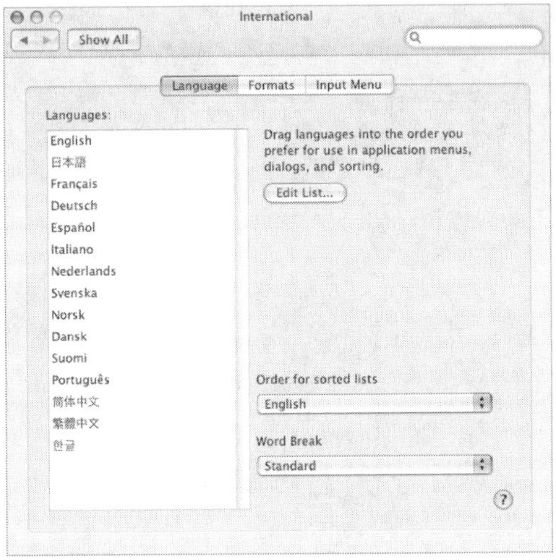

## To set preferred language options

1. In the International preferences pane, click the Language button (**Figure 53**).

2. To set the preferred order for languages to appear in application menus and dialogs, drag languages up or down in the Languages list (**Figure 54**).

3. To set sort order for text, choose an option from the Order for sorted lists pop-up menu.

4. To set word break behavior, choose an option from the Word Break pop-up menu.

## ✔ Tips

- You can edit the Languages list. Click the Edit button in the Language pane (**Figure 53**) to display a dialog sheet like the one in **Figure 55**. Turn on the check boxes beside each language you want to include in the list and click OK.

- The changes you make to the Languages list in step 2 take effect in the Finder the next time you restart or log in. Changes take effect in applications (**Figure 56**) the next time you open them.

- A *script* is a writing system or alphabet.

**Figure 53** The Language pane of the International preferences pane.

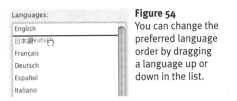

**Figure 54**
You can change the preferred language order by dragging a language up or down in the list.

**Figure 55** Turn on check boxes for the language you want to include in the Languages list.

**Figure 56** Changing the language of an application's menus and dialogs is as easy as dragging the language to the top of the Languages list (**Figure 54**). Here's TextEdit in German (Deutsch).

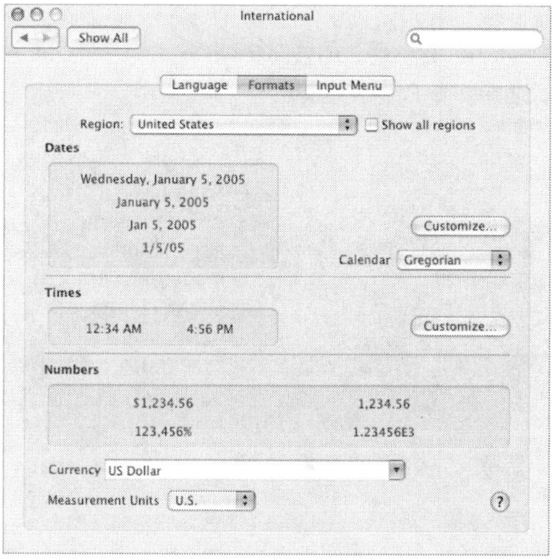

**Figure 57** The Formats pane of the International preferences pane.

## To set the date, time, & number formats

1. In the International Preferences pane, click the Formats button (**Figure 57**).

2. Choose an option from the Region pop-up menu.

3. To customize the date or time format, click the Customize button in the appropriate area of the dialog. In the dialogs that appear (**Figures 58** and **59**), use the pop-up menu to specify which format you want to customize, then drag elements into the edit area to set the format. Repeat this process for each format you want to customize and click OK.

4. To change the currency format, choose an option from the Currency pop-up menu.

5. To change the measurement unit, choose an option from the Measurement Units pop-up menu.

## ✔ Tips

- Changes in this pane affect how dates, times, and numbers are displayed throughout Mac OS X and applications.

- The sample dates, times, and numbers in the Formats pane (**Figure 57**) show the effect of your changes.

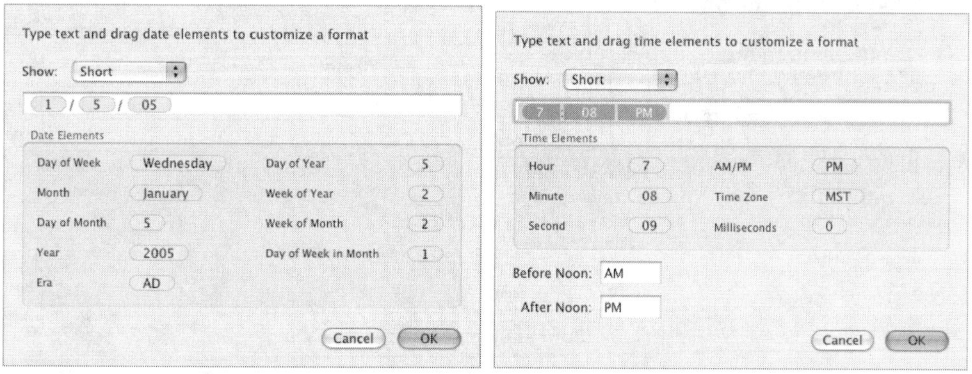

**Figures 58 & 59** Use these dialogs to customize the date (left) and time (right) formats.

## To create & customize an input menu

1. In the International Preferences pane, click the Input Menu button (**Figure 60**).

2. Turn on the check boxes beside each input method or keyboard layout you may want to use with Mac OS X. If more than one item is selected, an Input menu appears on the menu bar (**Figure 61**).

3. Choose an Input source option:

   ▲ **Use one input source in all documents** requires you to use the same input source for all documents you create during a session with an application.

   ▲ Allow a different input source for each document enables you to choose a different input source for each document you create during a session with an application.

4. To toggle the display of the input menu, set the Show input menu in menu bar check box.

## ✔ Tips

■ To switch from one keyboard or input method to another, select an item from the Input menu (**Figure 61**) or press ⌃ ⌘ Option Spacebar to cycle through all options on the menu, one at a time.

■ The Input menu may also appear on the menu bar when you use the Special Characters command in an application.

■ I explain how to use the Character palette in **Chapter 11**.

**Figure 60** The Input Menu pane of the International preferences pane.

**Figure 61**
An input menu appears on the menu bar, with all the language options you selected.

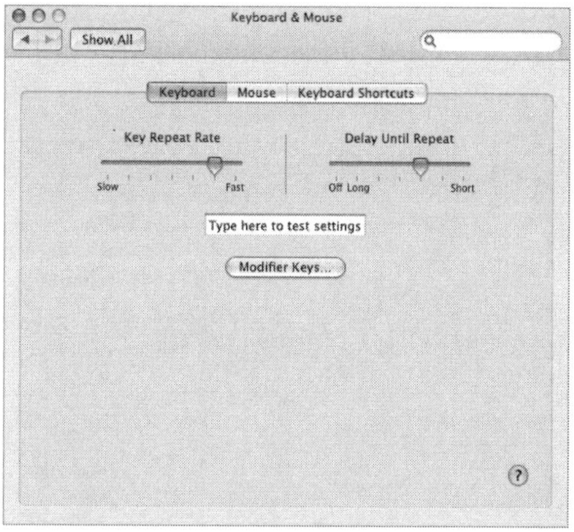

Figure 62 The Keyboard pane of the Keyboard & Mouse preferences pane.

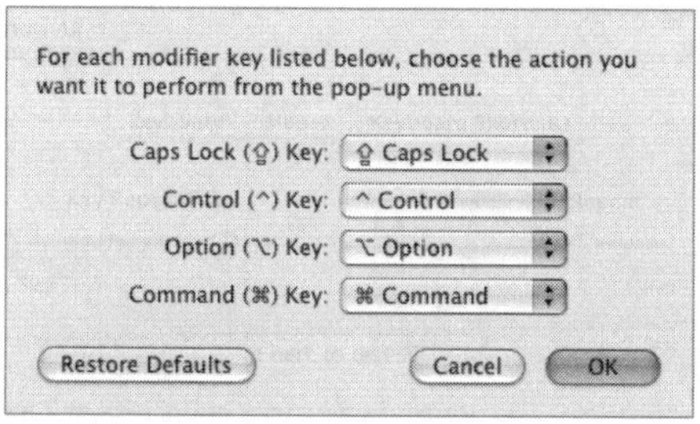

Figure 63 Use this dialog to change the behavior of modifier keys.

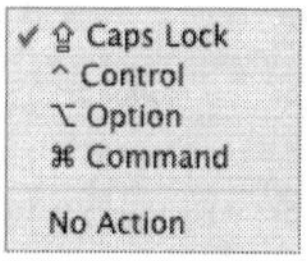

**Figure 64**
This pop-up menu enables you to make a modifier key work like a different modifier key.

# Keyboard & Mouse

The Keyboard & Mouse preferences pane enables you to customize the way the keyboard and mouse **(or trackpad)** work. Options can be set in three panes: Keyboard **(Figure 62)**, Mouse **(Figure 65)**, and Keyboard Shortcuts **(Figure 66)**.

## ✔ Tip

- If you have a wireless keyboard or mouse attached, you may see an additional button labeled Bluetooth. Click this button to configure your input device.

## To set keyboard options

1. In the Keyboard & Mouse preferences pane, click the Keyboard button **(Figure 62)**.

2. Set options as desired:
   - ▲ **Key Repeat Rate** sets how fast a key repeats when held down.
   - ▲ **Delay Until Repeat** sets how long a key must be pressed before it starts to repeat.

3. Test your settings by typing in the test field at the bottom of the pane. If necessary, repeat step 2 to fine-tune your settings for the way you type.

4. To change the behavior of modifier keys such as ⌘, Option, and Control, click the Modifier Keys button. In the dialog that appears **(Figure 63)**, use the pop-up menus to set the action you want each key to perform and click OK.

## ✔ Tips

- Key Repeat settings are especially useful for heavy-handed typists.

- Why you'd want to change the behavior of modifier keys is beyond me. It would make a good April Fools joke, though.

## To set mouse speeds

1. In the Keyboard & Mouse preferences pane, click the Mouse button (**Figure 65**).

2. Set options as desired:

   ▲ **Tracking Speed** enables you to set the speed of the mouse movement on your screen.

   ▲ **Double-Click Speed** enables you to set the amount of time between each click of a double-click. You can test the double-click speed by double-clicking in the test area; make changes as necessary to fine-tune the speed.

## ✔ Tip

■ If you're just learning to use a mouse, try setting the tracking and double-click speeds to slower than the default settings.

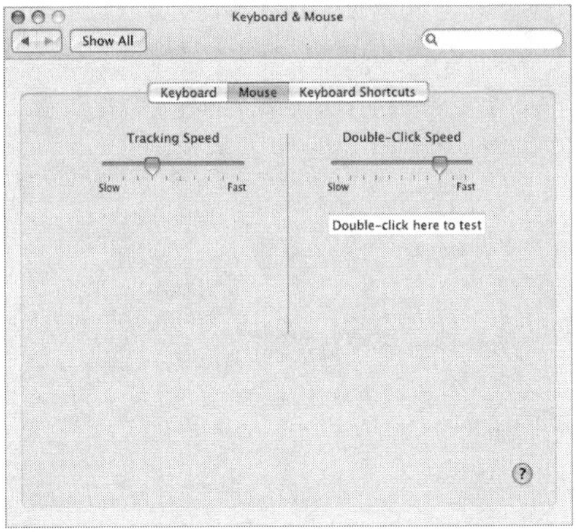

**Figure 65** The Mouse pane of the Keyboard & Mouse preferences pane.

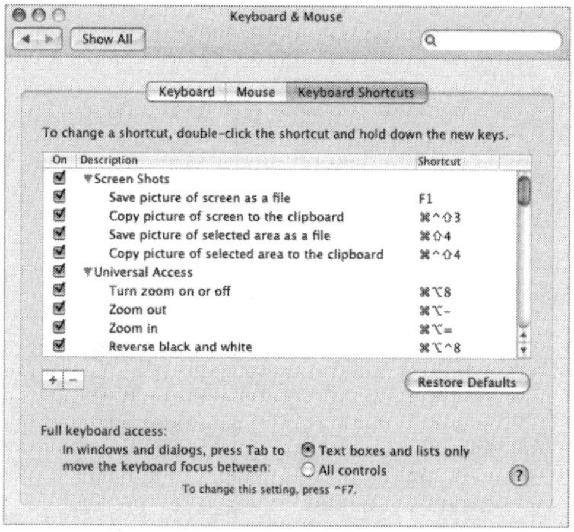

**Figure 66** The Keyboard Shortcuts pane of the Keyboard & Mouse preferences pane.

**Table 1**

| Full Keyboard Access Keys | |
| --- | --- |
| To do this | Press these keys |
| Turn full keyboard access on or off | Control F1 |
| Highlight the menu bar | Control F2 |
| Highlight the Dock | Control F3 |
| Highlight the active window or the window behind it | Control F4 |
| Highlight the toolbar | Control F5 |
| Highlight a tool palette, then each palette in order | Control F6 |
| Access all controls in the current dialog | Control F7 |

# To customize keyboard shortcuts

1. In the Keyboard & Mouse preferences pane, click the Keyboard Shortcuts button (**Figure 66**).

2. To enable or disable a specific keyboard shortcut, toggle the On check box beside it.

3. To change a keyboard shortcut, double-click the shortcut to select it, then hold down the new keys to change it.

4. To access an item with the keyboard (as well as the mouse), turn on the check box in the On column beside the item.

# ✔ Tips

- You can add custom shortcut keys for applications. Click the + button at the bottom of the list to get started.

- With full keyboard access enabled, you can use the shortcut keys in **Table 1** to activate onscreen items. Then use ↑, ←, →, ↓, Tab, and Return to select and accept items.

**CUSTOMIZING KEYBOARD SHORTCUTS**

# Print & Fax

The Print & Fax preferences pane (**Figures 67 and 68**) enables you to set options for printing and faxing from within applications. You can also set options in the new Sharing pane of the Print & Fax preferences pane to share your printers with others on your network.

## ✔ Tip

■ I cover printing and faxing in **Chapter 12**. That's where you can learn more about the Printer Setup Utility and Print Queues.

## To set printing options

1. In the Print & Fax preferences pane, click the Printing button to display its options (**Figure 67**).

2. To determine whether a listed printer should appear in the Printer pop-up menu in Print dialogs (**Figure 68**), toggle the In Menu check box beside the printer's name in the list.

3. To view the Print Queue for a printer, select its name in the printer list and click the Print Queue button.

4. To configure a printer, select its name in the printer list and click the Printer Setup button. This opens the Installable Options pane of the Printer Info window (**Figure 69**) in the Printer Setup Utility.

5. Choose options in the two pop-up menus to set basic printing options:

   ▲ **Selected Printer in the Print Dialog** (**Figure 70**) is the default printer. If you have a preferred printer, choose its name. The Last Printer Used option always defaults to the last printer used.

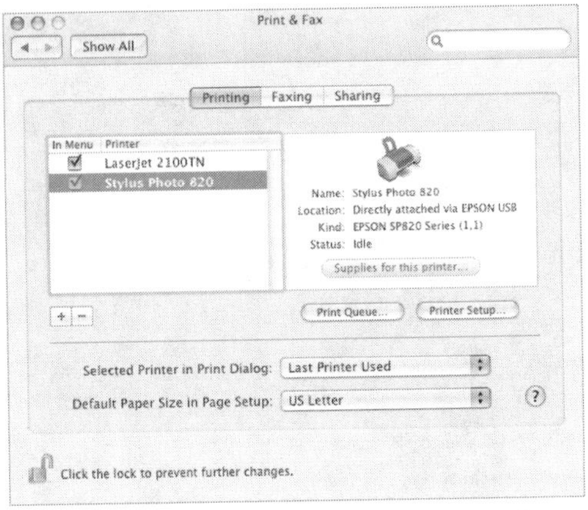

**Figure 67** The Printing pane of the Print & Fax preferences pane.

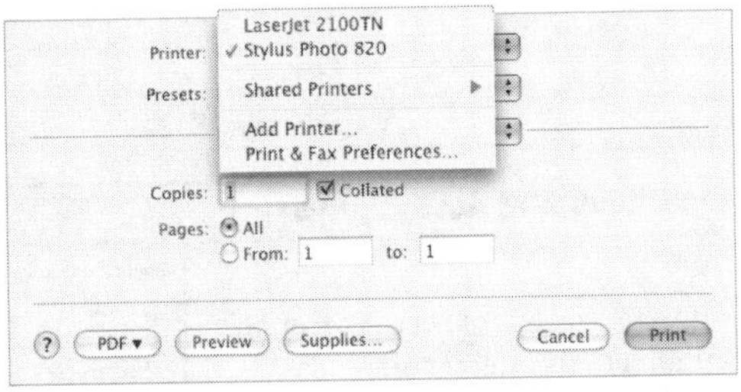

**Figure 68** The Printer pop-up menu in Print dialogs includes all printers for which you have turned on the In Menu check box.

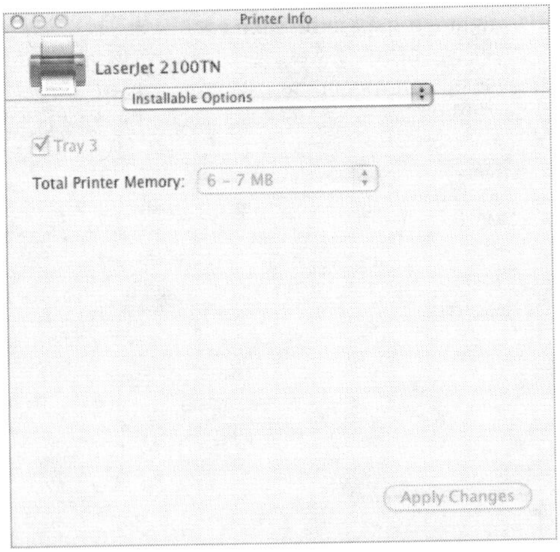

**Figure 69** Okay, so there aren't many installable options for my LaserJet 2100TN. If you're wondering why they're gray, its because this is a shared printer and cannot be changed by the eMac accessing it here.

SETTING PRINTING OPTIONS

✓ Last Printer Used

LaserJet 2100TN
Stylus Photo 820

**Figure 70** Use this menu to specify which printer should be the default printer.

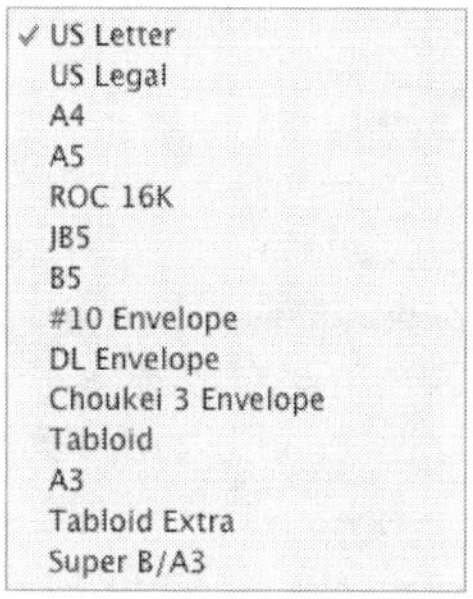

✓ US Letter
US Legal
A4
A5
ROC 16K
JB5
B5
#10 Envelope
DL Envelope
Choukei 3 Envelope
Tabloid
A3
Tabloid Extra
Super B/A3

**Figure 71**
Use this menu to set the default paper size. (Hmm. I'm fresh out of Choukei 3 envelopes—whatever *they* are.)

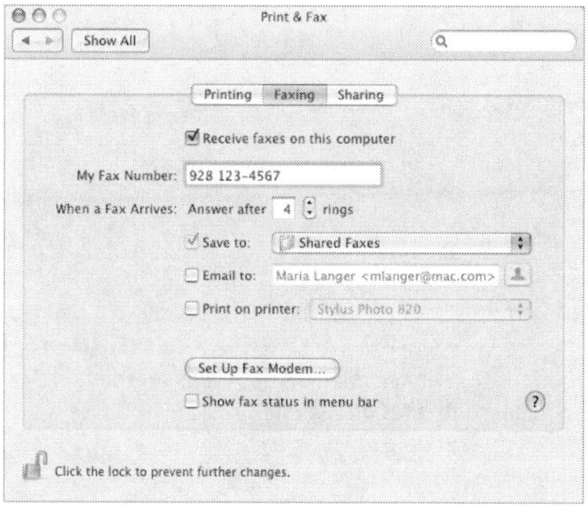

**Figure 72** The Faxing pane of the Print & Fax preferences pane.

▲ **Default Paper Size in Page Setup** (**Figure 71**) is the default paper size in the Page Setup dialog. Choose an option from the pop-up menu. The options that appear vary depending on the default printer.

## ✔ Tips

- You can click the + or − button beneath the printer list to add a printer or remove a selected printer. I tell you more about adding printers with the Printer Setup Utility in **Chapter 12**.

- Clicking the Supplies for this printer button displays a page on the Apple Store's Web site where you can find printer supplies.

## To set up your computer to receive faxes

1. In the Print & Fax preferences pane, click the Faxing button to display its options (**Figure 72**).

2. Turn on the check box marked Receive faxes on this computer.

3. Set other options as desired:
   ▲ **My Fax Number** is the fax phone number that will appear in fax headers.

   ▲ **Answer after** is the number of rings before the computer answers the phone.

   ▲ **Save to** enables you to choose a folder in which faxes should be saved. The options are Faxes and Shared Faxes, but you can choose Other Folder and use the dialog that appears (**Figure 34**) to choose a different folder.

*Continued on next page...*

**SETTING UP TO RECEIVE FAXES**

*Continued from previous page.*

▲ **Email to** tells your computer to e-mail a copy of the fax to the address you enter in the box.

▲ **Print on printer** tells your computer to print the fax on the printer you choose from the pop-up menu.

4. To configure your fax modem, click the Set Up Fax modem button. This displays the Fax List window in the Printer Setup Utility (**Figure 73**). Select your fax modem in the list and click the Show Info button to display its Printer Info window (**Figure 74**). Make changes as desired and close both windows to save them.

## ✔ Tips

■ To receive faxes, your computer must have a modem that is connected to a telephone line.

■ If your computer shuts down or goes to sleep, it cannot receive faxes.

■ Your fax modem may not appear in the Fax List window until after you have sent a fax.

■ I explain how to send faxes from your computer in **Chapter 12**.

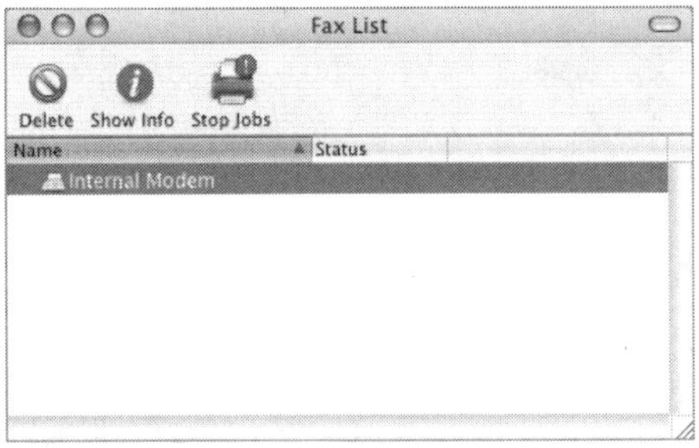

**Figure 73** The Fax List window of the Printer Setup Utility, with my internal modem selected.

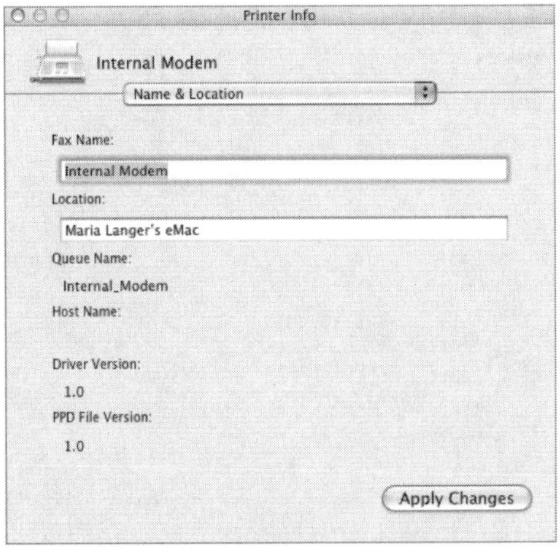

**Figure 74** As you can see here, there aren't many options to "set up." Mac OS does most of the fax modem configuration for you.

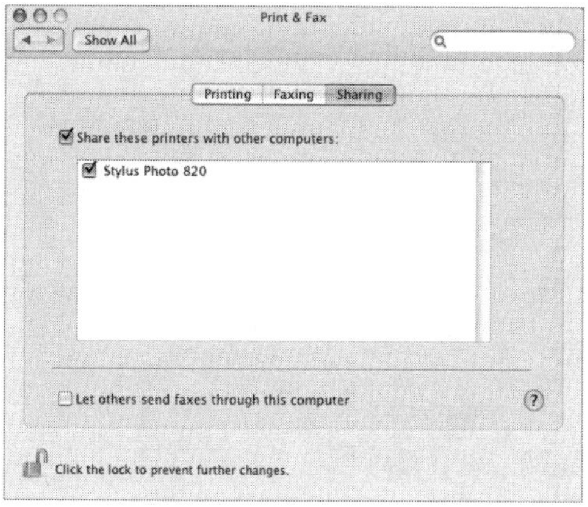

**Figure 75** Use the Sharing options to set up printer and fax modem sharing.

## To share your printers & fax modem

1. In the Print & Fax preferences pane, click the Sharing button to display its options (**Figure 75**).

2. Turn on the Share these printers with other computers check box.

3. Toggle the check boxes beside each printer in the list to specify which printer(s) should be shared.

4. To allow other network users to send faxes from your computer, turn on the Let others send faxes through this computer check box.

## ✔ Tips

- Turning on the Share these printers check box in step 2 is the same as turning on the Printer Sharing check box in the Services options of the Sharing preferences pane. I tell you more about that in **Chapter 12**.

- The Sharing options of the Print & Fax Preferences pane makes it possible to share some printers but not others.

- The ability to share your fax modem with network users is brand new in Mac OS X 10.4.

**SHARING YOUR PRINTERS & FAX MODEM**

# QuickTime

The QuickTime preferences pane enables you to set options that control the way QuickTime works. The pane's options are broken down into five groups of settings:

◆ **Register (Figure 76)** enables you to enter your QuickTime Pro registration code, which unlocks powerful QuickTime features.

◆ **Browser (Figure 80)** controls the way QuickTime works with your Web browser.

◆ **Update (Figure 81)** enables you to update or install Apple or third-party QuickTime software.

◆ **Streaming (Figure 83)** lets you specify a speed for streaming or downloading QuickTime content.

◆ **Advanced (Figure 85)** enables you to specify a music synthesizer to play Quick-Time music and MIDI files and set other more advanced options.

## ✔ Tips

■ The QuickTime preferences pane appears when you choose QuickTime Preferences from within the QuickTime Player application.

■ Using QuickTime Player is covered in **Chapter 8**.

**Figure 76** Use the Register options to enter, edit, and check registration information.

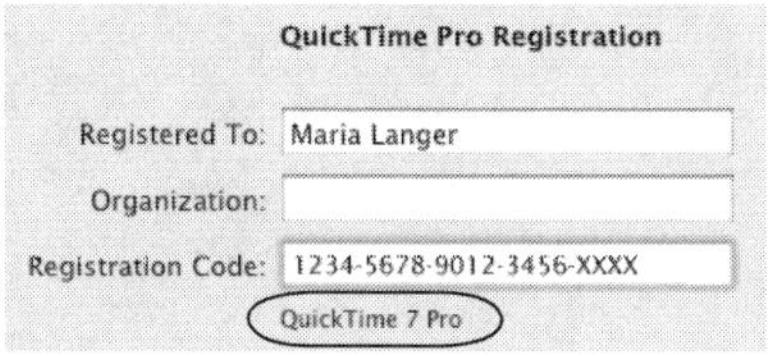

**Figure 77** Your registration code is confirmed after you enter it.

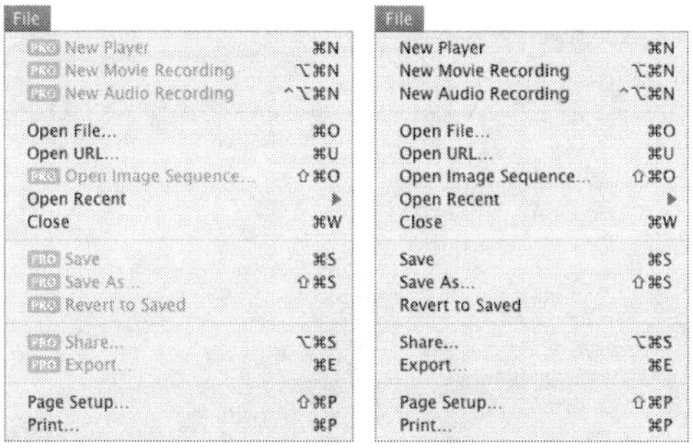

**Figures 78 & 79** Here's an example of the file menu in QuickTime Player (left) and QuickTime Player Pro (right). As you can see, QuickTime Pro offers many additional commands—in this one menu alone!

## To upgrade to QuickTime Pro

1. In the QuickTime preferences pane, click the Register button to display its options (**Figure 76**).

2. Click Buy QuickTime Pro.

   *or*

   If you already have a QuickTime Pro key, skip ahead to step 4.

3. Your Web browser launches, connects to Apple's Web site, and displays the Apple Store home page. Follow the links and instructions onscreen to purchase a QuickTime Pro key. Then switch back to System Preferences.

4. In the Register pane (**Figure 76**), enter your registration information in the appropriate boxes.

   When you move the insertion point to another field, your computer checks the registration code you entered and displays a message beneath it to confirm that it has been accepted (**Figure 77**).

## ✔ Tips

- A QuickTime Pro upgrade adds features to the QuickTime Player software, including the ability to edit and save QuickTime files. **Figures 78** and **79** show an example of how the File menu looks for both versions of the program.

- As this book went to press, an upgrade from QuickTime to QuickTime Pro was only $29.99. If you do any video editing in QuickTime format, I think it's worth it!

UPGRADING TO QUICKTIME PRO

# To set QuickTime Browser options

1. In the QuickTime preferences pane, click the Browser button (**Figure 80**).

2. Set options as desired:

   ▲ **Play movies automatically** plays QuickTime movies automatically as they are downloaded to your Web browser. With this option turned on, the movie will begin to play as it downloads to your computer. With this option turned off, you'll have to click the Play button on the Quick-Time controller to play the movie after it has begun to download.

   ▲ **Save movies in disk cache** saves a copy of downloaded movies in your Web browser's disk cache whenever possible. This makes it possible to replay the movie at another time without reloading it.

   ▲ **Movie Download Cache Size** is maximum amount of disk space the movie disk cache can occupy. Drag the slider to increase or decrease the amount. How you should set this depends on how much free space you have on disk; the more space you have, the bigger the cache can be. This option cannot be changed unless the Save movies in disk cache option is enabled.

3. To clear the current movie download cache, click the Empty Download Cache button.

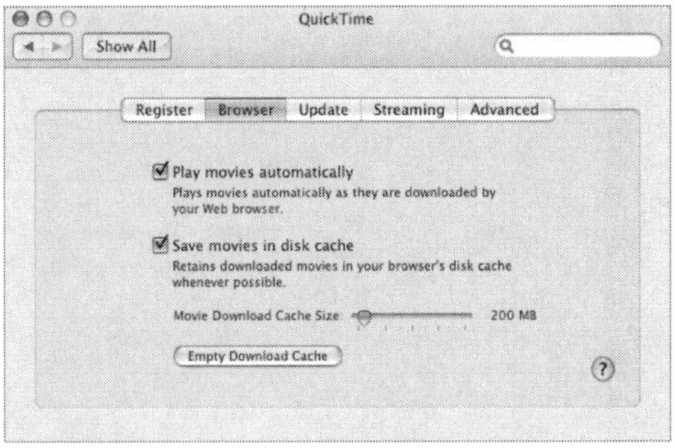

**Figure 80** The Browser options of the QuickTime preferences pane.

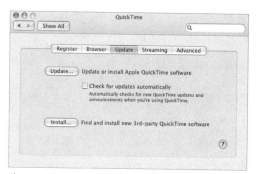

**Figure 81** The Update options of the QuickTime preferences pane.

**Figure 82** You can find third-party software that works with QuickTime on Apple's Web site.

## To update QuickTime software

1. In the QuickTime preferences pane, click the Update button (**Figure 81**).

2. Click a button to update or install QuickTime software:

   ▲ **Update** launches a QuickTime Updater application, which goes online and checks for QuickTime updates. If it finds any, it prompts you to install them. If it doesn't, it just quits.

   ▲ **Install** displays the QuickTime Components Web page on Apple's Web site (**Figure 82**) so you can research and download third-party software that works with QuickTime.

3. Follow the instructions that appear onscreen to update QuickTime or install component software.

## ✔ Tips

■ You must have an Internet connection to update QuickTime or download third-party QuickTime software with this feature.

■ If you turn on the Check for updates automatically check box (**Figure 81**), your computer automatically checks for updates when you work with QuickTime and displays update information when an update is available.

## To set QuickTime streaming options

1. In the QuickTime preferences pane, click the Streaming button (**Figure 83**).

2. Choose the speed at which you connect to the Internet from the Streaming Speed pop-up menu (**Figure 84**).

3. To enable QuickTime to play streamed media without delay, turn on the Enable Instant-On check box and use the slider to indicate the length of delay before streaming media begins playing.

## ✔ Tip

■ If you connect to the Internet in a variety of ways, you can leave the Streaming Speed pop-up menu set to Automatic. Your computer will make adjustments as necessary when it streams QuickTime content from the Internet.

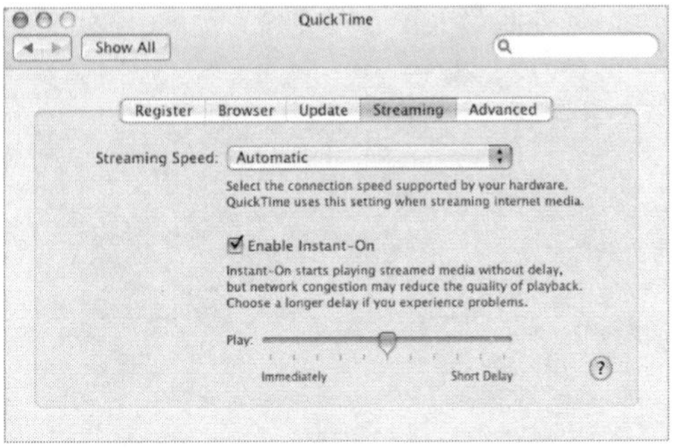

**Figure 83** The Streaming options of the QuickTime preferences pane.

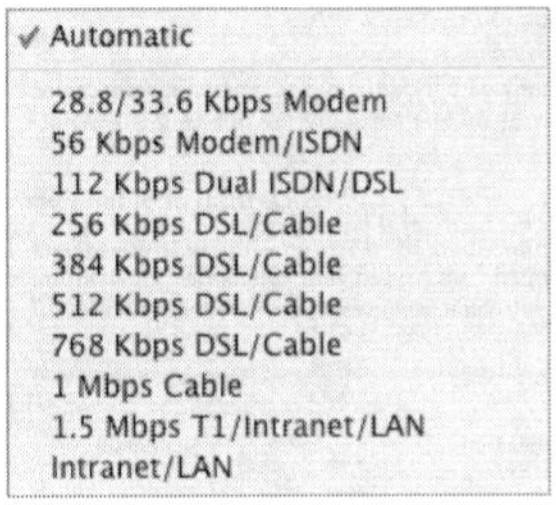

**Figure 84**
The Streaming Speed pop-up menu.

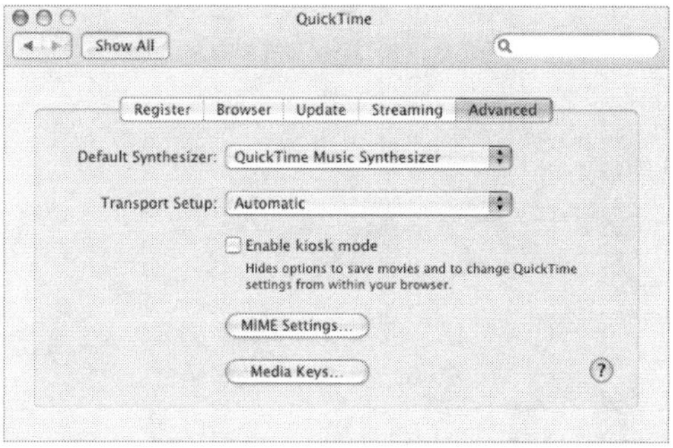

**Figure 85** The Advanced options of the QuickTime preferences pane.

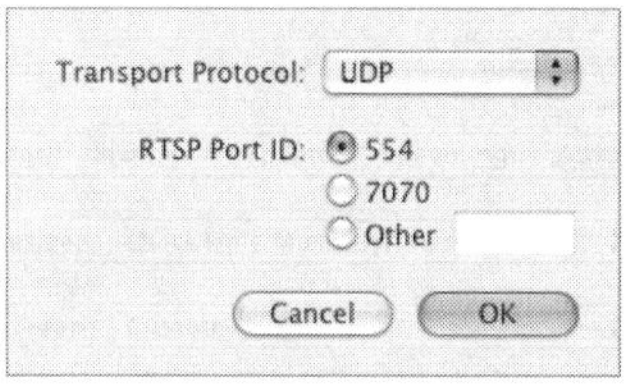

**Figure 86** If necessary, you can set network options to assure that QuickTime streamed content can be viewed.

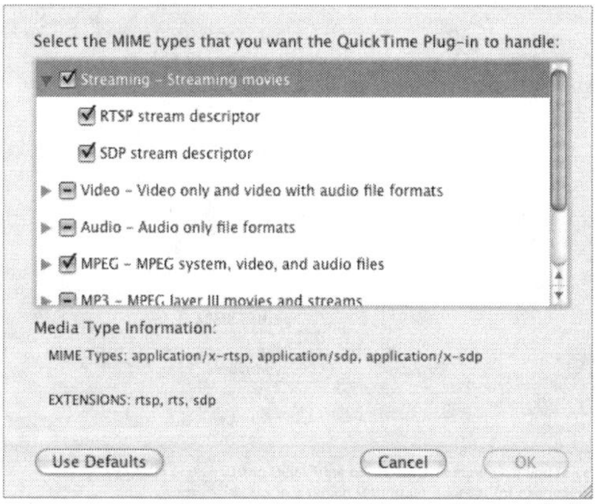

**Figure 87** Use this dialog to specify the types of documents that should be handled by QuickTime.

# To set Advanced QuickTime options

1. In the QuickTime preferences pane, click the Advanced options (**Figure 85**).

2. Set options as desired:

   ▲ **Default Synthesizer** is the synthesizer that will be used for MIDI music playback. The options that appear in the menu vary depending on the synthesizers installed in your computer; if you have not installed any synthesizers, the only option will be QuickTime Music Synthesizer.

   ▲ **Transport Setup** enables you to set up a custom network protocol for viewing streamed QuickTime content. To create a custom setup for firewall compatibility, choose Custom from the pop-up menu, set options in the dialog sheet that appears (**Figure 86**), and click OK.

   ▲ **Enable kiosk mode** hides the options to save movies and to change QuickTime settings from within your Web browser. With this option turned off, you can hold down [Control] and click a QuickTime movie to display a contextual menu with commands for working with the movie or QuickTime settings.

3. To associate document types with Quick-Time, click the MIME Settings button. Then use the dialog that appears (**Figure 87**) to turn on check boxes beside the document types that QuickTime should handle. (You can click a triangle to display options beneath it.) When you're finished, click OK.

*Continued on next page...*

**SETTING ADVANCED QUICKTIME OPTIONS**

*Continued from previous page.*

4. To enter media keys for secured Quick-Time content, click the Media Keys button. Then use the dialog that appears (**Figure 88**) to add, modify, or remove media keys and click OK.

## ✔ Tips

- QuickTime can import Standard MIDI, General MIDI, and Karaoke MIDI format files.

- The Audio MIDI Setup application, which you can find in the Utilities folder inside the Applications folder, enables you to fine-tune a MIDI setup for use with Mac OS X.

- If you're not sure what the Transport Setup option should be and QuickTime is working fine on your computer, don't change this option! If it ain't broke, don't fix it.

- Media keys are only required to view secure QuickTime content. You can find out how to get a media key for content when you access the content.

**Figure 88** This dialog lists your QuickTime media keys—if you have any. (I don't!)

SETTING ADVANCED QUICKTIME OPTIONS

**Figure 89** The Update Software options of the Software Update preferences pane.

# Software Update

The Software Update preferences pane (**Figure 89**) enables you to configure the Mac OS software update feature. This program checks Apple's Internet servers for updates to your Apple software—including Mac OS and other installed Apple applications and utilities—and enables you to download and install them.

## ✔ Tip

■ You must have an Internet connection to update Mac OS X software with this feature.

## To set automatic update options

1. In the Software Update preferences pane, click the Update Software button (**Figure 89**).

2. Turn on the Check for updates check box.

3. Use the pop-up menu to specify how often your computer should check for updates: Daily, Weekly, or Monthly.

4. To automatically download important updates without asking you, turn on the check box labeled Download important updates in the background.

## ✔ Tip

■ When your computer checks for updates and finds one or more, it displays a window like the one in **Figure 91**. Follow the instructions in step 2 on the next page to install software or dismiss the window.

## To manually update software

1. In the Update Software tab of the Software Update preferences pane (**Figure 89**), click Check Now.

   Your computer connects to the Internet and checks Apple's servers for updates (**Figure 90**).

2. When the check is complete, if updates are available, the Software Update window appears (**Figure 91**). It contains information about whether any updates are available.

   ▲ To install updates, turn on the check boxes beside them. Then click the Install *n* Item(s) button. Follow any additional instructions that appear onscreen.

   ▲ To quit Software Update without installing updates, click the Quit button.

## ✔ Tips

■ You can learn about an update before you install it by selecting it in the top half of the window to display a description in the bottom half of the window (**Figure 91**).

■ If you don't install a listed update, it will appear in the Software Update window (**Figure 91**) again the next time you check for updates. To remove it from the list without installing it, select it and choose Update > Ignore Update and click OK in the confirmation dialog that appears.

■ Updates may require that you provide an administrator password before installation. If so, an Authenticate dialog will appear. Enter administrator login information as prompted and click OK.

■ To view a log of installed updates, click the Installed Updates tab in the Software Update preferences pane (**Figure 92**).

**Figure 90** A progress bar appears in the bottom of the Software Update preferences pane while your computer checks for updates.

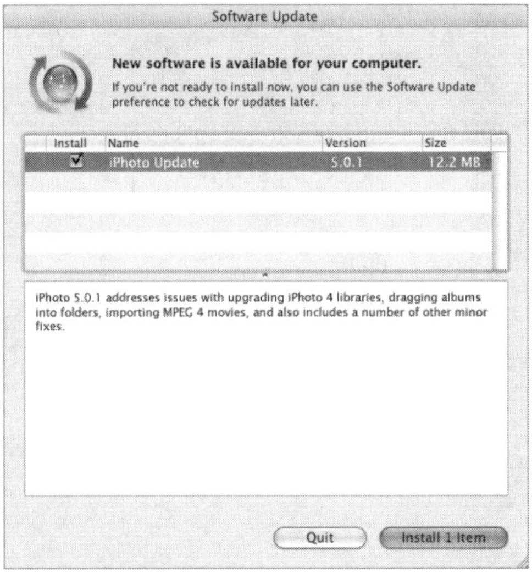

**Figure 91** A list of software updates appears in the Software Update window.

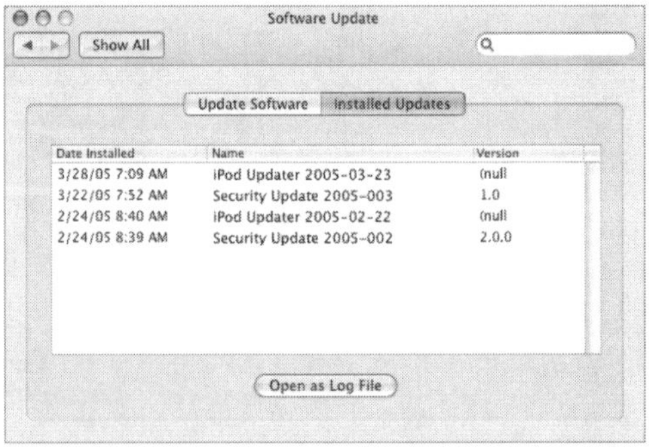

**Figure 92** The Installed Updates pane of the Software Update preferences pane shows a log of recent software update installations.

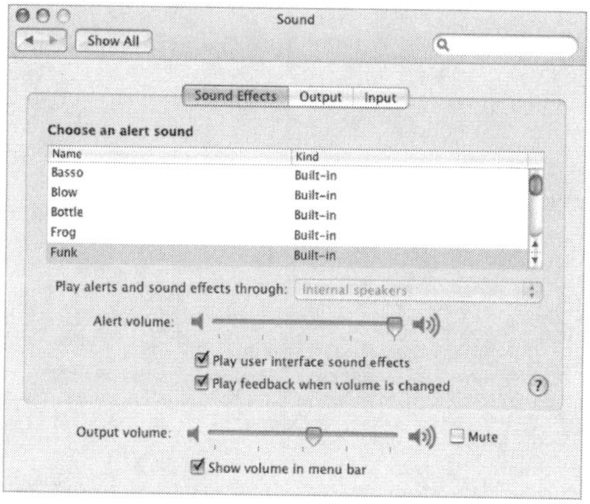

**Figure 93** The Sound Effects options of the Sound preferences pane.

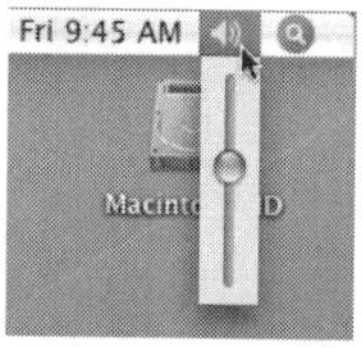

**Figure 94**
The Sound volume menu appears in the menu bar beside the menu bar clock.

# Sound

The Sound preferences pane enables you to set options to control the system and alert sounds, output device, and input device.

Sound settings can be change in three panes:

◆ **Sound Effects (Figure 93)** lets you set options for alert sounds and sound effects.

◆ **Output (Figure 95)** allows you to set the output device and balance.

◆ **Input (Figure 96)** enables you to set the input device and volume.

## ✔ Tip

■ The options that appear in the Sound preferences pane vary depending on your computer and the devices connected to it. The figures on these pages show options on an eMac.

## To set system volume

1. Display any tab of the Sound preferences pane **(Figure 93, 95, or 96)**.

2. Set options in the bottom of the window:

   ▲ **Output volume** is the system volume. Drag the slider to the left or right.

   ▲ **Mute** keeps your computer quiet.

   ▲ **Show volume in menu bar** displays a sound volume menu in the menu bar **(Figure 94)**.

## ✔ Tips

■ The output volume is the maximum volume for all sounds, including alerts, games, QuickTime movies, and iTunes music.

■ Each time you move and release the Main volume slider in step 2, an alert sounds so you can hear a sample of your change.

■ The Sound volume menu appears on the right end of the menu bar **(Figure 94)**. To use the menu, click to display the slider and drag it up or down. You can rearrange the menus on the right end of the menu bar by holding down ⌘ while dragging them.

## To set sound effects options

1. In the Sound preferences pane, click the Sound Effects button (**Figure 93**).

2. To set the alert sound, select one of the options in the scrolling list.

3. Set other options as desired:

   ▲ **Play alerts and sound effects through** enables you to set the output device for alert and sound effect sounds. (This option may not be accessible if the Sound preferences pane includes an Output tab.)

   ▲ **Alert volume** is the volume of alert sounds. Drag the slider to the left or right.

   ▲ **Play user interface sound effects** plays sound effects for different system events, such as dragging an icon to the Trash.

   ▲ **Play feedback when volume is changed** enables you to hear the volume each time you change it.

## ✔ Tips

■ With the Play feedback when volume is changed check box turned on, each time you move and release the slider or select a different alert sound, an alert sounds so you can hear a sample of your change.

■ Alert volume depends partly on the main volume setting, which is discussed on the previous page. An alert sound cannot be louder than the main sound.

■ Volume keys, when present, are located above the numeric keypad on keyboards. Not all Macintosh keyboards include volume keys.

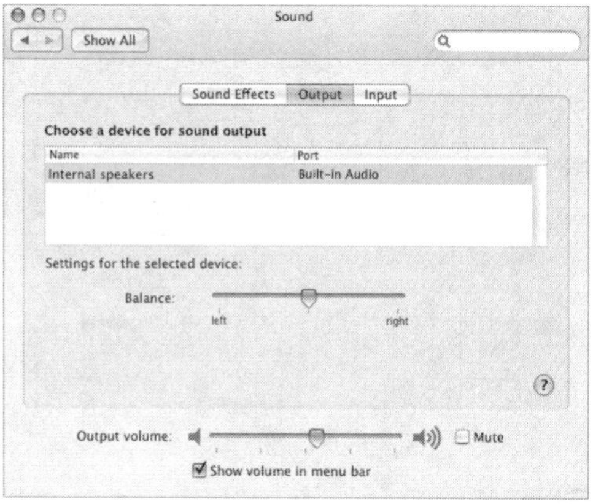

**Figure 95** The Output options of the Sound preferences pane.

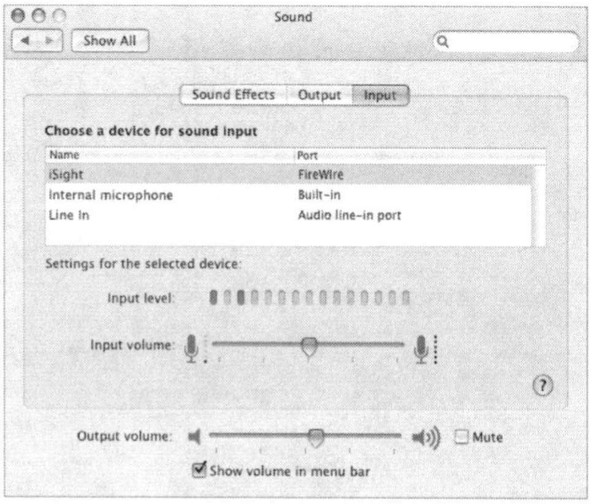

**Figure 96** The Input options of the Sound preferences pane.

## To set output device options

1. In the Sound preferences pane, click the Output button (**Figure 95**).

2. To set the output device, select one of the options in the scrolling list.

3. To set the speaker balance for the selected device, drag the Balance slider to the left or right.

## ✔ Tip

- Each time you move and release the slider, an alert sounds so you can hear a sample of your change.

## To set input device options

1. In the Sound preferences pane, click the Input button (**Figure 96**).

2. To set the input device, select one of the options in the scrolling list.

3. To set the input volume for the selected device, drag the Input volume slider to the left or right. The further to the right you drag the slider, the more sensitive the microphone will be.

## ✔ Tips

- Input device and volume are especially important if you plan to use Mac OS X's speech recognition features. I discuss speech recognition later in this chapter.

- The Input level area of the Input tab (**Figure 96**) graphically represents the current volume levels, including the peak level. You might find this helpful when setting the Input volume.

**SETTING INPUT & OUTPUT DEVICE OPTIONS**

# Speech

Mac OS X's Speech preferences pane includes two groups of options:

◆ **Speech Recognition** lets you enable and configure speech recognition features.

◆ **Text to Speech** allows you to set the default system voice and enable and configure talking alerts and other spoken items.

In this section, I explain how to set up and use these features.

## ✔ Tips

■ Speech recognition requires a sound input device, such as a built-in or external microphone or an iSight camera.

■ The speech recognition feature works best in a relatively quiet work environment.

## To enable & configure speech recognition

1. In the Speech preferences pane, click the Speech Recognition button (**Figure 97**).

2. Select the On radio button.

3. A dialog sheet may appear with instructions for using Apple Speakable Items (**Figure 98**). If this is your first time using this feature, read the contents of the dialog and click Continue to dismiss it.

   The round Feedback window appears (**Figure 99**).

4. If necessary, click the Settings button to display its options (**Figure 97**).

**Figure 97** The Settings options for Speech Recognition in the Speech preferences pane.

**Tips for Success with Spoken Commands**

• Position yourself in front of the microphone, hold down the listening key (esc by default) for about 1 second, then speak a command in a clear, normal voice. Try "what time is it?"

• The round feedback window shows the microphone sound level. Try to speak so that the level is primarily in the green area.

• If speech recognition seems to be unresponsive or inaccurate, press the "Calibrate..." button in the "Listening" tab of the Speech Preferences Panel and follow the instructions.

• The commands that you can speak are listed in the Speech Commands window. To open, say "Open Speech Commands window" or click on the triangle at the bottom of the round speech feedback window.

Continue

**Figure 98** This dialog sheet provides brief instructions for using Apple Speakable Items.

**Figure 99**
The Feedback window.

**Figure 100**
Use this pop-up menu to choose the device you'll use to talk to your computer.

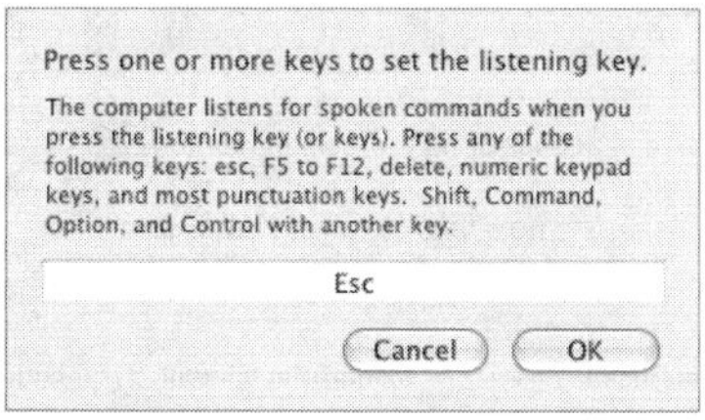

Press one or more keys to set the listening key.

The computer listens for spoken commands when you press the listening key (or keys). Press any of the following keys: esc, F5 to F12, delete, numeric keypad keys, and most punctuation keys. Shift, Command, Option, and Control with another key.

Esc

Cancel    OK

**Figure 101** Use this dialog to enter a new listening key.

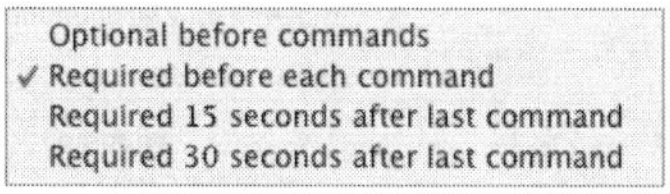

Optional before commands
✓ Required before each command
Required 15 seconds after last command
Required 30 seconds after last command

**Figure 102** This pop-up menu enables you to specify how the keyword should be used for listening.

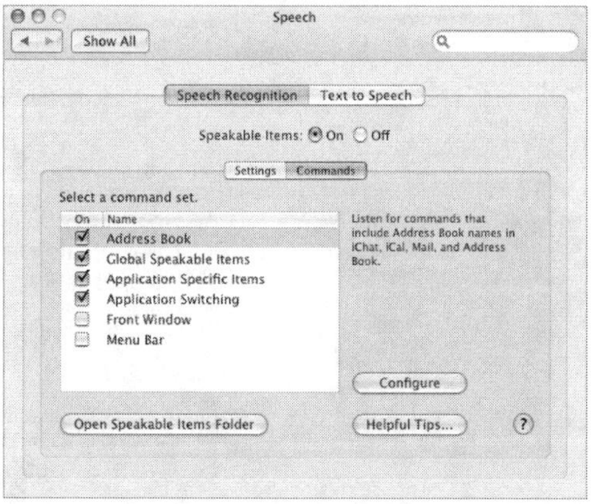

Speech

◀ ▶  Show All                          🔍

Speech Recognition   Text to Speech

Speakable Items: ◉ On ○ Off

Settings   Commands

Select a command set.

| On | Name |
|---|---|
| ☑ | Address Book |
| ☑ | Global Speakable Items |
| ☑ | Application Specific Items |
| ☑ | Application Switching |
| ☐ | Front Window |
| ☐ | Menu Bar |

Listen for commands that include Address Book names in iChat, iCal, Mail, and Address Book.

Configure

Open Speakable Items Folder    Helpful Tips...    (?)

**Figure 103** The Commands options for Speech Recognition in the Speech preferences pane.

5. Set options and click buttons as desired:

▲ **Microphone (Figure 100)** is your sound input device.

▲ **Listening key** is the keyboard key you must press to either listen to spoken commands or toggle listening on or off. By default, the key is Esc. To change the key, click the Change Key button, enter a new key in the dialog that appears (**Figure 101**), and click OK.

▲ **Listening method** enables you to select how you want your Mac to listen for commands. **Listen only while key is pressed** requires you to press the listening key to listen. **Listen continuously with keyword** tells the computer to listen all the time. If you select this option, you can choose an option from the Keyword is pop-up menu (**Figure 102**) and enter a keyword for your computer to recognize commands.

▲ **Upon recognition** instructs your computer how to acknowledge that it has heard the command. **Speak command acknowledgement** tells your computer to repeat the command. **Play this sound** enables you to choose a sound for acknowledgement.

6. Click the Commands button to display its options (**Figure 103**).

7. Turn on the check box beside each command set you want your computer to recognize.

*Continued on next page...*

*Continued from previous page.*

## ✔ Tips

- An external microphone—especially one on a headset—will work more reliably than a built-in microphone, such as the one on the front of the computer.

- Clicking the Calibrate button in the Settings pane (**Figure 97**) displays a dialog like the one in **Figure 104**, which you can use to test and adjust microphone volume.

- For best results, either set the Listening method to Listen only while key is pressed or require the computer name before each spoken command. Otherwise, your computer could interpret background noise and conversations as commands.

- The description of a command set appears in the Commands pane when you select the command set in the list (**Figure 103**).

- You can set options for some command sets. Select the command set in the Commands pane (**Figure 103**) and click the Configure button. A dialog appears with options you can set (**Figure 105**).

- Clicking the Open Speakable Items folder button in the Commands pane (**Figure 103**) opens a Finder window that includes all Speakable Items commands Mac OS X can recognize (**Figure 106**).

- Each user has his or her own Speakable Items folder, which can be found at /Users/*username*/Library/Speech/ Speakable Items.

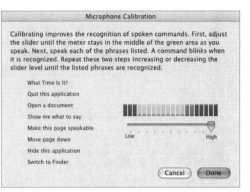

**Figure 104** This dialog enables you to test and adjust the microphone volume.

**Figure 105** This example shows how you can configure the Address Book command set to recognize just certain people in your Address Book.

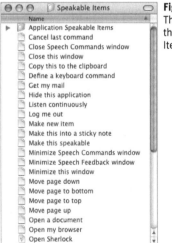

**Figure 106** The contents of the Speakable Items folder.

**Figure 107**
When your computer recognizes a spoken command, the command appears above the Feedback window.

**Figure 108**
When a command has feedback, the response appears beneath the Feedback window.

## To use Speakable Items

1. If your computer is configured to listen with a listening key, hold down the listening key and speak the command you want your computer to perform.

   *or*

   If your computer is configured to listen continuously, speak the command you want your computer to perform. If the keyword is required before or after the command, be sure to include it.

2. If your computer understands the command, it will acknowledge it with voice and/or sound and the command will appear above the Feedback window (**Figure 107**). The command is executed (if possible).

   *or*

   If your computer did not understand the command, nothing happens. Wait a moment and try again.

## ✔ Tips

- The Speakable Items folder (**Figure 106**) contains preprogrammed Speakable Items. Each file corresponds to a command. Say the file name to issue the command.

- The Application Speakable Items folder inside the Speakable Items folder (**Figure 106**) contains Speakable Items commands that work in specific applications.

- If it is not possible to execute a command, nothing will happen after the command appears above the Feedback window. For example, if you use the "Close this window" command and no window is active, nothing will happen.

- If the command you issued results in feedback (for example, the "What Time Is It?" command) and you set up speech recognition to speak feedback, your computer displays (**Figure 108**) and speaks the results of the command.

- To add a Speakable Item, use AppleScript to create a script for the command. Save the script as a compiled script in the appropriate location in the Speakable Items folder. Be sure to name the script with the words you want to use to issue the command. AppleScript is discussed in **Chapter 20**.

USING SPEAKABLE ITEMS

## To set Text to Speech options

1. In the Speech preferences pane, click the Text to Speech button (**Figure 109**).

2. Select one of the voices in the System Voice list (**Figure 110**).

3. To change the speed at which the voice speaks, use the Speaking Rate slider.

4. To test the settings, click the Play button.

5. To speak alerts, turn on the Announce when alerts are displayed check box. Then click the Set Alert Options button, set options in the dialog that appears (**Figure 111**), and click OK:

   ▲ **Voice** enables you to choose the System Voice or another voice.

   ▲ **Phrase** (**Figure 112**) is text that should be spoken before the alert.

   ▲ **Delay** is the amount of time that should elapse between when the dialog appears and the alert is spoken. Use the slider to set the delay.

6. To get a verbal alert when an application needs your attention, turn on the Announce when application requires your attention check box. (Normally, the icon for an application needing attention bounces in the Dock.)

7. To have your computer speak selected text, turn on the Speak selected text when the key is pressed check box. Then use the dialog sheet that appears (**Figure 113**) to press the keystroke you want to use to speak or stop speaking selected text and click OK. You can change the keystroke by clicking the Set Key button to display this dialog sheet again.

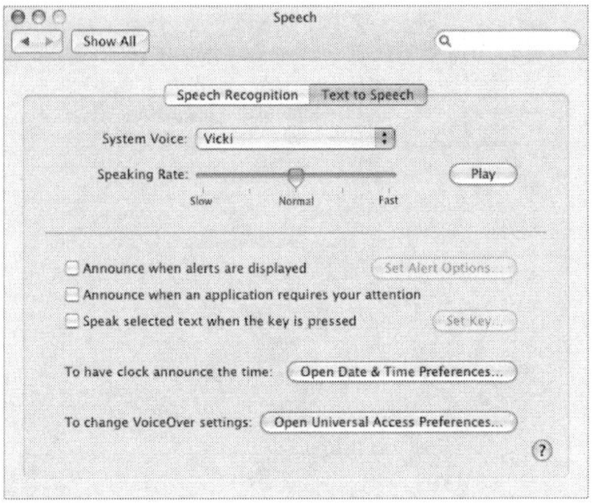

**Figure 109** The Text to Speech options of the Speech preferences pane.

**Figure 110**
Mac OS X comes pre-configured with these voices. (I bet you didn't know so many people were living inside your computer, waiting to talk to you.)

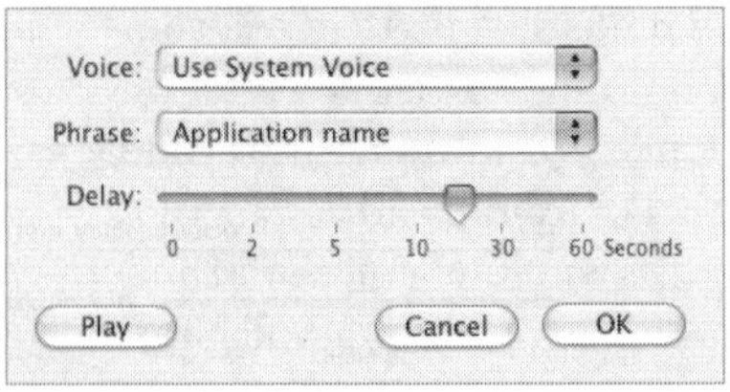

**Figure 111** Use this dialog to set options for the way your computer speaks alert items.

**Setting Text to Speech Options**

**Figure 112**
As this pop-up menu indicates, your computer can be very polite when it tells you about alerts.

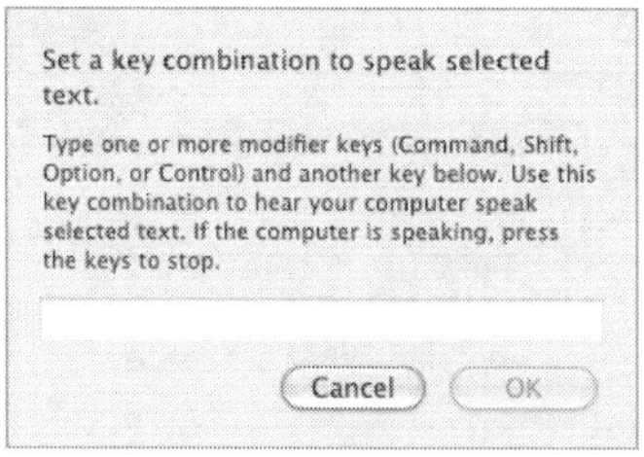

---

Set a key combination to speak selected text.

Type one or more modifier keys (Command, Shift, Option, or Control) and another key below. Use this key combination to hear your computer speak selected text. If the computer is speaking, press the keys to stop.

Cancel    OK

**Figure 113** Use this dialog sheet to specify a keystroke that will speak or stop speaking selected text.

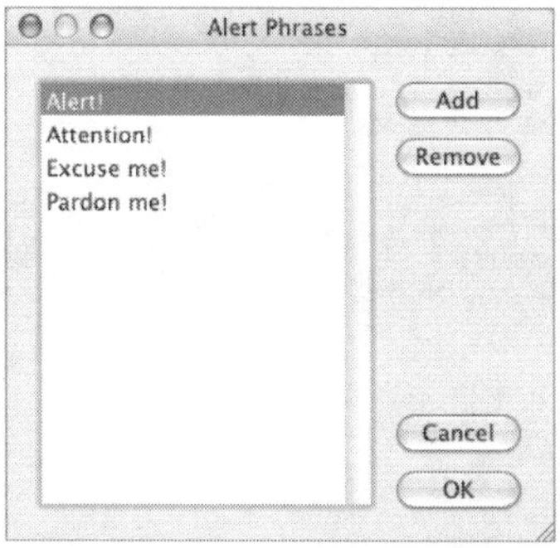

---

Alert Phrases

Alert!
Attention!
Excuse me!
Pardon me!

Add
Remove

Cancel
OK

**Figure 114** You can customize the way your computer alerts you by editing the Alert Phrases it uses.

## ✔ Tips

- As you try some of the voices, you'll see that the novelty voices are more fun than practical.

- The settings you make in the Text to Speech pane affect any application that can speak text.

- In step 5, you can choose Edit Phrase List from the Phrase pop-up menu (**Figure 112**) to display the Alert Phrases dialog (**Figure 114**). Click the Add or Remove buttons to add a new phrase or remove a selected one. When you're finished, click OK to save your changes.

- To speak the time, click the Open Date & Time Preferences button. This displays the Date & Time preferences pane. Click the Clock button and set Announce the time options (**Figure 27**). I tell you about the Date & Time preferences pane earlier in this chapter.

- To change VoiceOver settings, click the Open Universal Access Preferences button. This displays the Seeing options of the Universal Access preferences pane (**Figure 117**), which I discuss later in this chapter. I tell you about VoiceOver in **Chapter 22**.

# Startup Disk

The Startup Disk preferences pane (**Figure 115**) enables you to select a startup disk and, if desired, restart your computer. You might find this helpful if you want to start your computer under Mac OS 9.2 or from a bootable CD or DVD disc, such as a Mac OS installer disc.

The new Target Disk Mode feature of Mac OS X 10.4 makes it possible for your computer's hard disk to be used as an external hard disk when connected to another computer via FireWire cable. You can enable this option in the Startup Disk preferences pane, too.

## ✔ Tips

- Starting your computer under Mac OS 9.x is discussed in **Chapter 18**.

- Mac OS X enables you to have multiple System folders on a single disk or partition. Startup Disk is the tool you use to select which System folder should be used at startup.

- To decide "on the fly" which startup disk to use, hold down the (Option) key at startup to display icons for each startup disk or folder. Click the one you want and click the forward arrow to complete the startup process from the disk you selected.

- Holding down the ⒸC key while a bootable disc is inserted in your computer usually starts the computer from the System folder on that disc.

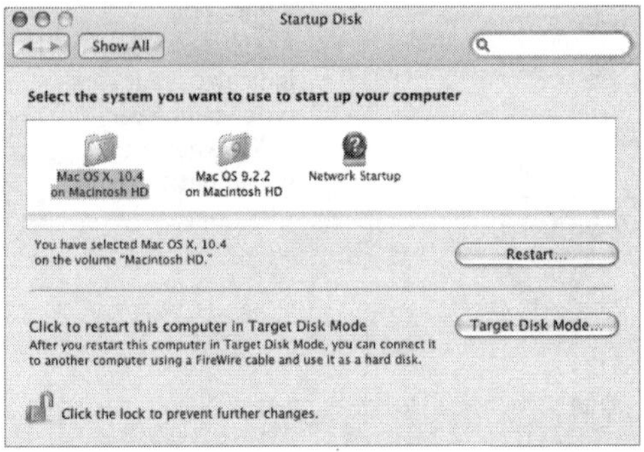

**Figure 115** The Startup Disk preferences pane.

**Figure 116** This dialog appears when you click the Target Disk Mode button.

## To select a startup disk

1. Display the Startup Disk preferences pane (**Figure 115**).

2. Click the icon for the startup folder or disk you want to use.

3. To immediately restart your computer, click the Restart button.

   *or*

   Quit System Preferences. Click the Change button in the confirmation dialog sheet that appears to save your change.

## ✔ Tips

- If you choose Network Startup in step 2, your computer will look for a NetBoot startup volume when you restart. This makes it possible to boot your computer from a Mac OS X server on the network. Do not select this option unless a NetBoot volume is accessible; doing so could cause errors on restart.

- If you do not immediately restart your computer with the new startup disk selected, that disk will be used the next time you restart or start up.

## To use target disk mode

1. Use a FireWire cable to connect your computer to another computer.

2. In the Startup Disk preferences pane (**Figure 115**), click Target Disk Mode.

3. Read the information in the dialog sheet that appears (**Figure 116**).

4. Click Restart.

## ✔ Tip

- When you're finished using your computer in target disk mode, press its power button.

# Universal Access

The Universal Access preferences pane enables you to set options for making your computer easier to use by people with disabilities.

Universal Access's features can be set in four different tabs:

◆ **Seeing (Figure 117)** enables you to set options for people with visual disabilities.

◆ **Hearing (Figure 119)** allows you to set options for people with aural disabilities.

◆ **Keyboard (Figure 120)** lets you set options for people who have difficulty using the keyboard.

◆ **Mouse (Figure 122)** enables you to set options for people who have difficulty using the mouse.

## To enable access for assistive devices

1. Display any pane of the Universal Access Preferences pane (**Figure 117, 119, 120, or 122**).

2. Turn on the Enable access for assistive devices check box.

## ✔ Tip

■ A screen reader is an example of an assistive device.

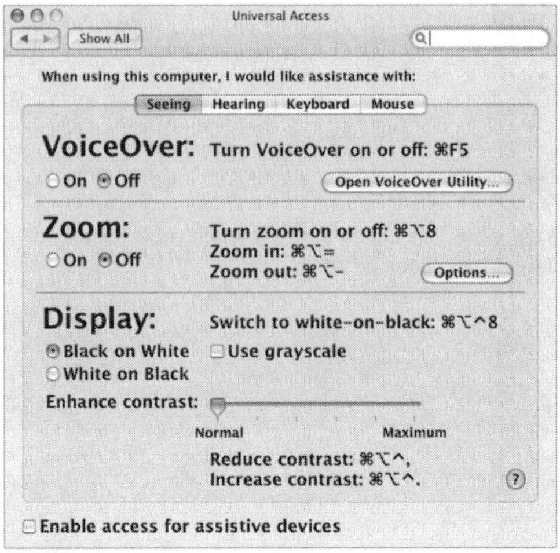

**Figure 117** The Seeing pane of the Universal Access preferences pane. Why is the text so big here? Because people who need this feature need it because they have trouble seeing.

**Figure 118** As odd as it may seem, some people find this image easier to see than the standard black on white image.

## To set Seeing options

1. In the Universal Access preferences pane, click the Seeing button (**Figure 117**).

2. Set options as desired:
   - ▲ **VoiceOver** enables you to turn Mac OS X's new VoiceOver feature on or off. I tell you about VoiceOver in **Chapter 22**.
   - ▲ **Zoom** enlarges the part of the screen you are pointing to when you press the zoom in key combination: ⌃ ⌘ Option =.
   - ▲ **Display** enables you to set black on white or white on black (**Figure 118**) screen display or convert color to grayscale. You can drag a slider in this area to enhance or reduce contrast.

## ✔ Tips

- ■ The keystrokes that are required to use some of these features appear in the preference pane.

- ■ Clicking the Open VoiceOver Utility button launches the VoiceOver Utility, which you can use to fine-tune VoiceOver settings.

- ■ You can click the Options button to set additional options for using the Zoom feature.

- ■ Other options in the Displays preferences pane (**Figure 40**) may help you set your computer monitor so you can see it better. I tell you about the Displays preferences pane earlier in this chapter.

SETTING SEEING OPTIONS

## To set Hearing options

1. In the Universal Access preferences pane, click the Hearing button (**Figure 119**).

2. To visually display an alert sound, turn on the Flash the screen when an alert sound occurs check box.

3. To change the volume, click the Adjust Volume button. Then use the Sound preferences pane (**Figure 93**), which I discuss earlier in this chapter, to adjust the volume.

## ✔ Tip

■ Clicking the Flash Screen button shows you what the screen will look like when visually displaying an alert sound. Try it and see for yourself.

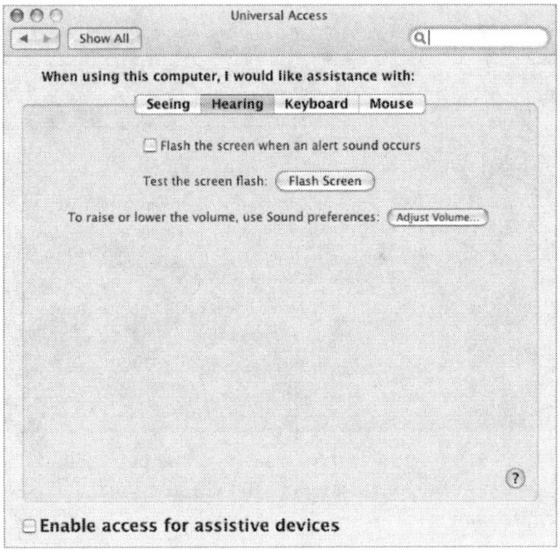

**Figure 119** The Hearing options of the Universal Access preferences pane.

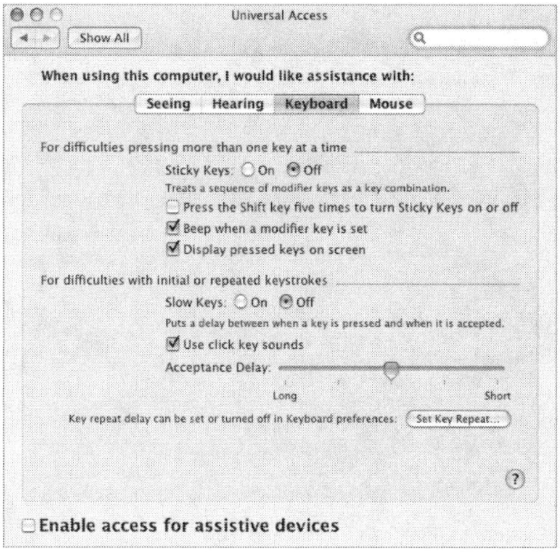

Figure 120 The Keyboard pane of the Universal Access preferences pane.

**Figure 121**
Universal Access can show you which keys you pressed—in this example, ⌘ ⌘ and (Shift).

## To enable & configure Sticky Keys & Slow Keys

1. In the Universal Access preferences pane, click the Keyboard button (**Figure 120**).

2. To enable Sticky Keys, select the On radio button beside Sticky Keys. Then set options as desired:

   ▲ **Press the Shift key five times to turn Sticky Keys on or off** enables you to toggle Sticky Keys by pressing (Shift) five times.

   ▲ **Beep when a modifier key is set** plays a sound when a modifier key you press is recognized by the system.

   ▲ **Display pressed keys on screen** shows the image of the modifier key on screen when it is recognized by the system (**Figure 121**).

3. To enable Slow Keys, select the On radio button beside Slow Keys. Then set options as desired:

   ▲ **Use click key sounds** plays a sound when a key press is accepted.

   ▲ **Acceptance delay** enables you to adjust the amount of time between the point when a key is first pressed and when the keypress is accepted.

## ✔ Tips

■ Sticky Keys makes it easier for people who have trouble pressing more than one key at a time to use modifier keys, such as (Shift), ⌘ ⌘, and (Option).

■ Slow Keys puts a delay between when a key is pressed and when it is accepted by your computer. This makes it easier for people who have trouble pressing keyboard keys to type.

■ Clicking the Set Key Repeat button displays the Keyboard preferences pane (**Figure 62**), which is discussed earlier in this chapter, so you can set other options for making the keyboard easier to use.

## To enable & configure Mouse Keys

1. In the Universal Access preferences pane, click the Mouse button (**Figure 120**).

2. To enable Mouse Keys, select the On radio button. Then set options as desired:

   ▲ **Press the option key five times to turn Mouse Keys on or off** enables you to toggle Mouse Keys by pressing [Option] five times.

   ▲ **Initial Delay** determines how long you must hold down the key before the mouse pointer moves.

   ▲ **Maximum Speed** determines how fast the mouse pointer moves.

3. To make the mouse easier to see, drag the Cursor Size slider to the right. The mouse pointer gets bigger.

## ✔ Tips

■ To move the mouse with Mouse Keys enabled, hold down a key on the numeric keypad. Directions correspond with the number positions (for example, [8] moves the mouse up and [3] moves the mouse diagonally down and to the right).

■ Mouse Keys does not enable you to "click" the mouse button with a keyboard key. Full Keyboard Access, however, does. You can set up this feature with the Keyboard preferences pane (**Figure 62**); click the Open Keyboard Preferences button to open it.

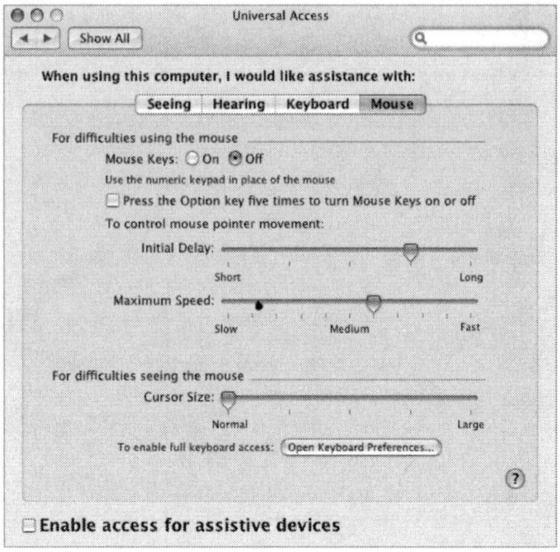

**Figure 122** The Mouse pane of the Universal Access preferences pane.

SETTING UP MOUSE KEYS

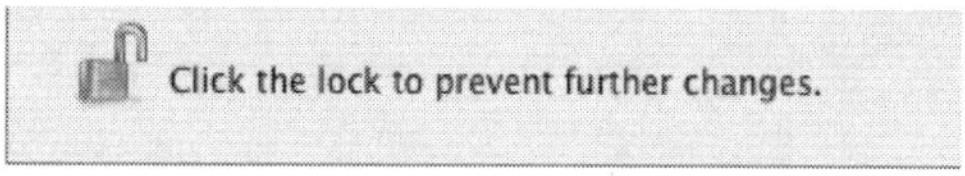

Click the lock to prevent further changes.

**Figure 123** When a preferences pane is unlocked, the padlock icon at the bottom of its window looks unlocked.

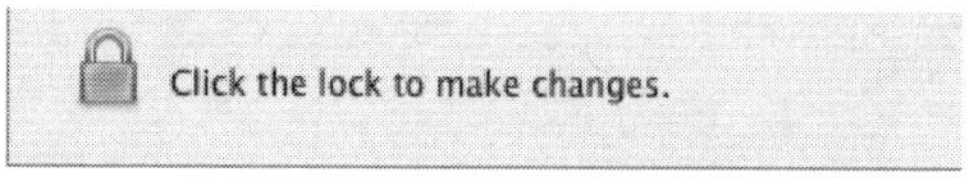

Click the lock to make changes.

**Figure 124** When a preferences pane is locked, the padlock icon at the bottom of its window looks locked.

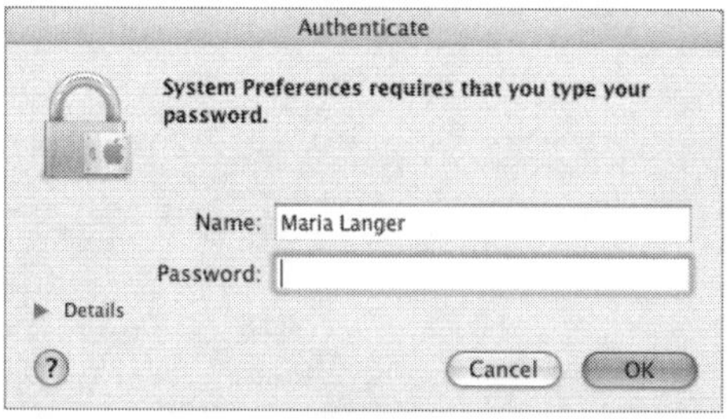

**Figure 125** Enter an administrator's user name and password in the Authenticate dialog to unlock the preferences pane.

# Locking Preference Settings

Most preferences panes include a lock button that enables you to lock the settings. Locking a preferences pane's settings prevent them from being changed accidentally or by users who do not have administrative privileges.

## To lock a preferences pane

Click the lock button at the bottom of a preferences pane window (**Figure 123**).

The button changes so that the icon within it looks like a locked padlock (**Figure 124**).

## To unlock a preferences pane

1. Click the lock button at the bottom of a locked preferences pane window (**Figure 124**).

2. Enter an administrator's name and password in the Authenticate dialog that appears (**Figure 125**) and click OK.

   The button changes so that the icon within it looks like an unlocked padlock.

# Mac OS Utilities

**Figure 1** The Utilities folder contains a bunch of utility applications for working with your computer and files.

## Mac OS Utilities

The Utilities folder inside the Applications folder (**Figure 1**) includes a number of utility applications you can use to work with your computer and its files.

This chapter covers the following utilities:

◆ **Activity Monitor** displays information about your computer CPU's workload.

◆ **Audio MIDI Setup** enables you to set options for audio and MIDI devices connected to your Macintosh.

◆ **ColorSync Utility** enables you to check and repair ColorSync profiles and to assign profiles to hardware devices.

◆ **Console** displays technical messages from the system software and applications.

◆ **Digital Color Meter** enables you to measure and translate colors on your display.

◆ **Disk Utility** allows you to check, format, partition, and get information about disks, as well as create and open disk image files.

◆ **Grab** enables you to capture screen images and save them as image files.

◆ **Grapher** lets you create static or animated graphs of formulas.

◆ **Installer** enables you to install software.

*Continued on next page...*

*Continued from previous page.*

◆ **Migration Assistant** enables you to transfer data from another Mac.

◆ **System Profiler** provides information about your Mac's installed software and hardware.

◆ **VoiceOver Utility** enables you to configure the new VoiceOver feature of Mac OS X.

This chapter also explores one of the seldom used features of Mac OS X: application services.

## ✔ Tips

■ This chapter does not cover the following utilities, which are discussed elsewhere in this book:

▲ Printer Setup Utility, in **Chapter 12**.

▲ Airport Admin Utility, Airport Setup Assistant, Bluetooth File Exchange, and Network Utility, in **Chapter 16**.

▲ Keychain Access, in **Chapter 17**.

▲ Terminal, in **Chapter 19**.

■ Coverage of Directory Access, Java, Net Info Manager, and ODBC Administrator is beyond the scope of this book.

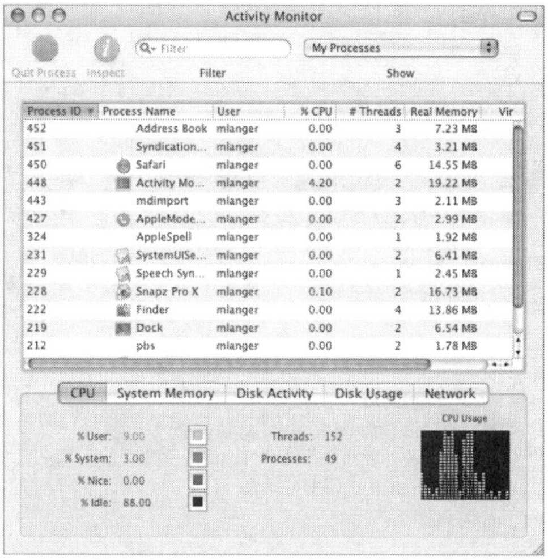

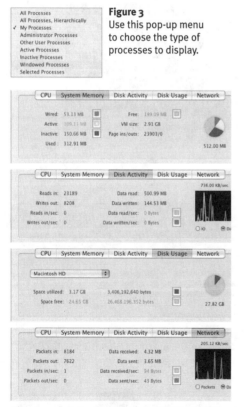

**Figure 2** The Activity Monitor window shows a list of all processes running on your computer.

**Figure 3**
Use this pop-up menu to choose the type of processes to display.

**Figures 4, 5, 6, & 7** The bottom half of the Activity Monitor window can show System Memory, Disk Activity, Disk Usage, and Network information.

# Activity Monitor

Activity Monitor enables you to get information about the various processes running on your computer. It also displays, in graphical format, CPU activity, memory usage, and disk and network statistics. You may find this information helpful if you are a programmer or network administrator or you are trying to troubleshoot a computer problem.

## ✔ Tip

■ A *process* is a set of programming codes that performs a task.

## To monitor computer activity

1. Open the Activity Monitor icon in the Utilities folder (**Figure 1**). The Activity Monitor window appears (**Figure 2**).

2. To view only specific types of processes, choose an option from the pop-up menu at the top of the window (**Figure 3**). The list of processes in the top half of the window changes accordingly.

3. Click a button at the bottom of the window to view other information:

   ▲ **CPU** (**Figure 2**) displays CPU activity.

   ▲ **System Memory** (**Figure 4**) displays RAM usage.

   ▲ **Disk Activity** (**Figure 5**) displays disk access activity.

   ▲ **Disk Usage** (**Figure 6**) displays free and utilized disk space. Use the pop-up menu to choose other available disks.

   ▲ **Network** (**Figure 7**) displays network activity.

## ✔ Tip

■ To sort processes in the Activity Monitor window (**Figure 2**), click the column you want to sort by. You can reverse the sort order by clicking the same column again.

MONITORING COMPUTER ACTIVITY

## To display other monitor windows

Choose an option from the Window menu or its Show Floating CPU Window submenu (**Figure 8**):

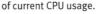

◆ **Activity Monitor** displays the Activity Monitor window (**Figure 2**).

◆ **CPU Usage** displays a graphical representation of current CPU usage (**Figure 9**).

◆ **CPU History** displays a window with a chart of CPU usage over time (**Figure 10**).

◆ **Show Floating CPU Window** submenu commands (**Figure 8**) display a horizontal or vertical bar with a graphical representation of current CPU usage.

*Or*

Choose an option from the View menu's Dock Icon submenu (**Figure 11**).These commands display graphical representations of usage and activity in the Dock. **Figure 12** shows an example of the Dock with a Network Usage display icon.

## ✔ Tip

■ You can use the Update Frequency submenu under the Monitor menu to change how often monitor windows are updated.

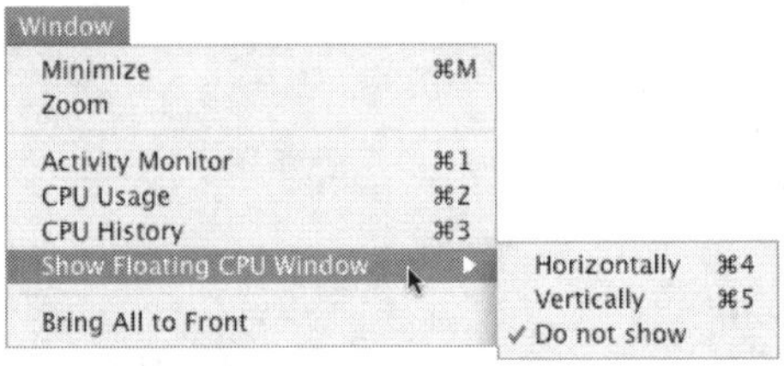

**Figure 8** The Window menu and its Show Floating CPU Monitor submenu.

 **Figure 9**
This tiny window displays a live, graphical representation of current CPU usage.

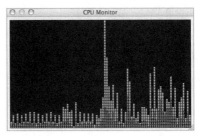

**Figure 10** This window displays CPU usage over time.

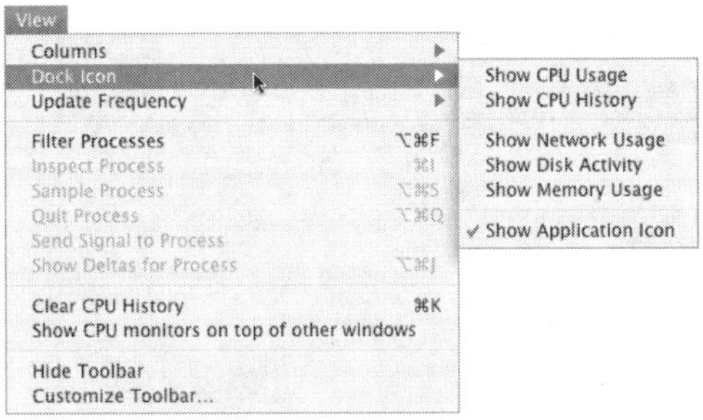

**Figure 11** The Dock Icon submenu offers options for displaying computer activity information in the Dock.

**Figure 12** Activity Monitor can display activity graphs, such as Network Activity, as an icon in the Dock.

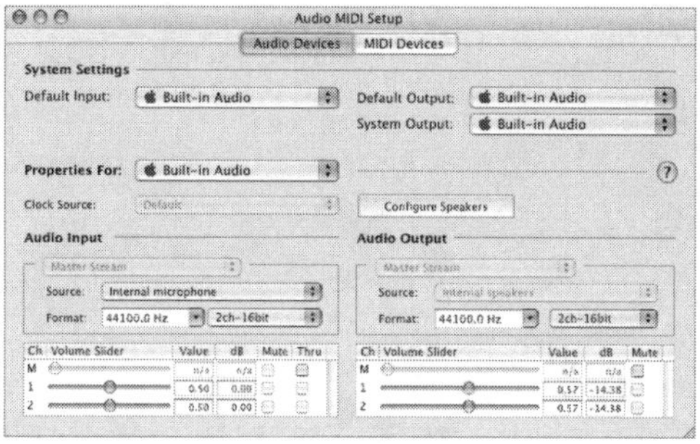

**Figure 13** The Audio Devices pane of Audio MIDI Setup.

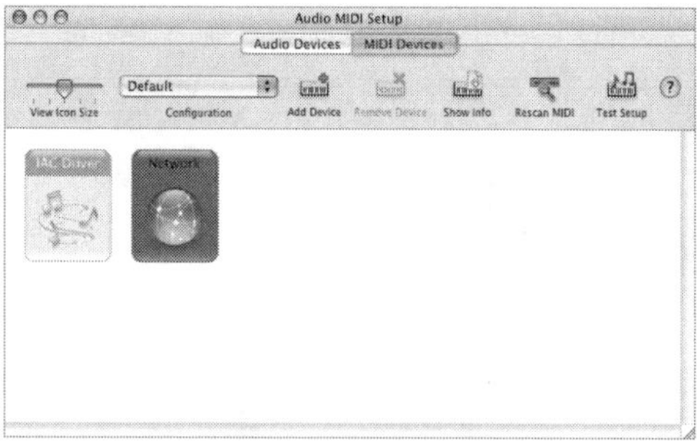

**Figure 14** The MIDI Devices pane of Audio MIDI Setup, before any devices have been added.

# Audio MIDI Setup

Audio MIDI Setup enables you to configure audio and MIDI devices for use with a MIDI music system. It offers two panes of settings:

◆ **Audio Devices (Figure 13)** enables you to configure input and output devices, including internal and external microphones and speakers.

◆ **MIDI Devices (Figure 14)** enables you to configure MIDI devices, such as MIDI keyboards and other instruments, that are connected to your Macintosh.

This section provides a quick overview of Audio MIDI Setup.

## ✔ Tips

■ If you don't use MIDI devices with your Macintosh, you probably won't ever need to use Audio MIDI Setup.

■ Some audio or MIDI devices require additional software to be used with your computer. Make sure any required drivers or other software is installed before setting audio or MIDI options.

## To configure audio devices

1. Open the Audio MIDI Setup icon in the Utilities folder (**Figure 1**).

2. Click the Audio Devices button in the Audio MIDI Setup window that appears (**Figure 13**).

3. Choose the devices you want to use and configure from the pop-up menus. Only those devices connected to your computer will appear in the menus.

4. Set other options as desired.

5. When you are finished, choose Audio MIDI Setup > Quit Audio MIDI Setup. Your settings are automatically saved.

# To configure a MIDI setup

1. Connect your MIDI interface device to your computer as instructed in its documentation and turn it on.

2. Open the Audio MIDI Setup icon in the Utilities folder (**Figure 1**).

3. Click the MIDI Devices button in the Audio MIDI Setup window that appears (**Figure 14**).

4. Click the Add Device button. A new external device icon appears in the window (**Figure 15**).

5. Double-click the new external device icon to display a dialog like the one in **Figure 16**.

6. Enter information about the device in the appropriate boxes. You may be able to use the pop-up menus to select a Manufacturer and Model.

7. To enter additional information about the device, click the triangle beside More Information to expand the dialog. Then use the Properties (**Figure 17**) and Ports (**Figure 18**) panes to enter information.

8. Click OK to save the device settings.

9. Repeat steps 4 through 8 for each device you want to add.

10. When you are finished, choose Audio MIDI Setup > Quit Audio MIDI Setup. Your settings are automatically saved.

## ✔ Tips

■ Your MIDI devices may appear automatically in step 3, depending on how they are connected.

■ Don't change default for a device unless you know what you're doing! Consult the documentation that came with the device if you need help.

**Figure 15**
An icon like this appears when you click the Add Device button.

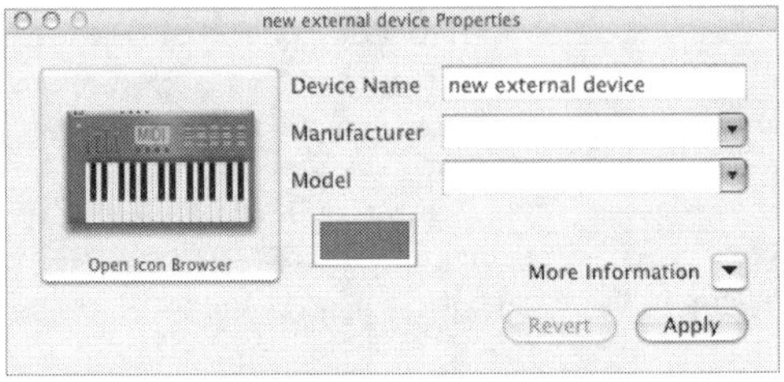

**Figure 16** Use this dialog to enter basic information about your MIDI device.

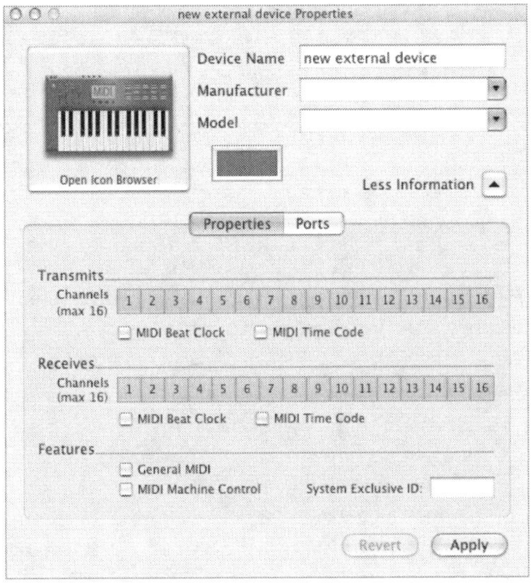

**Figure 17** Click the triangle beside More Information to expand the dialog sheet and set Properties...

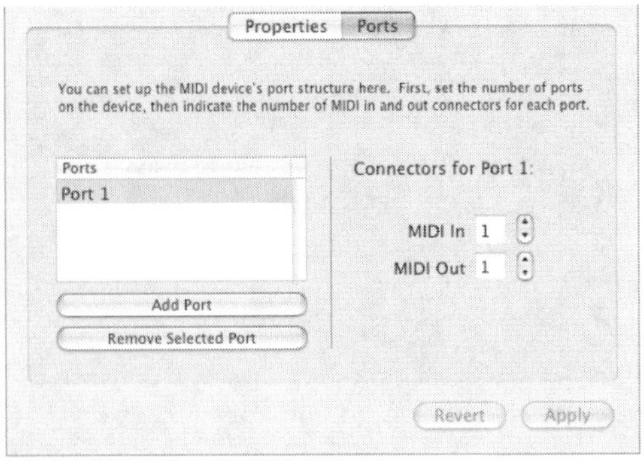

**Figure 18** ...and Ports options.

**Figure 19** When you first display the Profile First Aid pane of the ColorSync Utility, a window full of instructions appears.

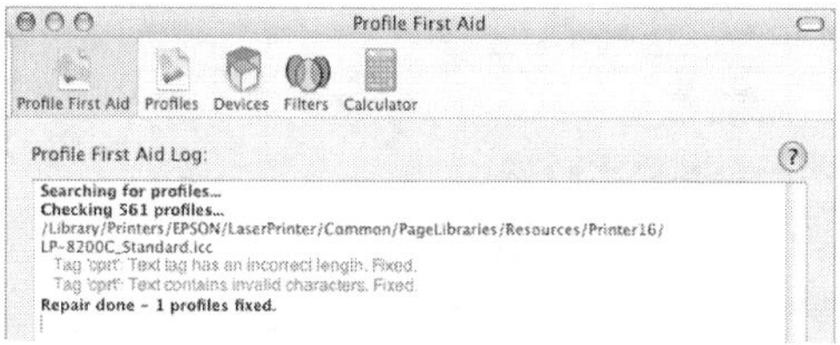

**Figure 20** Here's what the results of a profile repair might look like after repairing a profile.

# ColorSync Utility

ColorSync is an industry-standard technology that helps designers match the colors they see onscreen to those in devices such as scanners, printers, and imagesetters. For the average user, color matching may not be very important, but for a designer who works with color, correct reproduction makes it possible to complete complex projects on time and within budget.

In this section, I explain how to use the ColorSync utility to check ColorSync profiles and view profiles and devices.

## ✔ Tip

■ A complete discussion of ColorSync is far beyond the scope of this book. To learn more about ColorSync features and settings, visit www.apple.com/colorsync.

## To verify or repair ColorSync profiles

1. Open the ColorSync Utility icon in the Utilities folder (**Figure 1**).

2. In the window that appears, click the Profile First Aid icon (**Figure 19**).

3. Click Verify to check all installed profiles for errors.

   *or*

   Click Repair to repair any errors in installed profiles.

   ColorSync Utility checks or repairs installed profiles. When it's finished, it displays results in its window (**Figure 20**).

## ✔ Tip

■ Use this feature to check or fix ColorSync Profiles if you notice a difference between what you see on your monitor and what you see on printed documents.

ColorSync Utility

## To view lists of installed profiles, registered devices, & available filters

1. Open the ColorSync Utility icon in the Utilities folder (**Figure 1**).

2. Click an icon in the ColorSync Utility window's toolbar:

   ▲ **Profiles** displays a list of installed ColorSync profiles (**Figure 21**).

   ▲ **Devices** displays a list of registered ColorSync devices (**Figure 22**).

   ▲ **Filters** displays a list of available ColorSync filters (**Figure 23**).

3. If necessary, click triangles beside a folder pathname to view a list of the items in the folder (**Figures 21** and **22**) or settings for the item (**Figure 23**).

## ✔ Tips

■ A registered device is one that is recognized by the system software and has a ColorSync profile assigned to it.

■ Clicking the name of a profile or device displays information about it in the right side of the window, as shown in **Figures 21** and **22**.

■ You can change a device's profile by choosing an option from the Current Profile pop-up menu when the item is displayed (**Figure 22**).

■ The filters that are installed with Mac OS X 10.4 are locked and cannot be changed.

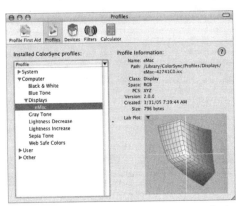

**Figure 21** The Profiles pane of ColorSync utility displays a list of all installed profiles. Click a profile to learn more about it.

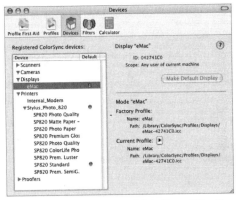

**Figure 22** The Devices pane of ColorSync utility displays a list of all registered devices. Click a device to learn more about it.

**Figure 23** The Filters pane of ColorSync Utility lists available filters.

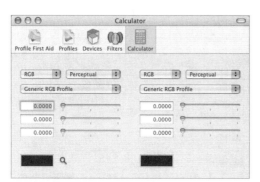

**Figure 24** The Calculator pane of ColorSync Utility enables you to convert color values.

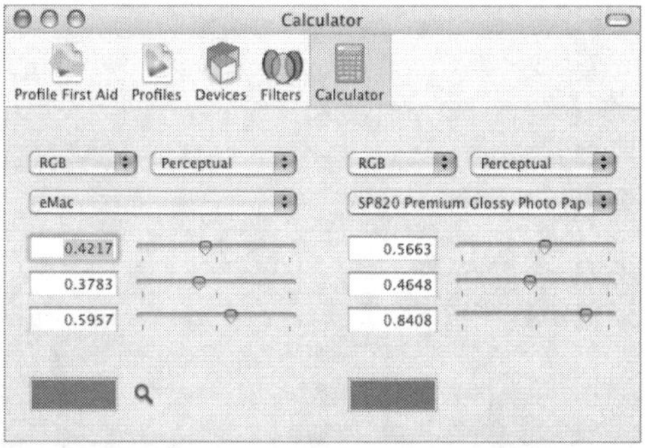

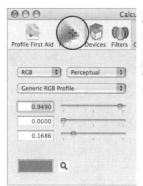

**Figure 25** This example shows a conversion from my monitor's profile to one of the profiles for my color printer.

**Figure 26**
You can click the magnifying glass icon and use a special cross-hairs pointer to get the color value of any pixel on the screen.

## To convert color values

1. Open the ColorSync Utility icon in the Utilities folder (**Figure 1**).

2. In the ColorSync Utility window that appears, click the Calculator icon (**Figure 24**).

3. On the left side of the window, use the pop-up menus to set the color space or profile you are converting from.

4. Use the sliders on the left side of the window to enter color values.

5. On the right side of the window, use the pop-up menus to set the color space or profile you are converting to.

   The converted color values appear on the right side of the window (**Figure 25**).

## ✔ Tip

- To find the color value for a pixel on your screen, click the magnifying glass icon to change the mouse pointer into a magnified cross-hairs pointer (**Figure 26**). Click the pixel you want to get the color values for to insert the values on the left side of the screen.

# To modify an image

1. Open the ColorSync Utility icon in the Utilities folder (**Figure 1**) to open ColorSync Utility.

2. Choose File > Open, or press ⌘O.

3. Use the Standard Open dialog that appears (**Figure 27**) to locate, select, and open an image file. The photo opens in its own window (**Figure 28**).

4. Use the pop-up menus at the bottom of the window to set options for the image. Click Apply after each change you want to apply. The appearance of the image changes accordingly.

5. To save the image with the changes applied, choose File > Save As, or press Shift ⌘S.

6. Set options in the Save As dialog that appears (**Figure 29**) and click Save.

## ✔ Tips

- I explain how to use the Open and Save As dialogs in **Chapter 7**.

- In step 4, if you set an option with the middle pop-up menu and don't like the results, choose None from that menu to revert back to the last time you clicked Apply.

- In step 6, you can choose from a number of popular image file formats (**Figure 30**).

- If you often use this feature to modify images, consider setting up an Automator workflow to get the job done. I tell you more about Automator in **Chapter 20**.

**Figure 27** Use a standard Open dialog to locate, select, and open an image to work with.

**Figure 28** The image appears in its own window.

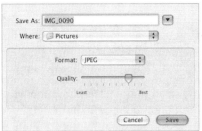

**Figure 29** Use a standard Save As dialog to save the modified image.

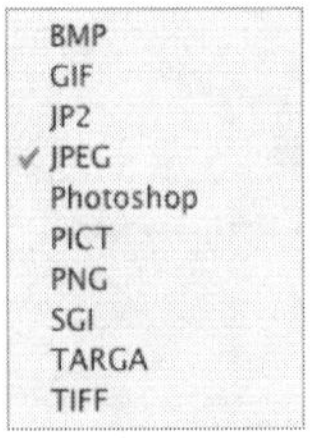

BMP
GIF
JP2
✓ JPEG
Photoshop
PICT
PNG
SGI
TARGA
TIFF

**Figure 30** ColorSync Utility supports most popular image file formats.

Figure 31 The console.log window records messages sent by Mac OS and its applications. (What may look like a bunch of gibberish to you and me can help a programmer or troubleshooter debug a Mac.)

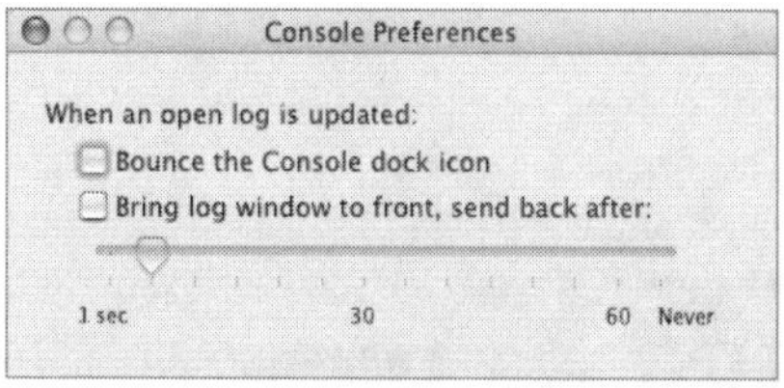

Figure 32 The Console Preferences window.

# Console

The Console application enables you to read messages from Mac OS X system software and applications. You might find this useful if you are a programmer or are troubleshooting a problem. (If not, you'll probably think it looks like a bunch of gibberish.)

## To view system messages

1. Open the Console icon in the Utilities folder (**Figure 1**).

2. The console.log window appears (**Figure 31**). Scroll through its contents to read messages.

## ✔ Tip

■ The most recent console.log entries appear at the end of the document.

## To set Console preferences

1. Choose Console > Preferences.

2. In the Console Preferences window (**Figure 32**), set options as desired:

   ▲ **Bounce the Console dock icon** bounces the log's icon in the Dock when a new message is recorded in the log.

   ▲ **Bring log window to front, send back after** brings the console.log window to the foreground when a new message is added. (Console must be running for this to work.) The window returns to the background after the number of seconds you specify with the slider has passed.

3. Click the close button to save your preference settings.

# DigitalColor Meter

The DigitalColor Meter (**Figure 30**) enables you to measure colors that appear on your display as RGB, CIE, or Tristimulus values. This enables you to precisely record or duplicate colors that appear onscreen.

## ✔ Tip

■ A discussion of color technology is far beyond the scope of this book. To learn more about how your Mac can work with colors, visit the ColorSync page on Apple's Web site, www.apple.com/colorsync/.

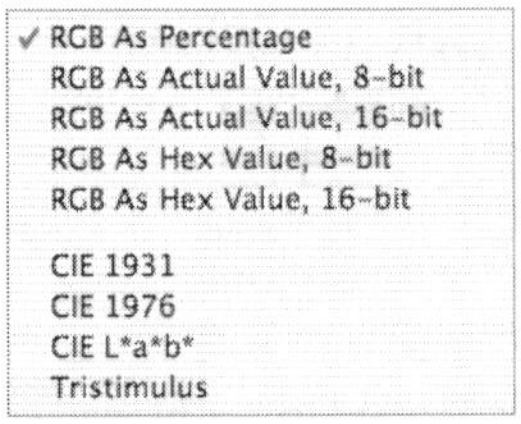

## To measure color values

1. Open the DigitalColor Meter icon in the Utilities folder (**Figure 1**) to display the DigitalColor Meter window (**Figure 33**).

2. Point to the color onscreen that you want to measure. Its values appear in the right side of the DigitalColor Meter window (**Figure 33**).

3. If desired, choose a different option from the pop-up menu above the measurements (**Figure 34**). The value display changes to convert values to that measuring system (**Figure 35**).

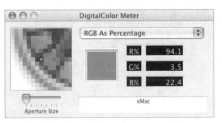

**Figure 33** The DigitalColor Meter can tell you the color of any area onscreen—in this case, one of the pixels in its icon.

**Figure 34** Choose an option to determine the system or units of the color measurement.

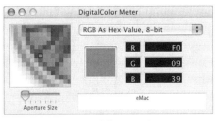

**Figure 35** Choosing a different color measurement option from the pop-up menu changes the way the color values appear.

**MEASURING COLOR VALUES**

Image

| Lock Position | ⌘L |
|---|---|
| Lock X | ⌘X |
| Lock Y | ⌘Y |
| Copy Image | ⌘C |
| Save as TIFF... | ⌘S |

**Figure 36** Use the Image menu to work with the sample image.

Color

| Hold Color | ⇧⌘H |
|---|---|
| Copy Color As Text | ⇧⌘C |
| Copy Color As Image | ⌥⌘C |

**Figure 37** Use the Color menu to work with sampled colors.

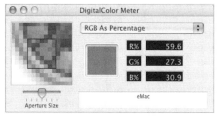

**Figure 38** By changing the aperture setting, you can sample more pixels. DigitalColor Meter automatically computes the average.

## ✔ Tips

■ You can use commands under the Image menu (**Figure 36**) to work with the color sample image that appears in Digital-Color Meter's window:

▲ **Lock Position** (⌃ ⌘L) prevents the image from moving.

▲ **Lock X** (⌃ ⌘X) allows only vertical changes in the color sample.

▲ **Lock Y** (⌃ ⌘Y) allows only horizontal change in the color sample area.

▲ **Copy Image** (⌃ ⌘C) copies the color sample image to the clipboard.

▲ **Save as TIFF** (⌃ ⌘S) saves the color sample image as a TIFF file.

■ You can use commands under the Color menu (**Figure 37**) to work with a selected color. (For best results, either use the command's shortcut key or choose Image > Lock Position [**Figure 36**] before using the Color menu's commands.)

▲ **Hold Color** (Shift ⌃ ⌘H) saves the color in the sample well until you choose the Hold Color command again.

▲ **Copy Color As Text** (Shift ⌃ ⌘C) copies the color information to the clipboard, where it can be pasted into other applications.

▲ **Copy Color As Image** (Option ⌃ ⌘C) copies the color information as a color sample to the clipboard, where it can be pasted into other applications.

■ You can change the amount of color that is sampled by dragging the Aperture Size slider to the right or left (**Figure 38**). A large aperture size will average the colors within it.

MEASURING COLOR VALUES

# Disk Utility

Disk Utility, as the name implies, is a utility for working with disks. Specifically, it can:

◆ Provide general information about a disk or volume.

◆ Verify and repair a disk or volume.

◆ Erase a selected disk or volume.

◆ Divide a disk into several volumes or partitions.

◆ Set up a RAID disk.

◆ Create a blank disk image, or a disk image from a file or a disk.

◆ Mount disk images as disks.

◆ Burn a disk image to CD-R or DVD-R.

◆ Restore a disk from a backup image.

In this part of the chapter, I explain how to use Disk Utility's most useful features.

## ✔ Tips

■ A *disk* is a storage device. A *volume* is a part of a disk formatted for storing files.

■ A *disk image* is a single file that contains everything on a disk. You can mount a disk image on your desktop just like any other disk.

■ I tell you more about mounting and unmounting disks in **Chapter 3**.

■ Disk images are often used to distribute software updates on the Internet.

■ Disk image files often include *.img* or *.dmg* filename extensions.

■ Disk Utility's RAID and Restore panes are not covered in this book. To learn more about this feature, enter a search phrase of *RAID* or *restore* in Mac Help and follow links that appear for specific instructions.

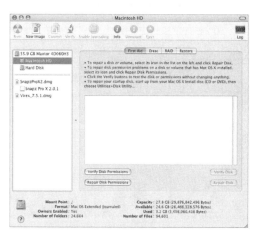

**Figure 39** Select the disk or volume you want to work with in Disk Utility's main window. The list includes physical disks and their volumes as well as disk image files you have created and saved on disk.

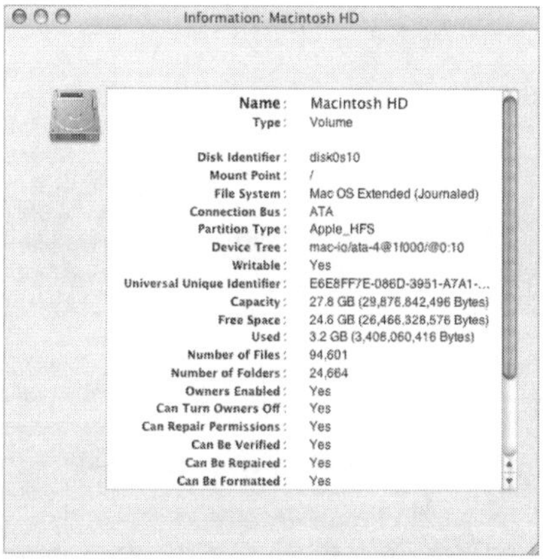

**Figure 40** This window shows information about one of the two volumes on my hard disk.

## To get information about a disk or volume

1. Open the Disk Utility icon in the Utilities folder (**Figure 1**).

2. In the Disk Utility window that appears, select the disk or volume you want information about. Some information about the item appears at the bottom of the window (**Figure 39**).

3. Click the Info button on the toolbar. A window with additional information appears (**Figure 40**).

## To verify or repair a disk or volume or its permissions

1. Open the Disk Utility icon in the Utilities folder (**Figure 1**).

2. In the Disk Utility window that appears, click the First Aid button.

3. Select the disk(s) or volume(s) you want to verify or repair (**Figure 39**).

4. Click the button for the action you want to perform:

   ▲ **Verify Disk Permissions** verifies file permissions on a Mac OS X startup disk or volume.

   ▲ **Repair Disk Permissions** repairs file permissions on a Mac OS X startup volume.

   ▲ **Verify Disk** verifies the directory structure and file integrity of any disk or volume other than the startup disk or volume.

   ▲ **Repair Disk** repairs damage to the directory structure of any volume other than the startup disk, as long as it is not write-protected.

*Continued on next page...*

**GETTING INFO, VERIFYING OR REPAIRING DISKS**

*Continued from previous page.*

**5.** Wait while your computer checks and/or repairs the selected disk or volume and its permissions. When it's done, it reports its results on the right side of the window (**Figure 41**).

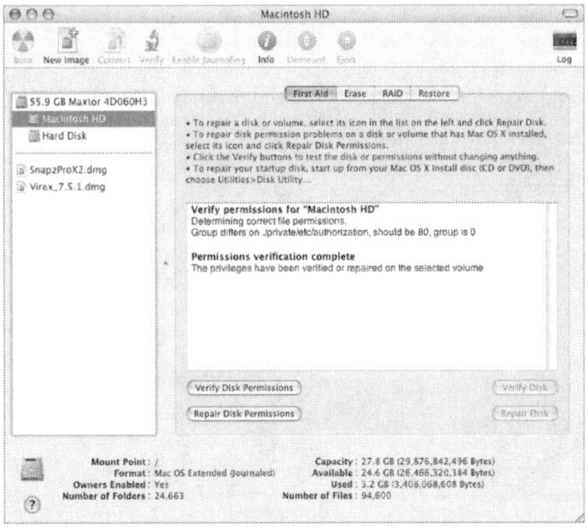

## ✔ Tips

■ Permissions determine how users can access files. If permissions are incorrectly set for a file, it may not be accessible by the users who should be able to use it. If permissions are really messed up, your computer might not work correctly.

■ The startup disk is verified and, if necessary, repaired when you start your computer.

■ To verify or repair your startup disk or volume, start your computer from the Mac OS X install disc. When the Installer launches, choose Installer > Disk Utility to run Disk Utility.

■ To select more than one disk or volume in step 3, hold down ⌥ ⌘ while clicking each item.

■ Disk Utility's First Aid feature cannot repair all disk problems. For severely damaged disks, you may need to acquire third-party utilities, such as Symantec's Norton Utilities or Alsoft's DiskWarrior.

**Figure 41** At the end of the verification (or repair) process, Disk Utility's First Aid feature reports results. In this example, Disk Utility found just one error in the permissions on my startup disk.

**VERIFYING OR REPAIRING DISKS**

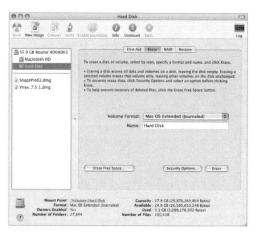

Figure 42 Use Disk Utility's Erase pane to erase a disk or volume.

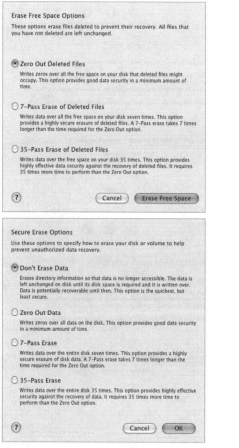

Figures 43 & 44 These dialogs offer more secure options for erasing a disk.

# To erase a disk or volume

1. Open the Disk Utility icon in the Utilities folder (**Figure 1**).

2. In the Disk Utility window that appears, click the Erase button.

3. Select the disk or volume you want to erase (**Figure 42**).

4. Set options for the volume:

   ▲ **Volume Format** is the format applied to the volume. Depending on what you are erasing, your options include Mac OS Extended (Journaled), Mac OS Extended, Mac OS Extended (Case-sensitive, Journaled), Mac OS Extended (Case-sensitive), Mac OS Standard, MS-DOS File System, and UNIX File System.

   ▲ **Name** is the name of the volume.

   ▲ **Mac OS 9 Drivers Installed** installs drivers on the disk so it can be read by computers running Mac OS 9.x. (This option is only available if you select a disk to erase.)

5. To specify how disk space occupied by deleted files should be erased, click the Erase Free Space button. Then select an option in the Erase Free Space Options dialog (**Figure 43**) and click OK.

6. To increase security and prevent the disk from being unerased, click the Security Options button. Then select an option in the Secure Erase Options dialog (**Figure 44**) and click OK.

7. Click Erase.

8. A dialog sheet like the one in **Figure 45** appears. Click Erase.

*Continued on next page...*

ERASING DISKS & VOLUMES

*Continued from previous page.*

9. Wait while your computer erases the disk or volume. A progress dialog appears as it works. When it's finished, an icon for the erased disk or volume reappears on the desktop.

## ✖ Caution!

■ Erasing a disk or volume permanently removes all data. Do not erase a disk if you think you will need any of the data it contains.

## ✔ Tips

■ You cannot erase the startup disk. (And that's a good thing.)

■ When you erase a disk, you replace all volumes on the disk with one blank volume. When you erase a volume, you replace that volume with a blank volume.

■ If you're not sure what volume format to choose in step 4, choose Mac OS Extended (Journaled). If you wanted one of the other formats, you'd know it.

■ To use a disk on a computer started with Mac OS 9, you must turn on the Mac OS 9 Drivers installed check box in step 4. With this option turned off, you can still use the disk in the Classic environment with Mac OS X. I tell you about Mac OS 9.x and the Classic environment in **Chapter 18**.

■ In steps 5 and 6, the explanations that appear beneath each option (**Figures 43** and **44**) should be enough information to help you decide which option is right for you.

■ If you're concerned about unauthorized persons recovering data from files you erase, be sure to check out the Secure Empty Trash command, which is covered in **Chapter 3**.

**Figure 45** A dialog like this appears to confirm that you really do want to erase the volume or disk.

**Figure 46** Use Disk Utility's Partition pane to set up partitions on a disk.

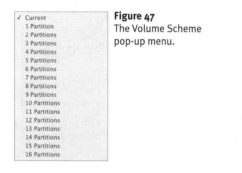

**Figure 47**
The Volume Scheme pop-up menu.

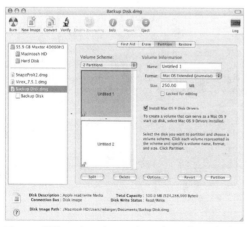

**Figure 48** When the volume scheme is set for multiple volumes, you can set options for each one.

# To partition a disk

1. Open the Disk Utility icon in the Utilities folder (**Figure 1**).

2. In the Disk Utility window that appears, click the Partition tab.

3. Select the disk you want to partition (**Figure 46**).

4. Choose an option from the Volume Scheme pop-up menu (**Figure 47**). The area beneath the pop-up menu changes (**Figure 48**).

5. In the Volume Scheme area, select a volume. Then set options in the Volume Information area as desired:

   ▲ **Name** is the name of the volume.

   ▲ **Format** is the volume format. The options may include Mac OS Extended (Journaled), Mac OS Extended, Mac OS Extended (Case-sensitive, Journaled), Mac OS Extended (Case-sensitive), Mac OS Standard, UNIX File System, and Free Space.

   ▲ **Size** is the amount of disk space allocated to that partition.

   ▲ **Locked for editing** prevents changes to the partition's settings.

   ▲ **Install Mac OS 9 Disk Drivers** enables the partition to be used as a Mac OS 9.x startup disk (if the computer supports starting from Mac OS 9.x).

6. Repeat step 5 for each partition.

7. Click Partition.

8. A warning dialog like the one in **Figure 49** appears. Click Partition.

*Continued on next page...*

*Continued from previous page.*

9. Wait while your computer erases the disk
   and creates the new partitions. When it's
   finished, icons for each formatted partition appear on the desktop.

## ✖ Caution!

- As warned in **Figure 49**, creating new
  volumes will erase all existing volumes,
  thus erasing data.

## ✔ Tips

- If you're not sure what volume format to
  choose in step 5, choose Mac OS
  Extended (Journaled). If you wanted one
  of the other formats, you'd know it.

- If you select Free Space as the format for
  any partition in step 5, that partition
  cannot be used to store files.

- You can also change the partition size in
  step 5 by dragging the divider between
  partitions in the Volume Scheme area
  (**Figure 50**).

- If you are partitioning removable media
  that may be used with non-Apple computers, before step 7, click the Options
  button in the Partition pane. Then choose
  PC Partition Scheme in the dialog sheet
  that appears (**Figure 51**) and click OK.

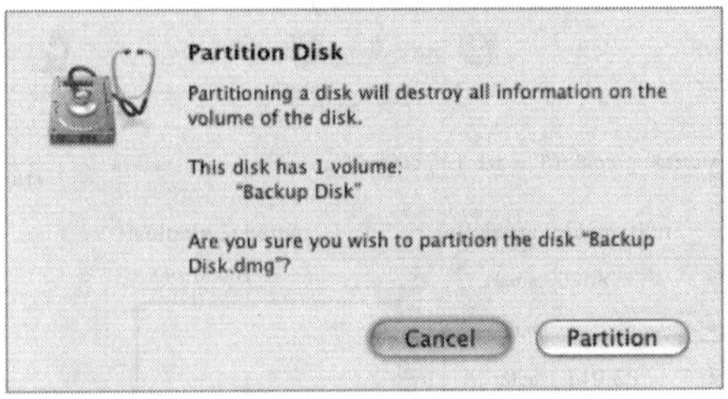

**Figure 49** If you're sure you want to change the
volume scheme, click Partition.

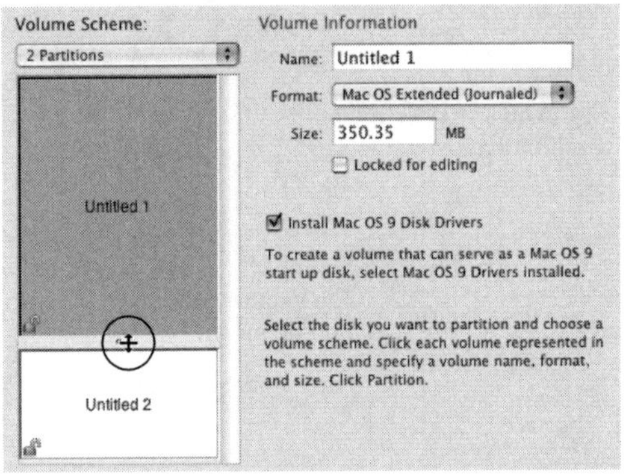

**Figure 50** Another way to change the size of the partition is to drag the divider between two partitions.

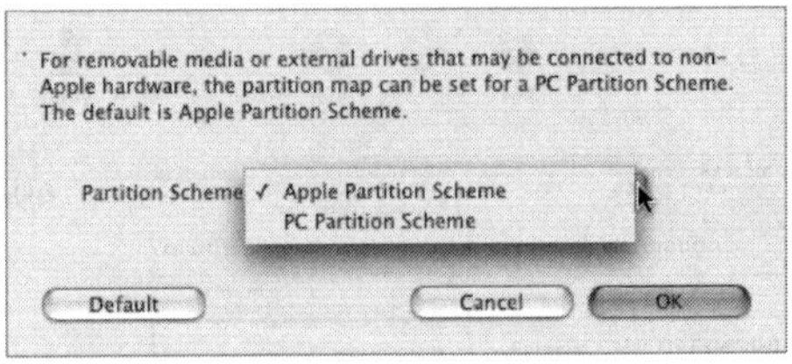

**Figure 51** When partitioning removable media, you
may need to set the Partition Scheme.

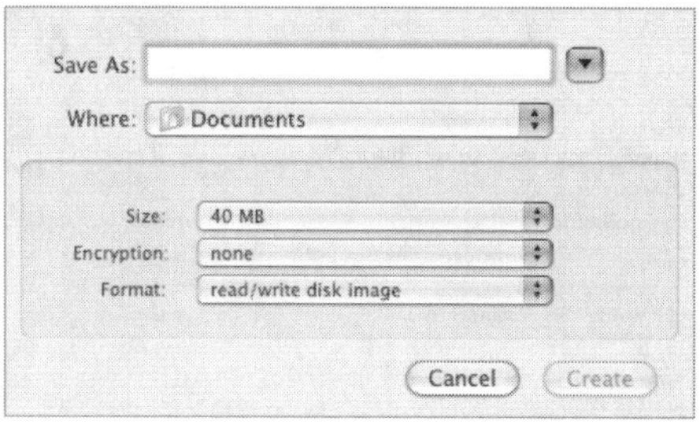

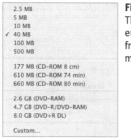

**Figure 52** Use a dialog like this to set options for a new disk image.

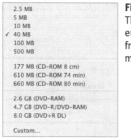

**Figure 53**
The Size pop-up menu enables you to select from a number of common disk sizes...

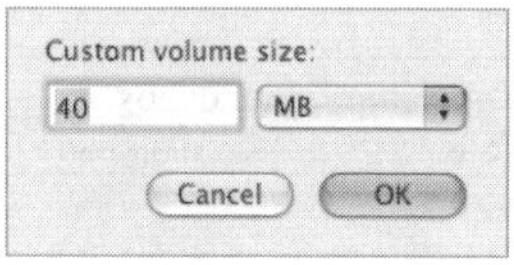

**Figure 54**
...or choose Custom and use this dialog to enter a custom size.

**Figure 55**
After creating the disk image, Disk Utility mounts it as a disk on your desktop. Here's the disk image created with the settings in **Figure 47**.

# To create a blank disk image file

1. Open the Disk Utility icon in the Utilities folder (**Figure 1**).

2. Click the New Image button in Disk Utility's toolbar.

3. In the top half of the dialog that appears (**Figure 52**) enter a name and specify a disk location in which to save the disk image file.

4. Set options in the bottom part of the dialog:

   ▲ **Size** is the size of the disk. Choose an option from the pop-up menu (**Figure 53**). If you choose Custom, use a dialog sheet (**Figure 54**) to set the size.

   ▲ **Encryption** is file encryption to apply to the disk image file. Choose an option from the menu. The selections are none and AES-128.

   ▲ **Format** refers to the type of disk image. Make sure read/write disk image is chosen.

5. Click Create. Disk Utility creates a disk image file to your specifications and mounts it on the desktop (**Figure 55**).

# ✔ Tips

■ The size of a disk image file is determined by the size specified in step 4.

■ Once you have created and mounted a blank disk image, you can copy items to it as if it were a regular disk. The items you copy to the disk are automatically copied into the disk image file. Copying files is discussed in **Chapter 2**.

## To create a disk image file from a folder

1. Open the Disk Utility icon in the Utilities folder (**Figure 1**).

2. Choose File > New > Disk Image from Folder.

3. Use the Select Folder to Image dialog that appears (**Figure 56**) to locate and select the folder you want to create a disk image of. Then click Image.

4. In the top half of the New Image From Folder dialog that appears (**Figure 57**), enter a name and choose a disk location for the image file.

5. In the bottom half of the dialog, set options as desired:

   ▲ **Image Format (Figure 58)** refers to the type of disk image.

   ▲ **Encryption** is file encryption to apply to the disk image file. Choose an option from the menu. The selections are none and AES-128.

6. Click Save. Disk Utility creates a disk image file containing the contents of the folder and mounts it on the desktop.

## ✔ Tips

■ The size of a disk image file is determined by the amount of data in the folder and the Image Format option you chose in step 5.

■ If you choose read/write from the Image Format pop-up menu (**Figure 58**), you can add files to the mounted disk image disk. Otherwise, you cannot.

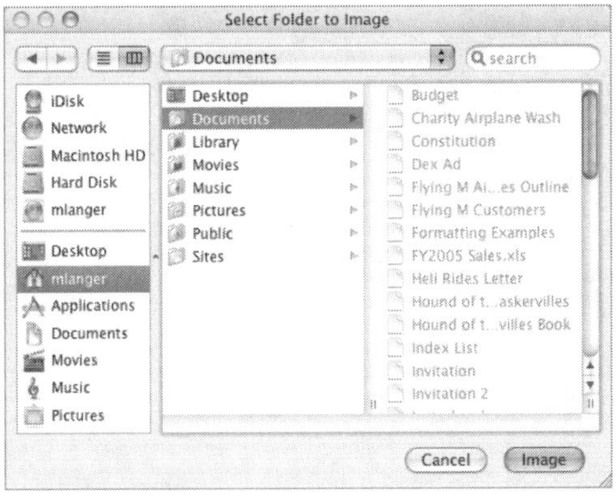

**Figure 56** Start by selecting the folder you want to create a disk image of.

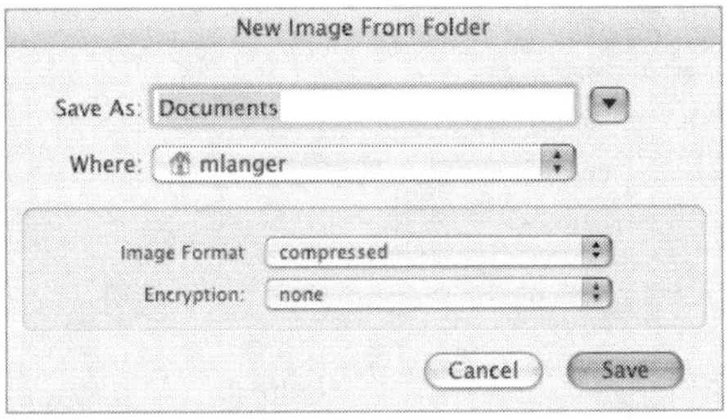

**Figure 57** Use the New Image From Folder dialog to set options for the image file.

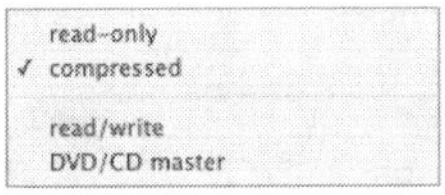

**Figure 58** The Image Format pop-up menu offers several options for the type of disk image file.

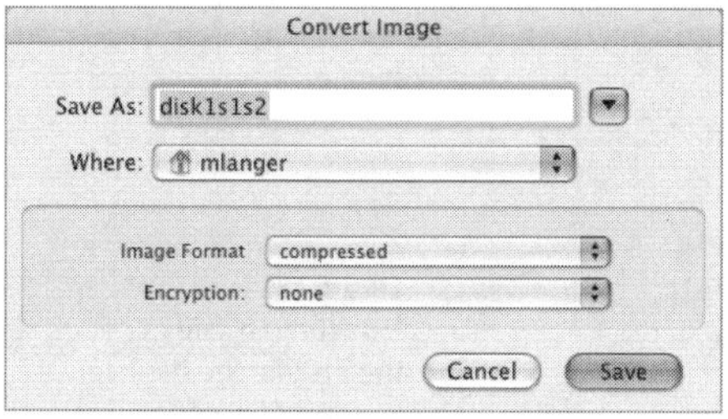

**Figure 59** Use the Convert Image dialog to set options for a disk image based on a disk.

## To create a disk image file from another disk

1. Open the Disk Utility icon in the Utilities folder (**Figure 1**).

2. On the left side of the window, select the volume you want to create an image of.

3. Choose File > New > Disk Image from *Disk Name*.

4. In the top half of the Convert Image dialog that appears (**Figure 59**), enter a name and choose a disk location for the image file.

5. In the bottom half of the dialog, set options as desired:

   ▲ **Image Format (Figure 58)** refers to the type of disk image.

   ▲ **Encryption** is file encryption to apply to the disk image file. Choose an option from the menu. The selections are none and AES-128.

6. Click Save. Disk Utility creates a disk image file containing the contents of the disk and mounts it on the desktop.

## ✔ Tips

■ The size of a disk image file is determined by the amount of data in the original disk and the Image Format option you chose in step 5.

■ If you choose read/write from the Image Format pop-up menu (**Figure 58**), you can add files to the mounted disk image disk. Otherwise, you cannot.

■ You cannot save a disk image file on the same disk you are creating an image of. For example, if you wanted to back up your hard disk to an image file, you must save that image to another disk.

## To mount a disk image

Double-click the disk image file's icon in the Finder (**Figure 60**).

*Or*

1. Open the Disk Utility icon in the Utilities folder (**Figure 1**).

2. Select the name of the disk image you want to mount in the list on the left side of the main window (**Figure 61**).

3. Click the Open button in the toolbar.

*Or*

1. Open the Disk Utility icon in the Utilities folder (**Figure 1**).

2. Choose File > Open.

3. Use the Select Image to Attach dialog that appears (**Figure 62**) to locate, select, and open the disk image file.

The disk image file's disk icon appears on the desktop and, if Disk Utility is open, in the list of disks and volumes (**Figure 63**).

## ✔ Tip

■ To mount an unmounted disk or partition, select it in the list on the left side of Disk Utility's main window and click the Mount button in the toolbar.

**Figure 60**
A disk image file's icon.

Virex_7.5.1.dmg

**Figure 61**
Select the name of the disk image file you want to mount.

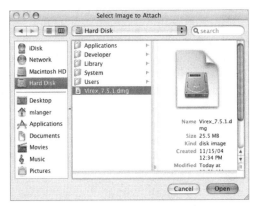

**Figure 62** Use the Select Image to Attach dialog to locate, select, and open a disk image file.

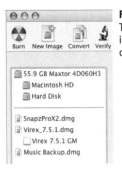

**Figure 63**
The disk image's disk icon appears in the list of disks and volumes.

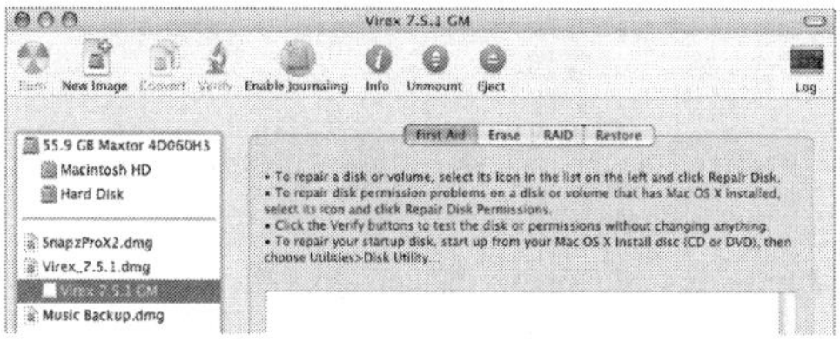

**Figure 64** Select the disk you want to unmount and click the Unmount button.

## To unmount a disk image, disk, or partition

In the Finder, drag the mounted disk icon to the Trash.

*Or*

1. In the Disk Utility main window, select the icon for the disk you want to unmount (**Figure 64**).

2. Click the Unmount button in the toolbar.

Although the icon disappears from the desktop, all of its contents remain in the disk image file.

## ✔ Tip

■ To eject removable media, you can select it on the right side of the window and click the Eject button in the toolbar (**Figure 64**).

## To burn a CD or DVD from a disk or disk image

1. Open the Disk Utility icon in the Utilities folder (**Figure 1**).

2. In the main Disk Utility window, select the disk you want to copy to CD or DVD (**Figure 61**). The disk can be a physical disk or a disk image.

3. Click the Burn button in the toolbar.

4. A dialog like the one in **Figure 65** appears. Insert a CD-R or DVD-R disc in your drive as instructed and click Burn.

   Wait while Disk Utility writes to the disc. A progress dialog like the one in **Figure 66** appears as it works.

5. When the disc finished, Disk Utility ejects the disc and displays a dialog like the one in **Figure 67**. Click OK.

## ✔ Tips

■ You must have a Combo Drive, Super-Drive, or compatible disc writer to create or "burn" CD or DVD discs.

■ If a disk image file that you want to burn to disc does not appear in the Disk Utility window, mount it as instructed on the previous page. Then follow these instructions.

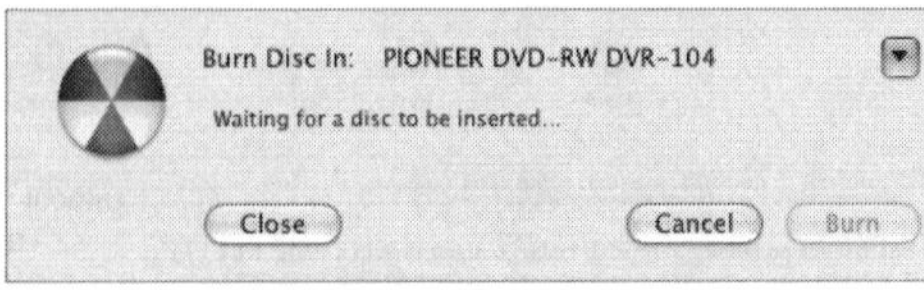

**Figure 65** A dialog like this one prompts you to insert a disc.

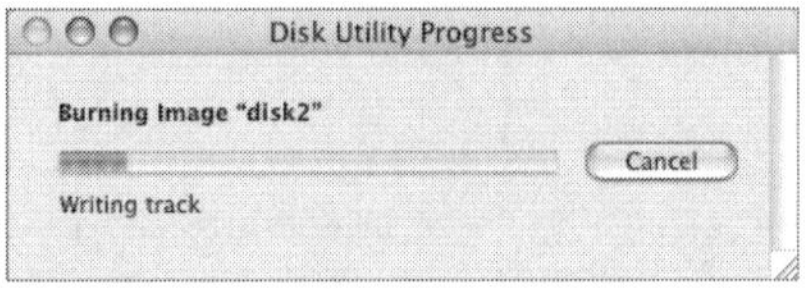

**Figure 66** Disk Utility displays a progress dialog as it creates the disc.

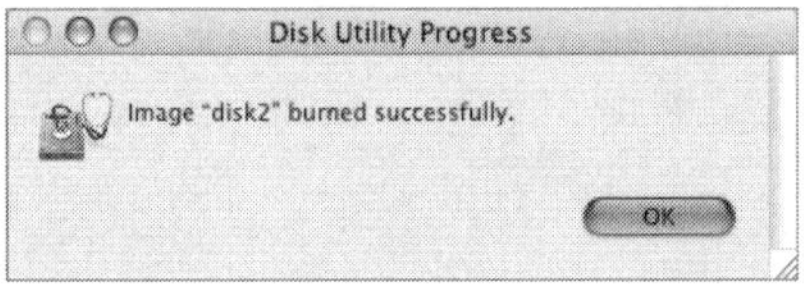

**Figure 67** A dialog like this appears when the disc is finished.

**Figure 68** If Grab is already running, click its icon in the Dock to make it active.

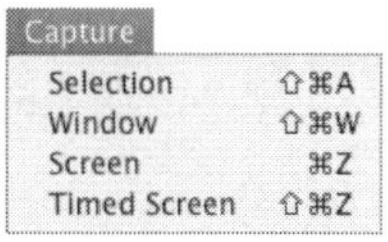

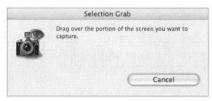

**Figure 69**
Grab's Capture menu.

**Figure 70** The Selection Grab dialog includes instructions for selecting a portion of the screen.

**Figure 71**
Use the mouse to drag a red rectangle around the portion of the screen you want to capture.

# Grab

Grab is an application that can capture screen shots of Mac OS X and its applications. You tell Grab to capture what appears on your screen and it creates a TIFF file. You can then view the TIFF file with Preview or any application capable of opening TIFFs.

## ✔ Tips

- You might find screen shots useful for documenting software—or for writing books like this one.

- Although Grab is a handy screen shot utility, it isn't the best available for Mac OS X. Snapz Pro X, a shareware program from Ambrosia Software, is far better. If you take a lot of screen shots, be sure to check it out at www.ambrosiasw.com.

## To create a screen shot

1. Set up the screen so it shows what you want to capture.

2. Open the Grab icon in the Utilities folder (**Figure 1**).

   *or*

   If Grab is already running, click its icon on the Dock (**Figure 68**) to make it active.

3. Choose an option from the Capture menu (**Figure 69**) or press its corresponding shortcut key:

   ▲ **Selection** (Shift ⌃ ⌘ A) enables you to capture a portion of the screen. When you choose this option, the Selection Grab dialog (**Figure 70**) appears. Use the mouse pointer to drag a box around the portion of the screen you want to capture (**Figure 71**). Release the mouse button to capture the screen.

*Continued on next page...*

CREATING SCREEN SHOTS

*Continued from previous page.*

▲ **Window** (Shift ⌃ ⌘ W) enables you to capture a window. When you choose this option, the Window Grab dialog (**Figure 72**) appears. Click the Choose Window button, then click the window you want to capture.

▲ **Screen** (⌃ ⌘ Z) enables you to capture the entire screen. When you choose this option, the Screen Grab dialog (**Figure 73**) appears. Click outside the dialog to capture the screen.

▲ **Timed Screen** (Shift ⌃ ⌘ Z) enables you to capture the entire screen after a ten-second delay. When you choose this option, the Timed Screen Grab dialog (**Figure 74**) appears. Click the Start Timer button, then activate the program you want to capture and arrange onscreen elements as desired. In ten seconds, the screen is captured.

4. Grab makes a camera shutter sound as it captures the screen. The image appears in an untitled document window (**Figure 75**).

5. If you are satisfied with the screen shot, choose File > Save (**Figure 76**) or press ⌃ ⌘ S and use the Save As dialog sheet that appears to save it as a file on disk.

*or*

If you are not satisfied with the screen shot, choose File > Close (**Figure 76**) or press ⌃ ⌘ W to close the window. In the Close dialog sheet, click Don't Save.

## ✔ Tip

■ You can create screen shots without Grab. Press Shift ⌃ ⌘ 3 to capture the entire screen or Shift ⌃ ⌘ 4 to capture a portion of the screen. The screen shot is automatically saved on the desktop as a PDF file.

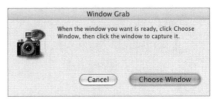

**Figure 72** The Window Grab dialog tells you how to capture a window.

**Figure 73** The Screen Grab dialog provides instructions for capturing the entire screen.

**Figure 74** The Timed Screen Grab dialog includes a button to start the 10-second screen grab timer.

**Figure 75**
The image you capture— in this case, a single icon in a window—appears in a document window.

**Figure 76**
Grab's File menu.

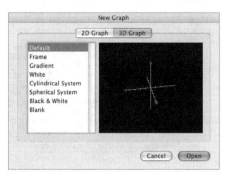

**Figure 77** The first step to graphing a formula is to choose a graph type in the New Graph dialog.

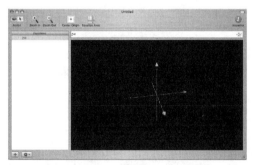

**Figure 78** An untitled document for a 3-D graph.

# Grapher

Grapher is a charting tool that can create static and dynamic 2-D and 3-D graphs based on formulas. Although Grapher appeared in earlier versions of Mac OS (as Graphing Calculator), Mac OS X 10.4 includes the first Mac OS X-compatible version.

I won't pretend to be an expert on Grapher because I'm not. Sure, I can tell you how to use it, but I can't tell you how it works to create all the cool graphs it can create. In fact, if you have a need for a tool like Grapher, you probably know a lot more about its use than I do. But in this section, I explain how to get started using it so you can experiment on your own.

## ✔ Tip

- Graphing Calculator has a fascinating history that might interest you if you like Apple trivia. To learn more about how and why it was written, fire up your Web browser and visit http://www.pacifict.com/story/.

## To graph a formula

1. Open the Grapher icon in the Utilities folder (**Figure 1**).

2. If necessary, choose File > New or press ⌃ ⌘ N to display the New Graph dialog (**Figure 77**).

3. Click a button near the top of the dialog to list either 2D or 3D document types.

4. In the list on the left side of the dialog, select the type of document you want. A preview appears in the right side of the dialog (**Figure 77**).

5. Click Open. An untitled window with an empty graph appears (**Figure 78**).

*Continued on next page...*

GRAPHING FORMULAS

*Continued from previous page.*

6. Type the formula you want to chart in the box at the top of the window.

7. Press Return. The formula's graph appears in the window and the formula is added to the Definitions list (**Figure 79**).

8. If desired, repeat steps 6 and 7 to add other formulas to the graph.

## ✔ Tips

- Once you've created a graph, you can save or print it using commands under the File menu (**Figure 80**). I tell you about saving files in **Chapter 7** and printing in **Chapter 12**.

- Grapher's Equation Palette (**Figure 81**) makes it a bit easier to enter complex formulas. To display it, choose Window > Show Equation Palette or press Shift ⌃ ⌘ E.

- Want to see some cool examples? Check out a few options under the Examples menu (**Figure 82**).

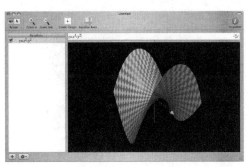

**Figure 79** Grapher can create animated, 3-D graphs like this one.

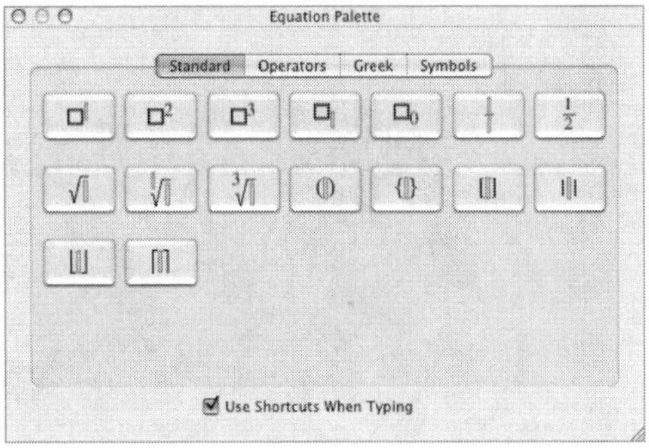

**Figure 80** You may find it easier to enter complex formulas with the Equation Palette.

**Figure 81** Grapher's File menu offers commands you can use with completed graphs.

**Figure 82** The Examples menu lists a bunch of cool sample graphs.

GRAPHING FORMULAS

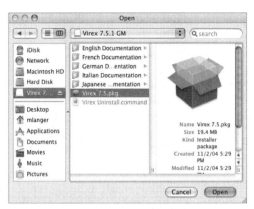

**Figure 83** Use this Open dialog to locate, select, and open an Installer document file.

# Installer

Installer enables you to install software in Apple Installer document files. In most cases, this program will launch automatically when you open an Installer document. You can, however, launch Installer and use its Open dialog to locate and open an installer document containing software you want to install.

## ✔ Tip

- Not all software uses Apple Installer document files. Some software has its own installer or uses the Vise installer.

## To install software with Installer

1. Open the Installer icon in the Utilities folder (**Figure 1**).

2. Use the Open dialog that appears (**Figure 83**) to locate and select the Installer document you want to install.

3. Click Open.

4. Follow the instructions that appear onscreen to install the software.

# Migration Assistant

Migration Assistant is a brand new utility that's part of Mac OS X 10.4. It enables you to copy user information from another Macintosh to the one you are using. This makes it possible to transfer your information from an old Mac to a new one or to add user accounts from another Mac.

The Migration Assistant is very easy to use. It provides clear instructions for completing every step and walks you through the process of copying user information. Simply double-click its icon to get started and follow the prompts. **Figures 84** and **85** show examples of the first two screens you'll encounter.

## ✔ Tips

■ The Mac OS X Setup Assistant may automatically perform the same tasks as the Migration Assistant, depending on your answers to questions during setup. I discuss the Mac OS X Setup Assistant in **Chapter 1**.

■ The Migration Assistant can only copy user information from a Macintosh connected via FireWire cable or from another volume or partition on the computer it is copying to.

■ The Migration Assistant requires that you authenticate as an Administrator when using it. This prevents unauthorized users from adding accounts to the computer.

■ Most users will never need to use the Migration Assistant.

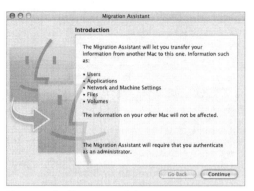

**Figure 84** The first screen of the Migration Assistant gives you a good idea of the kind of assistance it provides.

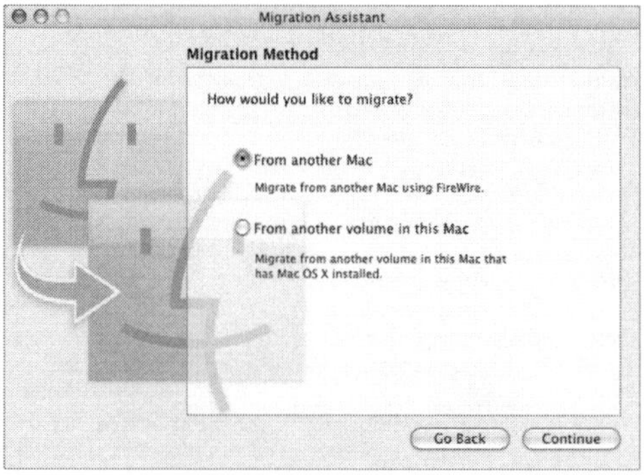

**Figure 85** The Migration Assistant can copy user account information from two sources.

**Figure 86**
Clicking the
More Info button
in this window
launches System
Profiler.

# System Profiler

The System Profiler application provides information about your computer's hardware, software, network, and logs. This information can come in handy when you are troubleshooting problems or just need to know more about the hardware and software installed on your computer.

## ✔ Tips

- System Profiler was known as Apple System Profiler and had a different interface in previous versions of Mac OS X.

- Clicking the More Info button in the About This Mac window (**Figure 86**) launches System Profiler.

## To view system information

1. Open the System Profiler icon in the Utilities folder (**Figure 1**).

2. In the Contents list of the System Profiler window, click the type of information you want to view (**Figures 87** through **89**).

3. The information appears in the window.

## ✔ Tips

- You can click a triangle to the left of an item in any System Profiler window to display or hide detailed information.

- Clicking an item in the top-right portion of a System Profiler window displays details about that item (**Figures 87** through **89**).

- You can use the File menu's Save and Print commands to save or print the information that appears in System Profiler. You might find this handy if you need to document your system's current configuration for troubleshooting or backup purposes.

**Figures 87, 88, & 89** Three examples of the information System Profiler can provide about your system.

# VoiceOver Utility

VoiceOver, a new feature of Mac OS X, is a built-in screen reader that helps visually impaired people use their computers. Once configured, VoiceOver enables you to hear descriptions of everything onscreen, move around the screen, select items, and read and manipulate text.

A complete discussion of VoiceOver is beyond the scope of this book. However, in this section, I introduce you to VoiceOver Utility, the application you use to configure VoiceOver.

## ✔ Tips

- VoiceOver can be enabled or disabled in the Universal Access preferences pane, which I discuss in **Chapter 21**.

- To learn more about configuring and using VoiceOver, open VoiceOver Utility and choose Help > VoiceOver Help. Then follow the links to get the information you need.

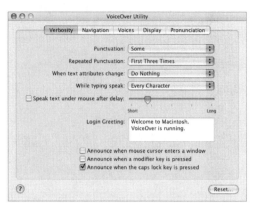

**Figure 90** The default settings in VoiceOver Utility's Verbosity pane.

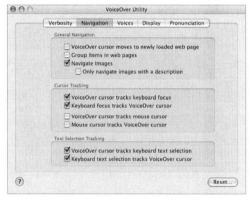

**Figure 91** The default settings in VoiceOver Utility's Navigation pane.

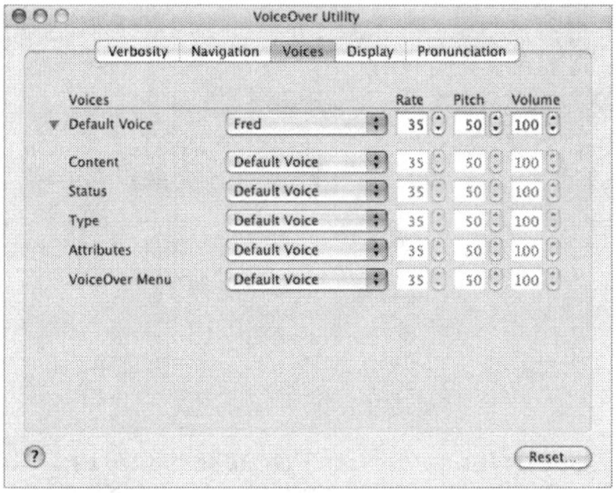

**Figure 92** The default settings in VoiceOver Utility's Voices pane. In this illustration, I've clicked the triangle beside the first row to display options for specific categories of spoken text.

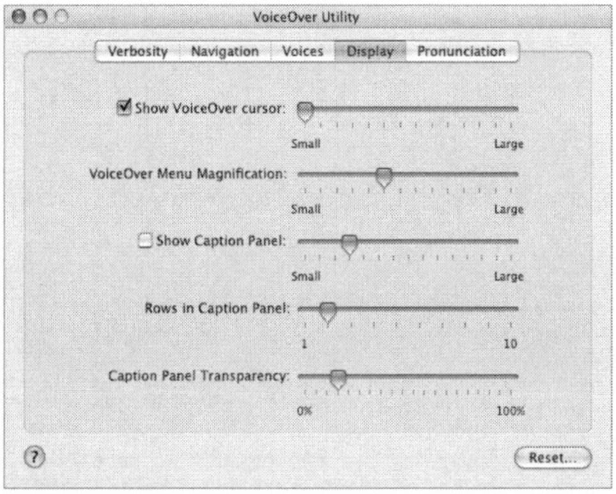

**Figure 93** The default settings in VoiceOver Utility's Display pane.

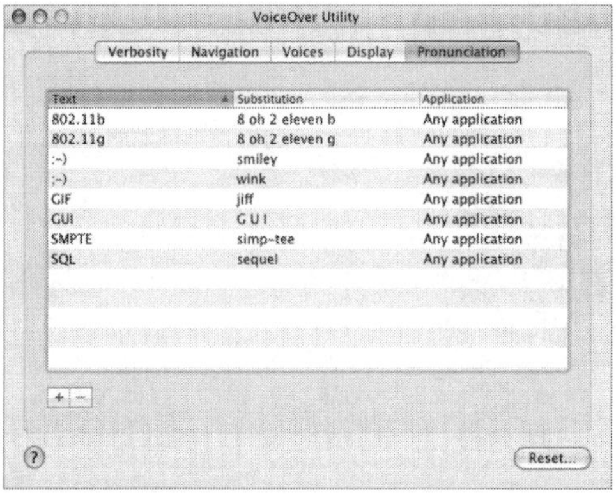

**Figure 94** The default settings in VoiceOver Utility's Pronunciation pane.

## To configure VoiceOver

1. Open the VoiceOver Utility icon in the Utilities folder (**Figure 1**).

2. The VoiceOver Utility window appears. Click buttons to set options in each of five categories:

   ▲ **Verbosity** (**Figure 90**) controls how much speaking VoiceOver does.

   ▲ **Navigation** (**Figure 91**) controls how VoiceOver moves and tracks the cursor and text selections.

   ▲ **Voices** (**Figure 92**) enables you to select the default voice and voices for various types of spoken text.

   ▲ **Display** (**Figure 93**) enables you to set the size of the VoiceOver cursor and menu magnification, as well as configure the Caption Panel.

   ▲ **Pronunciation** (**Figure 94**) lets you specify how VoiceOver should pronounce certain words, phrases, abbreviations, and acronyms.

3. Choose VoiceOver Utility > Quit VoiceOver Utility, or press ⌃⌘Q, to save your settings.

**CONFIGURING VOICEOVER**

**669**

# Application Services

Some Mac OS X applications provide services that enable you to use content from one application with another. The content can include text, graphics, or movies. For example, the services for Grab are available from within TextEdit (**Figure 95**)—this means you can use Grab to take a screen shot and have the image appear in your Text Edit document.

Although these application services have been available in Mac OS X since its original release, not all applications support it. As a result, the Services submenu, which offers access to application services, often contains dimmed menu commands. This feature of Mac OS X will become more useful as it is adopted by applications. Experiment with it to see what it can do for you!

## To use application services

Display the Services submenu under the application menu and choose the application and command you want.

For example, in **Figure 95**, to take a screen shot of the entire screen for placement in TextEdit, you'd choose TextEdit > Services > Grab > Screen. Grab would launch, take the screen shot, and insert it in your TextEdit document at the insertion point.

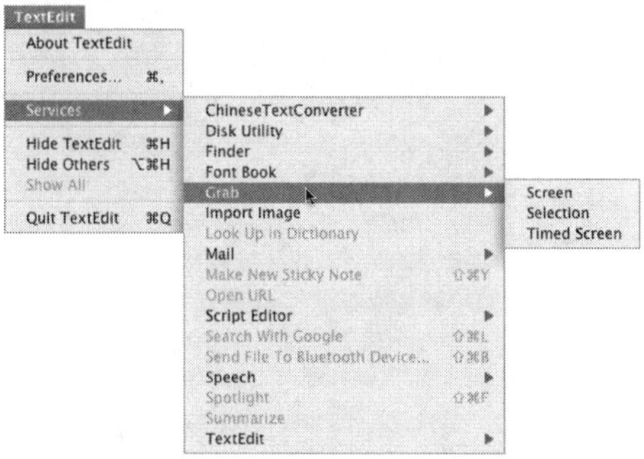

**Figure 95** The services for Grab are supported by TextEdit, enabling you to quickly and easily insert screen shots in a TextEdit document.

# Getting
# Help

## Getting Help

Mac OS offers two basic ways to get additional information and answers to questions as you work with your computer:

◆ **Help Tags** identify screen items as you point to them. This help feature is supported by many (but not all) applications.

◆ **Mac Help** uses the Help Viewer application to provide information about using Mac OS and Mac OS X applications. This Help feature, which is accessible through commands on the Help menu, is searchable and includes clickable links to information.

This chapter explains how to get help when you need it.

## ✔ Tip

■ You can find additional support for Mac OS, as well as Apple hardware and software, on Apple's Support Web site, www.apple.com/support/ or through the AppleCare channel of Sherlock. I tell you about the Internet in **Chapter 13** and about Sherlock in **Chapter 15**.

# Help Tags

Help Tags identify screen elements that you point to by providing information in small yellow boxes (**Figures 1**, **2**, and **3**).

## ✔ Tip

■ Help Tags are especially useful when first starting out with a new software application. Pointing at various interface elements and reading Help Tags is a great way to start learning about how an application works.

## To use Help Tags

Point to an item for which you want more information. If a Help Tag is available for the item, it appears after a moment (**Figures 1**, **2**, and **3**).

**Figure 1** A Help Tag in the Address Book main window,...

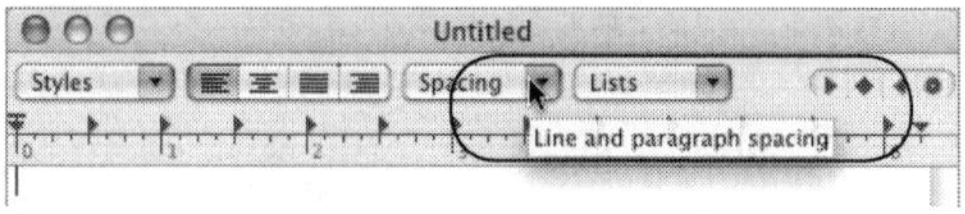

**Figure 2** ...in a TextEdit document window, ...

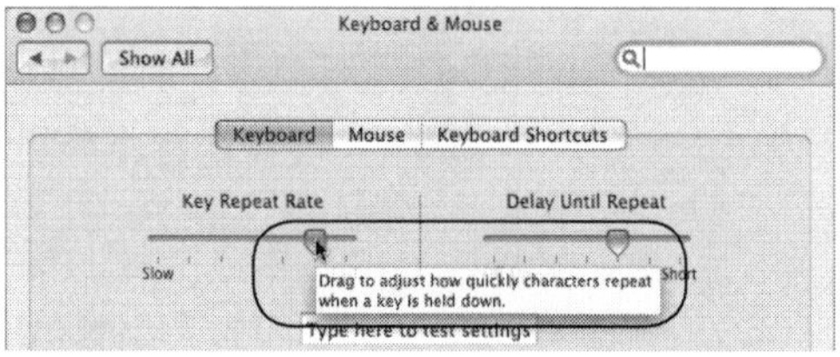

**Figure 3** ...and in a System Preferences pane window.

**Figures 4a, 4b, & 4c**
The Help command on Help menus for Finder (top), Address Book (middle), and TextEdit (bottom).

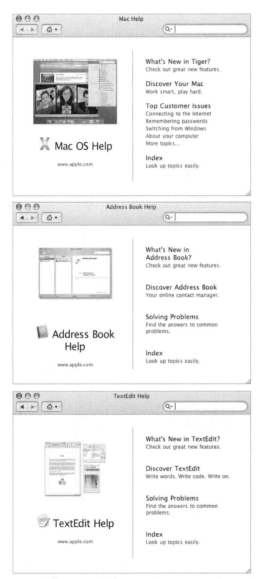

**Figures 5a, 5b, & 5c** The main Help windows for Finder (top), Address Book (middle), and TextEdit (bottom).

# Mac Help

Mac Help uses the Help Viewer application to display information about Mac OS or a specific application. It includes several features that enable you to find information—and use it—quickly:

◆ **Main Help window** usually provides clickable links to introductory information and a table of contents.

◆ **Search feature** enables you to search for topics containing specific words or phrases.

◆ **Links to related information** enable you to move from one topic to a related topic.

◆ **Links to applications** enable you to open an application referenced by a help topic.

◆ **Links to online information** enable you to get the latest information from Apple's Web site.

## ✔ Tips

■ Although this feature's generic name is Mac Help, help windows normally display the name of the application that Help is displayed for.

■ If you are connected to the Internet when you access Mac Help, the most up-to-date help information automatically appears.

## To open Mac Help

Choose Help > *Application Name* Help (**Figures 4a, 4b,** and **4c**), or press ⌃ ⌘ ?.

*Or*

Click the Help button in a window or dialog in which it appears.

The main Help window appears (**Figures 5a, 5b,** and **5c**).

MAC HELP

## To switch from one application's Help to another's

Choose an application from Help Viewer's Library menu (**Figure 6**). The contents of the Help window changes to display Help for the application you chose.

### ✔ Tips

■ The Library menu (**Figure 6**) makes it possible to open an application's Help without opening the application.

■ The applications that appear in the Library menu (**Figure 6**) vary depending on the applications for which you have viewed Mac Help. Each time you view Mac Help for an application, that application is added to the Library menu.

## To browse Mac Help

1. Click a link in a Help window. The window's contents change to view information about the item you clicked (**Figure 7**).

2. Continue clicking links to view related information (**Figures 8** and **9**).

### ✔ Tips

■ Links can be text or graphics. To find out if text is a link, point to it. The mouse pointer turns into a pointing finger (**Figure 7**).

■ You can backtrack through topics you have viewed by clicking the back button in the toolbar (**Figure 7**) or using the "breadcrumb" links that appear beneath the toolbar (**Figures 8** and **9**).

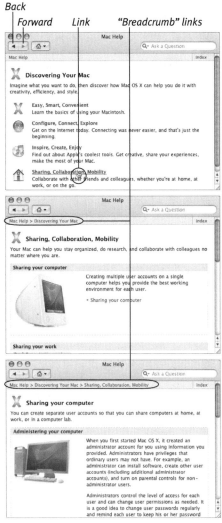

**Figure 6**
The Library menu is automatically populated with Help topics you have viewed.

*Back*
*Forward*   *Link*   *"Breadcrumb" links*

**Figures 7, 8, & 9** This series of windows show how you can click links to view information about topics in Mac Help—and navigate among windows.

Mac Help

Q▾ widget

**Figure 10** Enter a search word or phrase in the search box at the top of the Help window.

Search Results: widget

◄ ► ⌂▾                                    Q▾ widget

Title                                              Rank
▼ **Help Topics**
  ✗ Organizing widgets
  ✗ What is a widget?
  ✗ Getting more widgets
  ✗ Creating your own widgets
  ✗ Using Dashboard
  ✗ Customizing a Dashboard widget
  ✗ Using the Stickies widget
  ✗ Using the Address Book widget
  ✗ Using the Calculator widget
  ✗ Using the Dictionary widget
  ✗ Using the Tile Game widget

Found: 23 help topics                        Show

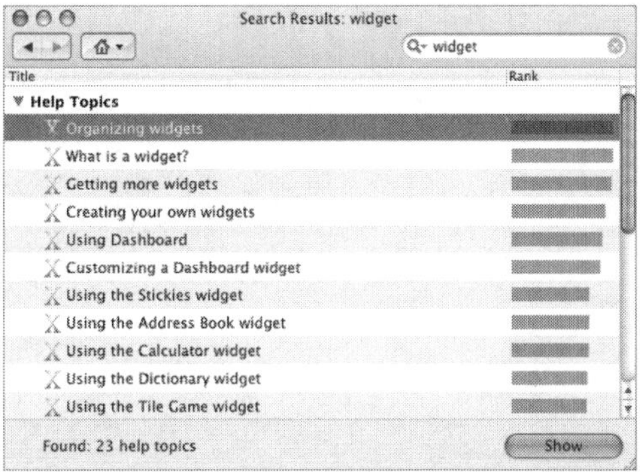

**Figure 11** A list of topics matching the search criteria appears.

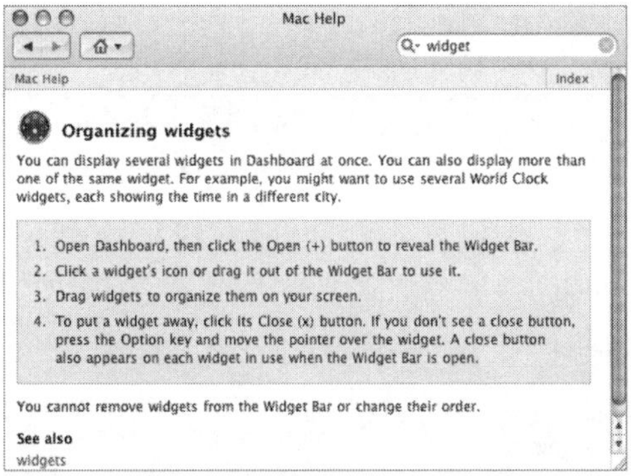

Mac Help

◄ ► ⌂▾                                    Q▾ widget

Mac Help                                        Index

🔘 **Organizing widgets**

You can display several widgets in Dashboard at once. You can also display more than one of the same widget. For example, you might want to use several World Clock widgets, each showing the time in a different city.

1. Open Dashboard, then click the Open (+) button to reveal the Widget Bar.
2. Click a widget's icon or drag it out of the Widget Bar to use it.
3. Drag widgets to organize them on your screen.
4. To put a widget away, click its Close (x) button. If you don't see a close button, press the Option key and move the pointer over the widget. A close button also appears on each widget in use when the Widget Bar is open.

You cannot remove widgets from the Widget Bar or change their order.

**See also**
widgets

**Figure 12** Clicking a link displays information as a Help topic.

## To search Help

1. Enter a search word, phrase, or question in the entry field at the top of the Help window (**Figure 10**) and press ⟨Return⟩.

2. After a moment, a Search Results window appears. Click a topic to display brief information about it in the bottom of the window (**Figure 11**).

3. Double-click a topic in the search results list or click the topic's name in the bottom of the window. The topic's information appears in the window (**Figure 12**).

## ✔ Tips

■ The bars in the Relevance column in the Search Results list (**Figure 11**) indicate how well the topics match your search word, phrase, or question. The bigger the bar, the more relevant the item.

■ You can click the Back button (**Figures 11** and **12**) to view previously viewed Help windows.

# Application Help

Many applications include extensive online help. The help features of various applications may look and work differently, so it's impossible to cover them in detail here. Most online help features, however, are easy to use.

## ✔ Tips

■ Some applications, such as the Microsoft Office suite of products, include an entire online manual that is searchable and printable.

■ Not all applications include online help. If you can't locate an online help feature for an application, check the documentation that came with the application to see if it has one and how you can access it.

## To access an application's online help

Choose a command from the Help menu within that application (**Figure 13**).

*Or*

Click a Help button within a dialog.

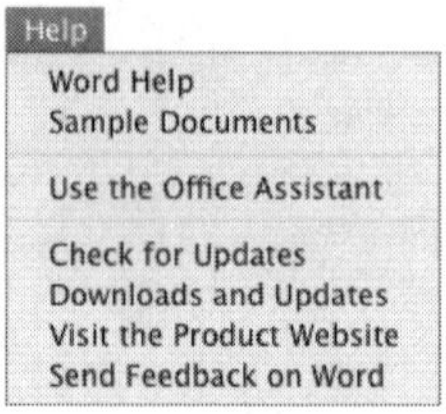

**Figure 13**
The Help menu in Microsoft Word 2004 offers a number of commands for getting onscreen help from within Microsoft Word or on the Microsoft Web site.

# Help & Troubleshooting Advice

Here's some advice for getting help with and troubleshooting problems.

◆ **Join a Macintosh user group.** Joining a user group and attending meetings is probably the most cost-effective way to learn about your computer and get help. You can find a users' group near you by consulting the Apple User Group Web site, www.apple.com/usergroups/.

◆ **Visit Apple's Web site.** If you have access to the Web, you can find a wealth of information about your computer online. Start at www.apple.com/support/ and search for the information you need.

◆ **Visit the Web sites for the companies that develop the applications you use most.** A regular visit to these sites can keep you up to date on updates and upgrades to keep your software running smoothly. These sites can also provide technical support for problems you encounter while using the software. Learn the URLs for these sites by consulting the documentation that came with the software.

◆ **Visit Web sites that offer troubleshooting information.** MacFixIt (www.macfixit.com) and MacInTouch (www.macintouch.com) are two excellent resources.

◆ **Read Macintosh magazines.** A number of magazines, each geared toward a different level of user, can help you learn about your computer: *Macworld* and *Mac Addict* are the most popular. Stay away from PC-centric magazines; the majority of the information they provide will not apply to your Macintosh and may confuse you.

*Continued on next page...*

**HELP & TROUBLESHOOTING ADVICE**

*Continued from previous page.*

◆ **Buy a good troubleshooting guide.**
I highly recommend *Mac OS X Help Line,
Tiger Edition,* a Peachpit Press book by
Ted Landau. I'm not recommending this
book because Peachpit or Ted asked me
to. I'm recommending it because I think
it's the best Mac OS X troubleshooting
book around.

# Menus & Keyboard Equivalents

## Menus & Keyboard Equivalents

This appendix illustrates all of Mac OS X's Finder menus and provides a list of corresponding keyboard equivalents.

To use a keyboard equivalent, hold down the modifier key (usually ⌘) while pressing the keyboard key for the command.

Menus and keyboard commands are discussed in detail in **Chapter 2**.

| | |
|---|---|
| About This Mac | |
| Software Update... | |
| Mac OS X Software... | |
| System Preferences... | |
| Dock | ▶ |
| Location | ▶ |
| Recent Items | ▶ |
| Force Quit... | ⌥⌘⌦ |
| Sleep | |
| Restart... | |
| Shut Down... | |
| Log Out Maria Langer... | ⇧⌘Q |

## Apple Menu

| | |
|---|---|
| Option ⌘ Esc | Force Quit |
| Shift ⌘ Q | Log Out |
| Option ⌘ D | Dock > Turn Hiding On/Off |

# Finder Menu

| | |
|---|---|
| �command ⌘ , | Preferences |
| Shift ⌘ Delete | Empty Trash |
| ⌘ H | Hide Finder |
| Option ⌘ H | Hide Others |
| Shift ⌘ Y | Services > Make New Sticky Note |
| Shift ⌘ * | Services > Script Editor > Get Result of AppleScript |
| Shift ⌘ L | Services > Search With Google |
| Shift ⌘ B | Services > Send File To Bluetooth Device |
| Shift ⌘ F | Services > Spotlight |

# File Menu

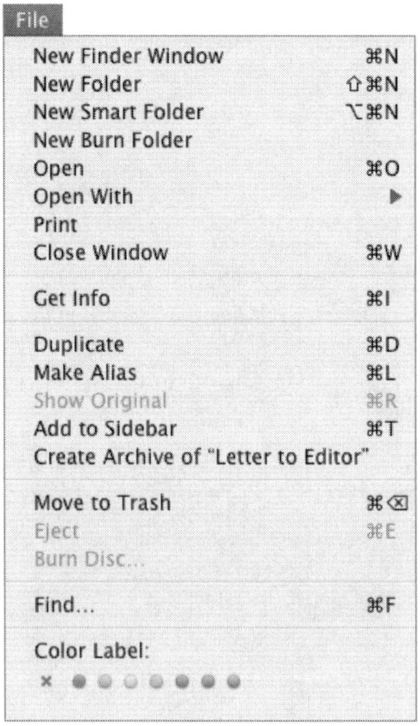

| | |
|---|---|
| ⌘ N | New Finder Window |
| Shift ⌘ N | New Folder |
| Option ⌘ N | New Smart Folder |
| ⌘ O | Open |
| ⌘ W | Close Window |
| Option ⌘ W | Close All |
| ⌘ I | Get Info |
| Option ⌘ I | Show Inspector |
| ⌘ D | Duplicate |
| ⌘ L | Make Alias |
| ⌘ R | Show Original |
| ⌘ T | Add to Sidebar |
| Shift ⌘ T | Add to Favorites |
| ⌘ Delete | Move to Trash |
| ⌘ E | Eject |
| ⌘ F | Find |

**Finder** menu

- About Finder
- Preferences...        ⌘,
- Empty Trash...        ⇧⌘⌫
- Secure Empty Trash
- Services              ▶
- Hide Finder           ⌘H
- Hide Others           ⌥⌘H
- Show All

**File** menu

- New Finder Window     ⌘N
- New Folder            ⇧⌘N
- New Smart Folder      ⌥⌘N
- New Burn Folder
- Open                  ⌘O
- Open With             ▶
- Print
- Close Window          ⌘W
- Get Info              ⌘I
- Duplicate             ⌘D
- Make Alias            ⌘L
- Show Original         ⌘R
- Add to Sidebar        ⌘T
- Create Archive of "Letter to Editor"
- Move to Trash         ⌘⌫
- Eject                 ⌘E
- Burn Disc...
- Find...               ⌘F
- Color Label:

FINDER & FILE MENUS

## Edit Menu

| | |
|---|---|
| ⌘Z | Undo |
| ⌘X | Cut |
| ⌘C | Copy |
| ⌘V | Paste |
| ⌘A | Select All |

## View Menu

| | |
|---|---|
| ⌘1 | as Icons |
| ⌘2 | as List |
| ⌘3 | as Columns |
| Option ⌘T | Show/Hide Toolbar |
| ⌘J | Show/Hide View Options |

## Go Menu

| | |
|---|---|
| ⌘[ | Back |
| ⌘] | Forward |
| ⌘↑ | Enclosing Folder |
| Shift ⌘C | Computer |
| Shift ⌘H | Home |
| Shift ⌘K | Network |
| Shift ⌘I | My iDisk |
| Shift ⌘A | Applications |
| Shift ⌘U | Utilities |
| Shift ⌘G | Go to Folder |
| ⌘K | Connect to Server |

**EDIT, VIEW, & GO MENUS**

## Window Menu

| | |
|---|---|
| ⌃ ⌘ M | Minimize |
| Option ⌃ ⌘ M | Minimize All |
| ⌃ ⌘ ` | Cycle Through Windows |

| Window |  |
|---|---|
| Minimize | ⌘M |
| Zoom | |
| Cycle Through Windows | ⌘ ` |
| Bring All to Front | |
| ✓ Applications | |
| Basics | |
| Documents | |

## Help Menu

| | |
|---|---|
| ⌃ ⌘ ? | Mac Help |

| Help | |
|---|---|
| Mac Help | ⌘? |

**WINDOW & HELP MENUS**

# Index

INDEX

INDEX

INDEX